2018–2019 TOWNSEND **PRESS**

Sunday School
Commentary

Based on the International Lessons Series

Writers: Dr. Cleo LaRue; Dr. Christopher Jackson; *Editors:* Rev. Wellington A. Johnson Sr.; Rev. Emmanuel Re *Qualitative Editor:* Tanae C. McKnight Murdic; *Associate Editor:* Regina Hoosier; *Copy Editor:* Yalemzewd Work *Layout Designer:* Royetta Davis; *Cover Designer:* Donn S. Jobe Sr.

ISBN: 978-1-939225-68-9

CONTENTS

Six-year Cycle v
List of Printed Texts vi
Preface vii
Acknowledgments viii
Know Your Writers ix

Fall Quarter, 2018—God's World and God's People

General Introduction 1

September: UNIT I—God Created the World
2   God Created the Heavens and Earth (Genesis 1:1-13) 3
9   God Created Plants and Animals (Genesis 1:14-25) 13
16 God Created People (Genesis 1:26-31; 2:4-7) 22
23 God Created the Family (Genesis 2:18-24; 4:1-2) 32
30 God Creates, Humans Sin (Genesis 3:8-17, 20-24) 41

October: UNIT II—God Destroys and Re-creates
7   Noah's Steadfast Faith (Genesis 6:9b-22) 50
14 God Is Always Working (Genesis 10:2; 11:10, 27, 31-32; 12:1-4) 59
21 Abraham and Sarah Birth God's People (Genesis 18:9-15; 21:1-7) 67
28 Isaac and Rebekah Continue the Legacy (Genesis 24:12-21, 61-67) 76

November: UNIT III—God Blesses and Re-creates Regardless
4   A Troubled Birth (Genesis 25:19-34) 85
11 Jacob Receives Isaac's Blessing (Genesis 27:5-10, 18-19, 21-29) 95
18 Jacob Forms a Relationship with God (Genesis 28:10-22) 104
25 God Blesses Jacob and Rachel (Genesis 30:22-32, 43) 114

Winter Quarter, 2018–2019—Our Love for God

General Introduction 123

December: UNIT I—*God Commands Our Love, Respect, and Obedience*
2   Love and Devotion (Deuteronomy 6:1-9) 125
9   Choose to Love and Serve God (Joshua 24:1-3 13-15, 21-24) 133
16 Love and Worship God (Psalm 103:1-17, 21-22) 142
23 Jesus: God's Loving Promise (Luke 1:26-31; 2:22, 25-35) 152
30 Modeling God's Love (Matthew 25:31-46) 161

January: UNIT II—*Loving God by Trusting Christ*
6   Hold Fast to God's Love (2 Thessalonians 3:1-5; 2 John 4-11) 169
13 Submit to God in Love (James 4:1-10) 177
20 Submit to God in Christ (Philippians 1:12-21) 187
27 Devote All to Christ (Philippians 2:1-11) 196

February: UNIT II—*Loving God by Trusting Christ*
3   Renounce Everything for Christ (Philippians 3:7-14) 205

UNIT III—*Love Songs that Glorify God*

10 Pondering God's Steadfast Love (Psalm 48:1-3, 9-14) 214
17 Praising God's Mighty Works (Psalm 66:1-9, 16-20) 223
24 Living with God's Loving Assurance (Psalm 91:1-8, 11-16) 232

Spring Quarter, 2019—Discipleship and Mission

General Introduction 241
March: UNIT I—*Call to Discipleship*

 3 Called to Humility and Hospitality (Luke 14:7-14) 243
10 A Costly Call (Mark 1:16-20; Luke 14:25-33) 251
17 Calling the Lost (Luke 15:11-24) 259
24 Calling to Salvation (Luke 19:1-10) 267

UNIT II—*Call to Ministry*
31 Called to Discipleship (Matthew 4:12-22) 275

April: UNIT II—*Call to Ministry*

 7 Call and Mission (Matthew 10:1-15) 284
14 Called to Remember (Matthew 26:1-13) 293
21 Called to Proclaim the Resurrection (Matthew 28:1-15) 301
28 Call and Commissioning (Matthew 28:16-20; Acts 1:6-8) 310

May: UNIT III—*The Spread of the Gospel*

 5 Called to Righteousness (Romans 3:21-31) 319
12 Called to Life in the Spirit (Romans 8:1-14) 327
19 The Call of the Gentiles (Romans 11:11-24) 335
26 Called to New Life in Christ (Romans 12:1-8) 344

Summer Quarter, 2019—Living in Covenant

General Introduction 353
June: UNIT I—*A Fulfilled Covenant*

 2 Jesus Institutes the New Covenant (Mark 14:17-24; Hebrews 8:6-7, 10-12) 355
 9 Jesus Seals the New Covenant (Mark 15:6-15, 25-26, 33-39) 365
16 The New Covenant's Sacrifice (Hebrews 9:11-22) 374
23 Hearts United in Love (Colossians 2:1-15) 383

UNIT II—*A Heartfelt Covenant*
30 Jesus Teaches about Right Attitudes (Matthew 5:1-12) 391

July: UNIT II—*A Heartfelt Covenant*

 7 Jesus Teaches about Fulfilling the Law (Matthew 5:13-20) 400
14 Jesus Teaches Us to Love One Another (Matthew 5:21-32) 408
21 Jesus Teaches about Transforming Love (Matthew 5:38-48) 417
28 Jesus Teaches about Spiritual Discernment (Matthew 7:1-6, 15-23) 426

August: UNIT III—*Covenant: A Personal Perspective*

 4 A Covenant between Friends (1 Samuel 18:1-5; 19:1-7) 435
11 A Mother-Daughter Covenant (Ruth 1:6-11, 14-18) 444
18 A Covenant to Marry (Ruth 3:1-6, 8-12, 16-18) 453
25 Marriage: A Covenant of Mutual Love (Ephesians 5:21-33) 462

2016–2022 SCOPE AND SEQUENCE—CYCLE SPREAD
ARRANGEMENT OF QUARTERS ACCORDING TO THE CHURCH SCHOOL YEAR, SEPTEMBER THROUGH AUGUST

Fall 2016 **GOD–SOVEREIGNTY** **Sovereignty of God** Isaiah; Matthew; Hebrews; Revelation	*Winter 2016–2017* **CREATION** **Creation: A Divine Cycle** Psalms; Luke; Galatians	*Spring 2017* **LOVE** **God Loves Us** Psalms; Joel; Jonah; John; Romans; Ephesians; 1 Peter; 1 John	*Summer 2017* **CALL** **God's Urgent Call** Exodus; Judges; Isaiah; Jeremiah; Ezekiel; Amos; Acts
Fall 2017 **COVENANT** **Covenant with God** Genesis; Exodus; Numbers; 1 Samuel; 2 Samuel; Nehemiah; Jeremiah; Ezekiel; 1 Corinthians; Titus; Hebrews	*Winter 2017–2018* **FAITH** **Faith in Action** Daniel; Matthew; Acts; Ephesians; Colossians; 1 Timothy; James	*Spring 2018* **WORSHIP** **Acknowledging God** Genesis; Exodus; Leviticus; 2 Chronicles; Psalms; Luke; John; 2 Corinthians; Hebrews; Revelation	*Summer 2018* **JUSTICE** **Justice in the New Testament** Matthew; Luke; Romans; 2 Corinthians; Colossians
Fall 2018 **CREATION** **God's World and God's People** Genesis	*Winter 2018–2019* **LOVE** **Our Love for God** Deuteronomy; Joshua; Psalms; Matthew; Mark; Luke; Philippians; 2 Thessalonians; James; 2 John	*Spring 2019* **CALL** **Discipleship and Mission** Matthew; Luke; Acts; Romans	*Summer 2019* **COVENANT** **Living in Covenant** Ruth; 1 Samuel; Matthew; Mark; Luke; John; Ephesians; Colossians; Hebrews
Fall 2019 **FAITH** **Responding to God's Grace** Genesis; Exodus; Numbers; Deuteronomy; 1 Samuel; 1 Kings; Luke; 2 Corinthians; Galatians; 1 Thessalonians; 1 Peter; 2 Peter	*Winter 2019–2020* **WORSHIP** **Honoring God** 1 Chronicles; 2 Chronicles; 1 Kings; Ecclesiastes; Matthew; Luke	*Spring 2020* **JUSTICE** **Justice and the Prophets** Esther; 1 Kings; Psalms; Isaiah; Jeremiah; Hosea; Amos; Micah; Habakkuk; Zephaniah; Zachariah; Malachi; Matthew; Mark; 1 Corinthians	*Summer 2020* **GOD–WISDOM** **Many Faces of Wisdom** Genesis; Leviticus; 1 Kings; Job; Proverbs; Ecclesiastes; Matthew; Mark; Luke; John; James
Fall 2020 **LOVE** **Love for One Another** Genesis; Leviticus; 1 Samuel; 2 Samuel; Luke; John; Acts; 1 Corinthians; James; 1 John; 2 John; 3 John	*Winter 2020–2021* **CALL** **Call in the New Testament** Isaiah; Matthew; Mark; Luke; John; Acts; Romans; 1 Corinthians; Hebrews; 2 Timothy	*Spring 2021* **COVENANT** **Prophets Faithful to God's Covenant** Exodus; Joshua; 1 Kings; 2 Kings; Ezra; Nehemiah; Isaiah; Jeremiah; Lamentations; Ezekiel; Amos; Jonah; Luke	*Summer 2021* **FAITH** **Confident Hope** Matthew; Mark; Luke; Romans; 2 Corinthians; Hebrews; 1 John
Fall 2021 **WORSHIP** **Celebrating God** Exodus; 2 Samuel; Ecclesiastes; Psalms; Mark; Luke; Acts; Revelation	*Winter 2021–2022* **JUSTICE** **Justice, Law, History** Genesis; Exodus; Deuteronomy; 2 Samuel; 1 Kings; Ezra; Job; Isaiah; Nahum; Luke	*Spring 2022* **GOD–LIBERATION** **God Frees and Redeems** Deuteronomy; Ezra; Matthew; John; Romans; Galatians	*Summer 2022* **CREATION** **Partners in a New Creation** Isaiah; John; Revelation

LIST OF PRINTED TEXTS

The Printed Scriptural Texts used in the 2018–2019 *Townsend Press Sunday School Commentary* are arranged here in the order in which they appear in the Bible. Opposite each reference is the page number on which Scriptures appear in this edition of the *Commentary*.

Reference	Page
Genesis 1:1-13	3
Genesis 1:14-25	13
Genesis 1:26-31	22
Genesis 2:4-7	23
Genesis 2:18-24	32
Genesis 3:8-17, 20-24	41
Genesis 4:1-2	33
Genesis 6:9b-22	50
Genesis 10:2	59
Genesis 11:10, 27, 31-32	59
Genesis 12:1-4	60
Genesis 18:9-15	67
Genesis 21:1-7	68
Genesis 24:12-21, 61-67	76
Genesis 25:19-34	85
Genesis 27:5-10, 18-19, 21-29	95
Genesis 28:10-22	104
Genesis 30:22-32, 43	114
Deuteronomy 6:1-9	125
Joshua 24:1-3 13-15, 21-24	133
Ruth 1:6-11, 14-18	444
Ruth 3:1-6, 8-12, 16-18	453
1 Samuel 18:1-5	435
1 Samuel 19:1-7	435
Psalm 48:1-3, 9-14	214
Psalm 66:1-9, 16-20	223
Psalm 91:1-8, 11-16	232
Psalm 103:1-17, 21-22	142
Matthew 4:12-22	275
Matthew 5:1-12	391
Matthew 5:13-20	400
Matthew 5:21-32	408

Reference	Page
Matthew 5:38-48	417
Matthew 7:1-6, 15-23	426
Matthew 10:1-15	284
Matthew 25:31-46	161
Matthew 26:1-13	293
Matthew 28:1-15	301
Matthew 28:16-20	310
Mark 1:16-20	251
Mark 14:17-24	355
Mark 15:6-15, 25-26, 33-39	365
Luke 1:26-31	152
Luke 2:22, 25-35	152
Luke 14:7-14	243
Luke 14:25-33	251
Luke 15:11-24	259
Luke 19:1-10	267
Acts 1:6-8	310
Romans 3:21-31	319
Romans 8:1-14	327
Romans 11:11-24	335
Romans 12:1-8	344
Ephesians 5:21-33	462
Philippians 1:12-21	187
Philippians 2:1-11	196
Philippians 3:7-14	205
Colossians 2:1-15	383
2 Thessalonians 3:1-5	169
Hebrews 8:6-7, 10-12	356
Hebrews 9:11-22	374
James 4:1-10	177
2 John 4-11	169

PREFACE

The *Townsend Press Sunday School Commentary*, based on the International Lessons Series, was developed consistent with the curriculum guidelines of the Committee on the Uniform Series, Education Leadership Ministries Commission, National Council of the Churches of Christ in the United States of America. Select Christian scholars and theologians—who themselves embrace the precepts, doctrines, and positions on biblical interpretation that we have come to believe—are contributors to this publication. By participating in Scripture selection and the development of the matrices for the Guidelines for Lesson Development with the Committee on the Uniform Series, this presentation reflects the historic faith that we share within a rich heritage of worship and witness.

The format of the *Townsend Press Sunday School Commentary* lessons consists of the following: the Unit Title, the general subject with age-level topics, Printed Text from the King James Version and the New International Version of the Bible, Unifying Lesson Principle, Objectives of the Lesson, Points to Be Emphasized, The Chronological Setting of the Lesson, The Geographical and Cultural Setting of the Lesson, Prominent Characters in the Lesson, Key Terms in the Lesson, Topical Outline of the Lesson—with the Biblical Background of the Lesson, Exposition and Application of the Scripture, Concluding Reflection (designed to focus on the salient points of the lesson), and the Home Daily Bible Readings. Each lesson concludes with a prayer.

The *Townsend Press Sunday School Commentary* is designed to be an instructional aid for persons involved in the ministry of Christian education. While the autonomy of the individual soul before God is affirmed, we believe that biblical truths find their highest expression within the community of believers whose corporate experiences serve as monitors to preserve the integrity of the Christian faith. As such, the Word of God must not only be understood, but it must also be embodied in the concrete realities of daily life. This serves to allow the Word of God to intersect in a meaningful way with those realities of life.

The presentation of the lessons anticipates the fact that some concepts and Scripture references do not lend themselves to meaningful comprehension by children. Hence, when this occurs, alternative passages of Scripture are used, along with appropriate content emphases, that are designed to assist children in their spiritual growth. There will, however, remain a consistent connection between the children, youth, and adult lessons through the Unifying Principle developed for each session.

We stand firm in our commitment to Christian growth, to the end that lives will be transformed through personal and group interaction with the Word of God. The challenge issued by the apostle Paul continues to find relevance for our faith journey: "Do your best to present yourself to God as one approved by him, a worker who has no need to be ashamed, rightly explaining the word of truth" (2 Timothy 2:15, NRSV). May we all commit ourselves to the affirmation expressed by the psalmist: "Your word is a lamp to my feet and a light for my path" (Psalm 119:105, NIV).

ACKNOWLEDGMENTS

The *Townsend Press Sunday School Commentary* is recognized as the centerpiece of a family of church-school literature designed especially to assist teachers in their presentation of the lessons as well as to broaden the knowledge base of students from the biblical perspective. Our mission has been and will always be to provide religious educational experiences and spiritual resources for our constituency throughout this nation, as well as many foreign countries. To achieve this end, the collaborative efforts of many people provide the needed expertise in the various areas of the production process. The editorial personnel, too numerous to list, approach their respective tasks with the dedication and devotion of those who serve God by serving His people. This *Commentary* is presented with gratitude to God for all those who desire a more comprehensive treatment of the selected Scriptures than is provided in the church-school quarterlies, and it is intended to be a complementary resource to the quarterlies.

This *Commentary* came into being as a result of employees with expertise in their assigned areas whose self-understanding is that of "workers together with God" and partners with those who labor in the vineyard of teaching the Word of God in order to make disciples and nurture others toward a mature faith.

Our gratitude is expressed to Dr. Cleo LaRue, expositor for the Fall and Spring Quarters, and Dr. Christopher Jackson, expositor for the Winter and Summer Quarters, for their devotion to the development of the respective lessons. These two writers bring diversity and a broad spectrum of ministerial, theological, and educational experience to bear on the exposition and application of the Scripture.

The task in which we are all involved would be meaningless and fruitless were it not for the many readers for whom this publication has been so diligently prepared. The faithfulness of our constituency has been enduring for more than a century, and we consider ourselves blessed to be their servants in the ministry of the printed Word—exalting the living Word, our Lord and Savior, Jesus Christ. We pray that God's grace will complement our efforts so that lives will be transformed within and beyond the confines of classroom interaction as the Spirit of God manifests Himself through the intersection of teaching and learning.

KNOW YOUR WRITERS

Dr. Cleo LaRue▼
Fall and Spring Quarters

Dr. Cleophus J. LaRue, Princeton Theological Seminary's Francis Landey Patton Professor of Homiletics, received his B.A. and M.A. degrees from Baylor University, and his M.Div. and Ph.D. degrees from Princeton Theological Seminary. He specializes in the theory and method of African-American preaching and worship. An ordained minister in the National Baptist Convention of America, LaRue is the former pastor of two churches in Texas as well as the former interim pastor of churches in Harlem and Jamaica Queens, New York. He is a frequent speaker at churches, seminaries, and conferences throughout the country, and is a member of the Academy of Homiletics.

A prolific author, Dr. LaRue has published several major publications. His latest work, *Toward a Deeper Understanding of Celebration in African American Preaching,* was released in Spring 2016. He has also written and/or edited the following works:

- *I Believe I'll Testify: The Art of African American Preaching* (Westminster John Knox Press, 2010)
- *More Power in the Pulpit: How America's Most Effective Black Preachers Prepare Their Sermons,* editor (Westminster John Knox Press, 2009)
- *The New Interpreter's Handbook of Preaching* (Nashville: Abingdon Press, 2008),

Co-editor with Paul Scott Wilson, Jana Childers, and John M. Rottman

- *This Is My Story: Testimonies and Sermons of Black Women in Ministry,* editor (Westminster John Knox Press, 2005)
- *Power in the Pulpit: How America's Most Effective Black Preachers Prepare Their Sermons,* editor (Westminster John Knox Press, 2002)
- *The Heart of Black Preaching* (Westminster John Knox Press, 1999)

LaRue is currently researching a volume entitled *Colored Preaching: The Shape of Proclamation in the Global South.*

LaRue received an honorary doctorate in 2003 from Coe College in Cedar Rapids, Iowa, and in 2012, Baylor University named him a Distinguished Alumnus of the school.

He has taken Princeton students on travel study courses to Asia, Africa, and Latin America. His most recent trips include travelling to Salvador, Brazil, and India.

For more than twenty years he has served on Princeton's faculty, and currently serves as the chairperson of the Practical Theology Department.

LaRue continues to lecture and preach throughout the United States. He has also spent time teaching homiletics in various settings on five continents.

He is married to Lori Neff LaRue and they reside in Princeton, New Jersey. His daughter, Coryell, resides in Houston, Texas.

Dr. Christopher Jackson▼
Winter and Summer Quarters

Dr. E. Christopher Jackson is a native of Chattanooga, Tennessee, the second son of Andrew and Christine Jackson. He received his Bachelor of Arts degree from the University of Tennessee–Knoxville. He completed his Master of Divinity degree at Southern Baptist Theological Seminary in Louisville, Kentucky, and his Doctor of Ministry degree at United Theological Seminary in Dayton, Ohio.

His ministry experience includes serving in campus ministry at the University of Tennessee–Knoxville and the University of Louisville. Full-time professional campus ministry positions include nine years at Lincoln University in Missouri and ten years at Tennessee State University, Fisk University, and American Baptist College in Nashville. He co-founded Creative Ministry Consultants, which provides seminars, counseling, and ministry consulting on a national basis. He served as Minister of Nurture at the Temple Church and as Adjunct Professor in Sociology at Tennessee State University, where he taught Courtship & Marriage and the Family. He currently serves as senior pastor of Nashville's Pleasant Green Missionary Baptist Church.

Dr. Jackson is an accomplished writer and the author of two books, internationally published by Zondervan Publishing House: *Straight Talk on Tough Topics*, and *The Black Christian Single's Guide to Dating and Sexuality*. He has also written extensively for the Sunday School Publishing Board and for LifeWay. He has been referenced in *Ebony* magazine and *Essence* magazine, and his newspaper column, "The Relationship Coach," appears weekly in the *Tennessee Tribune*.

He is married to Dr. Coreen D. Jackson, who is Director of the TSU Honors College. Their sons are Joshua, Juleon, and Jemiah. His special interests include music, drama, interpretive movement, reading, nature, visual arts, basketball, and photography. His international travels include West Africa, the Bahamas, Jamaica, Spain, Venezuela, and Belize. One of his primary objectives in life is to help other people to discover their life purposes. His personal mission statement is "To honor God, pursue purpose, and empower people through practical and creative ministries of teaching, writing, conferencing, and producing the arts." Above all, Jesus is the center of his joy.

God's World and God's People

GENERAL INTRODUCTION

In Genesis, the book of beginnings, God is revealed as the creator, sustainer, judge, and redeemer, who brought all things into being. The Fall quarter surveys the book of Genesis in developing sessions on God's creation of the universe, earth, and people. It also details how God continues to co-labor with sinful humanity in reconciling and re-creating order in all things.

Unit I, "*God Created the World,*" has five lessons. The first three lessons concentrate on God's creating the universe, earth, and people, and then declaring all things created good. Although God created and sustains all life, humankind is special to God and unique. Lesson 4 explores how God established the institution of marriage and the process of reproduction to populate the earth. Lesson 5 explains how humankind chose to do wrong and thus introduced sin into God's perfectly created world.

Unit II, "*God Destroys and Re-creates,*" has four lessons. Noah and his family are presented in the first two lessons as righteous followers of God, who help repopulate and restore the earth after the destruction caused by the great flood. The biblical couples Abraham and Sarah and Isaac and Rebekah, who worked with God in the cycle of continuing creation, are studied in the last two lessons of the unit.

Unit III, "*God Blesses and Re-creates Regardless,*" has four lessons. Lesson 1 explores how God blessed humble Isaac in enemy territory. The last three lessons of the unit consider how Jacob deceitfully obtained the blessing God had already destined for him, later established a right relationship with God, and finally was blessed by God to marry and produce children with the wife he loved and for whom he long labored.

September 2, 2018　　　　　　　　　　**Lesson 1**

GOD CREATED THE HEAVENS AND EARTH

ADULT/YOUTH

ADULT/YOUNG ADULT TOPIC: **Out of the Darkness**

YOUTH TOPIC: **The Beginning**

CHILDREN

GENERAL LESSON TITLE: **God Created the Heavens and Earth**

CHILDREN'S TOPIC: **A Great Creation**

DEVOTIONAL READING

Psalm 33:1-9

ADULT/YOUTH

BACKGROUND SCRIPTURE: **Genesis 1:1-13**

PRINT PASSAGE: **Genesis 1:1-13**

KEY VERSES: **Genesis 1:1-2**

CHILDREN

BACKGROUND SCRIPTURE: **Genesis 1:1-13**

PRINT PASSAGE: **Genesis 1:1-13**

KEY VERSE: **Genesis 1:1**

Genesis 1:1-13—KJV

IN THE beginning God created the heaven and the earth.

2 And the earth was without form, and void; and darkness was upon the face of the deep. And the Spirit of God moved upon the face of the waters.

3 And God said, Let there be light: and there was light.

4 And God saw the light, that it was good: and God divided the light from the darkness.

5 And God called the light Day, and the darkness he called Night. And the evening and the morning were the first day.

6 And God said, Let there be a firmament in the midst of the waters, and let it divide the waters from the waters.

7 And God made the firmament, and divided the waters which were under the firmament from the waters which were above the firmament: and it was so.

8 And God called the firmament Heaven. And the evening and the morning were the second day.

Genesis 1:1-13—NIV

IN THE beginning God created the heavens and the earth.

2 Now the earth was formless and empty, darkness was over the surface of the deep, and the Spirit of God was hovering over the waters.

3 And God said, "Let there be light," and there was light.

4 God saw that the light was good, and he separated the light from the darkness.

5 God called the light "day," and the darkness he called "night." And there was evening, and there was morning—the first day.

6 And God said, "Let there be a vault between the waters to separate water from water."

7 So God made the vault and separated the water under the vault from the water above it. And it was so.

8 God called the vault "sky." And there was evening, and there was morning—the second day.

9 And God said, "Let the water under the sky be

9 And God said, Let the waters under the heaven be gathered together unto one place, and let the dry land appear: and it was so.

10 And God called the dry land Earth; and the gathering together of the waters called he Seas: and God saw that it was good.

11 And God said, Let the earth bring forth grass, the herb yielding seed, and the fruit tree yielding fruit after his kind, whose seed is in itself, upon the earth: and it was so.

12 And the earth brought forth grass, and herb yielding seed after his kind, and the tree yielding fruit, whose seed was in itself, after his kind: and God saw that it was good.

13 And the evening and the morning were the third day.

gathered to one place, and let dry ground appear." And it was so.

10 God called the dry ground "land," and the gathered waters he called "seas." And God saw that it was good.

11 Then God said, "Let the land produce vegetation: seed-bearing plants and trees on the land that bear fruit with seed in it, according to their various kinds." And it was so.

12 The land produced vegetation: plants bearing seed according to their kinds and trees bearing fruit with seed in it according to their kinds. And God saw that it was good.

13 And there was evening, and there was morning— the third day.

UNIFYING LESSON PRINCIPLE: The wonders of the universe amaze even the keenest of human minds. Who is responsible for such marvelous and breathtaking creativity? Genesis 1 informs us that God is the Creator of all these marvelous wonders.

LESSON OBJECTIVES

Upon the completion of this lesson, the students will be able to do the following:

1. Know that God alone, through the divine spoken Word, created an amazing and wondrous universe.
2. Sense the importance of being a part of God's awesome creation.
3. Celebrate God's creation through praise and prayers of thanksgiving.

AGE-LEVEL POINTS TO BE EMPHASIZED

Teachers of ADULTS and YOUTH

—The book of Genesis provides two perspectives on creation: Genesis 1:1–2:4a and Genesis 2:4b–3:24. The first account encompasses the whole world, while the second is more intimate and takes place entirely in a garden in Eden.

—After creating the world in six days, God rested on the seventh, inaugurating the Sabbath as a day of rest and including it as part of the natural order (see Exodus 20:11).

—God's creative work was orderly and symmetrical. On days 1-3, God created day and night; sky and sea; and land and plants. On days 4-6, God populated these realms with stars and planets; birds and sea life; and land animals, including humans.

—Genesis brings together various strands of oral histories into a single written document. It contains archetypical stories similar to other creation stories in the region of the world from which it originates.

—Of the two Creation narratives in Genesis 1 and

2, the story in this session can be characterized as "creation by speaking."

—The "evening-morning" construction of days reflects the ancient worldview and continues to be practiced in Judaism today.

—Creation is an act of God that reflects God's choice to no longer be alone, to cooperate, to communicate, and to share in spite of the risks.

—Genesis 1 says that God created everything, but it is also an account of how God has structured creation in its ordered complexity.

Teachers of CHILDREN

—God created the heavens and earth out of nothing.

—On the first day, God created light, which was *day*, as distinguished from the dark, which was *night*.

—On the second and third days, God separated the waters in the heavens from the water under the heavens and called these creations *sky* and *seas*.

—Also, on the third day, God made dry land called *earth*, and vegetation, which reproduces itself.

—As God gave shape, organization, and function to creation, God evaluated it as good.

THE CHRONOLOGICAL SETTING OF THE LESSON

Genesis is a book about beginnings, from the beginnings of the universe and the various orderings of humankind to the beginnings of the people of Israel. It also witnesses to the beginnings of God's activity in the life of the world. Genesis stands at the beginning because creation is such a fundamental theological category for the entire canon (the authoritative list of books accepted as Holy Scripture). The placement of creation at the beginning of the Scriptures demonstrates that God's purposes with Israel, and with us, are universal in scope. God's work in redemption serves the entire creation, since it reclaims a creation that labors under the deep and pervasive effects of sin. It is also the case that the canonical placement makes clear that God's redemptive work does not occur in a vacuum; it occurs in a context that has been shaped in decisive ways by the life-giving, creative work of God. Redemption can never be understood as *ex nihilo* (out of nothing) without denigrating God's gifts given in creation.

THE GEOGRAPHICAL AND CULTURAL SETTING OF THE LESSON

The book of Genesis covers a vast amount of time, stretching from the beginning of the world down to about 1500 BC. The authors of the book of Genesis did not know much about this long history, nor did they care. They wished to sketch instead a few highlights about human origins that had a particular religious significance for Israel's view of life, and to record a few traditions about their own ancestors that would help them understand how they came to be a people and a nation called into covenant by the faithful God *Elohim*. In fact, 80 percent of Genesis is dedicated to the few founding patriarchs Abraham, Isaac, and Jacob, and only 20 percent to the remaining story of creation and life through the first two million years. However, that 20 percent is important because it tells the redemptive story of the faithful God and His steadfast love toward His creation.

Although Genesis has the first place in the Bible, it is by no means the first part to be written. Rather, it is the fruit of prolonged thought and reflection over several centuries. It is, however, the place to begin our biblical story. Its strong images and rich language explore the depths of human experience at its most mysterious—the awesome wonder of creation, the joys of life, the agony of sin, the fear of death, the human capacity for evil, the existence of God, and the questions about His patience and justice. These collections of remembrances and theological reflections that are found in Genesis help us to understand the purposive acts of a sovereign God in Israel's life and now in ours.

PROMINENT CHARACTER(S) IN THE LESSON

Elohim: a Hebrew word referring to gods in general and the most frequent Old Testament name for God. The origin of the word is unclear, although it may have derived from a root meaning "strength" or "power." The same or similar root may have been the source of the name *El*, of which some scholars believe *Elohim* to be the plural.

KEY TERMS IN THE LESSON

Darkness (verse 2)—Hebrew: *choshek* **(kho-shek'):** darkness; obscurity; night.
Day (verse 5)—Hebrew: *yowm* **(yome):** day; time; as a division of time.
Earth (verse 1)—Hebrew: *'erets* **(eh'-rets):** land; earth; whole earth.
Good (verse 4)—Hebrew: *towb* **(tobe):** good; pleasant; agreeable; precious.

Heaven(s) (verse 1)—Hebrew: *shamayim* **(shaw-mah'-yim):** heaven, heavens; visible heavens; sky.
Moved (verse 2)—Hebrew: *rachaph* **(raw-khaf'):** to have shaken or moved; "was hovering" (NIV).
Night (verse 5)—Hebrew: *layil* **(lah'-yil):** night; midnight; opposite of day.

TOPICAL OUTLINE OF THE LESSON

I. **Introduction**
   A. The Story of the Beginning
   B. Biblical Background

II. **Exposition and Application of the Scripture**
   A. God Is the Sovereign Creator of All that Exists
      (Genesis 1:1)
   B. God Transforms Chaos into Cosmos
      (Genesis 1:2)
   C. God Sovereignly Creates Light and Divides It from Darkness
      (Genesis 1:3-5)
   D. God Sovereignly Creates a Division for the Waters
      (Genesis 1:6-8)
   E. God Provides Fertility for the Earth
      (Genesis 1:9-13)

III. **Concluding Reflection**

I. INTRODUCTION

A. The Story of the Beginning

It is generally helpful to know how things started, and so the first book of the Bible sets out to tell us just that—the beginning of things. Genesis, or "in beginning," is a good name, for the book tells the beginning of all things connected with faith. *Genesis*, the name by which the book is commonly called, is transliterated from the Greek Septuagint and means "source, origin, ancestry, or birth." It must always be remembered that this book is interested in the beginning of the universe because of its religious value and its stress upon the sovereignty of God. Genesis neither emphasizes nor purports to explain matters of a scientific nature. Genesis does not seek to explain ***how*** God created, but ***why*** God created.

We find reported in Genesis the arrival of humankind, the entrance of sin into the world, the beginning of a redemptive plan, the inauguration of the Hebrew people and patriarchal society, and the beginning of institutional life as seen in the observance of the Sabbath. Though there is no stated purpose within the book itself, the name assigned to it is indicative of the general purpose of the book—to trace the beginnings of redemptive history. Genesis is an introduction to the story of redemption, which Christians believe reaches its climax in the New Testament. Genesis is designed as a "theological history" to show the origin of things—not from a detailed factual, scientific standpoint, but from a theological standpoint. Theology concerns itself with the study of God and His relation to humankind and the world.

If we try to read Genesis as a scientific document, we will come away disappointed. The opening chapters of Genesis alone are like nothing else in the Bible. Things happen in these chapters that are far removed not only from our own experiences, but also from the kinds of events described in the rest of the Bible. In Genesis, we find a forbidden tree, a snake that talks, a disgraced brother (Cain) who bears a mark that protects him from harm, a flood that covers the entire earth (including its highest mountains), and people who live to be nine hundred years old. Genesis is not history, nor is it science; it is a theological book that traces the beginnings of the redemptive purposes of God toward His creation. So, what are we to say of those who often perceive the book of Genesis as contradicting scientific fact? The Scriptures belong to the church. They contain what the church believes about the progressive revelation of God in human history. These Scriptures, when rightly understood, are our final source of authority in matters of faith and practice—whereas science, when properly conducted and applied, serves to amplify and elaborate on the gracious revelation that God gives to humankind through those Scriptures.

B. Biblical Background

The claim that God created the world and all that exists is a matter of faith, grounded in God's self-revelation. At this level, the opening chapters of Genesis are a confession of faith. In witnessing to God's creative activity, the biblical writers of Genesis made use of the available knowledge of the natural world. These chapters are prescientific in the sense that they predate modern science. If our view of the Bible insists that all information in it, of whatever sort, must correspond to scientific reality, then we will have to engage in all sorts of interpretive antics to try to bring Genesis in conformity to modern science. However, if we recognize that the writers of Genesis did not know everything about the world (for instance, the source of light or the age of the world), we can simply make note of that and move on. The Genesis text remains an indispensable theological resource that speaks powerfully to us about why God engaged in the creative acts found in Genesis.

The primary concerns of the book of Genesis are theological and kerygmatic (preaching). Those responsible for the material as we have it now were persons of faith concerned with speaking or reflecting on a word from God to other persons of faith. The voices of a living community of faith resound throughout these texts. Genesis was written with the problems and possibilities of a particular audience in view. The opening verses of this magnificent chapter form an awe-inspiring prologue to the book of Genesis. It is also significant that it has come to introduce the Old Testament and the whole of the Bible. It is the intended starting point of the biblical story.

With respect to the "why" of Genesis, the first chapter illuminates two theological affirmations. First, the sovereign creator God has a purpose and will for creation. The Creation exists only because of that will. The Creator continues to address the creation, calling it to faith response and glad obedience to His will. The creation has not been turned loose on its own, nor has it been given free reign for its own inclinations. However, the purposes of the Creator are not implemented in a coercive way or imposed as a tyrant might. The Creator loves and respects the creation. The freedom of creation is taken seriously by the Creator. Therefore, His sovereign rule is expressed in terms of faithfulness, patience, and sometimes anguish as He seeks to effect His will in the world He so loves.

Second, the creation, which exists only because of and for the sake of the Creator's purpose, has freedom to respond to the Creator in various ways. As the texts indicate, the response of creation to Creator is a mixture of faithful obedience and recalcitrant self-assertion. Both are present, though the negative response tends to dominate the narrative. Yet, God wills good and never gives up on His creation.

II. EXPOSITION AND APPLICATION OF THE SCRIPTURE

A. God Is the Sovereign Creator of All that Exists (Genesis 1:1)

IN THE beginning God created the heaven and the earth.

The first verse declares the message of the entire chapter in summary fashion: God created everything (verse 1). What is so striking about this great theological truth is that God (*Elohim*) is introduced simply as one who existed before anything in our universe. He is the very God of all creation and the universe in which it is set, and the reasons for His existence are known only to Himself. There is not a time when He was not, and there cannot be when He shall not be. God alone created the beauty of the earth.

The writer says succinctly and to the point that in the beginning, our God without beginning or end created. The verb used for "create" (*bara*) is used in Scripture exclusively in reference to the divine activity of God. Humans may make, form, or build, but when they "make" something, they take what already exists and simply refashion it in some form or another. However, when God creates He produces something new, fresh, and perfect. God created the heavens and the earth, signifying the whole universe. "Heaven" and "earth" indicate not only the heavens and the earth, but also everything in them. He did it all by Himself. The point of the opening verse is this: God is sovereign over all matter. Such sovereignty demands allegiance, for to acknowledge the Creator naturally leads to submission to Him. The Creator who creates creation affirms that God has a powerful purpose for His creation. Creation is not a careless, casual, or accidental matter.

B. God Transforms Chaos into Cosmos (Genesis 1:2)

And the earth was without form, and void; and darkness was upon the face of the deep. And the Spirit of God moved upon the face of the waters.

It is clear from the contents of verse 2 that something is drastically wrong at the outset. Two clauses set the circumstances as chaotic; the first says that the earth was "without form, and void." This key phrase indicates that the world must be shaped and populated by God before it can be pronounced as "good." The second clause reads, "darkness was upon the face of the deep" (verse 2). Darkness throughout the Bible represents evil and death; it is not conducive to life. This darkness covered the face of the deep, by which is meant the salty deep of the ocean or, figuratively, the abyss. Darkness is not a positive good; it is associated with everything we identify as destructive and productive of pain. Thus, it is dispelled by the first act of creation.

In the first part of Genesis 1:2, there is thus an ominous, uncomfortable tone. These two clauses describe not the results of divine creation, but chaos at the earliest stages of this world. In contrast to the first two clauses of verse 2, a third clause offers a positive thought: "the Spirit of God moved upon the face of the waters." The arena now is the life-giving water and not the chaotic, abyss-like deep. The activity of movement belongs to the Spirit of God. The verb used here means "flutter or fly," as an eagle stirring up the nest, fluttering over its young. In much the same way, the unformed, lifeless mass of the watery earth was under the care of the divine Spirit who hovered over it, ensuring its future development. God is the only source of anything that exists, and the ultimate will of God is for good and only good. Thus, He calls forth order out of disorder. God does not call the world to be chaotic, fragmented, or in conflict. In addition, He stays with it until it becomes as He wills it.

C. God Sovereignly Creates Light and Divides It from Darkness (Genesis 1:3-5)

And God said, Let there be light: and there was light.

And God saw the light, that it was good: and God divided the light from the darkness. And God called the light Day, and the darkness he called Night. And the evening and the morning were the first day.

At the beginning of the first day, the reader learns that the means of creation was the Word of God. The absolute control that God possesses over the cosmos (created order) is suggested by His first creative act, which is merely two words in Hebrew, translated "Let there be light," with an instantaneous result. God simply speaks and the cosmos responds. The word is power in itself, for there is no one to hear it and respond. There is no command; it is just God's spoken Word that has power.

Why is light the first thing created? Because light represents the presence of God Himself in the world. Also, light is associated with time. In the division of light from darkness, the day, which was the basic unit of time for the Jews, came into existence. Time itself was the result of God's first creative word. Thus, *darkness*—one of the symbols of formlessness, disorder, and threat to life—was brought under control on the first day. Although darkness was given a name and a time, God does not call it good. By creating light on the first day, God saw to it that light would restrict darkness even unto eternity. Moreover, light is called "good" by its Creator, meaning it is pleasing to God because it is suitable for His intended purposes. The idea of the word *good* is that the light is useful, fitting, and healthy. That which is good is conducive for and enhances life; so, light is good, not the darkness. Therefore, God affirms His sovereignty over both light and darkness by giving them names—*day* and *night*. In addition, with this, time begins.

The Bible shows repeatedly that light and darkness signify mutually exclusive realms, especially in spiritual matters of good and evil. Throughout Scripture, light is the realm of God and the righteous; darkness is the domain of the Evil One. Light represents that which is holy, pure, true, life-giving, and gladdening.

D. God Sovereignly Creates a Division for the Waters (Genesis 1:6-8)

And God said, Let there be a firmament in the midst of the waters, and let it divide the waters from the waters. And God made the firmament, and divided the waters which were under the firmament from the waters which were above the firmament: and it was so. And God called the firmament Heaven. And the evening and the morning were the second day.

Having no idea of infinite space, the writer of the book of Genesis thought the sky was something solid, either metal or ice, held up by pillars. This "dome" or "solid space" provided living space between the waters above (the source of rain and snow) and the waters on and below the earth. The sovereignty of God appears in this day's activity in His naming the space "heavens," or sky. Pagan mythology considered the heavens to be the dominion of the high gods. According to Genesis, however, God not only created this space, but also controlled it by making a division in it. The theological significance of this teaching involves Israel's confidence in the Lord as the supreme God of the heavens and their compliance with all the distinctions He made in His creation. The God who creates also has the power to name and to change what He has called into being. He hung the moon, the sun, and the stars in the sky, and He did it all by Himself.

E. God Provides Fertility for the Earth (Genesis 1:9-13)

And God said, Let the waters under the heaven be gathered together unto one place, and let the dry land appear: and it was so. And God called the dry land Earth; and the gathering together of the waters called he Seas: and God saw that it was good. And God said, Let the earth bring forth grass, the herb yielding seed, and the fruit tree yielding fruit after his kind, whose seed is in itself, upon the earth: and it was so. And the earth brought forth grass, and herb yielding seed after his kind, and the tree yielding fruit, whose seed was in itself, after his kind: and God saw that it was good. And the evening and the morning were the third day.

Genesis 1:9-13 witnesses a shift in God's way of creating; the earth itself participates in the creative process. On the third day, God caused the dry land to appear and the earth to flourish with vegetation. The emphasis now begins to shift from bringing order to bringing fullness. God decrees that fertile land appear through the gathering of water into reservoirs He called "seas." On the emerging dry land, God caused all manner of vegetation to appear—let the earth *vegetate*.

The decree for fertility stands in bold relief to ancient mythologies. Most ancient religions had rituals designed to induce the gods to produce crops and fruit. In contrast to such accounts of fertility, the writer of Genesis simply but powerfully says that God gathered the seas together and decreed that the fertile earth produce vegetation. Fertility is a self-perpetuating process decreed by God, the true Lord of life. There is no sea god, just the God who controls the seas. Vegetation does not result from some depraved pagan ritual; it results from the majestic Word of the sovereign Lord of creation.

III. CONCLUDING REFLECTION

The fact that the Creation account stands at the head of the canon (the official collection of biblical writings) is of considerable importance in conveying to us a message about God and His created order. The Bible purposely begins with a testimony to the universal activity of God. God's creative activity not only brought the world into being, but was also effectively engaged in the lives of individual peoples long before Israel came into being as a nation. The placing of the book of Genesis at the head of the biblical canon reflects the actual sequence of God's activity in the world. God was at work on behalf of the divine creational purposes long before Israel understood what this activity was all about. God's actions in the world achieve priority of place over human knowledge of what God has done. The position of Genesis 1–2 demonstrates that the sovereign God's purpose in redemption does not finally center on Israel alone. God as Creator has a purpose that spans the world, and since divine deeds are rooted in the divine will, God's redemptive activity reflected in creation must be understood to serve this universal intention. He is the God of all. He made us all and will redeem all who respond to His offer of redemption.

In addition, the goodness of the sovereign God's creation must always be of major interest to us. For example, those who believe that God created a good earth will be open to thoroughly enjoy all that He has given them. At the same time, they will be anxious to preserve it from the ravages of people who care nothing for what God has made and entrusted to humankind as His stewards. Those who believe God created everything good certainly will not be indifferent to developments which may serve to pollute and ruin, exterminate and defile all that He has made. Men and women who know they are created by God long to reflect something of His glory through lives of obedience and faith.

Mindful created people are grateful people. They are also people with a sense of wonder, for they cannot look dispassionately at humans or the beauty of the earth except that they see something of the Creator's handiwork. No person is insignificant, and no part of the created order is without meaning. This sense of awe and wonder makes created people worshippers, not only in the limited sense of attending church and singing praises, but also in the daily rounds of common tasks where we recognize that everything we do is done with His materials and time, and for His glory with the energy and skill His creative acts alone made available. Thanks be to God who has created all things!

Finally, the modern reader must confront the question of whether or not the book of Genesis is an adequate statement about creation for the contemporary times in which we live. We have learned truths about the origins, development, and nature of the world from modern science of which the biblical authors never dreamed. We are confronted with issues never faced by these authors, from the environment to the role of women. In seeking to address these issues in a responsible manner, we must go beyond the text and draw on insights from other parts of Scripture and from our own experience in and through which God continues to speak. At the same time, the opening chapters of Genesis will continue to provide the reader with an indispensable foundation for reflections on the images of God and the human, the relationship between God and the world He created, and human and nonhuman interrelationships. Genesis gives us a beginning knowledge of the God who made us, watches over us, sustains us, and redeems us.

PRAYER

Eternal God before whom the generations rise and fall, we give You thanks for Your wondrous acts of creation. We acknowledge Your sovereignty and care for that which You have so wonderfully created. We lift our hands and hearts to You in praise and adoration for the mighty things You have done to redeem us and to make us whole and complete. In Jesus' name we pray. Amen.

HOME DAILY BIBLE READINGS
(August 27–September 2, 2018)

God Created the Heavens and Earth
MONDAY, August 27: "In Your Suffering, Trust the Creator" (1 Peter 4:15-19)
TUESDAY, August 28: "Renewed by the Creator" (Colossians 3:8-11)
WEDNESDAY, August 29: "God Provides the Water" (Isaiah 41:17-20)
THURSDAY, August 30: "The Wind and Water Obey the Voice of Jesus" (Mark 4:35-41)
FRIDAY, August 31: "God Sends the Rain to Everyone" (Matthew 5:43-48)
SATURDAY, September 1: "God Is Great; God Is Good" (Psalm 33:1-9)
SUNDAY, September 2: "God Created the Heavens and Earth" (Genesis 1:1-13)

September 9, 2018   **Lesson 2**

GOD CREATED PLANTS AND ANIMALS

ADULT/YOUTH	CHILDREN
ADULT/YOUNG ADULT TOPIC: **Turn On the Lights!**	GENERAL LESSON TITLE: **God Created Light and Life**
YOUTH TOPIC: **Signs and Seasons**	CHILDREN'S TOPIC: **Light and Life**

DEVOTIONAL READING
Psalm 136:1-9

ADULT/YOUTH	CHILDREN
BACKGROUND SCRIPTURE: **Genesis 1:14-25**	BACKGROUND SCRIPTURE: **Genesis 1:14-25**
PRINT PASSAGE: **Genesis 1:14-25**	PRINT PASSAGE: **Genesis 1:14-25**
KEY VERSE: **Genesis 1:14**	KEY VERSES: **Genesis 1:16a, 21a**

Genesis 1:14-25—KJV

14 And God said, Let there be lights in the firmament of the heaven to divide the day from the night; and let them be for signs, and for seasons, and for days, and years:

15 And let them be for lights in the firmament of the heaven to give light upon the earth: and it was so.

16 And God made two great lights; the greater light to rule the day, and the lesser light to rule the night: he made the stars also.

17 And God set them in the firmament of the heaven to give light upon the earth,

18 And to rule over the day and over the night, and to divide the light from the darkness: and God saw that it was good.

19 And the evening and the morning were the fourth day.

20 And God said, Let the waters bring forth abundantly the moving creature that hath life, and fowl that may fly above the earth in the open firmament of heaven.

21 And God created great whales, and every living

Genesis 1:14-25—NIV

14 And God said, "Let there be lights in the vault of the sky to separate the day from the night, and let them serve as signs to mark sacred times, and days and years,

15 "and let them be lights in the vault of the sky to give light on the earth." And it was so.

16 God made two great lights—the greater light to govern the day and the lesser light to govern the night. He also made the stars.

17 God set them in the vault of the sky to give light on the earth,

18 to govern the day and the night, and to separate light from darkness. And God saw that it was good.

19 And there was evening, and there was morning—the fourth day.

20 And God said, "Let the water teem with living creatures, and let birds fly above the earth across the vault of the sky."

21 So God created the great creatures of the sea and every living thing with which the water teems and that

creature that moveth, which the waters brought forth abundantly, after their kind, and every winged fowl after his kind: and God saw that it was good.

22 And God blessed them, saying, Be fruitful, and multiply, and fill the waters in the seas, and let fowl multiply in the earth.

23 And the evening and the morning were the fifth day.

24 And God said, Let the earth bring forth the living creature after his kind, cattle, and creeping thing, and beast of the earth after his kind: and it was so.

25 And God made the beast of the earth after his kind, and cattle after their kind, and every thing that creepeth upon the earth after his kind: and God saw that it was good.

moves about in it, according to their kinds, and every winged bird according to its kind. And God saw that it was good.

22 God blessed them and said, "Be fruitful and increase in number and fill the water in the seas, and let the birds increase on the earth."

23 And there was evening, and there was morning—the fifth day.

24 And God said, "Let the land produce living creatures according to their kinds: the livestock, the creatures that move along the ground, and the wild animals, each according to its kind." And it was so.

25 God made the wild animals according to their kinds, the livestock according to their kinds, and all the creatures that move along the ground according to their kinds. And God saw that it was good.

UNIFYING LESSON PRINCIPLE: People's life experiences sometimes lead them to question whether the universe is ordered or unpredictably chaotic. How do the diverse parts of nature work together? Genesis 1 shares that God brought order to the universe He made, establishing the heavenly bodies and filling the sea, sky, and land with diverse and abundant life.

LESSON OBJECTIVES

Upon the completion of this lesson, the students will be able to do the following:

1. Explore the biblical writer's depiction of how God filled the universe with light and life.
2. Contemplate the ordered interrelatedness of God's creation and their place in it.
3. Become aware of the immensity and diversity of the physical universe.

AGE-LEVEL POINTS TO BE EMPHASIZED

Teachers of ADULTS and YOUTH

—While God created light on Day 1, apparent sources of light were not mentioned until Day 4.

—God created three broad categories of animals: those of the sea, the sky, and the land.

—Even though all animal life was included under the description of "good," some in each of these categories were later classified as clean (permitted as food) and unclean (not permitted as food). See Leviticus 11:1-19.

—Because God blessed them, animals had the ability to reproduce (verse 22).

—"The earth" participated with God in producing the land's animals (verse 24). The animals and the earth are also closely linked in the second Creation narrative; there, animals are made from the soil itself (Genesis 2:19).

—"It was good" carries a sense of satisfaction or measurable accomplishment—something delicious, acceptable, excellent, just right, as God intended. It is not a moral intention.

—Hebrew Scripture is largely the story of God's relationship with the people of Israel, but this origin narrative sets that important story in the larger context of creation of the universe and all that is.

—God orders the world with the "heavenly lights," providing day/night, months, years, and seasons. The same word for "seasons" is used for religious festivals in Hebrew, implying that God and creation work together on these.

Teachers of CHILDREN

—By proclamation, on the fourth day of Creation, God created the sun to light the earth by day and the moon and stars to provide light at night.

—God judged the lights that He created as good.

—By proclamation, on the fifth day of Creation, God created sky, sea, and land animals.

—God designed all animals so that they could reproduce their own kind.

—God instructed the animals that He created to reproduce plentifully.

—God judged the creation of sky, sea, and land animals as good.

THE CHRONOLOGICAL SETTING OF THE LESSON

The Old Testament does not attempt to write a history of Israel. Rather, it gives its witness to the work of God in establishing the nation. The Hebrews were the first ancient people to have a sense of history. Their contemporaries thought in cyclic terms and conceived of history as repeating itself. The Old Testament sees God as directing events toward the goal of the redemption of creation.

THE GEOGRAPHICAL AND CULTURAL SETTING OF THE LESSON

The Bible is a book of ancient origins. The first chapters tell us about the creation of the universe and of humankind, and of God and His dealings with humans from the beginning of the world. Further, the Bible has come to us in the setting of the ancient Near East. The Bible has to do primarily with the descendants of Abraham, God's chosen people. The people of the Bible reflect the culture that was their heritage and their setting. The way the people thought about God reflected the impact of their cultural heritage. Their concept of the material world as the immediate expression of God showed the impact of concept and practice. In the cultural setting of that day, Creation was viewed as having occurred over an indefinite period and having proceeded from the lower to the higher order of being. They believed God to be in charge of the creative process. Thus, there is no need to see Genesis and scientific theories as being in conflict with one another. Genesis was not written as a scientific paper. Genesis was written as witness to the fact that it is God who has made us, and we are His.

PROMINENT CHARACTER(S) IN THE LESSON

Elohim: a Hebrew word referring to gods in general and the most frequent Old Testament name for God. The origin of the word is unclear, although it may have derived from a root meaning "strength" or "power." The same or similar root may have been the source of the name *El*, of which some scholars believe *Elohim* to be the plural. (Note: This is repeated because the only prominent character in this lesson is God.)

KEY TERMS IN THE LESSON

Lights (verse 14)—Hebrew: *ma'owr* **(maw-ore'):** light; luminary.

Rule (verse 18)—Hebrew: *mashal* **(maw-shal'):** to rule; have dominion; reign; "govern" (NIV).

Set (verse 17)—Hebrew: *nathan* **(naw-than'):** to give; put or set.

Signs (verse 14)—Hebrew: *'owth* **(oth):** signs, signals; miracles.

Stars (verse 16)—Hebrew: *kowkab* **(ko-kawb'):** star; a star (as round or as shining).

Water(s) (verse 20)—Hebrew: *mayim* **(mah'-yim):** water; waters.

TOPICAL OUTLINE OF THE LESSON

I. **Introduction**
   A. The Creation of the Heavenly Bodies
   B. Biblical Background

II. **Exposition and Application of the Scripture**
   A. God Appoints Luminaries to Regulate Time (Genesis 1:14-19)
   B. God Creates Life in Sea and Sky (Genesis 1:20-23)
   C. God Creates Life for the Land (Genesis 1:24)
   D. God Saw Good in All that He Created (Genesis 1:25)

III. **Concluding Reflection**

I. INTRODUCTION

A. The Creation of the Heavenly Bodies

The Creation narrative is a document of faith. It is a quest for meaning and a statement of a religious position. Its quintessential teaching is that the universe is wholly the purposeful product of divine intelligence. It tells the story of the one self-sufficient, existing God who is a transcendent being outside of nature and who is sovereign over space and time. Genesis 1:3-25 covers five days of Creation. The structure of these verses is important, for it conveys a part of the theological message of the Creation narrative. Old Testament scholar Walter Brueggemann notes that the structure moves in a careful sequence:

Time: "there was evening and morning…"
Command: "God said, Let there be…"
Execution: "And it was so."
Assessment: "God saw that it was good."
Time: "there was evening and morning . . . ."

The time patterns in these verses reflect the good order of the created world under the serene rule of God. The rhetorical pattern reflects the movement of command and execution. God summons. It happens exactly as He commands. The design of the world is not autonomous or accidental. It is based on the will of God. Creation is in principle obedient to the will of God. Creation is what it is because God commands it. God gives permission for creation to be. It simply did not happen out of nowhere. All that we see and behold each day, all that unfolds before us in rhythmic beauty, come from the hands and the heart of the wonderful creator, God.

In Genesis 1:14-25, this sovereign God continues His task of filling the spheres of the physical cosmos as He now creates the luminaries (bodies that give light) to occupy the firmament of the sky: the sun, the moon, and the stars. Some would argue that the creation of the luminaries after that of vegetation is unnatural because plants are dependent upon sunlight for existence. However, for the writer of Genesis, light has existed since day 1, so this is not a problem.

God purposely made the luminaries on the fourth day, including the sun, moon, and stars. The objects created by God are not named as sun and moon, but rather "two great lights" (Genesis 1:16). While the writer says, "he made the stars also," significantly, no particular role is assigned to the stars. This silence constitutes a tacit repudiation of astrology. Our lives are not determined by the movement of the stars but, rather, by the purposeful acts of a loving Creator. In other ancient Near Eastern creation literature, luminaries are created as gods with personalities. In Mesopotamian culture, the sun was venerated as a god, and sun worship also featured in Israel's own previous history (see Ezekiel 8:16-18). The biblical writer of Genesis, however, is a rigid monotheist (an adherent of one God). Thus, the opening chapters of Genesis, as well as the Old Testament in general, refer to only one creator and one maintainer of all things—one God who created and transcends all cosmic matter.

To the Hebrews, the sun, moon, and stars were merely material entities called into being by God with a specific purpose. Their anonymity and unusually detailed description have the common purpose of emphasizing that the sun, moon, and stars are not divinities but simply the creations of the sovereign God who assigned to them specific purposes. The luminaries have essentially three functions: first, they separate day from night; second, they serve as signs for divisions of time, including seasons, days, and years; and third, they provide light for the earth. The guarded language of this chapter is intended to emphasize that these heavenly bodies are themselves merely a part of creation, with ironically one of their main functions being to ensure the proper worship of God. This fourth day, when the two great lights were called forth, is the midpoint of the seven days, which have both begun and will end by God's shaping of time.

God's creation of the luminaries on day 4 should evoke great wonder, praise, and thanksgiving on our part. In Psalm 136, the grand hymn of thanksgiving in the Old Testament, the psalmist directs our attention particularly to this creative day: Give thanks to Yahweh because He is good. Because of this creative work, Yahweh is worthy of our worship. Our destiny, our daily bread, our all in all are in His hands.

B. Biblical Background

A significant amount of space in the scriptural lesson for today is devoted to the creation of the sun and the moon in order to explain how they function. It is generally agreed that the sun and moon do not make their appearance until the fourth day so that the writer of Genesis can offer a critique of other existing religions. The heavenly bodies were worshipped in every religion except that of Israel's. The sun, moon, and Venus were often major deities in the pantheon (gods of other people), but not so in Israel. In the Genesis Creation narrative, the heavenly bodies (sun, moon, and stars) are certainly not deities, nor are they even essential for the existence of a habitable world. Their value is strictly defined and is limited to keeping time (see Genesis 1:14).

The calendar was very important to the priesthood, since it was the priests' responsibility to mark off the holy times and keep them sacred, and that interest appears here. Note especially the "seasons" which are mentioned in verse 14. They are not spring, fall, and the like, but the "appointed times," possibly in reference to the great pilgrimage feasts of Passover, Weeks, and Booths as well as other holy days. In some early Jewish traditions, New Year's Day always came on Wednesday, because that was when the calendar began with the appearance of these celestial timekeepers. In the writer's telling of the story of the world's beginning, time began with the creation of light on the first day; space for life was created on days 2 and 3; and timekeeping began in the middle of the week.

The sun and moon are such immense and obvious facts in the universal experience of the human race that it is natural that they should have entered often into religion. Solar myths were numerous. But here in these verses of Genesis is one of the many instances in which the Hebrew writer lifted up the instinctive conceptions of earlier peoples into a nobler faith. To the Hebrew, the sun and the moon are no longer mythical independent forces; they are now viewed as the handiwork of the one living God whose final work will be humankind. Next, God set about to provide for the populations that would enjoy His time and space—the fish of the sea, the winged fowl, and the living creatures of the earth (see Genesis 1:21).

II. EXPOSITION AND APPLICATION OF THE SCRIPTURE

A. God Appoints Luminaries to Regulate Time (Genesis 1:14-19)

And God said, Let there be lights in the firmament of the heaven to divide the day from the night; and let them be for signs, and for seasons, and for days, and years: And let them be for lights in the firmament of the heaven to give light upon the earth: and it was so. And God made two great lights; the greater light to rule the day, and the lesser light to rule the night: he made the stars also. And God set them in the firmament of the heaven to give light upon the earth, And to rule over the day and over the night, and to divide the light from the darkness: and God saw that it was good. And the evening and the morning were the fourth day.

The fourth day records how God created the luminaries—the sun, moon, and stars—to rule over the heavens. Luminaries have as their function to dominate the day and night, to serve as signs for the fixed seasons, and to rule over the heavens. The sun, moon, and stars are thus all God's creation, attesting to His glory and ruling over time by His decree. Not so in the mythology of the pagans. They thought of these heavenly bodies as objects of worship. We are so far removed from the world of Genesis that we can scarcely comprehend how revolutionary such a statement was—*that God made the two great lights*—uttered to those who were used to a universe whose heavens were peopled with gods, demons, and other evil spirits. In the prevailing superstition of that day, the sun, moon, and stars were thought to govern humankind's destiny as well as to determine their times and seasons. However, the writer of Genesis demotes these celestial bodies to pieces of created matter governing nothing except the sequence of light and darkness that God had already set in motion. Through this Creation narrative, Israel was taught to put her trust only in God, who created all these stars and planets by His Word. They must not give any credence or respect to the gods of the pagans (Vitter, 48).

Moreover, both earthly and heavenly bodies are all subject to the will of the Creator. They are witnesses to the glory of God and must not in any way be seen as overshadowing or shining in that glory. The brilliance of the sun, the moon, and the stars should direct the true believers' thoughts to the creator God. However, as Paul pointed out in the first chapter of the book of Romans, humans most often rejected the Creator and worshipped the creation. We are without excuse, for the writer of Genesis told us long ago that the one true God Yahweh was alone worthy of our worship, thanks, and praise. To look toward the heavens and see the great things God has done should prompt everyone to declare with the hymnist, "How great Thou art, how great Thou art."

B. God Creates Life in Sea and Sky (Genesis 1:20-23)

And God said, Let the waters bring forth abundantly the moving creature that hath life, and fowl that may fly above the earth in the open firmament of heaven. And God created great whales, and every living creature that moveth, which the waters brought forth abundantly, after their kind, and every winged fowl after his kind: and God saw that it was good. And God blessed them, saying, Be fruitful, and multiply, and fill the waters in the seas, and let fowl multiply in the earth. And the evening and the morning were the fifth day.

On the fifth day, God created all the living creatures that inhabit the seas and that fly across the skies. The word *create* is used here for the first time since Genesis 1:1, and it marks the appearance of living creatures. *Create* is a key word: a sign that what is happening now is a critical fresh stage in the orderly development of creation, and part of the deliberate intention of God (Amos, 10) This passage declares that life came into being by the direct command of God. Vegetation in not included here, for to the Hebrew mind, vegetation is not life.

The author of Genesis had a special interest in the sea creatures, however. The pagans worshipped the great sea creatures as dragons and monsters in rebellion that had to be subdued. In Canaanite and Babylonian mythology, great whales (sea monsters, verse 21) were considered as rivals of the gods who ruled the earth. They are not rivals of God, says Genesis. How could they be? If the sea swarms with life, it is by His command, and upon them rests the divine benediction to be fruitful and multiply. They are His creatures, just as are the living things of the land, the domesticated cattle, serpent life, and wild animals. The pagans may fear and venerate them as gods, but Israel knew that they were just another part of God's perfect and harmonious creation. God, not some pagan ritual, is the source of life and fertility (Ross, 111; Vawter, 43).

God's act of blessing is also a sign of the new stage that has been reached. Sea creatures and air creatures are blessed. Blessing at its core is connected with the love of and the gift of life. Life has always been important in Old Testament and Jewish culture; preservation of life supersedes even the Sabbath. God's presence is to be desired, precisely because in Him is the fullness of life. Animals (unlike plants) need to be blessed to ensure their ability to reproduce and thus continue the chain of life. So, in verse 22, blessing and the command to be fruitful are closely connected. Throughout Genesis, the author will repeatedly show us how this first command of God works itself out both in creation and in the world of human beings (Amos, 10).

C. God Creates Life for the Land
   (Genesis 1:24)

And God said, Let the earth bring forth the living creature after his kind, cattle, and creeping thing, and beast of the earth after his kind: and it was so.

On the final day of the physical creation, God forms the creatures that are to inhabit the dry land. There are two parts to this activity: first, God creates the animal kingdom, which includes livestock, creeping things, and wild animals. Second, humankind is formed. Three categories of animals are listed. The first describes large, four-footed domesticated animals. This is why the Hebrew word is usually translated as "cattle" or "livestock." The second category is creeping things, which refers to small animals. In addition, the third term, *beasts*, probably signifies wild animals. It is important to note that humankind never appears in any of these classifications. Humanity is not part of the animal world. The psalmist notes in Psalm 8 that God gave humans dominion over the beasts of the field.

Unlike the creatures of the sea and air, there is no pronouncement of a blessing on the land creatures. The absence of a blessing upon these categories of animals is striking. It may be owing to the fact that fish and fowl can proliferate without encroaching adversely upon humankind's environment, while the proliferation of animals, especially of the wild variety, could conceivably constitute a menace to humankind.

D. God Saw Good in All that He Created
   (Genesis 1:25)

And God made the beast of the earth after his kind, and cattle after their kind, and every thing that creepeth upon the earth after his kind: and God saw that it was good.

Genesis 1:25 repeats verse 24, with two significant changes. First, so that there is no confusion, it states that God is the primary source and cause of the creation of the animal kingdom. Second, the three categories of the animal kingdom are recapitulated in verse 25, but in a different sequence. The change in sequence is for the purpose of emphasizing the completion of the creative act. This is further accentuated by the statement "And God saw that it was good," a clause that also reflects the idea of completion (Currid, 84).

There are three main teachings behind this initial creative activity of God. First, God Himself—the true sovereign, wise, and personal God—stands behind creation. Second, the work of this true sovereign, wise, and personal God was an orderly work. Third, the creation was and is good, because it is the work of the God who is not only true, sovereign, wise, and personal, but also morally perfect.

Finally, the most obvious point of the first five days of creation is that God stands at the beginning of all things and is the one through whom all came into existence. Grammatically speaking, there is only one subject in all these verses: God Himself. Everything else is an object. Objects are acted upon. Light, air, water, dry land, vegetation, sun, moon, stars, fish, birds, land animals—all are objects in a creative process where God alone is the subject. In these verses, we are told that God saw, separated, called, made, and created. Moreover, before that, God spoke, which resulted in everything else that unfolded. When we are pleased with creation, as we should be, our praise should be directed to God who made all things, and not to creation itself. This is the first great dividing point between the religion of the Bible and most pagan religions. Pagans worship the object, but the Christian looks beyond the object to the God who made it and praises Him (Boice, 70-71).

III. CONCLUDING REFLECTION

In their symmetry and comprehensiveness, these verses affirm that God is the God of all creation. While much attention will be paid to the creation of humankind in the upcoming studies, today's lesson, with its focus on the God who creates the sun, moon, stars, plants, animals, and the fish of sea, is a reminder to us all that God is not totally preoccupied with human creatures. God has His own relation with the rest of creation. The others are also His faithful, valued, and obedient creatures. "It is good" is the repeated verdict pronounced over the creation. The first blessing in the Bible is not for humankind, but for the other creatures who have their own relation to God (Brueggemann, 31).

Earlier than the creation of humankind was the creation of sun, moon, stars, fish, and land animals. According to Genesis, humans are to have dominion over these. But it is not to be a brutal dominion. Humans are to delight in these as God did. To observe and study the majestic framework of the universe should lift and inspire our spirits. To stand in silence and watch the sunrise, or to walk out under the immense silence of the stars, should fill us with a sense of awe and wonder at the greatness of the creator God.

PRAYER

God of creation, we honor and praise Your name. Thank You for being not just the Creator, but most of all, our Father. In Jesus' name we pray. Amen.

HOME DAILY BIBLE READINGS
(September 3-9, 2018)

God Created Plants and Animals
MONDAY, September 3: "Creation, a Testament of God's Steadfast Love" (Psalm 136:1-9)
TUESDAY, September 4: "Jesus, Agent of God's Creation" (Hebrews 1:1-4)
WEDNESDAY, September 5: "All Creatures Depend on God" (Psalm 104:24-30)
THURSDAY, September 6: "Plants Witness to the Lord's Work" (Job 12:7-13)
FRIDAY, September 7: "Gifts from the Father of Lights" (James 1:17-18)
SATURDAY, September 8: "God Made All Creatures Clean" (Acts 11:5-9)
SUNDAY, September 9: "God Created Heavenly Lights and Animals" (Genesis 1:14-25)

September 16, 2018   **Lesson 3**

GOD CREATED PEOPLE

ADULT/YOUTH

ADULT/YOUNG ADULT TOPIC: Creation Is a Very Good Thing

YOUTH TOPIC: People Are Important

CHILDREN

GENERAL LESSON TITLE: God Created People

CHILDREN'S TOPIC: A Magnificent Creation

DEVOTIONAL READING
Psalm 103:1-5, 11-14

ADULT/YOUTH

BACKGROUND SCRIPTURE: Genesis 1:26–2:7

PRINT PASSAGE: Genesis 1:26-31; 2:4-7

KEY VERSE: Genesis 1:27

CHILDREN

BACKGROUND SCRIPTURE: Genesis 1:26–2:7

PRINT PASSAGE: Genesis 1:26-31; 2:4b-7

KEY VERSE: Genesis 1:26a

Genesis 1:26-31; 2:4-7—KJV

26 And God said, Let us make man in our image, after our likeness: and let them have dominion over the fish of the sea, and over the fowl of the air, and over the cattle, and over all the earth, and over every creeping thing that creepeth upon the earth.

27 So God created man in his own image, in the image of God created he him; male and female created he them.

28 And God blessed them, and God said unto them, Be fruitful, and multiply, and replenish the earth, and subdue it: and have dominion over the fish of the sea, and over the fowl of the air, and over every living thing that moveth upon the earth.

29 And God said, Behold, I have given you every herb bearing seed, which is upon the face of all the earth, and every tree, in the which is the fruit of a tree yielding seed; to you it shall be for meat.

30 And to every beast of the earth, and to every fowl of the air, and to every thing that creepeth upon the

Genesis 1:26-31; 2:4-7—NIV

26 Then God said, "Let us make mankind in our image, in our likeness, so that they may rule over the fish in the sea and the birds in the sky, over the livestock and all the wild animals, and over all the creatures that move along the ground."

27 So God created mankind in his own image, in the image of God he created them; male and female he created them.

28 God blessed them and said to them, "Be fruitful and increase in number; fill the earth and subdue it. Rule over the fish in the sea and the birds in the sky and over every living creature that moves on the ground."

29 Then God said, "I give you every seed-bearing plant on the face of the whole earth and every tree that has fruit with seed in it. They will be yours for food.

30 "And to all the beasts of the earth and all the birds in the sky and all the creatures that move along the

earth, wherein there is life, I have given every green herb for meat: and it was so.

31 And God saw every thing that he had made, and, behold, it was very good. And the evening and the morning were the sixth day.

.....

4 These are the generations of the heavens and of the earth when they were created, in the day that the LORD God made the earth and the heavens,

5 And every plant of the field before it was in the earth, and every herb of the field before it grew: for the LORD God had not caused it to rain upon the earth, and there was not a man to till the ground.

6 But there went up a mist from the earth, and watered the whole face of the ground.

7 And the LORD God formed man of the dust of the ground, and breathed into his nostrils the breath of life; and man became a living soul.

ground—everything that has the breath of life in it—I give every green plant for food." And it was so.

31 God saw all that he had made, and it was very good. And there was evening, and there was morning—the sixth day.

.....

4 This is the account of the heavens and the earth when they were created, when the LORD God made the earth and the heavens.

5 Now no shrub had yet appeared on the earth and no plant had yet sprung up, for the LORD God had not sent rain on the earth and there was no one to work the ground,

6 but streams came up from the earth and watered the whole surface of the ground.

7 Then the LORD God formed a man from the dust of the ground and breathed into his nostrils the breath of life, and the man became a living being.

UNIFYING LESSON PRINCIPLE: How the world and humans came to be is explored and questioned by many people. Where did people come from? According to the book of Genesis, God created people as the highest form of creation made in the image of God, and people are supported by all of God's creation.

LESSON OBJECTIVES

Upon the completion of this lesson, the students will be able to do the following:

1. Discern the biblical writer's message about the place of humanity in God's creation.
2. Value themselves and others as part of God's good creation.
3. Embrace God's call to practice good stewardship of the earth's abundance.

AGE-LEVEL POINTS TO BE EMPHASIZED

Teachers of ADULTS and YOUTH

—Genesis 1 establishes a hierarchy of authority. Humanity is divinely commissioned to govern other creatures on God's behalf, the ultimate purpose being that the whole earth should become the temple of God and the place of God's presence, and should display God's glory.

The nuanced meaning of "have dominion" is one of caregiving and nurturing. To "subdue" carries the connotation of continuing God's creative work by cultivating and developing it into something productive.

—Although God created humans on the sixth day with the other animals, God gave humans a special place among all living things. God made humans in the divine image and gave them "dominion" over all other living things—a charge to take care of creation in positive, creative ways.

—Being created in the image of God is more about having God's essential nature than about physical likeness.

—The words *subdue* and *have dominion* (verse 28) have become sticking points for those who fear that human activity has harmed the natural world more than it has helped.

—The language of verse 27 is a play on words in Hebrew: *adam*, a man, is made from dust, *adamah*. The "humanity from dust" imagery reminds us of our frailty and the fragility of life.

—The word for "God" in the chapter 1 Creation narrative is the more generic *Elohim*, but in chapter 2, both *Elohim* and *Yahweh* (the names God discloses to Moses) are used.

—In verse 5, we see that the earth is unproductive because God needs to do something (produce rain) and humans need to do something (cultivate), again pointing to the cooperative nature of creation.

Teachers of CHILDREN

—On the sixth day, God did the last act of Creation: the creation of humankind.

—Human beings were made "in the image of God," connoting that humans have the characteristics of God.

—God gave humankind "dominion," authority over nature; but, as God's representatives, a benevolent rulership can be inferred.

—God instructed humankind to "be fruitful and multiply," connoting biological reproduction.

—God gave humans and other animals the plants and fruit of the trees to eat.

—God judged everything that He had made to be good.

THE CHRONOLOGICAL SETTING OF THE LESSON

The basic theme of Genesis 1–2 undergirds the thinking of all the biblical writers. We must not interpret Genesis as a book containing separate stories, but as a book in which the various stories of the fathers have been combined in order to present a unified record of the work of God in this world. Chapter 1 opens with a glorious picture of God's creative acts and His charges and promises to humankind. The authors of Genesis have given accounts from two different traditions so as to give the full picture of what they believe happened in the beginning. Not only is God at work in His world, but He is also at work with a good purpose for humankind.

THE GEOGRAPHICAL AND CULTURAL SETTING OF THE LESSON

Reserved for His last act of creation was God's masterpiece—humankind. Destined to be the custodians of the earth and lords of all other living things, humans were to be the crowning glory of God's creative activity. For this reason, God lavished all His care upon the creature who was to be most like Himself. If humans were to have dominion over everything that had been made, then they would have to be similar to the One who had created all. They would need to reflect the divine nature and be able to understand the divine plan for the world. Just as animal life did not evolve from plant life, so humans did not evolve from the lower level of animal existence. The custodian of the universe was to be human, neither divine nor like the previously created animals. They would be created in the image and likeness of God and assigned the great work of dominion over all the earth.

PROMINENT CHARACTER(S) IN THE LESSON

Humankind (Hebrew: *adam*): a generic term for humankind; it never appears in Hebrew in the feminine or plural. In the first five chapters of Genesis, it is only rarely a proper name, Adam. The term encompasses both man and woman.

KEY TERMS IN THE LESSON

Created (1:27)—Hebrew: *bara'* (baw-raw'): to make; to create, shape, form.
Dominion (1:26)—Hebrew: *radah* (raw-daw'): to "rule" (NIV), have dominion, dominate, tread down.
Fruitful (1:28)—Hebrew: *parah* (paw-raw'): to bear fruit, be fruitful, branch off; increased.
Image (1:26)—Hebrew: *tselem* (tseh'-lem): image; likeness (or resemblance).

Man (1:26)—Hebrew: *'adam* (aw-dawm'): man; "mankind" (NIV); human being.
Seed (1:29)—Hebrew: *zera`* (zeh'-rah): seed, sowing; offspring.

TOPICAL OUTLINE OF THE LESSON

I. **Introduction**
    A. Humankind: The Crown of God's Labors
    B. Biblical Background

II. **Exposition and Application of the Scripture**
    A. God Creates Human Life (Genesis 1:26)
    B. God Ordained Sexuality (Genesis 1:27)
    C. Humankind as Ruler over Other Beings (Genesis 1:28)
    D. Humans and the Blessings of God (Genesis 1:29-31; 2:4-7)

III. **Concluding Reflection**

I. INTRODUCTION
A. Humankind: The Crown of God's Labors

On the first day, God created light and then distinguished the light from the darkness. On the second day, He created the heavens and separated the upper from the lower waters. On the third day, He separated the seas from the dry land and brought plants into existence. On the fourth day, God went back to the light and created the sun, the moon, and the stars, by which the seasons are determined. On the fifth day, He created the creatures of the seas and the fowls of the heavens. On the sixth day, God created the creatures of the land followed by the special creation of humankind.

Today's lesson begins by telling how God executed the special creation of humankind. The Scriptures do not say that humans were created in the image and likeness of the beasts. Rather, God said, "Let us make man in our image, and after our likeness." In their nature, person, and personality; in their moral and spiritual capacities; in their emotions, intellect, conscience, and will, humans stand apart from the lower brute creation. God begins with humankind's moral and spiritual nature and relates them to God.

Humans are placed on the stage of creation after all else has been formed. They are represented as the crown of God's labors. The creature called man (*Adam*) is formed in the image of God, in His likeness. These words reflect the Torah's abiding wonder over humankind's special stature in creation and over their unique intellectual capacity which bears the imprint of the Creator. Marveling at humankind's powers, the Bible finds them to be "a little lower than the angels" (Psalm 8:6). This likeness also describes humankind's moral potential. Humankind's nature is radically different from God's, but humans are capable of approaching God's actions—His love, His mercy, and His justice. Humankind becomes truly human as they attempt to do godly deeds. Humans also bear likeness to the Divine in their essential holiness, and by implication, in their dignity for all people. On the sixth day (see Genesis 1:31), all the land creatures are made, including human beings, as a way of acknowledging what people have in common with the other animals. No blessing is given until it can include the relationship between human beings and the other creatures. Six times the Bible says that God found His creation "good," but after humans were created He found it "very good" (Genesis 1:31).

B. Biblical Background

The first act of the sixth day sees the earth bringing forth land animals, as it had previously produced vegetation on the corresponding third day (see Genesis 1:11-12). The primary interest of the sixth day, however, is with the creation of humanity. Humans are distinguished from the rest of creation, and their significance is most heightened by God's command to make them "in our image, after our likeness" (Genesis 1:26).

While the text of Genesis 1 does not state explicitly what the image is, it does provide hints. If humans are in God's image, then there must be some analogy between God and humans. One such analogy is provided in Genesis 1:26b, with its granting of dominion over creation. God has just demonstrated His dominion by creating these creatures; the granting of human dominion over these same creatures is one way, perhaps the major way, in which human activity reflects the divine and thus indicates something of the "image of God" in humans. The blessing on humans in Genesis 1:28 adds two more elements. The first, "be fruitful and multiply, and fill the earth," is shared with the creatures of the sea and air. But the second, "subdue the earth," is a separate and uniquely human destiny. Thus, human subjugation of the earth and dominion over animals bear analogy with divine activity and represents at least part of the human condition of being in the image of God. Just as God previously created light (day 1) and then transferred this responsibility to the heavenly bodies of light—sun, moon, and stars—so here He transfers dominion over creation to human beings. This suggests that the "image of God" in humans refers not only to what humans are but also primarily to what they do.

II. EXPOSITION AND APPLICATION OF THE SCRIPTURE

A. God Creates Human Life
(Genesis 1:26)

And God said, Let us make man in our image, after our likeness: and let them have dominion over the fish of the sea, and over the fowl of the air, and over the cattle, and over all the earth, and over every creeping thing that creepeth upon the earth.

Before creating human beings, God took counsel—"Let us make man." This unique reference to God's reflecting in community before making something underscores both the importance and uniqueness of that humanity God was about to create. That community is either the plurality of the deity, or the heavenly council witnessed to in several other texts (see 1 Kings 22:19-22; Job 1:6-12). That God undertakes to consult underscores the importance He attached to the creation of humankind. The crowning point of creation is human life. Like the animals, humans were formed from the ground, given provision of food, and blessed with fruitfulness. However, humans are far more than animals. The Scriptures show that human life was set apart in relation to God by the divine plan ("let us make man"), by the divine pattern ("in our image"), and by the divine purpose ("let him have dominion").

With whom does God take counsel, and with whom does He share the "our" of the divine image and likeness in which He contemplates the creation of humans? These are longstanding questions to which no fully satisfactory answers have been given. Contrary to what some of the early fathers of the church thought, there are no allusions in these pronouns to the later Christian doctrine of a trinity of persons in the one Godhead. A more plausible thought is that when God employs the "let us" plural of majesty, this supposes that there is in Him such a fullness of being that He can deliberate with Himself just as several persons deliberate among themselves. We see the God who deliberates with Himself again in Hebrews 6:13: "For when God made promise to Abraham, because he could swear by no greater, he sware by himself." It is this same plurality of which the writer of Genesis speaks (Vawter, 53). Therefore, the plural in Genesis 1:26 should be considered as a plurality of majesty.

The next phrase, "after our image," expresses God's intent to mirror Himself to the world, to be an extension of His own dominion. The statement about the image of God (verses 26-27) must be understood in juxtaposition to Israel's resistance to any image of God. During the Exile, Israel resisted every effort to image God. Israel was at pains to affirm the otherness and transcendence of God. For the Israelites, there was only one way in which God could be imaged to the world, and that way was through human beings. This is the only creature, the only part of creation, which discloses to us something about the reality of God. This God is not known through any cast or molten image. God is known peculiarly through this human creature who exists in freedom—where power is received, decisions are made, and commitments are honored. God is not imaged in anything fixed, but He is imaged in the freedom of human persons to be faithful and gracious. This contrast between fixed images which are prohibited and a human image, which is affirmed, represents a striking proclamation about the creator God and humanness. The image of God in the human being is a mandate of power and responsibility.

B. God Ordained Sexuality (Genesis 1:27)

So God created man in his own image, in the image of God created he him; male and female created he them.

The Hebrew emphasizes the phrase "male and female" by placing it before the verb— "male and female created he them." This verse contains four important ideas: (a) It ascribes sexuality to God's design for humans. The distinctions of sexuality are ordained of God. If we imagine God as predominantly male or female, our picture is partial and distorted. (b) This reference to God's ordaining the distinctives of human sexuality sets the stage for God's blessing humans with fertility and commanding them to populate the earth. Sex is a gift from God! It is a gift to be shared between a husband and his wife. (c) This phrase establishes the fact that every male and female is made in the image of God. In the essence of our humanity, there is no qualitative difference between male and female. In other words, males are not a little more human or more reflective of God's image than females; we are all equally human in the creative hands of God. (d) We learn from this verse that God made humans as social creatures who discover their identities and destiny in relationships characterized by friendly and cordial relations with one another.

"Male and female" conveys that the basic reciprocating human relationship is between a man and a woman, but beyond that basic relationship, humans are to form communities in the broader world for sustaining and enriching their lives. God has so decreed that people need people, sensing that we are enriched through the establishment of deep bonds of friendship and love. We are all human and equal in the eyes of God, irrespective of race, ethnicity, or gender. Humanity exists in community, as one beside the other; there can only be anything like humanity and human relations where the human species exists in twos and in togetherness. Human beings must be seen as those whose destiny it is to live in community; people have been created to live with each other. Every deliberate detachment of male from female can endanger the very existence of humanity as determined by creation. God wills for us to engage in healthy, wholesome relationships with one another. We are to live out those bonds of friendship to God's honor and to God's glory.

C. Humankind as Ruler over Other Beings (Genesis 1:28)

And God blessed them, and God said unto them, Be fruitful, and multiply, and replenish the earth, and subdue it: and have dominion over the fish of the sea, and over the fowl of the air, and over every living thing that moveth upon the earth.

God further instructs humankind to subdue the earth and have dominion over every living thing that moves on the earth. Humanity is to exercise sovereignty over the rest of creation. The verb for "subdue" in Hebrew means "to subjugate." It is a word particularly associated with the rule of kings. Monarchs were to look after the welfare of the citizens. According to the ancient view, however, there is no suggestion of exploitation in this kind of rule; on the contrary, the king is personally responsible for the well-being and prosperity of those he rules. His rule serves the well-being of his subjects. That is what is meant here by humanity's rule over the rest of creation. Humankind is to serve and preside over the well-being of all the creatures over which they rule.

The words "to have dominion over" mean to be stewards, guardians, or caretakers who are answerable to God for the way in which they use His world. Although these commands empower humans to be masters of the animal kingdom—and by extension, of the earth—they do not give them the right to abuse or to kill animals wantonly. Nor do they ordain humans to rule imprudently by abusing the earth so that nature no longer supports various species. Such an abuse of authority would be a distortion of God's purpose, which includes working for the benefit of those under human authority. That God made animals and humans on the same day, and the fact that they belong to the same classification of living creature, attest to their closeness. Consequently, in promoting the welfare of animals, humans advance their own well-being. The power of dominion must be understood in terms of caregiving, even nurturing, but not exploitation. As the image of God, human beings should relate to the nonhuman as God relates to them—with love, care, and concern.

Humans are to aid in the task of bringing the world along to its fullest possible potential. The task of dominion does not have to do with exploitation and abuse. It has to do with securing the well-being of every other creature and bringing the promise of each to full fruition. It has been the tragedy of humankind's history that they thought they were given dominion over nature for their own benefit. Now humans are coming to realize that their dominion consists of the responsibility to help every aspect of nature to attain its highest goal. In a sense, humans are to join God in the awesome task of continuing the work of creation.

Finally, the Christian understanding of dominion must be discerned in the way of Jesus of Nazareth (see Mark 10:43-44). The one who rules is the one who serves. Lordship means servanthood. The human person is ordained over the remainder of creation for its profit, well-being, and enhancement. The role of the human person is to see to it that the creation becomes fully what the creator God willed it to be (Brueggemann, 33).

D. Humans and the Blessings of God
(Genesis 1:29-31; 2:4-7)

And God said, Behold, I have given you every herb bearing seed, which is upon the face of all the earth, and every tree, in the which is the fruit of a tree yielding seed; to you it shall be for meat. And to every beast of the earth, and to every fowl of the air, and to every thing that creepeth upon the earth, wherein there is life, I have given every green herb for meat: and it was so. And God saw every thing that he had made, and, behold, it was very good. And the evening and the morning were the sixth day . . . . These are the generations of the heavens and of the earth when they were created, in the day that the LORD God made the earth and the heavens, And every plant of the field before it was in the earth, and every herb of the field before it grew: for the LORD God had not caused it to rain upon the earth, and there was not a man to till the ground. But there went up a mist from the earth, and watered the whole face of the ground. And the LORD God formed man of the dust of the

ground, and breathed into his nostrils the breath of life; and man became a living soul.

God empowered humans with a special blessing in which He commanded them to be fruitful and multiply in order that they might fill the earth and subdue it. While the human capability to reproduce is inherent in the human physical constitution, fertility results from God's blessing. This belief differentiated Israel's understanding of fertility from that of its neighbors, who believed that fertility rites practiced at local shrines enabled their lands, flocks, and wives to produce abundantly.

In verses 30-31, we see that God preserves what He creates. What He brings into being He provides for its upkeep. Humanity is to have as food the seed and fruit of plants. Animals and birds are to have the leaves. At no point is anything (human being, animals, birds) allowed to take the life of another living being and consume it for food. The dominion assigned to the couple over the animal world does not include the prerogative to butcher. Instead, humankind survives on a vegetarian diet. Two features distinguish this last verse of the chapter from the preceding verses. First, "good" now becomes "very good." Second, while God saw what He made on each of the preceding five days in isolation, on the sixth day He saw all He made collectively. Both of these unique factors help to mark this sixth day as the highest point of God's creation thus far.

In Genesis 2:4-7, we are given some specifics as to how God created humankind. In the first chapter of Genesis, we are only given general assertions regarding the origin of human life, but in Genesis 2 we are told that God formed humans of the "dust of the ground." In Genesis 1:27, the writer makes it clear that humans were created as a distinct act of the Lord, which set them apart from other animals. But now, we have further clarification on what materials were used and how. We learn that existing earth particles were used to make humans, and that the Creator shaped or fashioned these ingredients into a physical specimen.

The verb translated "formed" (verse 7) is frequently used of the action of a potter, so humankind's creation is portrayed in terms of God's molding the clay soil into shape and then animating it. This image reveals a God who focuses closely on the object to be created and takes painstaking care to shape each one into something useful and beautiful. This means that humans were to be an integral part of the world itself, since they too were made of native dust and destined to return to the soil. God as potter shapes humans according to divine design. This combination of being made from clay and in the image of God, being made of the same substance as the earth, but made for dominion over it, constitutes a profound statement about human identity.

Also, for the first time God was given a personal name, Jehovah (*Yahweh*). Since the Supreme Being has taken such care in creating humans in chapter 2, we would expect Him to be understood as a personal God. Jehovah, this personal God, then breathes into the earthen vessel He has made the "breath of life" (Genesis 2:7). The eternal God has now shared His very life and being with humanity. The word for "breath" is *ruach*, the same as that for wind or spirit. Thus, we see that the Spirit that had earlier moved over the waters now moved over humans and took up residence within them. This life-giving Spirit is responsible for the unique nature of humans, causing them to reflect God's nature. The breath of God should not be confused with humankind's physically controlled inhaling and exhaling of air. Other animal life does this as well as humans. Here, it is well to note that the word translated "a living soul" (verse 7) is *nepesh* and means "a complete person." To be breathed into by God carries with it the idea of being physically endued with a quality of being which is beyond physical existence.

III. CONCLUDING REFLECTION

In the opening chapters of Genesis, we learn that humans occupy a special place in the hierarchy of creation and that they enjoy a unique relationship with God by virtue of their being the work of God's own hands, created in His own image and likeness. In one sense, humans bear the marks of divinity, for we are directly animated by God's own breath. But in another sense, we are reminded that humans are but dust taken from the earth, mere clay in the hands of the divine Potter. According to the will of God, we are and remain an odd mixture of dust and divinity. God alone is to be praised as our creator, redeemer, and sustainer. Thanks be to God.

PRAYER

Dear heavenly Father, help us never to forget that we are the products of Your creative hands. We give praise and thanks to You for the breath and life You have so graciously bestowed upon us. In Jesus' name we pray. Amen.

HOME DAILY BIBLE READINGS
(September 10-16, 2018)

God Created People

MONDAY, September 10: "God Glorified in the Heavens" (Psalm 104:1-4)

TUESDAY, September 11: "People Created in God's Likeness" (Ephesians 4:17-24)

WEDNESDAY, September 12: "Light of the Gospel" (2 Corinthians 4:1-6)

THURSDAY, September 13: "Living in the Light of God" (1 John 1:5-10)

FRIDAY, September 14: "Observe and Keep the Sabbath Holy" (Deuteronomy 5:12-15)

SATURDAY, September 15: "The Seventh Day, Hallowed and Blessed" (Genesis 2:1-3)

SUNDAY, September 16: "God Created People" (Genesis 1:26-31; 2:4-7)

September 23, 2018 — Lesson 4

GOD CREATED THE FAMILY

ADULT/YOUTH
ADULT/YOUNG ADULT TOPIC: **Relationships Are Important**
YOUTH TOPIC: **Where Do I Fit?**

CHILDREN
GENERAL LESSON TITLE: **God Created the Family**
CHILDREN'S TOPIC: **We Live in Families**

DEVOTIONAL READING
Leviticus 19:11-18

ADULT/YOUTH
BACKGROUND SCRIPTURE: **Genesis 2:18-24; 4:1-2**
PRINT PASSAGE: **Genesis 2:18-24; 4:1-2**
KEY VERSE: **Genesis 2:24**

CHILDREN
BACKGROUND SCRIPTURE: **Genesis 2:18-24; 4:1-2**
PRINT PASSAGE: **Genesis 2:18-24; 4:1-2**
KEY VERSE: **Genesis 2:18**

Genesis 2:18-24; 4:1-2—KJV

18 And the LORD God said, It is not good that the man should be alone; I will make him an help meet for him.

19 And out of the ground the LORD God formed every beast of the field, and every fowl of the air; and brought them unto Adam to see what he would call them: and whatsoever Adam called every living creature, that was the name thereof.

20 And Adam gave names to all cattle, and to the fowl of the air, and to every beast of the field; but for Adam there was not found an help meet for him.

21 And the LORD God caused a deep sleep to fall upon Adam, and he slept: and he took one of his ribs, and closed up the flesh instead thereof;

22 And the rib, which the LORD God had taken from man, made he a woman, and brought her unto the man.

23 And Adam said, This is now bone of my bones, and flesh of my flesh: she shall be called Woman, because she was taken out of Man.

Genesis 2:18-24; 4:1-2—NIV

18 The LORD God said, "It is not good for the man to be alone. I will make a helper suitable for him."

19 Now the LORD God had formed out of the ground all the wild animals and all the birds in the sky. He brought them to the man to see what he would name them; and whatever the man called each living creature, that was its name.

20 So the man gave names to all the livestock, the birds in the sky and all the wild animals. But for Adam no suitable helper was found.

21 So the LORD God caused the man to fall into a deep sleep; and while he was sleeping, he took one of the man's ribs and then closed up the place with flesh.

22 Then the LORD God made a woman from the rib he had taken out of the man, and he brought her to the man.

23 The man said, "This is now bone of my bones and flesh of my flesh; she shall be called 'woman,' for she was taken out of man."

24 Therefore shall a man leave his father and his mother, and shall cleave unto his wife: and they shall be one flesh.

.....

AND ADAM knew Eve his wife; and she conceived, and bare Cain, and said, I have gotten a man from the LORD.

2 And she again bare his brother Abel. And Abel was a keeper of sheep, but Cain was a tiller of the ground.

24 That is why a man leaves his father and mother and is united to his wife, and they become one flesh.

.....

ADAM MADE love to his wife Eve, and she became pregnant and gave birth to Cain. She said, "With the help of the LORD I have brought forth a man."

2 Later she gave birth to his brother Abel. Now Abel kept flocks, and Cain worked the soil.

UNIFYING LESSON PRINCIPLE: Humans often wonder what their purpose is in life and how they relate to all that is around them. What is our purpose and where do we fit in? According to the book of Genesis, God created families to support and care for one another and to care for all of God's creation.

LESSON OBJECTIVES

Upon the completion of this lesson, the students will be able to do the following:
1. Explore the teaching of Genesis concerning God's intention for families.
2. Affirm the gift of sexual differences as part of God's good creation.
3. Commit to relating to the members of one's family with mutuality and respect.

AGE-LEVEL POINTS TO BE EMPHASIZED

Teachers of ADULTS and YOUTH

—A paradox exists in that Adam was with God, yet Adam was alone. They were not equals. Adam needed a partner.

—Animals are created from the ground but are not said to receive God's breath (see 2:7, 19).

—The part of the body customarily translated "rib" (Genesis 2:21), out of which God made the second human, is actually uncertain, since the Hebrew term *tsela`* is not used anywhere else in reference to the human body.

—Genesis 2:23 introduces two new Hebrew terms: *ishshah*, which means "woman" or "wife,"

and *ish*, which means "man" or "husband." These two terms link the woman and man together biologically and socially. The Hebrew play on words emphasizes their likeness and compatibility.

—Verse 24 establishes the institution of marriage as having priority over the parent/child relationship.

—In Hebrew, the name *Cain* sounds like the verb for "given life to" or "created," a suitable name for the first human born.

—Woman's being called "helper" does not refer to her status. For example, God is called the "helper" of humanity, using the same Hebrew word. In this case, "helper" is not meant to imply a subordinate relationship with the man.

—Adam and Eve are intimately interconnected, and not just sexually; in every way, they are one flesh.

—Eve's reference to the Lord's help when Cain is born conveys a sense of optimism. The serpent may yet be overthrown by the offspring of the woman.

Teachers of CHILDREN

—After God created the first human, He decided to provide him help in caring for creation.

—God created all types of animals, and the first human gave each one a name.

—Since none of the animals created were suitable as a helper or partner for the first human, God created a woman made out of the flesh of the man.

—The marriage of man and woman, both as a physical and psychological unit that is organized as a separate kinship group, is substantiated in 2:24.

—The physical union of the first man and woman produced children, who became part of the first family.

—God created woman for a special relationship with man.

THE CHRONOLOGICAL SETTING OF THE LESSON

After the cosmic assertions of Genesis 1, the biblical text now focuses on human persons as the glory and central problem of creation. The destiny of human creation is to live in God's world, not in a world of its own making. The context of this world is laid out in rapid chronological order: A creature is formed from clay that is totally dependent upon God. There is the planting of a garden called Eden as a good place for the creature, and there is the identification of two trees—the Tree of Life and the Tree of the Knowledge of Good and Evil (see Genesis 2:4-17). God then creates woman and calls the woman and man into a loving relationship of mutuality and trust, togetherness and unity.

In His creative wisdom, God recognizes that the man needs a helper. God does not intend to be his helper. The "help" that the man needs and must have will be found among the "earthlings." That the helper must be creature not creator shows to what extent creation is left to its own resources and expected to honor its vocation, explore its freedom, and respect God-ordained prohibitions. Even though the helper would come from the earth, not just any helper would do. None of the known elements would suffice. There must be newness. The good news of the passage is that the well-being of the man requires a fresh creative act of God. The emergence of woman is as stunning and unpredicted as the previous emergence of the man. The woman is also God's free creation. The place of the garden is for this covenanted human community of solidarity, trust, and well-being. They are the beginning of the God-ordained family.

THE GEOGRAPHICAL AND CULTURAL SETTING OF THE LESSON

The place that God prepared for the first human to live in must have been exquisitely beautiful. Its very name, "Eden," is synonymous with paradise. The original meaning of the word is lost in obscurity. It may have been related to a Hebrew word denoting "bliss" or "delight," or it might have come from a Mesopotamian word that means simply "a plain." In any event, it was Eden that God planted—a garden where the first human couple was to make their first home. God made the man and woman as the crown and climax of His creative activity, as His highest and finest creations, as the particular objects of His special providence and care. In keeping with the intentional will of God, the man found his only suitable counterpart in woman, who together became the physical and spiritual progenitors of the entire human family.

PROMINENT CHARACTER(S) IN THE LESSON

Woman (*Genesis 2:23*): a fitting helper; a helper corresponding to the man.

KEY TERMS IN THE LESSON

Call (2:19)—Hebrew: *qara'* (kaw-raw'): "name" (NIV); to call, call out, recite, read, cry out, proclaim.

Cleave (2:24)—Hebrew: *dabaq* (daw-bak'): to cling, stick, stay close, cleave; joined; "is united" (NIV).

Formed (2:19)—Hebrew: *yatsar* (yaw-tsar'): maker; to form, fashion, frame.

Helper (2:18)—Hebrew: *`ezer* (ay'-zer): one who helps; help; succor; "help meet" (KJV).

Sleep (2:21)—Hebrew: *tardemah* (tar-day-maw'): deep sleep; trance.

Taken (2:22)—Hebrew: *laqach* (law-kakh'): to take, get, fetch, lay hold of, seize, receive, acquire.

TOPICAL OUTLINE OF THE LESSON

I. Introduction
  A. The Genesis Family versus the Modern American Family
  B. Biblical Background

II. Exposition and Application of the Scripture
  A. A Helper for the Man (Genesis 2:18)
  B. Dominion over the Animals (Genesis 2:19-20)
  C. God as Creator and Matchmaker (Genesis 2:21-23)
  D. The Two Become One (Genesis 2:24)
  E. The Result of Oneness (Genesis 4:1-2)

III. Concluding Reflection

I. INTRODUCTION

A. The Genesis Family versus the Modern American Family

The family of which the Bible speaks and the family of modern-day America are quite different in many ways. The Bible speaks of a man and a woman joined together in covenantal love that can only be severed by death. The children born of this union—often called a "traditional" family—know and feel the abiding love of two parents who care for them deeply and who desire to raise them in the nurture and admonition of the Lord. This classical traditional family—the kind imprinted on the American imagination by TV shows like *Leave It to Beaver* and *The Cosby Show*—has long since been left behind. In 1960, 37 percent of households included a married couple raising their own children. More than a half-century later, just 16 percent of households look like that.

Americans are putting families together later in life and in various ways. Today, the median age at first marriage is 29 for men and 27 for women, which is the highest in modern history. Mothers are also waiting longer to have children. In 1960, women ages

15 to 24 accounted for 40 percent of mothers with infants. By 2011, that number had dropped to 22 percent. Intermarriage among people of different races is also increasingly common. In 1980, just 7 percent of all marriages in the U.S. were between spouses of different races or ethnicities. In 2010, that share has doubled to 15 percent of all new marriages in America. Hispanics (26 percent) and Asians (28 percent) were most likely to "marry out," compared with 9 percent of whites and 17 percent of blacks. Families today are more blended and differently constructed. Nearly half (44 percent) of young people ages 18 to 29 have a stepsibling, while only 16 percent of those older than 65 have a stepsibling. More babies are born to unmarried mothers than ever before. Unmarried women accounted for 41 percent of births in a recent survey, up from just 5 percent in 1960.

Because of these changes, there is no longer one dominant family form in the United States. Parents today are raising their children against a backdrop of increasingly diverse and, for many, constantly evolving family forms. By contrast, in 1960, at the height of the post-World War II baby boom, there was one dominant family form. At that time, 73 percent of all children were living in a family with two married parents in their first marriage. By 1980, 61 percent of children were living in this type of family, and today less than half (46 percent) are. The declining share of children living in what is often deemed a traditional family has been largely supplanted by the rising shares of children living with single or cohabiting parents. The family envisioned by the writer of Genesis is not the only kind of family we will see in the modern world.

Although our families look quite different now, there are cords that bind us to the first family envisioned by God in the Garden of Eden. We, like they, have been created in the image and likeness of God. We have also been called to enter loving relationships bound by trust, fidelity, and mutual care and concern for the members of our families, our communities, church, and the world. Though we live in a fallen world and do not always measure up to what the creator God has called us to be, we are nonetheless called to be participants in loving, communal relationships. We, like the first family, continue to rely on God for our existence and continuing life. Moreover, we are committed to relationships that nurture and edify each member of the family based on the power and responsibilities that God has given to all humans in the creative act.

B. Biblical Background

Fellowship, friendship, and intimacy are basic needs of every human being, implanted in us by God Himself: "It is not good for the man to be alone" (Genesis 2:18, NIV). However, although animals and the man both came from the ground, animals can never provide for humanity the kind and degree of companionship they really require. The man's helper must be suitable for him. To allow Adam to perceive this for himself, God brought all the animals to Adam "to see what he would name them" (Genesis 2:19, NIV). As Adam gave each animal a name, he thereby demonstrated that he was in control of them, that he was their master. In so doing, he began to fulfill God's command given to him earlier: "rule over" them (Genesis 1:28).

Since none of the animals proved a suitable helper for Adam, God proceeded to make one for him. Genesis 2:21 describes the first case of controlled anesthesia in history: While Adam was sleeping, God took one of the man's ribs and made a woman from it. In Sumerian, one of the languages of Mesopotamia, the word "rib" also means "life." Something of that concept is also intended here: The woman comes into being out of the very life of the man. Life begets life. Surely much more is intended here as well. As many commentators have noted, the woman was not made from one of the bones in the man's head in order to make it possible for her to lord it over him; nor was she made from one of the bones in his foot in order to enable him to trample and crush her. On the contrary, she was made from one of the bones in his side so that they might share life together in mutual protection and concern and love and care. It is only sin that changed that original divine intention (see Genesis 3:16) and brought about the man's subjugation of woman in ways that are often cruel and unjust.

But how perfect was that original pristine relationship! In the Bible's second poem, Adam expressed his unbounded delight:

"This is now bone of my bones
And flesh of my flesh;
She shall be called "woman,"
For she was taken out of man."
(Genesis 2:23)

As in English, so also in Hebrew the words for "man" and "woman" sound very much alike. Even in themselves, they serve to help cement the one-flesh union—monogamy—that was the divine intention. One man would be united to one woman, and they would become one flesh (see Genesis 2:24) forever. In addition, in that primal state of innocence, their nakedness would cause them no shame.

II. EXPOSITION AND APPLICATION OF THE SCRIPTURE

A. A Helper for the Man
(Genesis 2:18)

And the Lord God said, It is not good that the man should be alone; I will make him an help meet for him.

The narrative begins with the striking announcement by God that the man is not yet as God had planned him to be. Everything thus far in Genesis that has been scrutinized by God has been given a positive assessment. Every situation has come through as either good or very good. For the first time, we encounter something that is not good: Adam is alone, and that state is not good. This emphatic negative contrasts with the verdict of Genesis 1:31— that everything was "very good." However, after the creation of male and female, there is no pronouncement of "very good." The idea here is that humans are recognized as social beings. Celibacy is undesirable. Since the idea of "good" describes that which is appropriate and fitting within the purpose of creation, humankind's being alone was not good because they could not do all that God had planned for humankind.

As Adam began to function as God's representative, naming the animals that God brought to him, he became very aware of his solitude. Being alone is a negative concept, for the full life is found in community. The tension of the man's incompleteness continued to build until God fulfilled his resolution of verse 18; God identified the problem with the state of creation and then moved to make the changes that would improve it. God makes Adam a "helper." Any suggestion that this particular word denotes one who has only an associate or subordinate status to a senior member is refuted by the fact that most frequently this same word describes Yahweh's relationship to Israel. "Helper" is not a demeaning term. The word essentially describes one who provides what is lacking in another, who can do what the other cannot do. The man was created in such a way that he needs the help of a partner. Or, we may say that human beings cannot fulfill their destiny except in mutual assistance.

B. Dominion over the Animals (Genesis 2:19-20)

And out of the ground the Lord God formed every beast of the field, and every fowl of the air; and brought them unto Adam to see what he would call them: and whatsoever Adam called every living creature, that was the name thereof. And Adam gave names to all cattle, and to the fowl of the air, and to every beast of the field; but for Adam there was not found an help meet for him.

Initially, God "formed" every animal and bird. Indeed, God did not simply create them, but "brought" them to the human in a kind of parade. This is a remarkable image of God. Twice God "brings" a creature—first the animals, then the woman—before the man. God thereby is placed at the service of the "good" of the human being, presenting creative possibilities before him. In addition, whatever the man called every living creature, that was its name. In Genesis 1, God bestows names only

on the cosmic creations—sun, moon, stars—phenomena connected with time and space. Here, God assigns the man the role of naming terrestrial animals, which is another way of expressing the bestowal of authority and dominion over them. To name a thing is to have power over it. Giving the creatures names (see Genesis 2:20) means relating to them, being responsible for them, and caring for them as far as is possible—rather than mastering them, destroying them, or being cruel to them. We are answerable to God for the way in which we relate to animals, who are our fellow creatures.

C. God as Creator and Matchmaker (Genesis 2:21-23)

And the Lord God caused a deep sleep to fall upon Adam, and he slept: and he took one of his ribs, and closed up the flesh instead thereof; And the rib, which the Lord God had taken from man, made he a woman, and brought her unto the man. And Adam said, This is now bone of my bones, and flesh of my flesh: she shall be called Woman, because she was taken out of Man.

God placed Adam into an abnormally heavy sleep, divinely induced. Such a sleep has here the dual function of rendering the man insensible to the pain of the surgery and oblivious to the work of God in his body. The mystery of the intimacy between husband and wife and the indispensable role that the woman ideally plays in the life of the man are symbolically described in terms of her creation out of his body. The rib taken from man's side thus connotes physical union and signifies that she is his companion and partner, ever at his side.

Genesis 1:22 says the Lord "brought her unto the man." God plays the role of attendant to the bride. He gives the man his wife He has created for him. Without a doubt, this verse conveys the idea that the institution of marriage is established by God Himself. The man's first recorded speech is a cry of ecstatic elation at seeing the woman. The corresponding sexual union between a man and a woman is God's gift for which we can rejoice. But this is one of God's gifts which is never more appreciated than on their wedding day when the couple commit themselves unconditionally to one another.

D. The Two Become One
(Genesis 2:24)

Therefore shall a man leave his father and his mother, and shall cleave unto his wife: and they shall be one flesh.

The idea of "one flesh" expresses the complete personal community of one man and one woman as a spiritual union. The fashioning of the woman from the man's body explains why his bond to his wife takes precedence over his ties to his parents. It accounts for the mystery of physical love and the intense emotional involvement of male and female, as well as for their commonality of interests. This God-ordained relationship is so powerful that it transcends ties of blood, the lifelong emotional bonds that connect child to parent. The man God created finds his full identity not in his associations with parents and siblings, but in his free and full commitment to a woman. Nowhere else does the Old Testament speak of "becoming one flesh," but expressions such as "you are my bone and my flesh" (see Genesis 29:14) are used to indicate the closest kind of interpersonal relationships. In addition, "the two become one flesh" does not merely speak of a sexual connotation; rather, it insists that the married couple become a new unit, socially and emotionally.

With the creation of the man and the wonderful creation of woman, his helpmeet, this section of the Creation sequence ends. God has formed humanity and provided for its life: food, freedom, and now family. This narrative, as it was told repeatedly in the faith community, has a carefully crafted flow that moves from a barren landscape to a fertile garden filled with life. And all of this comes to humanity as a gift from the hands of almighty God. Now thank we all our God!

E. The Result of Oneness
(Genesis 4:1-2)

AND ADAM knew Eve his wife; and she conceived, and bare Cain, and said, I have gotten a man from the Lord. And she again bare his brother Abel. And Abel was a keeper of sheep, but Cain was a tiller of the ground.

The focal point of this passage is so appropriate in its connection with the previous section (Genesis 2:24), where it is discussed that Adam and Eve became one flesh. The result of this oneness is seen in the first words of this passage: "And Adam knew his wife Eve." The idea of "knowing" in this context refers to sexual intercourse.

God had commanded our first parents, Adam and Eve, to "be fruitful, and multiply, and replenish the earth" (Genesis 1:28). They obeyed God's command and she conceived a child (Genesis 4:1a). We can only imagine how they felt and responded as they awaited the birth of their first child—the first of all naturally born humankind. Eve expressed her joy by declaring that her son was to be called Cain (Hebrew: *ganah*, meaning "acquire," "get," or "possess"), because she had gotten him from the Lord (Genesis 4:1b).

It is held among biblical scholars that Eve

believed Cain was to be the promised seed that God promised would deliver the human race (Genesis 3:15). The birth of Cain was followed by the birth of his brother, Abel (Genesis 4:2a).

III. CONCLUDING REFLECTION

In man and woman, there was an original equality but a difference in function (see Genesis 2:22). Adam expressed great pleasure with the woman. She was to be his first, last, and always. After he had looked at all the animals and had not found satisfaction, he found satisfaction in the woman. The perpetuation of this part of the blessing was to be found through monogamy. At times in the Old Testament, *polygamy* (being married to more than one person at a time) is apparently permitted; but the right state, as indicated here, is for each man to cleave to his wife.

Here, we have the beginnings of the family as God intended. Now joined in covenant with his wife, the husband and his spouse become one flesh. The man does not leave one family to start another family. What is being pinpointed here is solidarity. A man by himself is not one flesh. A woman by herself is not one flesh. The two became one, which is to say there was no barrier, physical or otherwise, between them. There was nothing before the Fall that drove a wedge between them. They were indeed one—created, blessed, and given authority by God.

No relationship in the world is so cohesive as that which exists between a man and a woman. So binding is it that at the outset of creation, God emphasized the responsibility involved in the cohabitation of the two parts of the generic species called *man* (see Genesis 2:23-24). The beasts, fowl, and fish were commanded to reproduce but without restriction, except that each should breed with its own kind. The man, however, was restricted to his sole female counterpart, with whom he was one flesh. The man and woman belong together, but not man and women or woman and men. Even at this early stage of human history, the institution of marriage was divinely sanctioned.

PRAYER

Eternal God, Thou before whom the generations rise and fall, we give You thanks for the blessings of love and companionship shared between a husband and his wife. In Jesus' name we pray. Amen.

HOME DAILY BIBLE READINGS
(September 17-23, 2018)

God Created the Family

MONDAY, September 17: "Becoming One Flesh" (Matthew 19:3-6)
TUESDAY, September 18: "Married and Devoted to the Lord" (1 Corinthians 7:1-7, 32-35)
WEDNESDAY, September 19: "Honor the Sanctity of Marriage" (Hebrews 13:1-6)
THURSDAY, September 20: "Cultivate Deep Mutual Love" (1 Peter 1:13-16, 22-23)
FRIDAY, September 21: "For the Sake of Your Prayers" (1 Peter 4:7-11)
SATURDAY, September 22: "Cain Ducks Responsibility for Abel" (Genesis 4:3-12)
SUNDAY, September 23: "The Family, Whole and Broken" (Genesis 2:18-24; 4:1-2)

September 30, 2018   **Lesson 5**

GOD CREATES, HUMANS SIN

ADULT/YOUTH
ADULT/YOUNG ADULT TOPIC: **Passing the Buck**
YOUTH TOPIC: **Prone to Disobey**

CHILDREN
GENERAL LESSON TITLE: **God Creates, We Disobey**
CHILDREN'S TOPIC: **Learn to Obey**

DEVOTIONAL READING
Psalm 51:1-12

ADULT/YOUTH
BACKGROUND SCRIPTURE: **Genesis 3**
PRINT PASSAGE: **Genesis 3:8-17, 20-24**
KEY VERSE: **Genesis 3:23**

CHILDREN
BACKGROUND SCRIPTURE: **Genesis 3**
PRINT PASSAGE: **Genesis 3:8, 14-17, 22-24**
KEY VERSE: **Genesis 3:13**

Genesis 3:8-17, 20-24—KJV

8 And they heard the voice of the LORD God walking in the garden in the cool of the day: and Adam and his wife hid themselves from the presence of the LORD God amongst the trees of the garden.

9 And the LORD God called unto Adam, and said unto him, Where art thou?

10 And he said, I heard thy voice in the garden, and I was afraid, because I was naked; and I hid myself.

11 And he said, Who told thee that thou wast naked? Hast thou eaten of the tree, whereof I commanded thee that thou shouldest not eat?

12 And the man said, The woman whom thou gavest to be with me, she gave me of the tree, and I did eat.

13 And the LORD God said unto the woman, What is this that thou hast done? And the woman said, The serpent beguiled me, and I did eat.

14 And the LORD God said unto the serpent, Because thou hast done this, thou art cursed above all cattle, and above every beast of the field; upon thy belly

Genesis 3:8-17, 20-24—NIV

8 Then the man and his wife heard the sound of the LORD God as he was walking in the garden in the cool of the day, and they hid from the LORD God among the trees of the garden.

9 But the LORD God called to the man, "Where are you?"

10 He answered, "I heard you in the garden, and I was afraid because I was naked; so I hid."

11 And he said, "Who told you that you were naked? Have you eaten from the tree that I commanded you not to eat from?"

12 The man said, "The woman you put here with me—she gave me some fruit from the tree, and I ate it."

13 Then the LORD God said to the woman, "What is this you have done?" The woman said, "The serpent deceived me, and I ate."

14 So the LORD God said to the serpent, "Because you have done this, Cursed are you above all livestock

shalt thou go, and dust shalt thou eat all the days of thy life:

15 And I will put enmity between thee and the woman, and between thy seed and her seed; it shall bruise thy head, and thou shalt bruise his heel.

16 Unto the woman he said, I will greatly multiply thy sorrow and thy conception; in sorrow thou shalt bring forth children; and thy desire shall be to thy husband, and he shall rule over thee.

17 And unto Adam he said, Because thou hast hearkened unto the voice of thy wife, and hast eaten of the tree, of which I commanded thee, saying, Thou shalt not eat of it: cursed is the ground for thy sake; in sorrow shalt thou eat of it all the days of thy life.

…..

20 And Adam called his wife's name Eve; because she was the mother of all living.

21 Unto Adam also and to his wife did the LORD God make coats of skins, and clothed them.

22 And the LORD God said, Behold, the man is become as one of us, to know good and evil: and now, lest he put forth his hand, and take also of the tree of life, and eat, and live for ever:

23 Therefore the LORD God sent him forth from the garden of Eden, to till the ground from whence he was taken.

24 So he drove out the man; and he placed at the east of the garden of Eden Cherubims, and a flaming sword which turned every way, to keep the way of the tree of life.

and all wild animals! You will crawl on your belly and you will eat dust all the days of your life.

15 "And I will put enmity between you and the woman, and between your offspring and hers; he will crush your head, and you will strike his heel."

16 To the woman he said, "I will make your pains in childbearing very severe; with painful labor you will give birth to children. Your desire will be for your husband, and he will rule over you."

17 To Adam he said, "Because you listened to your wife and ate fruit from the tree about which I commanded you, 'You must not eat from it,' Cursed is the ground because of you; through painful toil you will eat food from it all the days of your life."

…..

20 Adam named his wife Eve, because she would become the mother of all the living.

21 The LORD God made garments of skin for Adam and his wife and clothed them.

22 And the LORD God said, "The man has now become like one of us, knowing good and evil. He must not be allowed to reach out his hand and take also from the tree of life and eat, and live forever."

23 So the LORD God banished him from the Garden of Eden to work the ground from which he had been taken.

24 After he drove the man out, he placed on the east side of the Garden of Eden cherubim and a flaming sword flashing back and forth to guard the way to the tree of life.

UNIFYING LESSON PRINCIPLE: Irresponsible rebellion pervades our world. Why is disregard for rules, which are necessary for ordered life, so pervasive? Although God created a perfect place for Adam and Eve, their unwillingness to trust and obey God led to the Fall, making humanity prone to disobedience.

LESSON OBJECTIVES

Upon the completion of this lesson, the students will be able to do the following:

1. Discern how the events in Genesis 3 reflect the universal human experience of temptation and sin.
2. Regret the fractured relationship with God and others that our sins bring about.
3. Plan strategies for mending relationships that have been damaged by sin.

AGE-LEVEL POINTS TO BE EMPHASIZED

Teachers of ADULTS and YOUTH

—While the Serpent is never identified in this text as "Satan," many Bible students use Paul's reference in Romans 16:20 (crushing Satan under your feet) and John's reference to "that ancient serpent, who is called the devil and Satan" (Revelation 12:9) to so identify it.

—God told the man and woman that they would die if they ate from the forbidden tree (see Genesis 2:17). The death was not immediate. God's denying them access to the life-giving tree (see Genesis 3:22) was an act of grace, since an eternal life of the punishments prescribed would be unbearable.

—The ground God cursed was the same ground from which God made the humans (see Genesis 2:7) and that God gave them to farm.

—Although the pain of childbirth is sometimes described as "the curse," the only curses explicitly leveled in this passage were on the Serpent (verse 14) and on the ground (verse 17).

—The Serpent's question is designed to trick or entrap with its layer of truth and is addressed to the plural "you," implying that Adam is right there with Eve, if silent in this interchange.

—In God's questioning, God seeks confession. In God's sentencing, we see the effects on every created relationship.

—God's creating clothing for the woman and man is symbolic of continuing care and protection.

—Words like "the Fall" and "original sin" are applied to this text; but the story itself implies only temporal rather than more global consequences, though the relationships among creation and the Creator are distorted.

Teachers of CHILDREN

—The Serpent, who at the time of Creation had great knowledge and could talk, convinced the woman that she should eat fruit from a tree in the Garden, an act that God had forbidden.

—The woman was tempted because the fruit looked quite good to eat, and because the Serpent had convinced her that eating it would result in her having abilities that she was not given when she was created. ("You will be like God, knowing good and evil" [Genesis 3:5.])

—After the Serpent contradicted God's warning to the people about the results of eating from the tree, the woman not only ate the fruit from the tree herself, but she also gave some to her husband.

—They hid themselves from God because of their sin.

—As a result of the man and woman's disobedience, God made clothes for them from animal skins and sent them out of the Garden.

THE CHRONOLOGICAL SETTING OF THE LESSON

Up to this point, there had been unbroken fellowship with God. From chapter 3 on there is a picture of God's pursuing humanity, wooing them back. The Fall introduces us to humankind's need and God's grace. This story of sin provides the groundwork for all Christian theology. It shows the need for redemption, since humankind is unworthy to stand before God by virtue of their willful disregard of the boundaries of their creaturehood.

Regardless of whether or not humans are willing to accept responsibility for their sin, they are responsible for and in need of God's forgiveness.

THE GEOGRAPHICAL AND CULTURAL SETTING OF THE LESSON

The second part of Genesis 3 reports the effects of sin on the human race (see Genesis 3:8-24). It is therefore a natural extension of the first seven verses of the chapter, which report the temptation by Satan and the disobedience by Adam and Eve. Owing to their disobedience, humankind's entire way of being in the world is turned upside-down. Whereas before Adam and Eve had life, they now had death; where they had pleasure, they now would have pain; where they previously had abundance, they now had a meager sustenance by toil; previously they had perfect harmony with God and with each other, but now there was alienation and conflict. The passage falls into three sections: (1) the confrontation by the Lord, in which the sinners, hearing Him, fear and hide in the midst of the Garden; (2) the oracles (divine messages) of the Lord, in which the new order is declared for the Serpent, the woman, and the man; and (3) the provision of clothing from the Lord, in which the human instinct to cover guilt is superseded by the Lord's action.

PROMINENT CHARACTER(S) IN THE LESSON

Eve: living thing, propagator of life, wife of Adam.

KEY TERMS IN THE LESSON

Afraid (verse 10)—Hebrew: *yare'* **(yaw-ray'):** to fear, revere, be afraid.
Enmity (verse 15)—Hebrew: *'eybah* **(ay-baw'):** enmity; hatred.

Presence (verse 8 [KJV only])—Hebrew: *paniym* **(paw-neem'):** face; presence; countenance.
Serpent (verse 13)—Hebrew: *nachash* **(naw-khawsh'):** serpent; snake.
Sorrow (verse 16)—Hebrew: *'itstsabown* **(its-tsaw-bone'):** pain; labour; hardship; sorrow; toil; "pains" (NIV).
Voice (verse 8)—Hebrew: *qowl* **(kole):** voice; "sound" (NIV); noise.

TOPICAL OUTLINE OF THE LESSON

I. **Introduction**
   A. The Fall of Humankind
   B. Biblical Background

II. **Exposition and Application of the Scripture**
   A. The Lord Confronts Adam and Eve (Genesis 3:8-11)
   B. The Blame Game of Sinners (Genesis 3:12-13)
   C. The Serpent Answers to God (Genesis 3:14-15)
   D. The Punishment of the Man and Woman (Genesis 3:16-17)
   E. Salvation beyond the Fall (Genesis 3:20-24)

III. **Concluding Reflection**

I. INTRODUCTION

A. The Fall of Humankind

The third chapter of the book of Genesis deals with the sin of not just any man, but with the first man, and consequently the punishment is not directed simply to that individual but to humankind as a whole. Adam's sin consists of two levels: disobedience to a divine order, and eating fruit from the Tree of the Knowledge of Good and Evil (Tree of Knowledge). God specifically commanded humans not to eat of the Tree of Knowledge, but they were tempted and they ate. Though another tempted them, they could have and should have resisted the temptation. Their sin was a sheer act of disobedience, which demonstrates humankind's readiness to ignore the order of God and to succumb to seduction.

Why did God forbid humans to eat of the Tree of the Knowledge of Good and Evil (see Genesis 2:17)? When the Serpent persuaded Eve to eat of it, he said, "For God knows that in the day that you eat of it your eyes shall be opened and you shall be as God, knowing good and evil" (see Genesis 3:5). According to the Serpent, God forbade eating from the Tree of Knowledge in order to differentiate and to distance Himself from humans. When humans ate from the tree, God had no alternative but to banish them from the Garden of Eden to restore the difference between the eternity of God and the mortality of humans. The first sin of humans was therefore—in form and substance—the typical religious sin. God imposed restrictions on humans by subjecting them to commands and preventing them from becoming like God. Humans, in turn, sinned by failing to obey God's order; by eating from the Tree of Knowledge they hoped to become like God.

The broader concern here is how to live with the creation in God's world on God's terms. The assertion by the writer of Genesis is that recognizing and honoring boundaries leads to well-being in those who have been created by God. This lesson deals with human autonomy (self-direction) and the ways in which abuse of that autonomy leads to alienation and death, for self and for others. The freedom of human persons to enjoy life and the vocation of human persons to manage creation are set in the context of prohibitions set forth by God. What we are urged to engage in here is a relationship of trust between God and His created order.

The situation portrayed in the narrative is a very normal tension in life. We all live within boundaries, and at the same time we possess the power to cross those boundaries. Even though this drama comes to us as a story about a garden long ago, we know very well the tension between boundaries and our desire to cross them. We hear God's call to exercise the freedom to stay within the limits. We remember our experience of violating those limits. Together, we live with the consequences of such misuse of our power and freedom: thistles and thorns, pain, and oppression. This narrative does not end on a happy note, but it does leave the future open—open to celebrate God's act to replace a curse with blessing and judgment with grace.

B. Biblical Background

The transition from Genesis 1 to chapters 2 and 3 is truly astounding, not because of the difference in details, but because of the difference in spirit and outlook of the man and woman created by God. After the lofty act of Creation in chapter 1, chapters 2 (beginning at verse 4) and 3 reveal a disobedient act which resulted in the man's being reduced from his exalted height as a creature fashioned in God's image to a cursed being who must now pursue his sustenance. He is now a creature from dust consigned to return to dust (see 3:19).

In chapter 1, God finds everything "very good"; but chapters 2 and 3 show Adam and Eve's destiny in the world as bad and demonstrate the punishment of their transgression. In chapter 1, all is perfect at the hand of God; in chapters 2 and 3, the man, by his conduct, introduces perversion, which results in punishment for which he is doomed to carry a bitter burden for eternity. Chapter 1 proclaims perfection and harmony; chapters 2 and 3 raise the specter of disharmony and imperfection, embodied in humanity's sin and suffering, in his deceitful heart, and in his harsh state.

The harmony between the man and woman described in chapter 2 is shattered, and in the future women are not only destined to give birth in pain, but are humbled in status as compared to men (see Genesis 3:16). Moreover, God loses confidence in the man and banished him from the Garden of Eden. His new harsh lot is a punishment for his transgression in having eaten of the Tree of Knowledge, which was expressly forbidden by the Almighty. Humanity's experience of evil originates not in its destiny or in the will of God, but in the individual, and is a result of one's own sin.

Genesis 3 gives us a vivid picture of how sin entered the world. The ebb and flow of the events outlined in Genesis 3 have a striking symmetry all their own: (1) The Serpent tempts (see 3:1-5), then the woman sins, and finally the man (see 3:6). (2) Next, the Lord confronts them with their sin by speaking to them in the reverse order: first the man (see 3:9-12), then the woman (see 3:13), and finally the Serpent (see 3:14). (3) The Lord concludes this phase of His response to them by judging them in the same order in which they had sinned: first the Serpent (see 3:14-15), next the woman (see 3:16), and last of all the man (see 3:17-19). The chapter ends with one of the saddest scenes in all of Scripture: The Lord banishes the man and his wife from the Garden of Eden (see 3:22-24), where He had originally put them.

II. EXPOSITION AND APPLICATION OF THE SCRIPTURE

A. The Lord Confronts Adam and Eve (Genesis 3:8-11)

And they heard the voice of the Lord God walking in the garden in the cool of the day: and Adam and his wife hid themselves from the presence of the Lord God amongst the trees of the garden. And the Lord God called unto Adam, and said unto him, Where art thou? And he said, I heard thy voice in the garden, and I was afraid, because I was naked; and I hid myself. And he said, Who told thee that thou wast naked? Hast thou eaten of the tree, whereof I commanded thee that thou shouldest not eat?

We do not know how long Adam and Eve lived in the Garden of Eden in an unfallen state. However, as we read Genesis we gain the impression that the assault on them by Satan came quite early, before they had been confirmed in any good pattern of obedience.

Certainly, Satan had heard God's warning: "You are free to eat from any tree in the garden; but you must not eat from the tree of the knowledge of good and evil, for when you eat from it you will certainly die" (Genesis 2:16-17, NIV). Now Satan comes—immediately it seems—to suggest that God is not benevolent and that His word cannot be trusted.

The validity of the Word of God is the issue in Satan's temptation—for Satan's first words are phrased as a question designed to cast doubt on God's veracity: "Did God say you shall not eat of every tree of the Garden?" (see Genesis 3:1, Background Scripture). The origin of sin is involved in that speculation. Even though God gives the man and the woman all creation to enjoy, with but one exception—they must not eat from the Tree of the Knowledge of Good and Evil—Satan turns the one exception into a negative designed to cast doubt on God. Eve gives in to the temptation and Adam is soon to follow. The issue in this first part of the temptation is the integrity of the Word of God. Satan casts doubt on the goodness of God and whether God can be trusted. This is the first great revelation of sin's nature. Sin is unbelief. It is a rejection of God's good will and truthfulness, leading inevitably to an act of outright rebellion.

With their having eaten of the forbidden fruit, the curse that fell on both Adam and Eve resulted in the eyes of both of them being opened (see verse 7). The spiritual death they died that day was revealed in two ways: Their clean, clear consciences were tainted with shame—they had to cover parts of their bodies and their trust was forfeited; they tried to hide when they heard the voice of the Lord God as He walked in the Garden in the cool of the day (verse 8). What a wonderful sound that should have been; however, Adam and Eve were afraid, terrified. Even though sin separates, here we see the pursuing love of God. He would not leave them in their misery and nakedness. He would speak to them. God first called man when man was running away, and the Lord has been calling ever since. The fleeing sinner can never escape the pursuit of God's love.

B. The Blame Game of Sinners
(Genesis 3:12-13)

And the man said, The woman whom thou gavest to be with me, she gave me of the tree, and I did eat. And the Lᴏʀᴅ God said unto the woman, What is this that thou hast done? And the woman said, The serpent beguiled me, and I did eat.

How low sin brought the man is revealed in his first excuse. He is willing to hide behind the woman—the tender gift of God—and to throw blame from his own shoulders onto those of his wife. Adam's sin was far worse than that of Eve's, for she may have thought she was doing the right thing; she was improving the lot of her husband. However, Adam sinned in willful rebellion. Eve was the channel, not the cause, of his fall. God does not discuss with Adam his flimsy excuse, but He now demands an accounting of the woman. She is in the Fall as much as the man is. Sin in ignorance is nevertheless sin. Her shame was as great as that of Adam's. He sought to blame her and God; she sought to blame the Serpent. The Fall brought with it what is now an instinct to get out from under the blame.

C. The Serpent Answers to God
(Genesis 3:14-15)

And the Lᴏʀᴅ God said unto the serpent, Because thou hast done this, thou art cursed above all cattle, and above every beast of the field; upon thy belly shalt thou go, and dust shalt thou eat all the days of thy life: And I will put enmity between thee and the woman, and between thy seed and her seed; it shall bruise thy head, and thou shalt bruise his heel.

The Serpent, which had evidently been upright in posture, and with the gift of human speech, suddenly hears the doom of judgment. Because it had been the channel of Satan's office, it became a loathsome, crawling reptile. God was speaking also to Satan through the serpent, and this is why dust becomes the serpent's meat. To eat dust is to know defeat, and that is God's prophetic judgment upon the enemy. He will always reach for his desires and fall just short of them. There will be in the serpent continuous aspiration, but never attainment. The power of Satan is to be crushed (verse 15). He may rage for centuries, but his doom is sure. The Lord God has promised to make an end of him and will even bruise him under our feet. In the end, God will defeat sin; we simply await the declaration of His victory over Satan, the one who first beguiled Adam and Eve in the Garden.

D. The Punishment of the Man and Woman (Genesis 3:16-17)

Unto the woman he said, I will greatly multiply thy sorrow and thy conception; in sorrow thou shalt bring forth children; and thy desire shall be to thy husband, and he shall rule over thee. And unto Adam he said, Because thou hast hearkened unto the voice of thy wife, and hast eaten of the tree, of which I commanded thee, saying, Thou shalt not eat of it: cursed is the ground for thy sake; in sorrow shalt thou eat of it all the days of thy life.

By Adam and Eve's eating the fruit from the forbidden Tree of the Knowledge of Good and Evil, the human right to make decisions concerning human welfare is now done independently of God and in defiance of His norms. They have lost their innocence and must assume full responsibility for their actions. Accordingly, God now metes out punishment on each transgressor in turn, in the order of their original appearance on the scene. The snake is punished in the manner of how it maneuvers itself and in its contacts with human beings. The woman is doomed to suffer in childbearing (verse 16). In the beginning, they were told to be fruitful and multiply. Now, however, that fulfillment is to

be accompanied by pain and suffering. Intense pain in childbearing is unique to the human species and generally unknown to other female mammals.

The longest statement of divine rebuke and punishment is reserved for the man, for his is the greatest blame, since it was he who received directly from God the prohibition not to eat from the forbidden tree. His shifting of the blame to his wife is rejected. The sin of eating forbidden food results in complicating the production of goods. The man himself is not cursed, only the soil (verse 17). Dirt—the matter from which he sprang—now turns against him. His pristine harmony with nature is disturbed by his transgression. The man is fated to a life of arduous labor and toil. His backbreaking physical labor is regarded as the male equivalent of the labor of childbearing. The curse lies not in the work itself, but in the uncooperative nature of the soil, so that henceforth the wresting of survival from it entails continuous labor.

E. Salvation beyond the Fall (Genesis 3:20-24)

Adam named his wife Eve, because she would become the mother of all the living. The LORD God made garments of skin for Adam and his wife and clothed them. And the LORD God said, "The man has now become like one of us, knowing good and evil. He must not be allowed to reach out his hand and take also from the tree of life and eat, and live forever." So the LORD God banished him from the Garden of Eden to work the ground from which he had been taken. After he drove the man out, he placed on the east side of the Garden of Eden cherubim and a flaming sword flashing back and forth to guard the way to the tree of life.

To the woman's generic designation Adam adds a personal name that defines her destiny—Eve. Adam's naming of Eve is the beginning of hope (verse 20). Adam shows his restoration to God by believing the promise that the faithful woman will bear offspring that will defeat Satan. While this story is filled with death—judgment on the Serpent, painful labor, conflict of wills—a ray of hope remains in the promise that the seed of the woman who feels enmity toward the serpent will defeat the incarnation of evil (see verse 15).

Adam and Eve's "coverings" in verse 7 were only loincloths, inadequate to cover their shame. Now with the sacrifice of an animal, God constructs for them tunics that reach down to the knees or ankles (verse 21). With the sentence given, God does for the couple what they cannot do for themselves (verse 21). They cannot deal with their shame. However, God can, will, and does.

Another element of hope is found in the fact that the Garden was not locked or destroyed. The cherubim guarded the gate.

III. CONCLUDING REFLECTION

The major theological theme of this narrative encompasses the Lord's response to the disobedience of Adam and Eve. At first, the Lord interrogated the participants to obtain a confession. Then, He declared the new conditions of life in view of the presence of evil, conflict, pain, and death. Finally, He provided clothing for the humans and kept them away from the Tree of Life. The Lord once again is the sovereign and majestic subject of the narrative. Whereas His previous actions revealed Him as the Creator and Benefactor of the universe, this narrative demonstrated Him to be a compassionate judge of sinners.

In conjunction with this dominant theme, the passage clarifies the task and the hope of human beings. What must sinners do? They must confess their sin and trust in God's goodness for provisions of life. For what can sinners hope? They can look forward to release from the curse and anticipate the ultimate victory over evil. Sin has its consequences, but God is a loving God who wills to redeem His created order.

PRAYER

Eternal God, we confess to You that we are weak, finite, fallible creatures of the moment. We ask Your forgiveness for our sins, and we pray that You would strengthen us with Your tender-loving mercy and compassion. In Jesus' name we pray. Amen.

HOME DAILY BIBLE READINGS
(September 24-30, 2018)

God Creates, Humans Sin
MONDAY, September 24: "King David Gives In to Temptation" (2 Samuel 11:1-5)
TUESDAY, September 25: "Death by Adam; Life by Christ" (Romans 5:12-19)
WEDNESDAY, September 26: "Jesus Overcomes Temptation" (Matthew 4:1-11)
THURSDAY, September 27: "Removing the Stumbling Blocks to Temptation" (Mark 9:42-48)
FRIDAY, September 28: "Endure Temptation, Receive Crown of Life" (James 1:12-15)
SATURDAY, September 29: "The Serpent's Temptation" (Genesis 3:1-7)
SUNDAY, September 30: "The Sins of the First Humans" (Genesis 3:8-17, 20-24)

October 7, 2018 — **Lesson 6**

NOAH'S STEADFAST FAITH

ADULT/YOUTH
ADULT/YOUNG ADULT TOPIC: **A Faithful Following**
YOUTH TOPIC: **A Faithful Friend**

CHILDREN
GENERAL LESSON TITLE: **Noah's Steadfast Faith**
CHILDREN'S TOPIC: **Faith in Action**

DEVOTIONAL READING
Matthew 24:36-44

ADULT/YOUTH
BACKGROUND SCRIPTURE: **Genesis 6; 8:19**
PRINT PASSAGE: **Genesis 6:9b-22**
KEY VERSE: **Genesis 6:22**

CHILDREN
BACKGROUND SCRIPTURE: **Genesis 6; 8:19**
PRINT PASSAGE: **Genesis 6:9b-22**
KEY VERSE: **Genesis 6:9**

Genesis 6:9b-22—KJV

9 Noah was a just man and perfect in his generations, and Noah walked with God.

10 And Noah begat three sons, Shem, Ham, and Japheth.

11 The earth also was corrupt before God, and the earth was filled with violence.

12 And God looked upon the earth, and, behold, it was corrupt; for all flesh had corrupted his way upon the earth.

13 And God said unto Noah, The end of all flesh is come before me; for the earth is filled with violence through them; and, behold, I will destroy them with the earth.

14 Make thee an ark of gopher wood; rooms shalt thou make in the ark, and shalt pitch it within and without with pitch.

15 And this is the fashion which thou shalt make it of: The length of the ark shall be three hundred cubits, the breadth of it fifty cubits, and the height of it thirty cubits.

Genesis 6:9b-22—NIV

9 Noah was a righteous man, blameless among the people of his time, and he walked faithfully with God.

10 Noah had three sons: Shem, Ham and Japheth.

11 Now the earth was corrupt in God's sight and was full of violence.

12 God saw how corrupt the earth had become, for all the people on earth had corrupted their ways.

13 So God said to Noah, "I am going to put an end to all people, for the earth is filled with violence because of them. I am surely going to destroy both them and the earth.

14 "So make yourself an ark of cypress wood; make rooms in it and coat it with pitch inside and out.

15 "This is how you are to build it: The ark is to be three hundred cubits long, fifty cubits wide and thirty cubits high.

16 "Make a roof for it, leaving below the roof an

16 A window shalt thou make to the ark, and in a cubit shalt thou finish it above; and the door of the ark shalt thou set in the side thereof; with lower, second, and third stories shalt thou make it.

17 And, behold, I, even I, do bring a flood of waters upon the earth, to destroy all flesh, wherein is the breath of life, from under heaven; and every thing that is in the earth shall die.

18 But with thee will I establish my covenant; and thou shalt come into the ark, thou, and thy sons, and thy wife, and thy sons' wives with thee.

19 And of every living thing of all flesh, two of every sort shalt thou bring into the ark, to keep them alive with thee; they shall be male and female.

20 Of fowls after their kind, and of cattle after their kind, of every creeping thing of the earth after his kind, two of every sort shall come unto thee, to keep them alive.

21 And take thou unto thee of all food that is eaten, and thou shalt gather it to thee; and it shall be for food for thee, and for them.

22 Thus did Noah; according to all that God commanded him, so did he.

opening one cubit high all around. Put a door in the side of the ark and make lower, middle and upper decks.

17 "I am going to bring floodwaters on the earth to destroy all life under the heavens, every creature that has the breath of life in it. Everything on earth will perish.

18 "But I will establish my covenant with you, and you will enter the ark—you and your sons and your wife and your sons' wives with you.

19 "You are to bring into the ark two of all living creatures, male and female, to keep them alive with you.

20 "Two of every kind of bird, of every kind of animal and of every kind of creature that moves along the ground will come to you to be kept alive.

21 "You are to take every kind of food that is to be eaten and store it away as food for you and for them."

22 Noah did everything just as God commanded him.

UNIFYING LESSON PRINCIPLE: Faithfulness is a needed quality of life, but it is difficult to achieve. How can persons be faithful in difficult situations? Noah is an empowering example of someone who remained faithful to what God asked him to do, regardless of the opposing circumstances and consequences.

LESSON OBJECTIVES

Upon the completion of this lesson, the students will be able to do the following:

1. Remember Noah's faithfulness in obeying God's command to build the ark.
2. Repent of times when we have failed to follow God's instructions.
3. Embrace the calling to do what God commands despite the challenges this entails.

AGE-LEVEL POINTS TO BE EMPHASIZED

Teachers of ADULTS and YOUTH

—Noah is described as "blameless" (verse 9), a term often used to describe sacrificial animals (example: Exodus 12:5). This does not suggest that he was free from sin, but that he lived with integrity (see Psalm 15:2-5). The rabbis interpreted "blameless in his generation" to mean he was blameless relative to the wicked society around him: not perfect, but the best available candidate. That he "walked with

God" (verse 9) suggests an especially close relationship (see Genesis 17:1; 48:15; Micah 6:8).

—In Hebrew, Noah's ark is described with the same word (*teba*) as the basket Moses' mother used to hide her baby in the reeds of the Nile. A different term is used to describe the ark of the covenant.

—Noah is given a detailed set of instructions. For the narrator of the book of Genesis, the instructions themselves matter much less than the fact that Noah followed them (verse 22).

—Corruption in this story is said to extend to the earth itself. The earth as corrupt is noted six times.

—God's covenant with Noah's family is one-sided—God will protect them as promised because God is God.

—The corruption referred to in the text stems from violence among creation, which pollutes the earth—violence such as injustice, deeds that violate the lives of others, and so on.

—For the earth itself, the Flood is a kind of washing away of the corruption, where for "living things" it is a kind of purging of that which has gone awry.

Teachers of CHILDREN

—Humanity was evil and wicked, but God favored Noah.

—God decided to destroy the earth and everything in it due to its violence and corruption.

—God instructed Noah to construct an ark for the upcoming destruction of the earth.

—God's established covenant with Noah allowed Noah to bring his family onto the ark.

—The male or female of every creature would enter the ark and be kept alive.

—Noah did everything God commanded of him.

THE CHRONOLOGICAL SETTING OF THE LESSON

The literature of many ancient peoples contains stories of an earth-covering flood. Differences in culture, religion, and organization of the society shaped the stories as they were passed along. Indeed, the story in Genesis 6 shows evidence of being told and retold, written and rewritten through many generations. Central to this narrative is not exactly how many pairs of animals were taken aboard the ark or how many days the Flood lasted. Far more important for the Flood story is one's ability to answer this key question: "When God comes in judgment, can anyone survive?" The writer of Genesis wants to declare what the people who told this story repeatedly declared: that even when God executes such a terrible flood upon the earth, some people and animals will survive by God's grace. Why? Because God Himself will see to it!

THE GEOGRAPHICAL AND CULTURAL SETTING OF THE LESSON

The Flood narrative is widespread throughout the world. We can say at once that the Flood narrative, like the Creation narrative, is part of the common property of humanity. It is humankind's basic expression of its being in the world, of the threat to human existence and at the same time of its permanence. The biblical account of the Flood narrative begins in Genesis 6:9. It constitutes the third major section in the primeval history recorded in Genesis 1–11. It tells the story of the Flood that destroyed sinful humankind in the days of Noah. It describes the divine judgment on the human race that came because of their rebellion against God. However, it also tells the story of a man and his family who were given a way out of God's judgment through the man's obedience. The people of antiquity who heard this story believed with all their hearts that faithful obedience to the commands of God is the way back to God.

PROMINENT CHARACTER(S) IN THE LESSON

Noah: the hero and survivor of the great Flood; an exemplary righteous man who, with his family, was preserved from annihilation because of his faith in God and his obedience to the divine command.

KEY TERMS IN THE LESSON

Ark (verse 14)—Hebrew: *tebah* (tay-baw'): ark; vessel which Noah built.

Corrupt (verse 11)—Hebrew: *shachath* (shaw-khath'): to destroy, corrupt, go to ruin, decay.

Flood (verse 17)—Hebrew: *mabbuwl* (mab-bool'): flood; deluge; "floodwaters" (NIV). Noah's flood that submerged the entire planet earth under water for about a year.

Just (verse 9)—Hebrew: *tsaddiyq* (tsad-deek'): just; lawful; "righteous" (NIV).

Violence (verse 13)—Hebrew: *chamac* (khaw-mawce'): violence; wrong; cruelty; injustice.

Walked (verse 9)—Hebrew: *halak* (haw-lak'): to go, walk, come.

TOPICAL OUTLINE OF THE LESSON

I. **Introduction**
   A. The Judgment of the Flood
   B. Biblical Background

II. **Exposition and Application of the Scripture**
   A. Noah, God's Faithful Servant (Genesis 6:9b-12)
   B. Noah Obeys the Voice of God (Genesis 6:13-16)
   C. God Rewards Noah's Faithfulness (Genesis 6:17-21)
   D. The Fate of the Obedient (Genesis 6:22)

III. **Concluding Reflection**

I. INTRODUCTION

A. The Judgment of the Flood

This is one of the best-known events in the Bible. Indeed, even people who are largely ignorant of Scripture know something about Noah, his ark, and the great Flood, for the story has captured the imagination in a remarkable way. We find in Genesis 6 no intriguing characters like Eve or Cain, and there is not even any dialogue to enliven the story. God speaks several times, but Noah has nothing to say. Noah's virtues are listed and emphasized for us, but he is never presented as a fully rounded human being. Despite these things, something about this story has captured the imaginations of all kinds of people, notwithstanding the fact that the central figures are not fully formed and embraceable people.

The subject is a terrifying event—a worldwide catastrophe destroying almost every living thing—but it is told in a very restrained way. Our imaginations are given only a few clues concerning the emotional impact of the great Flood. The writer of Genesis concentrates instead on physical details: the construction of the ark, the animals that were saved, and how long it all took. The writer's decision to emphasize the ark rather than the drama of the storm and destruction will be seen to be not the result of his inability to tell a story effectively, but the result of an important theological choice. The story of the Flood is told not to emphasize the truth that God must judge the wickedness that corrupts His good earth, but to present the good news that in the midst of judgment, it is God's primary intention to save His people.

B. Biblical Background

The obvious theme of this narrative unit is divine judgment on sinners. The account shows God to be the judge of the whole earth, judging the wicked and the world in which they did the wickedness. In this judgment, God made distinctions between the righteous and the wicked, and also between the clean and the unclean (this is vividly portrayed in the animals chosen for the ark). The clean animals may have been for sacrificial purposes, showing that that which is clean belongs to God just as the righteous belong to God. A related theme is the deliverance from judgment by divine grace. God preserved His remnant from the Flood by prior announcement and special provision. In the eyes of the faithful, the fact that God sent the Flood and saved some from the Flood at the same time is a sign of hopefulness that God's judgments are always tempered with mercy.

II. EXPOSITION AND APPLICATION OF THE SCRIPTURE

A. Noah, God's Faithful Servant
(Genesis 6:9b-12)

Noah was a just man and perfect in his generations, and Noah walked with God. And Noah begat three sons, Shem, Ham, and Japheth. The earth also was corrupt before God, and the earth was filled with violence. And God looked upon the earth, and, behold, it was corrupt; for all flesh had corrupted his way upon the earth.

In the first eight verses of chapter 6, the writer of Genesis gave the distinct impression that there was no possible way to lift humanity out of its cesspool of existence and so change the course of history. The depravity was so deep, so pervasive, and so all-encompassing that destructive judgment was God's only option. God chose a dramatic intervention that nearly wiped all humankind from the face of the earth (see verse 7). God was ready to make His judgment complete, and yet Noah found favor in His eyes. Why did God approve of Noah? God saw in Noah what He wants to see in every person in every generation—a righteous person who lives in a blameless way before the community.

God saw wickedness everywhere and decided to destroy humankind, beasts of the field, creeping things, and the fowls of the air. However, it is Noah's faithful relationship with God that provided a channel through which God could start afresh. Even amidst the announced tragedy of the destruction of the world, one individual faithfully walked with God. It was Noah's walk with God that enabled a glimmer of hope in the midst of so much decay and deterioration.

Noah's godly life is described in three complementary ways in Genesis 6:9. Like John the Baptist (see Mark 6:20), Noah was a righteous man, satisfying the standards established for him by a holy God. He stood in a right relationship with God. Like Abraham (see Genesis 17:1), Noah was blameless, giving his contemporaries no excuse to criticize his conduct. To say that Noah was blameless is not to say that he was sinless, but rather that he was a person of high integrity. In addition, like Enoch (see Genesis 5:22), Noah walked with God, exhibiting in word and deed the closeness of his fellowship with God. All of these traits are exemplified by Noah's obedience to God's command to build an ark.

B. Noah Obeys the Voice of God (Genesis 6:13-16)

And God said unto Noah, The end of all flesh is come before me; for the earth is filled with violence through them; and, behold, I will destroy them with the earth. Make thee an ark of gopher wood; rooms shalt thou make in the ark, and shalt pitch it within and without with pitch. And this is the fashion which thou shalt make it of: The length of the ark shall be three hundred cubits, the breadth of it fifty cubits, and the height of it thirty cubits. A window shalt thou make to the ark, and in a cubit shalt thou finish it above; and the door of the ark shalt thou set in the side thereof; with lower, second, and third stories shalt thou make it.

Beginning in Genesis 6:13, the writer focuses on what has happened to the earth in the eyes of God. God informed Noah of the "end of all flesh." God deemed the earth to be corrupt (see verses 11a, 12a) because it was filled with violence; it stood over against the "good" God saw in chapter 1. The earth had not continued as it was created to be. Violence included lawlessness or injustice and a willful flouting of the moral order, manifested in deeds that violated the lives of others. Three times we are told how corrupt the earth had

become because of the entrance of sin into the human heart. Because violence and evil reign everywhere, God decided to destroy all humankind and to make Noah and his family the ancestors of a new humanity.

Due to the corruption of all flesh, God warned Noah that the Flood was coming and gave him 120 years to prepare a great ship (ark) for the saving of his family and every species of created animal life. During this time, Noah was also to preach to the pagan culture, that they too might have adequate warning. Noah must decide whether to obey God's command. He must decide if he has enough faith to trust God and begin to build an ark when not a cloud was in the sky.

This enormous ship was the vehicle that God would use to save the righteous few. The Hebrew word translated "ark" in the Flood story is used in the Old Testament almost exclusively to refer to Noah's ship. The ark (*tevah*) suggests a boxlike craft made to float on the water without rudder or sail or any other navigational aid. It does not use the services of a crew. The use of the ark was intended to emphasize that the fate of the occupants was to be determined solely by the will of God and not to be attributed in any way to the skill of humankind.

Noah faced a daunting task in constructing this enormous boat (five times longer than the *Mayflower*) and getting all the animals and necessary food on board in a short time. The ark's dimensions were truly remarkable for its time. It was 450 feet long, 75 feet wide, and 45 feet high (verse 15). Modern ocean liners rarely exceed twice the length of Noah's ark. To compare it with something perhaps more familiar to us, we observe that the ark was half as long as a football field. The writer of Genesis tells this story in a matter-of-fact way—for the key issue for the writer is whether Noah would obey the divine directive. He did indeed trust God enough to act on his faith and not his sight. He began building this humongous boat when there was no rain or even a sign of rain in the sky. Noah expected great things from God, and he attempted great things for God.

C. God Rewards Noah's Faithfulness (Genesis 6:17-21)

And, behold, I, even I, do bring a flood of waters upon the earth, to destroy all flesh, wherein is the breath of life, from under heaven; and every thing that is in the earth shall die. But with thee will I establish my covenant; and thou shalt come into the ark, thou, and thy sons, and thy wife, and thy sons' wives with thee. And of every living thing of all flesh, two of every sort shalt thou bring into the ark, to keep them alive with thee; they shall be male and female. Of fowls after their kind, and of cattle after their kind, of every creeping thing of the earth after his kind, two of every sort shall come unto thee, to keep them alive. And take thou unto thee of all food that is eaten, and thou shalt gather it to thee; and it shall be for food for thee, and for them.

Whatever the shape of the ark, its declared purpose was to provide sanctuary for eight people and thousands of animals throughout the crisis of the Flood. The devastating powers of the floodwaters would destroy all other life "under the heavens" (verse 17, NIV). Every creature that had the breath of life in it would die, but the Lord would keep alive Noah, his wife, their three sons, and their sons' wives (verses 19-20). The event of Noah's salvation from the Flood is used in the Bible to typify God's deliverance of all who trust in Him. This event also illustrates another important biblical principle: While God bestows His saving grace

and love on individuals, He is concerned about their families as well.

The word *covenant* appears for the first time in the Bible here in verse 18, and its context here seems to be God's intention to save Noah and those who go with him. "But with thee will I establish my covenant" (verse 18). The announcement of this covenant comes at the precise moment when all is dark as possible. In an act of mercy, God demonstrated to Noah that against all the odds there will be hope for the future for those who obey and serve God. In addition, the future will involve a concrete relationship between God and human beings. What is a covenant? A *covenant* is a promise of God to people with whom He is dealing in a special way. It signals a relationship in the context of an agreement. Admittedly, the covenant is not an agreement among equals. In this case, both members did not have responsibilities toward each other, for Noah had none specified toward God. Noah simply acted in obedience to what God had directed. In his covenant, the Lord showed intimacy and affection for Noah by revealing to him the plans necessary for him and his family to escape the coming deluge.

It would include the promise that such a destructive flood would never again wipe out all humankind. But implicit in its promise would also be the divine mandate to be fruitful and increase in number. The same command that God gave when He created humankind would also be necessary if the earth was to be repopulated after the Flood. The covenant assumes a right relationship, as do all of God's covenants in the Old Testament. The covenant probably refers to God's commitment to Noah and his family at that moment of danger. Noah could move into this horrendous experience surrounded by a promise from God that ensured a future relationship with Him and, by implication, the entire creation.

D. The Fate of the Obedient
(Genesis 6:22)

Thus did Noah; according to all that God commanded him, so did he.

Noah did all that God commanded him. His unquestioning obedience and unfaltering trust in God are stressed in verse 22. Of all the people in the Bible, Noah displayed the greatest faith, for until the great Flood it had never rained upon the earth. Rain was a thing not yet seen. Genesis 2:5-6 specifically states that God had not caused it to rain upon the earth, but a steam or mist would rise from the earth. What a fool Noah must have seemed to those around him when he warned of a change in nature that would be one of the greatest in geological history. He did not waver. In a world that had not known rain, he built a ship to prepare for a flood. True obedience consists not only in doing what one is told to do, but also in doing *all* that one is told to do. Noah did everything just as God commanded him to do, despite likely constant, daily ridicule. His faith held him steady in his obedient walk with God.

III. CONCLUDING REFLECTION

What is the importance of the Flood event for today's believers? Water is the most potent symbol of chaos, for in itself it has no form, and all other forms are swallowed up and disappear in it. Water has the power to engulf and extinguish life. It has been suggested that the experience of local floods, along with the personal awareness of the terror of drowning, are the factors largely responsible for the appearance of flood stories in many cultures. The potency of water as a symbol for the threat to all ordered life—the danger of the inbreaking of chaos—also may account for the popularity of these stories and may explain why Noah is one of the best-known biblical characters.

From time to time, well-ordered lives and stable communities are threatened by disaster, by a change for the worse so awful that chaos seems to be lurking at the edges of controlled, meaningful existence. Moreover, water continues to provide the most effective imagery for expressing those feelings. The Greek word for "cataclysm" or "worst disaster" originally meant "deluge." We speak of the feeling of being inundated, deluged, engulfed, and overwhelmed. We talk of barely keeping our heads above water and of sink-or-swim situations. The Flood—and specifically Noah's flood—in cultures influenced by the Bible has become another of those universal experiences in its appearance and impact on humankind. This Flood story makes a statement about Yahweh's dealings with humankind, even when they are under threat of extinction. God can be trusted to bring us out of chaotic situations that arise from time to time in our lives, even when our own unfaithfulness brings such trying times upon us.

What is most instructive for faith about this text is not its historical veracity, for this text is not primarily about amounts of water or pairs of animals or rainbows. But it is about the way God deals with His creation. The Flood story begins by bringing us face-to-face with the God of Israel. This God takes with uncompromising seriousness His own purposes for creation.

And He is impatient when those purposes are resisted or outright rejected. God holds an expectation for His world. When humanity goes astray from those purposes, God will judge humankind, but He will never abandon us. We can always turn to Him in repentance, seek His forgiveness, and be brought again into a right relationship with Him.

PRAYER

Dear heavenly Father, we are grateful that You have created us in Your own image and likeness. When we go astray from Your gracious purposes for our lives, we pray that You would forgive us and restore unto us the joy of our salvation. Grant unto us a spirit of faithful obedience. In Jesus' name we pray. Amen.

HOME DAILY BIBLE READINGS
(October 1-7, 2018)

Noah's Steadfast Faith

MONDAY, October 1: "The Lord's Sorrow for All Creation" (Genesis 6:1-8)

TUESDAY, October 2: "God Will Send a Great Flood" (Genesis 7:1-5)

WEDNESDAY, October 3: "Noah's Family Enters the Ark" (Genesis 7:6-10)

THURSDAY, October 4: "Wild and Domestic Animals Climb Aboard" (Genesis 7:11-16)

FRIDAY, October 5: "The Flood Destroys All Earthly Life" (Genesis 7:17-24)

SATURDAY, October 6: "Surviving People and Animals Disembark Ark" (Genesis 8:1-5, 13-19)

SUNDAY, October 7: "The Ark of Safety and Preservation" (Genesis 6:9b-22)

Fall Quarter 2018
Unit II: God Destroys and Re-creates
Children's Unit: God Destroys and Re-creates

October 14, 2018   Lesson 7

GOD IS ALWAYS WORKING

ADULT/YOUTH
ADULT/YOUNG ADULT TOPIC: Constantly Working
YOUTH TOPIC: Working Together

CHILDREN
GENERAL LESSON TITLE: Noah's Family Works with God
CHILDREN'S TOPIC: A Brighter Future Ahead

DEVOTIONAL READING
Hebrews 11:4-10

ADULT/YOUTH
BACKGROUND SCRIPTURE: Genesis 9–12
PRINT PASSAGE: Genesis 10:2; 11:10, 27, 31-32; 12:1-4
KEY VERSES: Genesis 12:2-3

CHILDREN
BACKGROUND SCRIPTURE: Genesis 9–12
PRINT PASSAGE: Genesis 11:27, 31; 12:1-5
KEY VERSE: Genesis 12:4a

Genesis 10:2; 11:10, 27, 31-32; 12:1-4—KJV

2 The sons of Japheth; Gomer, and Magog, and Madai, and Javan, and Tubal, and Meshech, and Tiras.

.....

10 These are the generations of Shem: Shem was an hundred years old, and begat Arphaxad two years after the flood.

.....

27 Now these are the generations of Terah: Terah begat Abram, Nahor, and Haran; and Haran begat Lot.

.....

31 And Terah took Abram his son, and Lot the son of Haran his son's son, and Sarai his daughter in law, his son Abram's wife; and they went forth with them from Ur of the Chaldees, to go into the land of Canaan; and they came unto Haran, and dwelt there. 32 And the days of Terah were two hundred and five years: and Terah died in Haran.

Genesis 10:2; 11:10, 27, 31-32; 12:1-4—NIV

2 The sons of Japheth: Gomer, Magog, Madai, Javan, Tubal, Meshek and Tiras.

.....

10 This is the account of Shem's family line. Two years after the flood, when Shem was 100 years old, he became the father of Arphaxad.

.....

27 This is the account of Terah's family line. Terah became the father of Abram, Nahor and Haran. And Haran became the father of Lot.

.....

31 Terah took his son Abram, his grandson Lot son of Haran, and his daughter-in-law Sarai, the wife of his son Abram, and together they set out from Ur of the Chaldeans to go to Canaan. But when they came to Harran, they settled there. 32 Terah lived 205 years, and he died in Harran.

NOW THE LORD had said unto Abram, Get thee out of thy country, and from thy kindred, and from thy father's house, unto a land that I will shew thee: 2 And I will make of thee a great nation, and I will bless thee, and make thy name great; and thou shalt be a blessing: 3 And I will bless them that bless thee, and curse him that curseth thee: and in thee shall all families of the earth be blessed. 4 So Abram departed, as the LORD had spoken unto him; and Lot went with him: and Abram was seventy and five years old when he departed out of Haran.	THE LORD had said to Abram, "Go from your country, your people and your father's household to the land I will show you. 2 "I will make you into a great nation, and I will bless you; I will make your name great, and you will be a blessing. 3 "I will bless those who bless you, and whoever curses you I will curse; and all peoples on earth will be blessed through you." 4 So Abram went, as the LORD had told him; and Lot went with him. Abram was seventy-five years old when he set out from Harran.

UNIFYING LESSON PRINCIPLE: Many tasks seem daunting or even impossible for mere human effort. How can mere humans accomplish such challenging and important work? We learn from the book of Genesis that God worked over many generations, from Noah to Abraham, in order to bring blessings to the entire world.

LESSON OBJECTIVES

Upon the completion of this lesson, the students will be able to do the following:

1. Discern the significance for the biblical writer of the genealogical record from Noah to Abraham.
2. Appreciate the generations-long process by which God intended to work in human history.
3. Celebrate how God has worked in one's own family to bring blessings to others.

AGE-LEVEL POINTS TO BE EMPHASIZED

Teachers of ADULTS and YOUTH

—After the Flood, God made a covenant with Noah and his family (Genesis 9:1-17). This covenant continues throughout the generations to God's new, more specific covenant with Abraham.

—Genesis 11:10-26 is one of ten genealogies found in the book of Genesis. It connects Noah's son Shem to Abram.

—Abram's journey to Canaan was started before his covenant with God, but his family stopped in Haran (in northern Mesopotamia; 11:31). God's call to leave home was a push to finish what Abram's family had already begun.

—Genesis 12:1-3 is considered a pivotal text in the book of Genesis and in the entire Pentateuch. God's promises to bless Abram and make him a great nation are themes that recur throughout the Bible.

—Abram was the same man who would later be called Abraham.

—The genealogy in chapter 11 traces Abraham back to Shem, whom God blessed in 9:26. Thus, the family line continues to be blessed and be a blessing to others.

—God's choice of Abram seems exclusive, but the goal is a most inclusive outcome—that all the families of the earth will be blessed.

—Although Abram is called to be a blessing to others, much rests on how they treat him. Those who are positive toward Abram will experience God's favor; the one who despises Abram will know God's displeasure. The text speaks of "those who bless" (plural), but of "the one who curses" (singular), emphasizing that many more will be blessed than cursed.

Teachers of CHILDREN
—Noah's descendant Terah, father of Abram, left Ur of the Chaldeans to move his family to Canaan.

—The Lord came to Abram and told him to move his family to another land.
—The Lord promised to bless Abram, his family, and his descendants.
—Abram obeyed God and left with his family and their possessions to go to an unknown land.
—When Abram left Haran, he was seventy-five years old.
—The family went to Canaan.

THE CHRONOLOGICAL SETTING OF THE LESSON

Genesis 10–11 represents a unique piece of intellectual activity in the ancient world, for they describe an effort to classify all the known peoples of the earth by their lands, languages, families, and nations. They also emphasize the existence of a unity binding all humanity together after the great Flood. All are children of one father, Noah, so there can be no differences in kind to separate humankind. Seventy nations are listed in these chapters. In the biblical world, the number "seventy" is typological—that is, it can be used for rhetorical effect to evoke the idea of totality. In light of this convention, that the offspring of Noah's sons totals seventy communicates God's completion of the restorative population process, and from a literary perspective it conveys the notion of the totality and completion of the human race. The naming of the peoples of the world is but another step in God's progressive revelation of continuing to bless those He has called into existence. Notable is the fact that Israel is nowhere mentioned in Genesis 10, not even in anticipation. Yet, God can clearly be seen laying the groundwork for the call to Israel to be His people in the upcoming chapters.

THE GEOGRAPHICAL AND CULTURAL SETTING OF THE LESSON

Chapter 11 begins the fourth list of names in the primeval history. While the Table of Nations explicitly intends to describe all the nations of the earth, the writer is careful to make sure that the table ends with Shem, one of the three sons of Noah. Five sons were born to Shem, and from this lineage would come Terah, the father of Abram. Abram was the only one of Terah's sons who would be the recipient of God's promise; through him the families of the world would be blessed. God continues to be on the move, working His will in the lives of His people.

PROMINENT CHARACTER(S) IN THE LESSON

Abram (Abraham): the son of Terah; husband of Sarah; and father of Isaac. Abraham was Israel's first great patriarch, and for Israel and Christianity he stands as the father of the faithful.

Lot: the son of Haran and nephew of Abraham.

Sarai (Sarah): wife of Abraham and the mother of Isaac. She is characterized as barren, a condition of humiliation. She is depicted as the mother of Israel, an example of God's faithfulness to His promise. Sarah died in Hebron at age 127.

Shem: the eldest son of Noah; progenitor of Abraham.

Terah: a descendent of Shem's; the father of Abram, Nahor, and Haran.

KEY TERMS IN THE LESSON

Begat (11:27 [KJV only])—Hebrew: *yalad* (yaw-lad'): bore, brought forth, beget; gender; travail.

Blessing (12:2)—Hebrew: *barakah* (ber-aw-kaw'): blessing, blessed; praise of God.

Days (11:32 [KJV only])—Hebrew: *yowm* (yome): day; time; year.

Generations (11:10)—Hebrew: *towladah* (to-led-aw'): descendants; results; proceedings; genealogies; "family line" (NIV).

Kindred (12:1)—Hebrew: *mowledeth* (mo-leh'-deth): kindred; birth; offspring; relatives; begotten; "your people" (NIV).

Went forth (11:31)—Hebrew: *yatsa'* (yaw-tsaw'): to go out, come out, exit, go forth; "set out" (NIV).

TOPICAL OUTLINE OF THE LESSON

I. Introduction
   A. God at Work throughout Human History
   B. Biblical Background

II. Exposition and Application of the Scripture
   A. God Repopulates the Earth with a Purpose (Genesis 10:2)
   B. From Shem to Abraham (Genesis 11:10, 27)
   C. A Promise Addressed to Emptiness (Genesis 11:31-32)
   D. The God Who Promises and Cannot Lie (Genesis 12:1-4)

III. Concluding Reflection

I. INTRODUCTION

A. God at Work throughout Human History

The genealogies found in Genesis 10 and 11 remain among the least satisfactorily studied passages in the book. When compared to the volumes produced on other sections of Genesis, the efforts to understand the structure and meaning of these passages have been sparse. At first glance, it does not appear that the genealogies are the stuff out of which exciting biblical insights can be had. Upon closer inspection of the text, however, the biblical student will find very important information. First, the genealogies give us a survey of the most significant descendants of the sons of Noah. They are intended to be a witness to the fulfillment of the divine commission to fill the earth (see Genesis 9:1). Additionally, this chapter demonstrates that all the nations of the earth came from one man, Noah—making all of us equal in the eyes of God and equal beneficiaries of the promises of God.

The more important lesson to remember is that Genesis 10 is a structured arrangement of the important nations of the world. The writer of the book of Genesis clearly is emphasizing the development of these nations in terms of their importance to Israel. Taking this passage in its context, one can see the hand of God at work in the nations of the earth. In His own time and in His own way, God is working out His purposes and plans for humankind. God has not left creation to its own devices, but He continues to guide and direct the affairs of humankind through His providential grace. Every nation, kindred, and tongue prospers under God's common grace.

B. Biblical Background

Genesis 10 and 11 may be heavy reading for a student of the Word today, but they offer a link to the purposive movement of God through the annals of history. From the new start for humankind by means of one family—Noah—these chapters take us to the life of Abraham, the man chosen to give rise to the race of people through whom the Redeemer was to come. Some of the names listed in the genealogies are meaningless to us today because of limited information from that period of history. Other names of nations are not found at all.

With the recording of the names of these ancient peoples, the universal history necessary to set the stage for what is to come has been completed. Beginning in Genesis 11:10, the record moves on to the purposes of Genesis. The writer first chronicled the descendants of the human family as a whole. The focus then moved to the lives of the patriarch of the chosen race. Now from Shem (see Genesis 11:10) come the descendants leading to Terah, the father of the man originally called Abram, and Abram's two brothers, Nahor and Haran.

Genesis 12 opens with the divine command to Abraham: "Get you of your country and from your kindred and from your father's house, unto the land that I will show you" (see verse 1). The phrase "the land I will show you" literally means, "the land I will make you see." The "seeing" of which God speaks is not by sight, but rather a seeing by faith. Before Abraham could see what God had for him, he must be willing to let go completely of what he already had. God never calls us *to* something without first calling us *away from* something. What Abraham was compelled to leave behind sharpened his sense of loss. To leave his country was not that difficult to do, for he was only a temporary visitor to Haran. However, to be asked to leave his kin and his father's house took exceptional faith, especially when one remembers that Abraham was still dealing with the disappointment of a barren wife.

The God who created the world and all the families therein chose one person, Abraham, to become the father of a great nation and a chosen people. He ordered him to leave the land of his birth for another land promised to the nation that would spring from his loins. And this He asked of Abraham when there was no child of promise in sight. God promised to make Abraham great and to bless all the families of the earth through him. Still, there was no promise of an heir in sight. By faith, Abraham struck out on his journey, trusting where he could not see and walking where he could not trace.

As God works His will in our lives, from time to time He chooses individuals upon whom He imposes particular tasks. Though the individual is confronted with great divine pressure, he or she can accept or refuse the mission. After the destruction of the earth in Noah's day, God is once again on the move to restore, to re-create, and to bless the nations of the world, but He chose to do it through one obedient person who must choose whether to respond to God in faith.

II. EXPOSITION AND APPLICATION OF THE SCRIPTURE

A. God Repopulates the Earth with a Purpose (Genesis 10:2)

The sons of Japheth; Gomer, and Magog, and Madai, and Javan, and Tubal, and Meshech, and Tiras.

The fact that seventy people are mentioned in this chapter (chapter 10) carries some significance for the writer of the book of Genesis. The number could signify that the entirety of the known world has been included and that all peoples share an ultimate unity despite the differences of language, race, and color. Japheth is mentioned in verse 2 perhaps because of the fact that he was the youngest son of Noah.

The listing of such a diverse group of people in chapter 10 becomes a natural extension of the Creation account. This entire chapter constitutes a theological witness to a common humanity shared by all. This multiplication of peoples across the face of the earth constitutes a fulfillment of the divine blessing and the divine command to fill the earth—to be fruitful and multiply.

B. From Shem to Abraham (Genesis 11:10, 27)

These are the generations of Shem: Shem was an hundred years old, and begat Arphaxad two years after the flood. . . . Now these are the generations of Terah: Terah begat Abram, Nahor, and Haran; and Haran begat Lot.

With the mentioning of the name of Shem, the focus of the biblical narration decisively narrows to concentrate upon one particular line of descent within the family tree of Shem. This line issues in Abraham, who is the tenth generation from Shem, just as Noah was the tenth generation from Adam. From a scriptural point of view, the birth of Abraham constitutes a turning point in human history. The author took care not to present Abraham's family line in isolation; instead, he set it in the midst of all the family units of the known world and, in so doing, kept the chosen line embedded in the life of the world. These are deep roots that Israel ought not to forget or set aside. God as creator has been active all the way with this line leading to Abraham. God chose Abraham, not to escape the world out of which he was hewn, but to return to it and bless the families of the world. The text mentions Terah's three sons because the posterity of each is to be connected with the fortunes of Abraham and his offspring.

This verse 27 also gives recognition to the culmination of a historic process of continuous divine selection that began with Adam's sons. God has been on the move not only to create and to judge, but also to restore and bless. Abraham and his family then became God's chosen vessels.

C. A Promise Addressed to Emptiness (Genesis 11:31-32)

And Terah took Abram his son, and Lot the son of Haran his son's son, and Sarai his daughter in law, his son Abram's wife; and they went forth with them from Ur of the Chaldees, to go into the land of Canaan; and they came unto Haran, and dwelt there. And the days of Terah were two hundred and five years: and Terah died in Haran.

Verse 30, which is part of the Background Scripture, is significant in this context. Theologically, it states a negative twice—"But Sarai was barren; she had no child." Twenty generations of genealogy have brought us to Abram, and it now seems that he is a person of no importance, for the story appears to end with him and Sarai. The writer of Genesis will hold nothing back regarding the seeming hopelessness of this couple to continue their long line of descendants. Indeed, it is the first piece of information he gives about them. In fact, it is the only thing we know about them until Abraham becomes the recipient of the promise.

It is a promise addressed to emptiness—"I will make of you a great nation" (Genesis 12:2, NRSV). The promise required descendants, and we have already been told that Sarai was barren; she had no child. The result of twenty generations of replenishing the earth is a childless couple whom God proposes to make a blessing to all the nations of this disturbed and suffering earth. Yet, contained in this promise addressed to barrenness is the way God chooses to bless the people of the earth: He will bring life out of barrenness and emptiness. This is what God will do in order to show that He alone is sovereign and filled with grace.

D. The God Who Promises and Cannot Lie (Genesis 12:1-4)

NOW THE LORD had said unto Abram, Get thee out of thy country, and from thy kindred, and from thy father's house, unto a land that I will shew thee: And I will make of thee a great nation, and I will bless thee, and make thy name great; and thou shalt be a blessing: And I will bless them that bless thee, and curse him that curseth thee: and in thee shall all families of the earth be blessed. So Abram departed, as the LORD had spoken unto him; and Lot went with him: and Abram was seventy and five years old when he departed out of Haran.

The starting point of Genesis 12 is the divine word to Abram (later renamed *Abraham*), calling him to leave his homeland and start a new nation that would bring blessing to the world. In later years as Israel reflected on its beginnings, it would learn by this account of the sojourn of Abraham and Sarah that their very existence as a nation was by God's election of one man who responded by faith. It would affirm to the nation that their beginnings were rooted in the will of God. Thus, in their own day, as they heard their call to leave Egypt and go with Moses to the land of Canaan to inherit the promises to the father, they would be reminded by this story that faith in God's promises would be demonstrated by obedience to God's call. And so it is with us. As we seek to discern God's will in our day and time, these narratives serve to remind us of what faith in the promises of God can do in our lives. God has a perfect track record of leading, guiding, and directing, and we can trust His promises. Abraham and Sarah bear witness to the faithfulness of the promises of God in their day and in ours.

In Abraham and Sarah's day, the message was that faith is demonstrated by obedience, but the circumstances in their story make this message even more powerful. Abraham's obedience was not a simple act of faith. He was advanced in years, probably prosperous and settled, but he was thoroughly pagan (one who has little or no religion) in his thinking and worldview. However, the Scriptures state that the Word of the Lord came to him—although we do not know how or in what form. When he heard the Word of the Lord, he left his world and his relatives to follow the command of God. Consequently, in the Scriptures he has become the epitome of faith. We should take care not to trivialize Abraham's great act of faith. What happened to Abraham was a life-altering act of faith.

When God revealed Himself to Abraham, Abraham responded with utter trust in almighty God, and it changed his life for the rest of his days. What we find in Genesis 12 is more than some historical account of a happening in the long ago; what happened here is the divine revelation of God to a human being He created in His own image and likeness. Abraham's great act of faith would have consequences for all of us, because it was through Abraham that God would bless all the peoples of the world. God revealed Himself to Abraham, and Abraham responded in faith. What about us? How will we respond to the divine initiative in our lives? How will we respond to the mighty workings of God in the world and for the world through us? Will we allow ourselves to be a channel of blessings, or will we turn a deaf ear and a blind eye to the movement of God among us in our day? Faith is the positive response of the total person to the initiatives of almighty God. A broken, hurting world desperately needs us to respond positively to God as He wills to work through us.

III. CONCLUDING REFLECTION

The gracious God's broad new strokes to bless the earth come suddenly and brilliantly upon the canvas of sacred history. The Lord had not spoken to His saints since His covenant with Noah, in which He resolved to bless the earth and forgive the evil ways of His creation (see Genesis 8:20–9:17). Now in Genesis 10 and 11, His creative word to bless the tribes and nations—which He has scattered—redirects the course of history. God moves now in the direction of blessings and fulfillment. Abraham comes on the scene as God moves from a nation to a family, a family whose offspring would bless the entire earth. With astounding suddenness, Abraham responded in obedience and faith to God's initiative to bless the world through him.

The creating God is still at work. His purposive acts are long range and play themselves out across the years. Sometimes it can appear that God is not present, or that He has left this world to its own design and desires. However, today's lesson reminds us that God is always working on behalf of His creation.

PRAYER

O Lord, with deep faith and utter dependence on You, help us to say yes to Your desire to be at work in our lives. In Jesus' name we pray. Amen.

HOME DAILY BIBLE READINGS
(October 8-14, 2018)

God Is Always Working
MONDAY, October 8: "Noah's Mandate: Fill the Earth" (Genesis 9:1-7)
TUESDAY, October 9: "God's Covenant with Noah and Animals" (Genesis 9:8-17)
WEDNESDAY, October 10: "Families and Nations Descended from Noah" (Genesis 9:18-19; 10:1-4, 6-8, 21-23)
THURSDAY, October 11: "The Lord Scatters the People" (Genesis 11:1-9)
FRIDAY, October 12: "Abram, Sarai, and Lot in Canaan" (Genesis 12:5-9)
SATURDAY, October 13: "Noah to Abraham, Faith in Action" (Hebrews 11:4-10)
SUNDAY, October 14: "God's Blessings—from Noah to Abraham" (Genesis 11:10, 27, 31-32; 12:1-4)

Fall Quarter 2018
Unit II: God Destroys and Re-creates
Children's Unit: God Destroys and Re-creates

October 21, 2018   Lesson 8

ABRAHAM AND SARAH BIRTH GOD'S PEOPLE

ADULT/YOUTH	CHILDREN
ADULT/YOUNG ADULT TOPIC: **Promises Give Hope**	GENERAL LESSON TITLE: **Trusting God's Promises**
YOUTH TOPIC: **A Promise Kept**	CHILDREN'S TOPIC: **Because I'm Happy**

DEVOTIONAL READING
Luke 1:26-38

ADULT/YOUTH	CHILDREN
BACKGROUND SCRIPTURE: **Genesis 18:9-15; 21:1-7**	BACKGROUND SCRIPTURE: **Genesis 18:9-15; 21:1-7**
PRINT PASSAGE: **Genesis 18:9-15; 21:1-7**	PRINT PASSAGE: **Genesis 18:9-15; 21:1-7**
KEY VERSE: **Genesis 21:1**	KEY VERSE: **Genesis 18:10**

Genesis 18:9-15; 21:1-7—KJV

9 And they said unto him, Where is Sarah thy wife? And he said, Behold, in the tent.

10 And he said, I will certainly return unto thee according to the time of life; and, lo, Sarah thy wife shall have a son. And Sarah heard it in the tent door, which was behind him.

11 Now Abraham and Sarah were old and well stricken in age; and it ceased to be with Sarah after the manner of women.

12 Therefore Sarah laughed within herself, saying, After I am waxed old shall I have pleasure, my lord being old also?

13 And the LORD said unto Abraham, Wherefore did Sarah laugh, saying, Shall I of a surety bear a child, which am old?

14 Is any thing too hard for the LORD? At the time appointed I will return unto thee, according to the time of life, and Sarah shall have a son.

Genesis 18:9-15; 21:1-7—NIV

9 "Where is your wife Sarah?" they asked him. "There, in the tent," he said.

10 Then one of them said, "I will surely return to you about this time next year, and Sarah your wife will have a son." Now Sarah was listening at the entrance to the tent, which was behind him.

11 Abraham and Sarah were already very old, and Sarah was past the age of childbearing.

12 So Sarah laughed to herself as she thought, "After I am worn out and my lord is old, will I now have this pleasure?"

13 Then the LORD said to Abraham, "Why did Sarah laugh and say, 'Will I really have a child, now that I am old?'

14 "Is anything too hard for the LORD? I will return to you at the appointed time next year, and Sarah will have a son."

15 Then Sarah denied, saying, I laughed not; for she was afraid. And he said, Nay; but thou didst laugh.

. . . . .

AND THE LORD visited Sarah as he had said, and the LORD did unto Sarah as he had spoken.

2 For Sarah conceived, and bare Abraham a son in his old age, at the set time of which God had spoken to him.

3 And Abraham called the name of his son that was born unto him, whom Sarah bare to him, Isaac.

4 And Abraham circumcised his son Isaac being eight days old, as God had commanded him.

5 And Abraham was an hundred years old, when his son Isaac was born unto him.

6 And Sarah said, God hath made me to laugh, so that all that hear will laugh with me.

7 And she said, Who would have said unto Abraham, that Sarah should have given children suck? for I have born him a son in his old age.

15 Sarah was afraid, so she lied and said, "I did not laugh." But he said, "Yes, you did laugh."

. . . . .

NOW THE LORD was gracious to Sarah as he had said, and the LORD did for Sarah what he had promised.

2 Sarah became pregnant and bore a son to Abraham in his old age, at the very time God had promised him.

3 Abraham gave the name Isaac to the son Sarah bore him.

4 When his son Isaac was eight days old, Abraham circumcised him, as God commanded him.

5 Abraham was a hundred years old when his son Isaac was born to him.

6 Sarah said, "God has brought me laughter, and everyone who hears about this will laugh with me."

7 And she added, "Who would have said to Abraham that Sarah would nurse children? Yet I have borne him a son in his old age."

UNIFYING LESSON PRINCIPLE: Because of past promises that were not fulfilled, we find it hard to trust future promises. What can help us have faith and confidence to depend on important promises that shape our lives? Although Abraham and Sarah had to wait a long time for God's promise of a son to be born to them to shape all people of the earth, God showed them that this promise was trustworthy.

LESSON OBJECTIVES

Upon the completion of this lesson, the students will be able to do the following:

1. Comprehend God's grace and power manifested in the birth of Isaac to Abraham and Sarah.
2. Appreciate the value of patience as God works out the divine will on His timetable, not ours.
3. Pray for faith to await God's promised blessings.

AGE-LEVEL POINTS TO BE EMPHASIZED

Teachers of ADULTS and YOUTH

—Hospitality is an enduring motif throughout Scripture, commended in this text as a practice toward humans and perhaps also God (even unawares).

—Abraham circumcised Isaac eight days after he was born because circumcision was the sign of the covenant for the nation that would come from Abraham (Genesis 17).

—The account of Isaac's birth emphasizes the great joy that accompanied Sarah with the birth of her son. Not only was she happy, but those around her were also joyful at the fulfillment of God's promise. The theme of laughter is revisited again in Genesis 21:1-7, culminating in the naming of Isaac, which means "he (God) laughs."

—The Genesis 21 verses seem to indicate divine intervention in Sarah's pregnancy; but God does not act alone in this but, rather, in partnership with Abraham and Sarah.

—Sarah's laughter is an external expression of Abraham's own internal response when God first promised to make of them a great nation. Often, many readers look down upon Sarah for laughing at the news given to her by the Lord, but they forget Abraham also fell down on his face and laughed when told he would have a son in his old age (see Genesis 17:15-17).

—Barrenness was a mark of shame for women at this time, and some even believed themselves to be cursed by God. This shame and lack of faith on Sarah's part is what compelled her to circumvent God's timing by having Abraham conceive a child with her slave, Hagar (see Genesis 16.).

—Isaac's birth occurred twenty-five years after its first promise, which is implied in Genesis 12:4 ("Abram was seventy-five years old").

Teachers of CHILDREN

—The Lord visited Abraham in the form of three men and told Abraham that his wife, Sarah, would have a son.

—Sarah listened behind the tent entrance when the Lord made the promise.

—Abraham and Sarah were very old and past child-bearing age.

—Sarah laughed to herself at the thought of her having a child at her old age.

—The Lord asked Abraham why Sarah laughed, and Sarah denied her laughter. The Lord told her that she did laugh.

—At the right time, the Lord came to Sarah and she conceived a son named Isaac, which means, "he (God) laughs."

THE CHRONOLOGICAL SETTING OF THE LESSON

God promised to make Abraham the father of a great nation—yet, Abraham was not even blessed with one son and heir. God also made Sarah a promise: "And I will bless her, and moreover I will give thee a son of her: yea, I will bless her, and she shall be a mother of nations" (Genesis 17:16, ASV). Yet, Abraham harbors doubts in his heart, and asks, "Shall a child be born unto him that is an hundred years old? and shall Sarah, that is ninety years old, bear?" (Genesis 17:17). Sarah laughs to herself when she hears this promise of a son to be born to her in her old age. In addition, when Sarah's name is first mentioned, it is stressed, "Sarai was barren; she had no child" (Genesis 11:30). Barrenness of the mother (Sarah) in the Bible is witness to the godly purpose and to the choice of the eventual destined child of the promise, Isaac. But the Lord spoke and Sarah conceived and bore Abraham a son in his old age, at the set time of which God had spoken to him (see Genesis 21:1-2). God fulfilled His Word and Isaac was born. It is stressed that the birth is wondrous, in that Abraham was a hundred years old. All the stories before the birth of the promised son reveal the supreme divine plan which is above nature and even beyond the comprehension of humankind. The hearers of this word are urged to have utter confidence in almighty God and to believe that He is able to fulfill His promises in every age to every generation.

THE GEOGRAPHICAL AND CULTURAL SETTING OF THE LESSON

In today's announcement of a promised heir to Abraham, the Lord of creation came in person to announce the time of the fulfillment of the promise. His words were laughed at, however, because they promised that which was humanly impossible. Nevertheless, the Lord set the time for the supernatural birth, for nothing was too incredible for the Lord. Basically, the passage forms an exhortation for the covenant people to believe that God can do the impossible. The promise to Sarah was the annunciation of an impossible birth. (Note that at the annunciation of the birth of Jesus, Mary likewise could not understand how such a thing could be, and it was more difficult in her case. God miraculously provided the long-awaited seed to her as well [see Luke 1:34].) When something similarly extraordinary is announced, our response is consistent with Sarah's—we are taken off guard; we wonder how these things can be; we look at it from the human side and laugh; and then out of fear, we deny that we laughed at a word from the Lord. The Lord expects His people to respond by faith and not doubt, for His Word is based on His nature. If the people of God (who enjoy covenantal fellowship with Him) fully believed what He said He would do—now or at any time in the history of the faith—their lives and their world would be very different.

PROMINENT CHARACTER(S) IN THE LESSON

Isaac: the name means, "He laughs." It was a name prenatally fixed by God. For this reason, Isaac is the only patriarch who does not undergo a name change.
Sarah: the wife of Abraham and mother of Isaac.

KEY TERMS IN THE LESSON

Bear (18:13 [KJV only])—Hebrew: *yalad* (yaw-lad'): to bear, bring forth, beget; gender; travail.
Heard (18:10)—Hebrew: *shama'* (shaw-mah'): to hear, listen to, obey; "was listening" (NIV).
Laugh (18:13)—Hebrew: *tsachaq* (tsaw-khak'): to laugh, mock, play.
Old (18:11)—Hebrew: *zaqen* (zaw-kane'): old; ancient; elder.
Visited (21:1 [KJV only])—Hebrew: *paqad* (paw-kad'): attended to; mustered; numbered; reckoned; visited; punished; appointed; looked after; cared for.
Wife (18:9)—Hebrew: *'ishshah* (ish-shaw'): woman; wife; female.

TOPICAL OUTLINE OF THE LESSON

I. **Introduction**
   A. Faith and Doubt
   B. Biblical Background

II. **Exposition and Application of the Scripture**
   A. An Incredible Promise (Genesis 18:9-12)
   B. Sarah's Laughter of Unbelief (Genesis 18:13-15)
   C. Fulfillment and Frustration (Genesis 21:1-2)
   D. Opportunities for Obedience (Genesis 21:3-7)

III. **Concluding Reflection**

I. INTRODUCTION

A. Faith and Doubt

Abraham and Sarah's case was a mixture of faith and doubt (see Genesis 18:9-15). This was especially true with respect to God's promise of the patriarch's seed through which the divine promise was to run. In Genesis 18, we find yet another word from God which will decisively change the world of Abraham and Sarah. Their world of barrenness is shattered by a new possibility that lies outside the reasonable expectation of their perceptual field. The story is constructed to present the tension between this mysterious speech of God (that comes as a promise) and the resistance and mockery of Abraham and Sarah who doubt the word and cannot believe the promise. Often, we stand before the promises of God and find those words to be beyond reason and belief in our own particular situations. Abraham and, especially, Sarah are not offered here as models of faith but as models of disbelief. For them, the powerful promise of God outdistances their ability to receive it.

Once again, this story points out to us just how difficult it is for us to trust in the promises of God. Faith is not a reasonable act which fits into the normal scheme of life. The promise of the Gospel is not a conventional piece of wisdom that is easily accommodated to everything else in our lives. Embracing the radical claims of God in our lives that often come to us as promises requires the shattering of long-held beliefs. Abraham and Sarah, owing to their barrenness, have become resigned to their closed future. They have accepted their feelings of hopelessness as normal. God's promise of an heir in their old age does not meet them in receptive hopefulness but, rather, in resistant helplessness. They reject the promise as nonsensical.

At the center of this passage is God's question to Sarah: "Is anything too hard for the Lord?" It is an open question, one that awaits an answer from Sarah and from us. It is the question which surfaces everywhere in the Bible. It is the fundamental question that every human being must answer before God, because how it is answered determines everything else.

If the question of the Lord is answered, "Yes, some things are too hard for God," then we have yet to trust Him completely. In some way, we are still counting on our own ingenuity and know-how. We continue to live in a closed universe where things are stable, reliable, and hopeless. On the other hand, if our answer is, "No, nothing is impossible for God," then that is the sign that we have fully entrusted our lives into God's hands. The writer of Genesis would have us to yield completely to the initiatives of God, for it is truly in Him that we live, move, and have our being. There are many things in life that we can work out on our own, but there are other things that we have to wait out and trust the promises of God to bring to pass. Sarah did indeed bear a son, but only after experiencing much heartache and frustration owing to her lack of faith.

B. Biblical Background

The divine promise of a child to be born to Abraham and Sarah in their old age unfolded in stages. First, in Genesis 15:4, Abraham was assured that his heir would be a natural-born son; then, in Genesis 17:16-21, he was assured that Sarah would bear this child. Now in Genesis 18:10, a time limit is set for the fulfillment of the promise—"I will surely return to you in due season, and your wife Sarah shall have a son." In this second announcement of a child, the focus is not so much on the announcement itself as it is on Sarah's response to the annunciation. The writer of Genesis reminds the listener of the ages of the couple and states that Sarah was past menopause or "after the manner of women." Sarah, laughing to herself, echoed that reminder with a probable touch of sarcasm. She wondered whether this announcement implied that she was to once again experience "pleasure" (Genesis 18:12). Perhaps Sarah's understanding of the problem included not only her menopause, but also Abraham's infertility or impotence. In any case, Sarah responded to the annunciation in the same way Abraham had, with laughter (see Genesis 17:17).

Nevertheless, the Lord was displeased not only with Sarah's laughter, but also with her subsequent denial that she had laughed. God responded to Sarah's laughter with two questions: "Why did Sarah laugh? Moreover, is anything too hard for the Lord?" We sometimes forget how powerful our God is. An angel had to remind Mary of the same truth concerning her own pregnancy and that of her aged kinswoman Elizabeth: "Nothing is impossible with God" (Luke 1:37). Can Mary, a virgin, conceive? Of course! Can an elderly woman become pregnant? Absolutely!

God's speech concluded with a repetition of the announcement of birth (see Genesis 18:14). The question "is anything too hard for the Lord?" (verse 14) constituted the key question for this story about an heir. The question is easy to answer abstractly for anyone in the family of Abraham. Of course, nothing is too hard for the Lord. However, what is easy to answer in theory becomes a different matter in the concrete human experience of barrenness. Neither Sarah nor Abraham answered the question. Abraham made no response, even though the question was put directly to him. Sarah avoided the question by denying she laughed.

God replied, "No, but you did laugh" (Genesis 18:15). The Bible does not gloss over the human failings of the ancient heroes.

II. EXPOSITION AND APPLICATION OF THE SCRIPTURE

A. An Incredible Promise
(Genesis 18:9-12)

And they said unto him, Where is Sarah thy wife? And he said, Behold, in the tent. And he said, I will certainly return unto thee according to the time of life; and, lo, Sarah thy wife shall have a son. And Sarah heard it in the tent door, which was behind him. Now Abraham and Sarah were old and well stricken in age; and it ceased to be with Sarah after the manner of women. Therefore Sarah laughed within herself, saying, After I am waxed old shall I have pleasure, my lord being old also?

We pick up this event when three divine visitors question Abraham as to the whereabouts of Sarah. The question seems rhetorical, for surely God knew Sarah's whereabouts. Sarah was not in sight when the visitors asked the question. They probably asked this question to give Abraham a clue that they were not ordinary men; though they were strangers, they knew Sarah was Abraham's wife. The question was intended to focus attention on the purpose of the visit. The promise is emphatically and specifically worded in verse 10: "I shall surely return to you this time next year, and Sarah your wife shall have a son." The Lord's return, meaning His intervention and determination to bless, signifies that the birth will be a divine provision. "I will surely return" is also a clear indication that the speaker is the Lord, since He alone can faithfully promise life out of barrenness and decay. Divine messengers deliver a divine promise, but Abraham and Sarah simply do not have sufficient faith to trust what appeared to be an impossible promise.

Sarah, who was inside her tent, overheard the remark. She discreetly stayed inside her tent, for since she was a married woman, custom said she should not display herself. The author has already noted that she was past the age of childbearing. The Hebrew literally reads, "Sarah no longer experienced the cycle of women" (Genesis 18:11). Her body is procreatively dead. She knew there was no way humanly possible that she could bear a child, so Sarah laughed within herself. Her laughter did not come from a sneering arrogance, for it was based on her physical condition. While she did not believe the event possible, she was much more reserved than Abraham had been, for when he first had heard the news "he fell upon his face, and laughed" (Genesis 17:17). Sarah's reaction is what would be expected, given the circumstances; she looked at the promise from her side and laughed. She could not see the promise through the eyes of faith.

B. Sarah's Laughter of Unbelief
(Genesis 18:13-15)

And the Lord said unto Abraham, Wherefore did Sarah laugh, saying, Shall I of a surety bear a child, which am old? Is any thing too hard for the Lord? At the time appointed I will return unto thee, according to the time of life, and Sarah shall have a son. Then Sarah denied, saying, I laughed not; for she was afraid. And he said, Nay; but thou didst laugh.

As assurance of His miraculous power, the Lord verbalized Sarah's secret thoughts. Sarah denied that she had laughed, but God assured her that He had heard her laughter: "You did laugh," said God. This is both a restorative rebuke and an assuring sign to Sarah: the one who reads her thoughts can also open her womb. While the laughter of disbelief might be considered normal for a woman of Sarah's age, it prompted one of the premier promises found in Scripture: "Is anything too hard for the Lord?" It is God who makes the promised future possible. God serves as the source of hope in situations where the way into the future seems entirely blocked. God gives shape to possibilities when all around us seems impossible. The active engagement of God in the midst of the problems of daily life opens the future to us rather than closing it down.

C. Fulfillment and Frustration
(Genesis 21:1-2)

AND THE Lord visited Sarah as he had said, and the Lord did unto Sarah as he had spoken. For Sarah conceived, and bare Abraham a son in his old age, at the set time of which God had spoken to him.

Genesis 21:1-7 tells the long-awaited fulfillment of the promise of a son. These verses could be classified as a birth report. The report forms the culmination of the preceding narratives, especially those that include the motif of laughter. The connection comes with the very first verse linking the fulfillment to the promise. The point to stress must be the fulfillment of the promise, or to put it another way, the reliability of the Word of the Lord. The verb translated "visited" in verse 1 describes a divine intervention in someone's life that shapes or alters his or her destiny. A survey of its range of usages will show that it can describe appointments to new positions, mustering of troops, intervening for blessing or for judgment, as well as any number of other activities. However, the word *visited* in this context signifies a divine intervention to bless Sarah, an intervention that would change not only her destiny, but also the destiny of the people of God for ages to come. God also intervenes in our lives today, sometimes to shape destiny, sometimes for judgment, and sometimes to reward our faith.

A *blessing* is defined as an action on the part of God that creates a condition of well-being in a person's life. Abraham and Sarah are blessed with a son in their old age. They do indeed live to see the fulfillment of their faith. Yet, because of previous doubts, it was an experience of fulfillment and frustration. As Jehovah had said, so it happened to Sarah. "For Sarah conceived, and bare Abraham a son in his old age" (verse 2). One may wonder why God delayed the event so long, twenty-five years after the first veiled promise was given (see Genesis 12:2). In a sense, it was a test of Abraham's faith. Furthermore, when the promise was fulfilled, there must be no question that it was God's doing alone. While Isaac's birth was not a virgin one, it was miraculous nonetheless. In accord with the Lord's Word, Isaac was named, and on the eighth day he was circumcised. What a time of rejoicing it was! This is reflected in Sarah's words, "God hath made me to laugh, so that all that hear will laugh with me" (Genesis 21:6). The former laughter of incredulity now gave way to the laughter of fulfillment.

D. Opportunities for Obedience (Genesis 21:3-7)

And Abraham called the name of his son that was born unto him, whom Sarah bare to him, Isaac. And Abraham circumcised his son Isaac being eight days old, as God had commanded him. And Abraham was an hundred years old, when his son Isaac was born unto him. And Sarah said, God hath made me to laugh, so that all that hear will laugh with me. And she said, Who would have said unto Abraham, that Sarah should have given children suck? for I have born him a son in his old age.

The name *Isaac* is repeated three times in three verses. The qualification "his son" also appears three times. The naming of his son and the performance of the rite of circumcision were acts of obedience to the Lord's previous commands. Abraham responded faithfully by naming his son Isaac, and by circumcising him. In spite of Abraham and Sarah's lack of belief, God delivered on His promise. Abraham responded in faithful obedience. In this section, Sarah alone spoke. She spoke of the fact that now she can laugh again and others too will laugh. Sarah credits God with changing her laughter of incredulity into joy. All will now laugh in joy and amazement with Sarah. She speaks of children (verse 7), implying that the fulfillment of God's promise will go even beyond Isaac to bless his offspring who are destined to bless the earth. Faith in the promises of God moves us far beyond the limitations of our own thoughts and aspirations. Knowing that nothing is impossible with God brings joy and laughter into our lives.

III. CONCLUDING REFLECTION

Never do Abraham and Sarah appear more like the rest of us than in Genesis 18:9-16; they simply could not believe that God's promise would come to pass as they considered the human limitations of their advanced ages. Sarah laughed the laughter of unbelief. And, indeed, Abraham had once been guilty of this same disbelieving laughter. The promise that was supposed to be from God seemed to her to be absurd. To have a general pious belief in God's existence was one thing; to trust that His power and grace could come directly into her life with a wonderful blessing was another. Why should she be simple-minded enough to believe that? Why should people in any time believe? Like Sarah, we may try to hide our most eager longings behind a laugh that tries to say, "You cannot fool me." In today's story, God's promise was fulfilled despite Sarah's skepticism, whether it originated from scorn or fear. But eventually, Sarah would cry out in great and wonderful happiness, "God hath made me to laugh, so that all that hear will laugh with me" (Genesis 21:6). Blessed laughter is the laughter that comes from one who has put his or her trust in almighty God and His promises, even when those promises seem distant, far off, and downright impossible.

While the final biblical testimony is convinced of God's ability to do the impossible, the question for us is whether we can reach the same conclusion. Is anything too hard for God in our lives? Is God's sovereign power limited to our expectations, or is God able to act above anything we could ask or think?

PRAYER

Teach us, O Lord, how to trust in Your promises. Give us the patience to await the realization of all those things You have promised in Your Word, and help us not to grow weary in well doing. In Jesus' name we pray. Amen.

HOME DAILY BIBLE READINGS
(October 15-21, 2018)

Abraham and Sarah Birth God's People
MONDAY, October 15: "God Honors Covenants with Abraham" (Psalm 105:1-11)
TUESDAY, October 16: "Hagar Births Abraham's Son, Ishmael" (Genesis 16:7-11, 15-16)
WEDNESDAY, October 17: "Gentiles Share in Abraham's Promise" (Galatians 3:6-9, 13-14)
THURSDAY, October 18: "Abram Believes God" (Genesis 15:1-6)
FRIDAY, October 19: "God's Covenant Extended through Isaac" (Genesis 17:15-22)
SATURDAY, October 20: "Abraham Hosts God's Messengers" (Genesis 18:1-8)
SUNDAY, October 21: "Child of Faith and Laughter" (Genesis 18:9-15; 21:1-7)

Fall Quarter 2018
Unit II: God Destroys and Re-creates
Children's Unit: God Destroys and Re-creates

October 28, 2018   **Lesson 9**

ISAAC AND REBEKAH CONTINUE THE LEGACY

ADULT/YOUTH
ADULT/YOUNG ADULT TOPIC: Make a Decision
YOUTH TOPIC: Say Yes!

CHILDREN
GENERAL LESSON TITLE: Isaac and Rebekah Continue the Legacy
CHILDREN'S TOPIC: Continuing the Legacy

DEVOTIONAL READING
Ephesians 5:21-33

ADULT/YOUTH
BACKGROUND SCRIPTURE: Genesis 24
PRINT PASSAGE: Genesis 24:12-21, 61-67
KEY VERSE: Genesis 24:61

CHILDREN
BACKGROUND SCRIPTURE: Genesis 24
PRINT PASSAGE: Genesis 24:15-21, 61-67
KEY VERSE: Genesis 24:67

Genesis 24:12-21, 61-67—KJV

12 And he said O LORD God of my master Abraham, I pray thee, send me good speed this day, and shew kindness unto my master Abraham.

13 Behold, I stand here by the well of water; and the daughters of the men of the city come out to draw water:

14 And let it come to pass, that the damsel to whom I shall say, Let down thy pitcher, I pray thee, that I may drink; and she shall say, Drink, and I will give thy camels drink also: let the same be she that thou hast appointed for thy servant Isaac; and thereby shall I know that thou hast shewed kindness unto my master.

15 And it came to pass, before he had done speaking, that, behold, Rebekah came out, who was born to Bethuel, son of Milcah, the wife of Nahor, Abraham's brother, with her pitcher upon her shoulder.

Genesis 24:12-21, 61-67—NIV

12 Then he prayed, "LORD, God of my master Abraham, make me successful today, and show kindness to my master Abraham.

13 "See, I am standing beside this spring, and the daughters of the townspeople are coming out to draw water.

14 "May it be that when I say to a young woman, 'Please let down your jar that I may have a drink,' and she says, 'Drink, and I'll water your camels too'—let her be the one you have chosen for your servant Isaac. By this I will know that you have shown kindness to my master."

15 Before he had finished praying, Rebekah came out with her jar on her shoulder. She was the daughter of Bethuel son of Milkah, who was the wife of Abraham's brother Nahor.

16 And the damsel was very fair to look upon, a virgin, neither had any man known her: and she went down to the well, and filled her pitcher, and came up.

17 And the servant ran to meet her, and said, Let me, I pray thee, drink a little water of thy pitcher.

18 And she said, Drink, my lord: and she hasted, and let down her pitcher upon her hand, and gave him drink.

19 And when she had done giving him drink, she said, I will draw water for thy camels also, until they have done drinking.

20 And she hasted, and emptied her pitcher into the trough, and ran again unto the well to draw water, and drew for all his camels.

21 And the man wondering at her held his peace, to wit whether the LORD had made his journey prosperous or not.

.....

61 And Rebekah arose, and her damsels, and they rode upon the camels, and followed the man: and the servant took Rebekah, and went his way.

62 And Isaac came from the way of the well Lahairoi; for he dwelt in the south country.

63 And Isaac went out to meditate in the field at the eventide: and he lifted up his eyes, and saw, and, behold, the camels were coming.

64 And Rebekah lifted up her eyes, and when she saw Isaac, she lighted off the camel.

65 For she had said unto the servant, What man is this that walketh in the field to meet us? And the servant had said, It is my master: therefore she took a vail, and covered herself.

66 And the servant told Isaac all things that he had done.

67 And Isaac brought her into his mother Sarah's tent, and took Rebekah, and she became his wife; and he loved her: and Isaac was comforted after his mother's death.

16 The woman was very beautiful, a virgin; no man had ever slept with her. She went down to the spring, filled her jar and came up again.

17 The servant hurried to meet her and said, "Please give me a little water from your jar."

18 "Drink, my lord," she said, and quickly lowered the jar to her hands and gave him a drink.

19 After she had given him a drink, she said, "I'll draw water for your camels too, until they have had enough to drink."

20 So she quickly emptied her jar into the trough, ran back to the well to draw more water, and drew enough for all his camels.

21 Without saying a word, the man watched her closely to learn whether or not the LORD had made his journey successful.

.....

61 Then Rebekah and her attendants got ready and mounted the camels and went back with the man. So the servant took Rebekah and left.

62 Now Isaac had come from Beer Lahai Roi, for he was living in the Negev.

63 He went out to the field one evening to meditate, and as he looked up, he saw camels approaching.

64 Rebekah also looked up and saw Isaac. She got down from her camel

65 and asked the servant, "Who is that man in the field coming to meet us?" "He is my master," the servant answered. So she took her veil and covered herself.

66 Then the servant told Isaac all he had done.

67 Isaac brought her into the tent of his mother Sarah, and he married Rebekah. So she became his wife, and he loved her; and Isaac was comforted after his mother's death.

UNIFYING LESSON PRINCIPLE: People often must face decisions that will change their lives forever. How can we make the most of the opportunities life gives us? Rebekah took initiative in answering the call to become the wife of Isaac and thus to play an important role in the unfolding of God's promises.

LESSON OBJECTIVES

Upon the completion of this lesson, the students will be able to do the following:

1. Understand how Rebekah seized the opportunity to become part of God's plan.
2. Joyfully welcome the possibilities God opens to them.
3. Say "yes" to the opportunities God provides them.

AGE-LEVEL POINTS TO BE EMPHASIZED

Teachers of ADULTS and YOUTH

—The words of Abraham at the beginning of Genesis 24 were his final words recorded in Genesis. With these words, Abraham commissioned his servant to travel to Abraham's homeland of Haran to find a wife for his son Isaac. Abraham did not want his son to marry into a family of the pagan Canaanites.

—Genesis 24 focuses greatly on the relationship between God's sovereignty and human free will. In Genesis 24:7-8, Abraham insisted that even though an angel would guide the servant's task, the woman who was to be Isaac's wife must make the choice herself.

—Many commentators note that Rebekah's actions parallel the actions of Abraham in Genesis 12:1-18, in which God called Abraham to leave his homeland and travel to a place God had chosen for him. In Genesis 24, Rebekah answered a similar call and made the decision to leave her family and move to Canaan to receive the blessings that had been bestowed upon Abraham earlier.

—The actions of Abraham's servant illustrate great faith on his behalf. He prayed to God for direction in determining who would be the right wife for Isaac, and he trusted God to answer his prayers. After having his prayers answered, the servant recognized God's provision and praised God (see Genesis 24:26-27).

—Rebekah's family accepted Abraham's servant. This shows that Rebekah's family served God (see Genesis 24:50-51).

—The servant brings evidence of Abraham's material wealth, but Rebekah's family is left to determine whether this is a sign of God's blessing or perhaps represents ill-gotten gain. Rebekah's family accepted Abraham's servant. This shows that Rebekah's family served God (see Genesis 24:50-51).

—God blesses the arrangement through the love that Isaac and Rebekah have for each other. In the wake of the sadness of Sarah's death, a joyful new generation emerges in the story of God's promise's being carried out.

Teachers of CHILDREN

—The servant prayed for Isaac's future wife to be revealed to him.

—While the servant was praying to God about a wife for Isaac, Rebekah, Isaac's cousin, appeared and was going down to the spring to fill her jar with water.

—The servant went to meet Rebekah and asked her for water from her jar. Rebekah offered him a drink of water and water for his camels.

—The servant watched her to learn if she was the wife the Lord had chosen for Isaac.

—Rebekah's family asked her if she would agree to marry Isaac and she agreed.

—Isaac welcomed Rebekah to his home; he married Rebekah and he loved her.

THE CHRONOLOGICAL SETTING OF THE LESSON

Abraham continued the promised legacy of being a blessing to the peoples of the world by arranging for the marriage of his son Isaac. The arrangements for that marriage are told in the form of a short story, more formally called a novella. The story begins with Abraham calling the servant to the task of obtaining a wife for Isaac from Abraham's kindred, the family Abraham had been directed to leave at the beginning of the saga (see Genesis 12:3). Abraham declared the inhabitants of Canaan disqualified as a source for a woman to become Isaac's wife. This would be a marriage kept within the family. Abraham sought to secure the servant's loyalty with an oath. Although the narrative shows us a resolute Abraham, the old man does not simply presume that the mission for a wife will succeed. He stipulates that if a suitable woman will not follow the servant back to Isaac, the servant is no longer obligated by the oath. Abraham acted toward the promise, but without any guarantee that any particular action would be successful.

THE GEOGRAPHICAL AND CULTURAL SETTING OF THE LESSON

Today's lesson begins on a note of thankfulness. Abraham recognizes that he has been blessed in all things. He has prospered in his possessions, and above all, he has a son. Now his most commanding hope is that Isaac should be rightly married and that the family inheritance be carried on. Isaac must not marry one of the Canaanites. It is the father's concern to find for him a bride of his own blood and lineage. Therefore, Abraham would send his devoted servant to seek for one in the land from which Abraham had come and in which his kindred dwelt.

The ancient custom of the father's finding his son a wife seems strange now to the modern way of falling in love, being engaged, and marrying. When the time had come for Isaac to marry, it was not Isaac who was to choose his bride. His father, the head of the family, would find the right one for him.

PROMINENT CHARACTER(S) IN THE LESSON

Eliezer: Abraham's most trusted servant, charged by Abraham to secure a wife for his grown son Isaac from among Abraham's relatives in Mesopotamia.

KEY TERMS IN THE LESSON

Appointed (verse 14)—Hebrew: *yakach* (yaw-kahh'): to have proved; decided; judged; rebuked; reproved; corrected; was right; "chosen" (NIV).

Drink (verse 14)—Hebrew: *shathah* (shaw-thaw'): to drink; banquet.

Hasted (verse 20)—Hebrew: *mahar* (maw-har'): to hasten; to be hurried, be anxious; "quickly" (NIV).

Kindness (verse 12)—Hebrew: *checed* (kheh'-sed): goodness; kindness; faithfulness.

"Make me successful" (verse 12)—Hebrew: *qarah* (kaw-raw'): to make happen; grant success to; "send me good speed" (KJV).

Peace (verse 21)—Hebrew: *charash* (khaw-rash'): to be silent; to be speechless; "without saying a word" (NIV).

Virgin (verse 16)—Hebrew: *bathuwlah* (beth-oo-law'): virgin; having never had sexual relations.

TOPICAL OUTLINE OF THE LESSON

I. **Introduction**
  A. The Choosing of a Bride
  B. Biblical Background

II. **Exposition and Application of the Scripture**
  A. The Believers' Responsibility to the Next Generation
     (Genesis 24:12)
  B. Arrival and Encounter at the Well
     (Genesis 24:13-14)
  C. A Rendezvous with Destiny
     (Genesis 24:15-21)
  D. The Lord Will Complete His Work
     (Genesis 24:61-67)

III. **Concluding Reflection**

I. INTRODUCTION

A. The Choosing of a Bride

The purpose of Genesis 24 is to explain how Isaac acquired his wife, Rebekah. The focus of the narrative is not on Abraham; after commissioning his servant, he receded into the background and did not even come on the scene for the marriage. Rather, the focus was on the servant of Abraham as he followed God's guidance to the wife of God's choosing. The emphasis of the chapter, then, is on the providential work of God in the circumstances of the faithful servant. This story is classified as a "guidance narrative," which is a narrative whose purpose is to attest to the hand of God in the life of a small community and thus in personal life.

Central to the development of the story is the idea of covenantal loyalty or steadfast love (*hesed*), both from the divine perspective and the human. Abraham acted with steadfast love in preparing for the future of the covenant through the marriage of Isaac and Rebekah. Eliezer acted with steadfast love in faithfully carrying out his responsibilities. And God demonstrated His sovereign steadfast love by guiding the servant to the proper place and ensuring that the mission did not fail.

With this understanding of steadfast love (*hesed*) at the heart of the story, the direction of the message is clear: it is about the providence of God in the lives of faithful people, ensuring the perpetuity of the covenant. Two considerations are important here. First, God is declared to be the sole cause of events in the story. The people in this event voice the author's convictions at this point. Second, God is deliberately behind the scenes, yet directing the people's actions. In this respect, the account is very similar to the book of Ruth. The story records no word from God, no miracle, no cultic contact, and no prophetic oracle; it does not even restate the Abrahamic covenant. It reports the hidden causality of God, sovereignly working through the circumstances of those who are acting in faith. The role of faith—expressed in personal prayer, trusting for divine guidance through the circumstances, and acting responsibly in anticipation of God's faithfulness—is predominant because God, though not visibly active, is no less at work behind the scenes to effect His will and prerogatives in the lives of His own.

This story, however, is more than an object lesson in divine guidance. It is a major part of God's program for covenantal blessing for those who trust Him and act in accordance with His will. Many potential setbacks are avoided because the participants in each scene take positive advantage of the initiatives of God in their lives at critical moments in their journey. Accordingly, many potential setbacks are avoided: the servant did not fail, the sign was not missed, Laban willingly agreed, and Rebekah gladly accepted. The Lord triumphed over all potential hazards and brought about compliance of all persons concerned. When opportunities open up for us to follow the plan that God has laid before us, we still must be willing to say yes to the providential movement of God in our lives. Rebekah is our example of how faith in God almighty can and will change our lives in ways we cannot even begin to imagine. We need only to trust Him.

B. Biblical Background

In this lengthy family story, the author focuses on the search for a wife for Isaac among family members back in the old country. In the course of this last story in which Abraham plays a role, interest passes to "master" Isaac (see Genesis 24:65). The story follows a pattern similar to that of Jacob and Rachel in Genesis 29:1-14—a meeting between a man and a woman at a well that results in a marriage.

In some sense, though, Rebekah rather than Isaac parallels Abraham; she continues the faithful response of leaving home and family that furthers God's purposes. Abraham initiates the journey by commissioning his servant to find a wife for Isaac (see Genesis 24:1-9), and Rebekah and her family respond (verses 28-61), resulting in the marriage of Rebekah and Isaac (verses 62-67).

Abraham's final days provide an occasion to note how God had filled his life with blessings. God had indeed kept the promise to him, a promise worked out largely through God's work as creator. Abraham now focuses on finding a proper wife for Isaac. Functioning with divine directive, he commissions the most senior of his servants for the task. He binds the servant with an oath to find a woman only among family members, not from among the resident Canaanites.

Having arrived at his destination, the servant prays that he will be successful in this venture, which would mean that God would show steadfast love (*hesed*) to Abraham—namely, manifest love in this particular way. Divine providence does not mean that the future is somehow predetermined or that human decision making can never frustrate the divine designs. The servant hopes he will be successful in securing a wife for Isaac, but he cannot be absolutely sure. He thus prays in a certain way that the woman to whom he will speak in a certain way will respond in such a way that he can be certain that she is the one God has chosen to be Isaac's wife. The author's description of Rebekah enables the readers to know that she will be Isaac's wife before the servant does (verses 15-16); the focus thus falls on the servant's faithful handling of the situation. When the anticipated conversation does occur, the servant does not know that this is the woman. Rather, he gazes at her in silence to learn whether the Lord had made his journey successful (verse 21). In other words, he deemed a period of reflection and observation necessary. He eventually gained the knowledge that Rebekah was the one. An inner certainty through God-given insight regarding the divine decision seems likely to have aided him.

II. EXPOSITION AND APPLICATION OF THE SCRIPTURE

A. The Believers' Responsibility to the Next Generation
(Genesis 24:12)

And he said O Lord God of my master Abraham, I pray thee, send me good speed this day, and shew kindness unto my master Abraham.

Abraham's commissioning the servant takes the form of a solemn oath by which the servant had to swear to find a wife from among the relatives who would be appropriate to the continuation of the covenant. The servant's concern was that such a woman might not be willing to go with him to Canaan. This tension would build throughout the narrative until the story was completed. The preliminary resolution to the servant's hesitancy is found in Abraham's conviction that God's angel would be sent before him. In short, Abraham places the success of the mission on divine intervention. With the success or failure of the mission left up to the providence of God, the servant executed the ancient oath, swearing to do his part. The servant played his part in God's plan for the chosen people. He trusted God to be at work through him and sought every opportunity to be obedient to God's will.

B. Arrival and Encounter at the Well
(Genesis 24:13-14)

Behold, I stand here by the well of water; and the daughters of the men of the city come out to draw water: And let it come to pass, that the damsel to whom I shall say, Let down thy pitcher, I pray thee, that I may drink; and she shall say, Drink, and I will give thy camels drink also: let the same be she that thou hast appointed for thy servant Isaac; and thereby shall I know that thou hast shewed kindness unto my master.

The servant's two prayers (found in Genesis 24:12, 17) bracket the developments at the well. Repetition in the opening prayer emphasizes the servant's petition that God act out of steadfast love and loyalty toward Abraham. The servant prayed to the God of his master for a favor for his master. The sign that the servant asked and the following scene have not been completely understood in their wisdom and refinement. Why should the solution depend upon a sign, and why did he not immediately approach the family? The reason is the same as for the oath in verse 3. The servant wanted to present his later request as God's will, which they could not refuse. The clever servant is worthy of his master. No task requires more delicacy and greater diplomacy than that of a matchmaker. Even a disguised refusal would be an insult. This way, he may be certain of acceptance. Not that the servant would be satisfied with any girl—he wanted Rebekah; it is she whom he would test. No other girl from Nahor's town would have suited Abraham, even if she had passed the test.

In his prayer, the servant stipulated the conditions by which he would identify the wife for Isaac. To meet the conditions, the woman must not just respond to his need for water, but to the thirst of the camels as well. Such action would be a model of hospitality, and indeed even of God's steadfast love. If the question would have merely been giving a drink to a poor, thirsty traveller, no girl could have refused. Yet, Abraham's first servant was not a poor wretch; he appeared as master of a large caravan, and as he was at a public well, he might expect the reply, "Please, help yourself." Besides, he had been at the well a good while. Parallels in ancient Jewish texts which have been preserved help to explain this scene. There, we find that respect is shown by younger persons to their elders through willingness to serve and courteously assist; the simplest service consists in offering a drink of water. The request of Abraham's servant is therefore a test of Rebekah's training and respect for elders.

C. A Rendezvous with Destiny
   ### (Genesis 24:15-21)

And it came to pass, before he had done speaking, that, behold, Rebekah came out, who was born to Bethuel, son of Milcah, the wife of Nahor, Abraham's brother, with her pitcher upon her shoulder. And the damsel was very fair to look upon, a virgin, neither had any man known her: and she went down to the well, and filled her pitcher, and came up. And the servant ran to meet her, and said, Let me, I pray thee, drink a little water of thy pitcher. And she said, Drink, my lord: and she hasted, and let down her pitcher upon her hand, and gave him drink. And when she had done giving him drink, she said, I will draw water for thy camels also, until they have done drinking. And she hasted, and emptied her pitcher into the trough, and ran again unto the well to draw water, and drew for all his camels. And the man wondering at her held his peace, to wit whether the Lord had made his journey prosperous or not.

A woman appeared even before the servant finished his prayer (verse 15). The writer of the book of Genesis tells us that she was a member of Abraham's family, beautiful, and unmarried (verses 15-16). Rebekah responded quickly to the need of the servant for a drink, and to the camels' thirst (verse 20). Here began one of the most winsome passages in Genesis. In most early societies, including the society of Israel, men were dominant and women were generally obscure. However, in the Old Testament, there are women who were significant, and one of them is Rebekah. After she had drawn water for Eliezer, she told him who her father is and that she knew her father would want to give this stranger and his camels shelter. Eliezer's wondering (verse 21) could not have been due to Rebekah. What he had seen in her gave no room for doubt on her account as to whether the Lord had made his journey prosperous. Rebekah sensed her rendezvous with destiny and would not let such an opportunity pass. She sensed that God was at work in her life in a unique way, and she was determined to open herself fully to the providential will of God.

D. The Lord Will Complete His Work
   ### (Genesis 24:61-67)

And Rebekah arose, and her damsels, and they rode upon the camels, and followed the man: and the servant took Rebekah, and went his way. And Isaac came from the way of the well Lahairoi; for he dwelt in the south country. And Isaac went out to meditate in the field at the eventide: and he lifted up his eyes, and saw, and, behold, the camels were coming. And Rebekah lifted up her eyes, and when she saw Isaac, she lighted off the camel. For she had said unto the servant, What man is this that walketh in the field to meet us? And the servant had said, It is my master: therefore she took a vail, and covered herself. And the servant told Isaac all things that he had done. And Isaac brought her into his mother Sarah's tent, and took Rebekah, and she became his wife; and he loved her: and Isaac was comforted after his mother's death.

This final section brings the narrative to its intended conclusion. The travellers entered the land of Canaan, Isaac came on the scene, and the couple became husband and wife. There is a slight building of tension when Rebekah first prepared to meet Isaac, but it dissolved as a matter of course. The Lord had guided the servant in all his ways, and so this culmination of the mission could only be reason for further praise and satisfaction, as no doubt the servant's report would have stressed again (verse 66).

It is important to note that Rebekah actually replaced Sarah by entering Sarah's tent. She would be the new matriarch of the clan, as Isaac would become the new patriarch. The fact that Abraham neither appears on the scene at this point nor is mentioned as the master (Isaac is now referred to as the servant's master in verse 65) suggests that this story formed a very important part of the succession of patriarchal and matriarchal figures. The theological significance of this succession is that Rebekah was the new matriarch of God's own choosing.

Believers can trust the Lord to give them guidance and success through His covenant faithfulness as they act responsibly in obedience to the covenant. It is the responsible pursuit of covenant obligations that God guides to completion.

Both sides of the matter of guidance are present in this story: human faithfulness and divine guidance based on divine faithfulness. The entire event concerned the Lord's guidance for a wife, but not just any wife; this marriage was essential to the work of God in the world. Prayer for guidance through the circumstances of our lives cannot come from a selfish motive; it must be for the will of God.

III. CONCLUDING REFLECTION

Entrusted with the responsibility of finding a bride for Isaac and trusting in the Lord's covenantal faithfulness and steadfast love to prosper his way, Abraham's servant faithfully and resolutely carried out his task under the providential guidance of the Lord, so that he acquired Rebekah to be Isaac's wife. Rebekah responded positively to the divine initiative of God in her life, and it transformed her life forever.

PRAYER

Dear God, help us to know when You are at work in our lives, and give us the strength and determination to respond positively to Your will and to Your way. In Jesus' name we pray. Amen.

HOME DAILY BIBLE READINGS
(October 22-28, 2018)

Isaac and Rebekah Continue the Legacy
MONDAY, October 22: "Mutual Love of Wives and Husbands" (Ephesians 5:21-33)
TUESDAY, October 23: "Inherit the Blessings of Marriage" (1 Peter 3:1-9)
WEDNESDAY, October 24: "Jacob Meets Rachel at the Well" (Genesis 29:1-14)
THURSDAY, October 25: "Searching for a Wife for Isaac" (Genesis 24:1-14)
FRIDAY, October 26: "Rebekah Becomes Isaac's Wife" (Genesis 24:45-51)
SATURDAY, October 27: "Rebekah Is Blessed for Her Commitment" (Genesis 24:54b-61)
SUNDAY, October 28: "Isaac and Rebekah—Joined in Love" (Genesis 24:12-21, 61-67)

Fall Quarter 2018
Unit III: God Blesses and Re-creates Regardless
Children's Unit: God Blesses and Re-creates Anyway

November 4, 2018   **Lesson 10**

A TROUBLED BIRTH

ADULT/YOUTH
ADULT/YOUNG ADULT TOPIC: **Sibling Rivalry**
YOUTH TOPIC: **All about Me**

CHILDREN
GENERAL LESSON TITLE: **A Troubled Birth**
CHILDREN'S TOPIC: **Brother versus Brother**

DEVOTIONAL READING
Matthew 16:13-20

ADULT/YOUTH
BACKGROUND SCRIPTURE: **Genesis 25:19-34**
PRINT PASSAGE: **Genesis 25:19-34**
KEY VERSE: **Genesis 25:23**

CHILDREN
BACKGROUND SCRIPTURE: **Genesis 25:19-34**
PRINT PASSAGE: **Genesis 25:19-34**
KEY VERSE: **Genesis 25:24**

Genesis 25:19-34—KJV

19 And these are the generations of Isaac, Abraham's son: Abraham begat Isaac:

20 And Isaac was forty years old when he took Rebekah to wife, the daughter of Bethuel the Syrian of Padanaram, the sister to Laban the Syrian.

21 And Isaac intreated the LORD for his wife, because she was barren: and the LORD was intreated of him, and Rebekah his wife conceived.

22 And the children struggled together within her; and she said, If it be so, why am I thus? And she went to enquire of the LORD.

23 And the LORD said unto her, Two nations are in thy womb, and two manner of people shall be separated from thy bowels; and the one people shall be stronger than the other people; and the elder shall serve the younger.

24 And when her days to be delivered were fulfilled, behold, there were twins in her womb.

Genesis 25:19-34—NIV

19 This is the account of the family line of Abraham's son Isaac. Abraham became the father of Isaac,

20 and Isaac was forty years oldwhen he married Rebekah daughter of Bethuel the Aramean from Paddan Aram and sister of Laban the Aramean.

21 Isaac prayed to the LORD on behalf of his wife, because she was childless. The LORD answered his prayer, and his wife Rebekah became pregnant.

22 The babies jostled each other within her, and she said, "Why is this happening to me?" So she went to inquire of the LORD.

23 The LORD said to her, "Two nations are in your womb, and two peoples from within you will be separated; one people will be stronger than the other, and the older will serve the younger."

24 When the time came for her to give birth, there were twin boys in her womb.

25 The first to come out was red, and his whole body was like a hairy garment; so they named him Esau.

25 And the first came out red, all over like an hairy garment; and they called his name Esau.

26 And after that came his brother out, and his hand took hold on Esau's heel; and his name was called Jacob: and Isaac was threescore years old when she bare them.

27 And the boys grew: and Esau was a cunning hunter, a man of the field; and Jacob was a plain man, dwelling in tents.

28 And Isaac loved Esau, because he did eat of his venison: but Rebekah loved Jacob.

29 And Jacob sod pottage: and Esau came from the field, and he was faint:

30 And Esau said to Jacob, Feed me, I pray thee, with that same red pottage; for I am faint: therefore was his name called Edom.

31 And Jacob said, Sell me this day thy birthright.

32 And Esau said, Behold, I am at the point to die: and what profit shall this birthright do to me?

33 And Jacob said, Swear to me this day; and he sware unto him: and he sold his birthright unto Jacob.

34 Then Jacob gave Esau bread and pottage of lentiles; and he did eat and drink, and rose up, and went his way: thus Esau despised his birthright.

26 After this, his brother came out, with his hand grasping Esau's heel; so he was named Jacob. Isaac was sixty years old when Rebekah gave birth to them.

27 The boys grew up, and Esau became a skillful hunter, a man of the open country, while Jacob was content to stay at home among the tents.

28 Isaac, who had a taste for wild game, loved Esau, but Rebekah loved Jacob.

29 Once when Jacob was cooking some stew, Esau came in from the open country, famished.

30 He said to Jacob, "Quick, let me have some of that red stew! I'm famished!" (That is why he was also called Edom.)

31 Jacob replied, "First sell me your birthright."

32 "Look, I am about to die," Esau said. "What good is the birthright to me?"

33 But Jacob said, "Swear to me first." So he swore an oath to him, selling his birthright to Jacob.

34 Then Jacob gave Esau some bread and some lentil stew. He ate and drank, and then got up and left. So Esau despised his birthright.

UNIFYING LESSON PRINCIPLE: We are often discouraged when our lives do not go smoothly but, instead, are disrupted by human conflict and struggle. How can our efforts amount to anything worthwhile when riddled with human frailty and error? Despite their selfish actions, God was present in the lives of Esau and Jacob.

LESSON OBJECTIVES

Upon the completion of this lesson, the students will be able to do the following:

1. Contrast the impulsiveness of Esau with the cunning and forethought of Jacob.
2. Long for human relationships in which selfish motives and ambitions are held in check.
3. Resolve to forgive family members who have taken advantage of us.

AGE-LEVEL POINTS TO BE EMPHASIZED

Teachers of ADULTS and YOUTH

—Esau did not take his birthright seriously.

It entitled him to a double share of the inheritance.

—Both Rebekah and Isaac are portrayed as people of prayer.

—Through Rebekah's long-term barrenness and later

childbirth, God's power in the lives of persons to effect His ultimate will is demonstrated.

—The story of Jacob and Esau describes the conflict between neighboring nations. Jacob represents Israel; Esau represents Edom. God said that one would be stronger (verse 23). At the time that the story was told, Edom was subject to Israel.

—The author of the story used Hebrew word play. The Hebrew term for "hairy" sounds like *Esau* (verse 25). The Hebrew term for "Jacob" sounds like *heel* (he was gripping Esau's heel, verse 26). Edom is so named because of Esau's fondness for red stew (verse 30).

—Sibling rivalry is a common theme in the book of Genesis (Cain and Abel, Isaac and Ishmael, Joseph and his brothers).

—Both Esau's and Jacob's actions and reactions in the birthright narrative reflect human flaws. While Jacob is opportunistic, Esau is hasty and present-focused.

—Rebekah and Isaac's experiences parallel those of the narrative of Sarah and Abraham in key ways (barrenness, journey, impatience with God's promise fulfillment, and so on).

Teachers of CHILDREN

—Isaac inherited everything from his father, Abraham, including God's promise to make his descendants a great nation.

—Isaac accepted the wife that was chosen for him by others.

—After pleading with God for children, God answered Isaac's prayer with the birth of twins.

—When the twins began to fight within Rebekah's womb, she inquired of God what was happening.

—God told Rebekah that she was carrying twins that would become rival nations.

—Favoritism produced more problems for the twins.

THE CHRONOLOGICAL SETTING OF THE LESSON

At this point, the writer of Genesis turned his full attention to Isaac. This is the account of Abraham's son Isaac (see Genesis 25:19). The account of Esau does not occur until Genesis 36:1; and not until Genesis 37:2 is found the account of Jacob. Though Isaac is little mentioned after Genesis 27, the title "the account of Abraham's son Isaac" is meant to cover the time when Isaac was at least the nominal head of the patriarchal family. His two sons' activities came at the time when he was technically in authority. At Genesis 25:19, the writer of Genesis enters a new phase of patriarchal history. With Abraham's death, the focus of the promise was passed to Isaac. There are times when the chronicle of God's movement with the patriarchs slows down to allow a microscopic look at one incident, such as we read in Genesis 24. So, too, Genesis 25:20 informed us that Isaac was forty when he married Rebekah, but just six verses later we learn that twenty years passed before Jacob and Esau were born. God moves in His own time to establish the promise through the seed of Isaac. That seed would come, however, with conflict and deceit.

THE GEOGRAPHICAL AND CULTURAL SETTING OF THE LESSON

We have now come to a major break in the book of Genesis. It is signaled by the telltale phrase, "This is the account of . . . ." (Genesis 25:19). For all intents and purposes, we have left the story of Abraham behind us, although his memory will continue to exercise a strong and beneficial influence over the people and events discussed in the rest of Genesis. The life of Abraham's grandson Jacob will now occupy our attention for the most part. In many respects, the personalities and activities of Jacob and Abraham provide quite a series of contrasts, as we shall see. The story of Jacob and Esau begins with a struggle, which sets the stage for a complex and difficult journey for everyone within this conflicted family. The problems and possibilities created by the interaction between God and this family constitute the essence of the story of Jacob and Esau.

PROMINENT CHARACTER(S) IN THE LESSON

Esau: the son of Isaac and Rebekah; elder twin brother of Jacob; traditional ancestor of the Edomites.

Jacob: the younger son of Isaac and Rebekah, and the twin brother of Esau; and husband of Leah and Rachel. Because Jacob is also called Israel, his twelve sons are the "sons of Israel" (Exodus 1:1).

KEY TERMS IN THE LESSON

Barren (verse 21)—Hebrew: `aqar (aw-kawr'): barren; sterile; "childless" (NIV).

Children (verse 22)—Hebrew: *ben* (bane): child; children; "babies" (NIV).

Enquire (verse 22)—Hebrew: *darash* (daw-rash'): to resort to, seek, seek with care, enquire, require; "inquire" (NIV).

Intreated (verse 21)—Hebrew: `athar (aw-thar'): to have prayed; entreated; supplicated; "prayed" (NIV).

Separated (verse 23)—Hebrew: *parad* (paw-rad'): to have separated; divided.

Stronger (verse 23)—Hebrew: `amats (aw-mats'): to be strong, alert, courageous, brave, stout, bold, solid, hard.

TOPICAL OUTLINE OF THE LESSON

I. **Introduction**
    A. The Saga of Jacob
    B. Biblical Background

II. **Exposition and Application of the Scripture**
    A. The Sovereign God and His Promises (Genesis 25:19-20)
    B. A Barren Wife Who Trusts God's Promises (Genesis 25:21)
    C. The Sovereign God Chooses (Genesis 25:22-23)
    D. The Naming of the Twins (Genesis 25:24-26)
    E. The Sale of the Birthright (Genesis 25:27-34)

III. **Concluding Reflection**

I. INTRODUCTION

A. The Saga of Jacob

This narrative is really about Jacob, and it is not a very flattering one. It presents Jacob in his crude and mixed motives. This grandson of the promise is a rascal compared to his faithful grandfather Abraham, or his successful father, Isaac. The writer of the book of Genesis knew that the purposes of God are tangled in a web of self-interest and self-seeking. Yet, we are guided through it with two affirmations being held in tension: First, God has chosen and destined Jacob in a special way. The initial designation of Jacob is difficult to understand (see Genesis 25:23). We are not told why God wills this reversal in birth order, but it is this designation that brings Jacob to well-being and prosperity. However, the one who has been chosen by God also lives a troubled life. In addition, this is the second reality which holds the narrative in tension. Jacob has conflicts with all those around him. At times, it is God's commitment to this troubled man that causes the conflict. But in the end, it is the same commitment from God that resolves the conflicts in his favor. The author knows that the election is a blessing and a burden. God works through Jacob's imperfections to bless the world.

B. Biblical Background

Genesis 25:19-34 introduces us to the patriarchal narratives pertaining to Isaac. The data about Isaac is exceedingly sparse. Much of what is preserved about him—his birth, circumcision, and marriage—is integrated into the biography of Abraham. Nothing is recorded of the first twenty years of Isaac's marriage. Only a few isolated events in his life are preserved in the literature, where he is eclipsed by the towering figure of his father, Abraham, and overshadowed by the dynamic, forceful personality of his son Jacob. Yet, Isaac is more than a mere transition between Abraham and Jacob, and the biblical account does contain unmistakable elements of individuality. Isaac's name, uniquely bestowed by God, is not changed; his pastoral wanderings are restricted to a narrow range and largely center around Beer-sheba; he is the only patriarch to engage in agriculture and the only one never to leave the Promised Land.

But the story of Isaac soon turns to the birth of Esau and Jacob and the rivalry between them. The narratives reveal the roots of the ancient belief that the bitter hostility that marked the later relationships between the peoples of Israel and Edom had its origin in the prenatal experience of their founding fathers Jacob and Esau, who were twins. This tradition is so extraordinary, given the long and bitter history of enmity between Israel and Edom, that it must reflect an authentic historical experience. The two peoples must have shared memories of an early common ancestry.

Family conflicts can have far-reaching consequences extending into personal, political, economic, and religious spheres. The conflict within this family will become more and more sharply evident as the narrative moves on. What will this mean for the future of God's people? Are seeds being sown in these dim recesses of history that will one day reap bitter fruit for the descendants of this family? What the people of God do with the conflicts with which they are inevitably presented will make a difference. Moreover, amid all of this intra-familial difficulty, what will become of the promises of God? Will they transpire as God intends? Neither the divine revelation nor the promises of God give a precise shape to the future. God will be faithful; that will never be in doubt. But what the recipients of the promise do and say along the way will make a difference regarding the shape of fulfillment.

II. EXPOSITION AND APPLICATION OF THE SCRIPTURE

A. The Sovereign God and His Promises (Genesis 25:19-20)

And these are the generations of Isaac, Abraham's son: Abraham begat Isaac: And Isaac was forty years old when he took Rebekah to wife, the daughter of Bethuel the Syrian of Padanaram, the sister to Laban the Syrian.

These opening verses show Isaac's connection to Abraham and the family, they compare Isaac to Abraham by mentioning the barrenness of his wife, and they also show how the promise moved to the next stage by the answer to prayer. In this narrative, the reader learns that the births of Esau and Jacob came by way of a supernatural provision. This seed of Abraham, as it came to be called, existed because the Lord miraculously brought it out of Rebekah's barren womb. It was therefore a creative act. It would also be appropriate to think here of the spiritual seed of Abraham in the New Testament. The people of God do not exist by natural birth but are born of the Spirit. They exist because God brought them into existence as His people. There is also a theological observation to be made of this emphasis on family connections in these opening verses (verses 19-20). Although Isaac was the son of Abraham, the heir of the promise, and although Rebekah was a carefully chosen bride, these facts are not sufficient to produce the next heir of the promised blessing; it would still take divine intervention.

B. A Barren Wife Who Trusts God's Promises (Genesis 25:21)

And Isaac intreated the Lord for his wife, because she was barren: and the Lord was intreated of him, and Rebekah his wife conceived.

Once again, we encounter the motif of the barren wife of the patriarch. In the present instance, Rebekah's inability to procreate was tinged with irony, for she had gone into her marriage with her family's hopeful blessing to procreate ringing in her ears (see Genesis 24:60). Now twenty years have passed, and the divine pledges that Isaac would be the progenitor (one who begins something) of a people remain unredeemed. Nevertheless, unlike Sarah and Abraham, Isaac and Rebekah do not resort to concubinage. Rather, they maintain their faith in God's Word and rely on the power of prayer (verse 21). The prolonged state of barrenness is profoundly meaningful in that it is ended by a deliberate act of divine providence, a clear sign that the resulting offspring are predestined to be the instruments of God's purposes. Barrenness here is not an occasion for anxiety, but for the sovereign grace of God to be made manifest. Isaac's generation also has to learn the lessons of faith and to understand that theirs is not a natural seed but, rather, a supernatural one. Unlike his father and mother, Isaac waited on and trusted in the promises of God concerning the offspring that would come from his body.

C. The Sovereign God Chooses
(Genesis 25:22-23)

And the children struggled together within her; and she said, If it be so, why am I thus? And she went to enquire of the Lord. And the Lord said unto her, Two nations are in thy womb, and two manner of people shall be separated from thy bowels; and the one people shall be stronger than the other people; and the elder shall serve the younger.

This section introduces the major tension of the narrative, the turmoil within the womb of Isaac's wife. The tension intensifies because Rebekah's pregnancy was an answer to prayer; something was wrong in the divine provision. Rebekah experiences an unusually difficult pregnancy. Instead of the normally gentle quickening, the fetal movements are spasmodic and she has fears of miscarrying. Not only is the report of the difficult pregnancy unique in biblical literature, but also the Hebrew uses an unusual verb—*rasas*—to describe the movement of the twins in her womb. It literally means "they crushed or thrust one another." This indicates more than a mild discomfort. The volatile movement she experienced foretold the future hostile relationship between these children who were about to be born.

Once again, Rebekah went to God in prayer (verse 22).

The report of the tension and the seeking of the Lord lead up to the main point of the passage: the oracle (divine speech) from the Lord. God revealed that two nations would come from her womb—meaning that the two sons would be the founders of great tribes—and that they would have conflict, with the elder becoming servant to the younger. (Down through her history, Israel would recall that the Lord had given her priority over Edom, one of her perennial enemies.) By sovereign election, God declared that the promised line would belong to Jacob, the younger son. Jacob thus owed his supremacy not to natural order or to human will, but to divine election. The theological themes of creation and election thus figure prominently in the development of the chosen people of God. The divine choice of Jacob also would become a source of the conflict that the patriarch would face. When God chose the younger over the elder, He upset the assumed order of society and prepared the way for opposition and antagonism. Moreover, Jacob and his mother would cling to this divine choice and attempt to achieve presumptuously what it has promised, thus adding to the conflict.

D. The Naming of the Twins
(Genesis 25:24-26)

And when her days to be delivered were fulfilled, behold, there were twins in her womb. And the first came out red, all over like an hairy garment; and they called his name Esau. And after that came his brother out, and his hand took hold on Esau's heel; and his name was called Jacob: and Isaac was threescore years old when she bare them.

Now comes the naming of the twins. The parents observed the unusual circumstances of the births and commemorated them in the naming. Esau's appearance—more like an animal of the field than an ordinary baby—prompted his naming (verse 25). This first child was red-brown, a description that significantly formed the basis of the sons of Esau, the Edomites. With the description of "hairy," there is an allusion to Mount Seir, where Esau later dwelt (see Genesis 36:8). The younger twin followed on the heels of his brother; his hand was seizing the heel (verse 26). The name *Jacob* was apparently chosen to retain the memory of the unusual activity of the infant. In the view of the parents, the seizing of the heel would have conveyed an affectionate thought. On later reflection, they would realize that the child was (in essence) struggling for the best starting position. Thus, Jacob's name would come in time to mean assailant, over-reacher, or deceiver.

This passage clearly teaches that Jacob and Esau were supernaturally provided to the barren woman, and that Jacob was unexpectedly elected over his older brother. We may thus conclude that the fulfillment of the promise was supernaturally provided by creation and election. Those who enjoy participation in God's program of blessing do so because they are the creation and the elect of God. That should encourage us to be kind and supportive of one another in our daily affairs and not be so quick to seek to undermine and discredit one another.

The beginning of two nations was thus acknowledged in the birth and naming of the twins. From the divine intervention of God in Rebekah's barrenness to the birth of her children, we learn that the nation of Israel was supernaturally intended. The primary emphasis is on sovereign grace, in that God was providing for the accomplishing of His program. In Romans 9:11-12, Paul used this passage in his discussion of election, explaining that the younger was chosen over the elder before their births. In election, God reverses the assumed order—for His ways are not our ways.

E. The Sale of the Birthright
(Genesis 25:27-34)

And the boys grew: and Esau was a cunning hunter, a man of the field; and Jacob was a plain man, dwelling in tents. And Isaac loved Esau, because he did eat of his venison: but Rebekah loved Jacob. And Jacob sod pottage: and Esau came from the field, and he was faint: And Esau said to Jacob, Feed me, I pray thee, with that same red pottage; for I am faint: therefore was his name called Edom. And Jacob said, Sell me this day thy birthright. And Esau said, Behold, I am at the point to die: and what profit shall this birthright do to me? And Jacob said, Swear to me this day; and he sware unto him; and he sold his birthright unto Jacob. Then Jacob gave Esau bread and pottage of lentiles; and he did eat and drink, and rose up, and went his way: thus Esau despised his birthright.

The struggle for preeminence between the twins, which commenced inside the womb, continued into adulthood. Jacob now seized an opportunity to persuade Esau, in a very clever way, into transferring the birthright to him. His desperate endeavors to obtain this end by means fair or foul can only be understood in terms of the privileges of the firstborn in that culture. The firstborn son along with the first fruits of the soil and the male firstling of the herd and the flock were considered to be possessed of a unique sanctity. They all belonged to God. The first male issue of the human womb was accorded a privileged position in the family and in the culture. The firstborn naturally ranked second only to the head of the family, the paterfamilias, whose successor he would automatically become.

What had appeared to be a trivial event at the birth of the twins became more obvious with this trickery. Here, Jacob and Esau show they developed according to their initial characteristics. The "red man" was overcome by his physical appetites for the "red stuff" and sold his birthright. The "heel grabber" cunningly overtook his brother and gained the birthright. Rebekah had surely told Jacob of the revelation God had given to her about the older serving the younger (verse 23), so Jacob was looking for the right time to usurp Esau's place. Jacob's opportunity came one day while he was cooking some lentil stew. Speculation is that in the stew with the lentils was added onions, rice, olive oil, and probably some cuts of meat. As its savory scent wafted in the air, an exhausted, ravenously hungry Esau approached Jacob requesting some of the red stew because Esau was famished (verse 30). Even before offering a bite, a cagey Jacob replied, "First sell me your birthright." A caring brother would have offered the soup requested. Jacob was not caring. He was callused and calculating. And Esau, with little concern for the future, had more anxiety about his current appetite.

While this narrative is primarily interested in explaining how the birthright became Jacob's possession, it also carries with it moral lessons as well. There are no winners in this encounter, even though Jacob comes away with the birthright. Neither brother is exemplary. On the one hand, we have a profane man, Esau, who considered the spiritual heritage of his birthright of little value and traded it for the lentil soup. Here is a description of a man who was controlled more by immediate appetite than long-term promise. On the other hand, we have the shrewd man, Jacob, who, although he regarded spiritual things highly, made the cause serve him through manipulation (verse 31).

The two are played off each other, for the point of tension in the story comes when the two brothers meet and exchange what they have. However, the entire narrative is slightly slanted against Esau's profanity, for it characterized Esau according to his impulsive nature and ended with a report of his despising his birthright. On the other hand, Jacob was devious and deceptive, determined to ignore custom. One must be careful not to justify Jacob's action simply because of his possible knowledge that God had ordained that he be over his brother. While this would have happened as prophesied, Jacob should not have taken advantage of his brother's condition. There is no immediate censure of Jacob in the Scripture text, but he later spent many anxious hours, even years, regretting what he had done, for in many ways his actions returned to haunt him.

III. CONCLUDING REFLECTION

This part of the Isaac-Rebekah narrative signals immediately that the people involved cannot be separated into good people and evil people. Both Jacob and Esau acted in ways that were sometimes worthy of praise and other times blame. Esau's entitlement as firstborn in the family was taken from him not because of his own sin, but by his opportunistic brother and the surprising reversal of custom that happens occasionally in God's world. Yet, Esau was not an innocent victim. He did not take sufficient care of his birthright. In addition, Jacob did not offer hospitality to his brother but used his brother's need to extort the family inheritance from Esau. Yet, the saga will later tell us that with all his faults, Jacob was chosen by God to carry the ancestral promise into the third generation.

We find in Isaac and Rebekah the same mixture of behavior. They were especially chosen by God for each other and as bearers of the promise (see Genesis 17–18; 21; 24). Yet, as parents, Rebekah and Isaac formed alliances with different children, coalitions that would prove destructive to the family.

We wish at times for a simple world in which the good people are chosen to carry God's blessing and the evil people are destroyed, either by God or by human agents of God's wrath. But the witness in the faith community is predicated in part on a very realistic understanding of human nature. There are no completely good people and completely evil people. If we look at the opportunistic Jacob and the careless Esau, we find they are us. The only separation between people that we can see clearly is between those who know themselves to be in need of God's forgiveness and those who do not. We must remember that we are all sinners saved by grace. We must also learn how to forgive and hold people accountable at the same time. It is in forgiving that wounds are allowed to heal and victim and victimized garner the strength to move on with life.

PRAYER

O Lord, in Your tender mercies hear our plea for forgiveness for the sins of omission and commission in our lives. Help us to become the kind of people You are calling us to be. Help us not to judge others, but keep us ever mindful of our own faults and failures. In Jesus' name we pray. Amen.

HOME DAILY BIBLE READINGS
(October 29–November 4, 2018)

A Troubled Birth

MONDAY, October 29: "Water Issue Resolved Peacefully, Peoples Blessed" (Genesis 26:6-22)

TUESDAY, October 30: "Jacob and Esau Reconcile, Families Blessed" (Genesis 33:4-11)

WEDNESDAY, October 31: "Too Late for Repentance" (Hebrews 12:14-17)

THURSDAY, November 1: "Commit to God's Love and Justice" (Hosea 12:2-6)

FRIDAY, November 2: "Differences Settled Peacefully" (Genesis 26:28-33)

SATURDAY, November 3: "God Blesses Ishmael and His Descendants" (Genesis 21:8-13; 25:17-18)

SUNDAY, November 4: "Different Traits Rooted in Conception" (Genesis 25:19-34)

Fall Quarter 2018
Unit III: God Blesses and Re-creates Regardless
Children's Unit: God Blesses and Re-creates Anyway

November 11, 2018 — Lesson 11

JACOB RECEIVES ISAAC'S BLESSING

ADULT/YOUTH
ADULT/YOUNG ADULT TOPIC: Deception in the Family
YOUTH TOPIC: Deception

CHILDREN
GENERAL LESSON TITLE: Jacob Receives Isaac's Blessing
CHILDREN'S TOPIC: Jacob Tricks Isaac

DEVOTIONAL READING
Psalm 24:1-6

ADULT/YOUTH
BACKGROUND SCRIPTURE: Genesis 27:1–28:5
PRINT PASSAGE: Genesis 27:5-10, 18-19, 21-29
ADULT KEY VERSE: Genesis 27:23
YOUTH KEY VERSE: Genesis 27:24

CHILDREN
BACKGROUND SCRIPTURE: Genesis 27:1–28:5
PRINT PASSAGE: Genesis 27:5-10, 18-19, 21-29
KEY VERSE: Genesis 27:24

Genesis 27:5-10, 18-19, 21-29—KJV

5 And Rebekah heard when Isaac spake to Esau his son. And Esau went to the field to hunt for venison, and to bring it.

6 And Rebekah spake unto Jacob her son, saying, Behold, I heard thy father speak unto Esau thy brother, saying,

7 Bring me venison, and make me savoury meat, that I may eat, and bless thee before the LORD before my death.

8 Now therefore, my son, obey my voice according to that which I command thee.

9 Go now to the flock, and fetch me from thence two good kids of the goats; and I will make them savoury meat for thy father, such as he loveth:

10 And thou shalt bring it to thy father, that he may eat, and that he may bless thee before his death.

.....

18 And he came unto his father, and said, My father: and he said, Here am I; who art thou, my son?

Genesis 27:5-10, 18-19, 21-29—NIV

5 Now Rebekah was listening as Isaac spoke to his son Esau. When Esau left for the open country to hunt game and bring it back,

6 Rebekah said to her son Jacob, "Look, I overheard your father say to your brother Esau,

7 "'Bring me some game and prepare me some tasty food to eat, so that I may give you my blessing in the presence of the LORD before I die.'

8 "Now, my son, listen carefully and do what I tell you:

9 "Go out to the flock and bring me two choice young goats, so I can prepare some tasty food for your father, just the way he likes it.

10 "Then take it to your father to eat, so that he may give you his blessing before he dies."

.....

18 He went to his father and said, "My father." "Yes, my son," he answered. "Who is it?"

19 And Jacob said unto his father, I am Esau thy first born; I have done according as thou badest me: arise, I pray thee, sit and eat of my venison, that thy soul may bless me.

.....

21 And Isaac said unto Jacob, Come near, I pray thee, that I may feel thee, my son, whether thou be my very son Esau or not.

22 And Jacob went near unto Isaac his father; and he felt him, and said, The voice is Jacob's voice, but the hands are the hands of Esau.

23 And he discerned him not, because his hands were hairy, as his brother Esau's hands: so he blessed him.

24 And he said, Art thou my very son Esau? And he said, I am.

25 And he said, Bring it near to me, and I will eat of my son's venison, that my soul may bless thee. And he brought it near to him, and he did eat: and he brought him wine and he drank.

26 And his father Isaac said unto him, Come near now, and kiss me, my son.

27 And he came near, and kissed him: and he smelled the smell of his raiment, and blessed him, and said, See, the smell of my son is as the smell of a field which the LORD hath blessed:

28 Therefore God give thee of the dew of heaven, and the fatness of the earth, and plenty of corn and wine:

29 Let people serve thee, and nations bow down to thee: be lord over thy brethren, and let thy mother's sons bow down to thee: cursed be every one that curseth thee, and blessed be he that blesseth thee.

19 Jacob said to his father, "I am Esau your firstborn. I have done as you told me. Please sit up and eat some of my game, so that you may give me your blessing."

.....

21 Then Isaac said to Jacob, "Come near so I can touch you, my son, to know whether you really are my son Esau or not."

22 Jacob went close to his father Isaac, who touched him and said, "The voice is the voice of Jacob, but the hands are the hands of Esau."

23 He did not recognize him, for his hands were hairy like those of his brother Esau; so he proceeded to bless him.

24 "Are you really my son Esau?" he asked. "I am," he replied.

25 Then he said, "My son, bring me some of your game to eat, so that I may give you my blessing." Jacob brought it to him and he ate; and he brought some wine and he drank.

26 Then his father Isaac said to him, "Come here, my son, and kiss me."

27 So he went to him and kissed him. When Isaac caught the smell of his clothes, he blessed him and said, "Ah, the smell of my son is like the smell of a field that the LORD has blessed.

28 "May God give you heaven's dew and earth's richness—an abundance of grain and new wine.

29 "May nations serve you and peoples bow down to you. Be lord over your brothers, and may the sons of your mother bow down to you. May those who curse you be cursed and those who bless you be blessed."

UNIFYING LESSON PRINCIPLE: Deceiving others is a way that some people get what they want. Does human deception erase the worth of human accomplishment? Even though the deception used by Rebekah and Jacob disrupted their family, God still worked through their situation to accomplish the planned and promised divine redemption of fallen humanity.

LESSON OBJECTIVES

Upon the completion of this lesson, the students will be able to do the following:

1. Identify how Jacob and Rebekah used deception to get what they wanted from Isaac.
2. Repent of times when they have decided to deceive others.
3. Commit to expressing their needs and desires to others in honest yet loving ways.

AGE-LEVEL POINTS TO BE EMPHASIZED

Teachers of ADULTS and YOUTH

—Rebekah urged Jacob to deceive in order to fulfill God's oracle (see Genesis 25:23).

—There were two parts to the blessing: prosperity and authority.

—Cultural tradition would not allow a blessing, once given, to be rescinded.

—The "blessing" discussed in this passage is to be distinguished from the "birthright" in Genesis 25:29-34. The birthright has to do with inheritance, while the blessing has to do with spiritual destiny.

—Rebekah's addition of the words "before the Lord" in verse 7 indicate that she believed she was doing as the oracle prescribed in helping Jacob take the birthright, which she understood to be God's will (Genesis 25:23).

—Jacob's slowness to follow Rebekah's direction is because he was concerned with the feasibility of her plan, not with its injustice or ethical problems.

—The power of Isaac's blessing was not magical but rather traditional, following accepted cultural conventions. We do not know that he could not have retracted it, but he did not.

Teachers of CHILDREN

—Rebekah devised a plan to trick Isaac into blessing Jacob, their younger son.

—Although Jacob was reluctant to follow his mother's plan, he gave in to her wishes.

—Jacob followed Rebekah's instructions to deceive his father, Isaac.

—Jacob and Rebekah were successful in deceiving Isaac, although Isaac was suspicious of what was going on.

—After blessing Jacob, Isaac realized he had blessed the wrong son, and Esau expressed anger at the loss of his blessing (Background Scripture).

THE CHRONOLOGICAL SETTING OF THE LESSON

The story of Abraham began with the divine command to uproot himself from his birthplace and to go to the Promised Land (see Genesis 12:1-3); the story of Jacob opened with his struggle with his twin brother, Esau, even before they were born. Jacob struggled in vain to be born first. Abraham's story continued with his fulfillment of the divine command (see Genesis 12:4-6), while Jacob's story described his opportunistic purchase of his brother Esau's birthright and the subsequent stealing of his elder brother's blessing (see Genesis 25:27-34; 27:27). These two introductory stories reveal an immense difference in the character and destiny of Abraham and Jacob. Abraham's life was mainly concerned with his contact with God; Jacob's life was concerned with an unending struggle with humanity. Abraham acted on God's command and asked nothing of his fellow men; Jacob was in a constant contest with men for his due, and more. Yet, Abraham and Jacob are both the principal ancestors of the people of Israel whose destiny and relations with God and with humans constitute the central theme of the Bible. With the story of Jacob's birth, we pass from one world to another, that together are the world of the book of Genesis, as they are that of the whole Bible. Jacob's life bears witness to the fusion of both worlds as he struggled not only with humans, but also with God. The Jacob saga began with two events: the purchase of the birthright in Genesis 25, and the stealing of the blessing through guile and trickery in chapter 27. His life is filled with pathos, much of it brought on by his own eagerness to advance himself at the expense of all others.

THE GEOGRAPHICAL AND CULTURAL SETTING OF THE LESSON

Jacob came out of his mother's womb clutching the heel of his older brother, and from that day forward he used every form of deceit to displace Esau as progenitor of the Hebrew people. Esau was the firstborn, and his status was by nature higher than Jacob's. However, Jacob is under no circumstances prepared to resign himself to this situation and employs every stratagem to deprive Esau of his privilege. He starts the struggle already as a fetus. The story of Rebekah's barrenness is told in one verse only (see Genesis 25:21), and her pregnancy is the opportunity to introduce the third of the ancestors—Jacob. His story begins with, "and the children struggled together within her" (Genesis 25:22), and although they struggle together, the context reveals that the main proponent is Jacob; Esau hardly participates; he receives the birthright and loses it with no fight. Only the loss of his blessing provokes an outcry: "He cried with a great and exceeding bitter cry" (Genesis 27:34). However, once the birthright and the blessing are gone, even though through trickery, Esau could not get them back. The culture and the time in which he lived so dictated it.

Jacob, on the other hand, is from the beginning the active party and contrives all possible ways to achieve his target. In the struggle between the two, one of whom possesses the advantage of precedence and the other ability and shrewdness, the latter succeeds. His reward for his guile will be that others will deal deceitfully with him. Because he had taken that which was not given him, others would deprive him whenever possible. Abraham always made concession and received much in return. Jacob took, and much was taken from him. Abraham's way is that of peace, but from the beginning Jacob embarked on a belligerent course—thus the path of struggle would be his lot in life. The trickery involved in the stealing of his brother's blessing continues the long line of deceit and betrayal that characterizes this family.

PROMINENT CHARACTER(S) IN THE LESSON

Esau: the son of Isaac and Rebekah; elder twin brother of Jacob; traditional ancestor of the Edomites.

Isaac: the second son of Abraham (first son of Sarah)—the son of promise.

Jacob: the younger son of Isaac and Rebekah, and the twin brother of Esau; and husband of Leah and Rachel. Because Jacob is also called Israel, his twelve sons are the "sons of Israel" (Exodus 1:1).

Rebekah: the wife of Jacob. She was instrumental in leading her son Jacob to trick her husband, Isaac, to give the birthright to Jacob.

KEY TERMS IN THE LESSON

Bless (verse 7)—Hebrew: *barak* **(baw-rak'):** to bless, kneel; "give . . . blessing" (NIV); the act or means of invoking or granting praise, goodness, and favor.

Bring (verse 7)—Hebrew: *bow'* **(bo):** to go in, enter, come, go, come in.

Father (verse 18)—Hebrew: *'ab* **(awb):** father of an individual.

Firstborn (verse 19)—Hebrew: *bekowr* **(bek-ore'):** firstborn; firstling.

Heard (verse 6)—Hebrew: *shama'* **(shaw-mah'):** to hear, listen to, obey; "overheard" (NIV).

Raiment (verse 27)—Hebrew: *lebush* **(leb-oosh'):** a garment; clothing; apparel; "clothes" (NIV).

Venison (verse 25)—Hebrew: *ayyal* **(ah-yawl'):** a hart, stag, deer; "game" (NIV).

TOPICAL OUTLINE OF THE LESSON

I. **Introduction**
   A. Blessed through Trickery and Deceit
   B. Biblical Background

II. **Exposition and Application of the Scripture**
   A. Stealing the Blessing through Cunning and Deception
   (Genesis 27:5-10)

   B. Families Deliberately Seeking to Harm One Another
   (Genesis 27:18-19)
   C. A Suspicious Father Preyed Upon by His Own
   (Genesis 27:21-26)
   D. A Blessing Received under False Pretense
   (Genesis 27:27-29)

III. **Concluding Reflection**

I. INTRODUCTION

A. Blessed through Trickery and Deceit

Why does God allow deceitful and treacherous people to prosper? This age-old question has baffled the faithful and stymied the learned throughout the ages. We want to believe that justice will prevail when people purposely lie, cheat, and steal their way through life. This becomes all the more difficult to accept when we find this sort of behavior going on in the households of faith. Among clergy and laity alike, there are those who have decided that the only way for them to get ahead is by trickery and deceit.

For some, the discovery of an unethical pastor who has been dishonest with his or her congregation is more than they can take, so they simply decide to leave the church and look for another, or some simply go home and drop out of church activities altogether. Others choose to stay and fight, but oftentimes when it seems their appeals to God for justice in the situation are going unheard, they decide to get down and dirty like those against whom they are complaining. In the end, an all-out church fight makes for a sordid affair where no one comes out of it unscathed. What do you do when you love your church and you find out that there are people in high places who are being less than honest in their dealings with the church? What options are open to you when you are dealing with people who are determined to act in unethical ways that lack integrity? In every instance of conflict caused by trickery and deceit, people of faith should seek to discern God's will in the situation. At the end of the day, Scripture declares that God's will shall prevail over all unjust situations.

In our lesson today, we find people who have chosen a path of deception for things God was already willing to grant in His purposive acts. This event is no compliment to either Rebekah or Jacob. Rebekah is the possessive mother who will stop at nothing to advance the future of her favored son. Jacob might allege that he had purchased the right of the firstborn, but this could never excuse his duplicity and deceit. Jacob was yet far from the strength of character he would manifest in keeping with his dignity as upholder of the promise given to Abraham. Mother and son thought they could lie and cheat their way to their desired goals with a stolen birthright and a blind blessing.

B. Biblical Background

God has always provided direction and enablement for His people to carry out their responsibilities in His covenantal program. Unfortunately, many people persist in handling them in their own earthly way. On the surface, it is the familiar story of how Jacob got the blessing by deceiving his father, Isaac, into thinking that he was Esau; but it is also the story of a family that fragments over the pursuit of spiritual blessings. This aspect of it makes it relevant to all who seek God's blessings. How do you come into that which you believe God has for you? Some wait with patience on that which God has promised, while others go out and pursue their hoped-for blessings by any means necessary.

Hebrews 12:16-17 simply declares that Esau sold his birthright and traded away the blessing. However, the details of this act reveal a tangled web. In fact, all the participants were at fault; Isaac, whether or not he knew of the earlier sale of the birthright, did know the revelation of God that the elder would serve the younger; yet, he set himself to thwart it by blessing Esau. Esau, in agreeing to the plan to be blessed by his father, Isaac, broke his oath to Jacob (see Genesis 25:33). Rebekah and Jacob, with a just cause, went about achieving it by deception—with no faith or love. Theirs would be the victory—although they obtained only what God declared Jacob would receive anyway—but they would reap the appropriate fruit of hatred and separation (Rebekah never saw her beloved Jacob again).

The conflict in the lifelong struggle between Jacob and Esau was greatly intensified with Jacob's grasping and trickery. He wanted what he believed belonged to him, but the manner in which he achieved the goal destroyed their relationship. Yet, the story is not just about Jacob; he alone did not destroy the family. Parental preference actually played a part also. Moreover, the entire scheme was made possible by the base level on which the family lived: brother plotting against brother; mother plotting against the elder son; and a father disobeying God's revelation as to which son would be the heir of the promise. The central lesson from this event is the transference of the blessing from the elder to the younger son. From beginning to end, the concern for the blessing predominates. Isaac sought to bestow it, and Esau wanted it. Rebekah heard about it and ensured that Jacob got it. Isaac unwittingly gave it to Jacob, and Esau was furious over having lost it. Finally, Isaac restated the blessing on Jacob in terms of the Abrahamic covenant.

II. EXPOSITION AND APPLICATION OF THE SCRIPTURE

A. Stealing the Blessing through Cunning and Deception
(Genesis 27:5-10)

And Rebekah heard when Isaac spake to Esau his son. And Esau went to the field to hunt for venison, and to bring it. And Rebekah spake unto Jacob her son, saying, Behold, I heard thy father speak unto Esau thy brother, saying, Bring me venison, and make me savoury meat, that I may eat, and bless thee before the Lord before my death. Now therefore, my son, obey my voice according to that which I command thee. Go now to the flock, and fetch me from thence two good kids of the goats; and I will make them savoury meat for thy father, such as he loveth: And thou shalt bring it to thy father, that he may eat, and that he may bless thee before his death.

Isaac, advanced in years, took steps to prepare his family for the future. Thus, he directed Esau to hunt for game and prepare his favorite food; then Isaac would give him a personal blessing. The provision of a meal constituted an essential part of the blessing ritual in the ancient Near East. Overhearing Jacob's request, Rebekah reported it to Jacob. Taking the initiative, she devised a ruse by which Jacob could receive the blessing, and she commanded him to help her.

This section of Scripture records the immediate reaction of Rebekah; through deception, Jacob would gain the blessing that was going to be given to Esau. What Jacob began by his cunning, his mother would complete through trickery. Rebekah apparently thought that the desperate situation of Isaac's desiring to bless his eldest son demanded desperate measures. She took matters into her own hands instead of trusting God to bring His revealed will to fruition concerning her youngest and favored son. If Jacob inherited his father's quiet nature, he also inherited his mother's cunning. As soon as Esau left on his hunt, Rebekah instructed Jacob to go and get two young goats, which she would prepare into a tasty meal. The full tragedy of this instance of parental favoritism gradually unfolded as they proceeded. Emphasized throughout the account is the phrase "just the way [Isaac] likes it" (verse 9). It stressed the fact that Rebekah and Jacob were taking advantage of Isaac's appetite for a certain kind of food to trick him.

What would have happened if Rebekah had not heard what Isaac was about to do, or what if she had done nothing? We may only speculate, but since God had already revealed that the heir would come through Jacob, surely God would have made a way for that to happen without Rebekah's plotting. We often get in God's way when we refuse to follow His leading. We do more harm than good when we deliberately choose to deceive and mislead people in the interest of our own well-being.

B. Families Deliberately Seeking to Harm One Another (Genesis 27:18-19)

And he came unto his father, and said, My father: and he said, Here am I; who art thou, my son? And Jacob said unto his father, I am Esau thy first born; I have done according as thou badest me: arise, I pray thee, sit and eat of my venison, that thy soul may bless me.

Another aspect of Jacob and his mother's trickery is that they took advantage of Isaac's blindness by dressing Jacob in Esau's clothes and putting the goatskins on Jacob's hand and neck to make him smell and feel like Esau (see verses 15-16). Jacob was hesitant to proceed with the scheme, not out of ethics, but out of fear (see verses 11-17). Since his brother was a hairy man, should his father feel Jacob's smooth skin the ruse would be discovered. Then, rather than bless him, he would curse him. However, Rebekah promised to take the fall if the plot went awry. Thus, to perpetuate the fraud, she went ahead with her deceptive plot against her husband and eldest son. Jacob, the deceiver par excellence, was tutored well by his equally deceitful mother. How sad, when parents who should be leading the way choose instead to participate in their children's folly.

C. A Suspicious Father Preyed upon by His Own
(Genesis 27:21-26)

And Isaac said unto Jacob, Come near, I pray thee, that I may feel thee, my son, whether thou be my very son Esau or not. And Jacob went near unto Isaac his father; and he felt him, and said, The voice is Jacob's voice, but the hands are the hands of Esau. And he discerned him not, because his hands were hairy, as his brother Esau's hands: so he blessed him. And he said, Art thou my very son Esau? And he said, I am. And he said, Bring it near to me, and I will eat of my son's venison, that my soul may bless thee. And he brought it near to him, and he did eat: and he brought him wine and he drank. And his father Isaac said unto him, Come near now, and kiss me, my son.

Now, Jacob approached his blind father, identifying himself as Esau. When Isaac asked how he had come so quickly, he said that God had enabled him to make a quick kill. Thus, he added a second lie to the first, even involving God in it (see verse 20). Evidently, the old man suspected trickery and asked to feel his son. When his hands touched the goat's hair, he said, "The voice is Jacob's voice, but the hands are the hands of Esau" (verse 22). This statement has become synonymous with deceit down through the ages. Still not satisfied, Isaac asked, "Art thou my very son Esau? And he (Jacob) said, I am" (verse 24). That was another lie! After Isaac had eaten, he tried one final test. He kissed his son and in so doing smelled the clothes Jacob was wearing—probably dirty and sweaty. This convinced him that it was Esau, so he gave him the much-sought-after blessing.

D. A Blessing Received under False Pretense
(Genesis 27:27-29)

And he came near, and kissed him: and he smelled the smell of his raiment, and blessed him, and said, See, the smell of my son is as the smell of a field which the Lord hath blessed: Therefore God give thee of the dew of heaven, and the fatness of the earth, and plenty of corn and wine: Let people serve thee, and nations bow down to thee: be lord over thy brethren, and let thy mother's sons bow down to thee: cursed be every one that curseth thee, and blessed be he that blesseth thee.

Isaac was suspicious from the start, and his suspicions remained until the end. Deprived of his eyesight, Isaac summoned to his aid the remaining senses of hearing, touch, taste, and smell. In demanding the meal, he imposed the test of taste. Even that sense failed him, for he mistook domesticated meat for wild game. The clothes of the shepherd reeked of the flock and the herd, while the hunter emitted the odor of the fields, which Isaac relished even more. After all, his hunting skills and outdoor prowess had endeared Esau to his father. This Rebekah and Jacob knew well. Now, fully convinced that Esau was standing before him, Isaac proceeded to communicate the decisive blessing, which really related to national destiny beyond simply the fate of an individual. The blessing is composed of three parts and contained assurances of fertility of the soil, of political and military preeminence, and of God's consummate protection. Jacob finally got what he wanted, consequences notwithstanding. Throughout the entire charade, Jacob lied repeatedly. He stole his brother's birthright and his blessing, but he would have no peace for years to come. The harm we do to others will visit us again in our own lives. Do not be deceived; God is not mocked, for you reap whatever you sow (see Galatians 6:7).

III. CONCLUDING REFLECTION

Jacob is the son before whom the future of the covenant lay—with the help of Rebekah. The recounting of the aforementioned events does not evoke positive feelings for either Rebekah or Jacob. If we feel anything toward them at all, it is probably a feeling of contempt. Our sympathies hardly lie with those who advance themselves through treachery and ill-gotten gains. Even though they were not perfect, our sympathies tend to run toward Isaac and Esau. However, Esau was not the son through whom God would work out His redemptive purposes for His chosen people. It is Jacob, the trickster, whom God decided to use as the heir of His promise. While Jacob's willingness to deceive and backstab his own kin disturbs us, the blessing of God has its way, whether we are attracted to or repelled by the conduit of the blessing. The author seems to have one single message in this narrative: Nothing can spoil God's plan to raise up a chosen people through whom He will save humanity.

But those who inject themselves in unhelpful ways into God's plan will have to answer for their misdeeds at some point in their lives.

Believing Jacob to be a cheat and a rascal who nonetheless received the blessing from God has occasioned both wonderment and hope on the part of the elect in every age: Why would God choose such a character? If God included Jacob, who then can be excluded? God uses ordinary people to advance His purposes on earth. Jacob's life should give us hope that no one is outside of blessing range in the eyes of God.

PRAYER

Our heavenly Father, we pray that You would enlighten our hearts as to Your will for our lives. Give us the patience to wait on that which You have promised to us. Remove from us all feelings of jealousy, envy, and cunning in our dealings with one another. Help us to trust the plan You have put forward for our lives. In Jesus' name we pray. Amen.

HOME DAILY BIBLE READINGS
(November 5-11, 2018)

Jacob Receives Isaac's Blessing

MONDAY, November 5: "Reject Deceit, Seek God's Face" (Psalm 24:1-6)

TUESDAY, November 6: "Live Openly and Honestly" (1 Peter 2:18-25)

WEDNESDAY, November 7: "Isaac Prepares to Bless Esau" (Genesis 27:1-4)

THURSDAY, November 8: "Rebekah Diverts Isaac to Bless Jacob" (Genesis 27:5-17)

FRIDAY, November 9: "Esau Loses Blessing; Is Exiled" (Genesis 27:30-40)

SATURDAY, November 10: "Jacob Charged to Marry Cousin" (Genesis 27:46–28:5)

SUNDAY, November 11: "Jacob Received Isaac's Blessing through Deceit" (Genesis 27:5-10, 18-19, 21-29)

November 18, 2018   Lesson 12

JACOB FORMS A RELATIONSHIP WITH GOD

ADULT/YOUTH
ADULT/YOUNG ADULT TOPIC: Finding Strength
YOUTH TOPIC: Weak Made Strong

CHILDREN
GENERAL LESSON TITLE: Jacob Forms a Relationship with God
CHILDREN'S TOPIC: A New Relationship for Jacob

DEVOTIONAL READING
Psalm 42:1-5

ADULT/YOUTH
BACKGROUND SCRIPTURE: Genesis 28:10-22
PRINT PASSAGE: Genesis 28:10-22
KEY VERSE: Genesis 28:15

CHILDREN
BACKGROUND SCRIPTURE: Genesis 28:10-22
PRINT PASSAGE: Genesis 28:10-22
KEY VERSE: Genesis 28:15a

Genesis 28:10-22—KJV

10 And Jacob went out from Beersheba, and went toward Haran.

11 And he lighted upon a certain place, and tarried there all night, because the sun was set; and he took of the stones of that place, and put them for his pillows, and lay down in that place to sleep.

12 And he dreamed, and behold a ladder set up on the earth, and the top of it reached to heaven: and behold the angels of God ascending and descending on it.

13 And, behold, the LORD stood above it, and said, I am the LORD God of Abraham thy father, and the God of Isaac: the land whereon thou liest, to thee will I give it, and to thy seed;

14 And thy seed shall be as the dust of the earth, and thou shalt spread abroad to the west, and to the east, and to the north, and to the south: and in thee and in thy seed shall all the families of the earth be blessed.

Genesis 28:10-22—NIV

10 Jacob left Beersheba and set out for Harran.

11 When he reached a certain place, he stopped for the night because the sun had set. Taking one of the stones there, he put it under his head and lay down to sleep.

12 He had a dream in which he saw a stairway resting on the earth, with its top reaching to heaven, and the angels of God were ascending and descending on it.

13 There above it stood the LORD, and he said: "I am the LORD, the God of your father Abraham and the God of Isaac. I will give you and your descendants the land on which you are lying.

14 "Your descendants will be like the dust of the earth, and you will spread out to the west and to the east, to the north and to the south. All peoples on earth will be blessed through you and your offspring.

15 And, behold, I am with thee, and will keep thee in all places whither thou goest, and will bring thee again into this land; for I will not leave thee, until I have done that which I have spoken to thee of.

16 And Jacob awaked out of his sleep, and he said, Surely the LORD is in this place; and I knew it not.

17 And he was afraid, and said, How dreadful is this place! this is none other but the house of God, and this is the gate of heaven.

18 And Jacob rose up early in the morning, and took the stone that he had put for his pillows, and set it up for a pillar, and poured oil upon the top of it.

19 And he called the name of that place Bethel: but the name of that city was called Luz at the first.

20 And Jacob vowed a vow, saying, If God will be with me, and will keep me in this way that I go, and will give me bread to eat, and raiment to put on,

21 So that I come again to my father's house in peace; then shall the LORD be my God:

22 And this stone, which I have set for a pillar, shall be God's house: and of all that thou shalt give me I will surely give the tenth unto thee.

15 "I am with you and will watch over you wherever you go, and I will bring you back to this land. I will not leave you until I have done what I have promised you."

16 When Jacob awoke from his sleep, he thought, "Surely the LORD is in this place, and I was not aware of it."

17 He was afraid and said, "How awesome is this place! This is none other than the house of God; this is the gate of heaven."

18 Early the next morning Jacob took the stone he had placed under his head and set it up as a pillar and poured oil on top of it.

19 He called that place Bethel, though the city used to be called Luz.

20 Then Jacob made a vow, saying, "If God will be with me and will watch over me on this journey I am taking and will give me food to eat and clothes to wear

21 "so that I return safely to my father's household, then the LORD will be my God

22 "and this stone that I have set up as a pillar will be God's house, and of all that you give me I will give you a tenth."

UNIFYING LESSON PRINCIPLE: In the midst of human turmoil, we grow weary and can lose sight of the purpose for our lives. How can we escape the confusion in order to refresh and reorient ourselves to get back on track? God created an opportunity for the weary Jacob to reconnect with his spiritual mission and resources so that he could begin his life's journey with renewed vigor.

LESSON OBJECTIVES

Upon the completion of this lesson, the students will be able to do the following:

1. Consider how Jacob's vulnerable situation led him to an encounter with God.
2. Affirm that God's strength is made manifest in human weakness.
3. Resolve to make room in their lives for times of spiritual retreat.

AGE-LEVEL POINTS TO BE EMPHASIZED
Teachers of ADULTS and YOUTH

—The angels in the dream are messengers but are not mediators for divine-human interaction.

The angels "ascending and descending" (verse 12) is an image of the connection between heaven and earth, between God and human beings. Jesus is the ultimate connection (John 1:51).

—Jacob is fleeing back to Haran to the land of his ancestors before God's covenant. Abraham was insistent that Isaac not go back there when the servant went to find him a wife.

—Jacob's vow to God does not condition God's keeping God's promise. The two are exclusive of each other. Jacob's vow (verses 20-22) is seen by some as bargaining with God: "If God does this, then I will do that (and if he doesn't, then I am not bound by the oath)." Others take it as more of a concession: "If (since, because) God will do this, then I will respond by doing that."

—Jacob awoke from the dream transformed into a man of faith—still flawed, but with a new faith in God.

—Jacob's name for the site, Bethel, means "house of God."

Teachers of CHILDREN

—Jacob honored his father's request not to choose a Canaanite wife.

—Jacob followed his father's instructions to seek a wife among his Uncle Laban's daughters.

—Jacob travelled from his home as instructed but had to spend the night in the open air.

—Jacob chose a stone for a pillow.

—Jacob dreamed that he saw a stairway that reached to heaven, with angels ascending and descending the stairway.

—The Lord spoke promises to Jacob.

THE CHRONOLOGICAL SETTING OF THE LESSON

When Jacob set out for Haran, he began his grandfather Abraham's journey in reverse. It is appropriate that this is the moment when the voice that once spoke to Abraham will finally speak to him. Up until now, God had never communicated with Jacob directly. Perhaps Jacob had even hoped to leave Yahweh behind in Canaan, along with all his family troubles. All that would now change as Yahweh confirmed to Jacob that he was indeed the bearer of the promise. These promises had enabled an infertile woman (Sarah) to bear a child (see Genesis 21); a homeless refugee (Isaac) to grow strong and wealthy (see Genesis 26); and one connected with the promise-bearing ancestor (Lot) to be rescued from disaster (see Genesis 19). In today's lesson, the emphasis of this divine revelation of promise falls on the promise of presence (see Genesis 28:15). This very ancient blessing on the traveller incorporates Jacob into the line of promise bearers. However, the most prominent promise in this narrative touches the fear and desire of a sojourner—divine presence, protection, and homecoming.

THE GEOGRAPHICAL AND CULTURAL SETTING OF THE LESSON

Jacob and Bethel have a special significance that connects with a theme woven through the book of Genesis. We have seen time and time again that Genesis is preoccupied with identifying various sacred places in Palestine with one or another of the patriarchs. Abraham built an altar to the Lord at Sichem in 12:7, and another near the plain of Mamre near Hebron in 13:8. Isaac built an altar at Bersabee to the Lord in 26:25. Jacob in the present story erects a memorial pillar at Bethel; later, he would build there an altar. And frequently throughout Genesis, we shall see similar stories identifying other sites with the worship of patriarchs. Thus, the place where Jacob slept (see Genesis 28:11) was probably a Canaanite (pagan) place of worship—that is to say, it was not a place kept for the worship of Yahweh only.

What Jacob would discover in his dream at the place where pagans had once worshipped their gods is a ladder to show that God is not separated from human beings. He would also see steps to remind him that communion between God and humans is possible. Perhaps this dream showed him another truth—namely, that God is present with us even when we are away from places where we have been accustomed to knowing His presence, like our homes and our places of corporate worship. Jacob was far away from home at this "place." He thought he could only find God in his hometown; thus, he was astonished to see that God was present and revealed Himself in a foreign country, even at a place once used for pagan worship.

PROMINENT CHARACTER(S) IN THE LESSON

Angels of God: beings used by God as messengers.
Jacob: the younger son of Isaac and Rebekah, and the twin brother of Esau; and husband of Leah and Rachel. Because Jacob is also called Israel, his twelve sons are called the "sons of Israel."

KEY TERMS IN THE LESSON

Ascending (verse 12)—Hebrew: *`alah* (aw-law'): to go up, ascend, climb.
Dreamed (verse 12)—Hebrew: *chalam* (khaw-lam'): to dream; "had a dream" (NIV).

Lighted (verse 11)—Hebrew: *paga`* (paw-gah'): encountered; met; "reached" (NIV); entreated; made intercession.
Seed (verse 13)—Hebrew: *zera`* (zeh'-rah): seed; sowing; offspring; "descendants" (NIV).
Sleep (verse 11)—Hebrew: *shakab* (shaw-kab'): to lie down.
Spread abroad (verse 14)—Hebrew: *parats* (paw-rats'): to spread, distribute; "spread out" (NIV).

TOPICAL OUTLINE OF THE LESSON

I.   **Introduction**
     A. Meeting God in Unexpected Places
     B. Biblical Background

II. **Exposition and Application of the Scripture**
     A. Encountering God on the Run (Genesis 28:10-11)
     B. A Life-altering Dream (Genesis 28:12-15)
     C. Awakened to a New Life in God the Father (Genesis 28:16-19)
     D. Jacob Makes a Vow to God (Genesis 28:20-22)

III. **Concluding Reflection**

I. INTRODUCTION

A. Meeting God in Unexpected Places

The clear revelation of God's gracious dealings with us when we deserve it the least can transform a worldly individual into a worshipper. Such a drama has been repeated throughout the history of the faith. Perhaps no story in Scripture illustrates this transformation as vividly as does Jacob's dream at Bethel. Before this experience, Jacob was a fugitive from the results of his sin, a troubled son in search of his place in life, a shrewd shepherd setting out to find a wife. After this encounter, however, he was a partner with God as a recipient of His covenant promises and a true worshipper. The transformation was due to God's intrusion into the course of his life.

The story unfolds quickly and dramatically. Being persona non-grata in Canaan after deceiving Isaac and receiving the blessing, Jacob fled to Haran until things settled down. At sundown, he stopped at a place and, taking one of the stones there, prepared to spend the night. In a dream, the Lord appeared to him from the top of an angel-filled stairway and confirmed that the blessing was indeed his. When Jacob awoke, he was afraid because he realized that the Lord was in that place; at dawn, he set up the stone as a memorial, named the place Bethel, "house of God," and vowed to worship there when he returned to his father's house in peace.

God often comes to us in surprising ways. His appearance in our lives is always an act of grace, for we do not deserve His blessings and His intervention at the critical junctures in our lives. God appeared before Jacob in a dream just after Jacob had been involved in one the most duplicitous schemes recorded in the Bible—the stealing of his brother's birthright and blessing. It is at such a low point in Jacob's life that God comes to him with a promise that He would neither leave nor forsake him. Thanks be to God, for indeed He has "promised never to leave, never to leave us alone."

B. Biblical Background

The biography of Jacob as an independent personality and a patriarch in his own right now begins. Having surreptitiously taken the blessing designed for Esau, Esau vowed to kill Jacob, but Jacob escaped his brother's wrath. It was now time for Jacob to leave. His mother Rebekah also desired for him to leave so that he could find a wife among her own family. Leaving the land is part of the realization of the promise God made to his grandfather Abraham, so Isaac added another blessing to speed Jacob on his way: "Arise to Paddan-Aram to the house of Bethuel your mother's father, and take you a wife from thence of the daughters of Laban your mother's brother. And God almighty bless you and make you fruitful, and multiply you, that you may be a congregation of peoples" (see Genesis 28:2-3).

Conflict and struggle will grow and continue throughout Jacob's days of wandering. However, at the particular moment of leaving the land, Jacob is extracted from his family turmoil to be transported into a different world, into the sphere of contact between humankind and God. Thus, Jacob went out from Beersheba and went toward Haran. He left his parents' house and birthplace to go alone to a distant land from which his grandfather Abraham had come to the land of Canaan. Years earlier, Abraham had made this journey in the opposite direction. The young Jacob makes this journey into the unknown by himself. He has no companion, but he has his father's blessings and his staff. Toward evening, he reached "the place." He takes some stones from the place to rest his head upon and to sleep on the mountain. In his loneliness on this holy mountain, he had a dream.

The home-loving favorite of an overprotective mother had become an exile, utterly alone and friendless, embarking on a long perilous journey that was to take him from Beer-sheba in southern Canaan to Haran in northern Mesopotamia. His character is to be tested and refined, his personality molded and transformed by the experience. In typical non-descriptive biblical style, the narrative provides no details about the adventures or the trials and tribulations of Jacob in the course of his trek; only the bare facts are mentioned—that he set out and that he arrived. However, the silence on the details of his trip is broken by the highlighting of a single, momentous encounter on the way, an encounter not with man but with God.

While Jacob slept unsuspectingly in this "place," he received a dream-revelation. It was customary throughout the ancient world for a devotee to sleep in the sacred precincts of a temple in order to induce the deity to reveal its will. However, this story about Jacob completely disassociates his experience from this pagan practice by stressing the wholly unplanned nature of his stopover, the complete anonymity of "the place," and the total unexpectedness of the theophany (the visible appearance of a deity). Here, God freely takes the initiative in revealing Himself to an amazed Jacob.

II. EXPOSITION AND APPLICATION OF THE SCRIPTURE

A. Encountering God on the Run (Genesis 28:10-11)

And Jacob went out from Beersheba, and went toward Haran. And he lighted upon a certain place, and tarried there all night, because the sun was set; and he took of the stones of that place, and put them for his pillows, and lay down in that place to sleep.

Jacob's deceitful act of stealing the blessing from his brother, Esau, was now complete. He left home with his father's blessing, which gave Jacob a shield of protection from Esau's interference. Isaac made no mention of the way Jacob had taken advantage of his failing eyesight and touch to snatch the blessing that ultimately in God's timing would have been his anyway. Perhaps Isaac had come to realize that God wanted him to give Jacob the blessing. Now Jacob was alone on the run. Jacob likely felt depressed and fearful as he left home. He had always preferred his home as opposed to the outdoors (see Genesis 25:27). Now he was forced to leave the place he loved because he had taken advantage of his brother and deceived his aging father. He must have been on the road for at least three days before he arrived in Bethel, for it was some sixty miles from his starting point.

This text stands as one of the pillars of the Jacob story, for at this, his lowest point thus far, God met Jacob as he fled to his parents' ancestral homeland and assured him that he is indeed an heir of the promise. This was the first time Jacob appeared by himself—without family, friend, or foe—thus, it represented a new beginning for the larger Jacob story. Jacob fled from the hatred and threats of his brother, Esau, seeming to reap the consequences of his own duplicity, and the future did not seem bright. At precisely this deeply vulnerable moment in his life, God appeared to him in a dream. He did not come in judgment but, rather, to confirm Jacob as the one chosen to carry on the promise. Why, some may ask, would God choose this time to bless a rogue like Jacob? Such an occasion is the proper time to remember that God never chooses people for what they are but for what they can become by the power of His grace. The story of Jacob's life should not be looked upon as an account of God's blessing wickedness but, rather, as an account of God's patient dealing with a sinful man until he became Israel, "fighter for God," or "striver with God."

B. A Life-altering Dream
(Genesis 28:12-15)

And he dreamed, and behold a ladder set up on the earth, and the top of it reached to heaven: and behold the angels of God ascending and descending on it.

And, behold, the LORD stood above it, and said, I am the LORD God of Abraham thy father, and the God of Isaac: the land whereon thou liest, to thee will I give it, and to thy seed; And thy seed shall be as the dust of the earth, and thou shalt spread abroad to the west, and to the east, and to the north, and to the south: and in thee and in thy seed shall all the families of the earth be blessed. And, behold, I am with thee, and will keep thee in all places whither thou goest, and will bring thee again into this land; for I will not leave thee, until I have done that which I have spoken to thee of.

In Jacob's dream, a stairway was set up on earth, and the top of it reached to heaven. The reader senses that more surprise and excitement is on the way because a dream generates the unexpected and the unusual. This dream is no exception. "Suddenly God's messengers (angels) are going up and down" the stairs (verse 12). The Hebrew word for "pathway" or "stairway" (*sullam*) suggests a stairway or path that connects the divine and human realms. The movement of the angels may have been intended to impress Jacob with their busy activity, looking after him and protecting him at a most vulnerable point in his life. Then just as suddenly, God appears and speaks. As we expect of dreams, the action does not move in a smooth sequence but irregularly jumps about. The jump to God's self-introduction immediately ties the dream to Jacob's heritage (verse 13). Indeed, the speech gave to Jacob the heritage of promise that his ancestors carried, the promise of land and an heir.

It may seem a bit surprising that God had nothing to say about the deceptive actions that had forced this journey upon Jacob. God's will had been done, albeit not in the best way. The Lord was most interested in starting afresh with Jacob, accepting—although not forgetting— what had happened. How uniquely like God!

He is always forgiving, always available, always ready to pick us up where we are, and always with us. Jacob needed acceptance and assurance, for he had lost his home, his possessions, and his inheritance. Esau had threatened his life, and for all he knew Esau might be pursuing him. Jacob needed direction for the future. God was there when Jacob needed Him most. God was faithful to Jacob, as He is with all who trust Him. Even when we fail miserably, God can be counted on to fulfill His promises in our lives. Sometimes, He blesses us *because of*, and at other times God blesses us *in spite of* what we do.

Truly, the God of the world and the God of the fathers is the same God who accompanied Jacob in his migration, guarding him from all harm, giving him security always: "And, behold, I am with thee, and will keep thee in all places whither thou goest" (verse 15a). The special destiny of Jacob brought out this element in God's being. Until this moment, God's promises to the fathers were that He would make a great nation of their seed and that He would give them the land. Here, however, God promised an individual that He would be with him to protect him wherever he went.

When men and women sense that God accompanies them, they derive a feeling of security that helps them to say, "Though I walk through the valley of the shadow of death, I will fear no evil: for thou art with me" (Psalm 23:4). The God of the world, the God of the people, and the God of the individual spoke here to Jacob, and He is the same God who speaks to us when He encounters us along the roadways of our lives and transforms us into the obedient followers He would have us to be.

C. Awakened to a New Life in God the Father (Genesis 28:16-19)

And Jacob awaked out of his sleep, and he said, Surely the Lord is in this place; and I knew it not. And he was afraid, and said, How dreadful is this place! this is none other but the house of God, and this is the gate of heaven. And Jacob rose up early in the morning, and took the stone that he had put for his pillows, and set it up for a pillar, and poured oil upon the top of it. And he called the name of that place Bethel: but the name of that city was called Luz at the first.

When Jacob awoke from his sleep, he realized that God must have been there even though he had been unaware of his presence at first (verse 16). Could there be a less likely place and time—so it had seemed to him—for God to manifest Himself? Jacob had come to one of the bleakest and most forbidding spots a person could have chanced upon. It was no pleasant meadow, no green oasis, and no sheltered valley. It was a hilltop of barren rock; its barrenness seemed to represent Jacob's lot in life at that moment. He was a fugitive, and he was afraid. His mother Rebekah had told him to go off for a few days, and then she would send and bring him home. However, Jacob may have had a better idea of the truth: that it would be no "few days" but a long time of punishing exile before he could ever dare to attempt to return home. Yet, despite his failings, there existed in Jacob's soul something to which God could speak. Jacob was capable of responding to more than the things of flesh and senses. He had a hunger to get his own life in touch with God.

His frightened response was that the place was awesome indeed, and he described it as "the house of God" and "the gate of heaven" (verse 17). When Jacob woke from his vision and felt that he had stood at the gate of heaven, there was first the sense of wonder and thanksgiving at the revelation of God's mercy; but then there swept over him an overwhelming awe: "How dreadful is this place" (verse 17). When a person is made to know that God has not forgotten him even though he has been a moral failure, there is the moment of rapturous exaltation, such as Jacob had when he saw the shining ladder and the angels; but when he remembered the holiness of God, he turned his face away from its intolerable light. Who can contemplate the difference between oneself and God and not bow down in agonizing unworthiness?

Waking up from this visitation by God, Jacob's *pillow* now becomes a *pillar*. He took the rock he had used as a headrest and set it up as a stone monument. After pouring oil on it to consecrate it, he gave the name "Bethel" to the town that had formerly been known as Luz (verse 19). When Jacob took the stone on which he had pillowed his head and set it up as a sacred thing, he followed an impulse that is as old and deep as humankind's religious experience. When people have had a spiritual experience, it is natural for them to think that the place where they had it and the things associated with it are in themselves holy. They want to enshrine the particular experience so that it may be not only remembered but also repeated.

D. Jacob Makes a Vow to God
(Genesis 28:20-22)

And Jacob vowed a vow, saying, If God will be with me, and will keep me in this way that I go, and will give me bread to eat, and raiment to put on, So that I come again to my father's house in peace; then shall the LORD be my God: And this stone, which I have set for a pillar, shall be God's house: and of all that thou shalt give me I will surely give the tenth unto thee.

Finally, Jacob made a vow that had several conditions attached to it. First, he promised God that if He would protect him while he was travelling, supply him with the basic necessities of life, and allow him to return home safely (verse 21), then the Lord would be Jacob's God and the pillar would be Jacob's house (in the sense that it would commemorate Jacob's meeting with God at Bethel). Last, but not least, Jacob promised to give to the Lord a tenth of everything he owned (verse 22). In summary, Jacob was promising God his life, his worship, and his possessions. Meeting God at Bethel was a critical step in Jacob's relationship with God. We might even call it Jacob's conversion. In this passage, the Lord transformed the ambitious *Jacob*—who had prevailed through his opportunism and malevolent cunning—into the ambitious *Israel*, who prevails through prayer to God and humble shrewdness in his dealings with his people.

God's love was not conditioned by what Jacob had done before his arrival at Bethel. Nevertheless God, as always, wanted a response from Jacob. It came! Jacob's affirmation of the Lord's being his God was a dramatic conversion experience. Many people choose not to admit their transgressions until they stand in the presence of a holy God, before whom they cannot hide their stained consciences. Jacob could have turned from God, but he chose to turn toward Him. One must be careful not to read Jacob's closing statement (verses 20-22) as an attempt to bargain with God. In reality, it was not that Jacob was so much choosing God at this time, as God was choosing him. Jacob likely felt that his actions had disqualified him. With that in mind, he said, "If God will be with me (despite what I have done), this I will do . . . ." Jacob was throwing himself before God's mercy.

III. CONCLUDING REFLECTION

The two most significant events in the life of Jacob were nighttime events where God appeared. The first was this dream at Bethel when he was fleeing from the land of Canaan—which, ironically, was his by virtue of the blessing. The other was his fight at Peniel, when he was attempting to return to the land. Each divine encounter was a life-changing event. In each of these encounters with God, there is instilled in the patriarch great expectations for the uncertain future. In this incident at Bethel, Jacob's vow expressed his anticipation for the future. God would now be with him and help him, even though he might be slow to realize it.

The promise of God's presence and protection would bring continued encouragement during the twenty years with Laban.

In his encounter with God at Bethel, Jacob realized that the one who desires to have the power of God must spend some time alone with God. Despite ourselves, we are who we are by the mercies of God. Even in our sinfulness, we can approach God with the confidence and assurance that He loves us and has a plan for our lives. He is slow to anger and quick with mercy. In addition, His love endures through all generations.

PRAYER

Dear Lord, teach us how to be open to the different ways You come into our lives. Allow us to live in hope that no matter what we have done, the promise of Your presence and protection is with us always. In Jesus' name we pray. Amen.

HOME DAILY BIBLE READINGS
(November 12-18, 2018)

Jacob Forms a Relationship with God
MONDAY, November 12: "Samuel Hears the Voice of God" (1 Samuel 3:1-9)

TUESDAY, November 13: "Elijah Meets God's Angel" (1 Kings 19:4-9)

WEDNESDAY, November 14: "The Lord Renews the Weary" (Isaiah 40:27-31)

THURSDAY, November 15: "A Great Priest for the People" (Hebrews 10:19-25)

FRIDAY, November 16: "Tithe to Support Levites and Community" (Deuteronomy 14:22-29)

SATURDAY, November 17: "Nathanael Will See Greater Things" (John 1:47-51)

SUNDAY, November 18: "Transformed by God's Visitation" (Genesis 28:10-22)

Fall Quarter 2018
Unit III: God Blesses and Re-creates Regardless
Children's Unit: God Blesses and Re-creates Anyway

November 25, 2018 — Lesson 13

GOD BLESSES JACOB AND RACHEL

ADULT/YOUTH
ADULT/YOUNG ADULT TOPIC: Amassing Wealth
YOUTH TOPIC: More than Enough

CHILDREN
GENERAL LESSON TITLE: God Blesses Jacob and Rachel
CHILDREN'S TOPIC: Jacob and Rachel Receive a Special Gift

DEVOTIONAL READING
Psalm 46

ADULT/YOUTH
BACKGROUND SCRIPTURE: Genesis 30
PRINT PASSAGE: Genesis 30:22-32, 43
KEY VERSE: Genesis 30:22

CHILDREN
BACKGROUND SCRIPTURE: Genesis 30
PRINT PASSAGE: Genesis 30:22-32, 43
KEY VERSE: Genesis 30:23

Genesis 30:22-32, 43—KJV

22 And God remembered Rachel, and God hearkened to her, and opened her womb.

23 And she conceived, and bare a son; and said, God hath taken away my reproach:

24 And she called his name Joseph; and said, The LORD shall add to me another son.

25 And it came to pass, when Rachel had born Joseph, that Jacob said unto Laban, Send me away, that I may go unto mine own place, and to my country.

26 Give me my wives and my children, for whom I have served thee, and let me go: for thou knowest my service which I have done thee.

27 And Laban said unto him, I pray thee, if I have found favour in thine eyes, tarry: for I have learned by experience that the LORD hath blessed me for thy sake.

28 And he said, Appoint me thy wages, and I will give it.

Genesis 30:22-32, 43—NIV

22 Then God remembered Rachel; he listened to her and enabled her to conceive.

23 She became pregnant and gave birth to a son and said, "God has taken away my disgrace."

24 She named him Joseph, and said, "May the Lord add to me another son."

25 After Rachel gave birth to Joseph, Jacob said to Laban, "Send me on my way so I can go back to my own homeland.

26 "Give me my wives and children, for whom I have served you, and I will be on my way. You know how much work I've done for you."

27 But Laban said to him, "If I have found favor in your eyes, please stay. I have learned by divination that the LORD has blessed me because of you."

28 He added, "Name your wages, and I will pay them."

29 And he said unto him, Thou knowest how I have served thee, and how thy cattle was with me.

30 For it was little which thou hadst before I came, and it is now increased unto a multitude; and the LORD hath blessed thee since my coming: and now when shall I provide for mine own house also?

31 And he said, What shall I give thee? And Jacob said, Thou shalt not give me any thing: if thou wilt do this thing for me, I will again feed and keep thy flock.

32 I will pass through all thy flock to day, removing from thence all the speckled and spotted cattle, and all the brown cattle among the sheep, and the spotted and speckled among the goats: and of such shall be my hire.

.....

43 And the man increased exceedingly, and had much cattle, and maidservants, and menservants, and camels, and asses.

29 Jacob said to him, "You know how I have worked for you and how your livestock has fared under my care.

30 "The little you had before I came has increased greatly, and the Lord has blessed you wherever I have been. But now, when may I do something for my own household?"

31 "What shall I give you?" he asked. "Don't give me anything," Jacob replied. "But if you will do this one thing for me, I will go on tending your flocks and watching over them:

32 "Let me go through all your flocks today and remove from them every speckled or spotted sheep, every dark-colored lamb and every spotted or speckled goat. They will be my wages."

.....

43 In this way the man grew exceedingly prosperous and came to own large flocks, and female and male servants, and camels and donkeys.

UNIFYING LESSON PRINCIPLE: Obstacles and loss often block our efforts to accomplish something worthwhile. How can we overcome these setbacks in order to live lives that count for good? God intervened to help Jacob overcome seeming defeat by not only gaining many possessions, but also escaping the wrath of a selfish and deceptive father-in-law.

LESSON OBJECTIVES

Upon the completion of this lesson, the students will be able to do the following:
1. Study how God provided for Jacob and his family.
2. Identify with Jacob's stormy relationship with his father-in-law.
3. Pray for God's intervention in our times of crisis.

AGE-LEVEL POINTS TO BE EMPHASIZED

Teachers of ADULTS and YOUTH

—Earlier, Jacob had been deceived when Laban substituted Leah for Rachel (Genesis 29:23). Now Laban continues to deceive by promising to give Jacob all the striped and speckled livestock to be born in his flock, but then removing the animals that would sire and bear such animals (Genesis 30:35).

—Like Rebekah and Sarah, Rachel was childless for a long time (probably at least seven years, per Genesis 30:19-22).

—Laban wanted Jacob to continue working for him because Laban had become wealthy through Jacob (Genesis 30:27).

—Verse 27 does not specify the manner of

divination Laban used, and divination is prohibited later when Israel receives the Law (see Leviticus 19:26; Deuteronomy 18:10; see also 1 Samuel 15:23).

—Jacob's dependence on "speckled and spotted sheep" (verse 32) to increase his wealth has been seen to reflect both scientific breeding principles and unscientific folklore tradition.

—Laban credits "divination" for his prosperity, but Jacob credits God's blessing.

—Jacob's cunning provides well for his families with the implication that God has blessed his efforts.

Teachers of CHILDREN

—Trusting God when nothing seems to be happening is difficult.

—The Lord eventually answered Rachel's prayers and gave her a child.

—Jacob made plans to return home with his wives and family.

—Laban tried to keep Jacob from returning home.

—Jacob made provisions to increase his wealth.

—Laban agreed to Jacob's proposition.

THE CHRONOLOGICAL SETTING OF THE LESSON

Jacob has now conscientiously discharged all his obligations to Laban. This coincides with the extraordinary birth of Joseph to his beloved Rachel. God's promise of numerous offspring has been abundantly fulfilled, and another milestone in Jacob's life has been reached. In accordance with the divine blessing at Bethel (see Genesis 28:15), the patriarch must now prepare to return home. God's promise would be further fulfilled in Jacob's life through the accumulation of wealth during his twenty-year stay in the land of his ancestors.

THE GEOGRAPHICAL AND CULTURAL SETTING OF THE LESSON

Women play an important role in the fulfillment of God's promise of land, seed, and blessing. The writer of the book of Genesis emphasizes the role of the women as mediators of the divine blessing in and through their bearing of children. Jacob, though prominent, remains deeply in the background as the voices and actions of the women fill these verses. In the midst of a patriarchal culture, the tradition gives women a central place in the story of the birth of the people of Israel. In addition, the use of God language by the women, both in connection with the birth of their children and with Jacob, attests to their personal faith, but also to their ability to engage in theological discussion and formulation. The women—Sarah, Rebekah, and Rachel—make confessions, not on the basis of some special revelation, but by the deep-down links they see between their experience and what they know their God to be about in the world.

Also, in the birth of Joseph we may see the hand of God at work on behalf of new life and families. This creative work of God remains indispensable for the history of the promise, for it enables the coming into being of persons to whom promises can be made and for whom they can be realized. God's promises are made on behalf of "families." God's most fundamental objective in making the promises to Abraham, Isaac, and Jacob—and Sarah and Leah and Rachel—is the blessing of families. Thus, the author places the birth of Israel as a community of faith within an admixture of familial conflict, human love and service, and ongoing divine blessing amidst human failure.

PROMINENT CHARACTER(S) IN THE LESSON

Joseph: the eleventh son of Jacob and the elder of Rachel's, his favored wife. Like Isaac and Jacob before him, Joseph was born to a formerly barren woman to whom God had shown compassion.

Rachel: the younger daughter of Laban; Jacob's second wife; and the mother of Joseph and Benjamin.

KEY TERMS IN THE LESSON

Add (verse 24)—Hebrew: *yacaph* (yaw-saf'): to add, increase, do again.

Bare (verse 23)—Hebrew: *yalad* (yaw-lad'): to bear, bring forth, beget; gender; travail; "gave birth" (NIV).

Favour (verse 27)—Hebrew: *chen* (khane): grace; charm; "favor" (NIV).

Opened (verse 22 [KJV only])—Hebrew: *pathach* (paw-thakh'): to be opened, be let loose, be thrown open.

Remembered (verse 22)—Hebrew: *zakar* (zaw-kar'): remembered; recalled; called to mind.

Served (verse 26)—Hebrew: `*abad* (aw-bad'): worked; served.

TOPICAL OUTLINE OF THE LESSON

I. Introduction
   A. Family Troubles and God's Provisions
   B. Biblical Background

II. Exposition and Application of the Scripture
   A. God Blesses His People by Removing Their Reproach (Genesis 30:22-24)
   B. God's People Can Anticipate His Continued Faithfulness (Genesis 30:25-26)
   C. The Enjoyment of God's Abundant Blessing (Genesis 30:27-32)
   D. Recipients of the Promise Trust in God's Faithfulness (Genesis 30:43)

III. Concluding Reflection

I. INTRODUCTION

A. Family Troubles and God's Provisions

This chapter continues the theme of sharp and deep levels of intrafamilial conflict and deception with the focus now on the family in the old country—Haran. The family in Haran more than matches the family in Canaan. They are chips off the same block; such familial tendencies run deep. At the same time, these ongoing family problems derive in many ways from Jacob's own duplicity in chapter 27. Jacob continues to reap the fruits of his own deception of Esau and, in the process, intensifies the problems in another community. How easy it would have been for the writer of Genesis to paint a rosy, idyllic picture of Israel's origins as a Garden of Eden-sort of beginning. However, the writer, with a grounded understanding of the human condition, knew that this would not be realistic. The more deeply the probe into Israel's past, the more the present looked like déjà vu. Yet, precisely because of this realistic look at human nature and divine action, readers can see themselves as if in a mirror, gaining new levels of self-understanding and being assured of God's continuing involvement in their lives.

At the same time, we see that human love and human service can counter human deception. We see in today's lesson how God makes use of human wisdom and ingenuity in effecting the divine purpose in and through this family. Both human beings and God act with favorable consequences, from the women (see Genesis 29:31–30:24) to Jacob (see Genesis 30:27, 30). Even people like Laban listen to God's voice and participate in the divine purposes (see Genesis 31:24). Jacob may not be entirely free of arrogance, but God extends abundant blessings through Jacob's service. God's blessings are always mediated, whether through created orders, human activity, or a combination thereof. Despite the many obstacles and hindrances Jacob had to overcome, God blessed him and his family in a marvelous way. No one can take away what God has for us. The psalmist expressed this providential care of God when he said, "Thou preparest a table before me in the presence of mine enemies" (Psalm 23:5a).

Prosperity can have one of two effects on people. Some view their success as a trust from God and put it to good use for Him. Others, however, see it as a personal accomplishment and the means to personal power. Such an independent, self-sufficient attitude is harmful to the faith, for it robs God of His honor by attributing the prosperity to human ingenuity. Sooner or later, believers—even those caught up in this worldly attitude—will acknowledge that their prosperity came from God. In Genesis 30, we have an unusual story about Jacob's acquiring great wealth at the expense of Laban. This clever man outwitted another opponent—or so it seemed. However, Jacob owed more to God in this successful venture than he realized at the time.

The point of the story, as Jacob's own interpretation of it will say, is God's sovereign blessing of the patriarch in accord with the promises. Jacob's blessing was far more than the expected food and clothing of Genesis 28:20; it was abundance in good measure.

B. Biblical Background

This section of Genesis opens and finds Rachel finally happy. She bore a son because God remembered her (see Genesis 30:22). The time span of misery for Rachel was likely the entire seven-year period of her marriage. Needless to say, she was glad her time had come. The name *Joseph* that she gives her child signified for her that "God has taken away my disgrace" (verse 23), and she followed the baby's naming with a prayer for the future: "May the Lord add to me another son" (verse 24).

The birth of Joseph coincided with the fourteenth year of labor Jacob had completed as a bride price for both Leah and Rachel. Jacob had hoped to complete his agreed-upon amount of labor in half the time. It was doubled because of Laban's trickery. In expressing his desire to leave for home, Jacob did not make demands but rather asked permission to leave: "Send me on my way . . . to my own homeland" (verse 25, NIV). Yet, it was a straightforward request without even a "please." The words could have been spoken tersely. However, Laban had come to realize that Jacob's departure would leave a huge hole in his operation and, furthermore, he had recognized how much the Lord had blessed him because of Jacob (verse 27).

Laban used both courtesy and cunning in replying to Jacob. He was most polite in ignoring Jacob's request to leave. Laban knew his present status was largely the result of Jacob's fourteen years of labor. So, he said to Jacob, "Name your wages and I will pay you" (verse 28). Jacob reminded Laban of the tremendous increase in animals that had occurred during the years Jacob had been in charge and how the Lord had blessed him wherever Jacob had been. But Jacob informed Laban that he was also interested in doing something for Jacob's own family. Laban quickly responded, "What shall I give you?" (verse 31, NIV). The reply indicated that he had no plans to give Jacob anything if he left. It would have been normal to give Jacob a parting gift; this was not in Laban's mind. Even after another six years of labor, Laban still laid claim to livestock belonging to Jacob by previous agreement: "[your] flocks are my flocks. All you see is mine" (Genesis 31:43, NIV). Only if Jacob stayed and continued to work would Laban offer him wages. Such a situation left Jacob with no choice but to stay, for he could not make it back home if he left with nothing.

At this point, Jacob appears to have learned that he had caused many of his own problems. They had come as punishments for what he had done in the past. It must be understood that God was not the source of the punishment. It was an automatic result of his deviousness. God never holds grudges after He forgives, but sin usually has its own consequences.

Jacob chose to continue working for Laban, and at a very modest wage. Their agreement was as follows: Jacob would go through the flock and separate all the irregularly colored sheep and goats; he would take for his wages all the multicolored animals. Laban readily agreed, obviously thinking his herds would grow four times faster in the future than those of Jacob's. In addition, to craftily ensure Jacob's wages would begin at nothing, before Jacob could go out into the field and claim his irregularly colored sheep, Laban went there first, removed them, and gave them to his sons. There was nothing Jacob could do about Laban's deceptive tactics. His only hope was to get spotted-colored offspring to have spotted animals. Though Jacob tried to influence the mating of the flocks through the use of fresh-cut poplar branches, it is clear that the Lord Himself saw to it that Jacob was rewarded (see Genesis 31:10-12).

Jacob's breeding method was applied in such a way as to ensure that the stronger offspring would be his, while the weaker would be Laban's. Jacob did not use deception as Laban had done; he simply applied his keen knowledge of animal husbandry and trusted the Lord to help him outwit Laban. Both Jacob and the author of Genesis knew that in reality, God was fulfilling the promise that He had made to Jacob at Bethel (see Genesis 28:13-15). It took Jacob many years and many hard knocks to finally recognize that God would take care of him minus all the trickery and deceit he felt he needed to use to get by.

II. EXPOSITION AND APPLICATION OF THE SCRIPTURE

A. God Blesses His People by Removing Their Reproach
(Genesis 30:22-24)

And God remembered Rachel, and God hearkened to her, and opened her womb. And she conceived, and bare a son; and said, God hath taken away my reproach: And she called his name Joseph; and said, The Lord shall add to me another son.

Finally, Rachel had a son of her own—Joseph. The report expresses a major triumph in Rachel's struggle; the birth of a son after a long period of unfruitfulness displayed divine intervention on behalf of the favorite wife of Jacob. With this name there is also a double word play, the first being an expression of joy loosely connected to the name by sound (*asap*), the second forming the motivation for the name Joseph (*yosep*): "May the Lord add [*yosep*] to me another son." Rachel, earlier haughty and impatient, now gave praise to God for taking away her reproach and prayed for another son from the Lord. After all, if a birth had broken the barrenness, more could follow. The name thus meant "May he add," or "may he increase."

With Rachel's pregnancy, we learn that God's choice to bless is not made by human standards. In fact, God characteristically works for things or people that humans reject—the downcast, the afflicted, the troubled, the oppressed, and the rejected. Those who find themselves in such predicaments can by faith rely on God, who in His sovereign plan will bless them. His blessing, however, cannot be gained by bargaining or striving. Whatever our lot in life—whether we are hated or ignored, oppressed or challenged, troubled or anxious—our attitude should not be one of jealousy, nor our efforts those of bitter rivalry. Rather, we must cultivate a wholehearted trust in God, waiting patiently for His blessing on us.

B. God's People Can Anticipate His Continued Faithfulness
(Genesis 30:25-26)

And it came to pass, when Rachel had born Joseph, that Jacob said unto Laban, Send me away, that I may go unto mine own place, and to my country. Give me my wives and my children, for whom I have served thee, and let me go: for thou knowest my service which I have done thee.

Jacob anticipates a new era in his life with his request to Laban to leave for his homeland. He had been with Laban for fourteen years of faithful service for his wives and his children. He clearly had kept his part of the bargain in an unfortunate situation. Now he was ready to return with his family to his homeland. God had given him a family; he now could look forward to the fulfillment of the promised blessing in the land.

By the terms of the original contract with Laban, Jacob's status was that of an indentured servant paying off a debt—in this case, the bride price for his employer's two daughters. Hence, Jacob is entitled to the philanthropy accorded one who leaves his master's house on completion of his term of service. Laban was reluctant to lose Jacob's skilled services, so he ignored the request to depart and pretended to understand Jacob's remarks as the opening bid in a haggle over the price of future service. Jacob's protracted service to Laban is a direct consequence of Jacob's deceit of Esau; Jacob fled because he stole the blessing, and this brings him to Laban and to his long service. Yet, God never left Jacob and continually promised to bless him and his household.

C. The Enjoyment of God's Abundant Blessing (Genesis 30:27-32)

And Laban said unto him, I pray thee, if I have found favour in thine eyes, tarry: for I have learned by experience that the LORD hath blessed me for thy sake. And he said, Appoint me thy wages, and I will give it. And he said unto him, Thou knowest how I have served thee, and how thy cattle was with me. For it was little which thou hadst before I came, and it is now increased unto a multitude; and the LORD hath blessed thee since my coming: and now when shall I provide for mine own house also? And he said, What shall I give thee? And Jacob said, Thou shalt not give me any thing: if thou wilt do this thing for me, I will again feed and keep thy flock. I will pass through all thy flock to day, removing from thence all the speckled and spotted cattle, and all the brown cattle among the sheep, and the spotted and speckled among the goats: and of such shall be my hire.

This part of the passage developed Jacob's decision to stay. Both he and Laban acknowledged that the Lord had blessed Laban because of Jacob. The acknowledgment of the Lord's blessing by the two men formed an interesting contrast. Laban observed that the Lord had prospered him through Jacob. He had enjoyed the prosperity while Jacob was with him and so concluded, through whatever means of perception he used, that God had done it. Jacob, on the other hand, simply stated that the Lord had blessed Laban because of him. The abundance that they recognized as God's blessing led them to a new agreement. Laban wanted Jacob to stay so that Laban might continue to prosper with this man, and Jacob agreed to stay because he was confident that the Lord would now provide for him, now that his

obligations toward Laban were completed. Jacob thus proposed a plan by which (ostensibly) he would gain little: he would receive the rare animals, the odd-colored livestock (verse 32). Laban agreed to this arrangement because he thought it would work only to his advantage. Nevertheless, both Laban and Jacob knew that the Lord was blessing Jacob's work, and in their own ways each man sought to obtain additional blessings from the Lord.

This time around, Jacob manages to "out-Laban" Laban. Last time there was a discussion about wages, Laban had managed to outmaneuver Jacob, but now the tables were turned (verse 31). Like his forebears Abraham (see Genesis 24:1) and Isaac (see Genesis 26:13), Jacob simply could not help but prosper. So, Jacob's wealth increased more and more, a clear clue that God's blessing was with him as much as it was with his more conventional ancestors. However, Jacob's success at outwitting Laban the cheater comes not from his folly this time but from God's grace.

D. Recipients of the Promise Trust in God's Faithfulness (Genesis 30:43)

And the man increased exceedingly, and had much cattle, and maidservants, and menservants, and camels, and asses.

"And the man increased exceedingly . . . ." (verse 43). This is the climax of the scene. The Hebrew verb for "increase" means, "To break out." It is the same verb used in God's promise at Bethel (see Genesis 28:14), showing that the promise had been fulfilled. Jacob bartered the strong sheep and goats for servants, camels, and donkeys. The sovereign God blessed Jacob's flock at Laban's expense despite the inexcusable cunning of both men. Jacob appeared to outwit Laban, balancing Laban's outwitting of Jacob, but he obtained his family (see 29:31–30:24) and wealth by God's sovereign grace. Even Laban had to concede that God's blessing was upon Jacob. God had committed Himself to this flawed man of faith. This narrative reinforces points that were relevant in the life of the Hebrew nation: that God does not forsake the cheat; that justice will finally be done; and that His promises to His people—here personified in Jacob, and embodied as land, protection, and blessing to the nations—will, despite all opposition, eventually triumph.

III. CONCLUDING REFLECTION

Everything in Jacob's life, no matter how small and ordinary, was overarched by the high purpose and providence of God. Owing to the infallible promises of God, Jacob became a wealthy man during his sojourn with Laban. He would return to Canaan with wives, a large family, and many possessions. What is more important, however, is what develops later; he was to return spiritually as well as materially enriched.

PRAYER

Dear God, we give You thanks for continuing to pour out upon us Your favor and daily blessings. We confess that we do not deserve them and therefore we are constantly reminded that all good and perfect gifts come down to us from above. In Jesus' name we pray. Amen.

HOME DAILY BIBLE READINGS
(November 19-25, 2018)

God Blesses Jacob and Rachel

MONDAY, November 19: "Jacob Marries Leah and Rachel" (Genesis 29:15-30)

TUESDAY, November 20: "Leah Gives Birth to Four Sons" (Genesis 29:31-35)

WEDNESDAY, November 21: "The God of Jacob Brings Victory" (Psalm 20)

THURSDAY, November 22: "Jacob Steals His Family from Laban" (Genesis 31:1-9)

FRIDAY, November 23: "Jacob and Laban Make Peace" (Genesis 31:43-50)

SATURDAY, November 24: "Rachel Gives Birth to Two Sons" (Genesis 30:22-24; 35:16-21)

SUNDAY, November 25: "Jacob Prospers at Laban's Expense" (Genesis 30:22-32, 43)

Our Love for God

GENERAL INTRODUCTION

This quarter's study begins with God's demands for our complete and undivided love, as shown in passages from the books of Deuteronomy and Psalms. It proceeds with our response to God's love in the advent of Christ, and the Epistles' interpretations of the nature and extent of our responses to God's love in Christ. It concludes with passages from three of the Psalms, expressing glorification of God.

Unit I, *"God Commands Our Love, Respect, and Obedience,"* has five lessons. The Deuteronomy passage contains a presentation of God's demand for total love and devotion. The session from the book of Joshua contains his faithful statement of love and reverence for a liberating God. In Psalm 103, David expresses love and glorification of God for God's creative, sustaining, and protective actions. Luke portrays the advent of Christ and human response to God's act of fulfillment of God's promise. We are challenged in the book of Matthew to love God through compassionate works.

Unit II, *"Loving God by Trusting Christ,"* has five lessons. Matthew continues to inspire trust in God for all things, while James encourages total submission to God in love. In his letter to the Philippians, Paul gives an interpretation of human devotion to God in Christ; promotes selfless devotion through exemplification of Christ's total submission to God in love; and encourages giving up everything for the sake of one's love for Christ.

Unit III, *"Love Songs that Glorify God,"* has three lessons. The quarter ends with Psalm 48, which focuses on a song of adoration for God's steadfast love; Psalm 66 focuses on part of a love song of praise to God for all His mighty works of goodness; and Psalm 91 closes this unit with a praise song to God for assurance of protection and comfort for those who love God.

And we know that in

ALL

things

GOD

works for the good of those
who love Him,
who have been called
according to His purpose.

ROMANS 8:28

December 2, 2018
Lesson 1

LOVE AND DEVOTION

ADULT/YOUTH
ADULT/YOUNG ADULT TOPIC: **Complete Devotion**
YOUTH TOPIC: **Love of a Lifetime**

CHILDREN
GENERAL LESSON TITLE: **Love and Devotion**
CHILDREN'S TOPIC: **Being Loving and Devoted**

DEVOTIONAL READING
Mark 12:28-34

ADULT/YOUTH
BACKGROUND SCRIPTURE: **Deuteronomy 6:1-9**
PRINT PASSAGE: **Deuteronomy 6:1-9**
KEY VERSE: **Deuteronomy 6:5**

CHILDREN
BACKGROUND SCRIPTURE: **Deuteronomy 6:1-9**
PRINT PASSAGE: **Deuteronomy 6:1-9**
KEY VERSE: **Deuteronomy 6:5**

Deuteronomy 6:1-9—KJV

NOW THESE are the commandments, the statutes, and the judgments, which the LORD your God commanded to teach you, that ye might do them in the land whither ye go to possess it:

2 That thou mightest fear the LORD thy God, to keep all his statutes and his commandments, which I command thee, thou, and thy son, and thy son's son, all the days of thy life; and that thy days may be prolonged.

3 Hear therefore, O Israel, and observe to do it; that it may be well with thee, and that ye may increase mightily, as the LORD God of thy fathers hath promised thee, in the land that floweth with milk and honey.

4 Hear, O Israel: The LORD our God is one LORD:

5 And thou shalt love the LORD thy God with all thine heart, and with all thy soul, and with all thy might.

6 And these words, which I command thee this day, shall be in thine heart:

7 And thou shalt teach them diligently unto thy children, and shalt talk of them when thou sittest

Deuteronomy 6:1-9—NIV

THESE ARE the commands, decrees and laws the LORD your God directed me to teach you to observe in the land that you are crossing the Jordan to possess,

2 so that you, your children and their children after them may fear the LORD your God as long as you live by keeping all his decrees and commands that I give you, and so that you may enjoy long life.

3 Hear, Israel, and be careful to obey so that it may go well with you and that you may increase greatly in a land flowing with milk and honey, just as the LORD, the God of your ancestors, promised you.

4 Hear, O Israel: The LORD our God, the LORD is one.

5 Love the LORD your God with all your heart and with all your soul and with all your strength.

6 These commandments that I give you today are to be on your hearts.

in thine house, and when thou walkest by the way, and when thou liest down, and when thou risest up.
8 And thou shalt bind them for a sign upon thine hand, and they shall be as frontlets between thine eyes.
9 And thou shalt write them upon the posts of thy house, and on thy gates.

7 Impress them on your children. Talk about them when you sit at home and when you walk along the road, when you lie down and when you get up.
8 Tie them as symbols on your hands and bind them on your foreheads.
9 Write them on the doorframes of your houses and on your gates.

UNIFYING LESSON PRINCIPLE: In the midst of life's challenges and uncertainties, people search for a foundation on which to make decisions. What is that foundation? In the book of Deuteronomy, God informed the Israelites that the basis for meeting all of life's circumstances is to love God absolutely, and Matthew recorded that Jesus repeated those instructions.

LESSON OBJECTIVES

Upon the completion of this lesson, the students will be able to do the following:
1. Explore the significance of the Shema (Deuteronomy 6:4-9) in both Jewish and Christian faith.
2. Aspire to love God with all their hearts, souls, and might.
3. Commit to pass on God's statutes and ordinances to others, especially to younger generations.

AGE-LEVEL POINTS TO BE EMPHASIZED

Teachers of ADULTS and YOUTH
—The great commandment on love is one of the most distinctive commands given by God.
—That the Lord alone is Israel's God leads to the demand for Israel's exclusive and total devotion to Him—"heart . . . soul . . . might." All Israelites in their total being are to love the Lord; "this is the greatest and first commandment" (Matthew 22:38).
—*Shema* is the Hebrew word for "Hear" that begins Deuteronomy 6:4.
—The Shema serves as a confession of faith in God.
—One's loving God with all his/her heart, soul, and might does not leave room for him or her to love the world or the things of the world.

Teachers of CHILDREN
—God gave Moses specific guidelines (commandments) to teach the Israelites.
—The Israelites were instructed to pass God's commandments on to future generations, using all opportunities possible.
—God expected obedience.
—The first and greatest commandment is to love God.
—Jesus reiterated the commandment given to Moses when the Pharisees asked Him to identify the greatest commandment.
—The second-greatest commandment is to love one's neighbor.

THE CHRONOLOGICAL SETTING OF THE LESSON

If the book of Exodus were written in approximately 1446 BC, then that would place the writing of the book of Deuteronomy in approximately 1406 BC. Support for Mosaic authorship is found in Deuteronomy 1:6, 9; 5:1; 27:1, 9; 31:1, 30; and 33:1. A direct reference to Mosaic authorship occurs in Deuteronomy 31:9, 24: "Moses wrote this law, and gave it to the priests the sons of Levi. . . . When Moses had finished writing the words of the law in a book . . . ." Consequently, even though the book is otherwise presented anonymously, many traditional scholars credit Moses with writing this book.

THE GEOGRAPHICAL AND CULTURAL SETTING OF THE LESSON

The plains of Moab serve as the geographical setting for the book of Deuteronomy. This is located on the east bank of the Jordan River across from the city of Jericho. After the older generation of the Israelites died, the new generation camped near the banks of the Jordan and waited for further instructions for crossing over into Canaan. Prior to their being able to cross over, the covenant between God and the people which had not been upheld by the older generation of Israelites had to be renewed by the new generation. This phenomenon illustrates the reality that every generation has the opportunity and responsibility to either embrace or reject the lifestyle and teachings of Jehovah God.

The Israelites lived a nomadic life, wandering through the wilderness for thirty-eight years. Although their relationship with God had been damaged through disobedience, it had not been terminated and God was still bound to fulfill the promise to give them the bountiful, plentiful land called *Canaan*. This arrangement stood strong because of God's unwavering love and the unconditional covenant of love between God and His people. Interestingly, although Deuteronomy displays God's unconditional nature, another aspect of God's simple complexity is His conditional relationship with the children of Israel. God's covenant emphasizes themes of monotheism, loyalty, justice, and transcendence. There are certain benefits available to God's people only if they are faithful to Him. The covenant between God and Israel is summed up in Deuteronomy 26:16-19. This covenant was to be reaffirmed as soon as Israel entered the Promised Land (see Deuteronomy 4:31; 5:2; 28:9-14) .

PROMINENT CHARACTER(S) IN THE LESSON

Noah: Noah was the firstborn son of Lamech. The name *Noah* means "relief" or "comfort" from all the hard work men have had to endure since the curse (see Genesis 5:29). God commanded Noah to build an ark, and in a display of grace God gave humans 120 years to repent before the floodwaters would come (see Genesis 6:3). When grace was ignored, flood waters covered the earth, and Noah and his family entered the ark—and only those eight survived the floodwaters.

KEY TERMS IN THE LESSON

Commands (verse 1)—Hebrew: *tsav* (tsawv): injunctions; "commandments" (KJV), precepts.

Day (verse 6)—Hebrew: *yohm* (yome): a literal day, or a period of time to be defined by associated words; "today" (NIV).

God (verse 3)—Hebrew: *elohim* (el-o-heem'): God; supreme divine being.

Hear (verse 4)—Hebrew: *shama* (shaw-mah'): to hear; heard; given heed.

Heart (verse 5—Hebrew: *lebab* (lay-bawb'): inner man; mind; will; heart.

Walk(est) (verse 7)—Hebrew: *halak* (haw-lak'): to go, come, walk; to travel.

Words (verse 6)—Hebrew: *dabar* (daw-baw'): speech; expression; "commandments" (NIV).

TOPICAL OUTLINE OF THE LESSON

I. **Introduction**
   A. The Covenant after the Storm
   B. Biblical Background

II. **Exposition and Application of the Scripture**
   A. Obedience Precedes Blessings
      (Deuteronomy 6:1-3)

   B. The Shema
      (Deuteronomy 6:4-5)
   C. Everlasting Commandments
      (Deuteronomy 6:6-9)

III. **Concluding Reflection**

I. INTRODUCTION

A. The Covenant after the Storm

After the catastrophic worldwide tragedy of the Flood, God offered renewed hope and strength for the people to rebuild their lives. Noah and his family had the unique opportunity of creating a new template for humanity. In many ways, although every generation is influenced by the previous generation, still each generation and each new family can start over and create a new life script to influence the families that will emerge from their family tree.

When tragedy strikes, we all have the choice of either giving up or looking up. Giving up leads to depression and defeat. Looking up leads to power and possibility. Noah and his family decided to look up to God for help and hope. They were rewarded by God in the form of a rainbow as a visual symbol to assure Noah and future generations that God would remember never to destroy the earth by water again.

B. Biblical Background

After the Flood, God made a covenant with Noah that even though the human heart is basically evil from the start, God would never destroy the world again. This displays God's tendency toward being a covenant-making and covenant-keeping God who is bound by His Word, regardless of the circumstances. A *covenant*, in this context, is an agreement between God and His people in which God makes promises and usually requires certain conditions to be met on behalf of the other party. In the Old Testament, in addition to Noah, God also made agreements with Abraham and Moses. In every covenant God makes with humanity, it is humanity who always gets the better end of the deal.

The responsibility of Noah and his descendants in the covenant process was to "be fruitful and increase in number and fill the earth." It is obvious in this command and in many others that there are marvelous built-in benefits of obeying God's instructions. Since the beginning of time, no one has ever been able to claim that their lives became worse rather than better after obeying commands and fulfilling their covenant agreement with God. One aspect of the divine nature of God is to be a giver. Consequently, all throughout Scripture as well as the experiences of the present, no one has ever been able to out-give God. Every deal God makes with His people always ultimately provides a greater benefit to the people than to God.

Built into God's covenant agreement were instructions for dietary provisions: "Everything that lives and moves about will be food for you. Just as I gave you the green plants, I now give you everything. But you must not eat meat that has its lifeblood still in it" (Genesis 9:3-4, NIV). God is concerned about not only the spiritual parts of life, but also its physical aspects. Ultimately, all aspects of life are interrelated and create a cause-and-effect situation with each other. Another aspect of the covenant dealt with the importance of righteous human interactions: "Whoever sheds human blood, by humans shall their blood be shed; for in the image of God has God made mankind. As for you, be fruitful and increase in number; multiply on the earth and increase upon it" (Genesis 9:6-7, NIV). God set a rainbow in the sky as a sign that the covenant between God and humanity would be fulfilled for future generations: "So God said to Noah, 'This is the sign of the covenant I have established between me and all life on the earth'" (Genesis 9:17, NIV).

II. EXPOSITION AND APPLICATION OF THE SCRIPTURE

A. Obedience Precedes Blessings
(Deuteronomy 6:1-3)

NOW THESE are the commandments, the statutes, and the judgments, which the Lord your God commanded to teach you, that ye might do them in the land whither ye go to possess it: That thou mightest fear the Lord thy God, to keep all his statutes and his commandments, which I command thee, thou, and thy son, and thy son's son, all the days of thy life; and that thy days may be prolonged. Hear therefore, O Israel, and observe to do it; that it may be well with thee, and that ye may increase mightily, as the Lord God of thy fathers hath promised thee, in the land that floweth with milk and honey.

The guidelines given by God for the people of God to obey are designated through a variety of terminology, including "laws," "commands," "decrees," "statutes," and "ordinances." An examination of some of the Hebrew words clarifies some of the differences between them.

The Hebrew word translated "commandments" usually refers to the extensive list of laws given by God in the books credited to Moses. This is also the Hebrew term usually used when God spoke directly in the Old Testament.

The Hebrew word translated "statutes" means "statute, prescription, rule, law, or regulation," and can refer to laws of nature (see Job 28:26; Jeremiah 5:22; 31:35-36). It can also refer to that which is allocated, rationed, or apportioned to someone (see Genesis 47:22; Exodus 29:28).

The Hebrew word translated "rules" refers to a judicial verdict or formal decree. In Mosaic Law, some legal types of rules would fall under this category.

Another Hebrew word translated "statutes/commands" refers to a particular law related to a festival or ritual, such as Passover (see Exodus 12:14), the Days of Unleavened Bread (see Exodus 12:17), or the Feast of Tabernacles (see Leviticus 23:41).

All four of these Hebrew words are used

"throughout the writings of Moses to refer to commands from God to be obeyed by God's people. Distinctions are sometimes made regarding one word from the other, yet the overall principle is one of obedience to all that the Lord commands, whether it's a general command, a prescribed law, a legal verdict, or a religious festival or ritual" (Doug McIntosh, in *Holman Old Testament Commentary on Deuteronomy,* p. 49).

It was critical for the children of Israel to be well steeped in the Law of the Lord prior to entering the Promised Land. The older generation had already departed in death, and this new group would be establishing a fresh precedent upon which successive generations would be able to build. This same important principle of foundation is repeated every time a new family unit is formed.

The phrase related to the fear of the Lord is found in several locations throughout Scripture. It is appropriate to recognize that those who fear the Lord have a continual awareness of Him, a deep reverence for Him, and sincere commitment to obey Him.

The phrase "flowing with milk and honey" is a metaphor describing abundance, goodness, God's blessings, and unlimited provision. Milk is related to nurture, sustenance, and fertility. Honey is related to sweetness and pleasant times. The word translated as "flowing" means "to stream forth or to gush." God's promise of such a land was enough to give the Israelites great hope for a bright future.

B. The Shema
(Deuteronomy 6:4-5)

Hear, O Israel: The Lord our God is one Lord: And thou shalt love the Lord thy God with all thine heart, and with all thy soul, and with all thy might.

This passage in Deuteronomy is the most fundamental Scripture in all of Judaism. It is the first prayer in the Jewish prayer book and the first prayer learned by a Jewish child. The Shema is one of only two prayers that are specifically commanded in the Torah (the other is Birkat Ha-Mazon—grace after meals). It is the oldest fixed daily prayer in Judaism, recited morning and night since ancient times. It consists of three biblical passages, two of which specifically say to speak of these things when you lie down and when you rise up. This commandment is fulfilled by including the Shema in the liturgy for *Ma'ariv* (evening services) and *Shacharit* (morning services). Traditional prayer books also include a Bedtime Shema, a series of passages including the Shema to be read at home before going to bed at night. The first part of the Shema begins with one of the best-known, most fundamental expressions of Jewish belief, and the one from which this prayer gets its name: *Shema Yisra'el* (Hear, Israel).

From a Jewish perspective, it was very important for Jehovah to be known and understood as the one and only true God, because that would provide the necessary distinction from the pagan concept of many false gods. The concept of exclusive worship of God is clearly stated in Exodus 20:3-6.

Throughout the Bible, the engagement of the heart is shown as being indispensable in the process of loving God. A pure heart is necessary for those who authentically worship God (see Psalm 24:4), and only those with pure hearts will eventually see God (see Matthew 5:8). In addition to loving God with our hearts, we are also to love God with our souls, which is the same thing as our spirits. The soul is the seat of our emotions and is capable of expressing both great sorrow and great joy.

The last category of loving God mentioned in the text is loving God with all our strength. "To love the Lord with all our strength means to love him 'exceedingly,' 'richly,' 'lavishly,' with reckless abandon out of simple devotion. In more practical terms, it means we are to love him 100 percent—to go all-out; to give it your best shot; if we fall down, to pick ourselves back up and keep going forward; to love him with all our might. Loving him with all our strength is to love with our resources, our abilities, and our time; to fully love him with what we find our hands to do, our eyes to see, our ears to hear, our feet to go, and our mouths to speak" (Greg Simas, gregsimas.org).

C. Everlasting Commandments (Deuteronomy 6:6-9)

And these words, which I command thee this day, shall be in thine heart: And thou shalt teach them diligently unto thy children, and shalt talk of them when thou sittest in thine house, and when thou walkest by the way, and when thou liest down, and when thou risest up. And thou shalt bind them for a sign upon thine hand, and they shall be as frontlets between thine eyes. And thou shalt write them upon the posts of thy house, and on thy gates.

No matter how important a particular life principle may be, time has a tendency to make us forget. That is why we must be truly intentional in maintaining our focus on life priorities that form the foundation of what ultimately matters in life. The contemporary culture is filled with negative distractions and even positive attractions that may be lawful but not expedient. Both negative and positive stimuli are capable of drawing our attention away from our optimum focus. When left to chance, cul-

ture consumes the best of our intentions, unless we exercise constant character correction and frequent reminders of purpose, direction, and destiny. This is accomplished through practices such as the following: "1) *Meditation*. God's Words must be laid up in our hearts, that our thoughts may be daily employed about them. 2) *The religious education of children*. Often repeat these things to them. Be careful and exact in teaching thy children. Teach these truths to all who are any way under thy care. 3) *Pious discourse*. Thou shalt talk of these things with due reverence and seriousness, for the benefit not only of thy children, but also of thy servants, thy friends, and companions. Take all occasions to discourse with those about thee, not of matters of doubtful disputation, but of the plain truths and laws of God, and the things that belong to our peace. 4) *Frequent reading of the Word*. God appointed them to write sentences of the Law upon their walls, and in scrolls of parchment to be worn about their wrists. This seems to have been binding in the letter of it to the Jews, as it is to us in the intent of it; which is, that we should by all means make the Word of God familiar to us; that we may have it ready to use upon all occasions, to restrain us from sin, and direct us in duty" (*Matthew Henry's Concise Commentary*, http://biblehub.com/commentaries/mhc/deuteronomy/6.htm).

III. CONCLUDING REFLECTION

As believers in God, we are called to demonstrate our love and commitment to God by a continual investment of our hearts, souls, minds, and strength. As parents and teachers, we are called to communicate and replicate our faith in the lives of our children and students through visual, verbal, and valuable investments of time and effort in planting spiritual seeds of truth into impressionable hearts. As children and students, we are called to pay close attention to the lessons taught by our parents and teachers with the realization that education is a lifelong process, and it is a wise thing to learn from those who have the benefit of more experience. There is a direct connection between the place of obedience and the place of blessings. With great wisdom, God has made sure that there are no shortcuts between obedience and blessings.

PRAYER

Hear, O Israel and all nations: The Lord our God, the Lord is one. Help us to love You with all our hearts, all our souls, all our minds, and all our strength. In Jesus' name we pray. Amen.

HOME DAILY BIBLE READINGS
(November 26–December 2, 2018)

Love and Devotion

MONDAY, November 26: "The Most Important Instruction" (Matthew 22:37-40)

TUESDAY, November 27: "Treat Your Neighbors Justly" (Leviticus 19:13-18)

WEDNESDAY, November 28: "Fulfilling the Royal Law" (James 2:8-13)

THURSDAY, November 29: "Don't Forget the Lord" (Deuteronomy 6:10-15)

FRIDAY, November 30: "Do What Is Right and Good" (Deuteronomy 6:16-19)

SATURDAY, December 1: "Fear the Lord and Live Rightly" (Deuteronomy 6:20-25)

SUNDAY, December 2: "The Lord Is God Alone" (Deuteronomy 6:1-9)

December 9, 2018   Lesson 2

CHOOSE TO LOVE AND SERVE GOD

ADULT/YOUTH
ADULT/YOUNG ADULT TOPIC: **Keep Your Promises**
YOUTH TOPIC: **Whom Will You Serve?**

CHILDREN
GENERAL LESSON TITLE: **Choose to Love and Serve God**
CHILDREN'S TOPIC: **Choosing to Love**

DEVOTIONAL READING
Psalm 81

ADULT/YOUTH
BACKGROUND SCRIPTURE: **Exodus 20:1-11; Joshua 24**
PRINT PASSAGE: **Joshua 24:1-3, 13-15, 21-24**
KEY VERSE: **Joshua 24:15**

CHILDREN
BACKGROUND SCRIPTURE: **Exodus 20:1-11; Joshua 24**
PRINT PASSAGE: **Joshua 24:1-3, 13-15, 21-24**
KEY VERSE: **Joshua 24:15b**

Joshua 24:1-3, 13-15, 21-24—KJV

AND JOSHUA gathered all the tribes of Israel to Shechem, and called for the elders of Israel, and for their heads, and for their judges, and for their officers; and they presented themselves before God.

2 And Joshua said unto all the people, Thus saith the LORD God of Israel, Your fathers dwelt on the other side of the flood in old time, even Terah, the father of Abraham, and the father of Nachor: and they served other gods.

3 And I took your father Abraham from the other side of the flood, and led him throughout all the land of Canaan, and multiplied his seed, and gave him Isaac.

.....

13 And I have given you a land for which ye did not labour, and cities which ye built not, and ye dwell in them; of the vineyards and oliveyards which ye planted not do ye eat.

14 Now therefore fear the LORD, and serve him in

Joshua 24:1-3, 13-15, 21-24—NIV

THEN JOSHUA assembled all the tribes of Israel at Shechem. He summoned the elders, leaders, judges and officials of Israel, and they presented themselves before God.

2 Joshua said to all the people, "This is what the LORD, the God of Israel, says: 'Long ago your ancestors, including Terah the father of Abraham and Nahor, lived beyond the Euphrates River and worshiped other gods.

3 '"But I took your father Abraham from the land beyond the Euphrates and led him throughout Canaan and gave him many descendants. I gave him Isaac."'

.....

13 '"So I gave you a land on which you did not toil and cities you did not build; and you live in them and eat from vineyards and olive groves that you did not plant.'

sincerity and in truth: and put away the gods which your fathers served on the other side of the flood, and in Egypt; and serve ye the LORD.

15 And if it seem evil unto you to serve the LORD, choose you this day whom ye will serve; whether the gods which your fathers served that were on the other side of the flood, or the gods of the Amorites, in whose land ye dwell: but as for me and my house, we will serve the LORD.

.....

21 And the people said unto Joshua, Nay; but we will serve the LORD.

22 And Joshua said unto the people, Ye are witnesses against yourselves that ye have chosen you the LORD, to serve him. And they said, We are witnesses.

23 Now therefore put away, said he, the strange gods which are among you, and incline your heart unto the LORD God of Israel.

24 And the people said unto Joshua, The LORD our God will we serve, and his voice will we obey.

14 "Now fear the LORD and serve him with all faithfulness. Throw away the gods your ancestors worshiped beyond the Euphrates River and in Egypt, and serve the LORD.

15 "But if serving the LORD seems undesirable to you, then choose for yourselves this day whom you will serve, whether the gods your ancestors served beyond the Euphrates, or the gods of the Amorites, in whose land you are living. But as for me and my household, we will serve the LORD."

.....

21 But the people said to Joshua, "No! We will serve the LORD."

22 Then Joshua said, "You are witnesses against yourselves that you have chosen to serve the LORD." "Yes, we are witnesses," they replied.

23 "Now then," said Joshua, "throw away the foreign gods that are among you and yield your hearts to the LORD, the God of Israel."

24 And the people said to Joshua, "We will serve the LORD our God and obey him."

UNIFYING LESSON PRINCIPLE: At critical junctures in life, people are forced to make life-changing decisions. How do they decide which path to take? When challenged by Joshua to serve God or other gods, the Israelites definitively chose to love and serve God.

LESSON OBJECTIVES

Upon the completion of this lesson, the students will be able to do the following:

1. Discern the importance of Joshua's challenge to choose whether to serve God or idols.
2. Repent of times we have failed to make God our highest priority.
3. Respond to Joshua's challenge to turn away from idols and serve God wholeheartedly.

AGE-LEVEL POINTS TO BE EMPHASIZED

Teachers of ADULTS and YOUTH

—Many centuries had passed between the call of Abram and the covenant renewal described in today's text.

—Shechem was located in a valley between Mounts Ebal and Gerizim, where the people under Joshua's leadership had previously renewed the covenant (see Joshua 8:30-35) in obedience to a command to do so (see Deuteronomy 11:29-30; 27:11-26).

—The Hebrew name *Joshua* is rendered in Greek as "Iesous," from which we get our English name *Jesus*.

—At the end of their conquest and before they began to live in the new land, Joshua gathered all of Israel at Shechem. Shechem had already played an important role in the history of God's people (see Genesis 12:6; 33:18-19; 35:4; 37:12-14) and would do so again (see Judges 9; 1 Kings 12:1).

—"Thus says the Lord": Joshua's utterance of these words further confirmed his status as the true successor to Moses (see Deuteronomy 34:9).

Teachers of CHILDREN

—Joshua helped the Israelites remember how God had shown them love, especially when they were in Egypt.

—The Israelites had been blessed with victories, land, vineyards, and olive yards for which they had not worked.

—Joshua declared his choice to serve the one true God rather than serve idols.

—Joshua challenged the Israelites to make a choice between worshipping the true God or idols.

—The Israelites made the choice to worship and obey God.

THE CHRONOLOGICAL SETTING OF THE LESSON

The setting for the book of Joshua begins in 1406 BC, when God commissioned Joshua to be the successor to Moses and to lead the children of Israel into the Promised Land. Also in 1406 BC, Rahab welcomed the spies; the Israelites crossed the Jordan; and they conquered Jericho. In 1405 BC, kings fought against Israel as the nation was on its quest to occupy the Promised Land, and the sun stood still. In 1399 BC, land was allotted among the tribes (see Joshua 13–22), and in 1375 BC, Joshua delivered his farewell address (see Joshua 23–24).

THE GEOGRAPHICAL AND CULTURAL SETTING OF THE LESSON

The book of Joshua highlights the possession of the land of Canaan and may be divided into three basic parts: (1) invasion or entrance, (2) conquest, and (3) possession or division of the land. This is the land that God promised to Israel through Abraham, Isaac, and Jacob, and now God was making good on that promise. "Joshua describes the military triumph of God's people through faith and obedience. However, unlike most military histories, in the book of Joshua the focus is on the commander's Commander, the Captain of the Lord's host (5:15). Repeatedly, as Joshua's name illustrates ('Yahweh saves'), the book demonstrates that Israel's victories were due to God's power and intervention" (Bible.org).

PROMINENT CHARACTER(S) IN THE LESSON

Joshua: Not only was Joshua the assistant to Moses, but he was also among the twelve spies who participated in the fact-finding mission into the land of Canaan. Only Joshua and Caleb returned with a faith-filled report that encouraged the people to trust God and possess the land. Joshua was a great warrior for God, and under his leadership the walls of Jericho came tumbling down. Through Joshua's great leadership, the Israelites were able to make it to the Promised Land.

KEY TERMS IN THE LESSON

Choose (verse 15)—Hebrew: *bachar* (baw-khar'): to choose, select.

Father (verse 2)—Hebrew: *ab* (awb): father; ancestor; family.

Gathered (verse 1)—Hebrew: *asaph* (aw-saf'): to gather, remove; "assembled" (NIV).

Land (verse 13)—Hebrew: *erets* (eh'-rets): earth; land.

Serve (verse 14)—Hebrew: *abad* (aw-bad'): to work, serve.

Took (verse 3)—Hebrew: *laqach* (law-kakh'): to take, take in hand.

TOPICAL OUTLINE OF THE LESSON

I. **Introduction**
    A. The Freedom to Choose
    B. Biblical Background

II. **Exposition and Application of the Scripture**
    A. Joshua Gathers the People
        (Joshua 24:1-3)
    B. Choose Ye This Day
        (Joshua 24:13-15)
    C. What Shall I Render?
        (Joshua 24:21-22)
    D. Absolute Obedience
        (Joshua 24:23-24)

III. **Concluding Reflection**

I. INTRODUCTION

A. The Freedom to Choose

Among the things that humanity does not choose to do is to be born. However, it is still the choice of humans to give birth to another—and when the latter is born, that choice is repeated. Since the Creation, God has given laws and ordinances to humanity to observe or to reject. Making the right choice is not always easy, and most significant choices also contain significant consequences.

The background for today's lesson is based on Exodus 20:1-11, and the Printed Text comes out of Joshua 24. These passages show us how some people chose to obey God and others faltered in that choice. Everyone at one time or another in life has had to make a choice between obeying God and obeying one's own selfish motives. This choice will continue to present itself as long as we shall live.

B. Biblical Background

The book of Joshua chronicles the fulfillment of the quest to possess the Promised Land. God's faithfulness is demonstrated, enemies are overcome, and God's miraculous deliverance is experienced. In Exodus 20, God gave the Ten Commandments to Moses on Mount Sinai, where He summoned and communed with Moses for forty days and then commanded Moses to communicate the Law to the whole people. This happened after the release of the children of Israel from Egypt. From verses 1-11, we see the passage addressing the first three commandments relating to the oneness of God, the prohibition of serving other gods, and the observance of the Sabbath day. It can be added that from the Garden of Eden after God created man and woman, He placed them there and gave them the formal restriction of not eating the fruit of the Tree of the Knowledge of Good and Evil (see Genesis 2:16-17). Again, we see a situation featuring choices and consequences.

In his speech, Joshua reminded the people of all the blessings of God from past generations. This was to bring them back to their origin and to refresh their memory about their inheritance. God also addressed their misconduct. The people of Israel publicly chose to serve God, but each had in secret the idols and false gods they worshipped once they were alone (see Joshua 24:14).

It is with a tone of warning and a bit of a threat that Joshua spoke to the people in verse 15 to help them to decide once and for all whom they wanted to serve. He even went further by distancing himself from disobedience when he declared, "As for me and my house, we will serve the LORD." He was exasperated and tired of the people who made choices, compromised them, regretted their bad choices, repented, were restored, and compromised them again. This same pattern of poor choices is repeated in marriages and relationships today. How many people in our society today forsake God and make poor choices which they later regret? The sure cure for the sickness of poor decision making is found in an obedient relationship with our Lord and Savior, Christ Jesus.

II. EXPOSITION AND APPLICATION OF THE SCRIPTURE

A. Joshua Gathers the People
(Joshua 24:1-3)

AND JOSHUA gathered all the tribes of Israel to Shechem, and called for the elders of Israel, and for their heads, and for their judges, and for their officers; and they presented themselves before God. And Joshua said unto all the people, Thus saith the LORD God of Israel, Your fathers dwelt on the other side of the flood in old time, even Terah, the father of Abraham, and the father of Nachor: and they served other gods. And I took your father Abraham from the other side of the flood, and led him throughout all the land of Canaan, and multiplied his seed, and gave him Isaac.

Joshua had a big task ahead of him in successfully filling the leadership shoes of his mentor, Moses. This example of an Old Testament leadership transfer helps us to understand the immense importance of grooming successors for pivotal roles. The great Myles Munroe insightfully deposited this gem of wisdom regarding leadership transfer: "True leaders don't invest in buildings. Jesus never built a building. They invest in people. Why? Because success without a successor is failure. So your legacy should not be in buildings, programs, or projects; your legacy must be in people." Every leader in the life of a church—from the pastor to the Sunday school teachers—should have an active plan for grooming someone else to occupy their role. This process is nothing more than discipleship in action, and it makes for a smart and spiritually strong ministry.

Joshua served as a mouthpiece for the voice of God and reminded the Israelites of the importance of worshipping only one God. Undoubtedly, the biggest threat to the strength and success of the children of Israel was the problem of idols and multiple gods. Historically, the God of the Israelites reserved some of His harshest criticism and chastisement for supposedly holy people who worshipped false gods and multiple gods. Consequently, the perpetual reminder for Israelites of the Old Testament as well as for the Jewish worshippers of today is the Shema: "Hear O Israel, the LORD your God, the LORD is One."

Polytheism is the belief in many gods. *Monotheism* is the belief in one God. The wording of the previous verse suggests that the father of Abraham was polytheistic. But Abraham is remembered in the Bible as the father of faith and the ancestor of the Israelites (see Genesis 12–24; Romans 4:1-12). According to Genesis,

> "God called him from his home in Mesopotamia to journey to the Promised Land, where God promised to multiply Abraham's offspring and make them into a great people and a blessing to the nations. The three major monotheistic religions—Judaism, Christianity, and Islam—call Abraham their father. The importance of Abraham to these religions raises many questions, both theological and historical. Was Abraham the first monotheist? The book of Joshua says that when God called Abraham from Mesopotamia, Abraham's family was polytheistic: they "served other gods" (Josh 24:2). But this topic does not come up in the stories about Abraham in Genesis. God calls Abraham and enters into a covenant with him and his family (Gen 12, Gen 15, Gen 17). This is an exclusive relationship between one god and a particular family. In the ancient world, these features belong to the category of family religion, in which the family god is often called

"the god of the father." In addition to the customs of family religion, ancient people also worshiped the gods of tribe, city, or state. In the stories of Abraham, however, the god of the father is also "God Most High, maker of heaven and earth" (Gen 14:19). In other words, the Abraham story shows the merger of family and state religion, yielding the worship of a single God. From the biblical perspective, Abraham was the first monotheist."[1]

B. Choose Ye This Day (Joshua 24:13-15)

And I have given you a land for which ye did not labour, and cities which ye built not, and ye dwell in them; of the vineyards and oliveyards which ye planted not do ye eat. Now therefore fear the LORD, and serve him in sincerity and in truth: and put away the gods which your fathers served on the other side of the flood, and in Egypt; and serve ye the LORD. And if it seem evil unto you to serve the LORD, choose you this day whom ye will serve; whether the gods which your fathers served that were on the other side of the flood, or the gods of the Amorites, in whose land ye dwell: but as for me and my house, we will serve the LORD.

Verse 13 accentuates the grace of God from an Old Testament perspective. It is easy to forget God's benefits to us, and we can easily take for granted the many rich gifts, privileges, and benefits that we enjoy through no merit of our own. That is why it is so important to "give thanks to the LORD, for He is good! For His mercy endures forever" (Psalm 107:1, NKJV). Sometimes, we have difficulty distinguishing between our needs and our greeds. Elizabeth Elliot helped to clarify this when she said, "God has promised to supply all our needs. What we don't have now, we don't need now." A heart of thanksgiving paves the way for receiving greater benefits in the future.

One of the ways to tell whether we have indeed made the choice to follow and obey the true and living God is whether we are willing to unreservedly relinquish any and every false god. There is no room, space, or place for holding on to mini-gods while also claiming the living God. Our devotion and dedication to God should be accompanied by great awe and respect, dedicated service, and faithful consistency. So-called dedication that is on again, off again is unacceptable in God's sight.

The Bible has much to say about choice. God could have created humanity pre-programmed to obey His will. The reason why that would not work is because it would not provide the opportunity to love God without being coerced to do so. Love and force do not coincide. Concerning choice, Deuteronomy 30:15-19 (ESV) records this:

> "See, I have set before you today life and good, death and evil. If you obey the commandments of the LORD your God that I command you today, by loving the LORD your God, by walking in his ways, and by keeping his commandments and his statutes and his rules, then you shall live and multiply, and the LORD your God will bless you in the land that you are entering to take possession of it. But if your heart turns away, and you will not hear, but are drawn away to worship other gods and serve them, I declare to you today, that you shall surely perish. You shall not live long in the land that you are going over the Jordan to enter and possess. I call heaven and earth to witness against you today, that I have set before you life and death, blessing and curse. Therefore, choose life, that you and your offspring may live."

C. What Shall I Render?
(Joshua 24:21-22)

And the people said unto Joshua, Nay; but we will serve the LORD. And Joshua said unto the people, Ye are witnesses against yourselves that ye have chosen you the LORD, to serve him. And they said, We are witnesses.

Sometimes, the quickest route to divine deliverance comes in the form of two little letters: *n-o*. How fortunate that the word *no* is not a complicated, multisyllable term that is difficult to pronounce. Even though this word is simple and uncomplicated, those who do not want to hear it often try to stretch it into meaning something else. But one's "no" should mean "no," and one's "yes" should mean "yes." Matthew 5:37 (NKJV) states, "But let your 'Yes' be 'Yes,' and your 'No,' 'No.' For whatever is more than these is from the evil one." First Kings 18:21 (NIV) records the occasion when Elijah went before the people and said, "How long will you waver between two opinions? If the LORD is God, follow him; but if Baal is God, follow him." Revelation 3:15-16 (NIV) asserts, "I know your deeds, that you are neither cold nor hot. I wish you were either one or the other! So, because you are lukewarm—neither hot nor cold—I am about to spit you out of my mouth."

Although the word *no* can be a very powerful word, this word alone is inadequate and must be paired with something powerful to replace whatever is being rejected. It may be great to "Just say no," but we need something stronger to which we choose to say "yes." We can say "yes" to God's best. We can say "yes" to sacrificially choosing God's way over any other way.

Every choice and every decision in life, whether positive or negative, comes with consequences and responsibilities.

When the people chose to serve the Lord, they also chose to accept any responsibility that might come with that choice, or the consequences of failing to serve Him.

D. Absolute Obedience
(Joshua 24:23-24)

Now therefore put away, said he, the strange gods which are among you, and incline your heart unto the LORD God of Israel. And the people said unto Joshua, The LORD our God will we serve, and his voice will we obey.

The assignment that Joshua had for the children of Israel after they chose to follow God was given in two simple parts: (1) obey the true God, and (2) throw away the false gods. The only way for the plan to work was for both parts of the plan to be activated. Contemporary culture places a high value on the concept of tolerance. But there is not a hint of tolerance from God's perspective when it comes to other gods. Similarly, there should be zero tolerance by a husband or wife when it comes to another man or woman receiving the same priority, attention, or privileges that are due one's spouse.

No specific instructions were given by Joshua as to how the foreign gods were to be discarded, but since many of the idols were physical and material in nature, they were likely treated like trash and refuse. Perhaps they were relegated to the dung heap, which would be roughly equivalent to our modern-day dump. In Deuteronomy 23:12-14 (NASB), we find this place described: "You shall also have a place outside the camp and go out there, and you shall have a spade among your tools, and it shall be when you sit down outside, you shall dig with it and shall turn to cover up your excrement. Since the LORD your God walks in the midst of your camp to deliver you and to defeat your enemies before you, therefore your camp must be holy; and He must not see anything indecent among you or He will turn away from you."

When it comes to worshipping other gods today, those gods may not come in the form of the idols of the Old Testament, but the same principle still applies: God desires for us to radically part ways with anything and anyone that distracts from absolute commitment and obedience to Him.

German theologian Dietrich Bonhoeffer spent two years in a Nazi concentration camp, but while there, he wrote extensively about his own faith and provided a powerful perspective for people around the world about the high cost of true discipleship. In his book *The Cost of Discipleship*, Dietrich Bonhoeffer posits that although salvation is free, discipleship is not cheap. "Cheap grace is the preaching of forgiveness without requiring repentance, baptism without church discipline, Communion without confession, absolution without personal confession. Cheap grace is grace without discipleship, grace without the cross, grace without Jesus Christ, living and incarnate" (Bonhoeffer, *The Cost of Discipleship*). In other words, no cross, no crown. Serving God would be easy if it were left up to our own fleshly parameters. But we cannot truly serve God on our own terms. Genuine spiritual service to God must be in line with divine obedience to God.

The word *covenant* comes from the Latin origin *con venire*, meaning "a coming together." It represents "two or more parties who come together to make a contract, agreeing on promises, stipulations, privileges, and responsibilities" (Biblestudytools.com). Obviously, any covenant is designed to be taken seriously and is more important than a contract. A covenant relationship is one in which certain terms are set, but each party looks out for each other.

III. CONCLUDING REFLECTION

Life is full of challenges and choices. Some of our choices are private, and other choices are made, seen, and known publicly. When we as believers publicly declare our commitment to serving God, we strengthen our resolve, and we also may inspire or encourage someone else. Every choice in life is impacted by the decision to serve God and God alone. As we practice discernment and eliminate things that may distract from our spiritual commitments, our determination to serve God will grow stronger.

PRAYER

Lord, grant us the strength to daily practice "putting away" false gods. Help us to replace that false god vacuum with an even stronger determination to serve only You, the true and living God. In Jesus' name we pray. Amen.

HOME DAILY BIBLE READINGS
(December 3-9, 2018)

Choose to Love and Serve God

MONDAY, December 3: "Rules on People Relating to God" (Exodus 20:1-11)
TUESDAY, December 4: "Rules on People Relating to People" (Exodus 20:12-17)
WEDNESDAY, December 5: "Keep the Faith and Live" (Joshua 23:2-6, 14-16)
THURSDAY, December 6: "Rescued from Egypt, Settled in Canaan" (Joshua 24:4-12)
FRIDAY, December 7: "We Promise to Serve God" (Joshua 24:16-21)
SATURDAY, December 8: "Covenant with God Confirmed" (Joshua 24:25-28)
SUNDAY, December 9: "Choose to Love and Serve God" (Joshua 24:1-3, 13-15, 21-24)

---

1. Ronald Hendel, "Abraham," Bibleodyssey.org.

December 16, 2018 — Lesson 3

LOVE AND WORSHIP GOD

ADULT/YOUTH	CHILDREN
ADULT/YOUNG ADULT TOPIC: Credit Where Credit Is Due	**GENERAL LESSON TITLE: Love and Worship God**
YOUTH TOPIC: Love Inspires Gratitude	**CHILDREN'S TOPIC: Worshipping with Thanks**

DEVOTIONAL READING
Psalm 86:1-7

ADULT/YOUTH	CHILDREN
BACKGROUND SCRIPTURE: Psalm 103:1-17, 21-22	**BACKGROUND SCRIPTURE: Psalm 103:1-17, 21-22**
PRINT PASSAGE: Psalm 103:1-17, 21-22	**PRINT PASSAGE: Psalm 103:1-17, 21-22**
KEY VERSE: Psalm 103:12	**KEY VERSE: Psalm 103:1**

Psalm 103:1-17, 21-22—KJV

BLESS THE LORD, O my soul: and all that is within me, bless his holy name.

2 Bless the LORD, O my soul, and forget not all his benefits:

3 Who forgiveth all thine iniquities; who healeth all thy diseases;

4 Who redeemeth thy life from destruction; who crowneth thee with lovingkindness and tender mercies;

5 Who satisfieth thy mouth with good things; so that thy youth is renewed like the eagle's.

6 The LORD executeth righteousness and judgment for all that are oppressed.

7 He made known his ways unto Moses, his acts unto the children of Israel.

8 The LORD is merciful and gracious, slow to anger, and plenteous in mercy.

9 He will not always chide: neither will he keep his anger for ever.

Psalm 103:1-17, 21-22—NIV

PRAISE THE LORD, my soul; all my inmost being, praise his holy name.

2 Praise the LORD, my soul, and forget not all his benefits.

3 who forgives all your sins and heals all your diseases,

4 who redeems your life from the pit and crowns you with love and compassion,

5 who satisfies your desires with good things so that your youth is renewed like the eagle's.

6 The LORD works righteousness and justice for all the oppressed.

7 He made known his ways to Moses, his deeds to the people of Israel:

8 The LORD is compassionate and gracious, slow to anger, abounding in love.

9 He will not always accuse, nor will he harbor his anger forever;

10 he does not treat us as our sins deserve or repay us according to our iniquities.

10 He hath not dealt with us after our sins; nor rewarded us according to our iniquities.

11 For as the heaven is high above the earth, so great is his mercy toward them that fear him.

12 As far as the east is from the west, so far hath he removed our transgressions from us.

13 Like as a father pitieth his children, so the LORD pitieth them that fear him.

14 For he knoweth our frame; he remembereth that we are dust.

15 As for man, his days are as grass: as a flower of the field, so he flourisheth.

16 For the wind passeth over it, and it is gone; and the place thereof shall know it no more.

17 But the mercy of the LORD is from everlasting to everlasting upon them that fear him, and his righteousness unto children's children.

.....

21 Bless ye the LORD, all ye his hosts; ye ministers of his, that do his pleasure.

22 Bless the LORD, all his works in all places of his dominion: bless the LORD, O my soul.

11 For as high as the heavens are above the earth, so great is his love for those who fear him;

12 as far as the east is from the west, so far has he removed our transgressions from us.

13 As a father has compassion on his children, so the LORD has compassion on those who fear him;

14 for he knows how we are formed, he remembers that we are dust.

15 The life of mortals is like grass, they flourish like a flower of the field;

16 the wind blows over it and it is gone, and its place remembers it no more.

17 But from everlasting to everlasting the LORD's love is with those who fear him, and his righteousness with their children's children.

.....

21 Praise the LORD, all his heavenly hosts, you his servants who do his will.

22 Praise the LORD, all his works everywhere in his dominion. Praise the Lord, my soul.

UNIFYING LESSON PRINCIPLE: People feel anxiety and confusion when they remember their personal failures and as they continually face life's trials. What consolation is there? The psalmist lists the many reasons why God's steadfast love inspires enthusiastic thanksgiving rather than dismay.

LESSON OBJECTIVES

Upon the completion of this lesson, the students will be able to do the following:
1. Consider the breadth and depth of God's care for us as expressed in Psalm 103.
2. Appreciate how God has provided comfort in past times of trouble.
3. Respond to God's consolation with worship and devotion.

AGE-LEVEL POINTS TO BE EMPHASIZED
Teachers of ADULTS and YOUTH
—This is a psalm of individual thanksgiving, occurring in Book IV of the five-book psalter. "Thanksgiving" differs from "praise" in that, while praise is offered to God simply because of who God is, thanksgiving is offered in response to specific things that God has done.

—This is one of seventy-three psalms that the psalter associates with David.

—Verses 1-5 indicate a soliloquy on God's goodness and mercy (*NRSV Study Bible*).

—This is a hymn of praise, celebrating the

abundant goodness and love of the Lord for His people. It is the first of four psalms reflecting on God's dealings with His people from Creation to Exile.

—*Pit* is another word for the "underworld" (*NRSV Study Bible*).

—Verses 6-14 indicate a recital of God's demonstrated love, protection, and forgiveness (*NRSV Study Bible*).

—Verses 15-18 indicate meditations contrasting human frailty and instability with God's steadfastness of purpose and eternality (*NRSV Study Bible*).

—Verses 19-22 indicate summons to the entire universe to join in praise of God (*NRSV Study Bible*).

Teachers of CHILDREN

—Psalm 103 is a psalm/song of praise and gratitude to God for God's favor.

—The psalmist expressed thanks for forgiveness, healing, redemption, God's love, justice, grace, and patience.

—If times are difficult, one can still identify blessings from God.

—Looking back at one's heritage can help reveal how God interacts with humans.

—The characteristics of God can be seen in the actions of God.

—God's love is everlasting.

THE CHRONOLOGICAL SETTING OF THE LESSON

The estimated date of writing for Psalm 103 is 1034 BC (according to blueletterbible.org) and is attributed to King David. He expressed awe, reverence, gratitude, and love for God in many psalms. Psalm 103 is a psalm of pure worship. Unlike most of David's psalms, this psalm contains no petitions for help or cries for deliverance. David focused on the Lord and His great blessings and overflows in worship. God's great goodness and our great need produce a response of heartfelt worship. The chronological setting for Psalm 103 is after 2 Samuel 12:15, when David had asked forgiveness for his sin of adultery with Bathsheba.

THE GEOGRAPHICAL AND CULTURAL SETTING OF THE LESSON

This psalm of David is attributed to his later years when he had a keener sense of sin and the importance of forgiveness. This psalm reflects exaltation of God written as a song on the Mount answering to his Redeemer's (Jesus Christ's) later Sermon on the Mount. The greatness and wonder of God is heralded to a new level in Psalm 103. Undoubtedly, David was familiar with accompaniment instruments such as the flute, harp, sacbut (sackbut), psaltery, dulcimer, and others. But David awakened all the melodies of heaven and earth in order to give honor and praise to the only true and living God.

Half-hearted, ill-conceived, unintelligent praises are not such as we should render to our loving Lord. If the law of justice demanded all our heart and soul and mind for the Creator, much more may the law of gratitude put in a comprehensive claim for the homage of our whole being to the God of grace" (*Psalms, Volume* 2, Charles Spurgeon). . . . It is instructive to note how the Psalmist dwells upon the holy name of God, as if His holiness were dearest to him, or, perhaps because the holiness or wholeness of God was to his mind the grandest motive for rendering to Him the homage of his nature in its wholeness. Babes may praise the divine goodness, but fathers in grace magnify His holiness (Charles Spurgeon).

PROMINENT CHARACTER(S) IN THE LESSON

The only characters in the text are David, the writer of this psalm, and the almighty God of David, who is the object of the psalm.
David: the youngest son of Jesse; chosen by God to succeed Saul as king over Israel and Judea. He was the author of numerous psalms of praise, penitence, etc., to God.

KEY TERMS IN THE LESSON

Benefits (verse 2)—Hebrew: *tagmul* (tag-mool'): benefits; bestowments.
Bless (verse 1)—Hebrew: *barak* (baw-rak'): to kneel, bless; "praise" (NIV).
Forgives (verse 3)—Hebrew: *salach* (saw-lakh'): to forgive, pardon; "forgiveth" (KJV).
Name (verse 1)—Hebrew: *shem* (shame): a name.

Redeems (verse 4)—Hebrew: *gaal* (gaw-al'): to redeem; acts as kinsman.
Righteousness (verse 6)—Hebrew: *tsedaqah* (tsed-aw-kaw'): honesty; righteousness; justice.

TOPICAL OUTLINE OF THE LESSON

I. Introduction
   A. Praising God in Difficult Times
   B. Biblical Background

II. Exposition and Application of the Scripture
   A. Praise the Lord, My Soul (Psalm 103:1-5)
   B. God's Character Traits (Psalm 103:6-10)
   C. Spiritual Similes (Psalm 103:11-14)
   D. Temporary versus Permanent (Psalm 103:15-17, 21-22)

III. Concluding Reflection

I. INTRODUCTION
A. Praising God in Difficult Times

We live in a time when a lot of persons seem to have lost their personality, purpose, and faith—a time when people seem to practice religion yet do not know entirely the one whom they worship. With men and women behaving as such, there seems to be a void that needs to be filled.

In this lesson that we will study, the psalmist stirred up himself and his own soul to praise and bless God (verses 1-2), not minding his present condition or predicament. This is a typical scenario of most people today, but unlike the psalmist, we tend to allow our predicament to get a better part of us. As we shall see in this study, it pays to praise despite our conditions, for in praise we find strength and purpose. We see the psalmist call for more devotion through praise. He begins to acknowledge God's favor to him, to believers in general, and to all good people to whom He is and will be just and kind and constant, and for His government of the world (verses 8-14). In praise, our faith is renewed, and we can extend to people around us the experience of forgiveness and compassion that we have received from God. In singing this psalm (that is, singing praises), as we shall further discover, we will learn that our hearts will be affected by the goodness of God and enlarged in love and thankfulness.

B. Biblical Background

The book of Psalms is one of the truly majestic and most exalting pieces of biblical literature. It is a collection of a total of 150 songs which are inspired by the Spirit of God, as is the rest of the Scriptures. While some of these passages celebrate the history of the nation of Israel, others tend to pronounce severe judgments upon those who set themselves as enemies of the Most High God. There are psalms which are also messianic in thrust; they point to the coming Messiah. Some psalms, though, simply lift a chorus of praise to the Creator. Psalm 103 may be the "Mount Everest" of praise psalms. It exalts the soul to breathtaking heights. According to the superscription—which is not a part of the inspired text, but is nonetheless very ancient—it is a psalm of David's. There is no reason to question David's authorship of this composition. We will examine this passage to understand the importance of praise even when the conditions and circumstances do not seem right or favorable.

The psalmist in this passage began with an exclamation of praise that he issued from the depths of his devout soul. "Bless Jehovah, O my soul; and all that is within me, bless his holy name" (verse 1, ASV). A newer version renders this as, "My soul, praise the Lord, and everything in me, praise His holy name" (Beck). This utterance reflects a burst of enthusiastic devotion in honor of the Lord (Yahweh)—the self-existent Being who has entered a covenant relationship with Israel. To bless the "holy name" of God is to praise the Lord for His intrinsic holiness (see Isaiah 6:3; Revelation 4:8). He is an utterly pure being in whom resides no sin (see Habakkuk 1:13; James 1:13).

The writer strains his entire being—everything "that is within" him—to express his feelings. He loves the Creator (God) intellectually, emotionally, and practically. There is some parallel in sentiment with the admonition to love God with the totality of one's being—heart, soul, mind, and strength (see Deuteronomy 6:5; Matthew 22:37; Mark 12:29-30).

Life presents all of us with dark periods in our lives—a period when we experience so much pain and agony that we feel as if we cannot go any further in life. Then, at some point during that dark period, we see "light at the end of the tunnel." We then find ourselves filled with thanksgiving and joy unspeakable and we burst forth in praise to our heavenly Father. This is that kind of experience in which the writer (David) finds himself.

Human beings are very forgetful creatures and the Bible is replete with admonitions to "remember," or, in the reverse format, "forget not." Some things are worthy of forgetting, especially when these things do not hold any positive value (see Philippians 3:13); one should ever hold mentally fresh, however, the fact of God's kindness. And so, David cautions that we should "forget not all his benefits" (verse 2). When the storms of life blow hardest, and it seems that all hope is lost, at that moment, we can witness true victory, strength, and courage when we recount the benefits of our

God. Elsewhere an inspired writer will ponder, "What shall I render unto the Lord for all his benefits toward me?" (Psalm 116:12).

In today's world, many are keenly conscious of those "benefits" associated with their employment. What sort of insurance do I have? What is my retirement package? How frequently do we contemplate, though, the "benefits" of our loving Father? In Psalm 103:3-5, five marvelous benefits are listed. How invigorating it is to reflect upon those blessings. They are expressed with the following verbs: forgives, heals, redeems, crowns, and satisfies.

The entire passage is full of God's amazing deeds. As a result, the psalmist extols God's righteousness, mercies, and love. Despite our iniquities, God always remains merciful and forgiving, a virtue that we must truly exhibit as God's dear children who walk in the light of His Word (verses 6-10; see Mark 11:25; Ephesians 4:32).

In conclusion of this passage (verses 21-22; see also Ephesians 5:17; Matthew 6:10), the psalmist admonishes all to bless God. He particularly referred to "all who do his will." It is very important to ensure that we understand and follow the will of the Creator. In and out of life's troubles, in time of plenty, in seasons of joy and sorrow, the will of the Lord should be sought and followed (see Luke 22:42). Finally, we are always to remember that we are the works of God's hands and are to be a praise to Him.

II. EXPOSITION AND APPLICATION OF THE SCRIPTURE

A. Praise the Lord, My Soul
(Psalm 103:1-5)

BLESS THE Lord, O my soul: and all that is within me, bless his holy name. Bless the Lord, O my soul, and forget not all his benefits: Who forgiveth all thine iniquities; who healeth all thy diseases; Who redeemeth thy life from destruction; who crowneth thee with lovingkindness and tender mercies; Who satisfieth thy mouth with good things; so that thy youth is renewed like the eagle's.

Psalm 103 is more suited for personal meditation than for scholarly investigation. David reaches into the recesses of his soul in order to obtain an opportunity for concentrated personal praise for the multiplicity of God's spiritual benefits toward him. Praise starts from the inmost heart and then progresses into the surrounding atmosphere. Praise that is not personal is either imitated or manufactured. The authenticity of public praise is then verified through the reality of private praise and worship. Performance without personal piety is lacking in substance.

Praise and worship that emanate from the soul is all-encompassing and includes every part of one's life and existence. The "soul" is not a separate entity within human beings; it is another way of saying a "living person." Man became a living soul when God combined the physical body with the breath of life. You do not have a soul; you are soul. The Hebrew word so rendered is *nepes*. It appears 755 times in the Old Testament. The King James Version uses 42 different English terms to translate it. The two most common renderings are "soul" (428 times) and "life" (117 times).

The psalmist describes as benefits the blessings that come along with having a personal relationship with God. A *benefit* is something that is good, positive, and advantageous. Benefits are desirable subsidiary services or perks that come with the primary asset as a package deal. Benefits can be easily overlooked when we do not spend enough time examining the fine print and nuances of a thing. The classic story is told about a low-income woman who always wanted to go on a cruise. Over time, she saved her nickels and dimes and whatever she could scrape together until finally she had enough to book the trip. At the welcome reception, she was greeted by the ship captain, who remarked to the woman that she reminded him of his own mother. Seven days passed, and the captain did not see the woman at breakfast, lunch, or dinner. As the passengers were headed off the ship at the end of the cruise, the captain saw the woman and remarked that he had not seen her at any of the meal times. The woman sheepishly explained to him that she knew she could not afford to eat in any of the fancy restaurants that she had seen in the brochure pictures, so she had brought cheese and crackers to eat in her room whenever the meal times arrived. Upon hearing that, the captain embraced the dear woman and with tears in his eyes, he explained to her that when she paid for the cruise, all the meals were a part of the benefits. Many people shortchange themselves in the process of being a disciple of Christ because they are not aware of their practical and spiritual benefits. Forgetting one's benefits can be a costly error.

Some of the benefits of a relationship with God are reflected in Galatians 5:22-23 (NIV): "But the fruit of the Spirit is love, joy, peace, forbearance, kindness, goodness, faithfulness, gentleness and self-control. Against such things there is no law." A way to be sure to remember the many benefits of God is to practice being thankful for everything in life. Since all good things come from God, there is a good chance that whatever we may be thankful for came from God.

One of the most underutilized benefits of a relationship with God is the gracious gift of forgiveness.

God's physical healing touch is another benefit of having a relationship with God. The Old Testament passage of Isaiah 53:4-5 (NIV) states, "Surely he took up our pain and bore our suffering, yet we considered him punished by God, stricken by him, and afflicted. But he was pierced for our transgressions, he was crushed for our iniquities; the punishment that brought us peace was on him, and by his wounds we are healed."

Wholehearted praise to God stems from God's holy history, God's trustworthy track record, and God's infinite faithfulness. God has a history of redemption, positional elevation, compassion, satisfaction, and renewal. To *redeem* is to make up for, to buy back, or to win back. To redeem means to make good or to fulfill. God elevates through opening the door for opportunities to excel in various areas of life. The compassion of God is endless, and His steadfast love never ceases. The reason why God's mercies never end is because they are new every morning. God is able to satisfy completely because our storage is attached to His rich and inexhaustible supply of resources.

Verse 5 highlights the fact that God satisfies our desires with good things. This is the opposite of the natural notion of one's satisfying his or her desires with bad things. When God satisfies our desires with good things, we prosper and live life on a higher level of divine wisdom. When we satisfy our own desires with bad things, we either die a little at a time or we may even die completely at one time. Many of our desires and needs are not inherently wrong in and of themselves; what makes a desire toxic is when it is fulfilled in an illegitimate manner. The graphic imagery of an eagle in flight was the one that the psalmist selected to illustrate the buoyant and life-giving effect of a God-filled desire. When we desire the things of God and we pursue the things of God, God then responds to our efforts by activating Matthew 5:6 (NIV): "Blessed are those who hunger and thirst for righteousness, for they will be filled."

B. God's Character Traits
(Psalm 103:6-10)

The LORD executeth righteousness and judgment for all that are oppressed. He made known his ways unto Moses, his acts unto the children of Israel. The LORD is merciful and gracious, slow to anger, and plenteous in mercy. He will not always chide: neither will he keep his anger for ever. He hath not dealt with us after our sins; nor rewarded us according to our iniquities.

Many people are familiar with the love of God, the mercy of God, and the blessings of God. But fewer people truly understand the righteousness of God and the justice of God for the oppressed. God has a very tender disposition toward those who are poor, hurting, marginalized, or deserted. This perspective is described in Psalm 146:7-9 (NIV): "He upholds the cause of the oppressed and gives food to the hungry. The LORD sets prisoners free, the LORD gives sight to the blind, the LORD lifts up those who are bowed down, the LORD loves the righteous. The LORD watches over the foreigner and sustains the fatherless and the widow, but he frustrates the ways of the wicked." God

always represents, assists, fights for, and helps those who cannot help themselves.

The psalmist had a personal relationship with God, and it showed in his thoughts, words, and deeds. David was not just acquainted with the historical acts or deeds of God; he was well-aware of the personal, intimate ways of God as well. The children of Israel witnessed many of the acts of God, but Moses knew God's ways. In order to have intimate knowledge of a person's ways, there must be time spent around and observation of the other person, and the observed person must be transparent—being his or her real self in real situations.

Armed with his intimate knowledge of God, the psalmist continued to expose several of God's traits in succession. Through reading this description, one is able to receive important, accurate insight regarding the character of God. The first traits listed in verse 8 are God's compassion and graciousness.

C. Spiritual Similes
(Psalm 103:11-14)

For as the heaven is high above the earth, so great is his mercy toward them that fear him. As far as the east is from the west, so far hath he removed our transgressions from us. Like as a father pitieth his children, so the LORD pitieth them that fear him. For he knoweth our frame; he remembereth that we are dust.

The emotional essence of this Scripture oozes from the verse like a melting vanilla ice cream cone on a hot summer day. The psalmist compares God's love for those who are obedient to the great distance between the heavens and the earth. This is pure poetry. Here, the medium of graphic description is used to convey the tremendous power and capacity of

God's love for the faithful. It is clear to see how these poetic words could be easily transposed into a musical message through song.

Transgressions are acts that go against a law, rule, or code of conduct. When we transgress God's law, we offend God and displease God through various acts of disobedience. But when we confess our sins and sincerely repent of our sins, God is faithful to forgive our sins and to cleanse us from all unrighteousness (see 1 John 1:9).

Human parents typically have a kind of love for their children like no other person can have. Parental love is instinctive love that cannot be extinguished, no matter what events or circumstances may occur in life. If human parents know how to give good gifts to their children, how much more does our heavenly father know how to give good gifts to His children (see Luke 11:13)? The wonder of God's love lies in the fact that God's love is not cancelled, weakened, or otherwise affected by our bad behavior. Our sins present opportunities for God's grace to be activated. God's grace is not based on our righteousness, but on God's love, mercy, and sacrificial forgiveness.

D. Temporary versus Permanent (Psalm 103:15-17, 21-22)

As for man, his days are as grass: as a flower of the field, so he flourisheth. For the wind passeth over it, and it is gone; and the place thereof shall know it no more. But the mercy of the LORD is from everlasting to everlasting upon them that fear him, and his righteousness unto children's children.... Bless ye the LORD, all ye his hosts; ye ministers of his, that do his pleasure. Bless the LORD, all his works in all places of his dominion: bless the LORD, O my soul.

In verse 15, the psalmist made a significant alteration in his perception and description of humanity. This time, instead of expressing an elevated depiction of humankind, he portrayed mere mortals as mere grass or wild flowers that are extremely temporary when seen in the grand scheme of life. These verses are quite reminiscent of the book of Proverbs, with a tendency toward sarcasm, aloofness, and dismissiveness. As in the book of Proverbs, verse 15 uses extreme imagery and metaphors for effect. In addition to the temporary nature of grass and wildflowers, another short-lived entity that people are compared to in this passage is the wind. Not much can be more transient than the wind, which is here one moment and gone the next. The wind blows away the grass or flowers; this phenomenon highlights the temporary nature of humanity, which is so fleeting. The temporary nature of life is a good reason not to waste time and to make sure that each day of our lives is utilized to the best of our ability.

Even though human life is short-lasting, the love of God is just the opposite: everlasting. This study in contrasts reveals the importance of capitalizing on a real relationship with the God who is everlasting. One of the great advantages of this is that our having a godly perspective on our temporary life helps us to stop wasting time. When we really get to know God, we begin to realize that every moment counts. This perspective also helps us to reject selfishness and to embrace kingdom-minded selflessness. When we live for kingdom causes, we understand that every day is another opportunity to be something, say something, do something, and build something that will last beyond our current culture and our lifetimes.

Psalm 103 ends in a flurry of praise-laden exultations. The scene summoned by the psalmist reflects one massive praise party with participation by the angels ("heavenly hosts") along with all God's servants. There is a powerful sense of corporation, depth, and nexus that develops when God's people unite in sincerely expressing praise and adoration to God. Praise is not just proper within the confines of a sacred sanctuary. It is God's desire for praise to be both private and public, because God's power can be seen anywhere and everywhere all around the world.

III. CONCLUDING REFLECTION

God's amazing and unconditional love for us serves as a template for how we are called to love others. Part of God's love for us includes the extending of care and comfort to us in times of trouble. There is no emotional pit that is so deep that God cannot reach it. Such extreme love deserves a response from the recipients through unceasing praise and faithful devotion. As we serve God with all our hearts, souls, minds, and strength, we should praise God with all our being.

PRAYER

Lord God of heaven and earth, thank You for Your great mercy toward us. We praise You for Your limitless grace. Help us to honor You with lives that sacrifice for the good of others. In Jesus' name we pray. Amen.

HOME DAILY BIBLE READINGS
(December 10-16, 2018)
Love and Worship God

MONDAY, December 10: "Nothing Separates us from God's Love" (Romans 8:31-39)

TUESDAY, December 11: "An Answer in a Time of Trouble" (Psalm 86:1-7)

WEDNESDAY, December 12: "Let Me Walk in Your Truth" (Psalm 86:8-13)

THURSDAY, December 13: "Acts of God's Steadfast Love" (Nehemiah 9:16-21)

FRIDAY, December 14: "God Abounds in Steadfast Love" (Exodus 34:1-7)

SATURDAY, December 15: "God Forgives and Loves People" (Numbers 14:13-20)

SUNDAY, December 16: "The People Bless the Lord" (Psalm 103:1-17, 21-22)

December 23, 2018   Lesson 4

JESUS: GOD'S LOVING PROMISE

ADULT/YOUTH

ADULT/YOUNG ADULT TOPIC: **Waiting Is Rewarded**

YOUTH TOPIC: **Keeping a Promise**

CHILDREN

GENERAL LESSON TITLE: **Jesus: God's Loving Promise**

CHILDREN'S TOPIC: **A Promise Fulfilled**

DEVOTIONAL READING
Isaiah 49:1-7

ADULT/YOUTH

BACKGROUND SCRIPTURE: **Luke 1:26-31; 2:21-35**

PRINT PASSAGE: **Luke 1:26-31; 2:22, 25-35**

ADULT KEY VERSES: **Luke 2:30-31**

YOUTH KEY VERSE: **Luke 1:31**

CHILDREN

BACKGROUND SCRIPTURE: **Luke 1:26-31; 2:21-35**

PRINT PASSAGE: **Luke 1:26-31; 2:22, 25-35**

KEY VERSE: **Luke 1:35b**

Luke 1:26-31; 2:22, 25-35—KJV

26 And in the sixth month the angel Gabriel was sent from God unto a city of Galilee, named Nazareth,

27 To a virgin espoused to a man whose name was Joseph, of the house of David; and the virgin's name was Mary.

28 And the angel came in unto her, and said, Hail, thou that art highly favoured, the Lord is with thee: blessed art thou among women.

29 And when she saw him, she was troubled at his saying, and cast in her mind what manner of salutation this should be.

30 And the angel said unto her, Fear not, Mary: for thou hast found favour with God.

31 And, behold, thou shalt conceive in thy womb, and bring forth a son, and shalt call his name JESUS.

.....

22 And when the days of her purification according to the law of Moses were accomplished, they brought him to Jerusalem, to present him to the Lord.

Luke 1:26-31; 2:22, 25-35—NIV

26 In the sixth month of Elizabeth's pregnancy, God sent the angel Gabriel to Nazareth, a town in Galilee,

27 to a virgin pledged to be married to a man named Joseph, a descendant of David. The virgin's name was Mary.

28 The angel went to her and said, "Greetings, you who are highly favored! The Lord is with you."

29 Mary was greatly troubled at his words and wondered what kind of greeting this might be.

30 But the angel said to her, "Do not be afraid, Mary; you have found favor with God.

31 "You will conceive and give birth to a son, and you are to call him Jesus."

.....

22 When the time came for the purification rites required by the Law of Moses, Joseph and Mary took him to Jerusalem to present him to the Lord.

25 And, behold, there was a man in Jerusalem, whose name was Simeon; and the same man was just and devout, waiting for the consolation of Israel: and the Holy Ghost was upon him.

26 And it was revealed unto him by the Holy Ghost, that he should not see death, before he had seen the Lord's Christ.

27 And he came by the Spirit into the temple: and when the parents brought in the child Jesus, to do for him after the custom of the law,

28 Then took he him up in his arms, and blessed God, and said,

29 Lord, now lettest thou thy servant depart in peace, according to thy word:

30 For mine eyes have seen thy salvation,

31 Which thou hast prepared before the face of all people;

32 A light to lighten the Gentiles, and the glory of thy people Israel.

33 And Joseph and his mother marvelled at those things which were spoken of him.

34 And Simeon blessed them, and said unto Mary his mother, Behold, this child is set for the fall and rising again of many in Israel; and for a sign which shall be spoken against;

35 (Yea, a sword shall pierce through thy own soul also,) that the thoughts of many hearts may be revealed.

25 Now there was a man in Jerusalem called Simeon, who was righteous and devout. He was waiting for the consolation of Israel, and the Holy Spirit was on him.

26 It had been revealed to him by the Holy Spirit that he would not die before he had seen the Lord's Messiah.

27 Moved by the Spirit, he went into the temple courts. When the parents brought in the child Jesus to do for him what the custom of the Law required,

28 Simeon took him in his arms and praised God, saying:

29 "Sovereign Lord, as you have promised, you may now dismiss your servant in peace.

30 "For my eyes have seen your salvation,

31 "which you have prepared in the sight of all nations:

32 "a light for revelation to the Gentiles, and the glory of your people Israel."

33 The child's father and mother marveled at what was said about him.

34 Then Simeon blessed them and said to Mary, his mother: "This child is destined to cause the falling and rising of many in Israel, and to be a sign that will be spoken against,

35 "so that the thoughts of many hearts will be revealed. And a sword will pierce your own soul too."

UNIFYING LESSON PRINCIPLE: Some people wait a long time for a promise to be kept. What assurance do we have that God's promise about salvation will be kept? God's angel spoke to Mary, and the Holy Spirit spoke through Simeon, to declare that in Jesus, God was sending a Savior and keeping the promise.

LESSON OBJECTIVES

Upon the completion of this lesson, the students will be able to do the following:

1. Remember how God spoke to Mary and through Simeon about Jesus, the promised Savior.
2. Ponder the love of God as revealed through the coming of Jesus.
3. Share testimonies about the significance of Christ's birth for one's personal faith.

AGE-LEVEL POINTS TO BE EMPHASIZED

Teachers of ADULTS and YOUTH

—"Jesus" comes from the Greek form of the Hebrew name *Joshua,* which means "the Lord will save," or "God is salvation."

—*Simeon* probably means "He (God) has heard." In rabbinical tradition, the name is interpreted as "He who listens (to the words of God)."

—Simeon's prayer, the *Nunc dimittis,* hinted that Jesus' ministry would include the non-Jewish world and, therefore, fit within Luke's theme of universal salvation.

—Reference to "a light for revelation to the Gentiles" echoes the words of Isaiah 49:6; "Glory to your people Israel" echoes the words of Isaiah 49:3.

—Matthew 1:21 provides a theological explanation of the meaning of the name *Jesus.*

—Nazareth (verse 26) was a culturally and economically insignificant village.

—Led by the Holy Spirit, Simeon confirmed the fulfillment of God's promise of the work of Jesus.

Teachers of CHILDREN

—Mary was told by an angel that she would be the vessel used by God to deliver the promised Messiah.

—Mary was part of God's divine plan to bring salvation to all of humanity.

—Mary gave birth to Jesus, who was God's Son.

—The name *Jesus* means "Savior" in the Greek language.

—Jesus' earthly parents followed the Jewish law of purification and presented Jesus to God.

—Simeon recognized the baby Jesus as the promised Messiah when Jesus was brought to the Temple.

THE CHRONOLOGICAL SETTING OF THE LESSON

The gospel of Luke is the longest book in the New Testament. Even though the other Gospels report many of the same events, more than half of Luke contains information that is found nowhere else.

Without Luke, certain periods of Christ's life and ministry would be unknown to us. Luke alone gives certain important chronological notations (2:1; 3:2; 3:23). Luke has a greater focus on individuals than do the other gospels. For example, Luke mentions thirteen women not found in the other gospels. It can also be said that Luke's gospel has more comprehensive range than the others. It begins with the announcements concerning the births of John the Baptist and Jesus and ends with a reference to the ascension of Christ. (*Luke: The Gospel of the Gentiles,* https://bible.org/seriespage/silence-shattered-luke-11-38)

THE GEOGRAPHICAL AND CULTURAL SETTING OF THE LESSON

Luke appears to have been a Gentile physician who was writing his gospel to Theophilus, an official of some kind who was also a Gentile. This makes Luke's gospel unique in its Gentile perspective. Theophilus was called "most excellent" (see Acts 23:26; 24:3; 26:25) and appears to have been an upstanding, well-respected man within the community.

Luke's gospel comes from firsthand, eyewitness accounts. Luke also tells us about his sources and informs us that while "he was not a witness to all these events, he has obtained his information from eye witnesses and 'servants of the Word' (v. 2). Eye witnesses would include individuals such as Mary, and the 'servants of the Word' would be the apostles, who were God's accredited witnesses (cf. Acts 1:21-22; 2:32; 6:2, 4; Heb. 2:3-4). The Book of Luke is therefore one which can greatly bless and benefit us in our Christian lives. Let us approach our study of Luke with eager anticipation" (*Luke: The Gospel of the Gentiles*, https://bible.org/seriespage/silence-shattered-luke-11-38).

PROMINENT CHARACTER(S) IN THE LESSON

Elizabeth: the cousin of Mary (mother of Jesus).
Gabriel: a messenger angel.
Joseph: the husband of Mary and earthly father of Jesus.
Mary: the physical mother of Jesus, and the only woman to give birth as a virgin.

KEY TERMS IN THE LESSON

Angel (1:26)—Greek: *aggelos* (ang'-el-os): an angel; a messenger; generally a (supernatural) messenger from God; an angel; conveying news or behests from God to men.
Betrothed (1:27)—Greek: *mnésteuó* (mnace-tyoo'-o): "espoused" (KJV); betrothed; asked in marriage; "pledged to be married" (NIV).
Blessed (2:34)—Greek: *eulogeó* (yoo-log-eh'-o): spoke well of; praised.

Consolation of Israel: refers to the coming of the Messiah.
Greetings (1:28)—Greek: *chairó* (khah'-ee-ro): to rejoice; to be glad; a salutation ("hail" [KJV]).
Favor (1:30)—Greek: *charis* (khar'-ece): grace; kindness; a gift or blessing brought to man by Jesus Christ; favor; gratitude; thanks; "favour" (KJV).
Jesus (1:31)—Greek: *Iésous* (ee-ay-sooce'): Jesus; the Greek form of "Joshua"; the name of the Messiah.

TOPICAL OUTLINE OF THE LESSON

I. Introduction
    A. Jesus Is Born
    B. Biblical Background

II. Exposition and Application of the Scripture
    A. Highly Favored (Luke 1:26-31)
    B. The Wait Is Over (Luke 2:22, 25-26)
    C. Child of the Promise (Luke 2:27-32)
    D. Child of Dual Destiny (Luke 2:33-35)

III. Concluding Reflection

I. INTRODUCTION

A. Jesus Is Born

The announcement of the birth of Jesus started the series of mysterious events which, to this day, humankind has still not deciphered. First, there is the account of Mary, the mother of our Lord, Jesus. Although we are not to pray *to* her or ascribe any divine nature or attribute to her, yet we ought to praise God for her being a vessel of honor counted worthy to give birth to our Lord and Savior so that He could fulfill His mandate on earth.

The passage opens with a timeframe referring to six months after the conception of John as recorded in the earlier part of the passage—as John was to be the forerunner of Christ who would announce Him to the people (see Luke 1:26). Christ was born miraculously and mysteriously, and thus the angel Gabriel was sent to communicate this great news to Mary. The angel's greeting to Mary confirmed that she was specially chosen and favored by the Most High to attain the honor that Jewish women had so long desired. This wondrous salutation and appearance troubled Mary.

Jesus was conceived in Mary, a virgin betrothed to Joseph, in a time when women were meant to be properly married before bearing children. Luke 1:26-31 narrates the conception process of Jesus and highlights certain similarities to the birth of John the Baptist, who was the forerunner of Jesus. Even today, the birth of any child usually brings great joy and celebration to the entire family, and this joy is shared with extended family, friends, and people all around.

B. Biblical Background

The announcement to Mary that there would be a Virgin Birth establishes a parallel to John's birth and shows a number of announcements of births in the Old Testament. But the mood of this passage seems to be very different from that of the account of Zechariah. Calmness, simplicity, and honesty ruled the exchange during the conversation between Mary and Gabriel. In the case of Zechariah, he was in the midst of performing his duties as priest before the whole nation in its religious center. The announcement came to Mary, the future child bearer, privately. If these events had been designed by humans, glamour, feasting, and a huge public celebration would probably have accompanied the announcement and birth of Jesus. But God, in His wisdom, chose to use an average young woman and announced His intentions in a most subdued manner. God's promise arrived in an unadorned package of human innocence without any glamor, far away from any palace or throne. The promised Messiah who would wipe away the sins of the world (see John 1:29) entered human life at the level of everyday human experience with everyday kind of people.

Mary and the Angel's Arrival

God once again took the utmost noble initiative when He sent the angel Gabriel to Galilee, which is a location some forty-five to eighty-five miles north of the city of Jerusalem. God's announcement came to Mary, a betrothed virgin. God would bring an unexpected addition into her newly forming family.

The chaste character of Mary is highlighted by the angel's description of her as being a virgin. This clearly shows that Jesus was fathered by the Holy Spirit (verses 34-35), and the human Davidic connection of Jesus which is the tie to the royal line is also noted in verse 27. Luke's portrait of Mary is significant. Mary is a model believer, taking God at His Word, in sharp contrast to Zechariah who doubted (verses 37-38). She is favored of God (verse 30), thoughtful (verse 29; 2:19, 51), obedient (verse 38), believing (verse 45), worshipful (verse 46), and a faithful follower of God's law (2:22-24). It must also be emphasized here, however, that despite all these qualities seen in Mary, God's choice of her to bear this holy child came totally from His grace rather than from any inherent merit or quality that she possessed. Mary was the object of God's unmerited, graciously provided goodness. Her description as being one who had found favor with God (verse 30) makes it very clear that God acted on her behalf and not because of her.

The Presentation of Jesus

Jesus was born into a Jewish family, and, as was customary, His parents observed the Law of Moses regarding childbirth, circumcision, and other rituals (see Genesis 17:10-14; Deuteronomy 4:44-45). Luke carefully points out that Jesus had His roots in the Old Testament. He also points out that the Good News of Jesus was also for the whole world; yet, there was something quite unsettling about Jesus. He was going to cause a crisis in Israel, and Luke emphasizes these points in this passage.

Luke shows that the story of Jesus was confirmed by two prophets at that time; Simeon and Anna spoke of Jesus under the inspiration of the Holy Spirit. It is therefore correct to say that "the Law and the Prophets" confirmed Jesus to be the Messiah (see Luke 16:16; Acts 28:23). We also see Simeon, who—just like Zechariah and Elizabeth and Joseph and Mary, as well as the prophetess Anna a little later (verses 36-38)—represented the best in Israel at the time, spending his days in the Temple and waiting for the Messiah as a devout and righteous man. When God makes a promise, we ought to wait patiently to see its fulfillment, as Simeon was waiting for the consolation of Israel. This is the promise of comfort and restoration proclaimed to the exiles in Isaiah 40:1-2. Simeon saw the Messiah and Savior of the world in the child he was holding. He also told so much more of the child, which seemed strange to Joseph and Mary and caused them to desire to know more about the future of their Son (see Luke 2:27-35).

II. EXPOSITION AND APPLICATION OF THE SCRIPTURE

A. Highly Favored
(Luke 1:26-31)

And in the sixth month the angel Gabriel was sent from God unto a city of Galilee, named Nazareth, To a virgin espoused to a man whose name was Joseph, of the house of David; and the virgin's name was Mary. And the angel came in unto her, and said, Hail, thou that art highly favoured, the Lord is with thee: blessed art thou among women. And when she saw him, she was troubled at his saying, and cast in her mind what manner of salutation this should be. And the angel said unto her, Fear not, Mary: for thou hast found favour with God. And, behold, thou shalt conceive in thy womb, and bring forth a son, and shalt call his name Jesus.

Other than Michael, the only other angel specifically mentioned in the Bible is *Gabriel*. The name means "God is my strength," or "mighty one." Although Gabriel is not called an archangel, he is a high-ranking angel and seems to be a messenger angel. His job is to receive important messages from the presence of God and relay them to the people in the kingdom of God.

Gabriel's announcement occurred in Nazareth. Nazareth was the place where Jesus spent His boyhood and early ministry years until He was about thirty years old. After moving to Capernaum, Jesus returned to Nazareth to teach in the synagogue of Nazareth twice but was rejected both times. On one occasion, the townspeople were so angry at Jesus that they tried to throw Him off a cliff. In Mark 6:4-6 (NIV), Jesus gives His perspective on this situation: "Jesus said to them, 'A prophet is not without honor except in his own town, among his relatives and in his own home.' He could not do any miracles there, except lay his hands on a few sick people and heal them. He was amazed at their lack of faith."

One definition of the word *favor* is "demonstrated delight." God's favor can be described as "tangible evidence that a person has the approval of the Lord."

Any time God is with us, we can safely say that we are favored. Matthew 1:23 (NIV) expresses this concept well: "'The virgin will conceive and give birth to a son, and they will call him Immanuel' (which means 'God with us')."

One can only imagine the mental and emotional overload experienced by Mary at the moment of this monumental announcement. The physical appearance of an angel alone would have been enough to unnerve any normal person. In addition, the information that the angel revealed to Mary was absolutely astounding and completely life-transforming. It is no wonder that Mary was troubled by the unusual greeting given by the angel. Not only was Mary going to give birth while still a virgin, but she was also going to become the mother of the Savior of the world.

B. The Wait Is Over
(Luke 2:22, 25-26)

And when the days of her purification according to the law of Moses were accomplished, they brought him to Jerusalem, to present him to the Lord; . . . And, behold, there was a man in Jerusalem, whose name was Simeon; and the same man was just and devout, waiting for the consolation of Israel: and the Holy Ghost was upon him. And it was revealed unto him by the Holy Ghost, that he should not see death, before he had seen the Lord's Christ.

Many years before the birth of Jesus, God through Moses enacted some complex ceremonial laws that were applied to the people, and part of those laws were related to childbirth. Leviticus 12:1-7a (NIV) reflects the specifics of this law:

The LORD said to Moses, "Say to the Israelites: 'A woman who becomes pregnant and gives birth to a son will be ceremonially unclean for seven days, just as she is unclean during her monthly period. On the eighth day the boy is to be circumcised. Then the woman must wait thirty-three days to be purified from her bleeding. She must not touch anything sacred or go to the sanctuary until the days of her purification are over. If she gives birth to a daughter, for two weeks the woman will be unclean, as during her period. Then she must wait sixty-six days to be purified from her bleeding. When the days of her purification for a son or daughter are over, she is to bring to the priest at the entrance to the tent of meeting a year-old lamb for a burnt offering and a young pigeon or a dove for a sin offering. He shall offer them before the LORD to make atonement for her, and then she will be ceremonially clean from her flow of blood.'"

The name *Simeon* means "the God-receiver." Simeon was serving in the Temple as Joseph and Mary entered to comply with the requirements of Moses to show up on the fortieth day after Jesus' birth. The phrase "waiting for the consolation of Israel" is related to "the redemption of Jerusalem" (see Luke 2:38; 24:21) and "the kingdom of God" (Luke 23:51). This consolation involves the coming of the Messiah (see Luke 2:26) and the revealing of salvation for all nations (see Luke 2:29-32) (BibleStudyTools.com).

C. Child of the Promise
(Luke 2:27-32)

And he came by the Spirit into the temple: and when the parents brought in the child Jesus, to do for him after the custom of the law, Then took he him up in his arms, and blessed God, and said, Lord, now lettest thou thy servant depart in peace, according to thy word: For mine eyes have seen thy salvation, Which thou hast prepared before the face of all people; A light to lighten the Gentiles, and the glory of thy people Israel.

Jewish culture and tradition called for several ceremonies soon after the birth of a baby, including the following: a) *Circumcision*: Circumcision, or removal of the foreskin of a male child's genitals, was performed (see Luke 2:21); b) *Naming:* A child was traditionally named after a relative or named according to a character trait or birth circumstance (see Luke 1:59); c) *Redemption of the firstborn:* A firstborn son was presented to God one month after birth, and the ceremony included a symbolic "buying back" from God in order to acknowledge God's ultimate ownership; d) *Purification of the mother:* For forty days after the birth of a son and eighty days after the birth of a daughter, the mother was considered ceremonially unclean and could not enter the Temple. At the end of this time, an animal offering was brought, and the priest would declare the mother to be clean. (*NIV Life Application Study Bible*)

Simeon had obviously waited on this day for many years with no sign of fulfillment of the expectation and hope. Sometimes, we place time limits on God and become impatient if God has not moved by the time we feel He should have moved. No doubt many catastrophes have been avoided because God did not grant us what we wanted when we wanted it. Waiting on God builds our faith in God, and we learn to trust God without knowing all the answers. When we wait patiently on the Lord, we are able to renew our strength.

This celebratory passage by Simeon is called "Simeon's Song" or *Nunc Dimittis* in Latin, because those are the first words of its translation (English: "Now you dismiss"). After a long wait, Simeon was finally able to see the Messiah and his tremendous sense of relief is seen in the words of his song. Now he could die in peace.

D. Child of Dual Destiny
(Luke 2:33-35)

And Joseph and his mother marvelled at those things which were spoken of him. And Simeon blessed them, and said unto Mary his mother, Behold, this child is set for the fall and rising again of many in Israel; and for a sign which shall be spoken against; (Yea, a sword shall pierce through thy own soul also,) that the thoughts of many hearts may be revealed.

Even though Joseph and Mary had been told by the angels before Jesus' birth that they would have a special child who would deliver the world, they were still amazed by the statement made by Simeon that he had finally seen the Messiah. This was indeed much more than a mere coincidence; this was one of many confirmations that were to come that this was no ordinary baby.

Simeon's statement to Mary was not generic but designer. It was not a simple, general blessing but a complex, mixed personal blessing. Simeon's blessing accurately articulated the tumultuous trajectory that the life of Jesus would take. The highs would be wonderfully high, but the lows would be woefully low. The joyful and amazing acknowledgment by Simeon was tempered by his prediction of pain. As was her custom, Mary undoubtedly treasured those things in her heart.

III. CONCLUDING REFLECTION

Mary was a woman with strong faith who was willing to be used by God. Joseph does not usually receive much notice or credit as the earthly father of Jesus, but from all indications he was a faithful father who loved his wife, raised his son, and supported his family. It is important today to celebrate faithful fathers, caring mothers, healthy marriages, and functional families. The Christmas season can be a wonderful time to sow seeds of support for strong families and to make plans for the intentional nurturing of marriages and family relationships throughout the year.

PRAYER

Dear God, thank You for sending Jesus into the world to bring light and love into the world and to bring peace and good will to all of humanity forevermore. May the joy You bring spread into our families and make a difference throughout the entire year to come. In Jesus' name we pray. Amen.

HOME DAILY BIBLE READINGS
(December 17-23, 2018)

Jesus: God's Loving Promise

MONDAY, December 17: "The Birth of John Promised" (Luke 1:11-16)

TUESDAY, December 18: "The Lord Was with John" (Luke 1:57-66)

WEDNESDAY, December 19: "Let It Be According to Your Word" (Luke 1:32-38)

THURSDAY, December 20: "Joseph Obeys the Lord" (Matthew 1:18-25)

FRIDAY, December 21: "Anna Speaks of Child Jesus" (Luke 2:36-38)

SATURDAY, December 22: "Angels Announce Good News to Shepherds" (Luke 2:8-14)

SUNDAY, December 23: "Testimonies to the Promised Savior" (Luke 1:26-31; 2:22, 25-35)

December 30, 2018 — Lesson 5

MODELING GOD'S LOVE

ADULT/YOUTH
ADULT/YOUNG ADULT TOPIC: **Everyone Matters**
YOUTH TOPIC: **Loving the Marginalized**

CHILDREN
GENERAL LESSON TITLE: **Loving as God Loves**
CHILDREN'S TOPIC: **Loving by Sharing**

DEVOTIONAL READING
James 2:14-26

ADULT/YOUTH
BACKGROUND SCRIPTURE: **Matthew 25:31-46**
PRINT PASSAGE: **Matthew 25:31-46**
KEY VERSE: **Matthew 25:40**

CHILDREN
BACKGROUND SCRIPTURE: **Matthew 25:31-46**
PRINT PASSAGE: **Matthew 25:31, 33-46**
KEY VERSE: **Matthew 25:40**

Matthew 25:31-46—KJV

31 When the Son of man shall come in his glory, and all the holy angels with him, then shall he sit upon the throne of his glory:

32 And before him shall be gathered all nations: and he shall separate them one from another, as a shepherd divideth his sheep from the goats:

33 And he shall set the sheep on his right hand, but the goats on the left.

34 Then shall the King say unto them on his right hand, Come, ye blessed of my Father, inherit the kingdom prepared for you from the foundation of the world:

35 For I was an hungred, and ye gave me meat: I was thirsty, and ye gave me drink: I was a stranger, and ye took me in:

36 Naked, and ye clothed me: I was sick, and ye visited me: I was in prison, and ye came unto me.

37 Then shall the righteous answer him, saying, Lord, when saw we thee an hungred, and fed thee? or thirsty, and gave thee drink?

Matthew 25:31-46—NIV

31 "When the Son of Man comes in his glory, and all the angels with him, he will sit on his glorious throne.

32 "All the nations will be gathered before him, and he will separate the people one from another as a shepherd separates the sheep from the goats.

33 "He will put the sheep on his right and the goats on his left.

34 "Then the King will say to those on his right, 'Come, you who are blessed by my Father; take your inheritance, the kingdom prepared for you since the creation of the world.

35 "'For I was hungry and you gave me something to eat, I was thirsty and you gave me something to drink, I was a stranger and you invited me in,

36 "'I needed clothes and you clothed me, I was sick and you looked after me, I was in prison and you came to visit me.'

37 "Then the righteous will answer him, 'Lord, when did we see you hungry and feed you, or thirsty and give you something to drink?

38 When saw we thee a stranger, and took thee in? or naked, and clothed thee?

39 Or when saw we thee sick, or in prison, and came unto thee?

40 And the King shall answer and say unto them, Verily I say unto you, Inasmuch as ye have done it unto one of the least of these my brethren, ye have done it unto me.

41 Then shall he say also unto them on the left hand, Depart from me, ye cursed, into everlasting fire, prepared for the devil and his angels:

42 For I was an hungred, and ye gave me no meat: I was thirsty, and ye gave me no drink:

43 I was a stranger, and ye took me not in: naked, and ye clothed me not: sick, and in prison, and ye visited me not.

44 Then shall they also answer him, saying, Lord, when saw we thee an hungred, or athirst, or a stranger, or naked, or sick, or in prison, and did not minister unto thee?

45 Then shall he answer them, saying, Verily I say unto you, Inasmuch as ye did it not to one of the least of these, ye did it not to me.

46 And these shall go away into everlasting punishment: but the righteous into life eternal.

38 "'When did we see you a stranger and invite you in, or needing clothes and clothe you?

39 "'When did we see you sick or in prison and go to visit you?'

40 "The King will reply, 'Truly I tell you, whatever you did for one of the least of these brothers and sisters of mine, you did for me.'

41 "Then he will say to those on his left, 'Depart from me, you who are cursed, into the eternal fire prepared for the devil and his angels.

42 "'For I was hungry and you gave me nothing to eat, I was thirsty and you gave me nothing to drink,

43 "'I was a stranger and you did not invite me in, I needed clothes and you did not clothe me, I was sick and in prison and you did not look after me.'

44 "They also will answer, 'Lord, when did we see you hungry or thirsty or a stranger or needing clothes or sick or in prison, and did not help you?'

45 "He will reply, 'Truly I tell you, whatever you did not do for one of the least of these, you did not do for me.'

46 "Then they will go away to eternal punishment, but the righteous to eternal life."

UNIFYING LESSON PRINCIPLE: Responsible people are pulled in a multitude of directions in trying to take care of themselves and their families. Why, then, would one extend effort beyond self and family? Jesus teaches His disciples that loving acts to the forsaken and needy are really demonstrations of love to Him.

LESSON OBJECTIVES

Upon the completion of this lesson, the students will be able to do the following:

1. Investigate how the parable of the sheep and the goats applies to the lives of adults.
2. Affirm the presence of Christ in every human being, including those considered "the least."
3. Find ways to serve the poor and outcast by addressing their physical and emotional needs.

AGE-LEVEL POINTS TO BE EMPHASIZED

Teachers of ADULTS and YOUTH

—Understanding this text can come about only by keeping it in context with other passages about salvation by grace. This passage is not assurance of salvation via deeds of kindness; such deeds are a response of the grace of God to us.

—The righteous are surprised because they were not trying to gain God's favor; they have simply lived lives modeled after Jesus and in accord with God's purposes.

—Matthew places great emphasis on the importance of obeying God's commands (see, for example, Matthew 7:21-27). This emphasis is echoed in passages such as James 1:22-27.

—Are the "members of [Jesus'] family" to be understood as oppressed Christians or as oppressed people generally?

—First-century Judaism held various opinions about the end times and the possibility of life after death.

—The book of Matthew, as well as other books of the Bible (see Isaiah 2:1-4; 66:18; Joel 3; Micah 4:1-3) address the "gathering of the nations."

—In this passage, as well as in others (see Psalm 100:3; Matthew 9:36; 10:16), *sheep* is another name used by Jesus for God's people.

—"The least of these" and "members of my family" refer to disciples on a mission for Jesus (see also Matthew 10:40-42; 12:46-50; 18:6-14).

Teachers of CHILDREN

—The Scripture describes what will happen at the time of judgment and separation based on one's behavior toward others.

—Meeting the needs of others translates into loving acts toward Jesus.

—Everyone will be held accountable for the deeds done or undone for the sake of helping others.

—Jesus reminds the people that their mistreatment of others is a reflection of how they treat Him.

—Jesus expects people to care for one another.

THE CHRONOLOGICAL SETTING OF THE LESSON

Various research estimates the composition of the book of Matthew to have been accomplished somewhere between AD 50 and AD 100. If the gospel of Mark was written first, then Matthew must have a later date (and vice versa). Most scholars accept the hypothesis that both Matthew and Luke used Mark as a source for various reasons. Matthew contains about 90 percent of Mark's material; Luke contains about 60 percent (blueletterbible .org). Most researchers believe that Matthew was written in either Palestine or Syria, because of its Jewish nature. Most lean toward Antioch of Syria, because many in the early church dispersed there (see Acts 11:19, 27).

THE GEOGRAPHICAL AND CULTURAL SETTING OF THE LESSON

The book of Matthew was essentially written to a Jewish audience. Matthew focused on the fulfillment of the Old Testament and quoted from it some sixty-two times, which is more than any other Gospel writer. "Matthew uses the phrase, 'kingdom of heaven' (the only author, in fact, to use this phrase), which can be considered as a 'reverential Jewish expression,' a term appropriate to a Jewish audience. His purpose in writing to the Jews was to show them that Jesus of Nazareth was the expected Messiah, and both his genealogy and his resurrection were legitimate proofs of this. [Matthew] was a tax collector, probably stationed on a main trade route near Capernaum where he would have collected tolls for Herod Antipas from commercial traffic. Additionally, being a tax collector might better qualify Matthew for his role as an official recorder of the life and actions of Christ. After the resurrection, there is no other mention of him in the New Testament" (blueletterbible.org). The major theme in the book of Matthew is that of Jesus as the Messiah. Other minor themes include the kingdom of heaven, the conflict between Jesus and the religious leaders, Jesus as the fulfiller of the Law, and the King who will return in the clouds.

PROMINENT CHARACTER(S) IN THE LESSON

Goats: Goats are much more aggressive than sheep and have the horns to go along with that aggression. Sheep are compliant animals and have no equipment for fighting.

Sheep: Sheep were primary sources for food and were used for sacrifices. In biblical literature, sheep are often compared to God's people.

Shepherd: Shepherds were the tenders of the sheep and were responsible for finding places where sheep could graze and for protection of the sheep from predators.

KEY TERMS IN THE LESSON

Glory (verse 31)—Greek: *doxa* (dox'-ah): honor; renown; glory splendor; divine quality; the unspoken manifestation of God.

Goats (verse 32)—Greek: *eriphos* (er'-if-os): young goats.

Inherit (verse 34)—Greek: *kléronomeó* (klay-ron-om-eh'-o): to inherit; to obtain, acquire; "take your inheritance" (NIV).

Prison (verse 39)—Greek: *phulaké* (foo-lak-ay'): a guarding; guard; watch; a watching; keeping guard; prison; imprisonment.

Sheep (verse 32)—Greek: *probaton* (prob'-at-on): a sheep.

Shepherd (verse 32)—Greek: *poimén* (poy-mane'): a shepherd; hence met: of the feeder, protector, and ruler of a flock of men.

TOPICAL OUTLINE OF THE LESSON

I. **Introduction**
   A. Watch How You Treat People
   B. Biblical Background

II. **Exposition and Application of the Scripture**
   A. The Sheep and the Goats (Matthew 25:31-34)
   B. Mandate for Missions (Matthew 25:35-43)
   C. The Least of These (Matthew 25:44-46)

III. **Concluding Reflection**

I. INTRODUCTION

A. Watch How You Treat People

Here in this parable of the judgment, we see Jesus changing the time of waiting for the Son of Man from mere anticipation to an important and selfless act of care for our neighbors and those who are in need. Earlier during their discourse, Jesus had warned the disciples about asking when the Son of Man shall come (see Matthew 24:3-4, 36), and in this final parable of the passage, we do not hear an "if" but a very confident "when," regarding the coming of Christ. When the disciples would later receive the Great Commission (see Matthew 28:18-20), they would more clearly understand the Son of Man as being seated on His throne to judge all the people and nations. This Messiah, as exalted King (see Matthew 25:34), now exercises judgment, separating the sheep from the goats.

In this passage, it can be seen that the righteous are invited to share in the "blessings" of the kingdom prepared for them by the Father from the beginning—while the wicked ones are sent to their father, the devil, along with his angels.

As seen emphasized in this passage, the judgment is based upon how the thirsty, the hungry, the naked, the stranger, the prisoner, and the sick have been treated in the time of waiting. While we wait for the Son of Man, this parable encourages us to utilize the time of waiting for caring for our neighbors and the needy rather than concentrating on the time of the coming of the Son of Man. Judgment will be based on our actions, and not just on our faith.

B. Biblical Background

This teaching of our Lord Jesus on the final judgment is a challenge to every Christian and disciple/follower of Jesus. We are challenged to be true representatives of God's kingdom in a world where morals and love seem to continue to diminish daily. This teaching opens with images highlighting Christ's kingship. The Son of Man's coming in glory reminds us of the images from Daniel's revelation in Daniel 7:13-14 and also brings to mind all other places where Jesus revealed the forthcoming judgment in Matthew 24:30-31 and 26:64.

Earlier in chapter 24, Jesus had privately warned His disciples of dark days ahead. It would be a time when false prophets will become numerous, and those who are not strong in the faith will lose their faith. Jesus further told His disciples that the suffering which will be experienced in the dark days will be interrupted by the Son of Man's coming with power and great glory (see 24:30). When the Son of Man comes, He will send His angels to gather all the elect for judgment (see 24:31). This passage marks the end of Jesus' parables discourse (24:1–25:46).

With the Son of Man being shown as seated with His angels, He is called the King and shall execute His judgment (25:34). Jesus Christ's being shown as King is quite fearsome in this text. He gathers all the nations of this world before Him to behold His glory and majesty.

From the throne, King Jesus says that His sheep are blessed by the Father and uses His authority to separate these individuals from the "goats." The sheep (representing good) receive the place of honor and also inherit God's kingdom (25:34). The "blessed ones" here are those who have demonstrated their faithfulness by performing various acts of loving-kindness. The call as Christians to care for the poor and the disadvantaged amongst us through various ways can be found repeatedly throughout the Scriptures, but Jesus in His ministry exhibited this gesture everywhere He went.

Jesus says that whenever the righteous visit the sick or imprisoned, give food to the hungry, welcome a stranger, or clothe the naked, they act in kindness toward Jesus Himself. The righteous did these things and did not know they were doing them unto Christ. And for those who failed to see the needs of the less privileged, their neglect proved they have never seen or known Jesus and have not followed in His footsteps.

II. EXPOSITION AND APPLICATION OF THE SCRIPTURE

A. The Sheep and the Goats
(Matthew 25:31-34)

When the Son of man shall come in his glory, and all the holy angels with him, then shall he sit upon the throne of his glory: And before him shall be gathered all nations: and he shall separate them one from another, as a shepherd divideth his sheep from the goats: And he shall set the sheep on his right hand, but the goats on the left. Then shall the King say unto them on his right hand, Come, ye blessed of my Father, inherit the kingdom prepared for you from the foundation of the world.

In other places in Scripture where the metaphor of a shepherd is utilized, the shepherd is usually protective, self-sacrificing, and loving (see John 10:14). In this instance, however, the shepherd is seen as executing a sentence of judgment as indicated by the separation.

This passage describes the last judgment. At that time, humanity will inherit the fruit of their lives—which will be either eternal joy or perpetual pain. Although on earth the ungodly and the godly dwell together, in the great day of reckoning when the thoughts and intents of our hearts will be revealed, Jesus Christ, the great shepherd, will determine the outcome of the holy and unholy.

B. Mandate for Missions
(Matthew 25:35-43)

For I was an hungred, and ye gave me meat: I was thirsty, and ye gave me drink: I was a stranger, and ye took me in: Naked, and ye clothed me: I was sick, and ye visited me: I was in prison, and ye came unto me. Then shall the righteous answer him, saying, Lord, when saw we thee an hungred, and fed thee? or thirsty, and gave thee drink? When saw we thee a stranger, and took thee in? or naked, and clothed thee? Or when saw we thee sick, or in prison, and came unto thee? And the King shall answer and say unto them, Verily I say unto you, Inasmuch as ye have
done it unto one of the least of these my brethren, ye have done it unto me. Then shall he say also unto them on the left hand, Depart from me, ye cursed, into everlasting fire, prepared for the devil and his angels: For I was an hungred, and ye gave me no meat: I was thirsty, and ye gave me no drink: I was a stranger, and ye took me not in: naked, and ye clothed me not: sick, and in prison, and ye visited me not.**

The first two needs of hunger and thirst addressed in this passage are needs that are basic for human survival. Even in contemporary society (in almost any sizable city), there are individuals who are homeless and who publicly plead for money for food.

In verses 35-36, there are six specific needs that are addressed and supplied. It seems as though the persons who are in need did not necessarily initiate the requests for assistance, but the help was given simply because the needs became apparent to the givers. In addition to meeting the basic needs of food and drink, the third need met was less physical and more hospitable. Anyone who has ever visited a new and unfamiliar place can easily identify with the feeling of appreciation when shown kindness by a person from that new environment. Indeed, it is like receiving life-giving water when in the midst of an emotional desert.

The fourth issue in the passage addresses the physical exterior need for clothing. Most people nowadays have too many clothes rather than not enough clothes. Many closets are storage containers of clothes that are too small, too old, no longer in style, wearable but not appealing, and even clothes with the tag still attached. Still, in the midst of this abundance there are people today who are in need of proper clothing. Even if there is no great need in your immediate area, there are many in need of clothing who share our planet.

The fifth need expressed is people's need for care while sick. People who care for someone when he or she is sick often win a friend for life. People with illnesses were often targeted by Jesus for the administration of miracles. While many people may not have the ability and medical expertise to heal the sick, sometimes a kind word or gesture goes a long way to help a sick person move toward a healing place.

The sixth and final need met is the visitation of those who are incarcerated.

The questions posed by the righteous in verses 37-39 are genuine because their efforts to feed the hungry, help the stranger, clothe the needy, help the sick, and visit the prisoner were not done for recognition or for some kind of spiritual credit from God. The assistance they gave was rendered out of sincere love motivated by a heart like God's heart.

In this passage, the King represents the God-figure who draws a line of direct association between the downtrodden and the Divine. Throughout Scripture, the heart of God for the poor is reflected: "The LORD is [the poor's] refuge" (Psalm 14:6); "You deliver the weak (poor) from those too strong for them" (see Psalm 35:10); "With righteousness shall he judge the poor, and reprove with equity for the meek of the earth" (Isaiah 11:4a); "the blind see, the lame walk, the lepers are cleansed, the deaf hear, the dead are raised, to the poor the gospel is preached" (Luke 7:22); the heartbeat of God's way is that Jesus "emptied himself, taking the form of a slave," becoming "obedient to the point of death" and is raised by God's glory (see Philippians 2:1-11). This is made even clearer: "For you know the generous act of our Lord Jesus Christ, that though he was rich, yet for your sakes he became poor, so that by his poverty you might become rich" (see 2 Corinthians 8:9). God's way, and therefore our way in the world, is not through our supposed power but through the vulnerability of servanthood, identification, and friendship. A key way in serving the poor is to be there with them in solidarity and not only to give them gifts (Northumbriacommunity.org).

The penalty for ignoring the downtrodden is as significant as the blessings for embracing and assisting them. Although to ignore the plight of the needy is a sin of omission, the ramifications are still severe.

C. The Least of These
(Matthew 25:44-46)

Then shall they also answer him, saying, Lord, when saw we thee an hungred, or athirst, or a stranger, or naked, or sick, or in prison, and did not minister unto thee? Then shall he answer them, saying, Verily I say unto you, Inasmuch as ye did it not to one of the least of these, ye did it not to me. And these shall go away into everlasting punishment: but the righteous into life eternal.

The social perspective of Jesus is antithetical to the world's culture and value system. One might wonder why Jesus was so invested in the welfare of the helpless. The following excerpt sheds light on this question:

Cultures throughout history, including Jesus' and ours, have assumed that those with more—more power, more money, more prestige—are the ones who most deserve our attention. And here Jesus is saying nope, it's those with less, those who occupy the least powerful, least noticeable rungs on culture's ladder who deserve our attention. Those who are hungry, naked, imprisoned, vulnerable. He goes a step farther to say that these vulnerable people aren't merely co-citizens of the world who need our help, but that they are *Jesus himself*. Christians are fond of saying that we are Christ's hands in the world. But in Matthew 25, Christ's hands are not the ones offering a cup or a meal or a coat; Christ's hands are the ones reaching out in desperate need to be filled.[1]

The connection of Jesus to "the least of these" should also be reflected in our own connection to *the least of these*. When God's priorities become our priorities, we will then be on the right road toward actualizing the part of the Lord's Prayer that states, "Thy kingdom come, Thy will be done on earth as it is in heaven."

III. CONCLUDING REFLECTION

Part of our assignment as disciples of Jesus Christ is to recognize the needs around us and act to address that which is in our power to address. Even though we are called to make a difference within our own circle of family and friends, we are also called to be missionaries and to extend care beyond our immediate parameters. Service to the poor may involve attending to physical needs, emotional needs, financial needs, or spiritual needs. The Word of God identifies the positive consequences for merciful behavior as well as the negative consequences for ignoring genuine needs. We may say we have faith, but faith without works is dead. The best way to serve others is to treat it as if we were serving Jesus Himself.

PRAYER

Lord, please forgive us for the times when we have neglected to serve others and thus have neglected to serve You. As we end this year and begin another one, please give us eyes that see the world as You see the world so that we can serve the world as we serve You. In Jesus' name we pray. Amen.

HOME DAILY BIBLE READINGS
(December 24-30, 2018)

Modeling God's Love
MONDAY, December 24: "Live by Faith" (Habakkuk 1:2-4; 2:1-4)

TUESDAY, December 25: "Rewards for Hospitality" (Matthew 10:40-42)

WEDNESDAY, December 26: "Welcoming Children" (Mark 9:33-37)

THURSDAY, December 27: "Wait, the Lord Will Come" (1 Thessalonians 4:13-18)

FRIDAY, December 28: "Keep Awake and Ready" (Matthew 25:1-13)

SATURDAY, December 29: "Multiply God's Gifts" (Matthew 25:14-30)

SUNDAY, December 30: "Inherit the Kingdom" (Matthew 25:31-46)

---

1. http://www.patheos.com/blogs/ellenpainterdollar/2015/07/who-exactly-are-the-least-of-these/#

January 6, 2019   Lesson 6

HOLD FAST TO GOD'S LOVE

ADULT/YOUTH	CHILDREN
ADULT/YOUNG ADULT TOPIC: **Steadfast Love**	GENERAL LESSON TITLE: **Hold Fast to God's Love**
YOUTH TOPIC: **Steadfast Love**	CHILDREN'S TOPIC: **Desire God**

DEVOTIONAL READING
John 15:12-17

ADULT/YOUTH	CHILDREN
BACKGROUND SCRIPTURE: **2 Thessalonians 2:13– 3:5; 2 John 4-11**	BACKGROUND SCRIPTURE: **2 Thessalonians 2:13– 3:5; 2 John 4-11**
PRINT PASSAGE: **2 Thessalonians 3:1-5; 2 John 4-11**	PRINT PASSAGE: **2 Thessalonians 3:1-5; 2 John 4-11**
KEY VERSE: **2 John 6**	KEY VERSE: **2 John 6a**

2 Thessalonians 3:1-5; 2 John 4-11—KJV

FINALLY, BRETHREN, pray for us, that the word of the Lord may have free course, and be glorified, even as it is with you:

2 And that we may be delivered from unreasonable and wicked men: for all men have not faith.

3 But the Lord is faithful, who shall stablish you, and keep you from evil.

4 And we have confidence in the Lord touching you, that ye both do and will do the things which we command you.

5 And the Lord direct your hearts into the love of God, and into the patient waiting for Christ.

.....

4 I rejoiced greatly that I found of thy children walking in truth, as we have received a commandment from the Father.

5 And now I beseech thee, lady, not as though I wrote

2 Thessalonians 3:1-5; 2 John 4-11—NIV

AS FOR other matters, brothers and sisters, pray for us that the message of the Lord may spread rapidly and be honored, just as it was with you.

2 And pray that we may be delivered from wicked and evil people, for not everyone has faith.

3 But the Lord is faithful, and he will strengthen you and protect you from the evil one.

4 We have confidence in the Lord that you are doing and will continue to do the things we command.

5 May the Lord direct your hearts into God's love and Christ's perseverance.

.....

4 It has given me great joy to find some of your children walking in the truth, just as the Father commanded us.

5 And now, dear lady, I am not writing you a new command but one we have had from the beginning. I ask that we love one another.

a new commandment unto thee, but that which we had from the beginning, that we love one another.

6 And this is love, that we walk after his commandments. This is the commandment, That, as ye have heard from the beginning, ye should walk in it.

7 For many deceivers are entered into the world, who confess not that Jesus Christ is come in the flesh. This is a deceiver and an antichrist.

8 Look to yourselves, that we lose not those things which we have wrought, but that we receive a full reward.

9 Whosoever transgresseth, and abideth not in the doctrine of Christ, hath not God. He that abideth in the doctrine of Christ, he hath both the Father and the Son.

10 If there come any unto you, and bring not this doctrine, receive him not into your house, neither bid him God speed:

11 For he that biddeth him God speed is partaker of his evil deeds.

6 And this is love: that we walk in obedience to his commands. As you have heard from the beginning, his command is that you walk in love.

7 I say this because many deceivers, who do not acknowledge Jesus Christ as coming in the flesh, have gone out into the world. Any such person is the deceiver and the antichrist.

8 Watch out that you do not lose what we have worked for, but that you may be rewarded fully.

9 Anyone who runs ahead and does not continue in the teaching of Christ does not have God; whoever continues in the teaching has both the Father and the Son.

10 If anyone comes to you and does not bring this teaching, do not take them into your house or welcome them.

11 Anyone who welcomes them shares in their wicked work.

UNIFYING LESSON PRINCIPLE: Effective personal relationships are often thwarted by destructive forces. What can counteract these forces? Paul and John instructed believers to walk steadfastly in the love of God by loving one another and following God's commandments.

LESSON OBJECTIVES

Upon the completion of this lesson, the students will be able to do the following:

1. Grasp what Paul and John said about the importance of holding fast to God's love.
2. Aspire to love others as an expression of their love for God and God's commandments.
3. Embrace the responsibility of relating to fellow believers in a genuinely Christian manner.

AGE-LEVEL POINTS TO BE EMPHASIZED

Teachers of ADULTS and YOUTH

—The confidence Paul expressed to the Thessalonians is similar to that which he expressed to those in Corinth (see 2 Corinthians 7:16) and Galatia (see Galatians 5:10).

—Paul specifically requested prayer for evangelistic success (2 Thessalonians 3:1). Whatever hardships Christians may endure (see 1 Thessalonians 3:2-3a; 2 Thessalonians 1:4), Paul's overriding concern was for the spread of the Gospel.

—Prayer was essential to strengthen both Paul and the Thessalonians to continue to lead their lives following God's commandments.

—Second John 7 implies a plurality of antichrists versus the only Christ. This plurality is explicit in 1 John 2:18.

—The idea of abiding "in the teaching" found in 2 John 9 is similar to those found in 1 Timothy 2:15 and 2 Timothy 3:14.

—In 2 John 9, "teaching of Christ" (*didachē tou Christou*) can be translated either "teaching about Christ" (objective genitive) or "Christ's teaching" (subjective genitive).

Teachers of CHILDREN

—Paul requested prayer so that he could share God's message and be protected from evil.

—Paul was confident of the faithfulness of God.

—Paul was confident in the obedience of the people.

—Paul wanted the people to feel God's love.

—Obedience to God requires that we love others.

—Disobedience is a sign of not loving God.

THE CHRONOLOGICAL SETTING OF THE LESSON

Researchers hold to Paul's authorship of the book of 2 Thessalonians. It was probably penned around AD 51 or 52 in Corinth, after Silas and Timothy had returned from delivering the book of 1 Thessalonians. Second Thessalonians is very similar to 1 Thessalonians and probably was written about six months after the first letter. The situation in the church seems to have been much the same (Biblica.org).

THE GEOGRAPHICAL AND CULTURAL SETTING OF THE LESSON

Paul's second letter to the Thessalonians (the book of 2 Thessalonians) appears to have been written just a few months, possibly a year, after 1 Thessalonians. This would place the writing of the epistle during Paul's extended stay in Corinth on his second missionary journey (see Acts 18:11) sometime around AD 53 (*Blue Letter Bible*).

The book of 2 John, one of the shortest writings in the New Testament, deals with the problem of itinerant teachers whose words the Elder judges to be false (verse 10) because it denies that Jesus Christ has come in the flesh (verse 7; compare 1 John 4:2). He warns his readers against sharing in the wicked work (verse 11) of these teachers (by accepting their beliefs or aiding their propaganda in any way). These false teachers have gone out into the world (verse 7; 1 John 2:18-19), indicating that they are former church members who have now left the fold and probably are trying to win others to their teaching. Anyone familiar with 1 John will recognize that 2 John encapsulates the situation and problems that lie behind 1 John. But 2 John adds no substantially new content (Biblegateway.com).

KEY TERMS IN THE LESSON

Faith (2 Thessalonians 3:2)—Greek: *pistis* **(pis'-tis):** faith; belief; trust; confidence; fidelity; faithfulness.

Hearts (2 Thessalonians 3:5)—Greek: *kardia* **(kar-dee'-ah):** hearts; minds; character; inner selves; will; intention; center.

Lord (2 Thessalonians 3:3)—Greek: *kurios* **(koo'-ree-os):** lord; master; sir; the Lord.

Pray (2 Thessalonians 3:1)—Greek: *proseuchomai* **(pros-yoo'-khom-ahee):** to pray; to petition, make a request.

Steadfastness (2 Thessalonians 3:5)—Greek: *hupomoné* **(hoop-om-on-ay'):** endurance; "patient waiting for" (KJV); "perseverance" (NIV).

Word (2 Thessalonians 3:1)—Greek: *logos* **(log'-os):** word; speech; divine utterance; analogy; the expression of a thought; "message" (NIV).

TOPICAL OUTLINE OF THE LESSON

I. Introduction
  A. God's Revealed Truth
  B. Biblical Background

II. Exposition and Application of the Scripture
  A. Process of Perseverance
    (2 Thessalonians 3:1-5)

  B. Walk in the Truth
    (2 John 4-7)
  C. Maintain Your Progress
    (2 John 8-11)

III. Concluding Reflection

I. INTRODUCTION

A. God's Revealed Truth

Paul began his letter with giving thanks to God for the glorious future of the believers in Thessalonica, which is described in 2 Thessalonians 2:13-14. This was, in strong contrast to the perishing future, described in verses 10-12. The believer's future here is described from both the viewpoint of people's personal responsibility and God's sovereign activity. We see a very beautiful balance in these verses that is so many times missed as Bible scholars discuss the issues concerning God's sovereign election in salvation and human responsibility. In the two aforementioned verses, the apostle Paul described to us the necessity and fact of both these elements in our salvation. God's election without our responsibility, or our responsibility without God's election, represents a perspective in which not only is God's truth missed, but also the issue becomes one-sided and blown out of proportion, making the Scripture imbalanced.

The Scripture teaches both truths, and this passage by the apostle Paul among others is one of the proofs of that fact. Until we grow into the realization that our own wisdom and intelligence are inadequate, we will continue to distort what Scripture teaches on such issues. We must always be ready to listen to God's greater wisdom rather than our limited human knowledge. Jesus referred to this wisdom when He prayed to God in this manner: "You have hidden these things from the wise and learned, and revealed them to little children" (Luke 10:21b, NIV). Paul was a balanced Christian with a balanced ministry. This becomes even more evident as he brings his letter to a close. He moves from prophecy to practical Christian living. We see him turn from the negative (Satan's lies) to the positive (God's truth), and from warning the people to giving thanks to God through prayer.

B. Biblical Background

In 2 Thessalonians 2, there were rumors that had spread through the church in Thessalonica concerning Paul's teaching about end times, which caused significant distress among them. The texts here were chosen to frame the chapter and the discussion in a very enlightening way. Here, we see Paul's purpose in the chapter, as stated in verses 2 and 15. It encouragingly declared that they (the Thessalonian believers) should "not become easily unsettled or alarmed." Instead, they should "stand firm and hold fast to the teachings" given to them by Paul in person. What was occurring in this church was not a mild questioning about how things might work out but a strong doubt of theology and God's Word that was already leaving much destruction among them. This doubt about God's Word started based on the teaching of Paul while he was with them. They were also surprised by this new teaching which brought fear of having their foundation pulled out from underneath them. They were scared, paralyzed, and uncertain as to what to believe as well as, from that, how to act.

Paul spent some time attempting to correct the teaching that had gone so wrong, but the significance of this is that he spent more time and effort encouraging this congregation to have faith and to stand firm. This makes one wonder how churches generally handle the teaching about the end times. For some churches and preachers, it becomes an obsessive fascination. Paul's focus was on reminding them that certain things need to happen first, so they ought to trust God and continue doing good rather than obsessing about the end. Paul did not avoid teaching about the end times. To him, it was a means of encouragement. To him, all is grace.

In this letter, Paul showed how his confidence did not rest in human plans, programs, promotion, or personalities. His confidence rested in the Lord, and so should ours. As he began to bring this epistle to a close with chapter 3, we see a wonderful model which shows his confidence for his need and whatever he might face as an unending trust in the Lord, His faithfulness and provision, and His powerful Word. Jesus emphatically said, "On this rock I will build My church, and the gates of Hades shall not prevail against it" (Matthew 16:18, NIV). While God uses frail human instruments in accomplishing His work on earth, the ultimate accomplishment of the work depends on the work and faithfulness of the Lord and His Word.

Our modern tendency is to plan and act quickly rather than to pray and wait on God's timing, leading, work, strength, and provision. This is how we are to exercise wisdom and humility as we put our trust in God, our Savior. Again, the apostle here provides us with a model that is not just for ministry alone, but for life as well.

II. EXPOSITION AND APPLICATION OF THE SCRIPTURE

A. Process of Perseverance
(2 Thessalonians 3:1-5)

FINALLY, BRETHREN, pray for us, that the word of the Lord may have free course, and be glorified, even as it is with you: And that we may be delivered from unreasonable and wicked men: for all men have not faith. But the Lord is faithful, who shall stablish you, and keep you from evil. And we have confidence in the Lord touching you, that ye

both do and will do the things which we command you. And the Lord direct your hearts into the love of God, into the patient waiting for Christ.

Paul's primary focus in this passage was to make sure that God's truth was disseminated quickly and in a manner that commanded the respect that it so rightfully deserved (verse 1). This message was not a matter of being able to "take it or leave it," but it was urgent enough to be expedited. The urgency of the message is due to the importance of the message, which is a matter of life and death. Since the message is so important, it must be honored and esteemed accordingly.

Verse 2 in our text echoes a phrase from the Lord's Prayer (or the Disciples' Prayer), which is "deliver us from evil." God does not promise to deliver us from the *presence* of evil, but God does promise to deliver us from the *power* of evil. We are called to be in the world, but not of the world. We are not called to be *thermometers* that reflect the environment, but we are called to be *thermostats* that control and influence the environment. We influence the environment when we act as salt and light in our communities and allow our lights to spiritually illuminate the world around us.

One of the basic benefits of the believer is God's protection from evil. Second Timothy 4:18 records this (in essence): "the Lord will certainly deliver and draw me to Himself from every assault of evil. He will preserve and bring me safe unto His heavenly kingdom. To Him be the glory forever and ever." The Christian's job is to stand and persevere. God's job is to protect and assist the believer in the midst of the battle.

When we think of someone's heart (verse 5), it is usually not in terms of the heart's being able to be turned in a specific direction. However, this is the imagery utilized in verse 5 as well as in other locations in Scripture. Proverbs 21:1 (NIV) states, "In the LORD's hand the king's heart is a stream of water that he channels toward all who please him." The intent of this heart metaphor is to emphasize God's ultimate control over the will of humanity.

B. Walk in the Truth
(2 John 4-7)

I rejoiced greatly that I found of thy children walking in truth, as we have received a commandment from the Father. And now I beseech thee, lady, not as though I wrote a new commandment unto thee, but that which we had from the beginning, that we love one another. And this is love, that we walk after his commandments. This is the commandment, That, as ye have heard from the beginning, ye should walk in it. For many deceivers are entered into the world, who confess not that Jesus Christ is come in the flesh. This is a deceiver and an antichrist.

The key phrase in verse 4 is "walking in the truth," which is an indication of one's operating his/her life in accordance with the will and ways of almighty God. To walk in truth is to reject the self-directed life in favor of the God-directed life. Two verses which correspond with this concept are Psalm 86:11 (NKJV)—"Teach me Your way, O LORD; I will walk in Your truth; Unite my heart to fear Your name"; and 3 John 4 (NIV)—"I have no greater joy than to hear that my children are walking in the truth."

The salutation directed to the "dear lady" (verse 5) is most likely a reference to a local church that is being addressed from a feminine perspective, not unlike one might refer to a country in the feminine gender. The request to love one another is a recurrent theme throughout the New Testament. Jesus loved people.

In verse 7, John warned against the false Gnostic teaching that since the Spirit is good and matter is evil, then Jesus could not have actually come in the flesh. Of course, this notion flies in the face of all the miracles done by Jesus as well as the crucifixion of Jesus. This is dangerous because it is a distortion of many things held holy in the walk of faith. This is another reason to have a firm grasp of the truth, so that no one is able to deceive with their wise-sounding-but-inaccurate words.

C. Maintain Your Progress
(2 John 8-11)

Look to yourselves, that we lose not those things which we have wrought, but that we receive a full reward. Whosoever transgresseth, and abideth not in the doctrine of Christ, hath not God. He that abideth in the doctrine of Christ, he hath both the Father and the Son. If there come any unto you, and bring not this doctrine, receive him not into your house, neither bid him God speed: For he that biddeth him God speed is partaker of his evil deeds.

When it comes to the concept of rewards, Scripture generally discusses them in two different categories. One category concerns the heavenly rewards that are laid up for the faithful in the afterlife. The second category of rewards has to do with earthly rewards which come from faithfulness and service to God and in ministry to others. "Eye has not seen, nor ear heard, nor have entered into the heart of man the things which God has prepared for those who love Him" (1 Corinthians 2:9, NKJV). God wants us always to walk by faith and not by sight. Maintaining faith during times of trials is expected, because trouble and hardship tend to test our true content. Our pressing through our problems proves that our faith is real and brings the promised rewards from God.

To fail in the area of faithfulness runs the risk of losing that for which we have so diligently worked. God deeply desires our full commitment to His truth. Not only does Jesus know the truth and speak the truth to others, but Jesus said that He is the essence of the truth (see John 14:6). Our commitment to examining ourselves to see if we are in the faith honors God and secures the reward that we will receive. "Examine yourselves to see whether you are in the faith; test yourselves. Do you not realize that Christ Jesus is in you—unless, of course, you fail the test?" (2 Corinthians 13:5, NIV).

Perseverance is an extremely important component in our walk with God (verse 9). God desires us to press through life's obstacles despite the distractions and discomforts that could possibly deter us from our destination. As we learn how to overcome obstacles, difficulties, trials, and tribulations, we will experience the joy of the Lord and the victory in Christ. "Let us not become weary in doing good, for at the proper time we will reap a harvest if we do not give up" (Galatians 6:9, NIV).

In verse 10, John explicitly instructed the faithful disciples to refrain from welcoming those who are identified as false teachers and who reject the authentic instruction being advanced by John and other true teachers of the Word of God and the way of Jesus Christ. Perhaps the rationale behind this instruction was that they could not afford to allow the false teaching to affect and infect the still-young church. John's instructions regarding the intentional social ostracizing of heretics was seemingly an effort to avoid the potential damage that could be posed to the purity of the Gospel message. From John's perspective, a serious and potentially damaging situation called for urgent actions on the part of the church.

False teaching is a very serious spiritual infraction and cannot be tolerated because it could breed a generation of pseudo-saints who have been fed falsehood and who are unable to distinguish between the truth and a lie. Even if various types of false teaching are widespread, that does not mean that it should be overlooked or treated lightly. Every believer who knows the truth has a responsibility to perpetuate the truth and to correct any spiritual or biblical falsehoods. As verse 11 suggests, our silence in the presence and knowledge of false teaching makes us just as guilty as the individual who teaches spiritual inaccuracies.

III. CONCLUDING REFLECTION

It is of utmost importance that we as believers in Christ make sure to walk in love and hold fast to God's Word. We cannot tell others how to walk if we are not walking in love ourselves. When we show love to others, we are replicating the love that God shows to us. Stepping up to this challenge, especially when the object is not so lovely, is a sure mark of spiritual maturity. As we learn how to exercise our God-given gift of discernment, we will clearly know how to distinguish between that which is good and that which is evil. As we pray for each other, hold each other accountable, and unite in spiritual oneness, we will reflect the love of Christ to the world and others will be drawn to Christ not just because of our words, but also because of our light.

PRAYER

Lord, make us instruments of Your love and peace. Let us make a difference in the world through standing boldly for Your truth. Even when others may not understand, let us still make a stand. In Jesus' name we pray. Amen.

HOME DAILY BIBLE READINGS
(December 31, 2018–January 7, 2019)

Hold Fast to God's Love

MONDAY, December 31: "Love as I Have Loved You" (John 15:12-17)

TUESDAY, January 1: "Live in Love and Light" (1 John 2:7-11)

WEDNESDAY, January 2: "Live by the Truth" (1 John 2:20-27)

THURSDAY, January 3: "Support Coworkers" (3 John 2-8)

FRIDAY, January 4: "Stand Firm in the Faith" (2 Thessalonians 2:13-17)

SATURDAY, January 5: "Do What Is Right" (2 Thessalonians 3:6-13)

SUNDAY, January 6: "Love God and One Another" (2 Thessalonians 3:1-5; 2 John 4-11)

January 13, 2019

Lesson 7

SUBMIT TO GOD IN LOVE

ADULT/YOUTH
ADULT/YOUNG ADULT TOPIC: Humility in Love
YOUTH TOPIC: Come Near

CHILDREN
GENERAL LESSON TITLE: Love and Obey God
CHILDREN'S TOPIC: Love and Obey

DEVOTIONAL READING
Proverbs 3:27-35

ADULT/YOUTH
BACKGROUND SCRIPTURE: James 4:1-10
PRINT PASSAGE: James 4:1-10
KEY VERSE: James 4:8

CHILDREN
BACKGROUND SCRIPTURE: James 4:1-10
PRINT PASSAGE: James 4:1-10
KEY VERSE: James 4:8a

James 4:1-10—KJV

FROM WHENCE come wars and fightings among you? come they not hence, even of your lusts that war in your members?

2 Ye lust, and have not: ye kill, and desire to have, and cannot obtain: ye fight and war, yet ye have not, because ye ask not.

3 Ye ask, and receive not, because ye ask amiss, that ye may consume it upon your lusts.

4 Ye adulterers and adulteresses, know ye not that the friendship of the world is enmity with God? whosoever therefore will be a friend of the world is the enemy of God.

5 Do ye think that the scripture saith in vain, The spirit that dwelleth in us lusteth to envy?

6 But he giveth more grace. Wherefore he saith, God resisteth the proud, but giveth grace unto the humble.

7 Submit yourselves therefore to God. Resist the devil, and he will flee from you.

James 4:1-10—NIV

WHAT CAUSES fights and quarrels among you? Don't they come from your desires that battle within you?

2 You desire but do not have, so you kill. You covet but you cannot get what you want, so you quarrel and fight. You do not have because you do not ask God.

3 When you ask, you do not receive, because you ask with wrong motives, that you may spend what you get on your pleasures.

4 You adulterous people, don't you know that friendship with the world means enmity against God? Therefore, anyone who chooses to be a friend of the world becomes an enemy of God.

5 Or do you think Scripture says without reason that he jealously longs for the spirit he has caused to dwell in us?

6 But he gives us more grace. That is why Scripture says: "God opposes the proud but shows favor to the humble."

7 Submit yourselves, then, to God. Resist the devil, and he will flee from you.

8 Draw nigh to God, and he will draw nigh to you. Cleanse your hands, ye sinners; and purify your hearts, ye double minded.	8 Come near to God and he will come near to you. Wash your hands, you sinners, and purify your hearts, you double-minded.
9 Be afflicted, and mourn, and weep: let your laughter be turned to mourning, and your joy to heaviness.	9 Grieve, mourn and wail. Change your laughter to mourning and your joy to gloom.
10 Humble yourselves in the sight of the Lord, and he shall lift you up.	10 Humble yourselves before the Lord, and he will lift you up.

UNIFYING LESSON PRINCIPLE: Destructive thoughts and desires lead to further destructive behavior. What can be done to break this cruel cycle? James asserts that loving and obeying God opens the door to God's blessings and frees us from conflicts and disputes.

LESSON OBJECTIVES

Upon the completion of this lesson, the students will be able to do the following:

1. Understand James's teaching about the source of conflicts and his prescription for avoiding them.
2. Repent of attitudes and behaviors that keep adults mired in conflicts and disputes.
3. Develop ways to draw near to God in humble submission.

AGE-LEVEL POINTS TO BE EMPHASIZED

Teachers of ADULTS and YOUTH

—James 4:6 quotes Proverbs 3:34.

—The adultery language of James 4:4 alludes to covenant unfaithfulness (compare Hosea 3:1).

—The inward battle of James 4:1 is also reflected in Romans 7:23 and 1 Peter 2:11.

—"The Scripture says" citation of James 4:5 is not a verbatim quote of any OT text, but reflects the thrust of Exodus 20:5; 34:14.

—The call to resist the devil is also found in 1 Peter 5:9.

—James reminds us that we cannot love the world and love God (Matthew 6:24 and 1 John 2:15-17).

Teachers of CHILDREN

—Believers should not fight one another to gain money or things.

—James explained that the sinful desires that are inside of everyone cause bad choices to be made.

—Sometimes Christians pray for the wrong things and for the wrong reasons.

—James explained that pleasures are good, but Christians should not allow pleasures to keep them from obeying God.

—Humility frees us from disobeying God and seeking worldly pleasures.

—God reaches out to believers in love and wants us to draw near.

THE CHRONOLOGICAL SETTING OF THE LESSON

If the book of James was written by James, the brother of Jesus, it would have been written sometime before AD 70. "James's probable purpose in [writing] is confirmed in the letter: to encourage suffering Christians in the face of hardship and to strengthen them for faithful Christian living. It would fit this historical setting that James would be writing primarily to poor Christians and that one of his goals would be to instruct and encourage them in the face of hardship at the hands of rich unbelievers. In speaking of the 'rich,' James would likely have in mind the unbelievers who were using their wealth as power to oppress the very vulnerable Christians" (*The IVP New Testament Commentary Series, James*, George M. Stulac, p. 195).

THE GEOGRAPHICAL AND CULTURAL SETTING OF THE LESSON

Jerusalem was probably the geographical origin of the book of James. The recipients of the book of James were probably Christian Jews who fled Jerusalem during the persecution of Stephen in Acts 7–8. James identified his audience as the "twelve tribes who are dispersed abroad" (see 1:1). The designation "twelve tribes" suggests a Jewish audience which could have been unconverted Jews, Christian Jews, or Hellenistic Jews.

The recipients are identified explicitly only in 1:1: "the twelve tribes scattered among the nations." Some hold that this expression refers to Christians in general, but the term "twelve tribes" would more naturally apply to Jewish Christians. Furthermore, a Jewish audience would be more in keeping with the obviously Jewish nature of the letter (e.g., the use of the Hebrew title for God, *kyrios sabaoth*, "Lord Almighty," 5:4). That the recipients were Christians is clear from 2:1; 5:7-8. It has been plausibly suggested that these were believers from the early Jerusalem church who, after Stephen's death, were scattered as far as Phoenicia, Cyprus and Syrian Antioch (see Ac 8:1; 11:19 and notes). This would account for James's references to trials and oppression, his intimate knowledge of the readers, and the authoritative nature of the letter. As leader of the Jerusalem church, James wrote as pastor to instruct and encourage his dispersed people in the face of their difficulties. ("Recipients," *NIV Study Bible, eBook, Red Letter Edition*)

KEY TERMS IN THE LESSON

Covet (verse 2)—Greek: *zéloó* **(dzay-lo'-o):** to be jealous; eager for; "desire" (KJV).

Envy (verse 5)—Greek: *phthonos* **(fthon'-os):** envy; a grudge; spite; "jealously longs for" (NIV).

Friendship (verse 4)—Greek: *philia* **(fil-ee'-ah):** friendship; affection; fondness; love.

Members (verse 1 [KJV only])—Greek: *melos* **(mel'-os):** limbs; members.

Quarrel (verse 2)—Greek: *polemeó* **(pol-em-eh'-o):** to make war, contend; "fight" (KJV); battle.

Receive (verse 3)—Greek: *lambanó* **(lam-ban'-o):** to receive, take; to get.

TOPICAL OUTLINE OF THE LESSON

I. **Introduction**
   A. The Path to Conflict
   B. Biblical Background

II. Exposition and Application of the Scripture
A. The Source of Conflict
   (James 4:1-3)
B. Lover of the World Equals Enemy of God
   (James 4:4-6)
C. Submit, Resist, Approach, Grieve, and Humble Yourself
   (James 4:7-10)

III. Concluding Reflection

I. INTRODUCTION
A. The Path to Conflict

There is always a false wisdom that comes from envy and selfish ambition which always produces disorder (James 3:16). To put it plainly, it leads to fighting. James, having known this, carried this argument bluntly to this next issue: What is the cause of fights and quarrels among you? In some other texts (Hebrews 11:34 is one), it refers to the actual armed conflict and carries a violent image with it. "Quarrels" in other literature is used only for battles without material weapons and so refers more to angry disputes. Here, James used these terms as a pair to make his question inclusive and pointed. It was not meant to be avoided. The fights among Christians is an outrageous evil, which is what James is addressing here. He is not talking about disagreements (healthy conflicts that should be expected in a church whose ministries are expanding). He is writing about fighting, which is "unspiritual, earthly, and of the devil" in origin, and he called its perpetrators "you adulterous people" (James 4:4). Such a serious matter urgently called for a serious response before it spread like wildfire. When we as Christians find ourselves embroiled in contentious disagreements with each other, we need to immediately examine what we are doing, making reference to this passage as James gives us great help by answering questions which are usually hard for us to face. What really is the cause of the fighting (see James 4:1)? (www.biblegateway.com/resources/commentaries/IVP-NT/Jas/What-Causes-Fights-You)

B. Biblical Background

One of the most decisive steps of faith in a believer's life is to deal honestly with what James says in this lesson's Print Passage. This requires tearing away from self-justification and then redirecting oneself toward self-examination. So often, Christians try to justify their roles in conflict in terms of the high ideals, the critical issues, and the infringed rights that we are supposedly defending. In this passage, James did not entertain any such talk. He went right to the fact that these fights are mostly about personal desires. This point is reminiscent of James 1:14, where he also refused to allow such excuses for temptation. People, he says, are tempted when they are drawn by their own "evil desire." Because of pleasures that we desire for ourselves, we get into fights. An important self-examining question for all Christians in conflict/fights is, "What are the personal desires that I am trying to protect or to gain?"

What James says could refer to conflict and fights in group relationships, such as within a church, with some maneuvering for positions of authority usually from a desire for status and admiration within the community, or to criticize others. This is equally applicable in individual relationships, such as marital conflict (constantly exchanging hurtful words) or carrying out sexual infidelity. These things happen in Christian churches and in Christian marriages. James also pointed out that this "desire" battle is within us. We should not be too quick to assume that James meant that our good and evil desires are battling against each other. Peter's use of the same verb shows the evil desires as warring not with each other, but against the Christian's own soul (see 1 Peter 2:11). James's point in 4:2 is, quite simply, that our desires lead to fighting because of our immorality in trying to get what we want. At the beginning of this verse, the verb "want" does not automatically signify one's evil desires. Luke (see Luke 22:15), using the same verb, has Jesus desiring to eat the Passover with His disciples. But this context here in the book of James clearly is negative and recalls James's theme of evil desire in James 1:14.

In James 4:2, then, James explained the answer he declared in the second half of 4:1 to the question which he posed in the first half of 4:1. By the structure, James implied that the quarrels and fights among the people are like murder, and he drew a direct connection between an unfulfilled coveting (the cause) and murderous fighting (the effect). Here, James laid bare the immorality of the motivation for our fights. He said that we fight because we are coveting and are not able to get what we covet. James made his point in two stages—and in each stage, he reflected a theological premise that God is graciously generous (stated in 1:5). This emphasis is on prayer and is another manifestation of James's consistent reliance on the grace of God.

God is pure and will have nothing to do with evil (as asserted in 1:13, 17). This formed the basis for the second part of James's point in the passage, stated in chapter 4:3: this is a warning that one may not expect God to answer his/her prayers when his/her motives are wicked. James warned against asking wrongly or wickedly; then James went on to further explain what the wrong motives are. Persons ask so they can spend on their pleasures and desires in 4:1.

The conclusion is for us to understand that our fights reveal a wrong relationship with God which manifests in our prayer lives. We either do not pray, because we do not trust in God's manifold grace—or we are praying with wrong motives, because we do not follow the purity of God. In all these, James again takes the Lord at His Word and applies it in full belief to a practical situation of life. For the Christian, conflict is not primarily about who is right and who is wrong. For the Christian, conflict is an opportunity to reveal spiritual maturity or spiritual immaturity. Like the references made to the judgment in 3:13-18, James's pattern of thought also parallels that of Jesus', as seen in the Sermon on the Mount (see Matthew 5–7).

II. EXPOSITION AND APPLICATION OF THE SCRIPTURE

A. The Source of Conflict
(James 4:1-3)

FROM WHENCE come wars and fightings among you? come they not hence, even of your lusts that war in your members? Ye lust, and have not: ye kill, and desire to have, and cannot obtain: ye fight and war, yet ye have not, because ye ask not. Ye ask, and receive not, because ye ask amiss, that ye may consume it upon your lusts.

James began this passage by posing to his readers a rhetorical question which he himself answered. What is the true source of the conflict among believers? Why are there church fights? Why is there conflict in the choir, division among the deacons, and misunderstanding throughout membership? The true source of the trouble is all too often simply our selfishness. When we insist on thinking and acting in a self-centered manner, our primary priority becomes the almighty "me." When we become centered on ourselves our vision becomes myopic, and our understanding becomes short-sighted. Selfishness closes our hearts to others, but unselfishness opens our minds to greater possibilities. This is a very strong natural tendency, because self-preservation is the first law of nature. Consequently, we must have a power stronger than ourselves in order to override this very strong natural tendency. We can begin to conquer the giant of selfishness by putting God first. Anything that comes before God is an idol, including ourselves. When we put God first, God is able to clarify our vision so that we can see perspectives and possibilities that are beyond ourselves. After putting God first, we will have the humility and the grace to esteem others above ourselves in a healthy way. Then we will be able to actualize the first commandment to love the Lord our God with all our hearts, minds, souls, and strength, and also to love our neighbor as we love ourselves.

In this context, the word *desire* (verse 2) means "to intently and solidly set one's heart, mind, focus, and will onto something." When our desire is extremely strong, and that desire is unfulfilled or hindered by someone or something, the outcome or reaction is to lash out physically, mentally, and/or metaphorically. The harsh word used in the text is to *kill* when we do not get our way. This word may be used in a literal way but is often exercised in a figurative manner. We figuratively kill others when we harbor hate in our hearts. Hate can cause quality relationships to die. Other ways that we figuratively kill each other can be through jealousy, gossip, unproductive arguments, and harsh words. The truth of the matter is that we do not always know what we truly need in life. We tend to gravitate toward what seems attractive, and we strive for empty trinkets that promise instant gratification but leave us with long-term emptiness.

Sometimes, the reason why we do not have what we need is because our motive was greed. God has promised to supply our needs, not our greeds. When God presents us with something that He knows we need and we stubbornly refuse to take it, we subconsciously stunt our growth. Like a child who shuns vegetables or bad-tasting medicine, when we say "no" to God we are rejecting a healthy future. When we consult and obey God regarding our decisions in life, we set the stage for wise outcomes and healthy choices. Even partial obedience is disobedience. Disobedience leads to disappointment. But there is no disappointment in life when we make the choice to wholeheartedly obey the divine guidelines of almighty God.

The only way that we can experience disappointment in life is if we have an expectation and that expectation is not met. When we ask God for something, the usual answer is either "Yes," "No," or "Wait." Everyone loves a "Yes," and it is wonderful when that does happen. But a "Yes" is not always feasible and is not always ultimately beneficial. When we receive a "No," sometimes that "No" may be just a stress test to check our attitude. A "No" could also be given to prevent us from hardship, heartache, or heartbreak. One of the answers God gives us that may seem frustrating is the response of "Wait." When we are told to wait, it often seems to mean that we may or may not receive what we have asked, but either way we will not receive the answer just now. That can be a very frustrating answer because we live in a quick-service environment that has made us accustomed to instant results. Fortunately, God is not a clone of contemporary culture and consequently, God does not operate on our time schedule.

B. Lover of the World Equals Enemy of God (James 4:4-6)

Ye adulterers and adulteresses, know ye not that the friendship of the world is enmity with God? whosoever therefore will be a friend of the world is the enemy of God. Do ye think that the scripture saith in vain, The spirit that dwelleth in us lusteth to envy? But he giveth more grace. Wherefore he saith, God resisteth the proud, but giveth grace unto the humble.

The term *adulterous people* essentially refers to a people who stray away from the God who is their spiritual husband and who choose to give their time, attention, and allegiance to other gods. The classic scriptural imagery for this concept is seen in the book of Hosea, named for the one who was told by God to marry a prostitute in order to graphically illustrate the painful experience of what it is like when your spouse leaves you to chase after another lover. Although we are called to be in the world, we are not called to be of the world or a part of the world. We are called to be beacons of light to a world that is dark. When we become part of the world, we set ourselves up as enemies of God. It is impossible to be both an enemy and a friend at the same time. That is why we are asked to choose this day who we will serve. We are further challenged to be either hot or cold rather than lukewarm.

Have you ever been jealous of someone or had someone be jealous of you? Jealousy has been commonly referred to as the green-eyed monster because of its capacity to wreak havoc. Although God can also be jealous, God's jealousy is not of the same makeup as human jealousy. Godly jealousy is a redemptive jealousy, just as the anger of Jesus aroused by the buyers and sellers in the Temple was more so a case of righteous indignation. We were made in the image of God. The next time you start to feel angry or jealous, it might be a good idea to check the anger source.

There are at least two different kinds of pride: Healthy pride and sickly pride. Healthy pride is the kind that enables one to do the best, look the best, and to give one's best in a particular situation. This has to do with good stewardship and management of one's spiritual and natural gifts and abilities. Examples of this would be one's taking pride in raising a family or in the thorough way that his/her work is done. Sickly pride would be the kind of pride where one minimizes another person in order to exalt his/her own self. Sickly pride is selfish pride that refuses to see the value in others and can only see the value in oneself. The other side of pride is humility. Humility receives its strength from God's grace. Humility is reflected in a mindset that allows a person to place others before self because it is God who enables promotion, advancement, provision, and favor. A humble perspective is an inner conviction that pleasing God is more important than living a life to please self.

C. Submit, Resist, Approach, Grieve, and Humble Yourself
(James 4:7-10)

Submit yourselves therefore to God. Resist the devil, and he will flee from you. Draw nigh to God, and he will draw nigh to you. Cleanse your hands, ye sinners; and purify your hearts, ye double minded. Be afflicted, and mourn, and weep: let your laughter be turned to mourning, and your joy to heaviness. Humble yourselves in the sight of the Lord, and he shall lift you up.

The word *submission* is a term that has often been misunderstood and has unfortunately and incorrectly been regarded in a negative light. To the uninformed, submission assumes a position of weakness, while aggression is thought to be a sign of strength. In the subject area of marriage, some wives reject the idea of submission because they see that as giving up all their rights. Perhaps this idea has materialized through some husbands who have misused their position of headship and have acted as terrible tyrants rather than servant leaders. The prefix of the word *submission* is "sub," which means "under." The suffix of the word is "mission," which means "a plan." Therefore, in a healthy, godly marriage, for a wife to be in submission is for the wife to be under the plan of her man. It is the hope that that plan comes from a man who is also submissive to God and to his wife in terms of being willing to lay down his life in order to protect her, provide for her, and serve her. One's submission, therefore, becomes powerful and productive when the source of his/her submission is God or is connected to God.

The second part of verse 7 addresses resistance. There are several practical ways to resist the devil. The first way is to respond with the Word of God. Each time Jesus was tempted by Satan in the desert, Jesus responded with the phrase, "It is written . . . ." That phrase was followed by an appropriate passage from Scripture. The Word of God is a spiritual weapon that we can use to conduct spiritual warfare. But we have to have the Word inside of us in order to bring the Word out of us. This concept is captured in Psalm 119:11 (NIV): "I have hidden your word in my heart that I might not sin against you." God's Word provides the power to avoid anything that is contrary to the will of God.

Another way to resist the devil is through prayer. Prayer sharpens our spiritual sensitivity and opens our spirits to receive power and divine influence to conquer evil. The weapon of prayer was also used by Jesus when He was in great anguish in the garden just before His arrest and crucifixion. Through prayer, Jesus conquered the fear of torture and death. He arrived at that crucial point when He surrendered His will to the will of the Father: "Nevertheless, not my will but Thy will be done."

There are many other ways to resist the devil, but two last ways to mention here are through partnership and persistence. *Partnership* is the intentional seeking of assistance, accountability, and mentorship to help you in the resistance against Satan, who constantly seeks footholds to climb over the spiritual walls of protection in our lives. When we join forces with other strong believers, our strength is magnified. "Where there is no counsel, the people fall; but in the multitude of counselors there is safety" (Proverbs 11:14, NKJV). Then there is persistence. If we do not stand for something, we will fall for anything. Galatians 6:9 declares, "And let us not be weary in well doing: for in due season we shall reap, if we faint not." After the armor of God is discussed in Ephesians 6:13, the exhortation ends with, "Therefore put on the full armor of God, so that when the day of evil comes, you may be able to stand your ground, and after you have done everything, to stand" (NIV).

Again, there is a trilogy of instructions in verse 8. We are instructed to come near, wash hands, and purify hearts. All three are necessary and related extensions of the previous statement. We cannot figuratively wash our hands unless we come near. And we cannot purify our hearts unless we first start with hands. The "coming near" represents the development of a devotional approach to holiness and hearing God's voice through spiritual surrender. The washing of our hands could include the elimination of any sinful word, deed, or habit from our lives. When we wash our ways, we align our lives to the will of God and the Word of God rather than to the curve of culture and the habits of humanity. The purification of our hearts deals more with the inner workings of our mental and emotional psyches. Our hearts must be clean so that our thoughts will be washed and our motives will be pure. Jesus declared that those with pure hearts are the ones who are blessed and who ultimately will see God.

There is a time for everything in life, and verse 9 addresses the time to grieve, mourn, and cry.

The sins to which the apostle refers are those which he had specified in the previous part of the chapter, and which he had spoken of as so evil in their nature, and so dangerous in their tendency. The word rendered 'be afflicted' means properly to endure toil or hardship; then to endure affliction or distress, and here means that they were to afflict themselves; that is, they were to feel distressed and sad on account of their transgressions. Comp. Ezra viii. 21. The other words in this clause are those which are expressive of deep grief or sorrow. The language here used shows that the apostle supposed that it was possible that those who had done wrong should voluntarily feel sorrow for it, and that, therefore, it was proper to call upon them to do it. (*Notes, Explanatory and Practical, on the General Epistles of James, Peter, John and Jude*, Albert Barnes, p. 86)

The heaviness, dejection, or sorrow that we feel when we sin is made possible by the presence of the Holy Spirit who guides us into all truth and who does not condemn us, but who convicts us of sin (*Barnes Notes on the Bible*).

It is our job to continually humble ourselves in God's presence (verse 10), and it is God's job to elevate us to our place of purpose. If we do God's job (elevation), then God must do our job (humble us). In order for a tree to grow tall, it must first have deep roots in order to support the weight of the tall tree. The greater the fruit, the lower the tree branch will bow. Deep-rooted humility produces elevated spiritual growth and fruit. We will have no real spiritual ability without true personal humility. As God gives us grace to be exalted, God also gives us the grace to stay humble in the midst of our elevation.

III. CONCLUDING REFLECTION

James's teaching about the source of conflicts and how to avoid them is as relevant today as it was when originally written. For the Christian, conflict is not just about who is right and who is wrong. For the Christian, conflict is an opportunity to reveal spiritual maturity

or spiritual immaturity. Mature disciples are called to repent for attitudes and behaviors that keep them immersed in conflicts and disputes. We are drawn closer to God not when we retaliate, but when we respond in humility and in submission to God. It does not help to dwell on the person who has wronged us. This only leads to destructive thoughts and destructive behavior. Rather than getting even, we should desire to get a solution to the conflict. As Christians, we should recognize and avoid behaviors and attitudes that make us friends of the world and enemies of God.

PRAYER

Dear God, help us to see the value of handling conflict from a spiritual perspective rather than from a fleshly perspective. As we interact with others, may the sweet perfume of Your fragrance be released in the atmosphere so that they may know that You were here. In Jesus' name we pray. Amen.

HOME DAILY BIBLE READINGS
(January 7-13, 2019)

Submit to God in Love
MONDAY, January 7: "One Teacher, Many Students" (Matthew 23:1-11)

TUESDAY, January 8: "Members Depend on Each Other" (1 Corinthians 12:19-26)

WEDNESDAY, January 9: "Solve Conflicts One to One" (Matthew 5:21-26)

THURSDAY, January 10: "Longing for God's Help" (Psalm 42)

FRIDAY, January 11: "Walk in Newness of Life" (Romans 6:1-14)

SATURDAY, January 12: "Boasting an Insult to God" (James 4:13-17)

SUNDAY, January 13: "A Godly Approach to Worldliness" (James 4:1-10)

January 20, 2019   Lesson 8

SUBMIT TO GOD IN CHRIST

ADULT/YOUTH	CHILDREN
ADULT/YOUNG ADULT TOPIC: **Good from Bad**	GENERAL LESSON TITLE: **Joyfully Tell Others**
YOUTH TOPIC: **Facing Challenges**	**of Christ**
	CHILDREN'S TOPIC: **Share Joy**

DEVOTIONAL READING
1 Peter 4:12-19

ADULT/YOUTH	CHILDREN
BACKGROUND SCRIPTURE: **Philippians 1:12-21**	BACKGROUND SCRIPTURE: **Philippians 1:12-21**
PRINT PASSAGE: **Philippians 1:12-21**	PRINT PASSAGE: **Philippians 1:12-21**
ADULT KEY VERSE: **Philippians 1:12**	KEY VERSE: **Philippians 1:18**
YOUTH KEY VERSE: **Philippians 1:21**	

Philippians 1:12-21—KJV

12 But I would ye should understand, brethren, that the things which happened unto me have fallen out rather unto the furtherance of the gospel;

13 So that my bonds in Christ are manifest in all the palace, and in all other places;

14 And many of the brethren in the Lord, waxing confident by my bonds, are much more bold to speak the word without fear.

15 Some indeed preach Christ even of envy and strife; and some also of good will:

16 The one preach Christ of contention, not sincerely, supposing to add affliction to my bonds:

17 But the other of love, knowing that I am set for the defence of the gospel.

18 What then? notwithstanding, every way, whether in

Philippians 1:12-21—NIV

12 Now I want you to know, brothers and sisters, that what has happened to me has actually served to advance the gospel.

13 As a result, it has become clear throughout the whole palace guard and to everyone else that I am in chains for Christ.

14 And because of my chains, most of the brothers and sisters have become confident in the Lord and dare all the more to proclaim the gospel without fear.

15 It is true that some preach Christ out of envy and rivalry, but others out of goodwill.

16 The latter do so out of love, knowing that I am put here for the defense of the gospel.

17 The former preach Christ out of selfish ambition, not sincerely, supposing that they can stir up trouble for me while I am in chains.

18 But what does it matter? The important thing is that in every way, whether from false motives or true,

pretence, or in truth, Christ is preached; and I therein do rejoice, yea, and will rejoice.

19 For I know that this shall turn to my salvation through your prayer, and the supply of the Spirit of Jesus Christ,

20 According to my earnest expectation and my hope, that in nothing I shall be ashamed, but that with all boldness, as always, so now also Christ shall be magnified in my body, whether it be by life, or by death.

21 For to me to live is Christ, and to die is gain.

Christ is preached. And because of this I rejoice. Yes, and I will continue to rejoice,

19 for I know that through your prayers and God's provision of the Spirit of Jesus Christ what has happened to me will turn out for my deliverance.

20 I eagerly expect and hope that I will in no way be ashamed, but will have sufficient courage so that now as always Christ will be exalted in my body, whether by life or by death.

21 For to me, to live is Christ and to die is gain.

UNIFYING LESSON PRINCIPLE: It is easy to become demoralized by difficult circumstances and adversaries. How can people maintain their joy? Paul willingly submitted to God's will and rejoiced that his sufferings had led to further proclamation of the Gospel.

LESSON OBJECTIVES

Upon the completion of this lesson, the students will be able to do the following:

1. Explore Paul's historical circumstances in this letter and his responses to them.
2. Forgive those who have sought to benefit from our own misfortune.
3. Look for opportunities to share in God's work in the world through Jesus Christ.

AGE-LEVEL POINTS TO BE EMPHASIZED

Teachers of ADULTS and YOUTH

—Philippians is considered one of Paul's "prison epistles," the others being Ephesians, Colossians, and Philemon. Paul also wrote the book of 2 Timothy while imprisoned, but that letter is categorized as one of the "pastoral epistles."

—Paul's credibility was an issue to those who supposed that a "suffering apostle" was a contradiction in terms.

—Philippians has been called Paul's "joy letter," with words such as *rejoice* and *joy* occurring about 4.2 times per thousand words—more than twice as frequently as in any of his other letters.

—The word translated "imperial guard" (*praitōrion*) in verse 13 can also signify a palace, as in Acts 23:35, where it is translated "headquarters."

—In verse 20, Paul feared being "put to shame" by failing to speak boldly about Christ. His honor was invested in his calling to be Christ's "apostle to the gentiles." He was willing even to suffer in prison rather than fail in this regard.

—Paul encouraged believers because those misusing the Word of God and contending with Paul were actually spreading the Gospel.

—Paul concluded that no matter why people are proclaiming Christ, the proclamation of Christ is taking place.

—In verse 21, Paul saw "living for Christ" as an end to his struggles and "dying is gain" as representing a sharing in Christ's resurrection.

Teachers of CHILDREN

—God gave Paul the special mission of sharing Christ with others.

—Paul was not ashamed to share the Gospel of Christ.

—Paul's being in prison did not stop him from sharing Christ, even with the Roman guards.

—Paul shared Christ because he loved God and he loved people.

THE CHRONOLOGICAL SETTING OF THE LESSON

The book of Philippians is traditionally believed to have been written during Paul's two-year prison stay in Rome after he appealed to Caesar in the court of Festus (see Acts 25:9-11; 28:16, 30). This "prison epistle" is only one of the writings produced by Paul during this period: AD 60–62, approximately ten years after Paul's first visit to Philippi. Other writings include Ephesians, Colossians, and Philemon. Paul also wrote the book of 2 Timothy while incarcerated, but that letter is categorized as one of the Pastoral Epistles.

THE GEOGRAPHICAL AND CULTURAL SETTING OF THE LESSON

Philippi is located in the northeastern portion of Greece (Macedonia). Paul arrived in this ancient city around AD 49, according to Acts 16:11-40. The religious life of those in Philippi was marked by very syncretistic practices, including the worship of the emperor (Julius, Augustus, and Claudius), the Egyptian gods Isis and Serapis, as well as many other deities. It was an important land route, and in 168 BC, Philippi became part of the Roman Empire after the Persians were defeated by Rome. Macedonia was divided into four districts, with Philippi being one of these districts.

When Paul came to the city around 49 CE, Philippi was an urban center at the eastern end of the plain, a few miles northwest from Neapolis. The people there were both Romans and Greeks and spoke predominantly Greek even though Latin was the official language. The church in Philippi was founded by the apostle Paul on his second missionary journey, recorded in Acts 16:1-40. Paul originally went to Macedonia because of a night vision described for us in Acts 16:9. In it Paul saw a man of Macedonia standing and asking that he come over to help them. Paul responded and so the gospel went triumphantly westward beginning in Philippi as the first city to be evangelized in Europe. (https://bible.org/book/export/html/6258)

KEY TERMS IN THE LESSON

Brothers and sisters (verse 12)—Greek: *adelphos* **(ad-el-fos'):** brothers/sisters; members of the same religious community, especially fellow Christians; "brethren" (KJV).

Chains (verse 13)—Greek: *desmos* **(des-mon'):** "bonds" (KJV); chains; imprisonment; strings or ligaments; an impediment, infirmity.

Christ (verse 13)—Greek: *Christos* **(khris-tos'):** Anointed One; the Messiah; the Christ.

Goodwill (verse 15)—Greek: *eudokia* **(yoo-dok-ee'-ah):** good-will (good-pleasure); favor; feeling of complacency of God to man; good-pleasure; satisfaction; happiness; delight of men; "good will" (KJV).

Gospel (verse 12)—Greek: *euaggelion* **(yoo-ang-ghel'-ee-on):** the Good News; the Gospel.

TOPICAL OUTLINE OF THE LESSON

I. Introduction
A. God Be Glorified above All
B. Biblical Background

II. Exposition and Application of the Scripture
A. Chained for Christ
(Philippians 1:12-14)

B. Motives for Preaching
(Philippians 1:15-18)
C. Let Christ Be Exalted
(Philippians 1:19-21)

III. Concluding Reflection

I. INTRODUCTION
A. God Be Glorified above All
As humans, we are frequently caught in scenarios where we want everything to go smoothly. If only we did not have the problems we do have. We often tell ourselves that if this or that did not happen then we would have become better Christians, would have lived an excellent Christian life, or would have witnessed without fear of any kind. This passage inspires us differently with its unique and rich experience. It makes us understand that despite our problems, challenges, and circumstances, Christ can be glorified in our lives. This is an important mindset for all Christians to embrace. This attitude should always be in us. Our preaching of the Gospel of Christ should not be based on our wishes or expectations, or on any unpleasant life experiences (see 2 Timothy 2:24-26).

B. Biblical Background
In 1:12, Paul writes to his beloved friends in Philippi from his jail cell. He tells them that what has happened to him has really served to advance the Gospel. This simply showed the perspective from which he viewed his challenges. He saw these things as agents that have promoted the Gospel he propagated. Paul was either held in a Roman building (see Acts 23:35) or was under house arrest as it seems (see Acts 28:16), but wherever he was being held, he certainly was not alone there—he was with a soldier (see Acts 28:16).

During this Roman era, Paul's imprisonment was not considered a penalty for a crime, but a sort of holding/detention process used to detain those awaiting trial or execution. Paul was presumably held in Rome awaiting his trial before Caesar, which was his right as a Roman citizen. While in prison, though guarded, he was allowed the freedom to receive guests (see Acts 28:17, 23, 30), and to carry out his teachings and preaching to those who visited him in prison (see Acts 28:17-31) and to the prison guards who attended to him. In keeping guard over Paul while he was in prison, many soldiers, no doubt, were converted and became Christians as a result. These new converts would in turn influence their entire unit, their families, and beyond. Whether or not they became Christians, they all knew that Paul's imprisonment was because of his confession and testimony for Christ, not because he was some kind of political prisoner or a criminal. This would be the reason why Paul said, "What has happened to me has actually served to advance the gospel" (1:12, NIV).

As humans, often we complain about our difficult situations. This was not true of Paul. He knew it was about Christ and the kingdom rather than about him. This allowed him to see progress rather than difficulties. This also encouraged the Roman Christians, as they saw in Paul an example of a person who was a faithful witness that was unafraid of any earthly consequences. They were so encouraged that if Paul could be an effective witness despite his peril, then they could also (1:14).

Paul had enemies who were Christians and tried to work against him. He was apparently criticized for his openness toward Gentiles and his willingness to baptize them, eat with them, and allow them leadership roles in the church (see Galatians 2:11-16). He was probably also criticized for his lack of oratorical skills (see 1 Corinthians 2:1) and for his unwillingness to be calm about his strong beliefs in the Gospel to the Gentiles. These people would preach out of envy and rivalry, and not out of a love for the lost souls or goodwill toward Paul.

On one hand, there is the bold and faith-filled witness; on the other hand, there is the selfish and ambitious witness. They might have intended to discredit Paul by making him feel bad, and they probably undercut his support within the Roman church. Paul, however, saw through their corrupt intentions and rejoiced. His goal was to see the Gospel being preached actively in Rome, without regard for the intentions with which it was preached. They were helping to accomplish his purpose. Paul's choice to rejoice in response to their actions characterized his attitude toward life. He was confident that he was in Christ who controls his destiny, in whose trust he could rest.

He was confident that through prayers for him and with the help of the Holy Spirit, he would be able to speak the Word clearly and boldly at his trial. His goal was that in the end, Christ receives glory. This more importantly becomes the reason for his seeming unconcern about his death versus his life. He was convinced that either way it went he would win personally—and God wins too.

II. EXPOSITION AND APPLICATION OF THE SCRIPTURE

A. Chained for Christ
(Philippians 1:12-14)

But I would ye should understand, brethren, that the things which happened unto me have fallen out rather unto the furtherance of the gospel; So that my bonds in Christ are manifest in all the palace, and in all other places; And many of the brethren in the Lord, waxing confident by my bonds, are much more bold to speak the word without fear.

Paul was aware of the fact that his bold stand for Jesus Christ would involve painful experiences that he would have to endure. He was exposed to a great many sufferings, which he recounted in 2 Corinthians 11:24-28:

> Of the Jews five times received I forty stripes save one. Thrice was I beaten with rods, once was I stoned, thrice I

suffered shipwreck, a night and a day I have been in the deep; In journeyings often, in perils of waters, in perils of robbers, in perils by mine own countrymen, in perils by the heathen, in perils in the city, in perils in the wilderness, in perils in the sea, in perils among false brethren; In weariness and painfulness, in watchings often, in hunger and thirst, in fastings often, in cold and nakedness. Beside those things that are without, that which cometh upon me daily, the care of all the churches.

Despite all these trying circumstances, Paul found it valuable to view them as avenues to advance the Gospel. Although persecution may seem utterly distasteful from the natural perspective, it can actually be a means of spreading the Gospel (see Acts 8:1).

The power and presence of the Gospel cannot be limited to beautiful sanctuaries with stately stained-glass windows. Everywhere the contagious Gospel appears, it begins the amazing work of radically transforming lives regardless of who or what that life represented in the past. The Gospel is no respecter of persons, and anyone who is open and willing can receive the love of God and be filled and empowered to serve.

Paul's reference to his chains (verses 13 and 14) is another referral to his imprisonment for the cause of Christ. When the other brothers and sisters in Christ saw how bravely Paul responded to his dire circumstances, that gave them more courage to make a bold stand for the Gospel without fear. No doubt, they reasoned that if Paul could still be courageous behind bars, surely they could be even more courageous in their freedom. *Coffman Commentaries on the Old and New Testament* underscores the significance of someone of Paul's stature and notability being permitted to freely continue preaching while still in custody for that very reason.

B. Motives for Preaching (Philippians 1:15-18)

Some indeed preach Christ even of envy and strife; and some also of good will: The one preach Christ of contention, not sincerely, supposing to add affliction to my bonds: But the other of love, knowing that I am set for the defence of the gospel. What then? notwithstanding, every way, whether in pretence, or in truth, Christ is preached; and I therein do rejoice, yea, and will rejoice.

Verse 15 focuses on the various motives for propagating the message of Jesus Christ. Not everyone has a right and pure motive for proclaiming the Gospel. The two listed in the text are envy and rivalry, and one can imagine how a person might be doing ministry or working close to a ministry because he/she is starstruck or is in competition with someone to see who can be the freshest, the wealthiest, the biggest, and the best. Other impure motives for ministry in contemporary society might be for the stroking of the ego or the accumulation of material and financial assets. It is important to note here that "the word *preach* is not to be taken here as implying that the different persons mentioned were what we call preachers of the Gospel: all that we can understand from St. Paul's use of the word is that they proclaimed Christ as the promised Messiah, espoused the Christian cause, and contended, whether in public or private, that this Jesus was the Christ; but nothing of this kind appears to have been intended in reference to the conversion of sinners" (*Clarke's Commentary on the Bible*, http://biblehub.com/niv/philippians/1-15.htm).

In verse 16, the phrase "the latter" refers to those who promote the Gospel out of goodwill, as was highlighted in verse 15. This motive stems from genuine love for God and others rather than selfishness. People with pure motives would understand and appreciate the sacrifice of Paul, who continuously placed himself in harm's way in defense of the Gospel.

Paul's imprisonment was part of God's overall plan to spread the gospel. Since Paul is God's instrument to bring the gospel before the very highest in the Roman government, these Christians will lovingly cooperate with God's plan. But hate, envy and self-interest are blind! Paul's rivals, preachers motivated by self, were completely blind to all of the above. These Christians did not begrudge Paul for the authority he exercised, the miraculous gifts he possessed or the fame he was gaining, because they realized that he was God's messenger to defend the gospel before the highest court in the land. In a sense, every Christian must be prepared to defend the gospel (1 Peter 3:15).[1]

The "former" (verse 17) refers to those who preach Christ out of envy and rivalry (verse 15). Some sick minds are so enamored with fame and notoriety that they have envy for someone who is imprisoned. For Paul, the motive for preaching the Word of God is not as important as the act and reality of preaching the Word.

Preaching with bad motives seemed better to Paul than no preaching at all.

Paul saw his purpose as defending the Gospel. . . . Paul viewed himself as "appointed" for the gospel. He knew his mission. He saw himself clearly in God's plan of world evangelism. Love finds its source in viewing things from God's perspective. The reason some Romans loved Paul was that they knew God had appointed him to advance the gospel. Love found its source in viewing things from God's perspective. (https://versebyversecommentary.com/philippians/philippians-17/)

Paul's primary concern was to advance and to elevate the Gospel. Motives for preaching and promoting the Gospel were secondary.

"Pretense" (verse 18, KJV) means to cover the real motive and present others with a false idea. This is an attempt to disguise true motives. . . . Paul did not condone their cunning. However, he did approve of their preaching Christ. Notwithstanding their motive, they were preaching the gospel. (https://versebyversecommentary.com/philippians/philippians-118/)

C. Let Christ Be Exalted (Philippians 1:19-21)

For I know that this shall turn to my salvation through your prayer, and the supply of the Spirit of Jesus Christ, According to my earnest expectation and my hope, that in nothing I shall be ashamed, but that with all boldness, as always, so now also Christ shall be magnified in my body, whether it be by life, or by death. For to me to live is Christ, and to die is gain.

The reference to the "Spirit of Jesus Christ" (verse 19) refers to the Holy Spirit, the Third Person of the Trinity. "He is 'the Spirit of Jesus Christ' because in the eternal relations within Deity He 'proceeds' from the Eternal Son, and is sent by Him (Joh. xv. 26) as well as by the Father (xiv. 16, 26), and is so one with Christ that where the Spirit comes Christ comes (xiv. 18). His whole work for and in the Church and the soul is essentially and entirely connected with the glorified Lord" (*The Cambridge Bible for Schools & Colleges: The Epistle to the Philippians,* p. 51).

In the latter part of the verse, the apostle summoned his great faith that had brought him thus far on the way. Despite his pitiful plight, Paul spoke with assurance that a way would be made even when there appeared to be no way. Life's circumstances were no match for the "power source" on which Paul relied, which was God's provision and the people's prayers. Paul believed in the spiritual formula of "fervent prayer + diligent work = victory over life's opposing circumstances." We are called to pray and work, then work and pray. When prayer will not get it, work will. When work will not get it, prayer will. When neither prayer nor work will get it, then forget it, because you do not need it anyway. No matter how things may look on the front end, God has the power to eventually deliver us on the back end.

Paul had no way to know what kinds of dangerous or painful situations to expect in the future. All he knew and all he had was the eager expectation and the blessed hope that through his ample faith in God and courage from within, Christ would be glorified. The bottom line in the life of a Christian must be the glory of God and the kingdom of God. This is the crucial instance experienced by Jesus in the garden on the evening of His arrest. The pain, torture, suffering, and humiliation that Jesus was about to experience were not on His personal wish list. In fact, the human side of Jesus would have preferred not to go through crucifixion, as was evident through His prayer recorded in Matthew 26:39 (NIV): "Going a little farther, he fell with his face to the ground and prayed, 'My Father, if it is possible, may this cup be taken from me. Yet not as I will, but as you will.'" Jesus did not want to die such a cruel death. But His love and respect for, and obedience to, God superseded His distaste for personal pain. Paul also reflected this perspective when he embraced whatever negative situation may have come, just as long as Christ was elevated through his life or even through his death.

How frustrating it must have been for Paul's antagonists in their attempts to break his will or to wound his spirit (verse 21). If they threatened to kill him, Paul just said, "To die is gain." If they threatened to let him live in jail, he replied, "To live is Christ." If they told him they were going to torture him, his response was, "For I reckon that the sufferings of this present time are not worthy to be compared with the glory which shall be revealed in us" (Romans 8:18). This attitude of being untouchable by life's circumstances made Paul a dangerous man in the eyes of his enemies. God desires for us that same level of being ultimately unaffected by the worries of the world.

III. CONCLUDING REFLECTION

There are times when life can deliver some difficult circumstances. Our commitment to

God and to the Gospel of Jesus Christ is not dependent on circumstances, but on our faith in the reliability of God and His Word. Our Christian witness depends on God, not on the imperfect vessels who deliver the witness. Even if some of those imperfect vessels deliver the Gospel while maintaining impure motives, the Gospel is still advanced. Believers should take every opportunity to share in God's work in the world through Jesus Christ. Even when suffering and misfortune are involved, God can still be glorified. We must pray for those who are persecuted for the sake of righteousness and even assist them in tangible ways when possible. We also must develop the spiritual discernment to recognize those who preach with selfish motives.

PRAYER

Dear Lord, when we encounter various trials in this life, please grant us the peace that surpasses understanding so that whatever happens to us in this life, we can honestly say, "It is well with my soul." In Jesus' name we pray. Amen.

HOME DAILY BIBLE READINGS
(January 14-20, 2019)

Submit to God in Christ

MONDAY, January 14: "God Sent Me to Preserve You" (Genesis 45:1-8)

TUESDAY, January 15: "The Spirit Rested on the Elders" (Numbers 11:24-30)

WEDNESDAY, January 16: "Apostles Are Fools for Christ" (1 Corinthians 4:8-13)

THURSDAY, January 17: "Sharing Life in Christ Now" (Philippians 1:22-26)

FRIDAY, January 18: "Believing in and Suffering for Christ" (Philippians 1:27-30)

SATURDAY, January 19: "Sharing God's Grace" (Philippians 1:3-11)

SUNDAY, January 20: "Telling the Good News" (Philippians 1:12-21)

1. *Mark Dunagan Commentary on the Bible: Philippians 1,* https://www.studylight.org/commentaries/dun/philippians-1.html

January 27, 2019   **Lesson 9**

DEVOTE ALL TO CHRIST

ADULT/YOUTH	CHILDREN
ADULT/YOUNG ADULT TOPIC: **Sacrificial Love**	GENERAL LESSON TITLE: **Serve Christ with Joy**
YOUTH TOPIC: **I Give Myself Away**	CHILDREN'S TOPIC: **Serving with Joy**

DEVOTIONAL READING
Psalm 119:65-72

ADULT/YOUTH	CHILDREN
BACKGROUND SCRIPTURE: **Philippians 2:1-11**	BACKGROUND SCRIPTURE: **Philippians 2:1-11**
PRINT PASSAGE: **Philippians 2:1-11**	PRINT PASSAGE: **Philippians 2:1-11**
KEY VERSE: **Philippians 2:3**	KEY VERSE: **Philippians 2:3**

Philippians 2:1-11—KJV

IF THERE be therefore any consolation in Christ, if any comfort of love, if any fellowship of the Spirit, if any bowels and mercies,

2 Fulfil ye my joy, that ye be likeminded, having the same love, being of one accord, of one mind.

3 Let nothing be done through strife or vainglory; but in lowliness of mind let each esteem other better than themselves.

4 Look not every man on his own things, but every man also on the things of others.

5 Let this mind be in you, which was also in Christ Jesus:

6 Who, being in the form of God, thought it not robbery to be equal with God:

7 But made himself of no reputation, and took upon him the form of a servant, and was made in the likeness of men:

8 And being found in fashion as a man, he humbled

Philippians 2:1-11—NIV

THEREFORE IF you have any encouragement from being united with Christ, if any comfort from his love, if any common sharing in the Spirit, if any tenderness and compassion,

2 then make my joy complete by being like-minded, having the same love, being one in spirit and of one mind.

3 Do nothing out of selfish ambition or vain conceit. Rather, in humility value others above yourselves,

4 not looking to your own interests but each of you to the interests of the others.

5 In your relationships with one another, have the same mindset as Christ Jesus:

6 Who, being in very nature God, did not consider equality with God something to be used to his own advantage;

7 rather, he made himself nothing by taking the very nature of a servant, being made in human likeness.

8 And being found in appearance as a man, he humbled

himself, and became obedient unto death, even the death of the cross.

9 Wherefore God also hath highly exalted him, and given him a name which is above every name:

10 That at the name of Jesus every knee should bow, of things in heaven, and things in earth, and things under the earth;

11 And that every tongue should confess that Jesus Christ is Lord, to the glory of God the Father.

himself by becoming obedient to death—even death on a cross!

9 Therefore God exalted him to the highest place and gave him the name that is above every name,

10 that at the name of Jesus every knee should bow, in heaven and on earth and under the earth,

11 and every tongue acknowledge that Jesus Christ is Lord, to the glory of God the Father.

UNIFYING LESSON PRINCIPLE: Personal interests and selfish ambitions can lead to controversies that threaten our relationships. How can people overcome their divisiveness? Paul commended the example of Christ, who humbly emptied Himself in order to serve God and others through His sacrifice.

LESSON OBJECTIVES

Upon the completion of this lesson, the students will be able to do the following:

1. Study the saving work of Christ as it is presented in the Christological hymn of Philippians 2:6-11.
2. Aspire to serve others by following Jesus' example of humility and sacrifice.
3. Grow in the ability to place the needs of others before our own.

AGE-LEVEL POINTS TO BE EMPHASIZED

Teachers of ADULTS and YOUTH

—The designation "kenotic theology" derives from verse 7. Christ "emptied" (*ekenōsen*) Himself, but just what that emptying entailed is a matter of great theological debate.

—Confession is an important biblical theme. The confession Paul speaks of here is not the admission of guilt but, rather, is the confession or affirmation of the lordship of Christ.

—The text presents Christ's two natures ("in the form of God" and "taking the form of a slave") as a paradox.

—In this passage, Paul focuses on being of one mind.

—Paul states four reasons to support this unity (verse 1).

—Based on the NRSV, the reference to selfish ambition (verse 3) recalls the actions of those

seeking to torment Paul in his imprisonment (1:17).

—According to the NRSV, Paul's use of singular poetic power presents the story of Christ's incarnation as a basis for humility and obedience.

—As a reward, God changed Christ's humility into Christ's exaltation.

—Jesus Christ became Lord, indicating Jesus' restoration to divine status and cosmic authority.

Teachers of CHILDREN

—Paul urged the Christians to be unified.

—Christ's example of putting others first is a model for us.

—Paul warns that being selfish can cause problems.

—Jesus gave up everything so that He could obey God and serve others.

—Paul states that Christians should live as Christ lived.

THE CHRONOLOGICAL SETTING OF THE LESSON

The early church was unanimous in its belief and support that the letter to the Philippians was indeed written by the apostle Paul (see Philippians 1:1). Internal proof of this is revealed through the many personal references of the author which align with what we know of Paul from other New Testament writings. References in the book of Philippians reveal that Paul wrote this letter from prison (see Philippians 1:13-14). Some biblical scholars believe that this imprisonment took place in Ephesus in AD 53–55. Others fix the place and time of writing in Caesarea around 57–59. The best evidence, however, favors Rome as the place of origin and the date as AD 61, which aligns with the account of Paul's house arrest in Acts 28:14-31. When Paul wrote the letter to the Philippians, he was not in the dungeon as he was when he wrote 2 Timothy. He was in his own rented house where for two years he was free to impart the Gospel to all who came to visit him. (https://www.biblica.com/resources/scholar-notes/niv-study-bible/intro-to-philippians/)

THE GEOGRAPHICAL AND CULTURAL SETTING OF THE LESSON

The city of Philippi was so named in honor of King Philip II of Macedon, who was the father of Alexander the Great. "It was a prosperous Roman colony, which meant that the citizens of Philippi were also citizens of the city of Rome itself. They prided themselves on being Romans (see Ac 16:21), dressed like Romans and often spoke Latin. No doubt this was the background for Paul's reference to the believer's heavenly citizenship (3:20-21). Many of the Philippians were retired military men who had been given land in the vicinity and who in turn served as a military presence in this frontier city. That Philippi was a Roman colony may explain why there were not enough Jews there to permit the establishment of a synagogue and why Paul does not quote the OT in the Philippian letter" (https://www.biblica.com/resources/scholar-notes/niv-study-bible/intro-to-philippians/).

KEY TERMS IN THE LESSON

Comfort (verse 1)—Greek: *paramuthion* (par-am-oo'-thee-on): comfort, consolation; an exhortation, persuasion, encouragement.

Compassion (verse 1)—Greek: *oiktirmos* (oyk-tir-mos'): pity, compassion, favor, grace, mercy; "mercies" (KJV).

Encouragement (verse 1)—Greek: *paraklésis* (par-ak'-lay-sis): exhortation; entreaty; encouragement; comfort; "consolation" (KJV).

Equal (verse 6)—Greek: *isos* (ee'-sos): equal, equivalent, identical; "equality" (NIV).

Fellowship (verse 1)—Greek: *koinónia* (koy-nohn-ee'-ah): participation, communion, fellowship; "common sharing" (NIV).

Joy (verse 2)—Greek: *chara* (khar-ah'): joy, gladness, a source of joy.

Obedient (verse 8)—Greek: *hupékoos* (hoop-ay'-ko-os): listening to; obedient; submissive.

TOPICAL OUTLINE OF THE LESSON

I. **Introduction**
   A. The Blessing of Like-mindedness
   B. Biblical Background

II. **Exposition and Application of the Scripture**
   A. Recipe for Fulfilled Joy (Philippians 2:1-2)
   B. Selfishness versus Humility (Philippians 2:3-4)
   C. The Jesus Mindset Is the Model (Philippians 2:5-8)
   D. Reward for Humility (Philippians 2:9-11)

III. **Concluding Reflection**

I. INTRODUCTION

A. The Blessing of Like-mindedness

As we study the second chapter of Philippians (2:1-11), we see further exhortations from Paul exhorting the Christians to display kindness, a humble spirit, and like-mindedness according to the example set by Jesus. As shown by the apostle Paul, kindness is the law of Christ's kingdom, a lesson of importance, and the life of his family. He also touches on the subject of brotherly love, and the many motives of brotherly love are also mentioned. When we experience the benefits of God's compassions, we also ought to be compassionate to one another. It is always the joy of ministers and indeed Christians to see like-minded people as it makes church life at-large more enjoyable. Christ came in the form of a man (verse 8) to humble us, so that we would not reflect a spirit of pride (see 1 Peter 5:6; Luke 14:11). We must, however, be sincere about our own faults and quick in observing our own defects but ready to tolerate and accommodate others. We must care kindly and compassionately for others and not be intruders in other men's matters. Neither inward peace nor outward peace can be enjoyed without humility.

B. Biblical Background

Paul begins here by reminding the Philippians of the blessings they have been given by Christ. He tells them, "If you have any encouragement from being united with Christ, if any comfort from his love, if any fellowship with the Spirit, if any tenderness and compassion . . . ." By saying this, he assumes that they have enjoyed all these as mentioned. Then follows the next part which is more of a call to action—"then make my joy complete by being like-minded, having the same love, being one in spirit and of one mind" (Philippians 2:2, NIV).

The apostle Paul was not just asking them to think like one another, as he further explained. He also wanted them to be likeminded with Christ—tender, comforting, encouraging, sharing, and compassionate as Christ is. He expressed his expectation of them to have the same kind of love which Christ has and has shown to people, both in attitude and goals. That surely is the only way to be united with one another in like mind. Paul's joy is complete when the Philippians put this into practice among them, for by then his gospel will have produced its fruit.

His major concern, he said, is to "do nothing out of selfish ambition or vain conceit" (verse 3). As Christians, it is expected of us not to be motivated by selfishness or pride, as they destroy unity and become the essence of sin. Rather, we should consider others as better than ourselves, in humility and compassion. Paul did not say others are better; he only encouraged the Philippians to consider them better, out of respect and like-mindedness. In reality, no one can actually be better, yet the unity of Christians and

Christianity must be built on considering others ahead of self. According to Paul's epistle, we may consider our own interests, but it is more important that we also look out for others. This is what Christianity and the way of Christ are truly about. Christ did not consider Himself first; rather, He considered the needs of others (see Isaiah 53:7).

The humility of Christ cannot be over-emphasized. In verses 5-7, Paul once again brought to light the humble nature of Christ when he urged his readers to have an attitude like Christ who, though is God in nature, did not emphasize His equality with God. Here, we see Paul extol in praises the person of Christ. In using those words, Paul reminded his readers of the example they are to follow—one who is divine, has the greatest honor, yet did not hold onto His rights and privileges. Although the Philippians had their rights as citizens of Rome, they were to focus on others and not themselves. Jesus, our perfect example, humbly and willingly set aside His rights in order to serve our needs even unto death (verse 8). In so doing, His humility was made complete. Having shown us a pattern of good works and a perfect example of humility and how to put others ahead of ourselves, Jesus was resurrected from the dead, and God exalted Him, giving Him the highest place and a name that is above every name. At the name of Jesus Christ, every knee should bow—all those in heaven and those on earth and those under the earth—and every tongue will confess that Jesus Christ is Lord, to the glory of God the Father (verses 9-11).

God says, "Before me every knee shall bow, every tongue shall confess" (see Isaiah 45:23). Paul tells us that because of His humility, Jesus is given the same honor as God. When we honor Jesus Christ, God is glorified. Jesus is seated in the highest place and is worthy of our worship and worthy of the name "Lord."

II. EXPOSITION AND APPLICATION OF THE SCRIPTURE

A. Recipe for Fulfilled Joy
(Philippians 2:1-2)

IF THERE be therefore any consolation in Christ, if any comfort of love, if any fellowship of the Spirit, if any bowels and mercies, Fulfil ye my joy, that ye be likeminded, having the same love, being of one accord, of one mind.

Paul's prerequisites for joy include several different ingredients that are highlighted throughout the chapter. The first necessary component for joy that is mentioned is being directly connected with Christ. This connection is absolutely necessary because without it we are operating in the flesh, and we will soon run out of energy and willpower. Jesus is the originator and the sustainer of genuine joy.

Everything else is a counterfeit. One contender to the throne is the common joy-imitator called happiness. Happiness is an emotional state of euphoria that is generally motivated by events, or happenings. Joy, however, is a more permanent emotion coming from God.

The second prerequisite for complete joy is God's love. Divine love distinguishes itself from human love, in that human love is limited and conditional, whereas God's love is unlimited and unconditional. Love and joy are close relatives, and when you have God's love you also experience God's joy. After love comes spiritual sharing and tender compassion. These specific characteristics are all just tributaries that freely flow from the wide river of God's inexhaustible love.

Once God's love is securely in place as a power source, joy is still not fully completed. This sense of completion refers to a spiritual state of progress and maturity that is beyond the basic entry-level minimum. Incomplete joy is a self-centered kind of joy that prospers only as long as one is able to get one's own way. But mature joy and complete joy see the bigger picture and can be satisfied even when things do not go your way—as long as the body at-large accomplishes its purpose and fulfills its destiny. Mature love and joy yield a harvest of one love, one spirit, and one mind. This state of unity is not necessarily uniformity. In the body of Christ, we do not have to be identical copies of each other in order to harmoniously coexist and even to thrive. A. T. Pierson described this spiritual state of unity with these words: "To a true child of God, the invisible bond that unites all believers to Christ is far more tender, and lasting, and precious; and, as we come to recognize and realize that we are all dwelling in one sphere of life in Him, we learn to look on every believer as our brother, in a sense that is infinitely higher than all human relationships. This is the one and only way to bring disciples permanently together. All other plans for promoting the unity of the Church have failed" (https://www.christianquotes .info/top-quotes/15-powerful-quotes-about-unity/#axzz59wINIfQT).

B. Selfishness versus Humility
(Philippians 2:3-4)

Let nothing be done through strife or vainglory; but in lowliness of mind let each esteem other better than themselves. Look not every man on his own things, but every man also on the things of others.

In Paul's detailed description of the nuances and components of corporate cooperation, we see a parallel picture of the fruit of the Spirit, which includes love, joy, peace, patience, kindness, goodness, faithfulness, gentleness, and self-control. Each spiritual fruit reflects evidence of the Holy Spirit's active presence in our daily lives. It is God's desire that we experience true sanctification.

These verses are written in the form of a command and forbid us to do anything or attempt anything that is motivated by the flesh, because in the flesh dwells no good thing. We are not to do anything while operating in a spirit or pattern that diminishes others while glorifying ourselves. Placing the needs and concerns of others before ourselves is not a naturally acquired tendency and requires God's spiritual influence and shaping to be successfully accomplished. But as we surrender to God's great guiding power, we will exhibit the ability to care more for others than ourselves. When this occurs, God will then providentially make sure that our own needs are fulfilled according to His riches in glory. This circle of care is often completed and accomplished within the atmosphere of true spiritual fellowship.

C. The Jesus Mindset Is the Model
(Philippians 2:5-8)

Let this mind be in you, which was also in Christ Jesus: Who, being in the form of God, thought it not robbery to be equal with God: But made himself of no reputation, and took upon him the form of a servant, and was made in the likeness of men: And being found in fashion as a man, he humbled himself, and became obedient unto death, even the death of the cross.

Within the body of Christ, there should be a distinct difference when compared to a regular human social group. In the fellowship of believers, we are held accountable by God for the way that we interact with each other. The Bible is filled with examples of the interactive relationships we should and should not have with each other. Scripture provides some positive examples of this interaction for us to observe and imitate. But Scripture also shares negative examples of believers who performed poorly and treated each other in ways that did not reflect love and dignity. From all these examples, we can learn what to do and what not to do.

While it is a good thing to learn from the positive interactions of fellow believers, the absolute sure way to fulfill God's expectations is to follow the example of Jesus in the ways that we think and act. "This was the highest example which could be furnished, and it would illustrate and confirm all the apostle had said of this virtue. The principle in the case is, that we are to make the Lord Jesus our model, and are in all respects to frame our lives, as far as possible, in accordance with this great example. The point here is, that he left a state of inexpressible glory, and took upon him the most humble form of humanity, and performed the most lowly offices, that he might benefit us" (*Barnes' Notes on the Bible*, http://biblehub.com/nasb/philippians/2-5.htm).

This phrase "made himself nothing" (verse 7) means that He "emptied (or, stripped) Himself of His glory by having taken on Him the form of a slave and having been made (or, born) in likeness of men" (*Ellicott's Commentary*). The "glory" is the "glory which He had with the Father before the world was" (see John 17:5; Philippians 1:14). He stripped Himself and took on the "form (or, nature) of a servant" of God. He resumed it for a moment in the Transfiguration and was crowned with it again at the Ascension.

Jesus exhibited the human side of Himself when the Word became flesh and dwelt among us, as reflected in John 1:14 (NIV): "The Word became flesh and made his dwelling among us. We have seen his glory, the glory of the one and only Son, who came from the Father, full of grace and truth." In the outward manifestation of the humanity of Jesus, there was "no form or comeliness," or "beauty, that they should desire Him" (Isaiah 53:2-3). "He became obedient," that is, to God's will, "even up to death." His death is not here only regarded as an atonement, for in that light it could be no pattern to us; but it is regarded as the completion of the obedience of His life (see Romans 5:19). Of that life as a whole, He said, "I came down from heaven, not to do mine own will, but the will of him that sent me" (John 6:38); and doing that will (see Hebrews 10:9-10) ended in "the offering of the body of Jesus Christ once for all." In this light, His death is the perfection of the suffering which, in consequence of the power of sin in the world, must be faced in doing the will of God (see 2 Timothy 3:12); in this light, we can follow it, and even "fill up what is lacking of the sufferings of Christ" (see Colossians 1:24).

D. Reward for Humility (Philippians 2:9-11)

Wherefore God also hath highly exalted him, and given him a name which is above every name: That at the name of Jesus every knee should bow, of things in heaven, and things in earth, and things under the earth; And that every tongue should confess that Jesus Christ is Lord, to the glory of God the Father.

Names are associated with power and significance. Among the Hebrews, when something was done in someone's name, it was an act of "utmost weight and potency," writes Orthodox Bishop Kallistos Ware.

Early Christians called upon the name of Jesus Christ for healing and deliverance. Always and everywhere the Church has celebrated the One whom God has "highly exalted" and to whom God has given "the name which is above every name, so that at the name of Jesus every knee should bend, in heaven and on earth and under the earth, and every tongue should confess that Jesus Christ is Lord." Those words (Phil. 2:5-11) are drawn from an ancient hymn and are quoted by Paul in his letter to the Philippians, written in the year 62." (*Society of Saint John the Evangelist,* "The Power of the Name of Jesus," David Vryhof, https://www.ssje.org/2017/01/01/the-power-of-the-name-of-jesus-br-david-vryhof/)

If every knee will eventually bow before the King of Kings (verse 10), one might wonder, Is this bowing down before God a thing that is coerced by God, or is it something that is done willingly and voluntarily? The act of physically bowing down is the universal sign of honor, respect, and humility. Whenever someone finds himself/herself in the presence of greatness and overwhelming power, the instinctive human reflex is to kneel and to bow. Nobody stands up straight when they are in the pathway of a tornado. Likewise, whenever God clearly speaks, whether through nature or through any other means, the knees must bow. Revelation 19:4 (NKJV) records that bowing is part of the regular activity in heaven: "And the twenty-four elders and the four living creatures fell down and worshiped God who sat on the throne, saying, 'Amen! Alleluia!'" If we all must bow to God eventually, it just makes good sense to get into practice now.

The term *Lord* is not just a formal name for Jesus. It is a title that describes the power and authority that belongs to God. The Hebrew prefix, *'adon,* means one possessed of absolute control. It denotes a master of slaves (see Genesis 24:14, 27), or a ruler of subjects (see Genesis 45:8). Due to a fearful reverence for the name *Jehovah,* the Jews, in reading their Scriptures, whenever that name occurred, always pronounced it "Adonai." The Greek word *kurios* refers to a supreme master. This term is invariably used for "Jehovah" and "Adonai" (Biblestudytools.com).

III. CONCLUDING REFLECTION

As long as there are people in the world, there will also be those who try to one-up others.

The defective gene of sin and selfishness often takes a terrible toll on human relationships. No marriage, no family, no church, no city, no race, or no country is exempt from this condition and its carnage. A personal relationship with Jesus Christ calls for us to be empowered by the Holy Spirit and thus to exhibit and reflect the personal characteristics of the Holy Spirit. As we interact with others, we set a good example or a bad example for those who are around us. When we claim Christ, but fail to reflect the fruit of the Spirit, our relationship with God becomes questionable. An intimate, obedient, growing, consistent relationship with God allows us to interact with other believers and to accomplish great things for the kingdom of God through being on one accord and of the same mind.

PRAYER

Lord, let the mind that was in Christ Jesus also be in us. As we interact with others, may the sweet fragrance of the Holy Spirit permeate our interactions and confirm to others that we have been with Jesus. In Jesus' name we pray. Amen.

HOME DAILY BIBLE READINGS
(January 21-27, 2019)

Devote All to Christ

MONDAY, January 21: "The Suffering Servant" (Isaiah 52:13–53:9)

TUESDAY, January 22: "Learning Godly Ways in Humility" (Psalm 119:65-72)

WEDNESDAY, January 23: "Message of the Good News" (1 Corinthians 15:1-11)

THURSDAY, January 24: "Learning Obedience through Suffering" (Hebrews 5:1-10)

FRIDAY, January 25: "Serve and Work for God's Pleasure" (Philippians 2:12-18)

SATURDAY, January 26: "Envoys of Ministry in Christ's Mission" (Philippians 2:19-30)

SUNDAY, January 27: "Your Call to Unity and Humility" (Philippians 2:1-11)

February 3, 2019   Lesson 10

RENOUNCE EVERYTHING FOR CHRIST

ADULT/YOUTH	CHILDREN
ADULT/YOUNG ADULT TOPIC: **Eyes on the Prize**	GENERAL LESSON TITLE: **Give Up All to Follow Christ**
YOUTH TOPIC: **Giving Everything Up**	CHILDREN'S TOPIC: **Personal Sacrifices**

DEVOTIONAL READING.
1 Corinthians 15:50-58

ADULT/YOUTH	CHILDREN
BACKGROUND SCRIPTURE: **Philippians 3:1-16**	BACKGROUND SCRIPTURE: **Philippians 3:1-16**
ADULT PRINT PASSAGE: **Philippians 3:7-14**	PRINT PASSAGE: **Philippians 3:7-14**
YOUTH PRINT PASSAGE: **Philippians 3:1-16**	KEY VERSE: **Philippians 3:7**
KEY VERSES: **Philippians 3:13-14**	

Philippians 3:7-14—KJV

7 But what things were gain to me, those I counted loss for Christ.

8 Yea doubtless, and I count all things but loss for the excellency of the knowledge of Christ Jesus my Lord: for whom I have suffered the loss of all things, and do count them but dung, that I may win Christ,

9 And be found in him, not having mine own righteousness, which is of the law, but that which is through the faith of Christ, the righteousness which is of God by faith:

10 That I may know him, and the power of his resurrection, and the fellowship of his sufferings, being made conformable unto his death;

11 If by any means I might attain unto the resurrection of the dead.

12 Not as though I had already attained, either were already perfect: but I follow after, if that I may apprehend that for which also I am apprehended of Christ Jesus.

Philippians 3:7-14—NIV

7 But whatever were gains to me I now consider loss for the sake of Christ.

8 What is more, I consider everything a loss because of the surpassing worth of knowing Christ Jesus my Lord, for whose sake I have lost all things. I consider them garbage, that I may gain Christ

9 and be found in him, not having a righteousness of my own that comes from the law, but that which is through faith in Christ—the righteousness that comes from God on the basis of faith.

10 I want to know Christ—yes, to know the power of his resurrection and participation in his sufferings, becoming like him in his death,

11 and so, somehow, attaining to the resurrection from the dead.

12 Not that I have already obtained all this, or have already arrived at my goal, but I press on to take hold of that for which Christ Jesus took hold of me.

13 Brethren, I count not myself to have apprehended: but this one thing I do, forgetting those things which are behind, and reaching forth unto those things which are before,

14 I press toward the mark for the prize of the high calling of God in Christ Jesus.

13 Brothers and sisters, I do not consider myself yet to have taken hold of it. But one thing I do: Forgetting what is behind and straining toward what is ahead,

14 I press on toward the goal to win the prize for which God has called me heavenward in Christ Jesus.

UNIFYING LESSON PRINCIPLE: People strive to enhance their standing before others by calling attention to their abilities and honors. What is the proper attitude toward our accomplishments? Paul told the Philippians that he willingly suffered the loss of his accomplishments press for the greater goal of gaining and being found in Christ.

LESSON OBJECTIVES

Upon the completion of this lesson, the students will be able to do the following:

1. Explore Paul's stated accomplishments and his purpose for sharing these with the Philippian believers.
2. Value their relationship with Christ above all other facets of their identity.
3. Learn to practice humble detachment from the credentials or accomplishments of which one could boast.

AGE-LEVEL POINTS TO BE EMPHASIZED

Teachers of ADULTS and YOUTH

—Verse 7 marks a transition from Paul describing what he previously viewed as great assets (verses 3-6) to what he came to realize were of relatively less value, even liabilities.

—The reference to becoming like Christ in His death in verse 10 probably refers to baptism as per Romans 6 and Colossians 2:11-15.

—Paul uses earthy language in this passage, saying he regards his past accomplishments as *skybalon* ("rubbish," verse 8). This word literally means "dung," "filth," or "refuse."

—Paul warned the Philippians against those who preached the necessity of circumcision, which meant they had to keep the laws of Judaism.

—The Pharisees were a group most concerned with the interpretation of the Jewish laws.

—Paul proclaimed that "righteousness [came] from God based on faith" (verse 9), which meant it was a free gift bestowed by God through the grace of Christ (see Romans 1:16–4:25).

—Paul's reference to "the goal" and "the prize" comes from popular sports, the Greek footraces, their finishing post, and the award to the winner (see verse 14; 2:16; 1 Corinthians 9:24-27).

Teachers of CHILDREN

—Paul reminded the Philippians to leave the past and wrong teachings behind.

—Paul warns believers against evildoers.

—Paul extols Christ as being excellent and supreme over all.

—Paul encourages Christians to grow spiritually.

—The righteousness and faith of God are experienced in the resurrection of Christ.

THE CHRONOLOGICAL SETTING OF THE LESSON

Prior to 359 BC, the city of Philippi was known as Krenides, the "The Little Fountains." In 359 BC, the city was annexed by Philip II, the father of Alexander the Great, and renamed after himself. Alexander made Philippi a great urban center of the east. It has been said that if Alexander the Great had not gone east, then Paul and the Gospel would not have gone west. The Greek language was made to be utilized on a widespread basis through the efforts of Philip and Alexander. In 146 BC, the city of Philippi came under the governorship of Rome and became one of its six primary provinces (Emeraldbible.com).

THE GEOGRAPHICAL AND CULTURAL SETTING OF THE LESSON

Philippi was located approximately ten miles northwest of Neapolis, which is present-day Kavalla in the heart of the Greek tobacco industry. It was well-known for its prosperous gold mining region, which is why Philip annexed the region of Macedonia. Philip financed his military pursuits with the gold yields from the region of Philippi. After 31 BC, when Philippi became a Roman colony, Philippi boasted all the privileges related to Rome and was considered somewhat of a "little Rome" planted outside of Italy. Most of the citizens were Romans, and they all exercised the legal, social, and religious rights thereunto pertaining to citizens of Rome with positions of praetors and local governors, which were officers that were usually only accorded to Roman colonies (Emeraldbible.com).

KEY TERMS IN THE LESSON

Faith (verse 9)—Greek: *pistis* **(pis'-tis):** faith; belief; trust; confidence; fidelity; faithfulness.

Gain(s) (verse 7)—Greek: *kerdos* **(ker'-dos):** gain; advantage; profit.

Knowledge (verse 8)—Greek: *gnósis* **(gno'-sis):** a "knowing" (NIV); doctrine; wisdom.

Loss (verse 7)—Greek: *zémia* **(dzay-mee'-ah):** damage; loss; detriment.

Power (verse 10)—Greek: *dunamis* **(doo'-nam-is):** might; power (miraculous); marvelous works; strength.

Righteousness (verse 9)—Greek: *dikaiosuné* **(dik-ah-yos-oo'-nay):** justice; justness; righteousness.

TOPICAL OUTLINE OF THE LESSON

I. **Introduction**
   A. Stand Firm
   B. Biblical Background

II. **Exposition and Application of the Scripture**
   A. My Gain Is Loss (Philippians 3:7-9)
   B. To Know Christ (Philippians 3:10-11)
   C. Pressing toward the Mark (Philippians 3:12-14)

III. **Concluding Reflection**

I. INTRODUCTION

A. Stand Firm

In chapter 3, the apostle Paul explained what rejoicing in the Lord is all about. His intentions are for us to understand and learn to derive our joy from our salvation, from our relationship with God, and from the service that follows. In the opening verse, the statement "rejoice in the Lord" summarizes Paul's intentions in chapter 3. The same is true for the statement "in this way stand firm in the Lord" in 4:1. This somewhat summarizes his entire message in chapter 3.

In the preceding chapters, Paul had already shown the people how he rejoiced in that the Gospel is being preached (see 1:18), and also how he was happy and rejoicing in his ministry (see 2:17). He further called them in 2:18 to rejoice with him. Paul, with his warm pastoral heart, does not delay in writing this out again so that they, and apparently, we, see Christ and the Gospel as our highest joy. In fact, he urged us to see it as our only reasonable boast and joy.

Paul furthermore exhorted his readers with a command to exhibit humility. He gave a negative example and three positive examples. He gave the command to rejoice in the Lord, and he gave the negative example of having confidence in the flesh in 3:2-7. He also gave the positive example in 3:9 of enjoying Christ's righteousness.

B. Biblical Background

In this passage, Paul gave his personal testimony about the posture of our confidence. He acknowledged his former pattern of putting confidence in his works, which were of no true benefit. According to Jeremiah 9:23, confidence in such things works against us and separates us from having confidence in Jesus Christ. Gaining more Christ control is the idea presented in verse 8. This idea simply shows that knowing Christ could refer to being redeemed and to being in God's family, as in Ezekiel 38:16, Jeremiah 24:7; 31:34, and Galatians 4:9. It can also refer to a rich, deep, and joyful personal closeness to God, as in Daniel 11:32 and 1 John 2:14; 5:20. In a few chosen words, Paul emphasizes what it is to rejoice in the Lord. He desires to experience the power of His resurrection more deeply. This is also what he prayed to happen in the lives of the Ephesian congregation in Ephesians 1:18-20.

Because Christ "humbled Himself, becoming obedient to death, even death on a cross," Paul stated that "God exalted Him, and gave Him a name that is above every name" (see Philippians 2:9). Having received more than a resurrection body, the Lord Jesus also attained His exaltation as a reward of His humble obedience. Paul, in this same manner, participates in His sufferings, to attain the resurrection of the dead. Paul's attaining the resurrection of the dead is in line with the exaltation of the Lord Jesus. Both are dependent upon suffering, humility, and obedience.

In verses 12-16, Paul once more stressed the need to focus on heaven and the higher calling of eternity. He went on to describe the zeal for his calling which can be described as a single-minded or complete focus, with which he pursued this status. We know, however, that he had not forgotten the past and would not allow himself to be distracted by such issues. Likewise, Paul did not embrace his old misguided efforts to justify himself through the Law or his more recent success in being devoted to Christ (as in verse 10). He would not rely on either of these because his focus is on the race which was before him.

Imagine how strenuous Paul's work was. He used terms like *strain*, *seize*, and *pursue*. These terms indicate hard work. In some ways, these terms might seem somewhat inappropriate for any discussion about receiving the free gift of eternal life. But what Paul is describing is the diligent work and suffering required, not to obtain citizenship in God's kingdom, but to gain resurrection. His desire is to reign with Christ our Savior in His kingdom. These are the things he was striving for with such single-minded diligence.

Paul referred to the prize as a crown in 1 Corinthians 9:25; 2 Timothy 2:5; and 4:8. It is called "the reward of an inheritance" in Colossians 3:24. In this context, Paul had no assurance that he would succeed. He wrote of the possibility of being disqualified in 1 Corinthians 9:27. In 2 Timothy 2:5, he reminded Timothy and indeed all believers that we need to compete according to the rules to win the crown. In 2 Timothy 4:7-8, we read that once Paul finished the race, he would receive a crown and further, that such a crown will be given to all who love God's appearing. These are not preconditions for salvation, but they are conditions for receiving a reward for hard work (Biblestudytools.com).

II. EXPOSITION AND APPLICATION OF THE SCRIPTURE

A. My Gain Is Loss
(Philippians 3:7-9)

But what things were gain to me, those I counted loss for Christ. Yea doubtless, and I count all things but loss for the excellency of the knowledge of Christ Jesus my Lord: for whom I have suffered the loss of all things, and do count them but dung, that I may win Christ, And be found in him, not having mine own righteousness, which is of the law, but that which is through the faith of Christ, the righteousness which is of God by faith.

It has been said that one person's trash is another one's treasure, and that beauty is in the eye of the beholder. These phrases are just other ways to say that various people place various value on different things.

Contemporary culture claims that the following items have value: wealth, sex appeal and physical appearance, fame, talent, expensive houses, cars, education, possessions, and position. Not much has changed since Paul's time of writing this text. After Paul added up everything in his lifetime credit column, the grand total equaled less than zero. Other translations replace the concept of "loss" with the word *dung* later in the passage. *Ellicott's Commentary* contends that this total is "not merely worthless, but worse than worthless," because "gaining all the world" tends to result in the loss of one's own soul. "St. Paul first applies this declaration to the Jewish privilege and dignity of which he had spoken. Then, not content with this, he extends it to 'all things' which were his to sacrifice for Christ."

It is difficult to understand and to concur with the rationale of counting all things as loss unless one's greatest joy is found in Jesus. Anyone who believes that there is more value in the material than the spiritual will continue to chase after the material and continue to be disappointed. The wise will seek first the kingdom of God and His righteousness, and everything else will be added.

The value and worth of some things lie in their rarity, their performance, or some other advantage they give to the one who possesses them (verse 8). A relationship with God helps us to remove the option of self-assertion and prideful independence, because no human can ever take credit for anything that is initiated by God. With great clarity and confidence, Paul artfully articulated the central aim, purpose, and mission of his life: "knowing Christ Jesus my Lord" (verse 8). "It is not everybody who dares to say what is his aim in life. We are ashamed to acknowledge even to ourselves what we are not at all ashamed to do. Paul knew his aim, and was not afraid to speak it. It was high and noble, and was passionately and persistently pursued. He tells us it here, and we can see his soul kindling as he speaks" (*Expositions of Holy Scripture: Second Corinthians, Galatians, and Philippians—Chapters: I to End. Colossians, Thessalonians, and First Timothy, Alexander MacLaren*). The purpose of life is to find and fulfill a life of purpose. Unfortunately, most people are born, live their lives, and die without ever truly discovering why they were born.

No matter what our specific purpose may be, our general, all-purpose spiritual assignment is found in Proverbs 3:5-6 (NIV): "Trust in the LORD with all your heart and lean not on your own understanding; in all your ways submit to him, and he will make your paths straight." Embracing our general spiritual assignment enables us to successfully discover and implement our individual mission in life. A life without God is a life of temporary distractions cluttered with worthless refuse.

Righteousness that is based on the Law is inadequate righteousness, because Law-based righteousness is tied to and dependent upon works (verse 9). Works are important, and ultimately works will emerge from a dedicated, obedient life. But our salvation comes by grace through faith. "For it is by grace you have been saved, through faith—and this is not from yourselves, it is the gift of God—not by works, so that no one can boast" (Ephesians 2:8-9, NIV). We are God's workmanship and we were created for good works in Christ, but those works are empowered through our relationship with God and not just through our own human efforts.

Prior to Paul's conversion, he sought to obtain self-earned, Law-based righteousness. In retrospect, he realized that all such efforts are utterly in vain.

All people by nature seek salvation by the law. They set up some standard which they mean to comply with, and expect to be saved by conformity to that. With some it is the law of honor, with others the law of honesty, with others the law of kindness and courtesy, and with others the law of God. If they comply with the requirements of these laws, they suppose that they will be safe, and it is only the grace of God showing them how defective their standard is, or how far they come from complying with its demands, that can ever bring them from this dangerous dependence. Paul in early life depended on his compliance with the laws of God as he understood them, and supposed that he was safe. When he was brought to realize his true condition, he saw how far short he had come of what the law of God required, and that all dependence on his own works was vain."[1]

B. To Know Christ
(Philippians 3:10-11)

That I may know him, and the power of his resurrection, and the fellowship of his sufferings, being made conformable unto his death; If by any means I might attain unto the resurrection of the dead.

This powerful Scripture is packed with spiritual depth and insight. At first glance, it may seem strange for the apostle Paul, who crafted three-fourths of the New Testament, to write a phrase desiring to know Christ. Paul's usage of the words "to know" reach beyond a casual, surface acquaintance. In *The Pulpit Commentary,* Dr. Wescott shares, "Knowledge expresses the apprehension of the truth by the whole nature of man. It is not an acquaintance with facts as external, nor an intellectual conviction of their reality, but an appropriation of them (so to speak) as an influencing power into the very being of him who knows them."

Three different levels of knowing Christ are articulated in the passage. Level 1 is an introductory level, and it is the power of His resurrection. The *Jamieson-Fausset-Brown Bible Commentary* identifies this level as one that empowers believers and focuses on "raising them up spiritually with Him, by virtue of their identification with Him in this, as in all the acts of His redeeming work for us (see Romans 6:4; Colossians 2:12; 3:1). The power of the Divine Spirit, which raised Him from literal death, is the same which raises believers from spiritual death now (see Ephesians 1:19-20), and shall raise their bodies from literal death hereafter (see Romans 8:11)."

Level 2 of knowing Christ gets more serious. This is the level of the fellowship of His sufferings. It identifies with Christ in His sufferings and death. This calls for the believer also to bear a cross after the example of Jesus Christ. Many stop short at this level because of their distaste for the discomfort of afflictions (see Colossians 1:24; Matthew 10:38; 16:24; 2 Timothy 2:11). Just as Jesus bore all our sufferings (according to Isaiah 53:4), so we participate in His.

Level 3 of knowing Christ is the harshest of them all. It is the level of being conformed to His death. This means we must be willing to put to death the things of the flesh in order to experience God's full and powerful life (see Romans 8:29; 1 Corinthians 15:31; 2 Corinthians 4:10-12; Galatians 2:20).

Paul did not end the three stages of knowing Christ with the stage of death, but paralleling the life of Jesus, Paul added the fourth stage of resurrection. The resurrection stage is Paul's ultimate goal, because this stage would result in perfect, unbroken knowledge of Christ and fellowship with Christ. In the text, it may sound like Paul had doubts about his attaining this stage when he used the word *somehow*. *The Expositor's Greek New Testament* offers this explanation:

> Paul knows by experience the difficulty of remaining loyal to the end, of being so conformed to Christ's death that the power of sin will not revive its mastery over him. So his apparent uncertainty here of reaching the goal is not distrust of God. It is distrust of himself. (*The Expositor's Greek Testament, Vol. III*, p. 456)

C. Pressing toward the Mark
(Philippians 3:12-14)

Not as though I had already attained, either were already perfect: but I follow after, if that I may apprehend that for which also I am apprehended of Christ Jesus. Brethren, I count not myself to have apprehended: but this one thing I do, forgetting those things which are behind, and reaching forth unto those things which are before, I press toward the mark for the prize of the high calling of God in Christ Jesus.

Paul is the first to harness his humility and to admit the fact that he had not yet arrived but was still in the process of becoming all that God would have him to be. Paul's use of the phrase "I was laid hold of by Jesus Christ" is how he described his conversion. He obviously did not see it coming, and possibly he would not have changed unless a hand had been laid upon him.

Paul spoke from the perch of a ripe-old age, and this notion of forgetting what lie behind applied to past blessings, past achievements, and even past sins. This statement provides insight into the content of Paul's character, as he advised all believers to be simultaneously oblivious and anticipatory. It almost sounds like a contradiction of terms to be both forgetful and remembering. But perfection in this focus lies in the direction of the focus. We cannot be successful in forgetting what lies ahead and anticipating what lies behind. When we walk forward while looking backwards, we risk running into unseen objects.

In spite of all his accomplishments, Paul refused to retire and to rest on his many laurels. He dared not even take a glance back (see Luke 9:62). Instead, he was in eager pursuit of perfection. Paul's idea of perfection was not in money, a mate, or material matters. For Paul, perfection was manifested in the fulfillment of God's calling on his life. The imagery of pressing toward the mark is borrowed from the Olympic games staged in Athens, Greece. Each runner would strain his/her muscles to the maximum with the hope of being the first to cross the line and claim the prize. For the Olympic runners, their prize was a laurel crown made of vines. But God offers a crown of life that will never fade. This focus on the spiritual prize rather than on earthly pursuits is reflected in the lyrics of the classic song "Only What You Do for Christ Will Last."

III. CONCLUDING REFLECTION

In life, we would do well to intentionally assess the relative values of things in light of God's perspective rather than our own. When we align our lives to the will of God, we find direction and energy for the long haul. A life lived pleasing God does not give us a guarantee to be problem-free. To the contrary, we are guaranteed some suffering, but we are also guaranteed to be supplied with the power to overcome any obstacle that life and circumstances may present. It is hoped that age, wisdom, and experience will teach us to wait upon the Lord and to be of good courage, knowing that God has promised to strengthen our hearts. As we develop spiritual maturity and discernment, we will begin to see all of life from a godly perspective in order to correctly evaluate the relative importance of spiritual and secular things.

PRAYER

Lord, thank You for the struggles of life, for in our struggles we gain strength. We trust You to walk with us through every phase and stage of our lives so that we may win in the end. In Jesus' name we pray. Amen.

HOME DAILY BIBLE READINGS
(January 28–February 3, 2019)

Renounce Everything for Christ

MONDAY, January 28: "A Matter of the Heart" (Romans 2:25-29)

TUESDAY, January 29: "Persistent Faith" (Mark 7:24-30)

WEDNESDAY, January 30: "Paul's Solid Credentials for Ministry" (2 Corinthians 11:21b-30)

THURSDAY, January 31: "Boast in Christ Jesus" (Philippians 3:1-6)

FRIDAY, February 1: "Live as Heavenly Citizens" (Philippians 3:17–4:1)

SATURDAY, February 2: "Guard Your Heart and Mind" (Philippians 4:2-9)

SUNDAY, February 3: "Be of the Same Mind" (Philippians 3:7-14)

---

1. *Barnes' Notes on the Bible,* http://biblehub.com/nasb/philippians/3-9.htm

February 10, 2019 | **Lesson 11**

PONDERING GOD'S STEADFAST LOVE

ADULT/YOUTH	CHILDREN
ADULT/YOUNG ADULT TOPIC: Some Things Never Change	**GENERAL LESSON TITLE: Praise God's Everlasting Love**
YOUTH TOPIC: It's a Love Thing	**CHILDREN'S TOPIC: An Everlasting Love**

DEVOTIONAL READING
Psalm 93

ADULT/YOUTH	CHILDREN
BACKGROUND SCRIPTURE: **Psalm 48:1-3, 9-14**	BACKGROUND SCRIPTURE: **Psalm 48:1-3, 9-14**
PRINT PASSAGE: **Psalm 48:1-3, 9-14**	PRINT PASSAGE: **Psalm 48:1-3, 9-14**
ADULT KEY VERSE: **Psalm 48:14**	KEY VERSE: **Psalm 48:9**
YOUTH KEY VERSE: **Psalm 48:9**	

Psalm 48:1-3, 9-14—KJV

GREAT IS the LORD, and greatly to be praised in the city of our God, in the mountain of his holiness.

2 Beautiful for situation, the joy of the whole earth, is mount Zion, on the sides of the north, the city of the great King.

3 God is known in her palaces for a refuge.

.....

9 We have thought of thy lovingkindness, O God, in the midst of thy temple.

10 According to thy name, O God, so is thy praise unto the ends of the earth: thy right hand is full of righteousness.

11 Let mount Zion rejoice, let the daughters of Judah be glad, because of thy judgments.

12 Walk about Zion, and go round about her: tell the towers thereof.

13 Mark ye well her bulwarks, consider her palaces; that ye may tell it to the generation following.

Psalm 48:1-3, 9-14—NIV

GREAT IS the LORD, and most worthy of praise, in the city of our God, his holy mountain.

2 Beautiful in its loftiness, the joy of the whole earth, like the heights of Zaphon is Mount Zion, the city of the Great King.

3 God is in her citadels; he has shown himself to be her fortress.

.....

9 Within your temple, O God, we meditate on your unfailing love.

10 Like your name, O God, your praise reaches to the ends of the earth; your right hand is filled with righteousness.

11 Mount Zion rejoices, the villages of Judah are glad because of your judgments.

12 Walk about Zion, go around her, count her towers,

13 consider well her ramparts, view her citadels, that you may tell of them to the next generation.

14 For this God is our God for ever and ever: he will be our guide even unto death.

14 For this God is our God for ever and ever; he will be our guide even to the end.

UNIFYING LESSON PRINCIPLE: In a world of constant change, nothing seems permanent or of abiding worth. What abides when everything else seems to be in flux? The psalmist pondered the steadfast, everlasting, and all-inclusive love of God while worshipping God in the Temple.

LESSON OBJECTIVES

Upon the completion of this lesson, the students will be able to do the following:
1. Analyze the psalmist's declarations about the value of worshipping God in the Temple.
2. Ponder how God's steadfast love is manifest in one's own life.
3. Plan ways to celebrate God's love through private and corporate worship.

AGE-LEVEL POINTS TO BE EMPHASIZED

Teachers of ADULTS and YOUTH

—Psalm 48:1 responds appropriately to the depiction of God's enthronement and the proclamation of God's universal sovereignty in Psalm 47 (verses 2, 5, 7-9).

—The word translated as "steadfast love," *hesed*, connects Psalm 48 to Exodus 15. It was God's guidance in "steadfast love" that delivered God's people through the Exodus; the people think about God's "steadfast love" in the Temple in Psalm 48. "Steadfast love" describes God's fundamental character.

—"Mount Zion" refers to the acropolis of Jerusalem on which the Temple stood. It is used poetically to refer to the city in its entirety. The rabbis taught that Mount Zion was the only mountain not covered by Noah's flood.

—Ancient Jews believed that God caused His name to dwell in the Temple (see Deuteronomy 12).

—Psalm 48 is a hymn to Zion, the place of God's peace.

—Instead of a historical battle, the verses refer to a symbolic gathering of kingdoms that rebel against the Lord's governance.

—The magnificence of Jerusalem stood as testament to God's power, so the nations capitulated.

—The Bible pictures Jerusalem as the place where believers will gather in the "last days" (Isaiah 2:2ff) and as the spiritual home of all believers where God will live among them (Revelation 21:2-3).

—The Temple buildings memorialize the Lord's steadfast love (Hebrew: *hesed*).

Teachers of CHILDREN

—Zion is understood to be both a literal and a symbolic dwelling place for God.

—Zion represents God's strength, power, and love to people of faith.

—God's love is unconditional and everlasting.

—God is the guide for the people of faith.

—God is the place for safety and protection.

THE CHRONOLOGICAL SETTING OF THE LESSON

The date of writing for Psalm 48 is unknown. It is evidently a song of triumph that some believe was written on the occasion of Jehoshaphat's victory (see 2 Chronicles 20). Others hold that it was at the time of Sennacherib's defeat, when his army laid siege to Jerusalem in Hezekiah's time (*Blue Letter Bible*). Several other psalms have titles that are similar to the title for this one, including Psalms 42, 44–49, 84–85, and 87–88.

THE GEOGRAPHICAL AND CULTURAL SETTING OF THE LESSON

It would be unwise to absolutely attribute this song to any one single event in Jewish history. The passage records "the withdrawal of certain confederate kings from Jerusalem, their courage failing them before striking a blow. The mention of the ships of Tarshish may allow us to conjecture that the Psalm was written in connection with the overthrow of Ammon, Moab, and Edom in the reign of Jehoshaphat" (http://www.sacred-texts.com/bib/cmt/tod/psa048.htm). From Psalm 48:4-8 the song records the confusion of Zion's foes, ascribing all the praise to God (see Psalm 48:9-11), extolling Zion, and proclaiming Jehovah to be God forevermore (biblestudytools.com).

KEY TERMS IN THE LESSON

Beautiful (verse 2)—Hebrew: *yapheh* (yaw-feh'): fair; beautiful.

Earth (verse 2)—Hebrew: *erets* (eh'-rets): earth; land.

Forever (verse 14)—Hebrew: *olam* (o-lawm'): long duration; antiquity; futurity; "for ever" (KJV/NIV).

God (verse 14)—Hebrew: *elohim* (el-o-heem'): refers to the one true God.

Greatly (verse 1)—Hebrew: *meod* (meh-ode'): very; muchness; force; abundance; "most" (NIV).

Rejoice(s) (verse 11)—Hebrew: *samach* (saw-makh'): rejoice; be glad.

TOPICAL OUTLINE OF THE LESSON

I. **Introduction**
   A. Songs of Praise
   B. Biblical Background

II. **Exposition and Application of the Scripture**
   A. The City of God (Psalm 48:1-3)
   B. Let the High Praise Begin (Psalm 48:9-11)
   C. The God beyond the Building (Psalm 48:12-14)

III. **Concluding Reflection**

I. INTRODUCTION

A. Songs of Praise

Psalm 48 sings the praises of Zion, the city of God and the city of the great King (48:1-2). This psalm is a companion to Psalms 46 and 47, which also proclaim God's victory over His enemies. The psalmist here affirms that God's magnificent rule belongs only to the godly ones who are the residents of Zion. Mount Zion represents the vision of God's kingdom. His kingdom is greater than Jerusalem, though it is given the visible expression/description of Jerusalem.

God delights in those who submit themselves to His rule and have chosen to establish His kingdom with them (see Psalm 132:13). Zion inspires God's people with hope, joy, adoration, and commitment to the great King. The "godly," here, refers to those ones who live and act in anticipation of the vision of Zion. This was the basis for praise, ethics, and evangelism (48:8-14). This vision of Zion as God's city and dwelling place is also not just for the Jews alone. The New Testament also makes reference and applies this Old Testament vision to the church (see Galatians 4:26; Ephesians 2:11-22).

B. Biblical Background

Psalm 48 tells about the Jewish vision of God's city and dwelling place, which is Zion. From the perspective of the New Testament, we may apply it to the church, which has been grafted in to believing Israel (see Romans 11:17-24). God promises here to establish Zion forever (see Psalm 48:8). Jesus also promised in Matthew 16:18 to establish His church forever. As God's temple, we are His dwelling place (see 1 Corinthians 3:16), and this concept allows Psalm 48 to have direct application to us.

Here, we see this psalm joyously proclaiming God's greatness, as seen in the splendor of His city and His miraculous deliverance from the hands of enemies. While most parts of this psalm would lead one to think that it primarily praises Zion's beauty, the first and last verses show that it is a psalm about God's greatness seen through His city. God's city is meant to proclaim the praise of His salvation to the earth and all generations.

Psalm 48 can be categorized into three parts. The first part shows that the purpose of God's city is to proclaim His holiness, power, greatness, joy, and grace (verses 1-3). God's greatness reaches far beyond the highest heaven, and we should worship Him with all our being. The psalmist further describes God's city as "His holy mountain" and adds that this mountain is beautiful to view. The world may think of holiness as boring, but the truth is that the God of the Bible is holy and beautiful (see Psalms 27:4; 96:6; Isaiah 33:17). This means that holiness refers to beauty, and as God's people we are to be holy just as He is holy (see Leviticus 11:44).

The second part shows God's deliverance of His city from powerful enemies (verses 4-8). Verse 4 tells how these kings joined together to assess the city and conquer it. They were already proud and confident, but then in verse 5 when they actually saw it, they were so amazed that they became terrified and had to flee in alarm. The psalmist describes their state of alarm. First, he says they are in anguish as a woman in childbirth (48:6). Second, he describes them like ships on the Mediterranean Sea, broken up by an east wind (48:7). Historically, the ships of Tarshish represented the strongest and largest ships of the time (see 1 Kings 10:22). But when God raises a powerful wind to deliver His city, the mighty ships become like matchsticks and are tossed and broken by the sea (see Ezekiel 27:25-27; Revelation 18:17-20). God uses such experiences to humble us and to showcase His great power. This absolutely should be the testimony of every true child of God. Our testimony can add to the story of others, proclaiming that the Lord of hosts is powerful and has rescued us from evil's destructive grasp and has placed us in His city, one which He will establish forever.

The third and final part shows that God deserves praise from His city for His great salvation. As we proclaim the Gospel of Christ, we must always tell of God's righteousness (see Acts 24:25). His mighty deliverances and mighty works would bring the earth and her people to trust in His might and saving grace. This is a divine gift of revelation to be known by every generation.

Psalm 48 shows us how the history and destiny of the people of God is connected with God Himself. God is our God, and this fact gives us a sense of peace when we are experiencing unpleasant circumstances. We have a sense of purpose to serve God's great cause of proclaiming His glory to every people and a greater sense of belonging as part of the city of this great King.

II. EXPOSITION AND APPLICATION OF THE SCRIPTURE

A. The City of God
(Psalm 48:1-3)

GREAT IS the LORD, and greatly to be praised in the city of our God, in the mountain of his holiness. Beautiful for situation, the joy of the whole earth, is mount Zion, on the sides of the north, the city of the great King. God is known in her palaces for a refuge.

Psalm 48 begins with a divine declaration regarding the undisputed greatness of almighty God. This declaration stood in direct contrast to the similar declarations of the Ephesian mob in Acts 19 that for hours shouted, "Great is Diana of the Ephesians," in tribute to the pagan idol who was so popular at that time in that region. This tribute to a foreign deity may seem strange to modern ears, but the principle is the same when we in contemporary times by our actions proclaim, "Great is my money," or "Great is my new car," or "Great is my technology." Whatever it is that we devote our best time and energy to becomes our god. Modern gods include the following:

1. **Materialism**—This god feeds our never-ending need for fulfillment through the acquisition of more "stuff." Our homes become filled with countless possessions. We are lulled into the false need to build bigger and bigger houses with more and more closet space in order to store all the things we buy, many of which still have the price tag attached and many of which are reflected on our unpaid credit card balances.

2. **Workaholism**—This god often takes the form of careers and jobs. Many people spend sixty to eighty hours a week working. On weekends and during vacations, our laptops are still active and our minds are whirling with thoughts of how to be more successful. In the meantime, our children are starved for love and attention.

3. **Naturalism and the power of science**—We reject God's description of how He created the world and we accept the concept of atheistic evolution. Through embracing the goddess of naturalism, we fool ourselves into thinking we have the power to indefinitely preserve the earth. We have the responsibility of stewardship of this world, but not guardianship—and certainly not ownership.

4. **Selfishness**—We exclude others and their needs in order to concentrate on our own desires. This is shown through indulgence in alcohol, drugs, and food. Wealthy countries

have unlimited access to alcohol and drugs, while poor countries struggle to meet the basic needs of food and clean water.

5. Fill in the blank—There is no limit to the ways that we create idols for ourselves. But no matter how hard we may try, there is simply no substitute for the power of Jehovah God (gotquestions.org).

When the text reads, "In the city of our God . . . in his holy mountain" (verse 1), these words are not intended to indicate the location where praise is due to God, but the place where God resides. The presence of God in His chosen city glorifies and secures the city like nothing else in heaven or upon earth could ever accomplish. In verse 3, God is even "in" the palaces of the nobles as "a refuge." Jesus Himself referred to Jerusalem as "the city of the Great King" (Matthew 5:35).

God also indwells the New Jerusalem, which is His holy church. After having already been identified as the Holy City in verse 1, Mount Zion is also described as beautiful and as being connected to joy. This connection may seem unusual because "the world does not think of holiness and joy in the same breath, unless to contrast them as opposites! But they always go together in the Bible. Some try to limit this to the joy of the whole land, meaning, the land of Israel, because there never has been a time when Jerusalem has been the joy of the whole earth" (https://bible.org/book/export/html/21949).

One of the challenging phrases to understand in this verse is the phrase "in the far north."

The NIV transliterates the Hebrew word for "north" as Zaphon, which was a pagan mountain north of Ugarit where Baal was worshipped. This line of interpretation argues that Israel borrowed from Canaanite and other pagan religions the idea that the supreme place where the gods reigned was a mountain in the north. But the Jews contended that the living and true God reigned in the north, on Mount Zion. (https://bible.org/book/export/html/21949)

But the point of the reference is that as representatives of the city of the great King, we should extend God's joy throughout the whole earth. In order to proclaim God's joy, we must actively experience it as we rejoice daily in God's great salvation. Thus, God's city should proclaim God's greatness, holiness, and joy (https://bible.org/book/export/html/21949).

The presence of God provides access to the power of God. As we stay connected to God's Spirit, we are able to display God's power and to live in this world, but not be of this world. This concept is illustrated by the ability of a life raft to float in the water, but not to be overcome by the water. As long as it remains on top of the water, it provides life. But as soon as it submerges, it could bring death. The way to live a life that impacts the world without allowing the world to impact us is reflected in the High Priestly Prayer of Jesus found in John 17:15-21. The first section of the psalm focuses on God's greatness, holiness, joy, and power. His power is especially displayed in the second section.

B. Let the High Praise Begin
(Psalm 48:9-11)

We have thought of thy lovingkindness, O God, in the midst of thy temple. According to thy name, O God, so

is thy praise unto the ends of the earth: thy right hand is full of righteousness. Let mount Zion rejoice, let the daughters of Judah be glad, because of thy judgments.

Spending time in an environment such as the Temple of God provides the type of atmosphere in which we may meditate on God's love that never fails. An atmosphere of corporate worship is a precious, powerful, and simultaneously delicate moment in the life of God's people when many people may be present, but it seems like just God and you.

Author Yinka Vidal wrote this very insightful commentary regarding worship:

> Worshiping God is not about dancing, preaching, praying, or even reading the Word of God. All those activities just mentioned can lead us into the worship realm. These rituals by themselves are not worship. In the church today, we go through the list of programs as Sunday rituals. Once the list is completed, we assumed that we have worshipped God. What is the difference in going to an opera, a concert, a movie theatre, or a ball game? There is no difference because those four activities are based on entertainment. Some people attend church services on Sunday as spectators. . . . Worshipping of God happens in an atmosphere we create with the help of the Holy Spirit that is conducive to the opening of the Portals of Heaven. Spiritual worship is the product of learning to walk in the Spirit of God. Without a walk in the Spirit of God, creating an atmosphere of spiritual worship is very difficult if not impossible.[1]

The writer equates the name of God with the praise of God, which is a sentiment also reflected in Psalm 145:3 (NIV)—"Great is the LORD and most worthy of praise; his greatness no one can fathom." In biblical times, names carried a great deal more significance than they seem to carry today. One's name reflected one's character. In this verse, we see that God's character and God's deeds are both extensive. Both of them reach unto the ends of the earth, which essentially means over all the regions known to the writer. His right hand is full of righteousness, and He has dealt out a righteous judgment by His hand, thereby showing how His hand is full of justice and judgment (*Pulpit Commentary*).

The righteousness of God is one of the most important characteristics of God. The righteousness of God is almost identical to the justice of God.

> When we say that God is just, we are saying that He always does what is right, what should be done, and that He does it consistently, without partiality or prejudice. The word just and the word righteous are identical in both the Old Testament and the New Testament. Sometimes the translators render the original word 'just' and other times 'righteous' with no apparent reason (cf. Nehemiah 9:8 and 9:33 where the same word is used). But whichever word they use, it means essentially the same thing. It has to do with God's actions. They are always right and fair. God's righteousness (or justice) is the natural expression of His holiness. If He is infinitely pure, then He must

be opposed to all sin, and that opposition to sin must be demonstrated in His treatment of His creatures. When we read that God is righteous or just, we are being assured that His actions toward us are in perfect agreement with His holy nature.[2]

Human righteousness is measured by conformity to an exterior moral and spiritual standard. God, however, has no exterior apparatus by which to measure and codify His righteousness.

The reason why the inhabitants of the Holy City are able to openly express their joy is because God's judgments are ultimately beneficial to anyone impacted by them. "Let the daughters of Judah be glad" (verse 11). The Hebrew word translated "towns" in other places literally means "daughters." "The daughters of Judah are not the maidens of Judah, though the fact that women were wont to celebrate victories with dance and song may have suggested the use of the expression, but the cities of Judah, which had been captured by Sennacherib (Isaiah 36:1), and therefore had special cause for rejoicing at his overthrow. Country towns are regarded as 'daughters' of the metropolis (Numbers 21:25; Joshua 17:11; 17:16)" (*Cambridge Bible for Schools and Colleges*).

C. The God beyond the Building (Psalm 48:12-14)

Walk about Zion, and go round about her: tell the towers thereof. Mark ye well her bulwarks, consider her palaces; that ye may tell it to the generation following. For this God is our God for ever and ever: he will be our guide even unto death.

Hebrew culture is inundated with instances in which each generation is reminded to extend the spiritual knowledge, awareness, and experiences from the current generation to the next. The importance of this phenomenon in Hebrew culture cannot be overemphasized. "After that whole generation had been gathered to their ancestors, another generation grew up who knew neither the LORD nor what he had done for Israel" (Judges 2:10, NIV). Moses passed the spiritual mantle on to Joshua in the Old Testament, and in the New Testament Paul passed the mantle of leadership and experience to Timothy. "We cannot assume [that] past faithfulness will continue or that future generations will be aware of the great historical legacy available to them. The passing on of our faith must continue to be refreshed with each generation. Each generation must be taught who God is, and what He has done for humankind. Through studying the life of Timothy, we will discover God has given us a model of how to pass on our faith to our children" (https://www.biola.edu/blogs/good-book-blog/2014/passing-on-our-faith-one-generation-to-another).

God is confirmed as the ultimate lifetime provider and protector. As long as we depend on God, God will never leave the eternal post of the ultimate defender. Once is not enough for God. Like a shepherd tending his sheep, God will exercise tender care and oversight to ensure our safe passage over the hills of life and through the valley of death. This guarantee of God's divine oversight is usually cast as a conditional promise, such as is found in Hebrews 13:5-6 (NIV): "Keep your lives free from the love of money and be content with what you have, because God has said, 'Never will I leave you; never will I forsake you.' So we say with confidence, 'The Lord is my helper; I will not be afraid. What can mere mortals do to me?'"

III. CONCLUDING REFLECTION

As worshippers, we are witnesses to God's character and will. Ancient Jewish people believed that God caused His name to dwell in the Temple, and they considered Jerusalem to be the center of the earth. However, as long as we worship God in spirit and in truth, regardless of geographical location, God is present in that place and in the heart, mind, and spirit of the one who worships. We can celebrate God's love through both private and corporate worship. Although Jerusalem will always be a special place for worship, the Word of God proclaims that the entire earth is the Lord's (see Psalm 24:1). Wherever we go, we become transportable temples because our very bodies are temples of the Holy Spirit, who is in us and whom we have received from God. We are not our own, but we have been bought with a price, so our aim becomes to glorify God everywhere we go.

PRAYER

Dear God, make us portable places of praise so that no matter where we may travel, Your Holy Spirit travels with us and You are glorified in everything that we may think, say, and do. In Jesus' name we pray. Amen.

HOME DAILY BIBLE READINGS
(February 4-10, 2019)

Pondering God's Steadfast Love

MONDAY, February 4: "Son of the Living God" (Matthew 16:13-20)

TUESDAY, February 5: "'I Am the Lord'" (Ezekiel 39:7-10)

WEDNESDAY, February 6: "Grow into a Precious Spiritual House" (1 Peter 2:1-8)

THURSDAY, February 7: "Majesty of God's Rule" (Psalm 93)

FRIDAY, February 8: "Rulers Astounded with the City of God" (Psalm 48:4-8)

SATURDAY, February 9: "Build Up Each Other in Worship" (1 Corinthians 14:26-33a)

SUNDAY, February 10: "Praise God's Steadfast Love in Worship" (Psalm 48:1-3, 9-14)

---

1. http://www.closerwalk.net/worship.htm
2. Richard L. Strauss, *The Joy of Knowing God* (New York: Loizeaux Brothers, 1984), 140.

February 17, 2019　　　　　　　　　　**Lesson 12**

PRAISING GOD'S MIGHTY WORKS

ADULT/YOUTH
ADULT/YOUNG ADULT TOPIC: Makes Me Want to Shout!
YOUTH TOPIC: Time for a Praise Break

CHILDREN
GENERAL LESSON TITLE: Praising God's Mighty Works
CHILDREN'S TOPIC: Rejoice! Rejoice!

DEVOTIONAL READING
Psalm 114

ADULT/YOUTH
BACKGROUND SCRIPTURE: Psalm 66
PRINT PASSAGE: Psalm 66:1-9, 16-20
ADULT KEY VERSE: Psalm 66:1
YOUTH KEY VERSE: Psalm 66:5

CHILDREN
BACKGROUND SCRIPTURE: Psalm 66
PRINT PASSAGE: Psalm 66:1-9, 16-20
KEY VERSE: Psalm 66:1

Psalm 66:1-9, 16-20—KJV

MAKE A joyful noise unto God, all ye lands:

2 Sing forth the honour of his name: make his praise glorious.

3 Say unto God, How terrible art thou in thy works! through the greatness of thy power shall thine enemies submit themselves unto thee.

4 All the earth shall worship thee, and shall sing unto thee; they shall sing to thy name. Selah.

5 Come and see the works of God: he is terrible in his doing toward the children of men.

6 He turned the sea into dry land: they went through the flood on foot: there did we rejoice in him.

7 He ruleth by his power for ever; his eyes behold the nations: let not the rebellious exalt themselves. Selah.

8 O bless our God, ye people, and make the voice of his praise to be heard:

9 Which holdeth our soul in life, and suffereth not our feet to be moved.

Psalm 66:1-9, 16-20—NIV

SHOUT FOR joy to God, all the earth!

2 Sing the glory of his name; make his praise glorious.

3 Say to God, "How awesome are your deeds! So great is your power that your enemies cringe before you.

4 "All the earth bows down to you; they sing praise to you, they sing the praises of your name."

5 Come and see what God has done, his awesome deeds for mankind!

6 He turned the sea into dry land, they passed through the waters on foot—come, let us rejoice in him.

7 He rules forever by his power, his eyes watch the nations—let not the rebellious rise up against him.

8 Praise our God, all peoples, let the sound of his praise be heard;

9 he has preserved our lives and kept our feet from slipping.

.....

16 Come and hear, all ye that fear God, and I will declare what he hath done for my soul.

17 I cried unto him with my mouth, and he was extolled with my tongue.

18 If I regard iniquity in my heart, the Lord will not hear me:

19 But verily God hath heard me; he hath attended to the voice of my prayer.

20 Blessed be God, which hath not turned away my prayer, nor his mercy from me.

16 Come and hear, all you who fear God; let me tell you what he has done for me.

17 I cried out to him with my mouth; his praise was on my tongue.

18 If I had cherished sin in my heart, the Lord would not have listened;

19 but God has surely listened and has heard my prayer.

20 Praise be to God, who has not rejected my prayer or withheld his love from me!

UNIFYING LESSON PRINCIPLE: People marvel at the legacies of those whose powerful influence has changed the world. What is the true measure of might? The psalmist praises the mighty works of God, the creator of the universe and the Savior of God's people.

LESSON OBJECTIVES

Upon the completion of this lesson, the students will be able to do the following:
1. Identify the mighty works for which the psalmist praises God.
2. Experience awe in contemplating God's works in creation and redemption.
3. Rejoice in the privilege of serving a mighty and powerful God.

AGE-LEVEL POINTS TO BE EMPHASIZED

Teachers of ADULTS and YOUTH

—This psalm is divided into three sections. The first section consists of verses 1-7, a hymn of praise of God. Verses 8-12 detail the trials of the people and their thankfulness for their subsequent deliverance. Verses 13-20 describe the thanksgiving of an individual person.

—Psalm 66 gives thanksgiving to God for help in times of danger.

—The psalmist describes God's activity as "awesome" (*yare'*; verses 3 and 5), the same adjective used in relation to God's activity in delivering Israel from Egypt (see Exodus 15:11).

—Verse 6 alludes to the crossing of the sea in Exodus 14:21-22 and to the similar miracle at the crossing of the Jordan River in Joshua 3:14-17.

—The psalmist reminded the people of how God rescued them during the Exodus (Exodus 14:21-22; Joshua 4:23), and encouraged them to continue to trust Him.

—To be "tried as silver" referred to how silver was refined by heat to remove impurities.

—The psalmist vowed to keep promises made during times of trouble.

—Praise is the outcome of God's deliverance.

Teachers of CHILDREN

—God is the Creator of the world and all that is within it.

—God is powerful even over enemies.
—God's rule and power are forever.

—God's people are expected to praise God.
—God hears prayers and shows mercy.

THE CHRONOLOGICAL SETTING OF THE LESSON

The exact origin and authorship of Psalm 11 is unknown. There is no specific evidence that David wrote it, yet there are also no clues that point to the assumption that he was not the author. Perhaps the most natural and obvious interpretation of Psalm 66:13-15 would be that "there is reference there to the temple; and if so, of course, the psalm must have been written by someone else. But it is not absolutely necessary to suppose that the temple is there referred to, for the language might be applied to the tabernacle as the 'house' or the place of the worship of God. There is, however, no positive evidence that it was composed by David, and it is impossible now to determine its authorship" (*Barnes' Notes on the Bible*, http://www.sacred-texts .com/bib/cmt/barnes/psa066.htm).

THE GEOGRAPHICAL AND CULTURAL SETTING OF THE LESSON

This psalm of thanksgiving is somewhat of an all-purpose psalm and was probably not composed for any particular special occasion. All people from every nation are invited to take part in unfettered praise to almighty God. The praise due to God is divided into three different categories: 1) For His sovereign dominion and power in the whole creation (verses 1-7). 2) For His favor to His people (verses 8-12). 3) "The psalmist praises God for his own experiences of his goodness to him in particular, especially in answering his prayers (ver. 13-20). If we have learned in every thing to give thanks for ancient and modern mercies, public and personal mercies, we shall know how to sing this psalm with grace and understanding" (*Commentary on the Whole Bible, Volume III*, https://www.ccel .org/ccel/henry/mhc3.Ps.lxvii.html).

KEY TERMS IN THE LESSON

Come (verse 5)—Hebrew: *halak* **(haw-lak'):** to go, come, walk.

Earth (verse 4)—Hebrew: *erets* **(eh'-rets):** land; earth.

Forever (verse 7)—Hebrew: *olam* **(o-lawm'):** long duration; antiquity; futurity; "for ever" (KJV).

Make (verse 2)—Hebrew: *sum or sim`* **(soom):** to put, place, set.

Song—Hebrew: *shiyr* **(sheer):** musical.

Works (verse 5)—Hebrew: *miph'al* **(mif-awl'):** work; "deeds" (NIV).

TOPICAL OUTLINE OF THE LESSON

I. Introduction
   A. The Power of Praise
   B. Biblical Background

II. Exposition and Application of the Scripture
   A. Unrestrained Praise (Psalm 66:1-3)
   B. Evidence of God's Greatness (Psalm 66:4-7)
   C. A Response to God's Glory (Psalm 66:8-9, 16-17)
   D. God's Grace and Mercy (Psalm 66:18-20)

III. Concluding Reflection

I. INTRODUCTION

A. The Power of Praise

Psalm 66 does not talk about Israel alone. It also has all the earth in view (verse 1). The psalmist understood that God is not just the God of Israel but the God of the whole world as well. Therefore, the psalmist called for good, appropriate, and joyful praise from everyone to God. He encouraged all to sing out to the honor of His name, and to do it in such a way that would make praises to God so glorious.

Praise requires concentrating on the thing, person, or deity that is being praised, while thanksgiving tends to focus on what a person has received. Thus, thanksgiving may become narrow and carried out with minimum depth of reflection. The psalmist then gives practical guidance on how to proceed with praise to God, saying specifically what they should say (verses 3-4). His intentions are not to make this methodical, but to help the heart that truly wants to praise God but needs some motivation and an example of how to praise God. Our praises begin with what we say to God and the words that we actually speak to Him. There is room for praise that is not yet spoken, as described in Psalm 65:1—but *spoken* praise must not be neglected.

The psalmist turned to the holy history of the Scriptures and remembered how God showed His power when He delivered Israel through the Red Sea (see Exodus 14:21) and through the River Jordan (see Joshua 3:14-16). The psalmist, here, could have picked anything to describe the wondrous works of God, but he chose those great events to show how God intervened for His people.

B. Biblical Background

God's work can never become old-fashioned. What God has been in ages past is what God still remains today. What God did in the past is what God can still do today. We can therefore allow our faith to ponder and reflect on all the records from the past and expect even greater works in the future.

The joy of Israel was in her God, and our joy should also be in the One who deserves our praise and trust. In giving our praises to God, it is important to note that it really is not about how much God has done for us that should stimulate our praise, but for who God is and what God has the capacity to accomplish. The psalmist called for all the earth to observe the great works of a great God and praise Him. God observes the nations, as they are His handwork. We should also look up to the One who continually watches over us (verse 7).

In verses 8-12, the psalmist gives more reasons for why God is to be praised. He repeats his exhortation to all the earth, exhorting them to praise the God of Israel. He further gives many more reasons to do so. Verse 8 urges us to proclaim God's praises and then lead others also to do the same. God has preserved and still preserves His people; He gives us life, health, wealth, and whatever earthly position we occupy, and thus deserves so much praise from us. The psalmist praised God for life and a secure position, but also pointed out the hardships of life. He further expressed his perception of hardships and testing with different scenarios (verses 10-12).

From verses 13-15, we see the psalmist praising God with sacrifices and through the paying of his vows. He is determined to praise God by obeying all of His commands regarding sacrifices and bringing them to God's altar. Burnt offerings were a common aspect of worship in Old Testament times. They demonstrated dedication or consecration to God. The psalmist had made God a promise to offer certain sacrifices in appreciation of God's work when he was in trouble. He did not want to sin by failing to fulfill these sacrifices. These promises he intended to fulfill were with generous, expensive sacrifices, and offering of multiple animals. He simply brought the best to God.

Verses 16-19 tell of how we ought to praise God with words, as shown by the psalmist. The psalmist's vows were not fulfilled through sacrifice alone; he also proclaimed God's goodness. His actions showed his intentions toward God. However, that did not take away the need for his mouth also to speak and proclaim God's praises. As he spoke to others about God's goodness, he equally described how he spoke to God.

It would be a huge mistake for anyone to think that God could be persuaded by mere sacrifices or vows. The psalmist did not just offer sacrifices; he gave God something which is also important in our worship—obedience. In giving his praise and offering his sacrifices, he made sure that he did not hold iniquity in his heart (verses 18-19).

The psalmist finally showed his appreciation of God's receiving his prayer and how it inspired praise to God. This is an important reminder that the answer to prayer does not come from what we deserve, but as a gift of love and mercy from God. The psalmist's final words of gratitude were not for the answered request alone, but also signified an unbroken relationship with God. The passage is completed by praising the mercy of God.

II. EXPOSITION AND APPLICATION OF THE SCRIPTURE

A. Unrestrained Praise
(Psalm 66:1-3)

MAKE A joyful noise unto God, all ye lands: Sing forth the honour of his name: make his praise glorious. Say unto God, How terrible art thou in thy works! through the greatness of thy power shall thine enemies submit themselves unto thee.

Psalm 66 wastes no time in addressing the central subject matter of the passage—praise! The initial focus on praise is not so much a command to shout for joy as it is an enthusiastic invitation for participation in praise. There is a time for quiet, reflective meditation, and there is also a time for unscripted, unashamed, unhindered adulation of almighty God. Psalm 66 makes it clear that this is that time.

"If praise is to be widespread, it must be vocal; exulting sounds stir the soul and cause a sacred contagion of thanksgiving. Composers of tunes for the congregation should see to it that their airs are cheerful; we need not so much noise, as joyful noise. God is to be praised with the voice, and the heart should go therewith in holy exultation. All praise from all nations should be rendered unto the Lord" (*Gill's Exposition of the Entire Bible*, http://biblehub.com/psalms/66-1.htm).

Various people have different ideas about the correct approach to praise. Should praise be eclectic, euphoric, and emotional? Or should praise be planned, coordinated, harmonic, and orchestrated? More important than the style of one's praise is the heart of one's praise. Just as effectual, fervent prayer avails much, so does the sincere, heartfelt praise matter much. Our praise becomes glorious to God when we give it our all without reservation. Sometimes this takes the form of well-planned, highly organized, orchestrated praise, and other times it may be a matter of a spontaneous and emotional outburst of sanctified celebration that streams from a sincere spirit.

There are times when God puts His power on display through the works of nature. Other times, God's power is seen through amazing miracles that occur in life.

If the terror of God can intimidate the believer, how much more can it make God's enemies cringe?

B. Evidence of God's Greatness
(Psalm 66:4-7)

All the earth shall worship thee, and shall sing unto thee; they shall sing to thy name. Selah. Come and see the works of God: he is terrible in his doing toward the children of men. He turned the sea into dry land: they went through the flood on foot: there did we rejoice in him. He ruleth by his power for ever; his eyes behold the nations: let not the rebellious exalt themselves. Selah.

Here in verse 4, the universality of the church is contemplated and previewed. Honoring God is not just for the Jewish nation but for every nation, every tongue, and every race of people. This sentiment is echoed in Psalm 150:6 (NIV): "Let everything that has breath praise the LORD. Praise the LORD." One may wonder how we can give specific praise to God in practical ways. The answer is this:

> Praise God with strong faith; praise him with holy love and delight; praise him with entire confidence in Christ; praise him with believing triumph over the powers of darkness; praise him by universal respect to all his commands; praise him by cheerful submission to all his disposals; praise him by rejoicing in his love, and comforting ourselves in his goodness; praise him by promoting the interests of the kingdom of his grace; praise him by lively hope and expectation of the kingdom of his glory. Since we must shortly breathe our last, while we have breath let us praise the Lord; then we shall breathe our last with comfort. (*Matthew Henry's Concise Commentary*, http://www.sacred-texts.com/bib/cmt/mhcc/psa150.htm)

Verse 5 is a personal invitation for spiritual investigation. The works of God and ways of God do not require so much defending as they deserve investigating. Most of the people who dismiss the importance and relevance of God are people who have never delved deeply into the essence of God and therefore are left to offer only empty, shallow conjectures based on their limited human personal experience and information. This principle is also emphasized in Psalm 34:8 (NIV): "Taste and see that the LORD is good; blessed is the one who takes refuge in him."

There are certain events in history that shape the mentality and spirituality of a people. One such event that has made an indelible impression on the life and faith of Judeo-Christian people is when God parted the Red Sea to allow the children of Israel to escape the pursuing armies of Pharaoh. This single event became the unmistakable indication to Israel and the enemies of Israel that this group of pilgrim people was indeed exceptionally and unmistakably favored by God. This event has been used to symbolize the way in which God is able to remove obstacles that stand in the way of individual dreams and spiritual progress.

Personification is used in verse 7 that attributes power to the watchful gaze of God. God's eternal energy force cannot be thwarted by the resistant actions of those who are rebellious. The rebellious are those who act contrary to the will of God and God's commandments. "The same power which God possessed and exerted for his people in ancient times, . . . and is as able and ready to act for them as ever he was . . . . *His eyes behold the nations*—He sees all their secret and subtle devices, and can and will defeat them, when he sees fit" (*The Holy Bible, Containing the Old and New Testaments (According to the Present Authorized Version)*, Joseph Benson, p. 833).

C. A Response to God's Glory (Psalm 66:8-9, 16-17)

O bless our God, ye people, and make the voice of his praise to be heard: Which holdeth our soul in life, and suffereth not our feet to be moved. . . . Come and hear, all ye that fear God, and I will declare what he hath done for my soul. I cried unto him with my mouth, and he was extolled with my tongue.

The psalmist presupposes that the reader shares a common relationship and connection with the God who is worthy to be praised. Regardless of ethnic background or national heritage, the God of Israel is not just for the Israelites but for everyone. "The Lord not only preserves our temporal life, but maintains the spiritual life which he has given to believers. By afflictions we are proved, as silver in the fire. The troubles of the church will certainly end well. Through various conflicts and troubles, the slave of Satan escapes from his yoke, and obtains joy and peace in believing: through much tribulation the believer must enter into the kingdom of God" (*Matthew Henry's Concise Commentary*, http://biblehub.com/commentaries/psalms/66-12.htm). The sound of praise is an auditory affirmation that God is a worthy recipient of our adulation.

The metaphor of "walking" is used as an indication of one's life. God has "put (or placed) us in a state of safety. The word rendered 'in life' means literally *among the living*. The word *soul* here is equivalent to *us—ourselves*; and the idea is, that he keeps us *among the living*. What is here said of this special deliverance is true of all men at all times, that they owe the fact that they are among the living to the care of God; or, it is because he *puts* them among the living, or *keeps* them alive" (*Notes, Critical, Explanatory,* and *Practical, on the Book of Psalms, Volume II*, Albert Barnes, p. 193).

The allusion to fear essentially refers to godly respect. Respect for God is a precondition for effectively hearing God. When we are willing to humbly stand under God, it is then that we begin to understand God. Another precondition for successfully hearing God is the condition of faith and belief as is shown in Hebrews 11:6 (NIV): "And without faith it is impossible to please God, because anyone who comes to him must believe that he exists and that he rewards those who earnestly seek him."

When God has done something for anyone, the blessing received is not complete until two things are accomplished. The first is that we give thanks to God because He is good and His mercy endures to all generations (see Psalm 107). The next step is when we declare to someone else about the goodness and greatness of God and what God has done for us.

This passage is a reflection of "one individual speaking on behalf of the nation, or uttering the sentiment of the people. At the same time, however, all this is language appropriate to an individual when recording his own experience. And he was extolled with my tongue—I praised him; I acknowledged his supremacy. I recognized my dependence on him, and looked to him as that God who had all things under his control, and who could grant me the deliverance which I desired" (*Barnes' Notes on the Bible*, http://www.sacred-texts.com/bib/cmt/barnes/psa066.htm).

At first glance, verse 17 seems like a contradiction in terms. How can a person cry out to God and simultaneously give praise to God?

But could it be that the writer was so confident of being heard that a song of praise was already by faith on his lips and ready to ring forth for all to hear? This is what happens when we combine our praise with our faith. These two entities should never be mutually exclusive.

D. God's Grace and Mercy (Psalm 66:18-20)

If I regard iniquity in my heart, the Lord will not hear me: But verily God hath heard me; he hath attended to the voice of my prayer. Blessed be God, which hath not turned away my prayer, nor his mercy from me.

Contrary to popular belief, although the love of God is unconditional, many of God's promises are conditional. For example, 2 Chronicles 7:14 (NIV) reads, "If my people, who are called by my name, will humble themselves and pray and seek my face and turn from their wicked ways, then I will hear from heaven, and I will forgive their sin and will heal their land." This promise is conditional. This conditional perspective is seen in verse 18, which states that known sin harbored in the heart effectively cancels the benefit of God's attention to our petition.

Never stop believing that God will hear your prayer. We may not always receive an immediate answer or the answer that we desire.

This powerful psalm of thanksgiving appropriately concludes in verses 10-20, with a euphoric pronouncement of special blessing for God's love toward us. God has extended such extravagant love and mercy. Who else would have thought to pray a prayer thanking God for not rejecting one's prayer? We can always find something new and different for which to give God thanks. We should never get tired of giving God thanks.

III. CONCLUDING REFLECTION

Only a fool would say that there is no God. One glance at a sunset or a newborn baby would be enough to convince the skeptic that there is a God. The heavens declare the glory of God and the reality that we as humankind did not create ourselves. There is a greater power that is in ultimate control of the universe; this powerful God periodically sends reminders of His capacity to produce peace in the midst of a storm and to bring life out of death. We offer praise to God in response to His mighty acts in creation and for His redemptive impact within our own lives and within the community. We look not to ourselves to save ourselves, but we look to the hand of God at work in every aspect of our lives to make a difference to the glory of God.

PRAYER

Dear God, thank You for making a difference in our lives, and may we never forget to give You the praise for all that You have done. In Jesus' name we pray. Amen.

HOME DAILY BIBLE READINGS
(February 11-17, 2019)

Praising God's Mighty Works

MONDAY, February 11: "In God I Trust" (Psalm 56:1-8)

TUESDAY, February 12: "God Listens to the Humble" (Luke 18:9-14)

WEDNESDAY, February 13: "Faith Tested by Fire" (1 Peter 1:3-7)

THURSDAY, February 14: "The Lord Is Near in Suffering" (James 5:7-12)

FRIDAY, February 15: "Crossing the Jordan on Dry Land" (Joshua 4:19-24)

SATURDAY, February 16: "God's Grace for Hard Testing" (Psalm 66:10-15)

SUNDAY, February 17: "Praise God for His Mighty Works" (Psalm 66:1-9, 16-20)

February 24, 2019   **Lesson 13**

LIVING WITH GOD'S LOVING ASSURANCE

ADULT/YOUTH	CHILDREN
ADULT/YOUNG ADULT TOPIC: **You're in Good Hands** YOUTH TOPIC: **Guaranteed Protection**	GENERAL LESSON TITLE: **Living under God's Protection** CHILDREN'S TOPIC: **A Protective Covering**

DEVOTIONAL READING
Romans 8:31-39

ADULT/YOUTH	CHILDREN
BACKGROUND SCRIPTURE: **Psalm 91:1-16** PRINT PASSAGE: **Psalm 91:1-8, 11-16** ADULT KEY VERSE: **Psalm 91:15** YOUTH KEY VERSE: **Psalm 91:2**	BACKGROUND SCRIPTURE: **Psalm 91:1-16** PRINT PASSAGE: **Psalm 91:1-8, 11-16** KEY VERSE: **Psalm 91:2**

Psalm 91:1-8, 11-16—KJV

HE THAT dwelleth in the secret place of the most High shall abide under the shadow of the Almighty.

2 I will say of the LORD, He is my refuge and my fortress: my God; in him will I trust.

3 Surely he shall deliver thee from the snare of the fowler, and from the noisome pestilence.

4 He shall cover thee with his feathers, and under his wings shalt thou trust: his truth shall be thy shield and buckler.

5 Thou shalt not be afraid for the terror by night; nor for the arrow that flieth by day;

6 Nor for the pestilence that walketh in darkness; nor for the destruction that wasteth at noonday.

7 A thousand shall fall at thy side, and ten thousand at thy right hand; but it shall not come nigh thee.

8 Only with thine eyes shalt thou behold and see the reward of the wicked.

Psalm 91:1-8, 11-16—NIV

WHOEVER DWELLS in the shelter of the Most High will rest in the shadow of the Almighty.

2 I will say of the LORD, "He is my refuge and my fortress, my God, in whom I trust."

3 Surely he will save you from the fowler's snare and from the deadly pestilence.

4 He will cover you with his feathers, and under his wings you will find refuge; his faithfulness will be your shield and rampart.

5 You will not fear the terror of night, nor the arrow that flies by day,

6 nor the pestilence that stalks in the dark-ness, nor the plague that destroys at midday.

7 A thousand may fall at your side, ten thousand at your right hand, but it will not come near you.

8 You will only observe with your eyes and see the punishment of the wicked.

11 For he shall give his angels charge over thee, to keep thee in all thy ways.

12 They shall bear thee up in their hands, lest thou dash thy foot against a stone.

13 Thou shalt tread upon the lion and adder: the young lion and the dragon shalt thou trample under feet.

14 Because he hath set his love upon me, therefore will I deliver him: I will set him on high, because he hath known my name.

15 He shall call upon me, and I will answer him: I will be with him in trouble; I will deliver him, and honour him.

16 With long life will I satisfy him, and shew him my salvation.

11 For he will command his angels concerning you to guard you in all your ways;

12 they will lift you up in their hands, so that you will not strike your foot against a stone.

13 You will tread on the lion and the cobra; you will trample the great lion and the serpent.

14 "Because he loves me," says the LORD, "I will rescue him; I will protect him, for he acknowledges my name.

15 "He will call on me, and I will answer him; I will be with him in trouble, I will deliver him and honor him.

16 "With long life I will satisfy him and show him my salvation."

UNIFYING LESSON PRINCIPLE: People often live in fear that misfortune will befall them. Where can we find protection from danger? The psalmist looked to God for protection in the midst of life's calamities.

LESSON OBJECTIVES

Upon the completion of this lesson, the students will be able to do the following:

1. Explore the diverse circumstances in which the psalmist perceived God's protection.
2. Feel grateful for God's protection in past times of difficulty.
3. Develop greater trust that God will protect them from danger in the future.

AGE-LEVEL POINTS TO BE EMPHASIZED

Teachers of ADULTS and YOUTH

—The powerful and moving profession of faith in Psalm 91:1-13 is followed by a divine affirmation of the psalmist's faith (verses 14-16).

—The psalmist expresses confidence in God's ability to protect us in all places, at all times, and in all circumstances.

—The devil quoted Psalm 91:11-12 when he tempted Jesus to throw Himself from the top of the Temple (see Matthew 4:6; Luke 4:10). Jesus refused, understanding that the promise

of divine protection is not intended to be used for personal advantage.

—Psalm 91 has been interpreted as a pilgrimage song sung by worshippers on their way to Jerusalem. It is a confession of trust that God will protect them on the journey and throughout their lives.

—This psalm is divided into two main parts. Verses 1-13 are a list of things that God will do. Verses 14-16 are a divine promise in the form of a response from God.

—This psalm is a song of trust in God as protector.

Teachers of CHILDREN

—The psalmist describes various forms of protection, both figuratively and literally.

—God's protection is expressed as an angel.

—The theme that righteousness prevails over the wicked is declared.

—God's safety and protection overcome fear.

—The psalmist trusted God to protect him and to keep him safe.

THE CHRONOLOGICAL SETTING OF THE LESSON

Specific authorship and date of this psalm are uncertain. Some scholars note that the many expressions used in the book are somewhat similar to those used by Moses in the book of Deuteronomy. They also suggest that the internal evidence of peculiar idioms may point toward Moses' being the possible composer. Perhaps the lives of Joshua and Caleb, who followed the Lord fully, would make good illustrations of the subject matter of this psalm. The tone of this psalm is encouraging and extremely motivational. It is easy to see how this psalm could have been useful when applied during times of personal and family crises, as well as in times of widespread national tragedy. Just as it was useful back then, it is just as useful in current times of personal challenge and community crisis.

THE GEOGRAPHICAL AND CULTURAL SETTING OF THE LESSON

Psalm 91 is probably intended as a psalm for public worship. "It has been attributed to Moses more often than to any of the other Old Testament writers. It could easily have been a psalm which was sung in the wilderness and may have been used by the Levites in their worship. There are five divisions to be noted in this psalm, each of which speaks of aspects of our walk with God" (http://www.johnrobertstevens.com/teachings/the-man-who-thoroughly-trusts-god-psalm-91/). There is no generation that is exempt from trouble, and the degree to which this psalm effectively addresses problems is why it is still relevant and has remained consistently effective.

KEY TERMS IN THE LESSON

Charge (verse 11)—Hebrew: *tsavah* (tsaw-vaw'): to lay charge (upon), give charge (to), "command" (NIV), order.

Day (verse 5)—Hebrew: *yomam* (yo-mawm'): daytime; by day; day.

Night (verse 5)—Hebrew: *layil* or *lel* or *layelah* (lah'-yil): night (as opposed to day); of gloom.

Pestilence (verse 3)—Hebrew: *deber* (deh'-ber): plague; murrain.

Refuge (verse 2)—Hebrew: *machaseh* (makh-as-eh'): shelter.

Reward (verse 8)—Hebrew: *shillumah* (shil-loo-maw'): requital; retribution; recompense; "punishment" (NIV).

Truth (verse 4)—Hebrew: *emeth* (eh'-meth): firmness; "faithfulness" (NIV).

TOPICAL OUTLINE OF THE LESSON

I. Introduction
   A. The Powerful Protection of God
   B. Biblical Background

II. Exposition and Application of the Scripture
   A. 100 Percent Protection (Psalm 91:1-4)
   B. No Fear (Psalm 91:5-8)
   C. Guard Duty (Psalm 91:11-13)
   D. Rescue and Rest (Psalm 91:14-16)

III. Concluding Reflection

I. INTRODUCTION

A. The Powerful Protection of God

Psalm 91 contains some of the most beautiful words written in the Bible, and it is filled with wonderful words of comfort. These words speak of God's protection of those who put their trust in Him and promise safety to those who trust in God even while many suffer destruction. This lesson explores the diverse circumstances in which the psalmist perceives God's protection. We should feel grateful for God's protection in past times of difficulty, and we should develop the faith and confidence that God will protect us from danger in the future.

In the New Testament, we find a related passage which sheds much light on the meaning and application of this psalm. At the temptation of Jesus in the wilderness, Satan quoted Psalm 91:11-12 to our Lord Jesus (see Luke 4:10-11 and Matthew 4:6). Since Psalm 91 promises deliverance from death and suffering, Satan tried to persuade Jesus to jump in belief that God would rescue Him. Jesus replied to him by referring to the Scripture which forbade testing the Lord God. He could have said much more than this, but He did not, and Jesus would later affirm that the promise of God written in Psalm 91 would be fulfilled through His suffering and death at Golgotha. God promises deliverance to all who would trust in Him, basically because Jesus suffered and was raised from the dead. This allowed victory over sin, death, and Satan. Psalm 91 was never an excuse for Jesus to avoid the Cross but was the reason why He went to the Cross. Psalm 91 is no guarantee that Jesus did not need to suffer on our behalf. His suffering is the reason why Christians and the saints are continually protected from and safeguarded in suffering.

B. Biblical Background

Psalm 91 begins with the strong statement of conviction that God is our refuge, our fortress, and our place of safety (verses 1-4). The psalm mentions two kinds of people with two different destinies and expectations from God. One group is made up of those who are delivered from destruction, and in the other group are those who are not delivered but, instead, are destroyed. Psalm 90, which comes immediately before our passage in this lesson, speaks of the suffering and short life that the godly experience as a result of living in a fallen and sinful world.

Psalm 90 then speaks of God's eternal nature and the very temporal nature of human beings. A thousand years with God is nothing, while a man sees seventy years as a long life even when these years are filled with sorrow and labor. This painfulness of life is explained by Moses (author of Psalm 91) as the result of the righteousness and holiness and the sinful nature of fallen humanity. The solution to this problem of pain and the hope of the believer is not in this life, but in the next. This solution will come with the Lord's return, as the psalm puts it, in the morning. This solution would not be found in the deliverance from death but, rather, in deliverance after death. Though not clearly stated in Psalm 91, it might be correct to infer that death itself is also a kind of deliverance for Christians. It removes us from the effects of sin, that of pain, suffering, and sorrow, and thus carries us into the eternal joy of the Lord's presence.

A Christian's deliverance from destruction is certainly not deliverance from the suffering, pain, and even death of this life. Rather, it is deliverance from the judgment of God, from the second death, and from eternal separation from God's presence.

Verses 14-16 of this psalm summarize any calamity that could happen to God's children and promise deliverance when they are placed in harmful circumstances. God promises to deliver them—to rescue, protect, and answer His children in their times of trouble. In addition to deliverance, He honors and satisfies them with long life (verse 14).

Psalm 91 is such a powerful passage, especially when used during a believer's time of crisis. It has the most assuring ending—as God says He will "show him (or her) His salvation." God is our refuge, our fortress, our shield, our buckler, and His love overshadows us and will bring us safely into heaven someday. God truly is our refuge and fortress, and we ought to trust continually in Him.

II. EXPOSITION AND APPLICATION OF THE SCRIPTURE

A. 100 Percent Protection (Psalm 91:1-4)

HE THAT dwelleth in the secret place of the most High shall abide under the shadow of the Almighty. I will say of the LORD, He is my refuge and my fortress: my God; in him will I trust. Surely he shall deliver thee from the snare of the fowler, and from the noisome pestilence. He shall cover thee with his feathers, and under his wings shalt thou trust: his truth shall be thy shield and buckler.

Psalm 91 begins with a guarantee of protection and spiritual security for the one who chooses to live under the authority, leadership, and direction of almighty God. The benefits of obedience to God include the avoidance of being overwhelmed by life's dangers and difficulties. This is not a specific promise of painlessness for the one who follows God. It is rather a general statement of encouragement to the believer that God will not withdraw ultimate protection from the faithful. "He shall not be disappointed of his hope, but shall find a quiet and safe resting place under the divine care. A *shadow*, in Scripture, often signifies protection. But there evidently seems to be an allusion to the most holy place in the tabernacle and temple, and to the outstretched wings of the cherubim covering the ark and mercy-seat . . . . And it is as if the psalmist had said, He shall dwell like the ark in the holy of holies, under the immediate shadow and protection of the Divine Majesty" (*Benson Commentary,* http:// biblehub.com/commentaries/psalms/91-1 .htm). Some people do not contemplate their need for protection until there is an urgent, threatening situation. Verse 1 encourages us to value God's protection prior to the onset of an emergency. Advance preparation is better than stress, tension, and apprehension.

The psalmist does a voluntary self-placement under the security, custody, and guardianship of a proven, trusted, and beloved enterprise. This experience of spiritual seclusion is not done through any type of force but is very much a voluntary decision and action by the believer who is assured that this is the right choice. The psalmist projects a serene sense of assurance in God's ability to provide and to protect regardless of the circumstances.

There is no subtle scheme or clever plot that can be devised against which God cannot ultimately provide protection and deliverance. The Spirit of God is able to protect us against any other spirit that might seek to distract us or to harm us. There are many different types of negative, troublesome circumstances against which God's covering can provide protection. "There is a deadly pestilence of error, we are safe from that if we dwell in communion with the God of truth; there is a fatal pestilence of sin, we shall not be infected by it if we abide with the thrice Holy One; there is also a pestilence of disease, and even from that calamity our faith shall win immunity if it be of that high order which abides in God, walks on in calm serenity, and ventures all things for duty's sake. Faith by cheering the heart keeps it free from the fear which, in times of pestilence, kills more than the plague itself" (*The Treasury of David*, https://www.biblestudytools.com/commentaries/treasury-of-david/psalms-91-3.html). Our walk with God is a matter of faith, and the degree of our healing is according to the measure of our faith (see Romans 12:3).

The literary device used in this verse is the opposite of personification. Instead of ascribing human characteristics to an inanimate object, the psalmist ascribes animalistic characteristics to almighty God. In the spirit of a parabolic metaphor, the psalmist appropriates the sense of protection provided by a mother hen for her chicks and applies it to the comfort and serenity made possible by God's guidance.

B. No Fear
(Psalm 91:5-8)

Thou shalt not be afraid for the terror by night; nor for the arrow that flieth by day; Nor for the pestilence that walketh in darkness; nor for the destruction that wasteth at noonday. A thousand shall fall at thy side, and ten thousand at thy right hand; but it shall not come nigh thee. Only with thine eyes shalt thou behold and see the reward of the wicked.

In Old Testament times, one of the most pervasive fears was the threat of marauding robbers who attacked at night (see Job 24:14-16; Jeremiah 49:9; Obadiah 1:5). The reference to the arrow that flies by day (verse 5) probably alluded to seasons of war during which armies attempted to devastate their opponents prior to coming into direct contact with them by launching a barrage of arrows to thin down the front lines of a battle or to hit random, unsuspecting targets on the other side of a fortress wall. In fearsome times like these, God's reassuring protection would be of great value. The presence of faith means the absence of fear.

A *pestilence* is defined as any sudden fatal epidemic (verse 6). This particular designation of the word in its biblical use generally indicates a divine visitation. The word is most frequently used in the prophetic books, is always associated with the sword and famine, and occurs twenty-five times in the books of Jeremiah and Ezekiel (https://www.biblestudytools.com/

dictionary/pestilence/). Since plagues are often spread invisibly through germs and exposure to some human, animal, or plant, it would be quite possible to go to bed as a healthy person and wake up as a very sick individual. The reference to the plague that destroys at midday could refer to the heat strokes that commonly occurred due to the lack of protection from the relentless desert heat (*Pulpit Commentary*). In spite of life's diverse array of common threats and problems, God promises to be a very present help in times of need.

This classic verse presents a powerful promise for those who walk in obedience to God and who trust in the grace of God. This verse is not to be applied universally in the sense that all godly people will avoid problems or physical illness. Some popular prosperity preachers sometimes seem to suggest that any Christian who suffers a sickness must somehow have a defect in their faith. God never promises a lifetime of perfect physical health or existence without death. In some instances, "when God sees death is more for his good than life, as it apparently is, when righteous men are taken away from the evil to come, as is said in Isaiah 57:1. In which case, though God doth not give the thing promised, yet he giveth a far greater mercy instead of it, and so fulfils his promise in the best sense, and with most advantage" (*Benson Commentary*, http://biblehub.com/commentaries/psalms/91-7.htm).

When God is our protector, there is no need to take matters into our own hands. When we accept God's protection, we transfer our rights for revenge to God. Romans 12:17-19 (NKJV) records, "Repay no one evil for evil. Have regard for good things in the sight of all men. If it is possible, as much as depends on you, live peaceably with all men. Beloved, do not avenge yourselves, but rather give place to wrath; for it is written, 'Vengeance is Mine, I will repay,' says the Lord."

C. Guard Duty
(Psalm 91:11-13)

For he shall give his angels charge over thee, to keep thee in all thy ways. They shall bear thee up in their hands, lest thou dash thy foot against a stone. Thou shalt tread upon the lion and adder: the young lion and the dragon shalt thou trample under feet.

Verse 11 may pose some difficulty for those who see it as a guarantee against pain. In Matthew 5:45 (NIV), we see that God "causes his sun to rise on the evil and the good, and sends rain on the righteous and the unrighteous." This means that on any given day, good or bad things could happen to good or bad people. Godly people are not exempt from problems, and unrighteous people are not denied perceived prosperity. The difference here is that although God's people may go into the proverbial fire, God's presence is guaranteed in the midst of the fire. Psalm 23:4 (NIV) accentuates this: "Even though I walk through the darkest valley, I will fear no evil, for you are with me; your rod and your staff, they comfort me."

In verse 12, the focus is still on divine protection, but this time the protection comes not through removal of the threat, but through elevation above the danger. Although the trouble in our lives may still exist, God's power can lift us to a place where the problems do not affect us.

God will do His job of protection as long

as we do our job of trusting. One of the strongest New Testament passages that verifies this principle is found in Philippians 4:6-7 (NKJV): "Be anxious for nothing, but in everything by prayer and supplication, with thanksgiving, let your requests be made known to God; and the peace of God, which surpasses all understanding, will guard your hearts and minds through Christ Jesus." The picture of protection in this psalm is that of a parent or nurse with children or infants who sometimes have to be picked up in order to be rescued from danger.

The reference to a snake (verse 13) is reminiscent of the New Testament reference to Mark 16:18a (NIV): "they will pick up snakes with their hands; and when they drink deadly poison, it will not hurt them at all." Obviously, these types of references are not meant to encourage or endorse the handling of snakes, but they continue to address the subject of divine protection and triumph over enemies. The psalmist simply chose some of the most feared animals in the animal kingdom to accentuate and contrast the blessing of safety in the midst of danger.

D. Rescue and Rest
(Psalm 91:14-16)

Because he hath set his love upon me, therefore will I deliver him: I will set him on high, because he hath known my name. He shall call upon me, and I will answer him: I will be with him in trouble; I will deliver him, and honour him. With long life will I satisfy him, and shew him my salvation.

In the earlier part of Psalm 91, the writer was speaking in the first person, but now God is introduced as the speaker and confirms the promises made. Reasons are provided for the constant care for all who trust and believe in Him. The promised reward for this trust is deliverance, recovery, security, stability, and shelter from life's storms. In this instance, acknowledgment of God's name is seen as synonymous with obedience to God's will. This is more than head knowledge; it is heart knowledge and personal experience with God. God is addressing those who are doers of the Word rather than hearers only.

Verse 14 displays the conditional interplay of God's unconditional love. Even though salvation is free, discipleship is costly and God's grace is not cheap. Although it is not God's will for any to perish, God will not force His love on anyone. Instead, God stands at the door of our lives and knocks because humanity was created with free will and the ability to accept Him or reject Him. Throughout the Bible, God offered His people choices: "This day I call the heavens and the earth as witnesses against you that I have set before you life and death, blessings and curses. Now choose life, so that you and your children may live" (Deuteronomy 30:19, NIV). The prescribed way to designate God as one's choice is to "call upon" Him. This call usually comes in the form of a prayer but can also materialize through a praise or a desperate plea. God's sheep know God's voice, and the Lord as the shepherd also knows the voice of the sheep. God extends the invitation to "Call to me and I will answer you and tell you great and unsearchable things you do not know" (Jeremiah 33:3, NIV).

God's answers (verse 15) are not empty greetings but include God's gracious presence, unseen support, dynamic deliverance, relevant righteousness, and profound honor. God grants the requests of those who ask in faith, and the responses are in line with our good and God's glory.

All throughout Psalm 91, the focus has been on physical protection by a spiritual source. The logical result of lifelong protection is long life. Obviously, not every follower of God is absolutely guaranteed to live a long time. *Matthew Pool's Commentary* has this take on the concept of promised long life: "With long life will I satisfy him; either in this world, when it is expedient for my service, and for his benefit; or, at least, in the next world, where he shall live to eternity in the blissful sight and enjoyment of God in glory" (http://biblehub.com/commentaries/psalms/91-16.htm). There is a subconscious expectation among some Christians that those who follow God cannot be touched by pain, problems, sickness, or death. The existence of this unrealistic expectation causes some Christians to doubt God or even to dislike God when something bad happens to someone who is considered to be good.

III. CONCLUDING REFLECTION

Psalm 91 is a powerful and moving profession of faith in the power of God to provide and to protect in all places and at all times. No doubt this passage must have given hope and help to those ancestors of African Americans who experienced the horrors of slavery, failed reconstruction, Jim Crow, and the civil rights struggle. The psalm is universally relevant for anyone who has ever been hurting or in trouble and longed for some sense of peace and relief. Believers are not insulated from pain and isolated from difficulty, but in the midst of our mess, God makes a magnificent promise: *I will never leave you or forsake you. Indeed, nothing will be able to separate us from the love of God* (see Romans 8:39).

PRAYER

Dear God, thank You for Your promise of protection in the middle of any circumstance. Let us always seek Your face and never take our eyes off You. In Jesus' name we pray. Amen.

HOME DAILY BIBLE READINGS
(February 18-24, 2019)

Living with God's Loving Assurance
MONDAY, February 18: "God Sustains and Cares for Jacob" (Deuteronomy 32:10-14)
TUESDAY, February 19: "Trust God; No Need to Fear" (Psalm 121)
WEDNESDAY, February 20: "The Lord Will Help You" (Isaiah 41:8-13)
THURSDAY, February 21: "God Overpowers Adversaries" (Nahum 1:2-8)
FRIDAY, February 22: "God's Protection through Oneness" (John 17:11-15)
SATURDAY, February 23: "Deliverance from Violent People" (Psalm 140:1-8)
SUNDAY, February 24: "Assurance of God's Protection" (Psalm 91:1-8, 11-16)

Discipleship and Mission

GENERAL INTRODUCTION

This quarter surveys several calls to ministry and the expectations of those called. Calls to service, as recorded in the gospels of Mark and Luke, are highlighted. We explore Paul's call to ministry, with special attention to the Roman church. On Easter Sunday, we examine Matthew's account of the Resurrection.

Unit I, "*Call to Discipleship*," has four lessons and highlights several aspects of what it means to be called by Jesus as a disciple. They include hospitality, counting the cost, reaching the lost, and salvation for all people.

Unit II, "*Call to Ministry*," has five lessons that explore the diverse ways in which Jesus' disciples were challenged to exercise their call to ministry: by witnessing to the Gospel message, acting with loving kindness, sharing the Resurrection story, and making new disciples through preaching, teaching, and baptism.

Unit III, "*The Spread of the Gospel*" (four lessons), begins with Paul's introduction of himself to the Jewish and Gentile Christians living in Rome. Paul affirms that the call to salvation is to Israel and to Gentiles. This call to salvation is a call to a life in the Spirit and involves a new life in Christ.

GO & MAKE DISCIPLES OF ALL NATIONS

March 3, 2019   Lesson 1

CALLED TO HUMILITY AND HOSPITALITY

ADULT/YOUTH
ADULT/YOUNG ADULT TOPIC: **Humility Is Good for You**
YOUTH TOPIC: **Sitting with the Lowly**

CHILDREN
GENERAL LESSON TITLE: **Called to Be Humble and Kind**
CHILDREN'S TOPIC: **Dare to Care and Share**

DEVOTIONAL READING
Luke 14:15-24

ADULT/YOUTH
BACKGROUND SCRIPTURE: **Luke 14:7-14**
PRINT PASSAGE: **Luke 14:7-14**
KEY VERSE: **Luke 14:11**

CHILDREN
BACKGROUND SCRIPTURE: **Luke 14:7-14**
PRINT PASSAGE: **Luke 14:7-14**
KEY VERSES: **Luke 14:13-14a**

Luke 14:7-14—KJV

7 And he put forth a parable to those which were bidden, when he marked how they chose out the chief rooms; saying unto them.

8 When thou art bidden of any man to a wedding, sit not down in the highest room; lest a more honourable man than thou be bidden of him;

9 And he that bade thee and him come and say to thee, Give this man place; and thou begin with shame to take the lowest room.

10 But when thou art bidden, go and sit down in the lowest room; that when he that bade thee cometh, he may say unto thee, Friend, go up higher: then shalt thou have worship in the presence of them that sit at meat with thee.

11 For whosoever exalteth himself shall be abased; and he that humbleth himself shall be exalted.

12 Then said he also to him that bade him, When thou

Luke 14:7-14—NIV

7 When he noticed how the guests picked the places of honor at the table, he told them this parable:

8 "When someone invites you to a wedding feast, do not take the place of honor, for a person more distinguished than you may have been invited.

9 "If so, the host who invited both of you will come and say to you, 'Give this person your seat.' Then, humiliated, you will have to take the least important place.

10 "But when you are invited, take the lowest place, so that when your host comes, he will say to you, 'Friend, move up to a better place.' Then you will be honored in the presence of all the other guests.

11 "For all those who exalt themselves will be humbled, and those who humble themselves will be exalted."

12 Then Jesus said to his host, "When you give a luncheon or dinner, do not invite your friends,

makest a dinner or a supper, call not thy friends, nor thy brethren, neither thy kinsmen, nor thy rich neighbours; lest they also bid thee again, and a recompence be made thee.

13 But when thou makest a feast, call the poor, the maimed, the lame, the blind:

14 And thou shalt be blessed; for they cannot recompense thee: for thou shalt be recompensed at the resurrection of the just.

your brothers or sisters, your relatives, or your rich neighbors; if you do, they may invite you back and so you will be repaid.

13 "But when you give a banquet, invite the poor, the crippled, the lame, the blind,

14 "and you will be blessed. Although they cannot repay you, you will be repaid at the resurrection of the righteous."

UNIFYING LESSON PRINCIPLE: People crave recognition and status but are never satisfied and always want more. How does one find true fulfillment in relationship to others? Jesus taught that demonstrating humility and extending unselfish hospitality bring fulfillment in this life and in the life to come.

LESSON OBJECTIVES

Upon the completion of this lesson, the students will be able to do the following:

1. Examine Jesus' teaching about humility and hospitality described in Luke 14:7-14.
2. Reflect on their own tendencies to seek honor and praise for selfish reasons.
3. Identify ways to give honor and respect to people who might be considered "unworthy" by popular standards.

AGE-LEVEL POINTS TO BE EMPHASIZED
Teachers of ADULTS and YOUTH

—Jesus was introducing a new teaching—the importance and rewards of crossing social boundaries, to include people already humbled by life's circumstances.

—In many cultures, honor equals power. Being exalted by others is okay, but self-exaltation is not (see Proverbs 25:6-7; Matthew 23:12; Luke 18:14; James 4:6; 1 Peter 5:5-6).

—Self-examination, discipline, and sacrifice are required in seeking to understand and follow the teaching of Jesus about humility and hospitality.

—These teachings of Jesus about true spiritual character in His followers fit well into His tendency of reversal of social practices typical of the times (see Matthew 5–7).

—The direct opposite of the humility Jesus teaches in these verses is exhibited by the mother of the sons of Zebedee and the disciples in Matthew 20:20-28.

—Luke 14:1-6 provides background and setting for this parable.

—In the Greco-Roman world, inviting someone of inferior status was acceptable, but inviting a crippled or poor person was not.

—It was already taught that God would reward those who helped the poor (see Proverbs 19:17).

Teachers of CHILDREN

—When invited to a celebration, show humility by leaving the best seats for special guests.

—Allow your host to decide who will have the best seats.

—Give your host an opportunity to honor you by seating you in the best location.

—Don't assume you are the most important person at a celebration.

—Issue invitations to special events to persons whose social locations are different from yours.

—Both guests and hosts are addressed in Jesus' story. All are responsible for hospitality.

THE CHRONOLOGICAL SETTING OF THE LESSON

Jesus' discourse in Luke 14:7-14 is given in the setting of a meal. More specifically, it relates to meals within the framework of invitations to dinner parties. The idea of a dinner party functions on three levels in this scene: (1) The dinner party as setting for Jesus' discourse; (2) Jesus' discourse about (human) dinner parties; (3) the dinner party as a metaphor for the joyful kingdom of God. The interplay between these three levels adds to the richness of this scene. The scene may reflect the custom of the symposium, a dinner and drinking party that included after-dinner speeches. The symposium could be the setting for philosophical discussion or merely for witty remarks. In Luke 14, however, Jesus alone is allowed to give a speech. The narrator is interested only in Jesus' discourse, leaving us with the impression that the others cannot match Jesus' wisdom.

THE GEOGRAPHICAL AND CULTURAL SETTING OF THE LESSON

The dinner at the Pharisee's house, mentioned earlier in Luke 14:1, is the setting of this passage. The scribes and the Pharisees had been watching Jesus closely, but now the tables were turned, and He began to watch them. According to the cultural norms of that day, seeking places of honor at dinner parties was quite typical behavior. Jesus, an invited guest at the dinner party, observed the other guests' jockeying to grab the seats closest to the host that would bestow on them the badge of highest ranking in the social order. The hosts arranged the couches in the dining area to reflect the order of the importance of the guests. Where one sat indicated one's rank relative to that of the other guests. Getting a good seat at the party said a lot about one's social standing in the community.

After observing the guests' stepping all over one another for the most prominent seats at the dinner party, Jesus took them to task for this widely practiced custom. He had already pronounced a woe on a group of Pharisees for their love of the seats of honor in the marketplaces (see Luke 11:43). He characterized them as those who seek righteousness in the sight of others. Much later, He would warn His disciples not to be like the scribes who parade about in long robes, desiring to be saluted with stately greetings in public, while seeking places of honor at banquets (see Luke 20:46). In our lesson today, Jesus witnessed a similar grab for honor and power in action—as the guests made a mad dash for the most prominent seats of honor as if it were a game of musical chairs.

PROMINENT CHARACTER(S) IN THE LESSON

Pharisees: persons comprising one of the parties within Judaism of the late Second Temple period, known for their exact observance of the Jewish religion.

KEY TERMS IN THE LESSON

Exalt (verse 11)—Greek: *hypsoō* (hü-pso'-ō): to lift up on high; to exalt; "exalteth" (KJV).

Humbled (verse 11)—Greek: *tapeinoō* (tä-pā-no'-ō): devoid of all haughtiness; "humbleth" (KJV).

Parable (verse 7)—Greek: *parabolē* (pä-rä-bo-lā'): an earthly story with a heavenly meaning.

Poor (verse 13)—Hebrew: *ebyown* (ev·yōn'); Greek: *ptōchos* (ptō-kho's):** destitute of wealth, influence, position, honor.

TOPICAL OUTLINE OF THE LESSON

I. Introduction
A. Lessons in Kingdom Etiquette
B. Biblical Background

II. Exposition and Application of the Scripture
A. The Eternal Perils of Vain Glory (Luke 14:7-9)
B. The Rewards of Humility (Luke 14:10)
C. The Dangers of Self-exaltation (Luke 14:11)
D. Whom You Invite Matters in the Kingdom (Luke 14:12-14)

III. Concluding Reflection

I. INTRODUCTION

A. Lessons in Kingdom Etiquette

We all know people who go out of their way to be seen in the company of influential and prominent people. Such people are all too inclined to spend money they do not have, buying things they do not need and trying to impress folks they do not even like.

Some go to great lengths to make sure people know they have achieved a certain status in life. They achieve this through loud voices, flamboyant clothing, or an endless competitive spirit. Some announce their social arrival through name dropping, always calling attention to the high and mighty with whom they come into contact. Others make an all-out effort to belong to the right clubs and organizations. They have to believe they are among the movers and shakers in their community, or else they feel deflated and insignificant. They engage in all kinds of fanfare to be seen in the company of the right people, at the right places, and at the right time. Such status seekers will go to great lengths to make sure they are in the in-crowd.

In today's lesson, Jesus thought that the way to be noticed is not necessarily by rubbing shoulders with the high and mighty nor in standing out in the crowd in exceptional ways. Jesus thought that exaltation comes from true humility and that in God's order of divine reversal, the first shall be last and the last shall be first. Honor and respect are achieved through humility in the eyes of God. In the rule and reign of God, those who exalt themselves will be humbled, and those who humble themselves will exalted. The way to honor is through humility and service to others.

B. Biblical Background

On a Sabbath day at an unspecified location on His journey toward Jerusalem, Jesus went for a meal in the home of one of the leading Pharisees. At this meal, the Pharisees were watching Him closely. Luke set the scene of a typical elite group in society, given to self-indulgent feasting. Jesus brought challenging words to their closed, self-absorbed world as He watched them choose the places of honor at the dinner, another feature of this self-absorbed, status-conscious elite group. The places assigned to a person at a dinner represented a public recognition of their status in the peer group of elite dinner guests. To be assigned a place of honor was very gratifying, but to be assigned a place that did not reflect one's own sense of status in the group could cause offense and put someone in a vile mood while he or she was reclining at dinner.

After observing them jockey for the best seats at the dinner party, Jesus told them a parable. He told them not to pick a seat in the place of honor when invited to a wedding feast, for someone more important may be invited and they would then, to their shame, have to take a lower place. Conversely, if they take a low place, then the host may invite them to take a higher place and then they would be honored in the sight of all at the table.

As the meal continues, the focus of the teaching turned to the kinds of people one should invite to such a gathering—the poor and hungry who have no way to return the favor. With this group in mind, Jesus issued another challenge to the elite, closed group at the Sabbath meal. He told the host that when he held a feast, to stop inviting friends, brothers, relations, and rich neighbors, and—instead of these four categories of people who could reciprocate the invitation—he should invite four different categories of people: the poor, the crippled, the lame, and the blind. These stereotypes of the poor make up the marginalized members of society as distinct from the wealthy dinner-party invitees who could reciprocate the invitations they receive.

II. EXPOSITION AND APPLICATION OF THE SCRIPTURE

A. The Eternal Perils of Vain Glory
(Luke 14:7-9)

And he put forth a parable to those which were bidden, when he marked how they chose out the chief rooms; saying unto them. When thou art bidden of any man to a wedding, sit not down in the highest room; lest a more honourable man than thou be bidden of him; And he that bade thee and him come and say to thee, Give this man place; and thou begin with shame to take the lowest room.

Jesus' advice to the guests at a dinner party to which He had been invited (verse 7) is called a *parable*, not because He told the guests an illustrative story, but to alert the reader that He was talking about more than dining etiquette at a banquet table. Jesus was a keen observer of human beings. In Jewish banquets, the guests were arranged in positions that put them nearer or farther away from the host, with a closer seat reflecting greater social status or honor by the host. When the invited guests chose the higher positions for themselves, without being placed there by the host, they showed that they thought they deserved the honorable position, or that this was how they wanted others to see them.

Jesus pointed out the unnecessary risk that they took in doing so, because someone more important than they might arrive and be given the high seat of honor nearest the host. The status seekers would then lose face by being asked to get up and take a position lower down the line of guests. It is far better to be publicly honored by being called to a higher position than to be called down to a lower position. In giving this example from real life, Jesus was not encouraging people to be falsely humble. Jesus' point was that the virtue of humility is a leading character trait in His kingdom—where the childlike and the humble are honored and the proudly self-righteous are shut out. Those who have been too proud to humble themselves before Christ will be publicly humbled by God, and those whom the world has treated with disdain for Christ's sake will be publicly exalted. Humility ultimately lifts us up, while pride eventually brings us down.

Dinners were regarded as barometers of one's prestige in the gathering and in the community. To be brought to public shame at such an occasion—by being asked down from the higher seat—would be almost unbearable to a social climber. Honor and shame were matters of life and death, and saving face was more important than garnering wealth.

Jesus wishes to wake up His audience to life-and-death issues that are truly life-and-death issues with eternal ramifications. If self-admiration and self-exaltation can lead to disastrous consequences at a dinner party in this world, it will lead to even more disastrous results in the final judgment.

B. The Rewards of Humility
(Luke 14:10)

But when thou art bidden, go and sit down in the lowest room; that when he that bade thee cometh, he may say unto thee, Friend, go up higher: then shalt thou have worship in the presence of them that sit at meat with thee.

Having seen the guests at the banquet possibly pushing and shoving in a scramble for the better seats, Jesus offered a lesson in humility. He alone is in a position to offer such advice, for while we are not told which place He had been given, we can be sure He would not have jostled anyone for a seat. In Luke 14:10, Jesus did not say that the invited guests should sit two or three places away from the most preferred seats but, rather, they should choose the farthest place down from the most preferred seats. Why? It is much better, says Jesus, to be asked to sit higher than to be called out and instructed by the host to take a lower seat. When called up to the higher seat, says Jesus, you will be honored in the presence of all who sit at the table with you. Jesus is admonishing the guests to "drop back into the lowest or last place."

In the eyes of God, not all behavior is commendable or praiseworthy. Using seating choices at dinner as an example, Jesus informs His hearers that God is not impressed by self-promoting behavior. In the kingdom of God, humility will ultimately rule the day, and such a posture finds favor with God. Jesus warns that the attempt to gain the place of honor can actually lead to its opposite: the shame of being moved to the lowest place. If you want to be honored, do not run for the highest place and risk being ordered to the lowest, but quietly seek out the lowest place with the possibility of being asked up to a higher one. In the eyes of Jesus, it is humility in our dealings with others that brings us honor.

C. The Dangers of Self-exaltation
(Luke 14:11)

For whosoever exalteth himself shall be abased; and he that humbleth himself shall be exalted.

The Gospel significance of Jesus' teaching

in this passage is made clear in these two additional concluding lines found in verse 11 (NASB): "For everyone who exalts himself will be humbled, and he who humbles himself will be exalted." Suddenly, we are far beyond the wedding feast. We are far beyond table manners, as good and as important as they are. We are far beyond social strategies of how to be honored instead of embarrassed. Suddenly, the teaching has been universalized to apply to all people, including us. Moreover, the teaching has been placed within the ultimate context of the final judgment—of eternal humiliation or exaltation. Self-exaltation and arrogance here in this world—such as unbelief in, rejection of, and disobedience to God—will be dealt with supremely harshly in the world to come. Self-humbling and service in this world—such as faith in, acceptance of, and obedience to Jesus Christ—will be dealt with very graciously in the world to come. The stakes are high. The Gospel contains both warning and promise. Which will it be for us?

D. Whom You Invite Matters in the Kingdom (Luke 14:12-14)

Then said he also to him that bade him, When thou makest a dinner or a supper, call not thy friends, nor thy brethren, neither thy kinsmen, nor thy rich neighbours; lest they also bid thee again, and a recompence be made thee. But when thou makest a feast, call the poor, the maimed, the lame, the blind: And thou shalt be blessed; for they cannot recompense thee: for thou shalt be recompensed at the resurrection of the just.

Initially, Jesus' teaching called into question the self-seeking agenda of His table companions at the dinner party, but more fundamentally, beginning with verse 12, He now went on to hint at a life-world in which honor was measured and granted along unforeseen lines. Having addressed the guests, Jesus now turned to the host. He, too, had acted poorly. How relatively easy and tempting to give a dinner for close friends, family members, or right neighbors. Guests like these are quite capable of returning the favor. How much more costly and genuine, said Jesus, it is to invite people with no social connections—the poor, disadvantaged, and ordinary. They cannot pay back in kind, so they are the real test of a person's generosity.

Thus, Jesus admonished the host that when he gives a meal not to invite friends, family, other relatives, or rich neighbors, but rather to invite the poor, the maimed, the lame, and the blind. Jesus was not forbidding one to invite one's family, friends, and neighbors to meals, but He was forbidding inviting them exclusively. The host was no less self-centered than the guests clambering over one another for the seats of honor if he invited only the honorable in his social circle who could reciprocate and bestow future benefits and honor on him. If his aim in inviting was merely to schmooze with the influential and well-connected in his own inner circle, then he was no better than those jockeying for seats of honor at his table.

Christian discipleship is not self-promotion but freedom from it, freedom from self-obsession itself. Our trust should be in the One who calls, for it is He who will bestow our personal identity and honor as well as our purpose and place in life.

The careful practice of humility in our relationship with others is essential to our coming to authentic knowledge of God. It is to this altogether new and higher standard of hospitality that Jesus calls us. The amazing graciousness of God toward us in Christ calls for a reciprocal graciousness toward those who have no obvious claim to it. Hospitality in the light of Christ is not part of social obligation or reciprocity. Rather, it is like our very forgiveness—part of our identification with His love for the unlovely and those who can never hope to reciprocate.

III. CONCLUDING REFLECTION

Jesus' counsel to His fellow guests and His host would seem to be advice on gracious living related to table etiquette and compiling guest rosters were it not for the climaxes in 14:11 and 14:14, which introduce what God will do in the final judgment. According to Jesus, God will humble those who exalt themselves, and exalt those who humble themselves. Additionally, God will repay on the day of resurrection those who include the poor and the outcasts to share in their feasts. These pronouncements make clear that Jesus' advice concerning worldly issues involving human preoccupations with honor and shame will have eternal ramifications. Rather than seeking kudos from humans, one should concentrate on honoring those whom God honors.

On a regular basis, believers are faced with two choices—one which has a negative consequence, and the other a positive benefit. Before acting, it is helpful to review the choices before us and to reflect upon these in light of the Gospel. It is easy for our actions to be determined by the mores of the dominant culture. In the eyes of Jesus, whoever promotes oneself or acts in expectation of repayment from others in a *quid pro quo* arrangement is far from living out the values of the kingdom. "How many of my daily actions are determined by an effort to make myself look good in the eyes of others? How much of my time and energy is devoted to promoting my career, my status, my place in the world?" This passage prompts us to pause and to reevaluate. "Is there a true north to my moral compass, or does it point in whatever direction I can attain the greatest personal benefit?"

PRAYER

Dear God, teach us the power of humility, and help us not to seek for the vainglory of the world. Teach us how to be the people You have called us to be, and may we find comfort and assurance in living the identity of those who have been called to follow You. In Jesus' name we pray. Amen.

HOME DAILY BIBLE READINGS
(February 25–March 3, 2019)

Called to Humility and Hospitality
MONDAY, February 25: "Wait to Enter the King's Presence" (Proverbs 25:2-7a)
TUESDAY, February 26: "Treat the Poor and Rich Impartially" (James 2:1-7)
WEDNESDAY, February 27: "Love and Pray for the Persecutor" (Matthew 5:43-48)
THURSDAY, February 28: "A Life Worthy of God's Call" (Ephesians 4:1-7)
FRIDAY, March 1: "Serving with Love on the Sabbath" (Luke 14:1-6)
SATURDAY, March 2: "The Great Dinner for All Peoples" (Luke 14:15-24)
SUNDAY, March 3: "Humility, the Right Path for Believers" (Luke 14:7-14)

March 10, 2019   Lesson 2

A COSTLY CALL

ADULT/YOUTH
ADULT/YOUNG ADULT TOPIC: **Counting the Cost**
YOUTH TOPIC: **Counting the Cost**

CHILDREN
GENERAL LESSON TITLE: **Following Jesus Is Costly**
CHILDREN'S TOPIC: **Paying the Cost**

DEVOTIONAL READING
Philippians 3:7-16

ADULT/YOUTH
BACKGROUND SCRIPTURE: **Mark 1:16-20; Luke 14:25-33**
PRINT PASSAGE: **Mark 1:16-20; Luke 14:25-33**
KEY VERSE: **Luke 14:27**

CHILDREN
BACKGROUND SCRIPTURE: **Mark 1:16-20; Luke 14:25-33**
PRINT PASSAGE: **Mark 1:16-20; Luke 14:25-33**
KEY VERSES: **Mark 1:17-18**

Mark 1:16-20; Luke 14:25-33—KJV

16 Now as he walked by the sea of Galilee, he saw Simon and Andrew his brother casting a net into the sea: for they were fishers.

17 And Jesus said unto them, Come ye after me, and I will make you to become fishers of men.

18 And straightway they forsook their nets, and followed him.

19 And when he had gone a little farther thence, he saw James the son of Zebedee, and John his brother, who also were in the ship mending their nets.

20 And straightway he called them: and they left their father Zebedee in the ship with the hired servants, and went after him.

.....

25 And there went great multitudes with him: and he turned, and said unto them,

26 If any man come to me, and hate not his father, and mother, and wife, and children, and brethren,

Mark 1:16-20; Luke 14:25-33—NIV

16 As Jesus walked beside the Sea of Galilee, he saw Simon and his brother Andrew casting a net into the lake, for they were fishermen.

17 "Come, follow me," Jesus said, "and I will send you out to fish for people."

18 At once they left their nets and followed him.

19 When he had gone a little farther, he saw James son of Zebedee and his brother John in a boat, preparing their nets.

20 Without delay he called them, and they left their father Zebedee in the boat with the hired men and followed him.

.....

25 Large crowds were traveling with Jesus, and turning to them he said:

26 "If anyone comes to me and does not hate father and mother, wife and children, brothers and sisters—

and sisters, yea, and his own life also, he cannot be my disciple.

27 And whosoever doth not bear his cross, and come after me, cannot be my disciple.

28 For which of you, intending to build a tower, sitteth not down first, and counteth the cost, whether he have sufficient to finish it?

29 Lest haply, after he hath laid the foundation, and is not able to finish it, all that behold it begin to mock him,

30 Saying, This man began to build, and was not able to finish.

31 Or what king, going to make war against another king, sitteth not down first, and consulteth whether he be able with ten thousand to meet him that cometh against him with twenty thousand?

32 Or else, while the other is yet a great way off, he sendeth an ambassage, and desireth conditions of peace.

33 So likewise, whosoever he be of you that forsaketh not all that he hath, he cannot be my disciple.

yes, even their own life—such a person cannot be my disciple.

27 "And whoever does not carry their cross and follow me cannot be my disciple.

28 "Suppose one of you wants to build a tower. Won't you first sit down and estimate the cost to see if you have enough money to complete it?

29 "For if you lay the foundation and are not able to finish it, everyone who sees it will ridicule you,

30 "saying, 'This person began to build and wasn't able to finish.'

31 "Or suppose a king is about to go to war against another king. Won't he first sit down and consider whether he is able with ten thousand men to oppose the one coming against him with twenty thousand?

32 "If he is not able, he will send a delegation while the other is still a long way off and will ask for terms of peace.

33 "In the same way, those of you who do not give up everything you have cannot be my disciples."

UNIFYING LESSON PRINCIPLE: People are always faced with choices between the comfortable, easy way, and the more helpful but challenging way. How do we make the right choice? Jesus challenged His hearers to count the cost and recognize the consequences of discipleship.

LESSON OBJECTIVES

Upon the completion of this lesson, the students will be able to do the following:

1. Summarize what Jesus said about counting the cost of being His disciple.
2. Appreciate how the demands of discipleship can force one to make some hard choices in life.
3. Recognize what one must be prepared to give up to be Christ's disciple.

AGE-LEVEL POINTS TO BE EMPHASIZED

Teachers of ADULTS and YOUTH

—In Jewish culture, to study under a rabbi was a great honor.

—Radical discipleship—putting Christ before family and possessions—is a difficult calling, especially for those who have much.

—"Hate" in this context signifies a relative lack of importance. Holding family and possessions to be more important than Christ is idolatry.

—Crucifixion was a cruel and terrible form of execution. Therefore, one's carrying his/her cross is a shocking image of self-sacrifice (see Luke 9:23).

—Faithfulness (choosing to follow Jesus even after

counting the cost) is a hallmark of committed discipleship.

—The ready response of the brothers Simon and Andrew and James and John to Jesus' call for their discipleship attests to the natural charisma of Jesus in His appeals to attract followers.

—Devoting all the property to the community was considered radical by early Judaic and Greco-Roman standards.

Teachers of CHILDREN

—Jesus' first four disciples were fishermen who left their trade and families to follow Jesus.

—Following Jesus is accompanied by personal sacrifices and hardships.

—Those who follow Jesus are reminded of the cost of being His disciples.

—True disciples willingly give first priority to their relationship with Jesus.

THE CHRONOLOGICAL SETTING OF THE LESSON

The structure of these narratives is very similar to the call of Elisha by Elijah in 1 Kings 19:19-21; this scene in the Old Testament is generally considered as the model that inspired Mark's narrative setting of the call of Jesus' disciples. Even though Mark may have been inspired by this Old Testament model, he did not want to present Jesus as the new Elijah, since the figure of Elijah is reserved for John the Baptist. Mark chose instead to illustrate the theme of the prophetic authority that belonged to Jesus as He called people away from their old way of life to a new life of service in following Him.

Various sayings in Luke 14:25-33 are similar to those in the book of Mark. Luke carefully constructed this charge to discipleship from Mark's gospel. Luke characterized discipleship as "coming to Jesus." The full significance of coming to Jesus is defined in terms of "hating" father and mother, wife, children, brothers, sisters, and even self. The call of Jesus takes precedence even over primary familial and marital relationships of life. In verse 27, coming to Jesus is defined in terms of bearing one's cross, an image of discipleship introduced earlier. The Cross (see Luke 9:23), an instrument of suffering and shame, epitomizes the sacrifices required of a disciple in following Jesus. Additionally, in verse 33, coming to Jesus is defined in terms of forsaking earthly possessions. Coming to Jesus, in other words, means acknowledging Jesus as the preeminent relationship in one's life, and one whose presence takes precedence over all things in life. Exclusive allegiance is what is required of all those who would follow Jesus.

THE GEOGRAPHICAL AND CULTURAL SETTING OF THE LESSON

The passages before us are among the most dynamic in the Gospels, but it should be remembered that these words were spoken to crowds that were already eagerly anticipating the early establishment of a kingdom. Excitement was beginning to run high, for it was obvious to all that Jesus was marching toward Jerusalem (see Luke 14:25). It is very possible that even as He walked, the Lord was able to hear the conversation of those who accompanied Him. They were convinced that the glory of the messianic kingdom was about to break over Israel, and therefore the Master felt constrained to correct their mistaken beliefs. He knew that the Cross was awaiting Him within the city to which He was journeying, and unless these eager people were prepared for what was to come, their faith would disintegrate.

Therefore, the theme of this passage is indisputably *the cost of discipleship*. Many writers have spiritualized the verses to make them mean many things, but the only thing obvious here is that Christ was warning people about making hasty decisions. Following Christ meant deliberation and very much determination. No one ever had a picnic on a cross. Probably the tower to which Christ referred was the usual tall tower often found in vineyards. This was a lookout tower from which the watchman could see any pilferer of the harvest.

The life of discipleship would make exacting demands upon all who decided to follow Christ. Consequently, prospective disciples were urged to count the cost, for ultimately the claims of the Cross would divide families, and even the dearest of earthly friends would oppose the dedicated Christian. Unless the disciples were willing to leave father and mother and friends—unless they were willing to go all the way with the Lord—it would be better not to start. In the truest and fullest sense of the term, half-hearted disciples were not disciples, for unless Christ possessed them completely, He did not possess them at all.

PROMINENT CHARACTER(S) IN THE LESSON

Andrew: a native of Bethsaida. He and John were Jesus' first converts. He brought his brother Peter to Christ.

James: the son of Alphaeus. He was called "The Little," perhaps because of his height.

Simon: later known as Peter; he was a partner in the fishing business with James and John. He was a native of Bethsaida and had a home in Capernaum. He was considered the "leader" among the disciples/apostles (the Twelve).

KEY TERMS IN THE LESSON

Cross (Luke 14:27)—Greek: *stauros* (stau-ro's): a well-known instrument of most cruel and ignominious punishment. To it were affixed among the Romans, down to the time of Constantine the Great, the guiltiest criminals.

Disciple (Luke 14:26)—Greek: *mathētēs* (mä-thā-tā's): a learner; pupil.

Hate (Luke 14:26)—Greek: *miseō* (mē-se'-ō): to detach, detest.

Peace (Luke 14:32)—Greek: *eirēnē* (ā-rā'-nā): the tranquil state of a soul assured of its salvation through Christ.

TOPICAL OUTLINE OF THE LESSON

I. **Introduction**
   A. Follow Me!
   B. Biblical Background

II. **Exposition and Application of the Scripture**
   A. Called into the Service of the Master (Mark 1:16-20)
   B. The Demands of Discipleship (Luke 14:25-27)
   C. The Cost of Discipleship (Luke 14:28-32)
   D. Discipleship as Total Surrender (Luke 14:33)

III. **Concluding Reflection**

I. INTRODUCTION

A. Follow Me!

What does it mean to be a follower of Jesus Christ in our day and time? And what does it mean to count the cost of discipleship in our day? What is the cost of Christian discipleship? And are we willing to consider it? How many times have we made a commitment to do something only to discover later that we bit off more than we could chew? What about those commitments we have made on the spur of a moment only to regret them later when we actually have to show up and do what we promised we would do? Jesus is urging all who would follow Him to count the cost of what it means to be one of His disciples. Unlike some contemporary preachers who make it sound easy to be a follower of Christ, Jesus actually did lay down some tough guidelines for people to follow. In fact, He urged us to count the cost before we say yes to following Him.

B. Biblical Background

In our lesson today, Luke returned to the journey motif. Because Jesus faced martyrdom in Jerusalem, His followers had to be prepared to leave everything behind and make their commitment to Jesus as complete and all-consuming as Jesus' own devotion to His mission. These sayings are addressed to the large crowds following Jesus. Their intent is to urge persons who are seeking to be disciples to consider first the demands of discipleship. Rather than trying to lure the unsuspecting into unconsidered commitments, Jesus warned the crowd in advance that the way of discipleship would not be easy. The three conditions laid down in this sequence of pronouncements are these: renouncing family ties that would prevent one from being a disciple; bearing one's cross; and forsaking possessions.

II. EXPOSITION AND APPLICATION OF THE SCRIPTURE

A. Called into the Service of the Master (Mark 1:16-20)

Now as he walked by the sea of Galilee, he saw Simon and Andrew his brother casting a net into the sea: for they were fishers. And Jesus said unto them, Come ye after me, and I will make you to become fishers of men. And straightway they forsook their nets, and followed him. And when he had gone a little farther thence, he saw James the son of Zebedee, and John his brother, who also were in the ship mending their nets. And straightway he called them: and they left their father Zebedee in the ship with the hired servants, and went after him.

From the beginning of this first part of Mark's gospel, Jesus appeared as an itinerant constantly on the move (verse 16). To accompany Him does not therefore issue in the entry into a school, but it comes down to adopting a kind of itinerant lifestyle just like His, which consists of unending travel on foot. The first to be called were Simon and Andrew, his brother; then James and John, both sons of Zebedee. The narrative does not tell us any more about these characters for now, except for the fact that they were fishermen.

The striking fact is that in all these call narratives, Jesus kept the initiative. He was the one who spotted the fishermen and called them while they were busy with their daily tasks. He was the one who set down the rules and requirements of discipleship. Jesus' manner is close to that of the angel of Yahweh's, who chose Moses when he was busy pasturing his little flock (see Exodus 3:1-2), or Gideon, who was busy threshing wheat (see Judges 6:11-12). It is also close to that of the prophet Elijah's, who threw his mantle onto Elisha while he was working (see 1 Kings 19:19).

The purpose of the call of the first disciples is only clarified through a metaphor: "I will cause you to become fishers of people" (see Mark 1:17). Unknown as such in the Old Testament or in rabbinic literature, the expression "fishers of people" is probably nothing other than a play on words; instead of fishing for fish, you will now fish for people! Jesus did not ask anything else of those He called other than for them to follow Him. The abandonment of their trade and their tools flowed from their adherence to Jesus, the itinerant (one who stays in a place for only a short amount of time).

James and John—the sons of Zebedee (verse 19)—together with Peter, formed the group of disciples mentioned most often by Mark, and apparently were the closest to Jesus. James and John's response to Jesus' call was as immediate as that of the first two disciples Peter and Andrew: they severed their family ties and left their father, Zebedee, in the boat with the hired men. The reference to "hired men" (verse 20) indicates that the brothers were by no means poor men. They were willing to leave all to follow Jesus. The description of their immediate response to the summons of Jesus conveyed vividly the authority and power which He exercised. Mark does not tell us whether these men had already met or heard of Jesus. The impression given by Mark, however, is that the personality and authority of Jesus were such that the four men responded to His call at their first meeting. By telling the story in this way, Mark not only impresses his readers with the authority of Jesus, but also reminds us that we too are called by Jesus to obey the same command.

B. The Demands of Discipleship (Luke 14:25-27)

And there went great multitudes with him: and he turned, and said unto them, If any man come to me, and hate not his father, and mother, and wife, and children, and brethren, and sisters, yea, and his own life also, he cannot be my disciple. And whosoever doth not bear his cross, and come after me, cannot be my disciple.

Here, Jesus again addressed the crowds about discipleship. In verses 26-33, there are three challenges to discipleship that end with a common refrain: "cannot be my disciple." These three verses refer to three kinds of sacrifice that disciples must be willing to make. Jesus had already talked about these three issues, but here His language was very sharp; for hating one's family, carrying one's cross, and taking leave of all of one's possessions are made explicit conditions of discipleship. In the early church, the travelling missionaries were most likely to make these sacrifices, but the believers who stayed at home might face circumstances in which these demands would be made of them as well.

There are a number of seeming anti-family sayings in Luke's gospel. However, the demand in verse 26 that one "hate" one's family is perhaps the strongest. In the ancient world, the terms *love* and *hate* referred less to emotions than to behavior. To *hate* was a Semitic expression that conveyed indifference to one and preference for another. The word *hate* is intended to convey the inestimable worth of a choice, not a malicious motive of a choice. The point of verse 26 is that good things—even things created and commended by God, such as father and mother and the honor due them—cannot be given precedence over Jesus. When the good rivals the best, then it must be hated. The saying reflects the reality of many first-century disciples, whose choice to follow Jesus alienated families.

The metaphor of bearing one's cross in verse 27 connotes the process of following Jesus through daily trials. What is sought after here is some understanding of constancy and steadfastness in following Jesus. In the words of the Book of Common Prayer, our commitment to following Christ is not something that we should enter into lightly or unadvisedly, but deliberately and in the fear of God. This deeply held commitment is also captured in one of the great hymns of the church: "I'm going through, and I'll pay the price whatever others do."

C. The Cost of Discipleship (Luke 14:28-32)

For which of you, intending to build a tower, sitteth not down first, and counteth the cost, whether he have sufficient to finish it? Lest haply, after he hath laid the foundation, and is not able to finish it, all that behold it begin to mock him, Saying, This man began to build, and was not able to finish. Or what king, going to make war against another king, sitteth not down first, and consulteth whether he be able with ten thousand to meet him that cometh against him with twenty thousand? Or else, while the other is yet a great way off, he sendeth an ambassage, and desireth conditions of peace.

In Luke 14:28-32, Jesus made a simple observation. A prudent person would not begin a project until being sure it can be finished. A man would not lay the foundation for a tower unless he was sure he could finish it (verses 28-30). A king would not go to war unless he had enough soldiers to defeat the opposing force. Similarly, God has not entered a redemptive process without being prepared to complete it, and Jesus did not set His face for Jerusalem without being prepared to face the sacrifice that would be required of Him there. Thus, no one should step forward as a disciple without being prepared to forsake everything for the sake of following Jesus.

The two parables move from the lesser to the greater consequence. In the first, the threat is merely that one may be embarrassed before one's neighbors. In the second, the consequence may be defeat at the hands of an enemy. The parable does not advocate building stronger armies; it illustrates the folly of one's embarking on a venture without being sure he/she can see it through to completion. Both questions are intended to elicit agreement from the audience because the answers are obvious; no one among us would do anything this imprudent. The obvious answers also draw in the entire audience, for if they answer the questions correctly, it helps them to see that they were all potential disciples if they were willing to make the radical commitment that Jesus required. In effect, Jesus was saying that a person who is willing to count the cost and pay the price can be one of His disciples. However, we should not say yes without seriously pondering the consequences of what a "yes" to Jesus will mean in our lives.

D. Discipleship as Total Surrender (Luke 14:33)

So likewise, whosoever he be of you that forsaketh not all that he hath, he cannot be my disciple.

Luke added the remark about getting rid of one's possessions to these two parables and thus brought them into line with his overall concern about attachment to possessions and how it is a hindrance to becoming Jesus' disciple and entering the kingdom of God. The building of the tower required the ability to commit all of one's wealth to the project. In like manner, preparing for war and suing for peace required one's honest assessment of his or her ability to withstand the superior force, just as the attraction of wealth is a superior force for working against discipleship and entry into the kingdom.

If one is truly to join Jesus on this journey,

then that person must say farewell to all he or she has (verse 33). This "leaving behind" is cast in the present tense, demarcating this condition not simply as a potential for which disciples must be constantly ready, but as characteristic of the disciple. The disciples of Jesus must put aside all competing securities in order that they might refashion their lives and identity according to the norms of the kingdom of God.

III. CONCLUDING REFLECTION

German theologian and martyr Dietrich Bonhoeffer captured Christ's stark demands for discipleship in this oft-repeated saying: "The cross is laid on every Christian. [It begins with] the call to abandon the attachments of this world. . . . When Christ calls a [human being], he bids him come and die." This radical obedience and absolute allegiance to Jesus may sound harsh and impossible to most contemporary Christians in the West. Yet, the history of the church is filled with those who have heard this call and responded with utter abandon. Martyrs like Polycarp and Perpetua laid down their lives, refusing the plea of family and friends to renounce their faith. Saints like Francis rejected worldly comforts for a life of Christian discipline. This is our story and our calling too. However, we are prone to lose the edge of our commitment; we are vulnerable to let other distractions erode our allegiance to Christ.

Discipleship consists of both giving and receiving. Not all are called to the same form of discipleship at all times. However, whatever form the call takes, all are called to Jesus absolutely and without reserve. Discipleship cannot be an expression of mere civil religion. It does not confuse the Gospel with ideologies or cultural norms, nor does it tailor the Gospel to our preferences and causes—even the most noble. It is the forsaking of all for Jesus.

PRAYER

Teach us Thy way, O Lord. Illumine our hearts and minds so that we may know the cost of what it means truly to follow You. Then we pray You would give us the strength to say yes to a life of dedicated commitment to Your will and to Your way. In Jesus' name we pray. Amen.

HOME DAILY BIBLE READINGS
(March 4-10, 2019)

A Costly Call

MONDAY, March 4: "Answering the Lord's Call of Discipleship" (Mark 4:10-20)

TUESDAY, March 5: "It's Hard to Enter the Kingdom" (Mark 10:23-31)

WEDNESDAY, March 6: "The Lord's Call and Family Conflict" (Matthew 10:34-39)

THURSDAY, March 7: "The Father Honors Those Who Follow" (John 12:20-26)

FRIDAY, March 8: "Suffering and Knowing Christ Jesus" (Philippians 3:7-16)

SATURDAY, March 9: "Faithful Witness through Suffering" (2 Corinthians 6:1-10)

SUNDAY, March 10: "Counting the Cost, Answering the Call" (Mark 1:16-20; Luke 14:25-33)

March 17, 2019 — Lesson 3

CALLING THE LOST

ADULT/YOUTH
ADULT/YOUNG ADULT TOPIC: **Lost and Found**
YOUTH TOPIC: **Lost and Found**

CHILDREN
GENERAL LESSON TITLE: **Jesus Calls the Lost**
CHILDREN'S TOPIC: **He's Looking for You!**

DEVOTIONAL READING
Ezekiel 34:11-16

ADULT/YOUTH
BACKGROUND SCRIPTURE: **Luke 15**
PRINT PASSAGE: **Luke 15:11-24**
KEY VERSES: **Luke 15:22, 24**

CHILDREN
BACKGROUND SCRIPTURE: **Luke 15**
PRINT PASSAGE: **Luke 15:11-24**
KEY VERSES: **Luke 15:22a, 24**

Luke 15:11-24—KJV

11 And he said, A certain man had two sons:

12 And the younger of them said to his father, Father, give me the portion of goods that falleth to me. And he divided unto them his living.

13 And not many days after the younger son gathered all together, and took his journey into a far country, and there wasted his substance with riotous living.

14 And when he had spent all, there arose a mighty famine in that land; and he began to be in want.

15 And he went and joined himself to a citizen of that country; and he sent him into his fields to feed swine.

16 And he would fain have filled his belly with the husks that the swine did eat: and no man gave unto him.

17 And when he came to himself, he said, How many hired servants of my father's have bread enough and to spare, and I perish with hunger!

18 I will arise and go to my father, and will say unto him, Father, I have sinned against heaven, and before thee,

19 And am no more worthy to be called thy son: make me as one of thy hired servants.

Luke 15:11-24—NIV

11 Jesus continued: "There was a man who had two sons.

12 "The younger one said to his father, 'Father, give me my share of the estate.' So he divided his property between them.

13 "Not long after that, the younger son got together all he had, set off for a distant country and there squandered his wealth in wild living.

14 "After he had spent everything, there was a severe famine in that whole country, and he began to be in need.

15 "So he went and hired himself out to a citizen of that country, who sent him to his fields to feed pigs.

16 "He longed to fill his stomach with the pods that the pigs were eating, but no one gave him anything.

17 "When he came to his senses, he said, 'How many of my father's hired servants have food to spare, and here I am starving to death!

18 "'I will set out and go back to my father and say to him: Father, I have sinned against heaven and against you.

20 And he arose, and came to his father. But when he was yet a great way off, his father saw him, and had compassion, and ran, and fell on his neck, and kissed him.

21 And the son said unto him, Father, I have sinned against heaven, and in thy sight, and am no more worthy to be called thy son.

22 But the father said to his servants, Bring forth the best robe, and put it on him; and put a ring on his hand, and shoes on his feet:

23 And bring hither the fatted calf, and kill it; and let us eat, and be merry:

24 For this my son was dead, and is alive again; he was lost, and is found. And they began to be merry.

19 "'I am no longer worthy to be called your son; make me like one of your hired servants.'

20 "So he got up and went to his father. But while he was still a long way off, his father saw him and was filled with compassion for him; he ran to his son, threw his arms around him and kissed him.

21 "The son said to him, 'Father, I have sinned against heaven and against you. I am no longer worthy to be called your son.'

22 "But the father said to his servants, 'Quick! Bring the best robe and put it on him. Put a ring on his finger and sandals on his feet.

23 "'Bring the fattened calf and kill it. Let's have a feast and celebrate.

24 "'For this son of mine was dead and is alive again; he was lost and is found.' So they began to celebrate.'"

UNIFYING LESSON PRINCIPLE: In our world, it is easy for people to lose their way. What is our responsibility to those who go astray? Jesus taught that those who are lost are loved by God and are to be valued, searched for, and welcomed back when they return.

LESSON OBJECTIVES

Upon the completion of this lesson, the students will be able to do the following:

1. Identify whom in contemporary life might be illustrated by the characters in the parable.
2. Sense God's grief over God's lost children as the father grieved over the lost son before the son's return.
3. Suggest a culturally appropriate means by which new converts can be rejoiced over as the father rejoiced over the returning son.

AGE-LEVEL POINTS TO BE EMPHASIZED

Teachers of ADULTS and YOUTH

—Jesus' welcoming sinners and the criticism He received for it (see Luke 15:1-2) provide the context of this parable.

—The mercy of the loving father is not dependent on some measure of the son's sinfulness, but on the son's repentance and return, and the condition of the father's heart.

—Jesus shows that God's love is all-embracing, unconditional, and seems to overflow for repentant sinners.

—In the parable of today's lesson, the father does not search for the younger son; the son comes back on his own. But in the two preceding parables, the shepherd searches for the lost sheep and the woman searches for the lost coin.

—The sense that Jesus suggested of God's grieving over His lost children as the father grieved over the lost son is a characteristic displayed throughout the Hebrew Bible, where God always was aggrieved over Israel's going astray or acts of disobedience (see Jeremiah, Isaiah, other prophets).

—The son insulted the father by asking for his inheritance before the father died.

—The son shamed himself and his father by wasting his money on dissolute living.

—It violated Jewish laws to eat "unclean" animals such as swine.

—The son realized that his disrespectful behavior affected his family.

—The father demonstrated unconditional love by running to meet his lost son.

—The robe, the ring, and the feast were symbols of the celebration of the father's love for his son.

Teachers of CHILDREN

—People ask God to give them what they want rather than what they need.

—Forgiveness is an important ingredient in a sinner's healing process.

—Parents, in an attempt to support their children's dreams, may enable their destruction.

—Loving parents rejoice and welcome their children back to the fold after they have gone astray.

—Jesus commands faith communities to welcome erring members and rejoice when they return to the fold.

THE CHRONOLOGICAL SETTING OF THE LESSON

During the time of Jesus' ministry, there were many parables He told to various audiences. In Luke 15, the third parable Jesus told is probably the best known of all three. Throughout the church's history, it has been admired and found helpful by countless people, even being the subject of religious art. It is full of profound insights into human beings and the way repentance and salvation work in human experience. It proves that Jesus was a master storyteller and perfectly understood the entire human condition. Although the parable has been strongly connected with one son—the Prodigal Son—it is more accurately a parable about a father who had two sons.

THE GEOGRAPHICAL AND CULTURAL SETTING OF THE LESSON

From two brief parables about the celebration of the lost and found—sheep and coins—Jesus turned to a more extended account of a lost and found son. To be sure, the stakes were significantly raised in this instance: the son lost was one of only two, compared with the one sheep of a hundred and one coin of ten in verses 3-10. The fact that today's lesson speaks of one of two sons contributes to the intrinsic interest of the narrative as well as to its dramatic appeal.

The point at which this third parable advances significantly beyond the framework of the earlier two is in its heightened attention to issues of kinship. As valuable as sheep and coins might be to a person, the loss and recovery of a son or daughter are of even greater importance. Critical to the development of this parable is how this loss and recovery are signified in familial terms. A younger son acknowledged his father as such but acted toward him in ways that were out of character, according to normal canons of familial behavior. This led eventually to his attempt to reframe their relationship as one of master and hired hand (see Luke 15:19)—a definition at odds with his father's persistence in continuing to recognize him as a member of the family. It is worth recalling that a primary image of God in the Lukan travel narrative has been God as Father, a portrait continued in this parable.

PROMINENT CHARACTER(S) IN THE LESSON

The Father: The father in this story/parable is not named in order for us to see the characteristics of this father which mirror the characteristics of God toward those who stray.

The Prodigal Son: It can be speculated that this Prodigal Son is not named because in a sense there is a "prodigal inclination" in many people; thus, we can all identify with him.

KEY TERMS IN THE LESSON

Famine (verse 14)—Greek: *limos* (lē-mo's): scarcity of harvest.

Journey (verse 13)—Greek: *apodēmeō* (ä-po-dā-me'-ō): to go (travel) into a far country; "set off for a distant country" (NIV).

Pigs (verse 15)—Greek: *choiros* (khoi'-ros): "swine" (KJV).

Riotous living (verse 13): living lavishly beyond one's means; living in a wild manner; "wild living" (NIV).

Sinned (verse 21)—Greek: *hamartanō* (hä-mär-tä'-nō): wandered from the law of God; violated God's law.

Squandered (verse 13)—Greek: *diaskorpizō* (dē-ä-skor-pē'-zō): scattered abroad; dispersed; "wasted" (KJV).

TOPICAL OUTLINE OF THE LESSON

I. **Introduction**
   A. Helping the Lost to Find Their Way
   B. Biblical Background

II. **Exposition and Application of the Scripture**
   A. A Premature Demand and an Untimely Departure
      (Luke 15:11-13a)
   B. High Living and Wasteful Spending
      (Luke 15:13b-14)
   C. Down but Not Out!
      (Luke 15:15-19)
   D. Returning with a Plea for Mercy
      (Luke 15:20-24)

III. **Concluding Reflection**

I. INTRODUCTION

A. Helping the Lost to Find Their Way

The Prodigal Son in today's lesson models for us what it looks like when people of high promise go astray. The loving father in the story models for us what we should do every time we have an opportunity to help people get their lives in order. Sometimes, it is a child who has been coddled and pampered too much who just cannot seem to get his or her act together. Other times it is an absent father, battered by life, who simply could not keep things together long enough to be the loving father that he needed to be to his children. Scripture teaches that we have a responsibility to help those who are struggling to make something of themselves, even when their wounds and hurts are self-inflicted. We too are called to throw open our loving arms to all who are struggling to find their way back home.

B. Biblical Background

This is a parable of a father with two sons. Normally, Jewish sons would stay with their fathers and serve under them in the family business, waiting until they died before inheriting a share of the family assets. In this story, the younger son brought forward his claim on his inheritance prematurely, no doubt deeply wounding the father in doing so. His attitude showed that he cared more about his inheritance than about his father. Nor did he choose to work his part of the property. Instead, he asked for it to be realized as capital, and upon receiving it immediately left home. How brokenhearted the father must have been in the face of his son's selfishness and insensitivity.

The younger son put as much distance between himself and the father as possible by travelling to a country far away from home. By choosing a far country, the younger son was choosing the life of a spendthrift over being guided by the hand of a loving father. He enjoyed himself in the far country with its alluring attractions and enticing entertainment, spending his money freely, indulging his senses to the fullest. He was glad to be free of the restraints and service of living with his father. However, the son burned up his whole inheritance just at a time when an economic recession was falling on that country. Jobs were scarce and none of his former friends, so ready to share his fortune when he was rich and generous, would help him now that he was the one in need. In survival mode, he hired himself out to a local farmer, to do the most menial jobs, like feeding pigs. He even reached the point where he envied the pigs because they were eating, and he was not. As he looked down upon those beasts in the pigpen—sometimes God cannot get our attention until we have fallen low enough—the Bible says he came to himself. In addition, when he came *to* himself he had a conversation *within* himself and decided that home was the best place for him. He arose from the depths of his despair and returned to the waiting arms of his father. A repentant son and a loving father are at the heart of this lesson today.

II. EXPOSITION AND APPLICATION OF THE SCRIPTURE

A. A Premature Demand and an Untimely Departure
(Luke 15:11-13a)

And he said, A certain man had two sons: And the younger of them said to his father, Father, give me the portion of goods that falleth to me. And he divided unto them his living. And not many days after the younger son gathered all together, and took his journey into a far country.

"There was a man who had two sons" (verse 11) sets up an expectation that there will be a contrast between the two boys. The first tension comes when the younger son demands—"give me"—his share of the inheritance. In Jesus' culture, as in our own, land ownership was a mark of stability and security. Land was something to protect and to keep intact, if possible, so that one could pass it along to one's children. The eldest son is supposed to have a double share of the inheritance, so in this story he should inherit two-thirds and his younger brother one-third. Sons did not normally demand their inheritance before the death of their father.

To ask for one's inheritance while the father is still alive is the equivalent of saying, "I wish you were already dead, but since you aren't, I can't wait any longer." The father met the son's impatience with patience and submitted to his request. Impudent, ungrateful, and rebellious sons were not unknown in the ancient world, but when they appeared, they usually came to a bad end. This younger son, like so many sons and daughters down through the ages, would have to learn the hard way that what you do to others you will see again in your life. Moreover, this lesson teaches that the comfort and security of home are often taken for granted until one leaves home.

The younger son gathered his earthly belongings and left home abruptly. This, no doubt, he did after making a quick deal to get as much cash as he could out of the sale of his inheritance. In a culture where all transactions involve lengthy negotiations, and where land sales are the most involved of all, "not many days" is simply too fast to have gotten a good price. The hard lessons of life are often learned through the bitter experiences of life.

B. High Living and Wasteful Spending
(Luke 15:13b-14)

and there wasted his substance with riotous living. And when he had spent all, there arose a mighty famine in that land; and he began to be in want.

The younger son went to the "far country" and spent his money by living large (verse 13b). "Riotous living" simply means he lived without control. Thus, the way he lived led to his impoverishment. His folly is a story replayed many times in the lives of the young, and others not so young. The young are expected to climb fool's hill at least once in their lives; the

hope is that it will become a lifelong learning experience for them. The Prodigal Son was a short-sighted spendthrift who lived only for today with little to no thought about what tomorrow would bring.

He lived in the moment, thinking the provisions from his father's particular grace would last forever. And then reality kicked in. When he had spent all, a famine came, and the boy had no family or resources on which to fall back (verse 14). Young and foolish, he had yet to learn that life is filled with unexpectedness. Even with the best of planning, life throws us a curve ball from time to time. Had he not spent all, he might have been able to ride out the depressed economy.

C. Down but Not Out!
(Luke 15:15-19)

And he went and joined himself to a citizen of that country; and he sent him into his fields to feed swine. And he would fain have filled his belly with the husks that the swine did eat: and no man gave unto him. And when he came to himself, he said, How many hired servants of my father's have bread enough and to spare, and I perish with hunger! I will arise and go to my father, and will say unto him, Father, I have sinned against heaven, and before thee, And am no more worthy to be called thy son: make me as one of thy hired servants.

Broke, hungry, and away from home, he "hired himself out" as a day laborer to a citizen of that region (verse 15), who promptly sent him into his fields to feed his pigs.

The Gentile owner of the pigs apparently valued his pigs more than he did the Prodigal Son who was looking after them. The Scriptures say the younger son would gladly have filled his belly with what he was feeding to the pigs—the sweet pulp of the carob tree (verse 16). At this point in his life, the boy is poor, separated from his family, separated from his faith, and starving far from home. He is so hungry that he would have eaten the pig's food if he could. The last part of verse 16 finds him at the bottom of the pit, and Jesus says, "And no one gave him anything." He got there by demanding everything that was coming to him and, in fact, he got it all, and it turned out to be far more than he expected.

The expression "came to himself" in verse 17 is a literal translation; it is used in other texts to mean something like coming to one's senses, especially when one has been under a delusion. The boy thought over his situation and decided he could do better than the situation he was in: "How many of my father's hired workers have more than enough food, while I am here perishing from hunger!" (see verse 17). Did he truly repent? On the positive side, he said the right words and walked in the right direction—"I will arise and go to my father" (verse 18). He had sinned against God and against his father, and he had started home to face the person he dishonored and damaged by leaving. He is to be given credit for coming to himself and returning home to his father. How deep his repentance runs will only become clear from what he does after being received so generously by his father.

D. Returning with a Plea for Mercy (Luke 15:20-24)

And he arose, and came to his father. But when he was yet a great way off, his father saw him, and had compassion, and ran, and fell on his neck, and kissed him. And the son said unto him, Father, I have sinned against heaven, and in thy sight, and am no more worthy to be called thy son. But the father said to his servants, Bring forth the best robe, and put it on him; and put a ring on his hand, and shoes on his feet: And bring hither the fatted calf, and kill it; and let us eat, and be merry: For this my son was dead, and is alive again; he was lost, and is found. And they began to be merry.

Having left his family, abandoned his religious heritage, lost his integrity, and now with his very existence threatened with starvation, the Prodigal Son came to his senses. He decided to return home hoping to be accepted back, not as a son, but as a servant. Like many who come to the point where they want to reconnect with injured family members and repair estranged relationships, the wasteful son practiced his speech—hoping to find the right words to achieve his goal. The rest depended on his father. While he was still a long way off, his waiting father was overjoyed to see him. The father's unwavering expectation reflected how much hope he still had for his son's return. When the son finally came into view, the father was filled with compassion. He ran to meet him, embraced him, and kissed him (verse 21). Without reprimand, indignation, or anger, the father received him back as a son. Before the disgraced son could even finish his prepared speech, the father interrupted him and proceeded to honor him with gifts and plans and grand celebrations.

Just as the younger son represents the wanderlust and sin in every heart, the father represents the God and Father of Jesus in His patience and love for all men and women who have gone astray in their lives. Like God, the father in this parable had never forgotten his erring son. As a result, the moment his son appeared on the horizon, the father immediately ran to welcome him back home, not in reproachful coldness, but with the warmest reunion. Not with "I told you so," but with "this my son was dead, and is alive again" (verse

24). This is a truly wonderful representation of the love of God for the world, and especially for all who come home again. It is also our model for the way in which we are to be reconciled to one another and how we are to give aid and succor to one another when we have not lived up to all that we could and should be.

III. CONCLUDING REFLECTION

A son left home, enticed by the false promises of his world. How attractive the far country of the world appears when people first set out for it, often when they are young and in pursuit of their dreams and promised pleasures. They begin by celebrating with other kindred spirits, exhilarating in the freedom of being their own person and following their own illusions, free from the moral restraints of family, church, and community. Many young people in the world today share in the outlook and behavior of the Prodigal Son. They desire to choose their own paths and experience the different options that the world has to offer. However, boom times never last, dreams fade, friends desert, and people discover for themselves the harsh realities of trying to succeed in a fallen and sometimes unfriendly world. Once out of blessing range, they truly come to understand Tina Turner's famous question, "What's love got to do with it?"

The Prodigal Son is everyone's story to some degree, whether we have lived far away from God or not. The truth be told, no one has to travel over the miles to be in a far country. It is not distance that separates us from God; it is spiritual alienation. Whenever we leave the loving arms of the Father and those who love us, we are in a far country, and that far country can be just up the street or no farther than the other side of town. Alienation respects no distance, but love knows no bounds. The loving Father represented in this parable, as well as in our lives, is eagerly awaiting all who have become alienated and estranged from Him.

PRAYER

Heavenly Father, we thank You for Your unconditional steadfast love. In trying days when our own selfish wills and misguided desires separate us from You, please do not leave us or forsake us. Help us to meet the people we need to meet on our way in life, and give us the confident assurance that we can always turn from our sins and come back to Your loving arms. In Jesus' name we pray. Amen.

HOME DAILY BIBLE READINGS
(March 11-17, 2019)

Calling the Lost

MONDAY, March 11: "Transformed by Christ into New Life" (Ephesians 2:1-10)
TUESDAY, March 12: "God Seeks the Scattered People" (Ezekiel 34:11-16)
WEDNESDAY, March 13: "God's Compassion for Straying People" (Hosea 11:1-4, 8-9)
THURSDAY, March 14: "Calling Sinners to Repentance" (Luke 3:12-13; 5:27-32)
FRIDAY, March 15: "Finding the Lost Sheep and Coin" (Luke 15:1-10)
SATURDAY, March 16: "A Plea for Understanding and Recognition" (Luke 15:25-32)
SUNDAY, March 17: "Family Members—Forgiven and Reconciled" (Luke 15:11-24)

March 24, 2019   Lesson 4

CALLING TO SALVATION

ADULT/YOUTH
ADULT/YOUNG ADULT TOPIC: Finding Acceptance
YOUTH TOPIC: Responding to the Call

CHILDREN
GENERAL LESSON TITLE: Jesus Calls the Lost to Salvation
CHILDREN'S TOPIC: Jesus Saves Me

DEVOTIONAL READING
1 Chronicles 16:8-13, 23-27

ADULT/YOUTH
BACKGROUND SCRIPTURE: Luke 19:1-10
PRINT PASSAGE: Luke 19:1-10
KEY VERSE: Luke 19:10

CHILDREN
BACKGROUND SCRIPTURE: Luke 19:1-10
PRINT PASSAGE: Luke 19:1-10
KEY VERSE: Luke 19:10

Luke 19:1-10—KJV

AND JESUS entered and passed through Jericho.

2 And, behold, there was a man named Zacchaeus, which was the chief among the publicans, and he was rich.

3 And he sought to see Jesus who he was; and could not for the press, because he was little of stature.

4 And he ran before, and climbed up into a sycamore tree to see him: for he was to pass that way.

5 And when Jesus came to the place, he looked up, and saw him, and said unto him, Zacchaeus, make haste, and come down; for today I must abide at thy house.

6 And he made haste, and came down, and received him joyfully.

7 And when they saw it, they all murmured, saying, That he was gone to be guest with a man that is a sinner.

8 And Zacchaeus stood, and said unto the Lord; Behold, Lord, the half of my goods I give to the poor; and if I have taken any thing from any man by false accusation, I restore him fourfold.

Luke 19:1-10—NIV

JESUS ENTERED Jericho and was passing through.

2 A man was there by the name of Zacchaeus; he was a chief tax collector and was wealthy.

3 He wanted to see who Jesus was, but because he was short he could not see over the crowd.

4 So he ran ahead and climbed a sycamore-fig tree to see him, since Jesus was coming that way.

5 When Jesus reached the spot, he looked up and said to him, "Zacchaeus, come down immediately. I must stay at your house today."

6 So he came down at once and welcomed him gladly.

7 All the people saw this and began to mutter, "He has gone to be the guest of a sinner."

8 But Zacchaeus stood up and said to the Lord, "Look, Lord! Here and now I give half of my possessions to the poor, and if I have cheated anybody out of anything, I will pay back four times the amount."

9 And Jesus said unto him, This day is salvation come to this house, forsomuch as he also is a son of Abraham. 10 For the Son of man is come to seek and to save that which was lost.

9 Jesus said to him, "Today salvation has come to this house, because this man, too, is a son of Abraham. 10 "For the Son of Man came to seek and to save the lost."

UNIFYING LESSON PRINCIPLE: Some people can be considered unacceptable, either because of their actions or because of stereotypes held by others. How does one find acceptance? Jesus recognized Zacchaeus's interest and honored him despite the grumbling of the crowd; Zacchaeus responded with overwhelming repentance.

LESSON OBJECTIVES

Upon the completion of this lesson, the students will be able to do the following:
1. Tell how Zacchaeus and Jesus ignored social taboos and how that resulted in new life for Zacchaeus.
2. Repent of sinful attitudes the learner may have held toward certain kinds of people.
3. Challenge the social or cultural stereotypes of people different from themselves and to make an effort to share Christ's love with others.

AGE-LEVEL POINTS TO BE EMPHASIZED

Teachers of ADULTS and YOUTH
—Hospitality was a strong practice in Israelite culture. Jewish religious traditions also adhered to strong boundaries concerning who was acceptable and who was not. Tax collectors, though Jewish, were considered to be collaborators with the Roman government, and therefore were treated as Gentiles.
—Jesus cared first about developing a relationship with Zacchaeus. Jesus did not tell Zacchaeus what to do about his career choice or the way he handled his affairs.
—This incident is an example of Jesus' tendency to challenge the social or cultural stereotypes and religious stigmas of the times; other examples include the story of the woman at the well in Samaria (see John 4:7-29), His encounter with the woman caught in adultery (see John 8:1-11), and the healing of the man born blind (see John 9:1-41).

—Zacchaeus's example shows that benefactors/participants in oppressive systems can change in the face of Jesus' grace and love.
—Tax collectors for the Roman government were not well liked in Jewish society.
—A chief tax collector had other tax collectors under him and contracted for sales and custom taxes.
—The sycamore tree was like a fig tree and easy to climb.
—Zacchaeus desired to see Jesus because he thought Jesus was important.

Teachers of CHILDREN
—A close encounter with Jesus will change lives.
—Jesus proved that He is an all-inclusive Savior who transforms the lives of sinners.
—Our bodies are holy temples, houses into which Jesus is awaiting our acceptance of His invitation to enter our hearts.
—Salvation causes those with grateful hearts to willingly make restorations to others above and beyond what is due.

—Tax collectors for the Roman government were not well liked in Jewish society.

—Zacchaeus desired to see Jesus because He thought He was important.

THE CHRONOLOGICAL SETTING OF THE LESSON

Luke's account of Jesus' entering the house of Zacchaeus is the last of Jesus' encounters with outcasts before His entry into Jerusalem. Earlier, Jesus was mocked as a friend of tax collectors and sinners (see Luke 7:34). In Luke's gospel, tax collectors functioned as the typical outcasts, those whom Jesus befriended. Roman officials, charged with the responsibility of collecting taxes throughout their region, contracted with local entrepreneurs to collect the prescribed taxes, tolls, tariffs, and customs fees in a given area. These entrepreneurs, the "chief tax collectors," were required to pay the contract in advance. They would then employ others to collect the taxes with the hope that the amount collected would yield a profit. The system was open to abuse, and Jews who collected taxes for the Romans were assumed to be dishonest and were hated by other Jews for their complicity with the despised Roman government.

THE GEOGRAPHICAL AND CULTURAL SETTING OF THE LESSON

From the start, Zacchaeus's occupation and socioeconomic status paint a negative picture of him for the first hearers of this story. He held the position of tax collector in Jericho, a much-despised occupation in Judea. The custom of the day held that whenever a tax collector entered a house all that was within it became unclean. This negative characterization of the position of tax collector was also found in other first-century witnesses. Repeatedly in the book of Luke, tax collectors are coupled with the generic category of "sinners." The epithet "rich" would also have been perceived negatively by the crowd in Jericho, since Zacchaeus's wealth would have been interpreted as something he most likely gained at the expense of others. His ill-gotten wealth would also have served as an important impediment to his salvation.

The third descriptor of Zacchaeus would also have been perceived as a negative quality: his diminished height. Why mention that Zacchaeus was short in stature? In ancient cultures, smallness in physical stature was generally seen as reflective of "smallness in spirit." Conversely, greatness of soul was associated with great physical stature. The widespread appeal to physical characteristics in that day suggests that the diminished stature of Zacchaeus would have been viewed as a laughable, perhaps despicable, character. It was thus a bold move on Jesus' part to invite Himself into the home of such a man. However, Jesus demonstrated with His invitation that just because Zacchaeus was a despised tax collector did not mean that he was to be excluded from the family of God. This parable functions to identify faith in improbable places among improbable people. Despised Zacchaeus trusted not in who he was but in who God was—the merciful one. For Luke, salvation by grace means that one can never feel religiously superior to another.

PROMINENT CHARACTER(S) IN THE LESSON

Publicans: Jewish tax collectors for the ancient Romans; regarded as outcasts and traitors among the Jews for having accepted such a position.
Zacchaeus: a chief tax collector in Jericho whose encounter with Jesus led to his salvation.

KEY TERMS IN THE LESSON

Abide (verse 5)—Greek: *menō* (me'-nō)**:** to remain; to tarry; "stay" (NIV).

Publican (verse 2)—Greek: *architelōnēs* (är-khē-te-lō'-nās): "tax collector" (NIV).

Sought (verse 3)—Greek: *zēteō* (zā-te'-ō): sought (in order to find out) by thinking, meditating, reasoning; enquired into; "wanted" (NIV).

Sycamore (verse 4)—Greek: *sykomorea* (sü-ko-mo-re'-ä): The biblical sycamore tree is a fig tree. It is a strong, wide-spreading tree standing 30-40 feet tall.

TOPICAL OUTLINE OF THE LESSON

I. Introduction
  A. The Priority of Saving the Lost
  B. Biblical Background

II. Exposition and Application of the Scripture
  A. An Encounter with Destiny
     (Luke 19:1-4)
  B. A Divine Invitation
     (Luke 19:5-6)
  C. A Hostile Crowd and a Generous Response to God's Saving Purpose
     (Luke 19:7-8)
  D. A Son of Abraham
     (Luke 19:9-10)

III. Concluding Reflection

I. INTRODUCTION

A. The Priority of Saving the Lost

James Truslow Adams's famous quote seems most fitting for today's lesson: "There is so much good in the worst of us, and so much bad in the best of us, that it ill behooves any of us to find fault with the rest of us." Jesus invited Himself into the home of Zacchaeus, a despised tax collector, known for cheating the local citizenry out of its money. One would expect this to be the last place for Jesus to spend His time in the closing days of His ministry. However, Zacchaeus is just the kind of person Jesus came into the world to save. Thus, Jesus is all too willing to lay aside custom and taboo and spend quality time with this man who has lots of bad about him, but also some good in him. Jesus does not give priority to that which is dark and sinful in Zacchaeus's life; instead, He focused on the hope of salvation that He brought to Zacchaeus on the day of their meeting. Zacchaeus responded to the Master's gracious visit by confessing his sins and promising to make restitution to all those he had dealt with unfairly in his past. Zacchaeus responded to Christ's offer of grace and came out of his house a changed man. Jesus' encounter with Zacchaeus is instructive for our faith today. We too are called upon to reach out to the lost and misguided in the name of Jesus Christ. Judgment of others belongs to God alone. Ours is to reach out in love to those who are lost and make every effort to lead them to the newness of life that can only be found in having a divine encounter with Christ Jesus.

B. Biblical Background

Many see this story as the heart of Luke's presentation of the mission of Jesus Christ.

Many of Luke's favorite themes are present in this story, such as the compassion of God, sin, repentance, and human recovery. The whole story makes for captivating reading, all the more so because it is true. Jesus appears here in His most attractive role as the gracious Redeemer of lost women and men.

The story is simply told: A very rich tax collector name Zacchaeus has heard that Jesus from Nazareth was heading through Jericho. Intrigued by what he had heard about this travelling rabbi, Zacchaeus ran ahead of the crowd and climbed a sycamore tree (an easy task because of its low branches). Zacchaeus was a small man and wanted a better vantage point to see Jesus. To his and everyone's surprise, Jesus halted right under where Zacchaeus was watching and invited him down so that he could entertain Jesus at his house. Gladly, Zacchaeus opened his home and hospitality to Jesus. The visit of Jesus brought an occasion of deep soul searching and change of heart for Zacchaeus. He used the occasion to confess his past corruption in his professional work and to make a clean start by promising compensations to those he had wronged. Jesus responded in kind by declaring that God's salvation had come to Zacchaeus's household. Zacchaeus was an example of those lost men and women Jesus as the Son of Man had come to seek and to save. This is one of the best-loved and most moving stories of the gospel of Luke. It sums up many of the most valuable lessons of salvation and the kingdom. It shows that Jesus continues to attract the interest of many people who are searching for answers to life's deepest questions and dilemmas. In addition, Jesus' taking the initiative to invite Himself to Zacchaeus's house demonstrates the truth that God seeks us out, even when we are not looking for Him. God pursues us in His love for us through Jesus Christ.

The fact that Zacchaeus held one of the most despised of professions in that day did not seem to bother Jesus. In His contact with Zacchaeus, Jesus demonstrates that God is no respecter of persons and that nothing can separate us from the love of God in Christ Jesus. Even though we may be among the greatest of sinners, when we repent of our sins and turn to God, He is faithful and just to forgive us of our sins and to cleanse us from all unrighteousness.

II. EXPOSITION AND APPLICATION OF THE SCRIPTURE

A. An Encounter with Destiny
(Luke 19:1-4)

AND JESUS entered and passed through Jericho. And, behold, there was a man named Zacchaeus, which was the chief among the publicans, and he was rich. And he sought to see Jesus who he was; and could not for the press, because he was little of stature. And he ran before, and climbed up into a sycamore tree to see him: for he was to pass that way.

This encounter with Zacchaeus took place while Jesus was passing through the town of Jericho. Zacchaeus was no tax underling like Levi (see Luke 5:27); he was a man of considerable wealth. The Romans auctioned off the collection of indirect taxes (tolls, tariffs, and customs) to the highest bidders, which may have been an individual or a group of individuals. By farming out the collection of these taxes, the Roman governor could count on receiving a fixed sum from the beginning of the year and thus reduce overhead expenses.

Because the tariffs were unfixed, this arrangement opened the door to fraud and abuse. The tax collector who won the right to collect the taxes for the Roman government could charge whatever he wanted in order to cover expenses and make a profit, but he would also have to bear any losses.

The term *chief tax collector* appears only here in the book of Luke. Zacchaeus was rich, presumably because he has raked in big payoffs, as Jericho was a significant import and export post. As a chief tax collector and a wealthy man, he represented the chieftain of sinners. Luke does not earmark wealth as categorically evil, but it poses a danger to discipleship that cannot be minimized. Despite his riches, Zacchaeus remained on the margins of society—disdained, if not hated, as a despicable, greedy, and laughable character. Classed with murderers and robbers, tax collectors were hated in the Jewish world. Jesus, knowing all of this about Jewish culture, called out to him with an invitation.

B. A Divine Invitation
(Luke 19:5-6)

And when Jesus came to the place, he looked up, and saw him, and said unto him, Zacchaeus, make haste, and come down; for today I must abide at thy house. And he made haste, and came down, and received him joyfully.

As Jesus passed through Jericho with the crowds surrounding Him, Zacchaeus wanted to know who He was, so he ran ahead and climbed a sycamore tree in order to see Jesus, who was about to pass that way. Although Zacchaeus was set to see Jesus, Jesus saw him first and addressed him by name—almost the same name, and evidently the same power with which the angel addressed Zechariah in the opening theophany of the gospel (see Luke 1:13): "Zacchaeus, make haste, and come down; for today I must abide at thy house" (verse 5). This is the only instance in the Gospels in which Jesus invited Himself into another person's presence or premises.

A self-invitation was not the norm in Judaism and verged on impropriety, but Jesus undoubtedly felt the occasion merited such an invitation. The injunction to "make haste, and come down" is urgent; the call of Jesus is not to be put off to a future time, but acted on *today*. Zacchaeus was a man of reputation, wealth, and power, but Jesus appealed to his person rather than his titles or offices. Zacchaeus came down at once and welcomed Jesus "joyfully." This sentence (verse 6) has only seven words in Greek, four of which are strong verbs, translated "hurried," "came down," "received," and "rejoiced." Zacchaeus heard Jesus' unusual invitation not as a judgment but as an occasion for joy—a very unusual response of a tax collector to a meeting with a Jewish rabbi!

Hearing about his position and wealth, the readers' first reaction to him would probably be negative. However, a fuller picture of Zacchaeus gives rise to a more sympathetic response. He was a short guy who decided to run ahead so that he could see Jesus. His energetic, enthusiastic response inspired others to overcome obstacles in their quest to encounter God's prophet. Unlike the rich young ruler in Luke 18:18-23 who walked away from Jesus sorrowful, wealthy Zacchaeus responded to Jesus differently and shows us that a rich man can be saved despite the encumbrances and false security that wealth often brings.

C. A Hostile Crowd and a Generous Response to God's Saving Purpose
(Luke 19:7-8)

And when they saw it, they all murmured, saying, That he was gone to be guest with a man that is a sinner. And Zacchaeus stood, and said unto the Lord: Behold, Lord, the half of my goods I give to the poor; and if I have taken any thing from any man by false accusation, I restore him fourfold.

Throughout Scripture, one sees an unwillingness on the part of some to accept the fact that the sovereign God will save any and all who trust in His name—rich and poor alike. As has happened before in Luke's story, those who saw Jesus heading to the home of Zacchaeus could not tolerate the Master's association with sinners, and so they "murmured," saying that Jesus had gone to be a guest of a man who is a sinner. However, a different scene was transpiring within the house. The grace of Jesus evoked a transformation within Zacchaeus; he stood and faced Jesus as he vowed, "Behold, Lord, the half of my goods I give to the poor; and if I have taken any thing from any man by false accusation, I restore him fourfold" (verse 8). Rising to his own defense, Zacchaeus answered the critics by pledging concrete actions as a sign of his conversion. This restoration was far more than the law required. His gracious act went beyond mere legalism. It indicates that Zacchaeus was a changed man.

Those who grumbled about Jesus' entering the home of Zacchaeus seemed unaware of the reason for which Jesus came into the world. He came to call sinners to repentance, and He was always ready to extend a measure of grace to those who expressed a willingness and a desire to draw closer to God. That is exactly the work we are called to do in our day—invite women and men to come to Christ and live life as it is meant to be lived in the presence of God almighty.

D. A Son of Abraham
(Luke 19:9-10)

And Jesus said unto him, This day is salvation come to this house, forsomuch as he also is a son of Abraham. For the Son of man is come to seek and to save that which was lost.

Jesus recognized the change in Zacchaeus when He said, "This day is salvation come to this house, forasmuch as he also is a son of Abraham" (verse 9). Zacchaeus might have been despised by his neighbors, but his profession had not cancelled his birthright. He was not so low that he could not respond to the grace of God. When was Zacchaeus actually saved? While he was in the tree? Between the limb and the ground? In his house? Who can say? However, saved he was. For that day, according to Jesus, salvation came to his house—for only salvation could produce such a change in Zacchaeus. The people were quite angry that Jesus could show such compassion and concern for this chief publican. Perhaps they expected Jesus to lecture Zacchaeus about the evil of his ways. There may have been some in the crowd who had been robbed by Zacchaeus through the levying of exorbitant taxes. However, Jesus did more than lecture him; He went into his home and won him to Himself. In addition, when He returned to the street, He presented them not with an indignant, conniving publican but with a redeemed tax commissioner, a philanthropist, and an honest man.

This is the business of Jesus, and it should be the business of all who follow Him. "For the son of man is come to seek and to save that which was lost" (verse 10). This narrative also demonstrates that no one is beyond the reach of the merciful Savior. It is for this reason that He came into the world. Custom and tradition must be cast aside in the interest of winning the lost to Jesus Christ.

III. CONCLUDING REFLECTION

In our lesson today, we find a rambunctious, engaging, and likable character. How easy it is to imagine this short, rather dignified fellow running through a hostile crowd and climbing a tree to see the one to whom his heart is drawn. His actions dramatize Augustine's spiritual insight addressed in this prayer to God: "You have made us for yourself, and our heart is restless until it rests in you." What is it that really satisfies the deepest longing of the human heart? Many paths have been tried, some running after great wealth, increased power, or acclaimed success; some pursuing personal projects that promote one's own well-being; and others striving after a kind of self-justifying perfection.

The Zacchaeus story invites us to reflect on the roads on which we have chosen to travel. What are we running after? Given the pace of life many lead, this running can almost be taken literally. Am I on the path that leads toward wholeness and salvation? If not, what course corrections do I need to take? What might it mean for us to accept Jesus' statement that He must dwell in our home?

It is also the case that different members of the Lukan audience could have heard different messages from this story. For outcasts like Zacchaeus, it could have been an affirmation of their right to belong to the people of God. For a community inclined to exclude, it could have been a challenging reminder of the meaning of Jesus' mission. For people with wealth, it could have provided a model—perhaps an ideal model that was seldom completely copied—of what conversion meant for people of means.

PRAYER

Dear Lord, help us ever to put our trust in You. Give us the wisdom and insight to see the good in others and to know that no one is beyond the reach of Your grace and mercy. Make us instruments of Your saving purposes, and use us to win others to Christ in a mighty way. In Jesus' name we pray. Amen.

HOME DAILY BIBLE READINGS
(March 18-24, 2019)

Calling to Salvation
MONDAY, March 18: "Laws of Confession and Restitution" (Exodus 22:1-3; Numbers 5:5-7)
TUESDAY, March 19: "Israel's Salvation and Commitment to God" (Deuteronomy 26:16-19)
WEDNESDAY, March 20: "'I Must Proclaim the Good News!'" (Luke 4:38-43)
THURSDAY, March 21: "'Let the Children Come to Me'" (Luke 18:15-17)
FRIDAY, March 22: "Entering the Kingdom of God" (Luke 18:18-30)
SATURDAY, March 23: "Blind Man Receives Sight and Salvation" (Luke 18:35-43)
SUNDAY, March 24: "Receiving Salvation, Correcting Injustice" (Luke 19:1-10)

March 31, 2019 — Lesson 5

CALLED TO DISCIPLESHIP

ADULT/YOUTH
ADULT/YOUNG ADULT TOPIC: **Purposeful Following**
YOUTH TOPIC: **Follow the Good Leader**

CHILDREN
GENERAL LESSON TITLE: **Called to Love and Follow Jesus**
CHILDREN'S TOPIC: **Follow the Leader**

DEVOTIONAL READING
Psalm 91

ADULT/YOUTH
BACKGROUND SCRIPTURE: **Matthew 4:12-22**
PRINT PASSAGE: **Matthew 4:12-22**
KEY VERSE: **Matthew 4:19**

CHILDREN
BACKGROUND SCRIPTURE: **Matthew 4:12-22; Mark 1:14-20**
PRINT PASSAGE: **Matthew 4:12-22**
KEY VERSE: **Matthew 4:22**

Matthew 4:12-22—KJV

12 Now when Jesus had heard that John was cast into prison, he departed into Galilee;

13 And leaving Nazareth, he came and dwelt in Capernaum, which is upon the sea coast, in the borders of Zabulon and Nephthalim:

14 That it might be fulfilled which was spoken by Esaias the prophet, saying,

15 The land of Zabulon, and the land of Nephthalim, by the way of the sea, beyond Jordan, Galilee of the Gentiles;

16 The people which sat in darkness saw great light; and to them which sat in the region and shadow of death light is sprung up.

17 From that time Jesus began to preach, and to say, Repent: for the kingdom of heaven is at hand.

18 And Jesus, walking by the sea of Galilee, saw two brethren, Simon called Peter, and Andrew his brother, casting a net into the sea: for they were fishers.

Matthew 4:12-22—NIV

12 When Jesus heard that John had been put in prison, he withdrew to Galilee.

13 Leaving Nazareth, he went and lived in Capernaum, which was by the lake in the area of Zebulun and Naphtali—

14 to fulfill what was said through the prophet Isaiah:

15 "Land of Zebulun and land of Naphtali, the Way of the Sea, beyond the Jordan, Galilee of the Gentiles—

16 "the people living in darkness have seen a great light; on those living in the land of the shadow of death a light has dawned."

17 From that time on Jesus began to preach, "Repent, for the kingdom of heaven has come near."

18 As Jesus was walking beside the Sea of Galilee, he saw two brothers, Simon called Peter and his brother Andrew. They were casting a net into the lake, for they were fishermen.

19 And he saith unto them, Follow me, and I will make you fishers of men.

20 And they straightway left their nets, and followed him.

21 And going on from thence, he saw other two brethren, James the son of Zebedee, and John his brother, in a ship with Zebedee their father, mending their nets; and he called them.

22 And they immediately left the ship and their father, and followed him.

19 "Come, follow me," Jesus said, "and I will send you out to fish for people."

20 At once they left their nets and followed him.

21 Going on from there, he saw two other brothers, James son of Zebedee and his brother John. They were in a boat with their father Zebedee, preparing their nets. Jesus called them,

22 and immediately they left the boat and their father and followed him.

UNIFYING LESSON PRINCIPLE: People can be settled in their ways but destined for greater purposes. How do people discover and respond to that higher calling? When Jesus called His first disciples, they responded by leaving their routine work to follow Him.

LESSON OBJECTIVES

Upon the completion of this lesson, the students will be able to do the following:

1. Tell how Peter, Andrew, James, and John accepted Jesus' call and the difference it made in their lives.
2. Reflect on how their lives would be different if they had not heard the call to follow Jesus.
3. Worship God for the blessings in their lives that have come because they follow Jesus.

AGE-LEVEL POINTS TO BE EMPHASIZED

Teachers of ADULTS and YOUTH

—Matthew quotes Isaiah 9:1-2 in condensed form (verses 15-16) to show that Jesus is the future ideal king, the Messiah. (In Isaiah, the "sea" is the Mediterranean; here, it is the Sea of Galilee.)

—"The kingdom of heaven has come near" (verse 17) is derived from Daniel 7:13-14, the salvation of all humanity through the exercise of the sovereignty of God's just rule.

—"Kingdom of heaven" is Matthew's way of speaking of the *kingdom of God*, to avoid using God's name, a Jewish sensibility of the time.

—"They left their nets" (verse 20). They had been wading out from the shore, throwing a casting net, and encircling the fish. Now they leave their business and means of livelihood to follow Jesus wherever He takes them, to learn His message, and to help in any way they are able.

—Jesus' proclamation, "Repent, for the kingdom of heaven has come near" (Matthew 4:17), is reflected in John the Baptist's earlier message (Matthew 3:1-2) and Jesus' later instructions on what His disciples were to proclaim (see Matthew 10:7, next week's lesson).

—Jesus adopted Capernaum as His own city after being rejected in Nazareth.

—Matthew describes Jesus' adoption of Capernaum as a fulfillment of Isaiah 9:1-2.

—Jesus' main message is about the arrival of the kingdom of God.

Teachers of CHILDREN

—Rabbis were sought out by would-be followers; they did not command people to be their disciples.

—Jesus' relocation from Nazareth to Capernaum was a purposeful act of self-determination, signaling the focus of His ministry to include Gentiles.

—The disciples Jesus called were busy when Jesus called them to change course.

—Matthew shows Jesus' power when His call of "Follow me" results in making disciples.

—Fishermen made good money near the city of Galilee and were important to the local economy.

—By abandoning their father's business, James and John risked being dishonored in their community.

THE CHRONOLOGICAL SETTING OF THE LESSON

Matthew sets the chronological scene of this narrative more carefully than Mark does, both by noting Jesus' removal from Nazareth to Capernaum and by giving it theological significance. The return of Jesus to Galilee functions as a hinge or bridge, bringing Matthew's introduction of Jesus to a close. Matthew uses a significant citation from Isaiah 9:1-2 to set the tone for the in-breaking of the kingdom as the mission of Jesus to Israel, beginning in Galilee. The consistent theme running through this whole section is the authority of Jesus and its impact. The demonstration of His authority begins with the immediate response of the disciples to His authoritative call to discipleship.

THE GEOGRAPHICAL AND CULTURAL SETTING OF THE LESSON

Jesus left Nazareth to make His home in Capernaum by the Sea of Galilee. He went there with the intent of forming His messianic community. He began by extending an authoritative call to four fishermen. Within this close-knit group of disciples, it will become clear that three of the four whose call is recorded first will form an inner circle, chosen to be with Jesus in moments of special significance, and mentioned by name from time to time. The rest of the Twelve receive little or no individual mention beyond the listing of their names in Matthew 10:2-4. The proximity here of the two pairs of brothers suggests that the four were already colleagues in the fishing business. The association of the mother of James and John with the other women at the Cross according to Matthew 27:56, as well as her intervention on their behalf in 20:20, has led some to suppose that the family of Zebedee was in some way related to Jesus' own family. Matthew does not indicate this. Rather, the suddenness with which Zebedee was left behind in the boat suggests his sons made an unpremeditated, spur-of-the-moment decision to follow Jesus.

PROMINENT CHARACTER(S) IN THE LESSON

Andrew: a fisherman who followed John the Baptist and then became one of the first disciples of Jesus; brother to Simon Peter.

James: an apostle of Jesus; a son of Zebedee, and the elder brother of John.

John: a son of Zebedee and the younger brother of James.

John (the Baptist): the son of the priest Zechariah and Elizabeth; forerunner of Jesus Christ.

Naphtali: the sixth son of Jacob. The territory named for him was located near the upper Jordan River.

Simon Peter: the most prominent of Jesus' twelve disciples.

Zebulun: the tenth son of Jacob. The territory named for him was located in the region of Galilee and shared a border with Naphtali.

KEY TERMS IN THE LESSON

Fishermen (verse 18)—Greek: *halieus* (hä-lē-yü's): "fishers" (KJV); catchers of fish.

Followed (verse 22)—Greek: *akoloutheō* (ä-ko-lü-the'-ō): joined one as a disciple; became or was a disciple.

Repent (verse 17)—Greek: *metanoeō* (me-tä-no-e'-ō): to change one's mind; to repent.

TOPICAL OUTLINE OF THE LESSON

I. Introduction
   A. Called to an Adventure in Jesus Christ
   B. Biblical Background

II. Exposition and Application of the Scripture
   A. The Light Dawns in Galilee (Matthew 4:12-16)
   B. The Founding of the Messianic Community (Matthew 4:17)
   C. The Command to Follow Jesus (Matthew 4:18-20)
   D. The Call of James and John (Matthew 4:21-22)

III. Concluding Reflection

I. INTRODUCTION

A. Called to an Adventure in Jesus Christ

The call story described in this lesson portrays a sudden and complete change of lifestyle involving "leaving" both work and family. Matthew understood discipleship as giving up everything to follow Jesus. Jesus' demands on His followers are uncompromising. While Matthew does not record the call of any others of the Twelve except Matthew, we are left to assume that all of them were similarly expected to give up everything to follow Jesus (as indeed Peter will assert in Matthew 19:27). The abortive call to the rich young ruler in Matthew 19:21-22 demonstrates the uncompromising nature of Jesus' call to discipleship; it is all or none when the Master calls!

The most prominent feature of these verses is the overwhelming authority of the call of Jesus. Matthew 4:18 recounts the normal, everyday activity of Simon Peter and Andrew. Jesus said, "Come on after me, and I will make you to be fishers of men" (see 4:19). In 4:20, they immediately left their nets and followed Him. The pattern of Jesus' powerful call was repeated with James and his brother, John; again, they responded immediately (see 4:21-22).

To what were the four fishermen responding? Jesus had just begun to proclaim, "Repent! For the kingdom of heaven is near" (see 4:17). The four believed, even if only with faltering faith, that Jesus' preaching was true! They began to acknowledge their need for conversion—their need to be saved—and they had begun to believe that through Jesus the promised kingly saving deeds of God have broken into Israel's history.

The fishermen left their former lives and followed Jesus. It is easy to find either too much or too little significance in this aspect of their response. On the one hand, commentators at times speak almost as if the disciples clearly understood at this point who Jesus was and what discipleship might personally cost them, and they were willing to pay that price. A quick reading of Matthew's gospel (or any of the Gospels) shows how wrongheaded it is to make that much of their response. The disciples did not yet fully understand who Jesus is or what He has come to do, and they understood neither what Christian discipleship is nor (in their case) what apostolic ministry would eventually cost them. Nor did they completely abandon everything in the sense of having nothing to do with their former lives. They still had houses and mothers-in-law (see Matthew 8:14-15), mothers (see 20:20-28), and presumably other relationships as well.

On the other hand, there can be no doubt that just as Jesus had begun to preach and to call disciples to Himself, so these disciples were given, through His preaching and call, the beginning of the understanding that none of their old priorities and relationships would ever be the same or would ever again possess primary importance. But the four do not know the implications of this as yet. There will be many occasions, even within the brief course of Matthew's gospel, when Jesus' disciples would know that they have not grasped or appropriated all the ramifications that His call will have for their lives. Nevertheless, the circumstances that define the beginning of discipleship with Jesus, which will go on characterizing that relationship for the fishermen (and for Jesus' disciples of all times and places), is the authority and primacy of His call to come to Him, to follow Him.

It is, after all, the reign of God that Jesus brought and announced. The great reality is that God's reign in Jesus has broken into a sinful world to reclaim and save it, and finally to renew it forever. Into that larger reality, individual men and women are claimed and called by Jesus, graciously and freely. No one, however, can come to Him without acknowledging His authority to call and to call unconditionally. He is the Lord. His call is "Come, follow me" (see Matthew 4:19).

B. Biblical Background

Notwithstanding its small size, this passage of Scripture represents a major piece of Matthew's introductory structure. The call of the first disciples is the beginning of the messianic community, the church. Jesus' baptism and temptation in Matthew 3 were not merely individualistic religious experiences of a "great man," but the recapitulation of the birth of Israel in the Red Sea and the wilderness testing; they lead to the formation of the new community, the Messiah's people.

Next to Jesus, interest in the gospel of Matthew is focused upon His disciples. Jesus called people to Himself. He did mighty works as the One who had authority, but His chief concern was to make God known as Father and to bring people to God. Jesus left a great body of teachings, but He was not content simply to bind people to His teachings. He gave Himself to His people, and He bound them to Himself.

The first clear indication of this is seen in the calling of the four fishermen.

That Jesus felt that He had the right to make demands upon people comes with force through all the traditions. He demanded the trust, love, obedience, and, if necessary, the lives of His followers. Of course, He gave Himself to them in the same radical way, even to His life at Golgotha. He offered more than example and teaching. He offered Himself. He demanded more than imitation and the acceptance of His teaching. He asked people to give themselves to Him. That some were willing thus to yield to His claims is proclaimed in today's lesson.

The Master-disciple relationship between Jesus and His disciples that is portrayed in Matthew is markedly different from that relationship as it is reflected, for example, in rabbinic literature. In rabbinic literature, a disciple was to choose his own master; and his first commitment was to the Law. Consequently, he could transfer from one master to another to acquire more knowledge of the Law. By contrast, Jesus did not wait for volunteers but selected His own disciples and confronted them with an unconditional demand. He required absolute allegiance to Himself, not merely respectful service. He did not call them to be His apprentices in the intellectual probing of the Torah, or to rehearse venerable religious traditions. He called fishermen to a new kind of fishing: they were to "fish for people."

II. EXPOSITION AND APPLICATION OF THE SCRIPTURE

A. The Light Dawns in Galilee
(Matthew 4:12-16)

Now when Jesus had heard that John was cast into prison, he departed into Galilee; And leaving Nazareth, he came and dwelt in Capernaum, which is upon the sea coast, in the borders of Zabulon and Nephthalim: That it might be fulfilled which was spoken by Esaias the prophet, saying, The land of Zabulon, and the land of Nephthalim, by the way of the sea, beyond Jordan, Galilee of the Gentiles; The people which sat in darkness saw great light; and to them which sat in the region and shadow of death light is sprung up.

This text is important because it marks a transition. It is the beginning of Jesus' ministry, and Matthew provided four scenes: Jesus preaching the reign of God; His return to Galilee; the calling of the disciples; and His demonstration of God's transforming reign in their midst through Jesus' teaching, preaching, and healing. John had been arrested. His work as forerunner of the Messiah was complete, and Jesus' own ministry began in earnest. Remarkably, Jesus dared to take up the very same message that got John arrested. "Repent, for the kingdom of heaven has come near" (verse 17). The word translated "arrested" literally means "handed over." It would appear at several junctures when Jesus is "handed over" (see Matthew 17:22; 20:18; 26:2), leading up to the point where He is to be "handed over to be crucified" (26:2).

When Jesus heard that John had been arrested, it says that He "withdrew" to Galilee. This is the same word used when Mary and Joseph were forced to flee with the baby Jesus under Herod's threat. The reader may be given to understand that Jesus is once again under threat. Going to Galilee is doubly significant. Galilee is the very heart of Israel. This location keeps faith with a priority of Jesus' mission, which is first to Israel (see 10:5). At the same time, it is a place referred to as "Galilee of the Gentiles," which signals the coming breakthrough of the mission to the "nations." Matthew quotes Isaiah 9:1-2: "the people who sat in darkness have seen a great light" (verse 16, NRSV). This is a text rich with messianic associations and expectations of a light that would enlighten the Gentiles in the messianic age. In its original context, this text refers to the situation of oppression after 722 BCE, when Assyria occupied Zebulun and Naphtali (in the region of Galilee) and exiled the leadership. Here, Matthew transposed the text from one situation of imperial aggression to another, as Israel now suffered under Rome's imperial control. The promise of the passage is that the rod of the oppressor would be broken through one who would embody God's reign of justice, righteousness, and peace.

B. The Founding of the Messianic Community (Matthew 4:17)

From that time Jesus began to preach, and to say, Repent: for the kingdom of heaven is at hand.

Up to now, Jesus had been largely a passive figure in Matthew's story, but with the words "From that time," the situation changed, as Jesus took the initiative. Up until this time, though briefly involved with John and others by the Jordan, Jesus had been presented as operating alone. However, it is significant that His first recorded action was to gather a group of followers who would commit themselves to a total change of lifestyle to join Jesus as His essential support group for the whole period of His public ministry.

From this point on, we shall not read stories about Jesus alone, but stories about Jesus and His disciples. Wherever He goes, they will go; their presence with Jesus, even if not explicitly mentioned, is assumed. While the Twelve would not be formally listed until Matthew 10:1-4, the stories from here on will assume a wider group of disciples than just the first four mentioned here.

These disciples would be the primary audience for Jesus' teaching and witnesses of His works of power, but they are also called to be His active helpers in the task of "fishing for people," as we shall discover in Matthew 10. The first time Jesus would be left alone after this point would be when the disciples eventually deserted Him in the garden of Gethsemane (see 26:56). Until then, Matthew's story is not only that of the Messiah, but also of the messianic community which is being formed around Him. The placing of this incident right at the beginning makes it clear that this was Jesus' intention. From that time, Jesus had begun to proclaim His message of repentance, surrounded by a supportive messianic community.

C. The Command to Follow Jesus (Matthew 4:18-20)

And Jesus, walking by the sea of Galilee, saw two brethren, Simon called Peter, and Andrew his brother, casting a net into the sea: for they were fishers. And he saith unto them, Follow me, and I will make you fishers of men. And they straightway left their nets, and followed him.

Etiquette required a rabbi's disciple to walk literally behind his teacher. However, when Jesus called Simon and Andrew to "come behind him" (verse 19), they would soon find that He is far from a conventional rabbi. This is true especially when we remember that those who wished to follow a rabbi generally took the initiative themselves, rather than being summoned in this way. What Jesus issued here is not even an invitation but, rather, a demand. Such a summons is more typical of a prophet than of a rabbi. Moreover, the task to which He was calling them is described not primarily as one of learning from a teacher, but of active fishing. The fishing metaphor follows naturally from the description of their previous occupation, but it left open the nature of what is to be caught from the fishing. Catching fish is not very pleasing to the fish—but catching people in the interest of the kingdom is an acceptable mode of fishing. Following Jesus' proclamation of repentance in view of the coming of God's kingship, it seems appropriate in this context to take the catching of fish in a positive sense, of recruiting new subjects to God's kingship. It is a metaphor that stands for the time of decision, and Simon and Andrew would have a role in bringing people to that decision. They would indeed become fishers of men and women.

The conclusion to the call story of Peter and Andrew ends with a remark on their sacrificial obedience: they immediately left their nets (verse 20). When the authoritative call of Jesus comes, there is not even time to say farewell to one's father. Peter and Andrew no longer belong first to kith and kin. They belong to Jesus from here on. Leaving their nets highlights the disciples' radical commitment. Renouncing their old life, not even taking time to bring in nets, they left all and followed Jesus. Their call was to homelessness. They were being ordered to deny self, to suffer the loss of their own lives and livelihood. Unlike the affluent or those who practiced trades to support themselves—for example, Paul the tentmaker—the disciples of Jesus must give full time and all energy to their work.

D. The Call of James and John
(Matthew 4:21-22)

And going on from thence, he saw other two brethren, James the son of Zebedee, and John his brother, in a ship with Zebedee their father, mending their nets; and he called them. And they immediately left the ship and their father, and followed him.

The two pairs of brothers are some distance apart. Matthew reported that Jesus saw the first two brothers (Simon and Andrew), and as He went from there He saw the other two (James and John). The first two were called away from their actual fishing—the second from repairing their nets. The call to these brothers was, of course, the same as that extended to the first pair of brothers. They responded with the same cheerfulness and readiness to serve (verse 22). Since their father was mentioned as being with them, Matthew remarked that they left him. Zebedee was not called to the ministry, but he consented to the call of his sons and remained behind. Therefore, he too believed in Jesus and rejoiced in the great work for which Jesus chose his sons. Even those who are not directly called to formal ministry can be a blessing to loved ones and friends who hear that call and respond positively. Loved ones can be a great means of encouragement and support.

III. CONCLUDING REFLECTION

One of the first things Jesus did at the beginning of His ministry was to call disciples. He formed an alternative community to share in the work of preaching and showing forth the reign of God. Most rabbis did not seek out their students but, rather, were sought by them. Here, by contrast, all the initiative rests with Jesus. He came to them, He saw them, and He called them to follow. It is worth noting that the calling was not a calling to worship Jesus and form a "cult of Jesus." It was not even a calling to accept Him as their personal Lord and Savior. They were called to follow Him, to walk in the way that He was walking as He proclaimed and made manifest the kingdom of heaven.

The passage follows a call and response and a transition to new identity format. In Peter, Andrew, James, and John, we see a prototype of all future followers who will respond to Jesus' call. Jesus called them, and they dropped everything and followed Him "immediately." They did not ask where He was going, and He did not tell them. There was no mention of their being apostles to hint at their future importance. Nor was there mention of what this calling would cost them. Did Peter and Andrew have any inkling that they might end up crucified?

The call for them is unexpected, disruptive, and intrusive. The disciples were called from other good and important things—from work that sustains them and from families that love them. This new commitment to follow Jesus wherever He leads may not break these relationships and obligations, but it will now take precedence. Before their encounter with Jesus, the disciples seemed peaceful and contented, living the lives of simple fisherfolk. But then, upon encountering Jesus, they found their hearts filled with the peace of God that surpasses all understanding. Therefore, they dropped their nets and followed Him. It is also notable that Jesus was here calling disciples from among the lower social ranks. Jesus' calling came first to some of the most vulnerable people. They were called out of their ordinary lives and ho-hum existence into God's service. They then receive an odd sort of promise: they would now become fishers of people. They joined God's great and gracious "dragnet" that took in all kinds of fish.

PRAYER

Dear heavenly Father, help us to respond in faith to Your call and claim upon our lives. Give us the courage to go immediately to the work You are assigning our hands to do. In Jesus' name we pray. Amen.

HOME DAILY BIBLE READINGS
(March 25-31, 2019)

Called to Discipleship
MONDAY, March 25: "Jethro Hears of the Egyptian Deliverance" (Exodus 18:1-9)

TUESDAY, March 26: "Sustained by God" (Deuteronomy 8:1-11)

WEDNESDAY, March 27: "God Speaks to Disciples" (Luke 9:28-36)

THURSDAY, March 28: "Well Pleased" (Matthew 3:11-17)

FRIDAY, March 29: "Tempted in the Wilderness" (Matthew 4:1-11)

SATURDAY, March 30: "Good News and Healing" (Matthew 4:23-25)

SUNDAY, March 31: "Called and Enabled for Ministry" (Matthew 4:12-22)

April 7, 2019   Lesson 6

CALL AND MISSION

ADULT/YOUTH	CHILDREN
ADULT/YOUNG ADULT TOPIC: **Summoned for Service**	GENERAL LESSON TITLE: **Jesus Calls Us to Witness**
YOUTH TOPIC: **Called for a Purpose**	CHILDREN'S TOPIC: **Be Helpful to Others**

DEVOTIONAL READING
Matthew 15:21-28

ADULT/YOUTH	CHILDREN
BACKGROUND SCRIPTURE: **Matthew 10**	BACKGROUND SCRIPTURE: **Matthew 10**
PRINT PASSAGE: **Matthew 10:1-15**	PRINT PASSAGE: **Matthew 10:1-15**
KEY VERSE: **Matthew 10:1**	KEY VERSE: **Matthew 10:1**

Matthew 10:1-15—KJV

AND WHEN he had called unto him his twelve disciples, he gave them power against unclean spirits, to cast them out, and to heal all manner of sickness and all manner of disease.

2 Now the names of the twelve apostles are these; The first, Simon, who is called Peter, and Andrew his brother; James the son of Zebedee, and John his brother;

3 Philip, and Bartholomew; Thomas, and Matthew the publican; James the son of Alphaeus, and Lebbaeus, whose surname was Thaddaeus;

4 Simon the Canaanite, and Judas Iscariot, who also betrayed him.

5 These twelve Jesus sent forth, and commanded them, saying, Go not into the way of the Gentiles, and into any city of the Samaritans enter ye not:

6 But go rather to the lost sheep of the house of Israel.

7 And as ye go, preach, saying, The kingdom of heaven is at hand.

8 Heal the sick, cleanse the lepers, raise the dead, cast out devils: freely ye have received, freely give.

Matthew 10:1-15—NIV

JESUS CALLED his twelve disciples to him and gave them authority to drive out impure spirits and to heal every disease and sickness.

2 These are the names of the twelve apostles: first, Simon (who is called Peter) and his brother Andrew; James son of Zebedee, and his brother John;

3 Philip and Bartholomew; Thomas and Matthew the tax collector; James son of Alphaeus, and Thaddaeus;

4 Simon the Zealot and Judas Iscariot, who betrayed him.

5 These twelve Jesus sent out with the following instructions: "Do not go among the Gentiles or enter any town of the Samaritans.

6 "Go rather to the lost sheep of Israel.

7 "As you go, proclaim this message: 'The kingdom of heaven has come near.'

8 "Heal the sick, raise the dead, cleanse those who have leprosy, drive out demons. Freely you have received; freely give.

9 Provide neither gold, nor silver, nor brass in your purses,

10 Nor scrip for your journey, neither two coats, neither shoes, nor yet staves: for the workman is worthy of his meat.

11 And into whatsoever city or town ye shall enter, enquire who in it is worthy; and there abide till ye go thence.

12 And when ye come into an house, salute it.

13 And if the house be worthy, let your peace come upon it: but if it be not worthy, let your peace return to you.

14 And whosoever shall not receive you, nor hear your words, when ye depart out of that house or city, shake off the dust of your feet.

15 Verily I say unto you, It shall be more tolerable for the land of Sodom and Gomorrha in the day of judgment, than for that city.

9 "Do not get any gold or silver or copper to take with you in your belts—

10 "no bag for the journey or extra shirt or sandals or a staff, for the worker is worth his keep.

11 "Whatever town or village you enter, search there for some worthy person and stay at their house until you leave.

12 "As you enter the home, give it your greeting.

13 "If the home is deserving, let your peace rest on it; if it is not, let your peace return to you.

14 "If anyone will not welcome you or listen to your words, leave that home or town and shake the dust off your feet.

15 "Truly I tell you, it will be more bearable for Sodom and Gomorrah on the day of judgment than for that town."

UNIFYING LESSON PRINCIPLE: When people have discovered a greater purpose in life, they may be uncertain of what to do with that discovery. Where can persons find directions for implementing that greater purpose to benefit others? Jesus gave the first disciples direction to heal and witness to the "lost" persons of their shared community.

LESSON OBJECTIVES

Upon the completion of this lesson, the students will be able to do the following:

1. Compare and contrast the disciples' mission in Matthew 10 with the mission of the church today.
2. Anticipate the challenges they will experience in attempting to fulfill Christ's mission for the church.
3. Prepare themselves for greater participation in Christ's mission for the church.

AGE-LEVEL POINTS TO BE EMPHASIZED

Teachers of ADULTS and YOUTH

—The listings of the Twelve in Matthew 10:2-4; Mark 3:16-19; Luke 6:13-16; and Acts 1:13 are consistent in that (1) Simon Peter is always listed first, (2) Philip is always listed fifth, and (3) James son of Alphaeus is always listed ninth; the three names under each of those three are always the same (with Judas Iscariot absent from Acts 1:13), although their ordering differs.

—The message the Twelve were to proclaim, "the kingdom of heaven has come near" (Matthew 10:7), is a consistent extension of Jesus' message (see Matthew 4:17, last week's lesson) and that of John the Baptist (see Matthew 3:1).

—The people of Sodom are condemned for their lack of hospitality in Ezekiel 16:49. Jesus says that failure to welcome His messengers invites a worse fate than failure to welcome the angels in Genesis 19.

—One's "shaking the dust from his/her feet" was a visual demonstration that one was finished with trying to communicate with or minister to someone. In Acts 13:51, Paul and Barnabas did that when they were driven out of the city of Antioch of Pisidia.

—This call to go only to the lost sheep of Israel was expanded in the Great Commission.

—Related to verse 12, the usual Jewish form of greeting was "Peace (*shalom*) be on this house."

Teachers of CHILDREN

—Jesus identified twelve followers whom He would train to minister to others.

—Jesus gave specific instructions to His followers as to where to go to minister.

—Jesus gave specific instructions as to what His followers were to do.

—Jesus' followers were to rely upon others for shelter and food.

—Those who showed hospitality to Jesus' followers would be blessed.

—Those who refused to show hospitality to Jesus' followers would be left alone.

THE CHRONOLOGICAL SETTING OF THE LESSON

A distinctive characteristic of the gospel of Matthew is that it includes long sections of the teachings of Jesus. There are five of these discourses in all; the first of these is the Sermon on the Mount (see 5:1–7:29), and the second is this section of instructions to the disciples as they are sent out as missionaries of the kingdom of heaven. Even though these teachings of Jesus are addressed to the twelve disciples, Matthew's original audience surely heard them as words intended to shape their own mission work. The aim of this section, then, is to instruct and encourage the disciples. They are to be about the urgent work of Jesus Christ. What they do and how people respond to what they do really counts. To accept the witness of the faithful church is, in effect, to receive Jesus Christ; to reject that faithful witness, on the other hand, is a dire loss, a lamentable missing of the treasure of the kingdom of heaven.

THE GEOGRAPHICAL AND CULTURAL SETTING OF THE LESSON

The people of Israel were comprised of twelve tribes from the lineage of Jacob and continued to be identified by tribe throughout their history. Thus, choosing twelve disciples would have been a symbolic act, communicating that Jesus was restoring and reconstituting Israel around Himself and His ministry. The authority that Jesus bequeathed to His twelve disciples was for the empowerment of their mission, which was to parallel His own. While their mission at this early stage was limited to Israel, a mission to "all nations" opened after His resurrection.

PROMINENT CHARACTER(S) IN THE LESSON

The Twelve: a group of disciples specially selected and instructed by Jesus to assist Him in His earthly mission.

KEY TERMS IN THE LESSON

Impure (verse 1)—Greek: *akathartos* (ä-kä'-thär-tos): not cleansed; "unclean" (KJV).

Lepers (verse 8)—Greek: *lepros* (le-pro's): persons with skin that is scaly, rough, affected with leprosy; "those who have leprosy" (NIV).

Samaritans (verse 5)—Greek: *Samaritēs* (sä-mä-rē'-tās): inhabitants of the city of Samaria.

Welcome (verse 14)—Greek: *dechomai* (de'-kho-mī): accept; "receive" (KJV).

TOPICAL OUTLINE OF THE LESSON

I. **Introduction**
   A. A Manual for Missionaries
   B. Biblical Background

II. **Exposition and Application of the Scripture**
   A. Commissioned and Sent Forth
      (Matthew 10:1)
   B. Called to Be Disciples—Sent Out as Apostles
      (Matthew 10:2-4)
   C. Instructions for Doing Ministry
      (Matthew 10:5-6)
   D. Empowered to Do Miraculous Things
      (Matthew 10:7-10)
   E. Travel Light and Trust in God
      (Matthew 10:11-15)

III. **Concluding Reflection**

I. INTRODUCTION

A. A Manual for Missionaries

At the outset of His ministry, Jesus called many persons to be His disciples, and from His disciples He chose His twelve apostles; they were to be His more intimate friends and witnesses, who were afterwards to become the messengers of the Gospel. The name *disciple* means "learner"; Jesus was with them and instructing them. After His ascension, they were to be independent teachers of others, and were to be called *apostles*, or those sent—messengers. There were at first those who had merely followed Him because they desired to learn more of Him; but now these were directly and specially appointed for a particular work. They had power to work miracles to convince the people that they were sent by God.

God has never called and sent anyone to do anything for Him, but He has qualified that person to do the work. All those whom He had called have in some measure been qualified to do the work for which they were called to do. We are not told here whether these twelve should use, at their own discretion, the power given to them or whether it would be used under the special promptings of the Holy Spirit. Moreover, we were not informed as to the limitations, if any, of the exercise of this authority. They had full authority to do that which the Lord wanted them to do.

Jesus called His twelve disciples. He did not draft them, force them, or ask them to volunteer; He chose them to serve Him in a special way. Jesus did not choose these twelve to be His disciples because of their faith; in fact, their faith often faltered. He did not choose them because of their talent and ability; no one stood out with unusual ability. The disciples represented a wide range of backgrounds and life experiences; we can also speculate that, apparently, they might have had no more leadership potential than those who were not chosen. The one characteristic they all shared was the willingness to obey Jesus.

Christ calls us today to do the same. He does not twist our arms and make us do something we do not want to do. We can choose to join Him or remain behind. When Christ calls us to follow Him in our day and time, how shall we respond? Shall we give Him only a halfhearted commitment or our whole hearts?

B. Biblical Background

Besides continuing His own itinerant ministry, Jesus now took another step of great importance, by actually sending out the Twelve who He had previously chosen for the twofold purpose of being with Him as His disciples and going forth from Him as His apostles. For the first and only time in the book of Matthew, the Twelve were called apostles. Of most of these twelve, we know remarkably little as individuals, though they soon came to be revered in the church, and legends about them multiplied without end. Several of them were given occasional parts to play in the gospel of John (Andrew, Philip, Thomas, and a second Judas besides the traitor). Thomas acquired a special place in the legends of the Syrian churches; he gave his name to two apocryphal Gospels (writings included in the Septuagint and Vulgate, but not in the Protestant Bible). It is believed that Thomas eventually travelled to India and founded there a Christian church which still exists in the southern part of the country. Peter alone can be said to be known to history in a serious way. He encountered Paul in Antioch and was known to travel with his wife (see Galatians 2:11-14); one of the factions at Corinth professed a particular allegiance to him (see 1 Corinthians 1:12). It is now generally agreed that he went to Rome and suffered martyrdom in the Neronian persecution.

II. EXPOSITION AND APPLICATION OF THE SCRIPTURE

A. Commissioned and Sent Forth
   (Matthew 10:1)

AND WHEN he had called unto him his twelve disciples, he gave them power against unclean spirits, to cast them out, and to heal all manner of sickness and all manner of disease.

Jesus had many disciples (learners), but He appointed twelve to whom He gave authority and special training. The twelve disciples had already joined Jesus (see Mark 3:14-19), but Matthew waited until writing his missionary discourse to introduce them in his gospel. This records the first time that Jesus sent them out on their own (verse 5). These men were His inner circle. Many people followed and listened to Jesus, but these twelve received the most intense training. We see the impact of these men throughout the rest of the New Testament. They started the Christian church. The Gospels call these men the "disciples" or the "Twelve." The choice of the Twelve is highly symbolic. The number "12" corresponds to the twelve tribes of Israel, showing the continuity between the old religious system and the new one based on Jesus' message. Jesus looked upon His mission as the gathering of the true people of God. These men were the righteous remnant (the faithful believers throughout the Old Testament who never abandoned God or His law) who would carry on the work the twelve tribes were chosen to do—to build the community of God.

The text explicitly tells us that Jesus was interested not only in proclaiming the kingdom, but also in demonstrating it. Thus, He gave His twelve authority over unclean spirits, to cast them out, and to cure every disease and every sickness (verse 1). In the Bible, God worked miracles most often in times of revival, times when He had raised up servants committed to His cause and full of faith. Jesus empowered the Twelve to perform such acts of mercy and compassion. Both Jesus' proclamation and practical acts of compassion went beyond what many Christians call ministry today. Our communities were ravaged by demonic forces, violence, injustice, and all kinds of human pain, while the church often remained irrelevant except to the few who venture through our doors. To follow Jesus' model of ministry, more Christians must stop simply going to church and learn rather to become the church among our communities in evangelism and ministry to social needs.

B. Called to Be Disciples—Sent Out as Apostles (Matthew 10:2-4)

Now the names of the twelve apostles are these; The first, Simon, who is called Peter, and Andrew his brother; James the son of Zebedee, and John his brother; Philip, and Bartholomew; Thomas, and Matthew the publican; James the son of Alphaeus, and Lebbaeus, whose surname was Thaddaeus; Simon the Canaanite, and Judas Iscariot, who also betrayed him.

The listing of the names of the disciples varies somewhat in the other Gospels (see Mark 3:16-19 and Luke 6:13-16). While Simon Peter heads each list, Judas Iscariot is always last, for he is the one who betrayed Jesus to His enemies and then committed suicide. All lists have as the first four the two sets of brothers—Peter and Andrew, James and John (verse 2). The second set of four names in each list includes Philip and Bartholomew,

Thomas and Matthew (verse 3). In the final set of four, only the infamous Judas Iscariot is well-known (verse 4). The disciples were all Jewish by ancestry and probably remained with that branch of Christianity after the church became increasingly Gentile in the second half of the first century. For that reason, our knowledge of their later lives comes primarily from tradition. Despite the common features of the disciples, however, the list indicates some diversity. To include a tax collector and possibly a revolutionary in the same band of disciples is noteworthy.

The list of Jesus' twelve disciples does not give us many details, probably because there were not many impressive details to tell. Jesus called people from all backgrounds and occupations—fishermen, religious activists, tax collectors. He called common people and uncommon leaders; rich and poor; educated and uneducated. Today, many people think that only certain people can follow Christ, but this was not the attitude of the Master Himself. God can use anyone, no matter how insignificant he or she appears. When you feel small and useless, remember that God uses ordinary people to do His extraordinary work. Any of us who struggle with whether we are adequate to carry out God's purposes in the world should recall that the first ambassadors Jesus called were wholly inadequate. God especially uses those who will recognize their own inadequacy, for those who suppose their own ability adequate for God's call usually end up depending on it instead of Him.

C. Instructions for Doing Ministry (Matthew 10:5-6)

These twelve Jesus sent forth, and commanded them,

saying, Go not into the way of the Gentiles, and into any city of the Samaritans enter ye not: But go rather to the lost sheep of the house of Israel.

Jesus sent out the twelve disciples on a mission to preach the coming of the kingdom (verse 7). He also empowered them to exercise authority over demons and sickness. Jesus gave specific instructions regarding the focus of their ministry: "Do not go among the Gentiles or . . . Samaritans" (verse 5, NIV). The Samaritans were a race that resulted from intermarriage between Jews and Gentiles after the Old Testament captivities (see 2 Kings 17:24). When the Jews returned from exile, they refused to allow the Samaritans to help them rebuild the Temple (see Ezra 4). As a result, the Samaritans developed their own religion, accepting only the Pentateuch as God's authoritative Word.

This did not mean that Jesus opposed evangelizing Gentiles and Samaritans; in fact, Matthew had already described Jesus' encounter with Gentiles (see 8:28-34), and John 4 recounts His conversation with a Samaritan woman. Jesus' command to "go rather to the lost sheep of Israel" (verse 6, NIV) means that the disciples should spend their time among the Jews. These words restricted the disciples' short-term mission to the south. Jesus came not to the Jews *only*, but to the Jews *first* (see Romans 1:16). God chose the Jews to tell the rest of the world about Him. Later, these disciples would receive the commission to "go and make disciples of all nations" (see Matthew 28:19). Jewish disciples and apostles preached the Gospel of the risen Christ all around the Roman Empire, and soon Gentiles were pouring into the church. The Bible clearly teaches that God's message of salvation is for all people, regardless of race, sex, or national origin.

D. Empowered to Do Miraculous Things (Matthew 10:7-10)

And as ye go, preach, saying, The kingdom of heaven is at hand. Heal the sick, cleanse the lepers, raise the dead, cast out devils: freely ye have received, freely give. Provide neither gold, nor silver, nor brass in your purses, Nor scrip for your journey, neither two coats, neither shoes, nor yet staves: for the workman is worthy of his meat.

The message to be proclaimed by the disciples is exactly the same as that of John the Baptist (see 3:2) and of Jesus Himself (see 4:17), though the call to repentance which explicitly introduces those earlier summaries is here left unspoken. Matthew takes the call to repentance for granted as the corollary of the coming of God's kingship (verse 7). The verbal message is to be complemented by actions which also correspond to Jesus' own miraculous activity; the four acts of deliverance specified are carefully worded to reflect the miracles in Matthew 8–9: cure the sick, raise the dead, cleanse the lepers, cast out demons (verse 8). Their mission was an extension of Jesus', and (with the exception of the calming of the storm) what He could do they were given the power to do too. Healing through divine power (even the curing of leprosy) was widely regarded as an appropriate activity of holy men, and even exorcism was an accepted part of the Jewish scene. Given Jesus' wide reputation already for such supernatural acts, people would have expected His representatives to do likewise.

The command to do these miracles without cost (verse 8b) can be translated "as a gift" (*dorean*). It can also mean "for nothing," or "without cause," but usually connotes generosity, in their case by not charging for services. Paul also made a point of not having charged for his missionary labors (see 2 Corinthians 11:7), in contrast with the common practice of itinerant philosophers and teachers who expected not just board and lodging, but fees as well. So, Jesus' disciples' having received the message of the kingdom of God free of charge through Jesus Himself means that they were to offer their services in both teaching and healing without expecting any material reward. The following verses show, however (verses 9-10), that unlike Paul they were to accept board and lodging, since they were to take no money with them to pay for it—for laborers deserve their food.

The essence of the instructions in these verses is to travel light by not making special provision for their material needs while on the mission. Here is an opportunity to exercise the practical trust in God's provisions that they had been taught. If the Son of Man has nowhere to lay His head (see Matthew 8:20), His representatives can expect no material security except in God. If they are not to go barefoot, basic clothing and equipment will be provided. Additional provisions are forbidden. Money will not be needed, since they can expect to receive appropriate hospitality en route. They will not need to carry belts or bags for their journey, but trust in the providential hand of God and those who love Him.

Pastors, teachers, and missionaries should not plan on getting rich by their pastoring or teaching. Full-time Christian workers deserve a reasonable wage for their labors, but rarely is it an enriching one; profit should not be of undue emphasis in any work they agree to do. The spirit of capitalism—maximum profit for minimum investment—has no place in the church's ministry. Jesus gave the disciples a principle to guide their actions as they ministered to others: "freely ye have received, freely give" (verse 8). The disciples had received salvation and the kingdom without cost, therefore they should give their time under the same principle. Because God has showered us with blessings, we should give generously to others of our time, love, and possessions. Jesus set the precedent for kingdom work: it was to be more humble than showy, more economically marginal than heavily endowed, more trustful in God than in upscale donors. All the basics would be supplied by well wishers en route, if necessary.

E. Travel Light and Trust in God (Matthew 10:11-15)

And into whatsoever city or town ye shall enter, enquire who in it is worthy; and there abide till ye go thence. And when ye come into an house, salute it. And if the house be worthy, let your peace come upon it: but if it be not worthy, let your peace return to you. And whosoever shall not receive you, nor hear your words, when ye depart out of that house or city, shake off the dust of your feet. Verily I say unto you, It shall be more tolerable for the land of Sodom and Gomorrha in the day of judgment, than for that city.

The disciples were expected to travel light because they would be able to rely on hospitality from strangers (the need to "make inquiries" indicates that the potential hosts were not yet known to the disciples [verse 11]). By this time, there were no doubt people in most Galilean villages who had been among the crowds following Jesus, and such sympathizers would likely be willing hosts for His disciples. The greeting of "Peace to this house" was no mere formality (verses 12-13). It was envisaged as an effective blessing which went out and took effect, provided that it was suitably received; if not, it would have no effect but would "return" like an uncashed check. Even human words uttered with intent and with God's sanction can be effective and irrevocable. To be willing hosts of such messengers is indeed a blessing, but to oppose them is to forfeit God's peace because to receive them is to receive Jesus, and to receive Jesus is to receive God.

Verses 14-15 recognize that not everyone will welcome Jesus' representatives, and some will actively oppose them. So, they are now prepared for what they must do if hospitality is refused. Shaking off the dust from one's feet is an obvious symbol of disassociation; they want nothing more to do with the place. It is also a ritual for failure which, once performed, allows for closure and the moving on to the next field of labor. Shaking off the dust that accumulated on one's sandals showed extreme contempt for an area and its people, as well as the determination not to have any further involvement with them. Pious Jews shook dust from their feet after passing through Gentile cities or territories to show their separation from Gentile influences and practices. When the disciples shook the dust from their feet after leaving a Jewish town, it would be a vivid sign that they wished to remain separate from people who had rejected Jesus.

III. CONCLUDING REFLECTION

Chapter 9 closes with Jesus' expression of compassion for the people. They were helpless and harassed. Their need was great, but the workers were few. In the final verse of chapter 9 (Matthew 9:38), Jesus charged the disciples to pray for God to send workers—as the need was great and the workers were few. The first verse of Matthew 10 finds the help summoned. The disciples were to become the answer to their own prayers. Here for the first time, twelve disciples are listed by name, and all are male. Much is made of the gender of the disciples in the resistance to women serving in ordained ministry. Less attention is drawn to the fact that all twelve were Jewish. Even though this list of twelve includes no women and no Gentiles, the final chapter of the book of Matthew will find women to be first in proclaiming the Resurrection, and the mission will extend explicitly to Gentiles. The Holy Spirit is steadily widening the circle.

PRAYER

Eternal God, give us a heart for missions and evangelizing Your Word. When we say yes to Your call, give us faith enough to trust in Your providential hand as we go about the business of Your kingdom. Bless the work You have assigned our hands to do. In Jesus' name we pray. Amen.

HOME DAILY BIBLE READINGS
(April 1-7, 2019)

Call and Mission
MONDAY, April 1: "Jeremiah: Prophet to the Nations" (Jeremiah 1:4-10)
TUESDAY, April 2: "Ananias Welcomes and Baptizes Saul" (Acts 9:10-19)
WEDNESDAY, April 3: "Paul Called by a Vision" (Acts 16:6-10)
THURSDAY, April 4: "Jesus Sends Out the Twelve" (Mark 6:7-13)
FRIDAY, April 5: "A Great Harvest, but Few Workers" (Matthew 9:35-38)
SATURDAY, April 6: "Handling and Surviving Persecution" (Matthew 10:16-25)
SUNDAY, April 7: "The Twelve—Chosen and Commissioned" (Matthew 10:1-15)

April 14, 2019   **Lesson 7**

CALLED TO REMEMBER

ADULT/YOUTH
ADULT/YOUNG ADULT TOPIC: **Remembering Good Deeds**
YOUTH TOPIC: **Remember This**

CHILDREN
GENERAL LESSON TITLE: **A Woman Is Kind to Jesus**
CHILDREN'S TOPIC: **Be Kind to Others**

DEVOTIONAL READING
Acts 2:29-39

ADULT/YOUTH
BACKGROUND SCRIPTURE: **Matthew 26:1-13**
PRINT PASSAGE: **Matthew 26:1-13**
KEY VERSE: **Matthew 26:13**

CHILDREN
BACKGROUND SCRIPTURE: **Matthew 26:1-13**
PRINT PASSAGE: **Matthew 26:1-13**
KEY VERSE: **Matthew 26:10**

Matthew 26:1-13—KJV

AND IT came to pass, when Jesus had finished all these sayings, he said unto his disciples,

2 Ye know that after two days is the feast of the passover, and the Son of man is betrayed to be crucified.

3 Then assembled together the chief priests, and the scribes, and the elders of the people, unto the palace of the high priest, who was called Caiaphas,

4 And consulted that they might take Jesus by subtilty, and kill him.

5 But they said, Not on the feast day, lest there be an uproar among the people.

6 Now when Jesus was in Bethany, in the house of Simon the leper,

7 There came unto him a woman having an alabaster box of very precious ointment, and poured it on his head, as he sat at meat.

8 But when his disciples saw it, they had indignation, saying, To what purpose is this waste?

9 For this ointment might have been sold for much, and given to the poor.

Matthew 26:1-13—NIV

WHEN JESUS had finished saying all these things, he said to his disciples,

2 "As you know, the Passover is two days away—and the Son of Man will be handed over to be crucified."

3 Then the chief priests and the elders of the people assembled in the palace of the high priest, whose name was Caiaphas,

4 and they schemed to arrest Jesus secretly and kill him.

5 "But not during the festival," they said, "or there may be a riot among the people."

6 While Jesus was in Bethany in the home of Simon the Leper,

7 a woman came to him with an alabaster jar of very expensive perfume, which she poured on his head as he was reclining at the table.

8 When the disciples saw this, they were indignant. "Why this waste?" they asked.

9 "This perfume could have been sold at a high price and the money given to the poor."

10 When Jesus understood it, he said unto them, Why trouble ye the woman? for she hath wrought a good work upon me.

11 For ye have the poor always with you; but me ye have not always.

12 For in that she hath poured this ointment on my body, she did it for my burial.

13 Verily I say unto you, Wheresoever this gospel shall be preached in the whole world, there shall also this, that this woman hath done, be told for a memorial of her.

10 Aware of this, Jesus said to them, "Why are you bothering this woman? She has done a beautiful thing to me.

11 "The poor you will always have with you, but you will not always have me.

12 "When she poured this perfume on my body, she did it to prepare me for burial.

13 "Truly I tell you, wherever this gospel is preached throughout the world, what she has done will also be told, in memory of her."

UNIFYING LESSON PRINCIPLE: People often long remember bad deeds done to them and forget good ones. Will the evil that is done to harm always outweigh the good? The woman with the alabaster jar performed an act of kindness to Jesus that will be remembered wherever the Good News is told.

LESSON OBJECTIVES

Upon the completion of this lesson, the students will be able to do the following:

1. Contrast the love of the woman with the disciples' response to her actions.
2. Appreciate the woman's preparation of Jesus for His coming death and burial.
3. Embrace the call to proclaim the death and resurrection of Jesus Christ despite ridicule or resistance.

AGE-LEVEL POINTS TO BE EMPHASIZED

Teachers of ADULTS and YOUTH

—Parallel accounts of Jesus' anointing in Bethany are Mark 14:3-9 and John 12:1-8. The person whom Matthew and Mark describe as "a woman" John identifies as Mary, sister of Martha.

—"All these things" (verse 1) refers to Jesus' end-times teachings in Matthew 24-25. As His crucifixion drew near, Jesus prepared His disciples for the eschatological upheavals His death and resurrection would bring.

—Verse 2 is a brief summary or reprise of the three Passion predictions in Matthew (16:21-28; 17:22-23; 20:17-19) and Mark (8:31-33; 9:30-32; 10:32-34).

—According to Deuteronomy 15:4, if the Israelites are faithful to God's commands (specifically regarding the remission of debts in 15:1-3), "there will . . . be no one in need among you." Does this suggest that Jesus' declaration "You always have the poor with you" is a critique of their obedience?

—In John 12:5, the cost of the woman's ointment is established as three hundred denarii. A denarius was a common daily wage. Allowing for Sabbaths and other holy days as well as days or weeks when work would simply not be available, this amount would easily represent a year's wage for an unskilled laborer.

—The action of the woman contrasts with the acts of the Jerusalem leaders in plotting to kill Jesus (see Matthew 26:1-4).

Teachers of CHILDREN

—Jesus shared with His disciples what would happen to Him in the future.

—Jesus' enemies plotted how they could kill Him and not upset the people.

—As Jesus was visiting a leper's house, a woman poured precious ointment on His head.

—Jesus' disciples became indignant over the woman's extravagant actions.

—Jesus commended the woman for her act of kindness.

—Jesus said that the woman's actions were acts of preparing His body for burial.

THE CHRONOLOGICAL SETTING OF THE LESSON

According to Matthew's arrangement of His material, three events lead up to the arrest and crucifixion of Jesus: (1) the plot of the chief priests and the elders to arrest and kill Jesus, (2) the anointing of Jesus at Bethany, and (3) the offer of Judas to betray Jesus. During Jesus' ministry, His opponents had regularly been the scribes and Pharisees who had previously plotted His death (see Matthew 12:14). The chief priests and elders introduced here are not really new; in all probability, they were the ones who in the birth story collaborated with King Herod in an early attempt to destroy the Messiah (see Matthew 2:3-4). In this passage, they do not even consider an investigation or fair trial, for they have already decided on Jesus' death. Matthew has so constructed this story that the reader already knows that the powerful words of Jesus and the purpose of God will overrule the plot of the Jewish leaders, and that Jesus will die on the day He has already designated by faithfully submitting to God's will rather than as a victim of their will.

At the very time the religious leaders were plotting to arrest and kill Jesus, another person was preparing for His death but in an entirely different way and with a different spirit. Even though Jesus was surrounded by enemies, Matthew's gospel demonstrates that God never leaves Himself without a witness. The lamp of witness may burn low, but it never burns out. There will always be a righteous remnant that will obey God.

THE GEOGRAPHICAL AND CULTURAL SETTING OF THE LESSON

Sandwiched between the scheming of the male authorities and the betrayal by a male disciple, the noble actions of an unnamed woman stands out as a gesture of faithful love, service, and discipleship. Having already said that the Gospel will be preached to all nations (see Matthew 24:14), Jesus will now go on to say that wherever it is preached the action of this woman will be told in her memory. In contrast to the plotting of the authorities and the treachery of Judas, there stands out in high profile the striking action of this woman who invaded the male space at the banquet, bringing an alabaster jar of precious ointment that she poured over the head of Jesus as He reclined at the table. For the woman of Bethany, it was a sacrifice of something very precious—the action of a devoted disciple demonstrating her faith in and love for Christ.

Anticipating the burial of Jesus, she became the first disciple to understand the significance of His death. She did beforehand what the disciples of John had done for their murdered master (see Matthew 14:12), and what the official male disciples of Jesus would fail to do for Him, as they would leave Him and flee. She prepared Him for a fitting burial, and interestingly Matthew will not say that the women's purpose in going to the tomb was to anoint the body with spices. For Matthew, that anointing had already taken place symbolically through this act of love on behalf of this unnamed woman.

PROMINENT CHARACTER(S) IN THE LESSON

Caiaphas: the high priest at the trial of Jesus.
High Priest: the performer of sacrifices offered to deity; the dispenser and interpreter of oracular messages from the divine realm.
Simon: a leper who lived in Bethany at whose home Jesus was anointed by a woman.

KEY TERMS IN THE LESSON

Alabaster jar (verse 7)—Greek: *alabastron* (ä-lä'-bä-stron): an oblong vessel made of alabaster in which unguents are preserved; "alabaster box" (KJV).

Anoint (verse 7)—Greek: *katacheō* (kä-tä-khe'-ō): to pour down upon; "poured on" (NIV); "poured . . . on" (KJV).

Indignant (verse 8)—Greek: *aganakteō* (ä-gä-näk-te'-ō): to be very displeased; "had indignation" (KJV).

Passover (verse 2)—Greek: *pascha* (pä'-skhä): the paschal sacrifice (which was accustomed to be offered for the people's deliverance of old from Egypt).

TOPICAL OUTLINE OF THE LESSON

I. Introduction
   A. The Anointing of Jesus
   B. Biblical Background

II. Exposition and Application of the Scripture
   A. Obedience to the Call of God (Matthew 26:1-2)
   B. Organized Religion Plots to Kill Jesus (Matthew 26:3-5)
   C. A Grateful Woman and a Jar of Perfume (Matthew 26:6-9)
   D. How Much Is Too Much? (Matthew 26:10-13)

III. Concluding Reflection

I. INTRODUCTION

A. The Anointing of Jesus

In today's passion announcement (see Matthew 26:1-2), Matthew reminds us that notwithstanding the power of those who plotted against Jesus, Jesus moved according to His Father's plan and not theirs. No matter how strong the forces arrayed against God's servants, God will ultimately fulfill His purposes. Jesus, our example and sacrifice, obeyed God's calling at great cost to Himself and provides a model for all others who would follow Him.

In one of the opening scenes of this section, a woman plays the role that women continue to play in the accounts of Jesus' death, burial, and resurrection: a foil that reveals the inadequate commitment of the male disciples. But more significant is that her sacrifice provides a stark contrast to Judas's determination to profit somehow from Jesus' demise (see Matthew 26:14-50), and his ultimate betrayal of Jesus to His enemies. That Jesus suffered at the hands of close associates and disciples should encourage us when we experience rejection from those we seek to help. That most of the male disciples failed to stand firm when Jesus needed them most challenges us to watch and pray that we may be ready for testing.

B. Biblical Background

The present passage narrates the story of an unnamed woman who anointed Jesus. The meaning of this Passion week anointing is a matter of debate. Anointing was a custom at feasts, including Passover, but it seems to be too much of a coincidence that Jesus was anointed during Passover week and then days later He was crucified as "king of the Jews." It is more probable that the woman's action was intended to be messianic. This definitely seems to be the way in which Jesus understood her act of anointing. The anointing took place at Bethany, about two miles opposite Jerusalem. Jesus' prophecy—that what the woman did would be told in remembrance of her—anticipated His vindication and the continued proclamation of His message and ministry. Otherwise, why would anyone recall the woman's generous act? Her act of devotion placed her into the heart of the Gospel story.

II. EXPOSITION AND APPLICATION OF THE SCRIPTURE

A. Obedience to the Call of God
(Matthew 26:1-2)

AND IT came to pass, when Jesus had finished all these sayings, he said unto his disciples, Ye know that after two days is the feast of the passover, and the Son of man is betrayed to be crucified.

"All these things" that Jesus had finished saying refers to His teaching about the kingdom, recorded in chapter 25 (verse 1). Matthew used this statement to signal the end of his record of teaching. Next, Jesus moved into the final days of His earthly ministry and to the act that He ultimately came to accomplish: death for sins. This was not a surprise to Jesus; in fact, He had already told His disciples on three different occasions that He would suffer and die (see Matthew 16:21-28; 17:22-23; 20:17-19). As if echoing these warnings, Jesus reminded His disciples that the time had come for these things to be fulfilled. That Jesus would die during Passover was deeply significant with respect to Jewish history. The Passover commemorated the night the Israelites were freed from Egypt (see Exodus 12), when God "passed over" homes marked by the blood of the lamb. This was the last great plague on Egypt when, in unmarked homes, the firstborn sons died. After this horrible disaster, Pharaoh allowed the Israelites to leave.

Annually, Hebrew families would celebrate the Passover meal, a feast with the main course of lamb. The sacrifice of a lamb and the spilling of its blood commemorated Israel's escape from Egypt when the blood of a lamb painted on their doorposts had saved their firstborn sons from death. This event foreshadowed Jesus' work on the Cross. As the spotless Lamb of God, His blood would be spilled in order to save His people from the penalty of death brought by sin. The original setting of the Passover and the ritual which had been developed for its observance were a perpetual reminder to Israel of what it meant to be the chosen people of God. This is the first time Jesus' death had been directly linked with the Passover, but the significance of the date would become an important part of the meaning of the Last Supper and of the explanation Jesus then gave of the purpose of His death.

B. Organized Religion Plots to Kill Jesus
(Matthew 26:3-5)

Then assembled together the chief priests, and the scribes, and the elders of the people, unto the palace of the high priest, who was called Caiaphas, And consulted that they might take Jesus by subtilty, and kill him. But they said, Not on the feast day, lest there be an uproar among the people.

The Jewish leaders (chief priests and the elders of the people) plotted secretly to kill Jesus. The opposition against Jesus had been rising for some time. His fame as a spiritual leader was widespread, as was His popular reputation as a prophet like John (see Matthew 21:26). His robust performance in debates with Pharisaic and other leaders in the Temple courtyard had not endeared Him to the religious authorities. These leaders had already decided that Jesus must die; they simply needed an opportunity to kill Him. Thus, they were summoned to a meeting by the high priest. It was not a formal meeting of the Sanhedrin Council (a council that functioned as the central judicial authority for Jews), but more on the order of an ad hoc planning group.

The leaders were afraid of Jesus' popularity, so they needed some sly way to arrest and convict Jesus and sentence Him to death. They sought by stratagem, by guile, by some snare, to accomplish their end secretly, without any public arrest of Jesus. It was the decision of the group not to destroy Jesus "during the feast, lest a tumult arise" (see verse 5). People had come to the feast from every nation where the Jews had been scattered; many of the people regarded Jesus as a prophet, and some as the Messiah. The chief priests and elders had seen that the people were on Jesus' side—hence, they did not wish to excite further prejudice in His favor; so,

their decision was to wait until after the Feast of the Passover when the people had dispersed from Jerusalem. Then they would put Jesus to death. Perhaps Judas's unexpected offer (see 26:14-26) caused them to move sooner than they had planned but, as this passage implies, all was proceeding according to God's timetable. God overruled their plan to wait for a more opportune time. The destined hour would arrive, and Jesus would be crucified at the Passover.

C. A Grateful Woman and a Jar of Perfume
(Matthew 26:6-9)

Now when Jesus was in Bethany, in the house of Simon the leper, There came unto him a woman having an alabaster box of very precious ointment, and poured it on his head, as he sat at meat. But when his disciples saw it, they had indignation, saying, To what purpose is this waste? For this ointment might have been sold for much, and given to the poor.

There is one bright interlude before the worst of the drama began. Jesus was staying in the home of "Simon the leper," who lived in Bethany, just outside Jerusalem. Simon did not have leprosy at this time, for lepers were forced to live separately from people because of the extreme contagiousness of the disease. As they sat at a meal, a woman came to Jesus with an alabaster jar of very costly ointment, and she poured it on His head (verse 7). An alabaster jar was a beautiful and expensive vase with a long, slender neck. The perfume inside the jar is described as pure nard, a fragrant ointment possibly imported from the mountains of India. This was pure and genuine ointment, thus very costly. The perfume may have been a family heirloom. The beautiful jar was broken, and the costly ointment poured on Jesus' head. It was a common custom at some Jewish meals for the honored guests to be anointed with oil, but it would not be expensive nard. This act of devotion by this unnamed woman, who is a heroine in this narrative, contrasts with the treachery of the villains—the religious leaders and Judas. The focus on an unnamed woman to the discomfiture of the disciples gives further expression to the Gospel principle that the last will be first and the first last—and prepares us for the final act of the story, when it will be Jesus' women followers rather than the men who stay with Him (see 27:55-56).

The immediate response of the disciples was anger at the "so-called" waste. Why this extravagance? Their objection was not unfounded. Rabbinic tradition mandated the selling of luxury items to provide for the poor. Almsgiving was an ongoing obligation that was especially emphasized during Passover week. This woman's gift to Jesus was worth a year's wages. Perfume such as this was used in burial rites because embalming was not the Jewish custom. Perfume covered the odor of the dead body. The disciples' pious protest hid their mixed reactions. They claimed to have felt moral outrage at the loss of resources for the poor. However, Jesus wanted them to understand that even concern for the poor must never be elevated over devotion to Him.

D. How Much Is Too Much?
(Matthew 26:10-13)

When Jesus understood it, he said unto them, Why trouble ye the woman? for she hath wrought a good work upon me. For ye have the poor always with you; but me ye have not always. For in that she hath poured this ointment on my body, she did it for my burial. Verily I say unto you, Wheresoever this gospel shall be preached in the whole world, there shall also this, that this woman hath done, be told for a memorial of her.

What for the disciples was "waste" was for Jesus a "lovely" gesture. When Jesus heard what was said, He asked, "Why trouble ye the woman? for she hath wrought a good work upon me" (verse 10). This unnamed woman was no doubt troubled by these murmurings against her, but she stood in silence attempting no defense; but the voice of Jesus whom she loved was raised in her defense. Jesus praised her work. "Good work" here implied more than what is ordinarily expressed by "good"; it meant noble or honorable. It was the act of a noble soul expressing a noble deed. It was a work of love which was done out of a pure desire to honor Jesus. In rebuking His disciples, Jesus said, "The poor you will always have with you, but you will not always have me" (verse 11, NIV). Jesus would not remain long with them; in fact, only two or three days more would He be with them. His disciples would have plenty of time and opportunities to aid the poor; the more that they helped the poor in the name of Christ, the greater blessings they would receive. The opportunity of making such expressions of love directly to Jesus would not occur again; but hereafter, they could express their love for Him through all generations by giving to the poor. Nothing in Jesus' words detracts from our ethical and social responsibility to assist the poor, which in our global economy is more pressing now than it was then. Jesus was simply saying that the opportunity to show Him such devotion would soon pass. However, the opportunity to show kindness to the poor would last to the end of the age.

Jesus added that the unnamed woman had done this to prepare His body for burial (verse 12). We do not know whether she had this in mind when she anointed Jesus, but Jesus ascribed to her act this interpretation. In ancient times, it was usual to anoint bodies with costly spices and perfumes. Therefore, her act anticipated this usage. Jesus then proclaimed that wherever this Gospel is preached in the whole world, what she had done would be told in remembrance of her (verse 13). Frequently, people do things with not the slightest intention of their deeds' being long remembered. This was true for this woman in our lesson today. However, Jesus memorialized her act and declared that wherever this Gospel about Him will be preached, reference to what this good woman did for Jesus will be made. The very thing that caused indignation among His disciples has become a memorial of love and service to Him. The disciples condemned her act, but Jesus honored and blessed it. The story of her good work has been told in every known tongue and continues to be told by a thousand tongues each and every day.

III. CONCLUDING REFLECTION

The unnamed woman in this anointing scene may not have set out to anoint Jesus' body for burial. She could have been simply showing great respect for the teacher she had come to love and admire. She may not have understood Jesus' approaching death any more than the disciples. She may have realized that something was going to happen to Jesus, for all knew He was in great danger, and thus she sympathized with Him and honored Him with the greatest gift she could give. Her unselfish act would be remembered forever. This has come true because we read about it today. While the disciples misunderstood Jesus' mission and constantly argued about places in the kingdom; and while the religious leaders stubbornly refused to believe in Jesus and plotted His death, this one quiet woman so loved Jesus and was so devoted to Him that she considered no sacrifice too great for her beloved Master. She is an example to all of what unselfish devotion to our Savior is like.

PRAYER

Eternal God, give us the wisdom to know when we are standing in the presence of Jesus. Help us to show our love for Jesus Christ through our own acts of love, service, and devotion to others. In Jesus' name we pray. Amen.

HOME DAILY BIBLE READINGS
(April 8-14, 2019)

Called to Remember

MONDAY, April 8: "The Original Passover Celebration" (Exodus 12:1-14)
TUESDAY, April 9: "Care for the Poor" (Luke 16:19-31)
WEDNESDAY, April 10: "Mary Anoints Jesus' Body for Burial" (John 12:1-8)
THURSDAY, April 11: "One Must Die for the Nation" (John 11:47-53)
FRIDAY, April 12: "Judas Negotiates the Handover of Jesus" (Matthew 26:14-16)
SATURDAY, April 13: "Jesus Celebrates the Last Passover Meal" (Matthew 26:17-29)
SUNDAY, April 14: "Jesus Defends the Woman's Beautiful Act" (Matthew 26:1-13)

Spring Quarter 2019

Unit II: Call to Ministry

Children's Unit: Called to Serve Jesus

April 21, 2019 (Easter)   Lesson 8

CALLED TO PROCLAIM THE RESURRECTION

ADULT/YOUTH	CHILDREN
ADULT/YOUNG ADULT TOPIC: **Go and Tell**	GENERAL LESSON TITLE: **Called to Proclaim**
YOUTH TOPIC: **Proclaiming Good News**	**the Resurrection**
	CHILDREN'S TOPIC: **Share Good News with Others**

DEVOTIONAL READING
1 Corinthians 15:12-22

ADULT/YOUTH	CHILDREN
BACKGROUND SCRIPTURE: **Matthew 28:1-15**	BACKGROUND SCRIPTURE: **Matthew 28:1-15**
PRINT PASSAGE: **Matthew 28:1-15**	PRINT PASSAGE: **Matthew 28:1-15**
ADULT KEY VERSE: **Matthew 28:10**	KEY VERSE: **Matthew 28:10**
YOUTH KEY VERSE: **Matthew 28:6**	

Matthew 28:1-15—KJV

IN THE end of the sabbath, as it began to dawn toward the first day of the week, came Mary Magdalene and the other Mary to see the sepulchre.

2 And, behold, there was a great earthquake: for the angel of the Lord descended from heaven, and came and rolled back the stone from the door, and sat upon it.

3 His countenance was like lightning, and his raiment white as snow:

4 And for fear of him the keepers did shake, and became as dead men.

5 And the angel answered and said unto the women, Fear not ye: for I know that ye seek Jesus, which was crucified.

6 He is not here: for he is risen, as he said. Come, see the place where the Lord lay.

Matthew 28:1-15—NIV

AFTER THE Sabbath, at dawn on the first day of the week, Mary Magdalene and the other Mary went to look at the tomb.

2 There was a violent earthquake, for an angel of the Lord came down from heaven and, going to the tomb, rolled back the stone and sat on it.

3 His appearance was like lightning, and his clothes were white as snow.

4 The guards were so afraid of him that they shook and became like dead men.

5 The angel said to the women, "Do not be afraid, for I know that you are looking for Jesus, who was crucified.

6 "He is not here; he has risen, just as he said. Come and see the place where he lay.

7 "Then go quickly and tell his disciples: 'He has

7 And go quickly, and tell his disciples that he is risen from the dead; and, behold, he goeth before you into Galilee; there shall ye see him: lo, I have told you.

8 And they departed quickly from the sepulchre with fear and great joy; and did run to bring his disciples word.

9 And as they went to tell his disciples, behold, Jesus met them, saying, All hail. And they came and held him by the feet, and worshipped him.

10 Then said Jesus unto them, Be not afraid: go tell my brethren that they go into Galilee, and there shall they see me.

11 Now when they were going, behold, some of the watch came into the city, and shewed unto the chief priests all the things that were done.

12 And when they were assembled with the elders, and had taken counsel, they gave large money unto the soldiers,

13 Saying, Say ye, His disciples came by night, and stole him away while we slept.

14 And if this come to the governor's ears, we will persuade him, and secure you.

15 So they took the money, and did as they were taught: and this saying is commonly reported among the Jews until this day.

risen from the dead and is going ahead of you into Galilee. There you will see him.' Now I have told you."

8 So the women hurried away from the tomb, afraid yet filled with joy, and ran to tell his disciples.

9 Suddenly Jesus met them. "Greetings," he said. They came to him, clasped his feet and worshiped him.

10 Then Jesus said to them, "Do not be afraid. Go and tell my brothers to go to Galilee; there they will see me."

11 While the women were on their way, some of the guards went into the city and reported to the chief priests everything that had happened.

12 When the chief priests had met with the elders and devised a plan, they gave the soldiers a large sum of money,

13 telling them, "You are to say, 'His disciples came during the night and stole him away while we were asleep.'

14 "If this report gets to the governor, we will satisfy him and keep you out of trouble."

15 So the soldiers took the money and did as they were instructed. And this story has been widely circulated among the Jews to this very day.

UNIFYING LESSON PRINCIPLE: Many people live with despair and hopelessness. What is the source of genuine hope, and who can offer that hope? Jesus called and continues to call disciples to share and celebrate the Good News of His resurrection and the hope it offers to the world.

LESSON OBJECTIVES

Upon the completion of this lesson, the students will be able to do the following:

1. Tell how the women's sorrow was turned to joy upon meeting the risen Christ.
2. Recall the joy that was present when they first accepted the Good News about Christ.
3. Commit to a greater involvement in telling others the Good News of Christ.

AGE-LEVEL POINTS TO BE EMPHASIZED

Teachers of ADULTS and YOUTH

—To Matthew's record that the women went "to see" the tomb (verse 1), Mark 16:1 and Luke 24:1 add that they were coming to bring spices to anoint Jesus' body.

—None of the Gospels describe the Resurrection, only the discovery of the empty tomb and some attendant details. Matthew gives more details than the others, alone mentioning the earthquake, the angel's rolling away the stone, and the fainting of the guards.

—The story the chief priests and elders devise would seem to be self-refuting. If the guards were asleep, how would they know it was the disciples who stole the body? Why didn't they seek to arrest the disciples and retrieve the body?

—Matthew also records an earthquake at the death of Jesus (27:50-54). In early Jewish and Christian thought, an earthquake could symbolize eschatological upheaval—either a herald of God's coming or an aspect of divine judgment.

—Both the angel (verse 7) and Jesus (verse 10) send word for the disciples to go to Galilee. Matthew's story is thus set to end where Jesus' public ministry began (2:22; 3:13; 4:12, 15).

—Another argument against the Resurrection is that the women went to the wrong tomb. If this is so, then why didn't the authorities go to the *right* tomb and produce Jesus' body?

Teachers of CHILDREN

—On the first day of the week, two women came to the tomb where Jesus was buried.

—The women discovered that the stone covering the door of the tomb was rolled away.

—The angel informed the women that Jesus (who was crucified) had risen, and that they (the women) were instructed to give Jesus' disciples the same message.

—While on their way to share the Good News with His disciples, the women met Jesus and worshipped Him.

—Jesus asked the women to tell His disciples that He would meet them in Galilee.

—The soldiers that guarded the tomb were paid to tell the lie that Jesus' disciples had stolen His body.

THE CHRONOLOGICAL SETTING OF THE LESSON

The Resurrection narrative begins with the empty-tomb account. This passage gains forcefulness by following immediately upon the story concerning the precautions taken by the Jewish authorities to guard against any intrusion into the tomb (see Matthew 27:62-66). The narrative presupposes the resurrection of Jesus, rather than giving an account of how or when it happened. What matters to all the Gospel writers is not when or how Jesus left the empty tomb, but the simple fact that now, all who believe in God can say with confidence and assurance each and every Sunday morning, "he is not here, he has risen as he said."

THE GEOGRAPHICAL AND CULTURAL SETTING OF THE LESSON

In Matthew 27:55-56, the reader learns of "many women" witnessing the Crucifixion from a distance, who had followed Jesus from Galilee and "provided for him." Three are identified specifically: "Mary Magdalene, and Mary the mother of James and Joseph, and the mother of the sons of Zebedee." That the women do at least witness from a distance sets them apart from the disciples, all of whom have fled. However, only two of the aforementioned women will go to the tomb to see the place where He lay. Mary Magdalene and the other Mary will play a crucial role in the Resurrection narrative. Having come to the site of Jesus' burial on the morning after the Sabbath, they witnessed the empty tomb, heard the angel's announcement of the Resurrection, and were present at Jesus' first resurrection appearance (see Matthew 28:1-10), but they also preceded the disciples in worshipping the risen Christ. Women were the last at the Cross and the first at the tomb. It was not uncommon for friends to come and wait by a tomb in case an apparently dead person should revive. This might continue as far as the third day. The effect of these visits was to confirm death. The women who came to perform this sad task of confirming death instead found themselves running for joy, announcing life. Waiting and watching in sadness, they became the first witnesses to the Resurrection. Once again, the last are first.

PROMINENT CHARACTER(S) IN THE LESSON

Angel: a spiritual being that serves God and supports humankind. According to Scripture, angels were created before human beings. In Job 38:7, their presence at the Creation of the universe is noted.

Mary Magdalene: She was one of the women who ministered to Jesus and contributed financially to Him and His disciples. She was present at the crucifixion and burial of Jesus, and was among the women who went to visit the tomb on Easter morning.

The Other Mary: the mother of James the Younger and Joses, and the wife of Cleophas. She was one of the women present when Jesus was crucified and buried, and who went on Easter morning to visit the tomb.

KEY TERMS IN THE LESSON

Angel (verse 2)—Greek: *aggelos* (ang'-el-os): a messenger from God.

Be afraid (verse 5)—Greek: *phobeō* (fo-be'-ō): to "fear" (KJV); to be seized with alarm.

Countenance (verse 3)—Greek: *prosopon* (pros-o-pon): the face; surface; "appearance" (NIV).

Sabbath (verse 1)—Greek: *sabbaton* (sä'b-bä-ton): the seventh day of each week which was a sacred festival on which the Israelites were required to abstain from all work.

TOPICAL OUTLINE OF THE LESSON

I. Introduction
    A. Christ the Lord Is Risen Today!
    B. Biblical Background

II. Exposition and Application of the Scripture
    A. The Faithful Visit to Jesus' Empty Tomb (Matthew 28:1-4)
    B. The Angel Tells the Women to Carry the Good News! (Matthew 28:5-7)
    C. Encountering the Risen Lord (Matthew 28:8-10)
    D. The Cover-up by the Priests (Matthew 28:11-15)

III. Concluding Reflection

I. INTRODUCTION

A. Christ the Lord Is Risen Today!

The resurrection of Jesus from the dead is the central fact of Christian history. On it the church is built; without it there would be no Christian church today. Jesus' resurrection is unique. Other religions have strong ethical systems, concepts about paradise and afterlife, and various holy books. However, only Christianity has a God who became human, literally died for His people, and was raised again in power and in glory to rule His church forever. Because Christ was raised from the dead, we know that the kingdom of heaven has broken into human history. Our world now has hope for redemption, and not just disaster. We also know that God's mighty power is at work—destroying sin, creating new lives, and preparing us for Jesus' second coming.

What great news we have for the world! Because of Christ's resurrection, we know that death has been conquered, and that all who believe on His name will be raised from the dead to live forever with Christ. It is the Resurrection that gives the church her authority to witness to the great things that God has done to save the world. The Resurrection is our constant reminder that those who put their trust in God shall never be disappointed. He is mighty to save, and He will do what He has promised. The Resurrection is our proof that sin and Satan will not have the last word in our lives. It is the Resurrection that helps us to find meaning even in great tragedy. No matter what happens to us as we walk with the Lord, the Resurrection gives us hope for the future. Because of the Resurrection we know that Christ is alive and ruling His kingdom. The power of God that brought Christ's body back from the dead is available to us to bring our morally and spiritually dead selves back to life, enabling us to change and to grow in Christ Jesus. Thanks be to God who gives us the victory on this Resurrection Day.

B. Biblical Background

In Matthew's gospel, the Resurrection narrative begins as dawn breaks: "After the Sabbath, as the first day of the week was dawning" (verse 1, NRSV). Matthew, like Mark, also recorded the coming of the two women to the Jerusalem tomb. They knew where the tomb was, and they went to see it. The Marcan details about what the women were intending to do are missing in the book of Matthew. There is no mention of buying spices, of preparing them as in Luke, or of intending to anoint the corpse. Matthew's account merely suggests a return to the graveside. The women are returning to grieve. At that point, the story takes a decisive turn.

The message given by the angelic figure is that there is no need to fear. The prophecies by Jesus of His own rising from the dead have been fulfilled. Furthermore, the message that He is risen is to be given to His disciples. He will await them in Galilee and will see them there (verse 7). In Matthew, that meeting will signal the beginning of a long history of mission and the new responsibilities of teaching and baptizing. The story that began with angelic messengers' quelling the fears of Joseph and making preparation for Emmanuel, "God with us," ends with angelic messengers quelling the fears of the women and making preparations for work in the presence of Emmanuel to the end of time.

II. EXPOSITION AND APPLICATION OF THE SCRIPTURE

A. The Faithful Visit to Jesus' Empty Tomb (Matthew 28:1-4)

IN THE end of the sabbath, as it began to dawn toward the first day of the week, came Mary Magdalene and the other Mary to see the sepulchre. And, behold, there was a great earthquake: for the angel of the Lord descended from heaven, and came and rolled back the stone from the door, and sat upon it. His countenance was like lightning, and his raiment white as snow: And for fear of him the keepers did shake, and became as dead men.

All the Gospels stress the significance of the women's being the first witnesses of the empty tomb. This is hardly likely to be a fictional invention, as it is in a society where women were not generally regarded as credible witnesses, especially as the singling out of the women for this honor detracts from the prestige of the male disciples. We have seen how Matthew 27:55-56 and 27:61 have prepared the ground for women's roles as guarantors of the reality of the Resurrection. It was now through them that the male disciples were to hear the news and to receive the instructions of their risen Lord. However, in Matthew their privilege was even more pronounced in that they were chosen to be the first to meet with the risen Jesus Himself. The male disciples must wait until they get to Galilee (and even then, some will doubt—see verse 17), but He revealed Himself to the women even in Jerusalem. It is Luke rather than Matthew who is generally regarded as placing special emphasis on the contribution of women to the origins of Christianity, but here Matthew gave them a place of honor which not even Luke can envisage.

Matthew reported that early on Sunday morning, as day was breaking, the women went to the tomb. The purpose of their visit "to see the tomb" (verse 1) sounds rather colorless, but Matthew chose not to mention their intention to anoint Jesus' body, perhaps because the anointing had already been done in advance (by the woman with the alabaster jar of perfume in Matthew 26:12). The earthquake, like that described in Matthew 27:51, added to the drama of the scene and to the sense of divine intervention. As the text of Matthew stands, we had an earthquake Friday afternoon when Jesus died, then another one early Sunday morning when Jesus rose from the dead. The first earthquake opened the tombs of some saints, but they did not venture forth until the second earthquake and the resurrection of Jesus Himself.

Whereas in Matthew 27:51 it was apparently the earthquake that opened the tombs, here in Matthew 28 the removal of the stone from Jesus' tomb is attributed not to the earthquake, but to the direct action of the "angel of the Lord" (verse 2), who rolled back the stone and sat on it. Whereas in Mark we are only told that the women saw "a young man dressed in a white robe sitting on the right side" (Mark 16:5, NIV); however, Matthew speaks explicitly of an angel whose appearance was like lightning, and his clothing white as snow. Reference to the "angel of the Lord" explains how it is that the women found the stone rolled away. A being of such awesome power and authority is not to be obstructed either by the size and weight of the stone or by the official seal of Rome, still less by a detachment of terrified guards. Note the irony that those assigned to guard the corpse themselves become "corpses," while the one they guarded is already alive. The attempt at human security has been neutralized, and the guards play no further part in the scene until they have to report to their superiors (verses 11-15). God raised Jesus from the dead and sent an angel to roll back the stone. God used the natural and supernatural world to bring about His redemptive purposes on our behalf.

B. The Angel Tells the Women to Carry the Good News!
(Matthew 28:5-7)

And the angel answered and said unto the women, Fear not ye: for I know that ye seek Jesus, which was crucified. He is not here: for he is risen, as he said. Come, see the place where the Lord lay. And go quickly, and tell his disciples that he is risen from the dead; and, behold, he goeth before you into Galilee; there shall ye see him: lo, I have told you.

The angel ignored the guards and spoke directly to the women—for whose sake He had apparently come—so that they could see inside the already-empty tomb and carry the message to Jesus' disciples. They, unlike the guards, had no need to be afraid. We have not been told of their reaction, but presumably they too were in awe of the supernatural visitor; but the angel reassured them, just as Jesus had reassured His disciples at the equally spiritual experience of the Transfiguration (see Matthew 17:7). The poignant description of Jesus as "the one who

has been crucified" (see verse 5) left no room for doubt of the real death of the one who is now alive again. The angel invited the women to look into the inner burial chamber and "see the place where he lay" (verse 6, NIV). However, the absence of the body from the place where it had been showed that His resurrection was no less real and physical than His death. It is explained simply by the fulfillment of Jesus' repeated predictions that one day He would "be raised" from the dead. However, little they may have understood what He meant at the time; now that the event has given substance to His words, they have them in their memory as a frame of reference for understanding this unprecedented occurrence.

The women were not only witnesses of the empty tomb, but they were also the chosen messengers to convey the amazing news to Jesus' male disciples. The women were told to remind the disciples of Jesus' bold promise in Matthew 26:32, the words of which are here closely echoed: "he is going ahead of you into Galilee." But now the corollary of His "going ahead" is spelled out: when they get to Galilee, they would see Him—not just an empty tomb, but a living Jesus. However, unlike the women, the male disciples must wait until Galilee before they would see Him. The disciples had deserted Jesus in the hour of trial, but the angel's words held hope of renewal and forgiveness. The disciples had deserted, but they were directed to meet Jesus in Galilee. This was exactly what Jesus had told them during the Last Supper—that He would go ahead of them into Galilee after His resurrection.

C. Encountering the Risen Lord
(Matthew 28:8-10)

And they departed quickly from the sepulchre with fear

and great joy; and did run to bring his disciples word. And as they went to tell his disciples, behold, Jesus met them, saying, All hail. And they came and held him by the feet, and worshipped him. Then said Jesus unto them, Be not afraid: go tell my brethren that they go into Galilee, and there shall they see me.

The women hurried from the tomb, realizing that they had seen the results of an awesome miracle in the empty tomb and had been in the presence of an angel. This revelation from God had filled them with a mixture of fear and joy (verse 8). They obeyed the angel's command and ran to the eleven disciples with the Good News of the empty tomb and Jesus' resurrection. As they ran from the tomb, Jesus Himself appeared in their path. The women took hold of His feet (a Near Eastern custom for a subject showing obeisance to a king) and worshipped Him, giving homage to their Savior, Lord, and King (verse 9).

Jesus' words in verse 10 largely repeated the reassurance and the message given to the women by the angel in verses 5-7. The result of this repetition is that the importance of the coming meeting in Galilee is further underlined. There is, however, one significant new element in this verse—the description of the male disciples as "my brothers." The phrase is not a new one, since Jesus had used it before. This time, however, it followed the abject failure of the Twelve to stand with Jesus when the pressure was on, a failure that was hardly less shameful because Jesus had predicted it in Matthew 26:31. But now it was time for the second half of that prediction to be fulfilled (see Matthew 26:32), and the Galilean meeting would eventually restore the family relationship that they must surely have thought had come to an end in Gethsemane.

D. The Cover-up by the Priests
(Matthew 28:11-15)

Now when they were going, behold, some of the watch came into the city, and shewed unto the chief priests all the things that were done. And when they were assembled with the elders, and had taken counsel, they gave large money unto the soldiers, Saying, Say ye, His disciples came by night, and stole him away while we slept. And if this come to the governor's ears, we will persuade him, and secure you. So they took the money, and did as they were taught: and this saying is commonly reported among the Jews until this day.

Matthew 28:11 invites the reader to compare two groups hurrying away from the tomb with a message to deliver: the women have a message of hope and victory for the disciples, while the guards have a message of confusion and failure for the chief priests. Jesus' resurrection was already causing a great stir in Jerusalem. A group of women was moving quickly through the streets, looking for the disciples, to tell them the amazing news that Jesus was alive. At the same time, guards were on their way, not to Pilate but to the chief priests. The guards, having been no more than passive spectators when the angel appeared and opened the tomb (verses 2-4), must now account for the failure of their watch. The very thing they were posted there to prevent had happened: Jesus' body has disappeared from the tomb. Instead of even considering that Jesus' claims had been true and that He truly was the Messiah risen from the dead, the chief priests and elders devised a plan and paid a bribe to the soldiers in order to explain away what had happened (verses 12-14). Apparently, the sum of money was worth it because the soldiers took it and did as they were instructed (verse 15).

The story concocted by the chief priests and

elders concerning the missing body of Jesus was still being circulated in the days of Matthew's writing of his gospel. Matthew wrote to counteract such a vicious lie. The disciples did not steal the body of Jesus; God raised Him from the dead. Matthew's statement, "this story is still told," brings to an end Matthew's defense of the Resurrection account. He has argued that the tomb was well guarded and that the disciples could not in fact have succeeded in illegally removing the body of Jesus. He further implied that the Jesus the women met in Matthew 28:9-10 was in fact bodily risen and not a spirit or phantom. Matthew's story is our story: Christ Jesus lives today!

III. CONCLUDING REFLECTION

One of the most significant factors in early Christian understanding of the Resurrection is the light it throws on the doctrine of God. The act of resurrection is always an act of God. Although Jesus claimed the power to take up His life again after laying it down (see John 10:18), the New Testament does not suggest that the Resurrection was an independent act of Christ. The power behind it was the power of God. Indeed, the resurrection of Christ is viewed as the supreme display of divine power.

It is the act by which the ceaseless round of death and corruption in human life has been checked. God has provided a way out of death into life, by raising His Son from death to life. The Resurrection is essentially a part of God's plan for the redemption of humankind.

Our task is to take this joyful news of what God has done for us in Christ Jesus and tell it to the entire world. We are indeed to be the bearers of great hope and great joy that come in knowing who Jesus is for us in our day and time. The angel's commission to the women to "go and tell" still applies in our day. Joyful Christians are commissioned to tell one another of the Resurrection every day. Every week in worship we tell each other the Resurrection story when we sing and confess our faith together.

PRAYER

Eternal God, our Father, on this glorious Resurrection Day we give You thanks for Jesus Christ, our example and perfect sacrifice. We thank You for the day, the very hour, He spoke peace to our souls and our redemption was made complete. Give us the strength and courage to tell this Good News to any and all we meet. In Jesus' name we pray. Amen.

HOME DAILY BIBLE READINGS
(April 15-21, 2019)

Called to Proclaim the Resurrection
MONDAY, April 15: "'I Am the Resurrection and the Life'" (John 11:17-27)
TUESDAY, April 16: "Judas Returns Money; Hangs Himself" (Matthew 27:3-10)
WEDNESDAY, April 17: "Jesus Crucified" (Matthew 27:32-44)
THURSDAY, April 18: "Guards Secure the Tomb" (Matthew 27:62-66)
FRIDAY, April 19: "Mary Meets Jesus Outside the Tomb" (John 20:11-18)
SATURDAY, April 20: "Reigning Triumphant with Christ" (Revelation 20:1-6)
SUNDAY, April 21: "'Meet Me in Galilee!'" (Matthew 28:1-15)

April 28, 2019   Lesson 9

CALL AND COMMISSIONING

ADULT/YOUTH
ADULT/YOUNG ADULT TOPIC: **A Job to Do**
YOUTH TOPIC: **Someone Is Calling You to Go**

CHILDREN
GENERAL LESSON TITLE: **Jesus Calls and Assigns His Disciples**
CHILDREN'S TOPIC: **Going on a Mission**

DEVOTIONAL READING
Colossians 3:12-17

ADULT/YOUTH
BACKGROUND SCRIPTURE: **Matthew 28:16-20; Acts 1:6-8**
PRINT PASSAGE: **Matthew 28:16-20; Acts 1:6-8**
ADULT KEY VERSES: **Matthew 28:19-20**
YOUTH KEY VERSE: **Matthew 28:19**

CHILDREN
BACKGROUND SCRIPTURE: **Matthew 28:16-20; Acts 1:6-8**
PRINT PASSAGE: **Matthew 28:16-20; Acts 1:6-8**
KEY VERSES: **Matthew 28:19, 20**

Matthew 28:16-20; Acts 1:6-8—KJV

16 Then the eleven disciples went away into Galilee, into a mountain where Jesus had appointed them.

17 And when they saw him, they worshipped him: but some doubted.

18 And Jesus came and spake unto them, saying, All power is given unto me in heaven and in earth.

19 Go ye therefore, and teach all nations, baptizing them in the name of the Father, and of the Son, and of the Holy Ghost:

20 Teaching them to observe all things whatsoever I have commanded you: and, lo, I am with you always, even unto the end of the world. Amen.

.....

6 When they therefore were come together, they asked of him, saying, Lord, wilt thou at this time restore again the kingdom to Israel?

Matthew 28:16-20; Acts 1:6-8—NIV

16 Then the eleven disciples went to Galilee, to the mountain where Jesus had told them to go.

17 When they saw him, they worshiped him; but some doubted.

18 Then Jesus came to them and said, "All authority in heaven and on earth has been given to me.

19 "Therefore go and make disciples of all nations, baptizing them in the name of the Father and of the Son and of the Holy Spirit,

20 "and teaching them to obey everything I have commanded you. And surely I am with you always, to the very end of the age."

.....

6 Then they gathered around him and asked him, "Lord, are you at this time going to restore the kingdom to Israel?"

7 And he said unto them, It is not for you to know the times or the seasons, which the Father hath put in his own power.

8 But ye shall receive power, after that the Holy Ghost is come upon you: and ye shall be witnesses unto me both in Jerusalem, and in all Judaea, and in Samaria, and unto the uttermost part of the earth.

7 He said to them: "It is not for you to know the times or dates the Father has set by his own authority.

8 "But you will receive power when the Holy Spirit comes on you; and you will be my witnesses in Jerusalem, and in all Judea and Samaria, and to the ends of the earth."

UNIFYING LESSON PRINCIPLE: When there have been dramatic changes in circumstances and in the roles of leadership, people are uncertain of their own roles and responsibilities. Where can they find direction and authority to act? The risen Lord commissioned the disciples, giving them authority and responsibility to continue and extend His mission and ministry throughout the world.

LESSON OBJECTIVES

Upon the completion of this lesson, the students will be able to do the following:

1. Compare and contrast Jesus' commission to the apostles on the mountain in Galilee (Matthew 28) with His commission on Mount Olivet (see Acts 1).
2. Take courage that Jesus is present with His disciples as they go into the world to make disciples.
3. Accept the commission to make disciples of all people.

AGE-LEVEL POINTS TO BE EMPHASIZED

Teachers of ADULTS and YOUTH

—The commission to the disciples, the third "go and tell" command (verses 19-20; cf. Matthew 28:7, 10) is expressed in rabbinical terms: go, make disciples, baptize, and teach.

—That some would doubt (verse 17) is surprising at this point in time. For that reason, many assume that this meeting included more than the apostles and, in fact, is the appearance to five hundred mentioned in 1 Corinthians 15:6.

—Matthew 28:19 is one of the few places in Scripture where an explicit trinitarian formula is found (others occur at 1 Corinthians 12:4-6; 2 Corinthians 13:13; Hebrews 9:14; etc.).

—Some interpreters note that "go" in verse 19 is a participle, not an imperative. The implication is that the command is along the lines of "*as you go*, make disciples. . . ." Others, however, say this is over-interpreting a grammatical construction that is better rendered simply "Go and make . . . ."

—Teaching disciples to obey everything Jesus has commanded is a fitting conclusion to the gospel of Matthew, which places such emphasis on the teaching ministry of Jesus and even arranges much of this material into five discrete teaching blocks.

Teachers of CHILDREN

—Jesus designated the place at which He would meet His disciples after His resurrection.

—Jesus' appearance to His disciples was met with worship and doubt.

—Jesus' final statement in Matthew's gospel affirmed His possession of all power.

—Jesus' instructions to His disciples were for them to teach and baptize in the name of the Father, the Son, and the Holy Spirit.
—The disciples' teaching was to include all the things commanded by Jesus.

—In Acts 1:8, Jesus informed the disciples that they would receive power after the Holy Spirit had come upon them, and they would be Jesus' witnesses in all the world.

THE CHRONOLOGICAL SETTING OF THE LESSON

The Resurrection narrative comes to its climax, as does the entire gospel of Matthew, in this its final majestic passage. The women have seen the empty tomb and have met the resurrected Jesus. It is assumed in the present passage that they relayed Jesus' message to the disciples, for now the latter are around in Galilee. Here, as promised, the risen Jesus appeared to them. And here they received their commission in the famous words that have become the hallmark of the gospel of Matthew. These final five verses (Matthew 28:16-20) not only conclude the passion-Resurrection narrative of chapters 26–28, but also serve as the conclusion to the entire Gospel. This passage is basic to the narrative framework of the entire Gospel, since it stresses authority and teaching—emphases found in every section of Matthew's gospel.

THE GEOGRAPHICAL AND CULTURAL SETTING OF THE LESSON

Jesus told His disciples before His death that He would be raised and would meet them in Galilee. The angel told the women to bear the message to the disciples that Jesus would meet them in Galilee; and then Jesus appeared to the women, telling them, "Go tell my brethren that they depart into Galilee and there they shall see me." Matthew now records that meeting. At this time, Jesus gave them the worldwide, time-lasting commission. All doubts had now been removed; all evidence was now before them, and they are now ready to receive this all-important commission. They would see that the death of Jesus would not end all, but that His death, burial, and resurrection constituted the essentials facts of the Gospel which they were to proclaim to the world. Their work, instead of ending, was just now beginning; their despair at the death of Jesus was turned into the glorious hope of the Gospel.

Those who are disciples of Jesus, and who have then been baptized into the name of the Father, the Son, and the Holy Spirit, are to be taught to observe all things which train and develop a child of God. Three things are commanded in the commission to be done—namely, (1) make disciples; (2) baptize those who are disciples; and (3) then teach them to be obedient to all the commands of God. Finally, there is a promise made to them in this charge: "And, lo, I am with you always, even unto the end of the world." This promise extends His spiritual presence and blessings to all who serve under His commission.

PROMINENT CHARACTER(S) IN THE LESSON

The Holy Spirit: The *Holy Spirit* or *Holy* Ghost is the third person (hypostasis) of the Trinity—the Trinity being the Triune God manifested as Father, Son, and *Holy Spirit*—each person itself being God. **The Resurrected Messiah:** For the earliest Christian preaching, it is the Resurrection that designates Jesus as the Christ, the Son of God. This is the point at which His reign as Messiah begins.

KEY TERMS IN THE LESSON
Authority (Matthew 28:18)—Greek: *exousia*

(eks-ü-sē'-ä): the power of authority (influence) and of right (privilege); "power" (KJV).

Doubted (Matthew 28:17)—Greek: *distazō* **(dē-stä'-zō):** wavered; had hesitation.

Witnesses (Acts 1:8)—Greek: *martys* **(mä'r-tüs):** persons who bear witness, testify.

Worshipped (Matthew 28:17)—Greek: *proskyneō* **(pros-kü-ne'-ō):** in the New Testament, by kneeling or prostration to do homage (to one) or make obeisance, whether to express respect or to make supplication; "worshiped" (NIV).

TOPICAL OUTLINE OF THE LESSON

I. Introduction
  A. The Hope and Promise of the Resurrection
  B. Biblical Background

II. Exposition and Application of the Scripture
  A. The Commissioning of the Eleven (Matthew 28:16)
  B. The Place of Doubt among the Faithful (Matthew 28:17)
  C. All Authority in Heaven and on Earth Has Been Given to Jesus (Matthew 28:18)
  D. Go Make Disciples! (Matthew 28:19-20)
  E. Empowered by the Spirit (Acts 1:6-8)

III. Concluding Reflection

I. INTRODUCTION

A. The Hope and Promise of the Resurrection

The risen Christ is central to the existence and proclamation of the church. There would be no Gospel if there had been no resurrection. The Resurrection, however, is not simply a datum of history, words about a past event. The Resurrection has enormous consequence for present Christian existence. It is the risen Jesus, to whom all authority in heaven and earth has been given, who here commissions His disciples and in effect the church of every period of history. The disciples are to go everywhere with the message of Good News in the name and authority of Jesus. Theirs is indeed an awesome responsibility—to go, make disciples of all nations, baptize, and teach. If left to their own devices and strength, the task would be overwhelming. Yet, they are not left alone in this assignment. The risen, enthroned Jesus promised to be with them in their fulfillment of it—not intermittently, but always.

Evidence of the truth of that promise is readily available in the narrative of the book of Acts, as well as in the history of the church, which has seen a network of believers around the world in every land of every race come into existence from what began just after the death of Jesus with but a handful of doubting, confused, and powerless disciples. The statements that frame the commission on either side concerning the authority and the presence of Jesus alone allow the church to continue in the world. Only the ongoing reality of these facts can continue to equip the church for her mission—a mission that will continue until the consummation of the age. The Great Commission on which Matthew ends his gospel remains one of the priceless treasures of the Christian church, providing comfort, strength, and hope until the final dawning of the eschaton (the biblical perspective concerning events to take place in the last days). This Good News of the kingdom will be proclaimed throughout the world as a testimony to what God has done for us in the resurrection of Jesus Christ.

B. Biblical Background

The resurrection of Jesus belongs to the very foundation of Christian faith and proclamation. By resurrection, no New Testament writer means simply a vision of Christ or a purely spiritual survival. They mean a *bodily* resurrection, whatever the transformation of that body may have been. Matthew alone placed Jesus' first appearance to the eleven disciples in Galilee. When the Eleven saw Jesus, they worshipped Him, but some doubted; however, there is no hint that the doubters were persons other than from the Eleven. The transparent honesty of the Gospels is reflected in these forthright confessions of the doubts of the apostles, and the case for the fact of the Resurrection and subsequent appearances is thereby strengthened. The disciples had not expected to see Jesus again, and both the reports of these appearances and His actual presence among them were almost too good to be true.

II. EXPOSITION AND APPLICATION OF THE SCRIPTURE

A. The Commissioning of the Eleven (Matthew 28:16)

Then the eleven disciples went away into Galilee, into a mountain where Jesus had appointed them.

In Matthew 28:11, Jesus took the imperfect number "11" and gave it a perfect vocation. The church that Jesus sends into the world is fallible, "elevenish," imperfect. Yet, Jesus used exactly such a church to do His perfect work. The eleven disciples commissioned by Jesus were not called leaders, church officers, or even apostles, but simply disciples. No complex church structure is visible in the Great Commission. The Eleven obeyed the angelic command relayed by the faithful women (verses 7, 10). The call to come to Galilee was the call to believe the Lord and His resurrection enough to make a trip. It was a call to trust Jesus almost in an Abrahamic way, for it was a call to come meet someone who might not be there. The faith of the disciples still had this element of risk, of daring to believe that the Lord will be at the end of the journey. In Matthew's gospel, faith is frequently simple obedience to Jesus' command.

By coming to Galilee, the disciples came to the place of Jesus' earthly ministry, and so they reconnected with the historical, pre-Resurrection Jesus—the Jesus to whom the Great Commission especially wanted to unite disciples. In this Galilean meeting, the disciples return to their beginnings, and at the same time and in the same place their lives now break out onto a worldwide horizon. Moreover, the fact that the disciples met Jesus in a group in Galilee and not, say, one by one in private, honors the church's simple meeting places and public worship services. This meeting says that the risen Jesus, like the historical Jesus, still meets disciples in a special way in the fellowship of believing people. Thus, in this verse there is a little doctrine of Christ and a little doctrine of the church. The Great Commission is nothing less than a summary of the whole gospel of Matthew.

B. The Place of Doubt among the Faithful (Matthew 28:17)

And when they saw him, they worshipped him: but some doubted.

In an effort to exclude the eleven disciples from having "doubted" (verse 17), some scholars have suggested that the phrase "they saw him" refers to more than just the eleven disciples—perhaps the "five hundred brothers" mentioned by Paul in 1 Corinthians 15:6. But the Matthean text does not allow for this; it says that among the eleven who saw Jesus, there were some who doubted—which means they had hesitations about believing in Jesus' resurrection. Quite possibly on their walk from Jerusalem to Galilee, lengthy discussions were held. Matthew may have been reporting some of the doubts and concerns still lingering in the minds of the eleven chosen disciples. Of course, they would eventually be fully convinced and believe.

It should not strike believers as odd that some of the disciples struggled with doubt. No Christian grows in faith without some doubt. Mother Theresa, the Catholic nun who dedicated her life to the poor of Calcutta, India, left behind a personal diary filled with doubts about her faith and her work among the poor. When doubts come we should not be discouraged; they are not a sign of sin or failure. They are a normal part of spiritual growth. In seasons of doubts concerning our faith, we should keep talking to thoughtful Christian friends and teachers. We should keep asking questions and looking for answers. We should keep praying.

God gave us a mind to discover His truth, and sometimes on the way to that truth we have to struggle with doubt until a breakthrough of unwavering faith comes.

C. All Authority in Heaven and on Earth Has Been Given to Jesus (Matthew 28:18)

And Jesus came and spake unto them, saying, All power is given unto me in heaven and in earth.

God gave Jesus authority over heaven and earth, a sweeping concept that implies divine status. He has "all authority"—that is, nothing is outside of His sovereign control. The major message here and in Matthew 28:20 is that Jesus, the one raised from the dead, has the authority of God Himself. During Satan's temptation of Jesus, Satan had offered "all the kingdoms of the world and their splendor" (Matthew 4:8, NIV). Jesus resisted the tempter, obeyed God to the point of horrible death, and was raised again in victory to receive all authority over heaven and earth—something Satan could never have given because it was never his in the first place.

From the risen Jesus the claim to have all authority has all-the-more-convincing power. The Resurrection serves as a vindication of the words and deeds of Jesus during His ministry. Now the resurrected (not resuscitated!) Jesus who appeared before the disciples is one who partakes of a new order of existence and who here anticipated His glorious exaltation at God's right hand (see Luke 24:51). It is accordingly the One who has "all authority in heaven and on earth" who now sends out His disciples to evangelize the world. This is to provide them in turn with authority and supply them with confidence as they go.

D. Go Make Disciples!
(Matthew 28:19-20)

Go ye therefore, and teach all nations, baptizing them in the name of the Father, and of the Son, and of the Holy Ghost: Teaching them to observe all things whatsoever I have commanded you: and, lo, I am with you always, even unto the end of the world. Amen.

This connection between the authority of Jesus and the fulfilling of the tasks now assigned to the disciples in Matthew's gospel and those who come after them is made plain in the connective, "therefore" (verse 19). Jesus' authority (verse 18) and His presence (verse 20) would empower His disciples to fulfill the commission He gave them. The disciples were to "go" and "make disciples." They were to go into all the world.

The universal authority of Jesus is the basis of the universal mission of the church. The word *disciple* means above all "learner" or "pupil." Interestingly enough, the usual missionary terms are not employed here: *preach, convert, win*, and so forth. Rather, they are told to make disciples. *To disciple* means "to make students of," "bring to school," and "educate." The word pictures students sitting around a teacher more than it does penitents kneeling at an altar—to make disciples is more of an educational process than an evangelistic concept, a school more than a revival. The word's prosaic character says in effect, "Work with people over a period of time in the educative process of teaching Jesus."

Only the one who has all authority can do the big things like win, convert, bring to repentance, or move a person to decision—that authority is Jesus' alone. However, disciples can, must, and will do the job within their power of "discipling" others—that is, they will spend prolonged time with people in the confidence that sooner or later the Lord Jesus will create in these people the decision to follow Him and be baptized. Effective witnessing is telling others about Jesus Christ and leaving the results to God.

Jesus' "all nations" gives disciples worldwide ambitions; it creates longings to see a universal spread of the mission, a worldwide renewal of the churches, and an international conversion among all peoples. Now after the death and resurrection of Jesus, for the first time the limitation of the Gospel to Israel is removed. The direct commission is given to take the message of Jesus to all nations, a task acknowledged and fulfilled by the early church. Now we finally arrive at the full inclusion of the Gentiles in the history of salvation.

The disciples are further told to "baptize" the new disciples (verse 19). Only Matthew records this command of Jesus, but the practice of the early church suggests its historicity. Yet now, the full-blown rite of Christian baptism is introduced without any indication that this is something new. For Matthew's readers, it was presumably so familiar as to need no explanation. "Baptizing them in the name of the Father, and of the Son, and of the Holy Ghost" (verse 19b)—it is one name with three names, one God in three persons. "Into the name of" comes from the world of banking and means "to the account of" or "into the possession of." Thus, by baptism, believers come onto the account and into the possession of the great God; baptized believers come under new management. They are transferred to a new "company"—into the fellowship of those who worship God the Father through listening to the teaching of Jesus Christ, His Son, by the drawing power of the Holy Spirit; they become members of the holy, catholic church and of God's own family. The reason why "baptizing" is put within the Great Commission is that it is more than an initiating ceremony; it is spiritual and effectual, empowering and connecting. We could appropriately paraphrase "baptizing them" by saying "empowering them into the possession of the loving Father, the life-giving teaching of the Son, and the power of the Holy Spirit."

The final element of the Great Commission is found in Jesus' instructions to the disciples to go teach. They are told to do what Jesus Himself did. In addition, indeed the gospel of Matthew provided the church with an excellent handbook containing that teaching. It is thus the peculiar responsibility of the church to hand on that teaching and to see to it that new disciples make it their way of life. The commission of the disciples is followed by a promise that must have cheered up the hearts of those to whom so much responsibility was being given. The promise of the Lord Jesus is, "I am with you always" (verse 20). Jesus, though not physically present among them, would not abandon them. He would be in their midst, though unseen, and would empower them to fulfill the commission He has given them. Those who receive the messengers of the Good News will receive Jesus Himself. Moreover, the promise of Jesus' continuing presence with them is not restricted to any special circumstances, nor is it made simply for the immediate future. He promised to be with them and with us "to the end of the age" (all the days until the consummation of the age).

E. Empowered by the Spirit (Acts 1:6-8)

When they therefore were come together, they asked of him, saying, Lord, wilt thou at this time restore again the kingdom to Israel? And he said unto them, It is not for you to know the times or the seasons, which the Father hath put in his own power. But ye shall receive power, after that the Holy Ghost is come upon you: and ye shall be witnesses unto me both in Jerusalem, and in all Judaea, and in Samaria, and unto the uttermost part of the earth.

When the disciples gathered after that first Resurrection Sunday, they did so as those who wait and question. What they know of what had happened in the Resurrection was the source of their hope but also of their yearning. They wanted Christ to fulfill His promise of restoration, to finish the work begun. When? they ask. As the recipients of their Lord's instruction and witnesses to His death and resurrection, they know the decisive battle has been fought and won—but not yet. Now, in the meantime, they wait as those who are still dependent upon the Father's faithfulness, those who have no control over the timetable of a beneficent God who graciously allows enough time to accomplish the work begun in Jesus. But their waiting is not empty-handed. They wait in hope as those who know their Master has been taken up where He is exalted at the right hand of God. The followers of Christ know that the one who served, taught, and loved them now rules them. But this knowledge is no smug inside knowledge for the privileged few. It is a knowledge which demands a witness. Thus, in the meantime they are given a job to do and will have power with which to do it. The time between the Resurrection and the restoration of the kingdom is the gracious interim for witness.

The coming of the Spirit would imbue them with the power to become effective witnesses for their Master. A *witness* is one who is able to give testimony based on knowledge. One must know Christ in order to bear witness to Him. An unbeliever, no matter how much he might have seen and heard Him, cannot qualify. The Resurrection was a key element in this testimony, and only believers had seen the risen Lord. "You will be my witnesses" (verse 8) is both prophecy and command. As prophecy, the disciples could count on its realization; as command, they were bound to sense the responsibility to make themselves obediently available. Implied in our Lord's words is the duty to make Him their message. In this gracious interim, there is work to be done; let the church be about that work in the meantime, secure in the promise that this Jesus, who was so dramatically taken from His disciples, shall return in the same way. Our duty as witnesses is to get all excited and go tell everybody that Jesus Christ is King!

III. CONCLUDING REFLECTION

With all authority in heaven and earth now given to Jesus, He commands us to tell others the Good News and make them disciples for the kingdom. We are to go—whether it is next door or to another country—and make disciples. It is not an option, but a command to all who call Jesus "Lord." We are not all evangelists in the formal sense, but we have all received gifts that we can use to help fulfill the Great Commission. As we obey, we have comfort in the knowledge that Jesus is always with us. "Always" literally means "all the days" and refers to the presence of Christ with each believer every moment. This would occur through the Holy Spirit's presence in believers' lives. The Holy Spirit would be Jesus' presence that would never leave them. Jesus continues to be with us today through His Spirit. Our job is to tell the whole world about Jesus!

PRAYER

We give You thanks, O God, for Your Son, Jesus, whom You sent to die for our sins. We give praise and thanks to You for raising Him to life anew with the promise that all who believe and trust His name shall one day rise into newness of eternal life. In Jesus' name we pray. Amen.

HOME DAILY BIBLE READINGS
(April 22-28, 2019)

Call and Commissioning
MONDAY, April 22: "A Place of Renewal" (Isaiah 2:1-4)
TUESDAY, April 23: "Body Building for Baptized Believers" (1 Corinthians 12:12-13; Colossians 3:12-17)
WEDNESDAY, April 24: "Lydia and Her Household Are Baptized" (Acts 16:11-15)
THURSDAY, April 25: "Jailer and His Household Are Baptized" (Acts 16:25-34)
FRIDAY, April 26: "Reaching New People" (Acts 18:5-11)
SATURDAY, April 27: "Matthias Chosen to Replace Judas" (Acts 1:12-17, 21-26)
SUNDAY, April 28: "Disciples: Called and Commissioned" (Matthew 25:16-20; Acts 1:6-8)

Spring Quarter 2019
Unit III: The Spread of the Gospel
Children's Unit: Called to Spread the Good News

May 5, 2019   **Lesson 10**

CALLED TO RIGHTEOUSNESS

ADULT/YOUTH	CHILDREN
ADULT/YOUNG ADULT TOPIC: Putting the Past Behind Us	**GENERAL LESSON TITLE: Called to Be Faithful and Loving**
YOUTH TOPIC: Do What's Right	**CHILDREN'S TOPIC: Telling the Good News**

DEVOTIONAL READING
John 10:1-11

ADULT/YOUTH	CHILDREN
BACKGROUND SCRIPTURE: Romans 3	**BACKGROUND SCRIPTURE: Romans 3**
PRINT PASSAGE: Romans 3:21-31	**PRINT PASSAGE: Romans 3:21-31**
KEY VERSES: Romans 3:24-25a	**KEY VERSE: Romans 3:22a**

Romans 3:21-31—KJV

21 But now the righteousness of God without the law is manifested, being witnessed by the law and the prophets;

22 Even the righteousness of God which is by faith of Jesus Christ unto all and upon all them that believe: for there is no difference:

23 For all have sinned, and come short of the glory of God;

24 Being justified freely by his grace through the redemption that is in Christ Jesus:

25 Whom God hath set forth to be a propitiation through faith in his blood, to declare his righteousness for the remission of sins that are past, through the forbearance of God;

26 To declare, I say, at this time his righteousness: that he might be just, and the justifier of him which believeth in Jesus.

27 Where is boasting then? It is excluded. By what law? of works? Nay: but by the law of faith.

Romans 3:21-31—NIV

21 But now apart from the law the righteousness of God has been made known, to which the Law and the Prophets testify.

22 This righteousness is given through faith in Jesus Christ to all who believe. There is no difference between Jew and Gentile,

23 for all have sinned and fall short of the glory of God,

24 and all are justified freely by his grace through the redemption that came by Christ Jesus.

25 God presented Christ as a sacrifice of atonement, through the shedding of his blood—to be received by faith. He did this to demonstrate his righteousness, because in his forbearance he had left the sins committed beforehand unpunished—

26 he did it to demonstrate his righteousness at the present time, so as to be just and the one who justifies those who have faith in Jesus.

27 Where, then, is boasting? It is excluded. Because of what law? The law that requires works? No, because of the law that requires faith.

28 Therefore we conclude that a man is justified by faith without the deeds of the law.

29 Is he the God of the Jews only? is he not also of the Gentiles? Yes, of the Gentiles also:

30 Seeing it is one God, which shall justify the circumcision by faith, and uncircumcision through faith.

31 Do we then make void the law through faith? God forbid: yea, we establish the law.

28 For we maintain that a person is justified by faith apart from the works of the law.

29 Or is God the God of Jews only? Is he not the God of Gentiles too? Yes, of Gentiles too,

30 since there is only one God, who will justify the circumcised by faith and the uncircumcised through that same faith.

31 Do we, then, nullify the law by this faith? Not at all! Rather, we uphold the law.

UNIFYING LESSON PRINCIPLE: People sense that evil actions negatively impact their lives. Who can make amends for evil behavior? Paul told the Romans that the blood of Christ atones for all our sin.

LESSON OBJECTIVES

Upon the completion of this lesson, the students will be able to do the following:

1. Summarize Paul's teaching about justification through grace, not through acts of Law keeping.
2. Rejoice that one's past sin need not be atoned for by heroic acts or strict observance of laws.
3. Give thanks to God for Jesus, our one and only perfect Savior.

AGE-LEVEL POINTS TO BE EMPHASIZED

Teachers of ADULTS and YOUTH

—The "righteousness of God" (verse 3) may have a double meaning—referring not only to the right, moral character of God (subjective genitive), but also to the right standing before God that God grants to believers through the blood of Christ (objective genitive).

—The biblical concept of "redemption" (verse 24; cf. Ephesians 1:7; Colossians 1:14) is illustrated in the description of the Old Testament Passover (Exodus 12–15).

—Verses 21-26 help to explain an important paradox of Christianity: How does a holy God maintain justice while at the same time demonstrating love by forgiving our sins?

—It is ironic that the Law, a source of much pride for the Jews, demonstrated the need for justification by faith, which leveled the playing field between Jews and Gentiles, thus removing any room for a sense of superiority of Jews above Gentiles.

—In verse 31, Paul attempted to dispel charges of antinomianism he knew would come. He further addressed the role of the Law in Romans 6–7.

Teachers of CHILDREN

—The Law and the Prophets spoke of a time when a Redeemer would come.

—All humankind falls under the trap of sin and there is no one on earth capable of bringing redemption.

—All people have the opportunity to be saved through the gift of grace and salvation through Jesus.

—The Law cannot make anyone righteous; righteousness is by way of Jesus alone.

THE CHRONOLOGICAL SETTING OF THE LESSON

Though Romans was not Paul's first letter, it now heads the list of his letters because the church came to regard it as his most important writing and made it the introduction to the whole collection of the letters claiming Paul as their author. We are not able to read the letter as its first recipients did, for it comes to us already interpreted by its placement in the canon. Its placement in the canon is intended to convey that this epistle is one of the greatest Christian writings. Its power has been demonstrated again and again at critical points in the history of the Christian church. Augustine of Hippo was converted by reading a passage from this letter, and Martin Luther's spiritual experience was shaped by his coming to grips with what Paul says in this epistle. But it is also the case that the humble believer can find inspiration and direction in these pages.

THE GEOGRAPHICAL AND CULTURAL SETTING OF THE LESSON

Although Christianity in Rome began among the Jews, owing to ongoing conflicts within the Jewish community, Emperor Claudius expelled the Jews from Rome. In their absence, Christianity became predominantly Gentile, perhaps primarily among those who had been "God fearers" (Gentiles attracted to Judaism but not converted to it). When the Christian Jews returned (along with other Jews), they found themselves marginalized and often at odds with Gentile believers over Torah observance, particularly over diet—because Gentile Christians customarily shared meals in conjunction with the Lord's Supper.

The authorship of the Romans letter is beyond serious dispute. All competent scholars agree that the letter was dictated to or composed by a scribe in the service of the apostle Paul during his third missionary journey. In this way, it is the conclusion to his missionary work in the eastern basin of the Mediterranean and the introduction to his future plans in the West, as well as his most detailed discussion of the Gospel. Around AD 57, Paul dictated this letter while at Cenchreae (the port near Corinth, mentioned in Romans 16:1); he was at a pivotal juncture in his mission (see Romans 15:19-23), when taking the fund to Jerusalem would conclude his work in the East and free him for a wholly new venture in the westernmost part of the Empire-Spain. For this new understanding, Paul hoped to have the support of the westernmost Christians, those in Rome, most of whom were Gentiles themselves.

PROMINENT CHARACTER(S) IN THE LESSON

Gentiles: non-Jews. Israelites were instructed to maintain strict separation from them in matters of religion, marriage, and politics.

Jews: In the Bible, Jews were called Hebrews or Children of Israel. The terms *Jew* and *Judaism* come from the tribe or kingdom of Judah. "Jew" now refers to all physical and spiritual descendants of Jacob (http://www.jewfaq.org-Judaism 101).

KEY TERMS IN THE LESSON

Justified (verse 24)—Greek: *dikaioō* (dē-kī-o'-ō): to declare; pronounce one to be just, righteous.
Propitiation (verse 25)—Greek: *hilastērion* (hē-lä-stā'-rē-on): that by which God is rendered propitious (i.e., by which it becomes consistent with His character and government to pardon and bless the sinner). "The propitiation does not procure his love or make him loving; it only renders it consistent for Him to [exercise] his love towards sinners" (*Easton's*); "sacrifice of atonement" (NIV).
Redemption (verse 24)—Greek: *apolytrōsis* (ä-po-lü'-trō-sēs): a releasing effected by payment of ransom; deliverance.

TOPICAL OUTLINE OF THE LESSON

I. Introduction
A. God's Righteousness and the Power of the Gospel
B. Biblical Background

II. Exposition and Application of the Scripture
A. Jesus Christ: God's Answer to Universal Sin (Romans 3:21)
B. From Condemnation to Justification (Romans 3:22-24)
C. Christ, the Redeemer of Humanity (Romans 3:25-26)
D. Grace: God's Unmerited Favor (Romans 3:27-31)

III. Concluding Reflection

I. INTRODUCTION

A. God's Righteousness and the Power of the Gospel

Romans is generally considered the central writing of the Pauline corpus for its subject matter as well as its length, power, and clarity of argument. Unlike those letters in which Paul responded to specific problems in virtual shorthand, Romans is an epistle both ample and magisterial. Paul had neither established the church in Rome (see Acts 28:14-15) nor ever met the Roman churches (see Romans 1:10-13). Therefore, he is careful throughout the letter not to assert the same role he sought to assume with the Corinthians (see 1 Corinthians 4:15), since he was neither a founder nor a father of the Roman churches. Paul's purpose in writing is practical and has to do with the future of his mission. Paul is at a juncture in his ministry marked by the completion of his attempt at the reconciliation of Jews and Gentiles through the collection for the poor Jewish saints in Jerusalem. With the symbolism of that enterprise in his mind, he writes to the Romans, preparing the way for them to become his new base of operations in the West, as Philippi had been for his Macedonian and Achaian mission (see Philippians 4:15; 2 Corinthians 11:9).

If Paul's purpose is so practical, why did he write so long and elaborate a letter? Since he was known to this church only by name, his understanding of the Gospel and of his mission needed to be expounded in detail. Before he could ask a new community to support his mission financially, he had to let it know what it would be backing. Romans is, therefore, Paul's letter of recommendation for Paul. For Paul to recommend his ministry is to recommend the Gospel in which he "boasts" (1:16). The Gospel of which Paul boasts speaks to the plight of the human condition as no other word could do.

Paul was on fire to preach the Good News of the gracious lordship of God expressed in Jesus Christ, and nowhere more so than in Romans. Because God as creator is Lord over the whole of created reality, reflections on that lordship encompass the full range of human problems, and nowhere is that more the case than in Romans. The fate and future of the

Jewish people; the role of the individual in the total sweep of history; the responsibilities of the citizen to the government of the country with which he or she may not always agree; the morality of actions in which adults engage, sexual, and otherwise—all these and more occupy Paul in his letter to the Christians in Rome. It could not have been otherwise because a letter to Rome was a letter to the political, military, and economic capital of Paul's world.

B. Biblical Background

In Romans 1:18–3:20, we learned that we cannot look to our collective past for any kind of comfort or salvific aid. Whatever our ancestry, whether Jewish or Gentile, it has distinguished itself principally by its resolute sinfulness and rebellion against God. Our past has left us the inheritance of being unacceptable to God through our separation from Him. The root of our problem is the human propensity to put non-gods in the place of God. Such idolatry clearly means the rejection of the Creator for a deity more pliable to our wishes. Thus, we face, in short, a problem. How are the results of the rejection of God to which we are heirs, and in which as heirs we participate, to be overcome? What hope is there for creatures who have rejected and alienated their Creator? What can we do in that situation? What will God do in that situation?

Jesus Christ, who is God's solution to the broken relationship with His creatures, is also our solution. In Jesus, God proves Himself faithful to His creation and invites us to be faithful to Him. In Jesus, God shows His willingness to maintain a positive relationship with rebellious humanity and to open the way for such rebels to enter into that relationship by trusting the God who offers it. In short, Paul's answer to our dilemma is Christ Jesus, who is God's demonstration of His righteousness and our hope of receiving righteousness. God's plan to save us from our addiction to sin unfolds in stages. Salvation has a history—past, present, and future—and the coming of Jesus marks a new stage in that plan.

The fact that these verses are placed after the discussion of human rebellion and divine abandonment is of high importance for understanding what Paul is getting at in these verses. By contrasting God's righteousness in Christ with God's abandonment of humanity to sin, Paul makes clear that God's gracious lordship which we ruptured by our idolatry is now to be restored through Christ. Thus, God's desire to reestablish a positive relationship with rebellious humanity is the counter-pole to His wrath visited on human unrighteousness.

Having made it devastatingly clear that all humankind is caught up in this sinfulness, Paul turns his attention in Romans 3:21-31 to the way sinfulness is overcome. It is central to his understanding of the Christian way that no human merit can ever avail before God, but that the death of Christ on the Cross changes all of that. For Paul, the death and resurrection of Christ is God's great divine act. Through this act, God justified humankind, which is to say, God brought humans into a right relationship with Himself through the death and resurrection of Jesus Christ. Before the coming of Jesus into the world, humans had no merit at all; our sins had disqualified us in the heavenly court. Because of what Christ has done, we can now face that court with assurance. The verdict that will be rendered on all believers is "not guilty." Such a verdict is only made possible through Jesus Christ!

II. EXPOSITION AND APPLICATION OF THE SCRIPTURE

A. Jesus Christ: God's Answer to Universal Sin (Romans 3:21)

But now the righteousness of God without the law is manifested, being witnessed by the law and the prophets.

For the first two-and-a-half chapters of Romans, Paul recounted the sad story of the ruin of the human race because of sin. Now he reached a new and glorious point in his letter. Instead of continuing to review the grim story of sin and God's wrath, he turned to the wonderful news of God's great grace to sinners through the Lord, Jesus Christ.

Paul's great turn from sin to grace began with two words—"But now" (Romans 3:21). The word *now* indicates that there has been a change in time or in history. Before, something bad had existed, "but now" that has changed. The contrast between then and now is a very great one for Paul. The reason is plain: The change between a past sad state of affairs and a glorious present state is one that Paul had experienced himself. It occurred on the Damascus Road. Before that event, Paul had been an enemy of Jesus Christ and His followers. He thought he was doing right, but the future apostle was actually in great darkness, ignorant of God and opposed to Him. It was on the road to Damascus that Jesus appeared to Paul, revealing Himself as the Son of God. From that day forward, Paul would come to see Jesus Christ as the lone hope of sinful humanity.

Paul spoke of this great historical change made possible through the coming of Jesus into the world, not so much as something that affected Him personally, but as something that God had done to provide for the whole of humanity. If God had not sent Jesus into the world, our present condition and future prospects would be bleak. They would be only what we have already found in Romans 1:18 through 3:20. We would be under wrath, in spiritual and moral decline, and without any possibility of helping or saving ourselves by human righteousness. "But now" things are different. There is hope because of what the Lord Jesus Christ has accomplished. The incarnation, life, death, and resurrection of Jesus have changed everything.

What changes is specifically behind Paul's "but now." The first change is the most obvious from our text. When Paul said, "But now a righteousness from God, apart from law, has been made known," it is clear that he was contrasting this with his earlier declaration about the wrath of God being revealed from heaven against all the godlessness and wickedness of humankind (see Romans 1:18). Before, the wrath of God was being revealed against us, "but now" the righteousness of God is being made known to us. If we do not understand that apart from Jesus Christ we are under God's wrath and destined for an eternity of judgment, we can hardly appreciate what God has done for us in providing salvation through Christ's atonement.

B. From Condemnation to Justification (Romans 3:22-24)

Even the righteousness of God which is by faith of Jesus Christ unto all and upon all them that believe: for there is no difference: For all have sinned, and come short of the glory of God; Being justified freely by his grace through the redemption that is in Christ Jesus.

The second change of the "but now" is from condemnation to justification. This is evident from the continuation of Romans 3, where Paul wrote, "There is no difference, for all have sinned and fall short of the glory of God, and all are justified freely by his grace (Romans 3:22b-24, NIV). Most people do not think of themselves as being under condemnation, obviously because the sentence hanging over them has not been fully executed. They are alive and well. Nevertheless, without Jesus Christ they are still under condemnation and will perish eventually. Jesus said God did not send Him into the world to condemn the world, but to save the world through Him (John 3:17-19). "But now" because of Christ's work, there can be justification rather than condemnation. There is justification "through the redemption that came by Christ Jesus" (Romans 3:24, NIV), but humans must be open to receiving it.

C. Christ, the Redeemer of Humanity (Romans 3:25-26)

Whom God hath set forth to be a propitiation through faith in his blood, to declare his righteousness for the remission of sins that are past, through the forbearance of God; To declare, I say, at this time his righteousness: that he might be just, and the justifier of him which believeth in Jesus.

The key term in Paul's explanation of how Christ came to redeem those who believe among humanity is rendered "propitiation" or "sacrifice of atonement" in the NRSV. When Adam sinned, he reaped the consequence of sin, which is death (see Romans 6:23). He instantly died spiritually, and his body began its decaying march toward the grave. In addition, the same is true for us: the penalty of our sin has become our overwhelming debt in the court of heaven. We stand before a Judge

whose wrath against sin must be satisfied. Paul declared the crucifixion of Jesus to be a public sprinkling of blood that satisfied the wrath of God, which demanded justice for humanity's sin. Given the nature of our sin, our only hope was to be declared righteous by the gracious gift of God. We received this gift through faith in Jesus Christ, who took God's punishment on our behalf, thus satisfying the heavenly court's requirement that justice be served.

The wrath of God calls for the just penalty of sin to be paid, and His wrath has been satisfied by the atoning death of His Son. Therefore, God is "just" because sin does not go unpunished, and He is the justifier because the death of His Son clears the way for Him to declare believers righteous without contradicting His own nature.

D. Grace: God's Unmerited Favor (Romans 3:27-31)

Where is boasting then? It is excluded. By what law? of works? Nay: but by the law of faith. Therefore we conclude that a man is justified by faith without the deeds of the law. Is he the God of the Jews only? is he not also of the Gentiles? Yes, of the Gentiles also: Seeing it is one God, which shall justify the circumcision by faith, and uncircumcision through faith. Do we then make void the law through faith? God forbid: yea, we establish the law.

Throughout this section, Paul has insisted that salvation comes only through Christ's death. He has said that we appropriate salvation only through faith, and he comes back to that thought now. He shows that there is no room for human boasting or the like, and that a right understanding of faith is necessary if we are to uphold the Law (verse 27). Boasting is the attitude of the worldly human being who seeks to establish his or her position independent of

God, and the only alternative to it (outside of faith) is despair. Boasting and faith are mutually exclusive. As long as human beings boast in their own deeds, it is impossible for them to trust in God's act of redemption. Humans are justified—that is, rightly related to God—only when they cease to boast and begin to believe.

The Old Testament specifically states that boasting before God was intolerable. But it also said that a special relationship existed between God and Israel. But if indeed God is one, as the Old Testament itself declares, then Paul argues that God is also the God of the Gentiles (verse 30). Thus, Jew and Gentile are equal before God, and neither is in a position to boast. Paul's argument is that for Jew and Gentile alike there is but one way to justification (a right relationship before God), and that is the way of faith alone.

III. CONCLUDING REFLECTION

The Good News in today's lesson begins with a clear understanding of the truth of our sin-sick condition: it is terminal. Fortunately, it is also curable. However, the deadly disease of sin cannot be treated with good nutrition and vigorous exercise—as good as those are. We need radical surgery. We are spiritually dead, and we need nothing less than a transplant. Paul's words in Romans 3:21-31 mark a crucial transition in his presentation of the Gospel. Having delivered the awful truth of our soul-decaying depravity, our willful rebellion against God, our pitiful attempts at self-improvement, our skewed moral compass, and our pathetic pride, the apostle turns us toward a hopeful truth: in Jesus Christ we have been justified—that is, brought into a right relationship with God our Father. Our right standing with God becomes a reality only when we accept God's gracious gift made possible through faith in Jesus Christ.

PRAYER

Most gracious God, our Father, we praise Your name for sending Jesus Christ into the world to save us from our sin. Help us ever to be mindful of this gracious act on Your part that puts us in a right relationship with You because of what Jesus Christ has done for us and for our salvation. In Jesus' name we pray. Amen.

HOME DAILY BIBLE READINGS
(April 29–May 5, 2019)

Called to Righteousness
MONDAY, April 29: "A God-given Task for Workers" (Ecclesiastes 3:9-17)
TUESDAY, April 30: "The Shepherd Lays Down His Life" (John 10:11-18)
WEDNESDAY, May 1: "The Value of the Law" (Romans 7:7-12)
THURSDAY, May 2: "The Purpose of the Law" (Galatians 3:19-29)
FRIDAY, May 3: "God Is Faithful and Fair" (Romans 3:1-8)
SATURDAY, May 4: "Jesus Brings True Justice" (Romans 3:9-20)
SUNDAY, May 5: "All Called to Righteousness" (Romans 3:21-31)

Spring Quarter 2019
Unit III: The Spread of the Gospel
Children's Unit: Called to Spread the Good News

May 12, 2019   Lesson 11

CALLED TO LIFE IN THE SPIRIT

ADULT/YOUTH
ADULT/YOUNG ADULT TOPIC: **Life without Guilt**
YOUTH TOPIC: **Walking Right**

CHILDREN
GENERAL LESSON TITLE: **Called to Live in the Spirit**
CHILDREN'S TOPIC: **Doing Things a New Way**

DEVOTIONAL READING
Romans 6:1-14

ADULT/YOUTH
BACKGROUND SCRIPTURE: **Romans 8**
PRINT PASSAGE: **Romans 8:1-14**
KEY VERSE: **Romans 8:1**

CHILDREN
BACKGROUND SCRIPTURE: **Romans 8**
PRINT PASSAGE: **Romans 8:1-14**
KEY VERSE: **Romans 8:14**

Romans 8:1-14—KJV

THERE IS therefore now no condemnation to them which are in Christ Jesus, who walk not after the flesh, but after the Spirit.

2 For the law of the Spirit of life in Christ Jesus hath made me free from the law of sin and death.

3 For what the law could not do, in that it was weak through the flesh, God sending his own Son in the likeness of sinful flesh, and for sin, condemned sin in the flesh:

4 That the righteousness of the law might be fulfilled in us, who walk not after the flesh, but after the Spirit.

5 For they that are after the flesh do mind the things of the flesh; but they that are after the Spirit the things of the Spirit.

6 For to be carnally minded is death; but to be spiritually minded is life and peace.

Romans 8:1-14—NIV

THEREFORE, THERE is now no condemnation for those who are in Christ Jesus,

2 because through Christ Jesus the law of the Spirit who gives life has set you free from the law of sin and death.

3 For what the law was powerless to do because it was weakened by the flesh, God did by sending his own Son in the likeness of sinful flesh to be a sin offering. And so he condemned sin in the flesh,

4 in order that the righteous requirement of the law might be fully met in us, who do not live according to the flesh but according to the Spirit.

5 Those who live according to the flesh have their minds set on what the flesh desires; but those who live in accordance with the Spirit have their minds set on what the Spirit desires.

6 The mind governed by the flesh is death, but the mind governed by the Spirit is life and peace.

7 The mind governed by the flesh is hostile to God; it

7 Because the carnal mind is enmity against God: for it is not subject to the law of God, neither indeed can be. 8 So then they that are in the flesh cannot please God. 9 But ye are not in the flesh, but in the Spirit, if so be that the Spirit of God dwell in you. Now if any man have not the Spirit of Christ, he is none of his. 10 And if Christ be in you, the body is dead because of sin; but the Spirit is life because of righteousness. 11 But if the Spirit of him that raised up Jesus from the dead dwell in you, he that raised up Christ from the dead shall also quicken your mortal bodies by his Spirit that dwelleth in you. 12 Therefore, brethren, we are debtors, not to the flesh, to live after the flesh. 13 For if ye live after the flesh, ye shall die: but if ye through the Spirit do mortify the deeds of the body, ye shall live. 14 For as many as are led by the Spirit of God, they are the sons of God.

does not submit to God's law, nor can it do so. 8 Those who are in the realm of the flesh cannot please God. 9 You, however, are not in the realm of the flesh but are in the realm of the Spirit, if indeed the Spirit of God lives in you. And if anyone does not have the Spirit of Christ, they do not belong to Christ. 10 But if Christ is in you, then even though your body is subject to death because of sin, the Spirit gives life because of righteousness. 11 And if the Spirit of him who raised Jesus from the dead is living in you, he who raised Christ from the dead will also give life to your mortal bodies because of his Spirit who lives in you. 12 Therefore, brothers and sisters, we have an obligation—but it is not to the flesh, to live according to it. 13 For if you live according to the flesh, you will die; but if by the Spirit you put to death the misdeeds of the body, you will live. 14 For those who are led by the Spirit of God are the children of God.

UNIFYING LESSON PRINCIPLE: Consequences of past actions, the reality of impending death, and a sense that we cannot undo past mistakes weigh heavily on the human spirit. Where does one find relief from these pressures? Paul assures us that those who are in Christ Jesus have life in the Spirit and are free from condemnation.

LESSON OBJECTIVES

Upon the completion of this lesson, the students will be able to do the following:
1. Contrast what Paul says about the flesh with what he says about the spirit/Spirit.
2. Sense the futility experienced by those who seek to have life but can draw only on the flesh to find it.
3. Tell what it means to "set the mind on the Spirit" and commit to have their minds thus set.

AGE-LEVEL POINTS TO BE EMPHASIZED
Teachers of ADULTS and YOUTH
—The "therefore" in verse 1 points back immediately to the victory described at the end of chapter 7, and also to Paul's whole argument

about salvation in Christ up to this point as he launches into a summary and conclusion to his argument.

—*Law* in verse 2 means "principle" and is not a reference to a specific written law as opposed to the Mosaic Law referred to in verses 3 and 4.

—Some believe that the fulfillment of the "just requirement of the law" is accomplished through the changed lives of believers saved by Christ. But it is more likely that this refers to the entire penalty of the Law (i.e., death; see Romans 6:23) being fulfilled through Christ's death on the Cross.

—Paul's mention of our relationship to the Holy Spirit ten times in verses 4-11 makes clear the importance of the Spirit's role in defeating ongoing sin in our lives.

—Living "according to the flesh" (verse 5) means living to satisfy our sinful, selfish desires. In Galatians 5:16-26, Paul describes in greater detail the struggle within believers between the "flesh" and the "Spirit."

—Verse 13 makes clear that as believers, we too must take an active role in the defeat of sin in our lives. God defeated sin through the work of Christ on the Cross while we battle our lingering sinful habits by the power of the Spirit.

Teachers of CHILDREN

—Believers are not condemned or punished because of salvation through Jesus Christ.

—The Law had no power to do what Jesus did.

—The Mosaic Law could not bring freedom from sin.

—The deliverance from sin came through Jesus' coming to earth as a human being. He was fully human and fully God.

—How does a person live when controlled by the sinful nature versus one controlled by the Spirit?

—Those who belong to Christ are not ruled by the sinful nature.

THE CHRONOLOGICAL SETTING OF THE LESSON

Of the letters of Paul which are generally recognized for their preeminence, the most important are undoubtedly Romans, 1 and 2 Corinthians, and Galatians; and of these four, the letter to the Romans can lay claim to a certain primacy. Not only is it the longest letter of Paul which has survived, but it is also the weightiest. All of Paul's letters were called forth by the needs of the churches he addresses and have the ad hoc character which true letters always have, and Romans is no exception in this regard; but this letter shows signs of having been composed with greater care than any of the rest. Thus, it comes nearer to being a systematic and inclusive statement of Paul's faith than any other of his known writings.

THE GEOGRAPHICAL AND CULTURAL SETTING OF THE LESSON

It has sometimes been argued that Paul's motive for making the letter to the Romans the occasion for a very in-depth description of his theological beliefs is his rather desperate need for their help in his mission to Spain. Paul was primarily interested in the Roman churches' giving large financial support to the Spanish mission. Rome must be the base of operations in the territories farther west, just as Antioch had been in the eastern and earlier phase of his work. Paul must therefore persuade the Roman church of the importance of his mission, and so he wrote with this purpose primarily in mind. For this reason, he emphasized the universal need of salvation in Christ and the universal ability, as well as the perfection of that salvation. He was not ashamed of the Gospel, and he wanted the Romans to share in his enthusiasm for it and his pride in it, so that they would support his effort to take it to the "barbarians" in the western part of the Empire.

PROMINENT CHARACTER(S) IN THE LESSON

Christ Jesus: Jesus is the spotless, sinless Son of God. He came to earth to "rescue" us from sin.
Holy Spirit: the mysterious power of God, conceived in the first place as the mode of God's activity, manifested especially in supernatural revelation to selected individuals—later identified with the personal presence of God and regarded as the distinctive endowment of His people.

KEY TERMS IN THE LESSON

Condemnation (verse 1)—Greek: *katakrima* (kä-tä'-krē-mä): to condemn, find guilty.
Flesh (verse 3)—Greek: *sarx* (sarks): used of natural or physical origin.

Holy Spirit (verse 2)—Greek: *pneuma* (pnyü'-mä): the third person of the triune God, the Holy Spirit—coequal, coeternal with the Father and the Son; "Spirit" (KJV/NIV).

TOPICAL OUTLINE OF THE LESSON

I. Introduction
   A. Life without Guilt and Shame
   B. Biblical Background

II. Exposition and Application of the Scripture
   A. Life in the Spirit (Romans 8:1-2)
   B. God's Action on Our Behalf (Romans 8:3-4)
   C. Flesh versus Spirit (Romans 8:5-11)
   D. Responsibilities and Privileges of Life in the Spirit (Romans 8:12-14)

III. Concluding Reflection

I. INTRODUCTION
A. Life without Guilt and Shame

Leonard Sweet, in *The Three Hardest Words in the World to Get Right*, tells the story of a physician who had been present at the bedside of dying patients too numerous to count. The physician reported that when people know that the end of their lives is near, there are eleven words they most wanted to hear:
- "I'll miss you."
- "Thank you."
- "I forgive you."
- "I love you."

If given a choice between these statements, they would choose to hear "I love you." And yet, according to Sweet, oftentimes those are the three most difficult words for people to say until death comes knocking on their door. Many people go through life feeling guilty over past words and deeds, and often feeling unloved because of it. Near death, the words they most want to hear are words that assure them that they are loved and forgiven.

Romans 8 is one of the most widely read chapters of the Bible, and its teachings about the way the Holy Spirit operates in enabling the believer to defeat the forces of evil has always been recognized as of the utmost importance. Paul was saying that on account of the actions of God, our guilt and shame have been removed and that a new and wonderful life opens before those who put their trust in Christ. This new life is completely dependent on the work of the Spirit of God. Paul's teachings are instructive for us today, for he reminds us that because of what God has done for us in Jesus Christ, we do not have to carry around burdens of guilt and feelings of lovelessness and hopelessness throughout our lives. We are a forgiven, redeemed, and restored people as a result of God's amazing grace.

B. Biblical Background

Romans 8 is without a doubt one of the best-known, best-loved chapters of the Bible. If in Romans 7 Paul has been preoccupied with the place of the Law, in Romans 8 his preoccupation is with the work of the Spirit. In chapter 7, the Law and its synonyms were mentioned thirty-one times, but the Holy Spirit only once—whereas in the first twenty-seven verses of chapter 8 the Spirit is referred to by name nineteen times. The essential contrast which Paul painted is between the weakness of the Law and the power of the Spirit—for over against indwelling sin, which is the reason the Law is unable to help us in our moral struggle, Paul now sets the indwelling Spirit, who is both our liberator now from "the law of sin and death" (Romans 8:2) and the guarantee of the Resurrection and eternal glory in the end (see Romans 8:11). Thus, the Christian life is essentially life in the Spirit—that is to say, a life which is animated, sustained, directed, and enriched by the Holy Spirit. Without the Holy Spirit, true Christian discipleship would be inconceivable, indeed impossible.

Paul's argument in Romans 8:1-14 was direct and to the point: deliverance from the struggle with sin and the guilty verdict of the Law comes to those who are in Christ Jesus. Jesus has both condemned sin and fulfilled the Law; those who remain in Him through faith are free. This freedom is not only a "freedom from," but it is also a freedom to operate in a new dimension, which Paul described as living according to the Spirit. Justification releases one from the condemnation of the past, while sanctification—a life controlled by God's Spirit—releases one from the power of unrighteousness. However, Paul counterbalances the work that God has done in Christ with the responsibility of believers to utilize that gift and have their minds set on what the Spirit desires. The divine initiative has provided the Spirit to control and energize the life of the believer.

II. EXPOSITION AND APPLICATION OF THE SCRIPTURE

A. Life in the Spirit
(Romans 8:1-2)

THERE IS therefore now no condemnation to them which are in Christ Jesus, who walk not after the flesh, but after the Spirit. For the law of the Spirit of life in Christ Jesus hath made me free from the law of sin and death.

The opening verses of chapter 8 mark a breakthrough into an atmosphere of freedom and life. Paul emerged from his grim account of humanity's helpless situation under the Law to outline the new possibility opened by the Spirit. His portrayal of the new possibility, however, explicitly responded to that former situation, since the contrast between what is possible when human beings "go it alone" and what is possible when they surrender to God remains central to his argument. The crucial difference in our new situation is indicated at the end of the first sentence: "in Christ Jesus" (verse 1). To be "in Christ" means to have been radically cut off through faith and baptism from the old, sin-dominated existence "in Adam," and to be living now in a sphere or context of salvation constituted by the power of the risen Lord.

This power of the risen Lord is, for Paul, the Spirit of God. Thus, "those in Christ" are those who live in the atmosphere of the Spirit and whose lives are thereby able to be shaped by its liberating power. With the power of the Spirit energizing their lives in this way, human beings are no longer on their own, locked into an unequal struggle with the power of sin (see Romans 7:7-25), the outcome of which must be "condemnation" (verse 1). On the contrary, the Spirit now brings them under the scope of God's power, where a right moral life becomes a possibility and the threat of condemnation is lifted. Thus, there is now no condemnation of those in Christ Jesus. When we walk in the Spirit, we walk in the grace of God, and our lives are no longer determined by sin, guilt, and shame. "For the law of the Spirit of life in Christ Jesus hath made me free from the law of sin and death" (Romans 8:2).

B. God's Action on Our Behalf (Romans 8:3-4)

For what the law could not do, in that it was weak through the flesh, God sending his own Son in the likeness of sinful flesh, and for sin, condemned sin in the flesh: That the righteousness of the law might be fulfilled in us, who walk not after the flesh, but after the Spirit.

The Law of God as given to Moses could not deliver us from sin and death, in contrast to the law of the Spirit. It was too weak because it depended upon weak human flesh for fulfillment. It demanded what the sinful human nature could not provide. To remedy this deficiency, God sent His own Son to provide an offering of atonement for sin (verse 3). Christ did not come in sinful flesh, but in the "likeness" of sinful flesh. Jesus Christ was fully human in all respects, but He did not have a sinful nature and did not commit sin.

Verse 4 presents the purpose for redemption: to fulfill the righteousness of the law "in us." The purpose of *justification* is *sanctification*. Jesus Christ came to do what the Law could not do—to give us power over sin, to enable us to meet the righteous requirements of the Law. God does not save us so that we can continue to sin and be excused. God saves us so that we can fulfill His original plan for humanity. He wants a holy people—people who can fellowship and commune with Him.

How can we fulfill the Law's requirements? We can only do so by walking after the Spirit and not after the flesh (sinful nature). We must live in daily dependence upon God's indwelling Spirit, looking to Him for guidance and power. We cannot rely upon the flesh. Instead of our trying by human effort to live up to the demands of an external law, the indwelling Spirit imparts to us internally the desire and power to live according to God's holy will. God does not give us inherent power over sin so that we can overcome sin on our own. Rather, God Himself becomes the power dwelling in us that overcomes sin.

C. Flesh versus Spirit
(Romans 8:5-11)

For they that are after the flesh do mind the things of the flesh; but they that are after the Spirit the things of the Spirit. For to be carnally minded is death; but to be spiritually minded is life and peace. Because the carnal mind is enmity against God: for it is not subject to the law of God, neither indeed can be. So then they that are in the flesh cannot please God. But ye are not in the flesh, but in the Spirit, if so be that the Spirit of God dwell in you. Now if any man have not the Spirit of Christ, he is none of his. And if Christ be in you, the body is dead because of sin; but the Spirit is life because of righteousness. But if the Spirit of him that raised up Jesus from the dead dwell in you, he that raised up Christ from the dead shall also quicken your mortal bodies by his Spirit that dwelleth in you.

According to the apostle Paul, there are two principles of living, two mindsets, two roads to follow: we can walk after the flesh or after the Spirit (verse 5). The first option is to live according to the flesh (sinful nature). This means obeying the flesh and letting it take control. Those who make this choice put their priorities on the flesh. They cater primarily to the needs and desires of the physical person, and they seek to gratify sinful lusts. They adopt the value system of the world and vie for worldly success, fame, wealth, material possessions, and power to the detriment of spiritual growth.

The second option is to live according to the Spirit. This means following the leading of the Spirit and letting the Spirit take control. Those who make this choice put their priorities on the will of God. They are sensitive to the Spirit. They seek first the kingdom of God and His righteousness. They are faithful in prayer, Bible study, church attendance, and support of and participation in the work of God. How can we tell which option we are choosing? We must evaluate our priorities, use of time, use of money, thoughts, attitudes, dress, actions, and amusements. In all things, we must judge our lives by the Word of God.

The word *carnal* means "fleshly"; "to be carnally minded" means to have the mind of the flesh. If we choose the first option—carnality—the result will be enmity against God and death. The carnal mind is totally contrary to God. It does not obey God's Law (verses 6-7). Verse 9 contrasts those who are "in" the flesh with those who are "in" the Spirit. Not only is this a contrast between the unregenerate and the regenerate but, as the context of the whole chapter indicates, it is a contrast between those who are controlled by the flesh and those who are controlled by the Spirit, whether they have been born again or not. If the Spirit dwells in us, we are in the Spirit and not in the flesh. The indwelling of the Spirit means more than talking in tongues, shouting, or exercising charismatic spiritual gifts; it means letting the Spirit control all aspects of our lives. The more we focus on our lives in the Spirit, the less inclined we are to pursue those things that bring hurt and pain to ourselves as well as to others. But even when we fall short, God has provided a way for us to be redeemed and restored in Christ Jesus.

D. Responsibilities and Privileges of Life in the Spirit
(Romans 8:12-14)

Therefore, brethren, we are debtors, not to the flesh, to live after the flesh. For if ye live after the flesh, ye shall die: but if ye through the Spirit do mortify the deeds of the body, ye shall live. For as many as are led by the Spirit of God, they are the sons of God.

We are debtors to the Spirit (verse 12). In view of what God has done and will do for us, we owe it to Him to live according to the Spirit and to kill the deeds of the flesh. The word translated "mortify" in the KJV means "to kill or put to death." It means that we must continually put to death the practices of the sinful nature. We can only do this by the power of the Holy Spirit. Only those who are being led by the Spirit of God are the sons and daughters of God. Salvation is not solely on a one-time past experience, but lifelong submission to the Spirit.

III. CONCLUDING REFLECTION

Paul reminds us in today's lesson that we must not take our new life in the Spirit for granted. The Christian life involves an ongoing conflict in which there are two sides. Christians are on the winning side, but we have a responsibility to fight even though we have died to sin and live to God. We fight by always being conscious of this battle between good and evil and by dismissing sinful thoughts, words, and deeds when they come our way. Paul had given similar teaching in Romans 6:11-14, but here in chapter 8 he added the important phrase "in the Spirit." Christians do not fight alone. The battle is theirs, but it is also God's. It is important to understand this teaching; it means that we need not despair because victory is certain. Our daily walk in the Spirit enables us eventually to overcome all those things that brought feelings of shame and guilt in days gone by. Through Jesus Christ, God has empowered us to walk in the Spirit.

By careful reasoning, scriptural quotations, appropriate illustrations, and finally a personal testimony, Paul has declared that a right standing with God comes not through any human endeavor to do good and thus measure up to God's holy standard, but rather through faith in His gracious gift. Paul has pointed out the immediate benefits of God's reconciling act for the believer: peace, joy, and a transformed identity.

PRAYER

Eternal God, we give You thanks for the victorious living that we lay claim to today because of what You have done for us in Christ Jesus. Teach us how to walk in the Spirit each and every day of our lives in order that we may grow closer to You and closer to being the redeemed people You have called us to be. In Jesus' name we pray. Amen.

HOME DAILY BIBLE READINGS
(May 6-12, 2019)

Called to Life in the Spirit
MONDAY, May 6: "Believers in Jesus Have Eternal Life" (John 5:19-24)
TUESDAY, May 7: "Spirit of Christ in Our Hearts" (Galatians 4:1-7)
WEDNESDAY, May 8: "The Resurrection of the Dead" (1 Corinthians 15:12-28)
THURSDAY, May 9: "Seeing Others through Christ" (2 Corinthians 5:16-21)
FRIDAY, May 10: "An Eager Longing" (Romans 8:18-25)
SATURDAY, May 11: "Sustained and Led by the Spirit" (Romans 8:26-30)
SUNDAY, May 12: "No Condemnation in Christ Jesus" (Romans 8:1-14)

Spring Quarter 2019
Unit III: The Spread of the Gospel
Children's Unit: Called to Spread the Good News

May 19, 2019   Lesson 12

THE CALL OF THE GENTILES

ADULT/YOUTH	CHILDREN
ADULT/YOUNG ADULT TOPIC: **Surrendering Pride**	GENERAL LESSON TITLE: **God Calls the Gentiles**
YOUTH TOPIC: **Called to Be Included**	CHILDREN'S TOPIC: **Everyone Is Welcome**

DEVOTIONAL READING
Romans 10:5-13

ADULT/YOUTH	CHILDREN
BACKGROUND SCRIPTURE: **Romans 11**	BACKGROUND SCRIPTURE: **Romans 11**
PRINT PASSAGE: **Romans 11:11-24**	PRINT PASSAGE: **Romans 11:11-24**
KEY VERSE: **Romans 11:18**	KEY VERSE: **Romans 11:22**

Romans 11:11-24—KJV

11 I say then, Have they stumbled that they should fall? God forbid: but rather through their fall salvation is come unto the Gentiles, for to provoke them to jealousy.

12 Now if the fall of them be the riches of the world, and the diminishing of them the riches of the Gentiles; how much more their fulness?

13 For I speak to you Gentiles, inasmuch as I am the apostle of the Gentiles, I magnify mine office:

14 If by any means I may provoke to emulation them which are my flesh, and might save some of them.

15 For if the casting away of them be the reconciling of the world, what shall the receiving of them be, but life from the dead?

16 For if the firstfruit be holy, the lump is also holy: and if the root be holy, so are the branches.

17 And if some of the branches be broken off, and thou, being a wild olive tree, wert grafted in among

Romans 11:11-24—NIV

11 Again I ask: Did they stumble so as to fall beyond recovery? Not at all! Rather, because of their transgression, salvation has come to the Gentiles to make Israel envious.

12 But if their transgression means riches for the world, and their loss means riches for the Gentiles, how much greater riches will their full inclusion bring!

13 I am talking to you Gentiles. Inasmuch as I am the apostle to the Gentiles, I take pride in my ministry

14 in the hope that I may somehow arouse my own people to envy and save some of them.

15 For if their rejection brought reconciliation to the world, what will their acceptance be but life from the dead?

16 If the part of the dough offered as firstfruits is holy, then the whole batch is holy; if the root is holy, so are the branches.

17 If some of the branches have been broken off, and you, though a wild olive shoot, have been grafted in among the others and now share in the nourishing sap from the olive root,

them, and with them partakest of the root and fatness of the olive tree;

18 Boast not against the branches. But if thou boast, thou bearest not the root, but the root thee.

19 Thou wilt say then, The branches were broken off, that I might be grafted in.

20 Well; because of unbelief they were broken off, and thou standest by faith. Be not highminded, but fear:

21 For if God spared not the natural branches, take heed lest he also spare not thee.

22 Behold therefore the goodness and severity of God: on them which fell, severity; but toward thee, goodness, if thou continue in his goodness: otherwise thou also shalt be cut off.

23 And they also, if they abide not still in unbelief, shall be grafted in: for God is able to graft them in again.

24 For if thou wert cut out of the olive tree which is wild by nature, and wert grafted contrary to nature into a good olive tree: how much more shall these, which be the natural branches, be grafted into their own olive tree?

18 do not consider yourself to be superior to those other branches. If you do, consider this: You do not support the root, but the root supports you.

19 You will say then, "Branches were broken off so that I could be grafted in."

20 Granted. But they were broken off because of unbelief, and you stand by faith. Do not be arrogant, but tremble.

21 For if God did not spare the natural branches, he will not spare you either.

22 Consider therefore the kindness and sternness of God: sternness to those who fell, but kindness to you, provided that you continue in his kindness. Otherwise, you also will be cut off.

23 And if they do not persist in unbelief, they will be grafted in, for God is able to graft them in again.

24 After all, if you were cut out of an olive tree that is wild by nature, and contrary to nature were grafted into a cultivated olive tree, how much more readily will these, the natural branches, be grafted into their own olive tree!

UNIFYING LESSON PRINCIPLE: Privileged people often feel superior to others. What is the corrective to such feelings of superiority? Paul warned the Gentile believers that their acceptance into grace must not make them feel superior to their Jewish brothers and sisters.

LESSON OBJECTIVES

Upon the completion of this lesson, the students will be able to do the following:

1. Explain Paul's metaphor of the olive tree with wild branches grafted in.
2. Recognize with humility the price that was paid in order for one to stand justified before God.
3. Repent of any arrogance they may have expressed against those who do not know Christ, as if their own standing were a matter of anything but the grace of God.

AGE-LEVEL POINTS TO BE EMPHASIZED

Teachers of ADULTS and YOUTH

—"Life from the dead" in verse 15 has drawn interpretations that are literal (to refer to the general resurrection) and metaphorical (to refer to a spiritual reawakening of Israel).

—Drawing from the language in Romans 9:32-33, Paul describes the Israelites' temporary fall as "stumbling" in verse 11.

—In verse 17, the metaphorical "broken branches,"

"olive tree," and "root" refer to Israel, and the wild "olive shoot" to the Gentiles. The broken branches represent the Israelites' unbelief in contrast to the shoot (Gentiles) that represents those who believe in Christ and are "grafted in" (supernaturally connected) to the covenantal family of God.

—Paul warns against boasting and pride in verse 18. He reminds the Gentiles that they are participants and recipients of God's blessings.

—In response to the statement in verse 19, verses 20-24 explain the engrafting process for both the Gentiles and the Israelites based on their faith and grace.

—Paul uses the metaphor of a tree's roots and branches to explain the relationship between Israel and Christ, and the inclusion of Gentiles in the covenantal family of God.

Teachers of CHILDREN

—A remnant of Jews believed Paul's words about Jesus, while many of the Jewish people did not accept Jesus.

—Paul explained that despite the Jewish people's unbelief and rejection of the Gospel, God did not reject them.

—Paul explains that in fact the Jewish people's rejection of the Gospel caused the furtherance of the Gospel; it was opened to the Gentiles.

THE CHRONOLOGICAL SETTING OF THE LESSON

In Romans 9–10, Paul taught that God is in control of all things, and that human beings are responsible to Him—those are two important truths we must not forget if we are to understand anything of how God works among us. However, Paul had not yet given a satisfactory answer to his chief problem: "What about all of God's promises to Israel—are they going to be fulfilled or not?" Paul faced this problem in today's lesson and gave a clear, reasoned solution to it.

THE GEOGRAPHICAL AND CULTURAL SETTING OF THE LESSON

We are entering a new section in Paul's overall argument in these verses. In Romans 11, Paul made four points that governed his thoughts throughout the remainder of the chapter. First, Israel had stumbled, but their stumble was not final. The unbelief of Israel would not be forever. Second, their stumble had a purpose: it would be used by God to bring salvation to the Gentiles. Third, the salvation of the Gentiles will lead in time to the

"fullness" of Israel. Fourth, the way this will happen is by the spiritual riches of the Gentiles making Israel jealous. The Jews will see what the Gentiles have, recognize that these spiritual blessings were intended for them, and long to possess them too. In the grand redemptive purposes of God, no one has a right to boast, for all of this is made possible through the salvific work of Jesus Christ.

PROMINENT CHARACTER(S) IN THE LESSON

Gentiles: (Comes from the Hebrew word *goyim* [usually in plural].) The word generally refers to all nations except the Jews. Over a period of time, as the Jews began more and more to pride themselves on their peculiar privileges, the word acquired unpleasant associations and was used as a term of contempt (*Easton Bible Dictionary*).

Israel: Israel is a group of people descended from Jacob's twelve sons. Jacob's name was changed to *Israel* by God.

KEY TERMS IN THE LESSON

Firstfruits (verse 16)—Greek: *aparchē* (ä-pär-khä'): to take away the first fruits of the productions of the earth which was offered to God; the first portion of

the dough, from which sacred loaves were to be prepared. Hence, the term used of persons consecrated
to God for all time.

Grafted (verse 17)—Greek: *egkentrizo* **(eng-ken-
trid'-zo):** engrafted by making a puncture to graft
a living shoot into another living plant (tree); refers
to God combining His two redeemed ethnic groups
(OT, NT believers) into one people.

Olive shoot (verse 17)—Greek: *agrielaios* **(ä-grē-
e'-lī-os):** of or belonging to the oleaster or wild olive;
"olive tree" (KJV).

Stumble(d) (verse 11)—Greek: *ptaiō* **(ptī'-ō):** to
err, make a mistake; to sin.

Transgression (verse 11)—Greek: *paraptōma* **(pä-
rä'p-tō-mä):** false step; go astray; err; "fall" (KJV).

TOPICAL OUTLINE
OF THE LESSON

I. Introduction
   A. The Continuing Role of Israel in God's
      Plan
   B. Biblical Background

II. Exposition and Application
of the Scripture
   A. Israel's Fall and the Riches of God's Grace
      (Romans 11:11-14)

   B. The Imminent Restoration of Israel
      (Romans 11:15)

   C. The Temporary Rejection of the Jews
      (Romans 11:16-17)

   D. No Room for Gentiles to Boast
      (Romans 11:18-22)

   E. The Danger of Taking God for Granted
      (Romans 11:23-24)

III. Concluding Reflection

I. INTRODUCTION
A. The Continuing Role of Israel in God's Plan

The exclusion of the great majority of Jews from the redemptive purposes of God manifested in the work and person of Jesus Christ is not permanent. Rather, it is the occasion
for the coming in of the Gentiles which, in its turn, is to have the effect of awakening the
unbelieving Jews to a realization of what they are missing and so to lead to their repentance.
Paul hoped that the very success of his mission to the Gentiles may contribute in this way
to the saving of some of his Jewish compatriots. In the meantime, the existence of those
Jews who already believe in Christ serves to sanctify the unbelieving majority.

We who are Gentiles are fortunate to have any part in the covenant promise made to
Abraham and his heirs. The fact that God used the rejection of the Jews to graft into His
plan believing Gentiles is cause for humility.

B. Biblical Background

In the eleventh chapter of Romans, Paul continued to express his concern about the
present state of Israel. He showed that the principle of the "remnant" was not new but has

been part of God's purpose and Israel's history throughout the ages (verses 1-6), as demonstrated by the Scriptures (verses 7-10). Paul explained that the rejection of Israel was not final, but temporary and partial (verses 11-12), and he made reference to the first-fruits offering (verse 16) and the grafting of olive branches (verses 17-21) to illustrate his argument.

These two images are significant, as they are both images from Exodus material. Instructions for the first-fruit offering of bread were given at Sinai in Leviticus 23:17, when the children of Israel were at the beginning of their journey to the Promised Land. Reference to the olive tree was made in Jeremiah 11:16-17 and in Hosea 14:4-6, where a promise of blessing was given for those who would be brought out of the predicted exile in Babylon.

Thus, the new Exodus motif emerges once again in Paul's argument. His reasoning is on two levels. First, he wished to show that a new exodus has taken place of which the church is the first fruit. There has not been a total break with the purposes of God as revealed in the Old Testament. This second picture was given to illustrate that Gentiles from many nations have been brought into the community of faith to receive the blessings promised to Abraham's children by virtue of sharing his faith.

II. EXPOSITION AND APPLICATION OF THE SCRIPTURE

A. Israel's Fall and the Riches of God's Grace (Romans 11:11-14)

I say then, Have they stumbled that they should fall? God forbid: but rather through their fall salvation is come unto the Gentiles, for to provoke them to jealousy. Now if the fall of them be the riches of the world, and the diminishing of them the riches of the Gentiles; how much more their fulness? For I speak to you Gentiles, inasmuch as I am the apostle of the Gentiles, I magnify mine office: If by any means I may provoke to emulation them which are my flesh, and might save some of them.

Verse 11 opens the section with a question that permeates the whole of the eleventh chapter of Romans: Has God rejected Israel completely because of the refusal on the part of some Jews to believe in Jesus Christ? Paul then gave the same emphatic answer throughout the entire chapter: God's rejection of Israel is not final. The Israelites have stumbled, but they are not beyond recovery; their predicament is not incurable. They have fallen temporarily, not permanently. In fact, the stumbling of Israel has set in motion a series of events that will lead to Israel's ultimate restoration. Through Israel's fall, salvation came to the Gentiles. Gentile salvation will provoke the Jews to jealousy so that they will again desire God's blessings.

The point we have reached at present is that by the Jews' stumble the Gentiles have come to be included within the scope of salvation (verse 12). While the details of this verse remain in some obscurity, Paul's main point is clear. Paul looks beyond the advantages conferred on Gentiles by the unbelief of Israel to the far greater end-time bliss that Israel's return will inaugurate. If Israel's fall brought the riches of God's grace to the Gentiles, how much more will Israel's reinstatement bring blessings to the world? Israel's fullness is the conversion of a large number of Jews (verse 12).

Verse 13 addresses the Gentiles in particular, who comprised the majority of the Roman church. Paul was divinely called to be an apostle to the Gentiles (see Romans 1:1) and made the most he could of his ministry to them. However, in ministering to the Gentiles, Paul hoped to save many of his fellow Jews (verse 14). The more he stressed his ministry to the Gentiles, leading them into God's blessings, the more he would arouse the Jews to envy, thus encouraging some of them to seek the same blessings of New Testament salvation. This restates the idea of verse 11, and in fact, the Greek text uses the same word as in verse 11, meaning "to provoke to jealousy."

B. The Imminent Restoration of Israel (Romans 11:15)

For if the casting away of them be the reconciling of the world, what shall the receiving of them be, but life from the dead?

In verse 15, Paul told the Roman Gentile Christians that they must not cast off the Jewish people as though they had no further purpose in the plans of God. Indeed, he reasoned that the real blessing of humankind through the Jewish people is yet to happen. If the Jews' casting off the Messiah brought salvation to the Gentiles, what will the Jewish return to the will of God bring? Paul said it would be wrong and foolish to discount the Jewish people with the assumption that they no longer had any place in the purposes of God. The expression of "life from the dead" echoes Ezekiel 37, the vision of the valley of dry bones where Israel was resurrected. It originally spoke, of course, of her return from exile. Its significance for our discussion on Israel's future is that only the remnant came back from the dead. The majority of the nation remained in exile and continued to suffer the consequences of the covenantal curses; they remained cut off from fellowship with God, for sadly, they chose to remain in a foreign land rather than to be faithful to their calling and the claims of Yahweh.

In saying that believing Israel would be part of redemptive history, Paul was suggesting that the resurrection of the Jewish people was taking place. If this is the imagery that Paul was alluding to in verse 15, he was arguing that in turning to the Messiah, Israel was being resurrected from spiritual death. She comes from exile, returning to God to worship Him. The fact that this is a present reality is evidenced by the growing number of Jews who, as a result of Yahweh's faithfulness to the covenant He made with Abraham, are now coming to Christ. What a glorious finale to human history! The promises of God are completely fulfilled so the whole of creation can have no doubt that He is to be worshipped as the covenant-keeping God.

C. The Temporary Rejection of the Jews (Romans 11:16-17)

For if the firstfruit be holy, the lump is also holy: and if the root be holy, so are the branches. And if some of the branches be broken off, and thou, being a wild olive tree, wert grafted in among them, and with them partakest of the root and fatness of the olive tree.

Paul pictured the temporariness of the Jews' rejection and the certainty of their restoration through two illustrations. The first is in verse 16 (NIV): "If the part of the dough offered as firstfruits is holy, then the whole batch is holy; if the root is holy, so are the branches." While we may wonder what is meant here, the Jews had no problem understanding it. Paul is referring to Old Testament offerings and sacrifices, and specifically the offering of the first fruits. In that offering, the priest took some of the dough from the larger lump and offered it to God. Paul reasoned that if the lump offered to God was acceptable, then the rest would naturally be as well. The first fruit was Abraham, the father of the Jewish nation, and he was accepted before God. Thus, it is natural for his descendants to be also accepted. Paul is making the point of how natural the Jews' return and acceptance by God will be. Put another way, "if the root is holy, so are the branches" (verse 16b, NIV). Israel's origins make her restoration the most natural thing.

In Romans 11:17-22, Paul extended this argument with the illustration of grafting branches onto an olive tree. The normal practice was to upgrade a wild olive tree by grafting healthy fruit-producing branches to it. While grafting does not affect the rest of the tree, the new branches become very productive. But here, Paul talks about grafting wild, fruitless branches onto a good tree—something he knew was contrary to nature (verse 24), but he wanted to make a point: If you were to cut out of an olive tree that is wild by nature, how much more readily will these natural branches be grafted into their own olive tree? Paul is simply saying that it would be so natural for Israel to return to health because she originally came from a productive tree. If God could engraft wild branches like you and me, how much more a natural branch?

D. No Room for Gentiles to Boast (Romans 11:18-22)

Boast not against the branches. But if thou boast, thou bearest not the root, but the root thee. Thou wilt say then, The branches were broken off, that I might be grafted in. Well; because of unbelief they were broken off, and thou standest by faith. Be not highminded, but fear: For if God spared not the natural branches, take heed lest he also spare not thee. Behold therefore the goodness and severity of God: on them which fell, severity; but toward thee, goodness, if thou continue in his goodness: otherwise thou also shalt be cut off.

Paul's concern was to stress to the Gentiles that they must not become arrogant toward the believing Jews in the congregation. At the heart of his concern is that the Gentile believers were beginning to look at their Jewish brothers and sisters with disdain, and their arrogance offended Paul deeply. He warned the Gentiles that their contempt for their Jewish brothers and sisters in the congregation was dangerous. Indeed, esteeming themselves over the Jews in the church would reverberate down through the generations to Abraham, the Jews' natural ancestor. Paul was determined that the Gentiles respect this patriarch of the Jews-Abraham. He was the one with whom God made His covenant to the eternal benefit of the Gentile nations. No one has the right to look down on any other person in the congregation, for we have all been saved by grace and not by works, heritage, and present-day connections.

The Gentiles, now a majority in the Roman church, were nonetheless totally dependent on the covenant which God made with Abraham and the promises made to him, because "Abraham believed the LORD, and he credited it to him as righteousness" (Genesis 15:6, NIV). In verse 19, Paul began to deal with the response he anticipated that the Gentile readers would make. He expected them to say something like, "God has put almost all of the Jews out of the covenant community, and we have replaced them. We were chosen and grafted into the tree in their place. We are the privileged people and they, the removed branches, have been abandoned." This was the very attitude of pride which took over the hearts of the Jews in the Old Testament and led to their downfall.

Paul acknowledged the claim of the Gentile believers concerning their status, as well as that of the unbelieving Jewish community as far as the new covenant blessings were concerned (verse 20). However, he warned the Gentiles of the danger of arrogance and of not being fearful of the living God, lest they become like the unbelieving Jews and fall under judgment. The reason Israel was brought under judgment was more than what the term *unbelief* implied. The term can also mean "unfaithfulness." Israel did not merely have a lapse of confidence in God but displayed a rebellious and determined turning away from God.

Paul had already told the Gentiles in Rome not to boast to their Jewish brethren. Now he tells them, "Do not become proud" (verse 20b), because he feared this attitude may lead to their own judgment. Paul's warning to the Gentiles in Rome was not that they would lose their salvation, but that they would experience the Lord's discipline. This would be exercised with the intention of bringing them back to Him in repentance and renewal. Paul had already implied that not all of the broken branches (the Jews) were discarded or consumed. The gardener (God) clearly preserved them so that He could, if He wished, graft them in again to the olive tree (the covenant community), thus reestablishing His covenant with them. Finally, in verse 20, Paul instructs the Gentiles to stand in awe (be afraid). Paul was concerned that unless they revere the Lord, their attitude may bring the Lord's chastisement.

Paul presented the inevitable logic of his reasoning with clarity and force. What right has the Gentile believing community to think that it will survive if the natural branches suffered chastisement for the same sin of arrogance (verse 22)? It is too easy for the Gentiles to think they are a special, privileged case whom God will excuse. Once they begin to think in such a way, they are in grave danger of being cast out of the covenant community as a consequence of the Lord's discipline.

E. The Danger of Taking God for Granted (Romans 11:23-24)

And they also, if they abide not still in unbelief, shall be grafted in: for God is able to graft them in again. For if thou wert cut out of the olive tree which is wild by nature, and wert grafted contrary to nature into a good olive tree: how much more shall these, which be the natural branches, be grafted into their own olive tree?

It is disturbingly easy to take the grace of God for granted; but Paul reminded his Gentile readers that the character of God has not changed. He was/is both stern and kind. He was/is kind to those who recognize their need and turn to Him in humble repentance. On such He pours His love and forgiveness without measure. But to those who are proud and arrogant, He sets Himself against them in judgment. He has always been such a God. Paul urged the Gentiles to remember this and not presume they have a relationship with a God who changes His character.

The Gentiles must not look down on the Jews as if they have been rejected by God forever. Far from God's having closed the door to the Jews, Paul asserts that they also can come in the blessings of the new covenant—not on the basis of merit or ancestry, but on the same basis as Abraham; that is, by faith. It is unbelief (unfaithfulness) which has caused the Jews to be cut off from their glorious destiny, but this destiny will be restored to them as soon as they exercise the same faith as their illustrious ancestors (verse 23).

Paul now brings his illustration of the olive tree to an end. His closing point is a further warning to the Gentile believers. It is as easy for God to reverse the position they are boasting about as it is for Him to restore believing Jews to their former place within the covenant community. This would not be difficult for God to do. Even in horticulture, it would be easier, more fruitful, and reliable to graft a previously cultivated branch back into its old cultivated tree than to graft in a branch from a wild tree. The latter process is notoriously unfruitful. Yet, this is what God did when He introduced the Gentiles into the new covenant community of faith. Paul wanted there to be no doubt among his Gentile hearers that their inclusion in the community was purely of grace. In our multicultural world where we mix and mingle with a host of people from every nation, kindred, and tongue, as these people find their way into the house of God, we must be open, welcoming, and affirming to their presence. We are all a part of the believing community by the gracious acts of God. None of us can claim a heritage or a history that sets us apart from any other members.

III. CONCLUDING REFLECTION

In this section, Paul placed Israel's unbelief in context. He showed that it has been the pattern of Israel's history throughout the Old Testament. How different her story would have been if she had truly believed and repented.

Yet, in spite of this unbelief, Paul insisted that the purposes of God still stand—Paul himself is living evidence that a believing remnant still exists, just as it existed throughout Israel's history. However, Paul feared that some Gentile believers in Rome were in danger of falling into Israel's sin of pride and unbelief (disobedience). He urged them not to boast that they have replaced Israel. He showed them that the Jews are the natural, cultivated, fallen branches of the olive tree, and that it would not be difficult for God to bring them back into the blessings promised to Abraham. After all, God had grafted the Gentiles into the tree as wild branches, so why could He not restore the natural branches to the site where they once grew?

PRAYER

We thank You, o God, for grafting us into the heritage, history, and promises You made to Israel. We are grateful for the mercy extended to those of us who were once excluded as outsiders but have now been brought into the covenant made with Abraham and confirmed through the death, burial, and resurrection of Jesus Christ, our Lord. In Jesus' name we pray. Amen.

HOME DAILY BIBLE READINGS
(May 13-19, 2019)

The Call of the Gentiles
MONDAY, May 13: "The Heritage Keepers" (Romans 9:1-5, 14-17)
TUESDAY, May 14: "A Light for the Gentiles" (Acts 13:44-49)
WEDNESDAY, May 15: "Life in Christ Jesus" (Colossians 2:1-10)
THURSDAY, May 16: "Testimony of God's Grace" (Acts 20:17-24, 32)
FRIDAY, May 17: "Israel's Rejection Is Not Final" (Romans 11:1-10)
SATURDAY, May 18: "All Peoples Saved by Faith" (Romans 11:25-36)
SUNDAY, May 19: "Salvation of the Gentiles" (Romans 11:11-24)

Spring Quarter 2019
Unit III: The Spread of the Gospel
Children's Unit: Called to Spread the Good News

May 26, 2019 — Lesson 13

CALLED TO NEW LIFE IN CHRIST

ADULT/YOUTH
ADULT/YOUNG ADULT TOPIC: **Giving One's All**
YOUTH TOPIC: **Set Apart to Serve**

CHILDREN
GENERAL LESSON TITLE: **Called to New Life in Christ**
CHILDREN'S TOPIC: **Let's Work Together**

DEVOTIONAL READING
Psalm 34:1-14

ADULT/YOUTH
BACKGROUND SCRIPTURE: **Romans 12**
PRINT PASSAGE: **Romans 12:1-8**
KEY VERSE: **Romans 12:1**

CHILDREN
BACKGROUND SCRIPTURE: **Romans 12**
PRINT PASSAGE: **Romans 12:1-8**
KEY VERSE: **Romans 12:2a**

Romans 12:1-8—KJV

I BESEECH you therefore, brethren, by the mercies of God, that ye present your bodies a living sacrifice, holy, acceptable unto God, which is your reasonable service.

2 And be not conformed to this world: but be ye transformed by the renewing of your mind, that ye may prove what is that good, and acceptable, and perfect, will of God.

3 For I say, through the grace given unto me, to every man that is among you, not to think of himself more highly than he ought to think; but to think soberly, according as God hath dealt to every man the measure of faith.

4 For as we have many members in one body, and all members have not the same office:

5 So we, being many, are one body in Christ, and every one members one of another.

6 Having then gifts differing according to the grace that is given to us, whether prophecy, let us prophesy according to the proportion of faith;

Romans 12:1-8—NIV

THEREFORE, I urge you, brothers and sisters, in view of God's mercy, to offer your bodies as a living sacrifice, holy and pleasing to God—this is your true and proper worship.

2 Do not conform to the pattern of this world, but be transformed by the renewing of your mind. Then you will be able to test and approve what God's will is—his good, pleasing and perfect will.

3 For by the grace given me I say to every one of you: Do not think of yourself more highly than you ought, but rather think of yourself with sober judgment, in accordance with the faith God has distributed to each of you.

4 For just as each of us has one body with many members, and these members do not all have the same function,

5 so in Christ we, though many, form one body, and each member belongs to all the others.

6 We have different gifts, according to the grace given

7 Or ministry, let us wait on our ministering: or he that teacheth, on teaching;

8 Or he that exhorteth, on exhortation: he that giveth, let him do it with simplicity; he that ruleth, with diligence; he that sheweth mercy, with cheerfulness.

to each of us. If your gift is prophesying, then prophesy in accordance with your faith;

7 if it is serving, then serve; if it is teaching, then teach;

8 if it is to encourage, then give encouragement; if it is giving, then give generously; if it is to lead, do it diligently; if it is to show mercy, do it cheerfully.

UNIFYING LESSON PRINCIPLE: People often engage in a "me first" way of thinking, which results in conflict and makes cooperation difficult. How do people learn to work together? Paul compares the church to a body and encourages believers to see themselves as individual members that work in sync with all the other members.

LESSON OBJECTIVES

Upon the completion of this lesson, the students will be able to do the following:

1. Relate Paul's teaching about being a living sacrifice to what he then says about being part of the body of Christ.
2. Appreciate the importance of one's using his or her gifts as both a sacrifice to the Lord and a responsible member of the body.
3. Analyze their gifts and abilities and commit those to the Lord for the good of the body of Christ.

AGE-LEVEL POINTS TO BE EMPHASIZED

Teachers of ADULTS and YOUTH

—The "therefore" of Romans 12:1 marks a shift from the doctrinal section of Romans (chapters 1–11) to the practical application of that doctrine (chapters 12–16).

—The concept of a "living sacrifice" (Romans 12:1) is a formal contradiction in terms.

—The phrase "spiritual worship" (*logikēn latreian*; verse 1) has been translated in a variety of ways: "reasonable service" (KJV), "true and proper worship" (NIV), and "true worship" (GNT).

—The Greek word *parakaleō,* meaning "to call aside, make an appeal," is used in verse 1 as an appeal in view of certain facts, and in verse 8 as an appeal by way of exhortation.

—The call to present oneself as a living sacrifice

is analogous to a dead animal sacrifice. It is a call (*parakaleō*) to serve God and obey God in a "newness of life."

—Serving sacrificially using one's body and by serving God through spiritual gifts requires a new way of thinking through the transformation of one's mind and through the empowerment of the Spirit.

—Paul lists spiritual gifts in this passage as well as in 1 Corinthians 12 and Ephesians 4.

Teachers of CHILDREN

—Paul encouraged believers to move beyond ritual worship.

—Paul called for believers to present themselves fully—their whole selves to God.

—The transformation that Paul called for is not outer but inner.

—A mind that is set on what God wants can know and prove God's will.

—Paul called for believers to have a mind that is filled with wisdom and not pride.

—Paul often used the body as a metaphor for the body of Christ. The many members of the physical body work together—so should members of the church.

THE CHRONOLOGICAL SETTING OF THE LESSON

It is something of a pattern with Paul to begin a letter with a strong doctrinal section and then follow with an exhortation to live out the Christian faith. When he used that pattern, he was and is saying that the Christian life is dependent on the great Christian doctrines. "Because these things are true, this is the kind of person you should be" is the line of reasoning. In a way, we can see that in Romans 8 and beyond. Paul is still concerned with justification by faith, for it is fundamental to him that the justified person does not live in the same way as the unrepentant sinner. Only when the power of sin is broken by what God did in Christ can ethical admonitions be effective. There can be no doubt that in these concluding chapters of Romans the way Christians live preoccupies the apostle to a far greater extent than in his earlier argument. There is little that is specific to Rome in most of what Paul is saying in this section—but since he had never been to Rome, this is not surprising. He evidently assumes that what applied to Christians generally applied to Roman Christians specifically.

THE GEOGRAPHICAL AND CULTURAL SETTING OF THE LESSON

The intended audience of Paul's letter was the believers in Rome. Information about the origins of this congregation (or congregations) is lost in history. However, the first suggestion of a group of believers in Rome comes from a New Testament reference combined with the historical records of Rome. The book of Acts reports that the Emperor Claudius had ordered all the Jews to leave Rome (see Acts 18:2). There is good reason to think that the Gospel had already arrived in Rome years before Paul's letter was sent. The fact that the letter was delivered in person to a group of individuals indicates that the government's earlier opposition to Jews in that city had largely subsided.

Little else is known about these believers in Rome, except what can be gleaned from the letter itself. It is clear that the church was composed of both Jews and Gentiles, and that disagreements on matters of doctrine and practice divided them. Paul himself had not been to Rome, although he expressed great eagerness to minister to them (see Romans 1:11). So, what prompted Paul to write this letter to the Romans? The most plausible explanation for the purpose of this letter is found in Paul's final remarks concerning an anticipated mission to Spain with a stopover in Rome. Even though the region of Spain was far to the west of Paul's main theater of operations, it represented a glorious opportunity for the further spread of the Gospel. Culture and learning were thriving in this region during the first century, and no doubt Paul's sense of indebtedness to the "non-Greeks" (Romans 1:14) extended all the way to the shores of the Atlantic Ocean.

PROMINENT CHARACTER(S) IN THE LESSON

Jesus Christ: Jesus is the spotless, sinless Son of God. He came to earth to "rescue" us from sin. It is through Him that we become united together as members of His church.

KEY TERMS IN THE LESSON

Conform(ed) (verse 2)—Greek: *syschēmatizō*

(sü-skhā-mä-tē'-zō): fashion(ed) oneself according to.

Gift (verse 6)—*charismata* (kuh-riz-muh-tuh): a divinely conferred gift or power.

Member(s) (verse 5)—Greek: *melos* (me'-los): a limb; a member of the human body.

Sacrifice (verse 1)—Greek: *thysia* (thü-sē'-ä): a sacrifice, victim.

Transformed (verse 2)—Greek: *metamorphoō* (me-tä-mor-fo'-ō): changed into another form.

TOPICAL OUTLINE OF THE LESSON

I. Introduction
   A. Grace and the Community of Faith
   B. Biblical Background

II. Exposition and Application of the Scripture
   A. Practical Exhortations for Christian Living (Romans 12:1)
   B. The Renewing of Our Minds (Romans 12:2)
   C. Grace and the Christian Community (Romans 12:3)
   D. The Church as One Body with a Multiplicity of Members (Romans 12:4-5)
   E. Gifts of Grace and the Christian Community (Romans 12:6-8)

III. Concluding Reflection

I. INTRODUCTION
A. Grace and the Community of Faith

Romans 1–11 can be described as the theological section of Paul's letter. In those chapters, he dealt with some hugely important issues. However, Christian living is not only about understanding theology but also about living it out, and it is to this that Paul turns in Romans 12. God saved His people to serve Him in truth and in holiness, qualities which Israel tragically failed to display. Living as faithful servants is obligatory, for we have been saved from the awful judgment that awaits those who are not in Christ. Like the Jews in the Exodus who benefitted from the death of the lamb, the church is saved as a result of the death of its paschal sacrifice, Jesus the firstborn and the Redeemer. Because of this, we are now challenged to commit ourselves to Christ and to His life-altering transforming process.

For this reason, Paul shifts his attention from the great doctrinal themes of justification by faith to the practical details of living out that new relationship. He builds a foundation for his pastoral instructions by once more calling the believers in Rome to become something more than they already were. Yes, they have been "justified through faith" (5:1), "set free from sin" (6:18), "released from the law" (7:6), and made "alive" in Christ (8:10). As the result of a divine act of grace, all God's blessings are theirs (and ours) as well. The only human contribution to that reality is faith in the promise of God.

In Romans 12, Paul appealed to believers in Rome to go beyond that inner reality to a conscious act of surrender and a "renewing of [the] mind" (12:1-2). The inner transformation now becomes an outward witness to others. This outward witness will set one apart from the world's way of thinking and behavior. A Christian is by nature a nonconformist. His or her conformity is defined in terms of being shaped by the pleasing and perfect will of God, not "the pattern of the world." How does this nonconformity express itself? It does so in acts of humility and love. Romans 12 demonstrates the essential connection between doctrine and life. These practical exhortations cover all aspects of the Christian life. In this chapter, Paul deals with the Christian's conduct as a member of the church—his relationship to God, to the corporate body, and to individuals.

B. Biblical Background

Diversity, not uniformity, is the mark of God's handiwork. It is so in nature; it is so in grace too, and nowhere more so than in the Christian community. Here are many men and women with the most diverse kinds of parentage, environment, temperament, and capacity. Not only so, but since they became Christians, they have been endowed by God with a great variety of spiritual gifts as well. Yet, because of and by means of that diversity, all can cooperate for the good of the whole. Whatever kind of service is to be rendered in the church, it is to be rendered heartily and faithfully by those divinely qualified, whether it be prophesying, teaching, admonishing, administering, making material gifts, visiting the sick, or performance of any other kind of ministry.

To illustrate what he meant, Paul used the figure of a human body, as he had already done in 1 Corinthians 12. Each part of the body has its own distinctive work to do, yet in a healthy body all the parts function harmoniously and interdependently for the good of the whole body. So should it be in the church, which is the body of Christ. This is not to be done in a spirit of competition, for each member of the body has a role to play and a function to fulfill. In a spirit of love, harmony, and mutuality, we offer our bodies to God as living sacrifices.

II. EXPOSITION AND APPLICATION OF THE SCRIPTURE

A. Practical Exhortations for Christian Living (Romans 12:1)

I BESEECH you therefore, brethren, by the mercies of God, that ye present your bodies a living sacrifice, holy, acceptable unto God, which is your reasonable service.

In verse 1, Paul urged the readers to establish a right relationship with God by consecrating themselves wholly. Paul used a favorite word—translated "beseech"—to phrase this as an exhortation instead of a command. The word *beseech* means "to exhort, entreat, appeal, plead, beg, urge." The exhortation is linked with the preceding doctrinal exposition by the word *therefore*, emphasizing the essential unity of doctrine and life. The purpose for doctrine is to produce consecrated lives. Specifically, the plea is based on the mercies of God, which include justification, sanctification, and other blessings from God's compassionate grace discussed in chapters 1–11. In view of these benefits of salvation, Christians are urged to respond in obedient consecration. It is important to note that we do not earn salvation by consecration and moral reform. To the contrary, the mercies of God freely bestowed upon us in salvation motivate, enable, and issue forth in holy living. It is the mercies of God that move humans to offer God what is essentially a sacrifice of thanksgiving.

Christians are to present their bodies to God. The Greek word translated as "present" here means "to yield, offer, dedicate." By implication, this includes soul and spirit, for we can only offer up the body by consent of the inner person, and the inner person can only serve God through the body. Attempting to serve God in the mind or spirit alone is not enough; our service to God must produce an actual transformation of our physical behavior. The Christian is to be a living sacrifice. This is Old Testament language, but with a significant difference. The Old Testament sacrificial animal was forced to give up its ordinary pursuit, while we are urged to sacrifice these things voluntarily and not through death but through continued life. We trade the old life of self-will for new abundant life in the will of God. God asks for living human sacrifice—people who live their lives totally dedicated and committed to Him. This, says the apostle, is our reasonable service. The primary meaning of the Greek word translated "reasonable" is "rational, logical, intelligent, reasonable, expected." Consecration to God is only to be expected after all the mercies He has bestowed on us.

B. The Renewing of Our Minds
(Romans 12:2)

And be not conformed to this world: but be ye transformed by the renewing of your mind, that ye may prove what is that good, and acceptable, and perfect, will of God.

In verse 2, the passage moves from a passive definition of *consecration* to an active one.

Verse 1 focuses on the gift of ourselves to God; verse 2 speaks of the activity—the life transformation—this involves. First, there is the negative aspect. We must not be conformed to this world. The word translated "conformed" means "to be fashioned after or patterned after." The word for "world" connotes the temporal customs or patterns of worldly society. In other words, we are not to imitate the ways of the world. Not only does this involve worldly activities and dress, but it also involves worldly value systems, standards of success, modes of operation, and lifestyles.

Positively speaking, we are to let ourselves be transformed by the renewing of our minds. The renewing of our minds describes the process of growing in grace, being sanctified (set apart for service), and becoming progressively more Christ-like in every way. It means taking on the mind of Christ, learning how to think according to spiritual principles, and evaluating life by heavenly standards. This comes by implanting the Word of God through reading, studying, meditating, and listening, as well as by communing with God in prayer and worship. With this kind of spiritual transformation and renewing we can test, approve, or discover God's will. Each one of us can know and do God's will if we will consecrate ourselves. In so doing, we will find God's will to be good (for us), acceptable or pleasing (to Him), and perfect (in every way). We must seek to do God's will at all costs, and this verse tells us it will be at once good, acceptable, and perfect.

C. Grace and the Christian Community
(Romans 12:3)

For I say, through the grace given unto me, to every man

that is among you, not to think of himself more highly than he ought to think; but to think soberly, according as God hath dealt to every man the measure of faith.

Paul turns now to the kind of conduct that should characterize Christians in their relations with other believers. It was just as easy for them as it has been for Christians throughout the centuries to have wrong ideas about themselves and those they meet, and to fail in their Christian performance accordingly. The apostle proceeds to outline some considerations that Christians should always have in mind. He referred to the way believers should act toward other Christians as well as the way they should behave toward those outside the church.

Christian community is an essential aid in renewing our minds and transforming our actions. It is so non-optional that Paul spends the rest of this chapter describing how we need to think about and function within community. This section (verses 3-8) begins with a negative and a positive admonition. In urging the Romans not to think more highly of themselves than they ought (verse 3), Paul is concerned with the attitude and behavior of those who promote their own importance at the expense of others. The cultural context in which this warning against arrogance must be understood is the athletic rivalry in the Mediterranean world where individuals and groups of roughly equal status endlessly compete with one another. It was commonplace for people in the Greco-Roman world—Rome especially—to scorn anyone perceived to be lower in wealth and honor; this was one consequence of the pronounced social stratification of this culture. Paul wanted to snuff out such behavior in the church before it could get started by telling his addressees not to harbor the thoughts that stimulate the attitude just

mentioned—namely, that they are superior to others whom they imagine they can despise and reject. Instead, they are to think in a moderate way, which here entails controlled and sober thoughts about others.

There is a tendency to make this and the following verses refer to people holding official positions in the church. This is probably misguided, for we know little about what offices existed in the church at the time Paul wrote. However, since a good deal of what he says applies to all believers, there is no reason to think that he was referring to office holders only. All who are included in the household of faith should be careful in how they treat one another.

D. The Church as One Body with a Multiplicity of Members
(Romans 12:4-5)

For as we have many members in one body, and all members have not the same office: So we, being many, are one body in Christ, and every one members one of another.

A number of times in Scripture, the church is likened to one body with its multiplicity of members (see 1 Corinthians 10:17; 12:12-30; Ephesians 1:23). Evidently, the thought of the basic unity underlying considerable diversity made a deep appeal. Paul also has lists of "gifts" in the church in other places (see 1 Corinthians 12:4-11; Ephesians 4:7-11). The point he is making is that different members of the church have different gifts, all of which have their place. Each should use whatever gift he or she has to the fullest extent. Paul recognized that while it takes many members to make up the body, they do not all have the same function. Our physical body is certainly a unit, with all the members contributing to the good of the whole. But equally certain is that there is a wide variety of function that goes into making up that one body (verse 4).

In the same way, we, the many, are one body in Christ. Paul does not speak of "the body of Christ" as in Ephesians and Colossians, but of "one body in Christ" (verse 5). The point here is the unity of the members of the body, even in their diversity. This unity is brought about by the fact that they are all in Christ. Their diversity in their unity does not reduce them to a drab uniformity.

E. Gifts of Grace and the Christian Community (Romans 12:6-8)

Having then gifts differing according to the grace that is given to us, whether prophecy, let us prophesy according to the proportion of faith; Or ministry, let us wait on our ministering: or he that teacheth, on teaching; Or he that exhorteth, on exhortation: he that giveth, let him do it with simplicity; he that ruleth, with diligence; he that sheweth mercy, with cheerfulness.

Romans 12:6 takes note of the fact that different members of the church have different offices and gifts, just as body parts have different functions. For this reason, we dare not compare ourselves among ourselves, but we should recognize a diversity of functions and acknowledge the value of the various members of the body. We must seek to identify our particular gifts and exercise them according to God's grace in us for the benefit of the body as a whole. Instead of seeking to do every possible task in the body, we should concentrate on the particular functions God has given us and perform them well. The Greek word for "gifts" here is *charismata*, the same word used of the nine spiritual gifts in 1 Corinthians 12:4-11. Neither of these lists is meant to be exhaustive, but they are rather representative of the ways

that God uses individuals in His church. Paul's readers learn that the context in which they are not to despise other Christ followers is concerning the way "gifts" are distributed among the faithful. Some gifts appear to be natural talents strengthened by the Spirit, whereas others are unique abilities following conversion. They are and remain gifts, however. True to their name, they are spiritual endowments for ministry within Christ's body; they are not our possessions or status builders. They should not be used in a game of one-upmanship in an attempt to lord over other members of the body.

Prophecy stands at the head of the list. Paul devoted an entire chapter to prophecy in 1 Corinthians 14 and regarded it as a decisive gift because of its close relationship to the proclamation of the Word. *Prophecy* may suggest to our ears the predicting of future events, and it sometimes entails this element, but it primarily concerns offering guidance from the Spirit and God's Word for the church in particular circumstances (verse 6). The second gift, *serving*, is in Greek *diakonia* (from which *deacon* is derived). It literally means "to wait on tables," or service rendered to another. How interesting that this gift would precede the prestigious gift of teaching. This undoubtedly is due to the remembrance of Jesus Himself, who exalted service of others over self. A third gift is *teaching*. The prophet interprets the Gospel according to the Spirit's direction in given circumstances, but the teacher, through knowledge of and reflection on the revelation of God, instructs the church in the whole counsel of God. A further gift includes *encouragement* or *exhortation* (verse 8). The term literally depicts someone who is called alongside another as a helping companion.

Verse 8 concludes with virtues rather than offices. The gift of *giving* is to be practiced generously. Likewise, leaders are to govern diligently. The Greek word might be translated "with haste," that is, not begrudgingly, but readily and eagerly. By ministering cheerfully, the servant of God liberates those whom he or she serves. Four of the seven gifts in verses 6-8 relate to what the church traditionally has called the diaconate (those who serve others both within and outside the church). Faced with burgeoning social ills and suffering, with a Gospel which is increasingly marginalized, the various ministries of the church afford numerous opportunities to reach the least of these—those who for whatever reason no longer hear the Gospel from the church. In so doing, the church bears witness to the world that Jesus did not come to be served, but to serve and to give His life as a ransom for many. This should be our focus as we use our gifts both as a sacrifice to the Lord and as a responsible member of the body.

III. CONCLUDING REFLECTION

In view of all that God has accomplished for His people in Christ, how should His people live? They should present themselves to God as a "living sacrifice" consecrated to Him. The animal sacrifices of an earlier day have been rendered forever obsolete by Christ's self-offering, but there is always room for the worship rendered by obedient hearts. Instead of living by the standards of a world at discord with God, believers are exhorted to let the renewing of their minds by the power of the Spirit transform their lives into conformity with God's will. Doctrine is never taught in the Bible simply that it may be known; it is taught in order that it may be translated into practice. It is also worthy of note that the ethical admonitions of this and other New Testament epistles, whether Paul's or not, bear a close resemblance to the ethical teachings of Jesus Christ recorded in the Gospels. There is an impressive list of parallels that can be drawn between Romans 12 and the Sermon on the Mount.

PRAYER

We give You thanks, O God, for the privilege of offering our bodies to You as living sacrifices. Do not let us become haughty in our offerings and keep before us the importance of a loving community free of competition and strife in the exercise of our gifts as we contribute to the body. In Jesus' name we pray. Amen.

HOME DAILY BIBLE READINGS
(May 20-26, 2019)

Called to New Life in Christ

MONDAY, May 20: "Trust and Honor God" (Proverbs 3:1-12)
TUESDAY, May 21: "The Gift of Love" (1 Corinthians 13)
WEDNESDAY, May 22: "Lifestyle of Christian Believers" (Luke 6:27-36)
THURSDAY, May 23: "Seek Peace and Pursue It" (Psalm 34:1-14)
FRIDAY, May 24: "Genuine Love for Each Other" (Romans 12:9-15)
SATURDAY, May 25: "Living Together in Harmony" (Romans 12:16-21)
SUNDAY, May 26: "A Living Sacrifice" (Romans 12:1-8)

Living in Covenant

GENERAL INTRODUCTION

This quarter will teach how Jesus fulfilled the Law—in the sense that it was given full meaning. Jesus emphasized the deep, underlying messages of the Gospel, and this same message is continued through the apostle Paul and the writer of the book of Hebrews. Relationships of faith empower us to live the covenant and spread the Gospel message.

Unit I, *"A Fulfilled Covenant,"* contains four lessons that reveal a new sign of the covenant for Jewish and Gentile believers, as recorded in the books of Matthew, Mark, Luke, Hebrews, and Colossians. During the celebration of the Passover, Jesus explained to the disciples that He would initiate a new covenant through His death. Paul explains that the sign of the covenant is now a relationship of the heart between God and God's people, not circumcision.

Unit II, *"A Heartfelt Covenant,"* has five lessons and gives new meaning and purpose to the Law. According to Matthew, Jesus began teaching the Law in a way that gave life to the hearer and doer. Unlike other teachers of the Law, Jesus preached the transforming righteousness of the kingdom. Jesus challenged the mere external observance of God's law without internal transformation.

Unit III, *"Covenant: A Personal Perspective,"* has four lessons. It focuses on personal relationships between people as recorded in the books of 1 Samuel, Ruth, and Ephesians. Ultimately, those relationships pave the way for the Messiah. After Christ established the New Testament church, relationships between people have been based on relationship with Christ Jesus. These relationships continue the work of Christ Jesus by spreading the Gospel message.

God's New Covenant

Jeremiah 31:31-34

*I will write my law
on their hearts
and minds.*

June 2, 2019   Lesson 1

JESUS INSTITUTES THE NEW COVENANT

ADULT/YOUTH	CHILDREN
ADULT/YOUNG ADULT TOPIC: Making Promises	**GENERAL LESSON TITLE: Jesus Makes a**
YOUTH TOPIC: Better Promises	**New Promise**
	CHILDREN'S TOPIC: Celebrate the New Promise

DEVOTIONAL READING
Jeremiah 31:31-34

ADULT/YOUTH	CHILDREN
BACKGROUND SCRIPTURE: Mark 14:12-31;	**BACKGROUND SCRIPTURE: Mark 14:12-31;**
Hebrews 8	**Hebrews 8**
PRINT PASSAGE: Mark 14:17-24;	**PRINT PASSAGE: Mark 14:17-24;**
Hebrews 8:6-7, 10-12	**Hebrews 8:6-7, 10-12**
KEY VERSE: Hebrews 8:6	**KEY VERSE: Hebrews 8:10**

Mark 14:17-24; Hebrews 8:6-7, 10-12—KJV

17 And in the evening he cometh with the twelve.

18 And as they sat and did eat, Jesus said, Verily I say unto you, One of you which eateth with me shall betray me.

19 And they began to be sorrowful, and to say unto him one by one, Is it I? and another said, Is it I?

20 And he answered and said unto them, It is one of the twelve, that dippeth with me in the dish.

21 The Son of man indeed goeth, as it is written of him: but woe to that man by whom the Son of man is betrayed! good were it for that man if he had never been born.

22 And as they did eat, Jesus took bread, and blessed, and brake it, and gave to them, and said, Take, eat: this is my body.

23 And he took the cup, and when he had given thanks,

Mark 14:17-24; Hebrews 8:6-7, 10-12—NIV

17 When evening came, Jesus arrived with the Twelve.

18 While they were reclining at the table eating, he said, "Truly I tell you, one of you will betray me—one who is eating with me."

19 They were saddened, and one by one they said to him, "Surely you don't mean me?"

20 "It is one of the Twelve," he replied, "one who dips bread into the bowl with me.

21 "The Son of Man will go just as it is written about him. But woe to that man who betrays the Son of Man! It would be better for him if he had not been born."

22 While they were eating, Jesus took bread, and when he had given thanks, he broke it and gave it to his disciples, saying, "Take it; this is my body."

23 Then he took a cup, and when he had given thanks, he gave it to them, and they all drank from it.

he gave it to them: and they all drank of it.
24 And he said unto them, This is my blood of the new testament, which is shed for many.

.....

6 But now hath he obtained a more excellent ministry, by how much also he is the mediator of a better covenant, which was established upon better promises.
7 For if that first covenant had been faultless, then should no place have been sought for the second.

.....

10 For this is the covenant that I will make with the house of Israel after those days, saith the Lord; I will put my laws into their mind, and write them in their hearts: and I will be to them a God, and they shall be to me a people:
11 And they shall not teach every man his neighbour, and every man his brother, saying, Know the Lord: for all shall know me, from the least to the greatest.
12 For I will be merciful to their unrighteousness, and their sins and their iniquities will I remember no more.

24 "This is my blood of the covenant, which is poured out for many," he said to them.

.....

6 But in fact the ministry Jesus has received is as superior to theirs as the covenant of which he is mediator is superior to the old one, since the new covenant is established on better promises.
7 For if there had been nothing wrong with that first covenant, no place would have been sought for another.

.....

10 "This is the covenant I will establish with the people of Israel after that time, declares the Lord. I will put my laws in their minds and write them on their hearts. I will be their God, and they will be my people.
11 "No longer will they teach their neighbor, or say to one another, 'Know the Lord,' because they will all know me, from the least of them to the greatest.
12 "For I will forgive their wickedness and will remember their sins no more."

UNIFYING LESSON PRINCIPLE: People often make promises to one another in seeking lasting, committed relationships. How can one be assured that a relationship will last? In the books of Mark and Hebrews, Jesus is affirmed as the one through whom God's new everlasting covenant is fulfilled.

LESSON OBJECTIVES

Upon the completion of this lesson, the students will be able to do the following:

1. Tell how Jesus is the initiator of the new covenant predicted by the prophets and illustrated in the Lord's Supper.
2. Appreciate their standing and relationship with Christ because of the new covenant.
3. Approach the Lord's Supper with greater reverence and awe for the Christ of the new covenant.

AGE-LEVEL POINTS TO BE EMPHASIZED

Teachers of ADULTS and YOUTH

—The earliest account of the institution of the Last Supper is found in 1 Corinthians 11:23-26. Other accounts are found in Matthew 26:26-30 and Luke 22:14-23.

—Jesus' prediction that one of the disciples would betray Him can be read in numerous ways. Was He threatening, warning, bluntly stating a fact, lamenting, or issuing a final appeal?

—The words of institution, "This is my body" and "This is my blood," echo the words of the Passover liturgy: "This is the bread of affliction which our ancestors ate in the land of Egypt."

—The writer of Hebrews announces in 8:1-2 that his "main point" is Jesus as the High Priest of the heavenly sanctuary. This is the "more excellent ministry" that authorizes Jesus to mediate the "better covenant" that the writer describes (verse 6).

—The declaration of Christ's more excellent ministry (verse 6) is in direct contrast to verse 4: "Now if He were on earth, He would not be a priest at all" (NASB).

—The new covenant is explained as that foretold in Jeremiah 31:31-34. This passage is quoted in Hebrews 8:7-13, the longest quotation from the Old Testament in the New.

Teachers of CHILDREN

—The Passover and the Feast of Unleavened Bread were celebrated during the week that Jesus celebrated the Last Supper with His disciples.

—Passover is the observance of God's freeing the Israelites from Egypt.

—The Feast of Unleavened Bread is a seven-day celebration that commemorates the Israelites' flight from Egypt.

—Jesus establishes a new covenant from God that lives inside of us.

—As Jesus eats His last meal with His disciples, He announces that one of the disciples will betray Him.

—Jesus gives thanks for the bread, representing His broken body—and the cup, representing His shed blood.

THE CHRONOLOGICAL SETTING OF THE LESSON

The gospel of Mark was probably written approximately AD 55–59 and is likely one of the first New Testament books written. Whereas Matthew was written with a primarily Jewish audience in mind, Mark primarily targeted Gentile Roman believers. Mark wanted the people to know that Jesus Christ was the servant of the Lord and the Savior of the world. Knowing this would help to strengthen their faith, even though they faced severe persecution. Although the gospel of Mark does not name its author, it is unanimously concluded by the early church fathers that Mark was the writer. According to 1 Peter 5:13, Mark was an associate of the apostle Peter's. He received from Peter firsthand information regarding the events and teachings of Jesus, and Mark preserved the information in written form (gotquestions.org).

The book of Hebrews must have been written prior to the destruction of the Jerusalem Temple in AD 70, because there is no mention of the Temple's destruction and the ending of the Jewish sacrificial system. In addition, the author consistently uses the Greek present tense when speaking about the Temple (biblia.com).

THE GEOGRAPHICAL AND CULTURAL SETTING OF THE LESSON

It is generally agreed that Mark is the John Mark of the New Testament, mentioned in Acts 12:12. His mother was a wealthy and prominent Christian in the Jerusalem church, and the church possibly met in her home. Mark joined Paul and Barnabas on their first missionary journey but not on the second, because of a strong disagreement between the two men about Mark (see Acts 15:37-38). However, near the end of Paul's life, he called for Mark to be with him (see 2 Timothy 4:11).

Although it is unclear regarding the authorship of the book of Hebrews, there are some clear indications regarding the intended audience for the writing. The original audience was Jewish. Hebrews 1:1 (NIV) states, "In the past God spoke to our forefathers through the prophets at many times and in various ways." The original audience of Hebrews was spiritually immature, based on the description in Hebrews 5:12 (NIV): "Though by this time you ought to be teachers, you need someone to teach you the elementary truths of God's word all over again." A history of suffering is another characteristic of the book of Hebrews: "Remember those earlier days after you had received the light, when you endured in a great conflict full of suffering. . . . So do not throw away your confidence; it will be richly rewarded" (Hebrews 10:32, 35, NIV). (thirdmill.org)

PROMINENT CHARACTER(S) IN THE LESSON

Son of Man: The term Jesus preferred to use in referring to Himself. This term is also unique to Mark's gospel.

Twelve Disciples: the twelve men Jesus chose to partner with Him and be trained to carry on the work of spreading the Gospel of Jesus Christ.

KEY TERMS IN THE LESSON

Covenant (Mark 14:24)—Greek: *diathéké* (dee-ath-ay'-kay)**:** "testament" (KJV); will; covenant.

Cup (Mark 14:23)—Greek: *potérion* (pot-ay'-ree-on)**:** a drinking cup; the contents of the cup; fig: the portion which God allots.

Man (Mark 14:21)—Greek: *anthrópos* (anth'-ro-pos)**:** a man; one of the human race.

Ministry (Hebrews 8:6)—Greek: *leitourgia* (li-toorg-ee'-ah)**:** a service; a ministry; a charitable gift.

Saddened (Mark 14:19)—Greek: *lupeó* (loo-peh'-o)**:** pained; grieved; vexed; "sorrowful" (KJV).

Said (Mark 14:18)—Greek: *legó* (leg'-o)**:** (a) say; spoken; I meant, mentioned, told; (b) I called, named, especially in the pass.; (c) I told, commanded.

Take (Mark 14:22)—Greek: *lambanó* (lam-ban'-o)**:** to receive, get, take, lay hold of.

TOPICAL OUTLINE OF THE LESSON

I. **Introduction**
   A. Parting Thoughts and Actions
   B. Biblical Background

II. **Exposition and Application of the Scripture**
   A. Betrayal Prediction (Mark 14:17-21)
   B. The Last Supper (Mark 14:22-24)
   C. A Superior Covenant (Hebrews 8:6-7)
   D. Forgiveness and Removal of Sin (Hebrews 8:10-12)

III. **Concluding Reflection**

I. INTRODUCTION

A. Parting Thoughts and Actions

Mark 14 opens with preparation for the meal of the evening and the plot to arrest Jesus (see 14:1). The description of this meal and the imagery presented deeply illustrates the deliverance of the Israelites from captivity (see Exodus 12:21-28). This meal also signifies a new life—based on Christ's death and resurrection—which would be available to all who would believe in Him. The preparation and setting for this meal are detailed in Mark 4:12-16, where the disciples had gone out to locate and prepare the venue for the meal as instructed by Jesus. The evening had come, and Jesus arrived with His disciples to the venue (see 14:17). This was immediately followed by the feast proper and Jesus' mysterious words concerning the one who would betray Him (see 14:18). As the night gradually unfolded, the disciples were worried about Jesus' words (see 14:19). Jesus then gave clues as to the identity of the betrayer: "It is one of the twelve, one who is dipping bread into the bowl with me" (see 14:20).

Written around AD 30, chapter 14 is the longest chapter in Mark's gospel, with seventy-two verses. It contains the plot to kill Jesus, Jesus' anointing by a woman, the Last Supper, His predictions of His betrayal, and Peter's denials of Him.

B. Biblical Background

During the course of the meal, Jesus took bread, blessed it, broke it, and gave it to His disciples (see 14:22). He also took the cup (which had also been blessed) and gave it to His disciples. Receiving the blessed bread and wine, the instructions and words that came with them possibly could have left the disciples wondering what might happen next, because Jesus said, "I tell you, I will never again drink of the fruit of the vine until that day when I drink it new in the kingdom of God" (see 14:23-25). Here, Jesus instituted Holy Communion, which is still widely practiced in Christianity today.

God's Redemption and Atonement

Hebrews can be described as a connector of the Old Testament and the New Testament. The Old Testament covenant is quite different from that of the New, yet many Christians understand God in terms of Old Testament Law rather than through the fuller revelation of New Testament grace. The book of Hebrews explains how Jesus became the mediator and guarantor of a new and better covenant.

In verse 6 of our text, we see a warning against walking away from the truth of God's Word and becoming reprobate. When there is a falling away, it becomes almost impossible to come to faith, and this subjects Christ to shame. Verse 7 compares Jesus and the priest Melchizedek. Abraham paid honor to Melchizedek, paying tithes to him and bringing the Levitical priesthood blessing upon Abraham. In the same way, Jesus was also a priest like Melchizedek—as neither of them was from the tribe of Levi. A change in lineage also brought about a change in law. Jesus had proven His priesthood through showing the world His indestructible life through His death and resurrection.

The first covenant was a good beginning but was ultimately inadequate. The new covenant is based on God's power and not on man's ability. The new covenant is also based on better promises and is guaranteed by a better high priest, Jesus Christ (see Hebrews 8:6). When a covenant was made, it was sealed by the blood of many bulls (see Exodus 24:3-8). In the same fashion, blood was a necessity to solidify and seal the new covenant that God had made with humanity. Jesus did it by shedding His blood on the Cross, thus establishing the promise. Here, Jesus once more fulfills His promise made to the disciples in Mark 14. Jesus is the guarantor of the new covenant, which is far better than anything the children of Israel experienced in the Old Testament. This covenant promise is available to anyone who believes in the saving grace of God through Christ.

II. EXPOSITION AND APPLICATION OF THE SCRIPTURE

A. Betrayal Prediction
(Mark 14:17-21)

And in the evening he cometh with the twelve. And as they sat and did eat, Jesus said, Verily I say unto you, One of you which eateth with me shall betray me. And they began to be sorrowful, and to say unto him one by one, Is it I? and another said, Is it I? And he answered and said unto them, It is one of the twelve, that dippeth with me in the dish. The Son of man indeed goeth, as it is written of him: but woe to that man by whom the Son of man is betrayed! good were it for that man if he had never been born.

The atmosphere must have been extremely tense in the room when Jesus dropped the bombshell revelation that somebody within their own tightly knit group would be the very one to disloyally betray His leader and Lord. Obviously, Jesus was not seeking to win any popularity contests when He made this startling statement, because He minced no words and figuratively went for the jugular. When we read such a starkly worded statement, two things come to the humanly thinking mind: First, could not Jesus have used a bit more verbal tact in this situation? Surely, He could have at least taken the disciple aside to speak to him privately rather than exposing the brother in front of the whole group. But, Jesus had no time to waste and verbalized the truth so that prophecy might be fulfilled (see Zechariah 11:12-13). A second reaction to Jesus' bold and troubling words might be, "What a shame! And how could someone supposedly so close to Jesus dare betray Him to the Roman authorities who wanted to kill Him?" Such a deed seems almost too terrible to conceive, until we start to ask ourselves if there have been times when we have betrayed Jesus through choosing money over Jesus by refusing to tithe. Have we ever denied Jesus by being outwardly committed to Jesus but inwardly rebellious and unbelieving? Have we ever stood strong for the things of the world but shrunk back and rejected the love of God? If the answer to any of these questions is yes, then we too have in some ways also betrayed the Savior.

When the disciples heard that one of them would betray Jesus, they were visibly disappointed. But instead of investigating each other, they began to quiz Jesus and to ask Him about themselves in an effort to distance themselves from the accusation rather than to make arrangements for Jesus' safety. It is important for everyone to examine themselves to see what lies within the heart. Psalm 139:23 (NIV) aligns with this concept: "Search me, God, and know my heart; test me and know my anxious thoughts." Socrates further illuminated this concept when he declared, "The unexamined life is not worth living."

It takes more than a casual tour of the heart to discover the roots of our unrighteousness. All sin has one root that is based on selfishness. But when we commit one sin, it is easier for others to follow.

> Sins are gregarious, as it were; they 'hunt in couples.' . . . The roots of all sin are in each. Men may think that they are protected from certain forms of sin by temperament, but identity of nature is deeper than varieties of temperament. The greatest sins are committed by yielding to very common motives. Love of money is not a rare feeling, but it led Judas to betray

Jesus. Anger is thought to be scarcely a sin at all, but it often moves an arm to murder. Temptations to each sin are round us all. We walk in a tainted atmosphere. There is progress in evil. No man reaches the extreme of depravity at a bound. Judas's treachery was of slow growth. So still there is the constant operation and pressure of forces and tendencies drawing us away from Jesus Christ. We, every one of us, know that, if we allowed our nature to have its way, we should leave Him and 'make shipwreck of faith and of a good conscience.' The forms in which we might do it might vary, but do it we should."[1]

The bowl to which Jesus referred (verse 20) was a common bowl used by everyone at the dinner. The purpose of Jesus' making the announcement revealing the betrayer was not necessarily to identify one specific person, because many of the disciples had dipped into the dish.

Jesus acknowledged that His own death had been predicted and prophesied hundreds of years prior to His birth. Such is the power of God's prescribed plan put into place prior to the foundation of the world. Although the actions of Judas were known before he committed them, this does not mean that he had no choice in the matter. Just because a parent knows a child will disobey a rule even before the choice is manifested does not mean that the parent made the child choose to do wrong. Likewise, the action by Judas came from an impure heart and selfish motives. Since this choice was made by Judas independently and

without divine coercion, for this reason Judas bears full guilt and is liable for full punishment for his choice.

The gravity of this scenario and the consequences for his actions are driven home by Jesus' statement that it would be better to have never been born than to play such a crucial part in bringing the Savior to the Cross. It would be "better not to have lived at all than to have lived and died ill. Existence is no blessing, but a curse, to him who consciously and willfully defeats the purpose of his existence" (*The Gospel of Mark*, John Schultz, p. 161).

B. The Last Supper
(Mark 14:22-24)

And as they did eat, Jesus took bread, and blessed, and brake it, and gave to them, and said, Take, eat: this is my body. And he took the cup, and when he had given thanks, he gave it to them: and they all drank of it. And he said unto them, This is my blood of the new testament, which is shed for many.

These are the words that are typically spoken in churches throughout the world at the sacred moment of Holy Communion. The physical symbol of the broken bread was to be a forever reminder regarding the tortured body of Jesus. When we eat the bread, we are figuratively ingesting the body of Christ. This simple yet powerful act serves to remind us of God's portable presence that has become a part of us and which we carry everywhere we go. This is an intimate statement of oneness that is in some ways comparable to the act of physical oneness between a husband and a wife. This ceremonial act of Holy Communion took place at the close of the Paschal supper while they were still reclined at the table. Most likely, the bread would have been unleavened bread. The central point of the experience is the spiritual oneness involved along with our remembering Jesus' supreme sacrifice.

Like the bread in verse 22, the cup filled with wine represented the blood of Jesus (verse 23). In today's times, when we think of someone being a part of our family, we speak of being related to each other by blood. This is a similar family-oriented mindset and spirit of being related by blood that is represented by the presence of the cup. Participation in communion suggests that we and Jesus are blood relatives.

> Frequent mention is made of his precious blood as the price of our redemption. How comfortable is this to poor repenting sinners, that the blood of Christ is shed for many! If for many, why not for me? It was a sign of the conveyance of the benefits purchased for us by his death. Apply the doctrine of Christ crucified to yourselves; let it be meat and drink to your souls, strengthening and refreshing your spiritual life. It was to be an earnest and foretaste of the happiness of heaven, and thereby to put us out of taste for the pleasures and delights of sense. (*The Miniature Commentary; Being Short Comments on Every Chapter of The Holy Bible: Matthew to Revelation*, p. 91).

C. A Superior Covenant
(Hebrews 8:6-7)

But now hath he obtained a more excellent ministry, by how much also he is the mediator of a better covenant, which was established upon better promises. For if that first covenant had been faultless, then should no place have been sought for the second.

Christ is the mediator of the new covenant by virtue of His substitutionary death on the Cross. The bottom line in the message conveyed by verse 6 is that the new covenant is better than the old covenant. The covenant was a solemn agreement between an offended God and the offending sinners. God promised pardon and life to those who fulfilled the conditions of the covenant, and they in turn would receive the benefits of the covenant. These benefits were "more spiritual, clear, comprehensive, and universal than those of the Mosaical covenant" (*A Biblical and Theological Dictionary*, Richard Watson, p. 832). Some of the benefits of the new covenant include forgiveness, justification by faith, the Holy Spirit, eternal life, and power over the enemy and over our flesh.

The first covenant was created and intended for the time and the people that it served. If the old covenant had been adequate, there would not have been a need for a new one. Since the old covenant was unable to adequately provide the many benefits previously mentioned, there had to be an update, a reboot—a new and improved version. This updated version was not free or cheap but came at a very high cost. The price paid for the new covenant was Christ's death on a cross. Since such a high price was paid for the new covenant, we dare not take it lightly but should demonstrate our appreciation by obedience to its mandates and adherence to its dictates.

D. Forgiveness and Removal of Sin
(Hebrews 8:10-12)

For this is the covenant that I will make with the house of Israel after those days, saith the Lord; I will put my laws into their mind, and write them in their hearts: and

I will be to them a God, and they shall be to me a people: And they shall not teach every man his neighbour, and every man his brother, saying, Know the Lord: for all shall know me, from the least to the greatest. For I will be merciful to their unrighteousness, and their sins and their iniquities will I remember no more.

Some covenants focus on the exterior elements of physical, tangible matter. But the new covenant focused on the inner matters of the heart. "The grand uniqueness of the Christian system is, that it regulates the conscience and the principles of the soul rather than external matters. It prescribes few external rites, and those are exceedingly simple, and are merely the proper expressions of the pious feelings supposed to be in the heart; and all attempts either to increase the number of these rites, or to make them imposing by their gorgeousness, have done just so much to mar the simplicity of the gospel, and to corrupt religion" (*Barnes' Notes on the Bible*, http://biblehub.com/commentaries/barnes/hebrews/8.htm). This new living law contained new living power to overcome the external forces of hindrance. This new law was not written on tablets of stone but on the tablet of the heart.

Perhaps the chief benefit of the new covenant is the privilege of knowing God. Following the Crucifixion, the veil of the Temple was torn, symbolically announcing the end of the stark and mysterious separation between God and humanity. Now we are able to come boldly before the throne of grace that we may obtain mercy and find grace to help in times of need (see Hebrews 4:16). To know God is to become acquainted with God. To become acquainted with God is to learn God's character, tendencies, and will. But, "It does not mean that all persons, in all lands, would then know the Lord—though the time will come

when that will be true; but the expression is to be limited by the point under discussion. That point is not that the knowledge of the Lord will fill the whole world, but that all who are interested in the new dispensation will have a much more full and clear knowledge of God than was possessed under the old. . . . Christians have a much more perfect knowledge of God and of his government than could have been learned merely from the revelations of the Old Testament" (*Barnes' Notes on the Bible*, http://biblehub.com/commentaries/barnes/hebrews/8.htm).

Here, we see highlighted another great benefit of the new covenant: forgiveness. There are many different kinds of potential sins that can be committed in this life. All of them are instances of falling short of God's glory. Some sins are by commission, and others are by omission. But through the new covenant, God has the power to wipe our slate clean of sins of the past, present, and future. This is possible through the mercy of God at work in the lives of God's people and even with those who are not yet officially God's people.

Since both covenants could not coexist simultaneously, one of the covenants (the old) had to decrease and the other covenant (the new) had to increase. In Matthew 5:17 (NIV), Jesus said, "Do not think that I have come to abolish the Law or the Prophets; I have not come to abolish them but to fulfill them." The abolition of the Law would have been catastrophic because it serves as a foundation of the new covenant. The new covenant is a clarification of the old covenant. Jesus addressed this concept and figuratively illustrated this in Matthew 9:16-17 (NIV) when He declared, "No one sews a patch of unshrunk cloth on an old garment, for the patch will pull away from the garment, making the tear worse. Neither do people pour new wine into old wineskins. If they do, the skins will burst; the wine will run out and the wineskins will be ruined. No, they pour new wine into new wineskins, and both are preserved."

of respect and appreciation for the sacrifice of Christ. The old covenant was like a tutor to help get us started and move toward greater things in the life of the Spirit. We stand in confident relationship with God made possible through Christ. May we forever resist the temptation to allow anyone or anything to damage our new covenant with God.

III. CONCLUDING REFLECTION

Jesus is the great initiator of the new covenant. We are called to remember His work to make the new covenant possible every time we partake of the Lord's Supper. This revelation alone should be enough to help us to approach the Lord's Supper with a greater sense

PRAYER

Dear God, thank You that through the new covenant we have greater access to You. Thank You for loving us enough to move us from having a "slave" relationship to the point of calling us "friend." In Jesus' name we pray. Amen.

HOME DAILY BIBLE READINGS
(May 27–June 2, 2019)

Jesus Institutes the New Covenant

MONDAY, May 27: "The Original Passover Celebration" (Deuteronomy 16:1-8)

TUESDAY, May 28: "Triumphal Entry into Jerusalem" (Mark 11:1-10)

WEDNESDAY, May 29: "Preparation for the Passover Meal" (Mark 14:12-16)

THURSDAY, May 30: "The Heart-centered New Covenant" (Jeremiah 31:31-34)

FRIDAY, May 31: "The Lord's Supper Shared with Disciples" (Luke 22:14-23)

SATURDAY, June 1: "Clean Feet, Clean Hearts" (John 13:2b-7)

SUNDAY, June 2: "Jesus Institutes the New Covenant" (Mark 14:17-24; Hebrews 8:6-7, 10-12)

---

1. *MacLaren's Commentary: Expositions of Holy Scripture*, biblehub.com

June 9, 2019   Lesson 2

JESUS SEALS THE NEW COVENANT

ADULT/YOUTH	CHILDREN
ADULT/YOUNG ADULT TOPIC: **Restored Relationships**	GENERAL LESSON TITLE: **Jesus Seals the New Promise**
YOUTH TOPIC: **Restoring Relationships**	CHILDREN'S TOPIC: **A Restored Relationship**

DEVOTIONAL READING
Psalm 22:1-8, 21b-28

ADULT/YOUTH	CHILDREN
BACKGROUND SCRIPTURE: **Mark 14:32-50; 15**	BACKGROUND SCRIPTURE: **Mark 14:32-50; 15**
PRINT PASSAGE: **Mark 15:6-15, 25-26, 33-39**	PRINT PASSAGE: **Mark 15:6-15, 25-26, 33-39**
KEY VERSE: **Mark 15:39**	KEY VERSE: **Mark 15:39**

Mark 15:6-15, 25-26, 33-39—KJV

6 Now at that feast he released unto them one prisoner, whomsoever they desired.

7 And there was one named Barabbas, which lay bound with them that had made insurrection with him, who had committed murder in the insurrection.

8 And the multitude crying aloud began to desire him to do as he had ever done unto them.

9 But Pilate answered them, saying, Will ye that I release unto you the King of the Jews?

10 For he knew that the chief priests had delivered him for envy.

11 But the chief priests moved the people, that he should rather release Barabbas unto them.

12 And Pilate answered and said again unto them, What will ye then that I shall do unto him whom ye call the King of the Jews?

13 And they cried out again, Crucify him.

14 Then Pilate said unto them, Why, what evil hath he done? And they cried out the more exceedingly, Crucify him.

Mark 15:6-15, 25-26, 33-39—NIV

6 Now it was the custom at the festival to release a prisoner whom the people requested.

7 A man called Barabbas was in prison with the insurrectionists who had committed murder in the uprising.

8 The crowd came up and asked Pilate to do for them what he usually did.

9 "Do you want me to release to you the king of the Jews?" asked Pilate,

10 knowing it was out of self-interest that the chief priests had handed Jesus over to him.

11 But the chief priests stirred up the crowd to have Pilate release Barabbas instead.

12 "What shall I do, then, with the one you call the king of the Jews?" Pilate asked them.

13 "Crucify him!" they shouted.

14 "Why? What crime has he committed?" asked Pilate. But they shouted all the louder, "Crucify him!"

15 Wanting to satisfy the crowd, Pilate released

15 And so Pilate, willing to content the people, released Barabbas unto them, and delivered Jesus, when he had scourged him, to be crucified.

.....

25 And it was the third hour, and they crucified him. 26 And the superscription of his accusation was written over, THE KING OF THE JEWS.

.....

33 And when the sixth hour was come, there was darkness over the whole land until the ninth hour. 34 And at the ninth hour Jesus cried with a loud voice, saying, Eloi, Eloi, lama sabachthani? which is, being interpreted, My God, my God, why hast thou forsaken me? 35 And some of them that stood by, when they heard it, said, Behold, he calleth Elias. 36 And one ran and filled a spunge full of vinegar, and put it on a reed, and gave him to drink, saying, Let alone; let us see whether Elias will come to take him down. 37 And Jesus cried with a loud voice, and gave up the ghost. 38 And the veil of the temple was rent in twain from the top to the bottom. 39 And when the centurion, which stood over against him, saw that he so cried out, and gave up the ghost, he said, Truly this man was the Son of God.

Barabbas to them. He had Jesus flogged, and handed him over to be crucified.

.....

25 It was nine in the morning when they crucified him. 26 The written notice of the charge against him read: THE KING OF THE JEWS.

.....

33 At noon, darkness came over the whole land until three in the afternoon. 34 And at three in the afternoon Jesus cried out in a loud voice, *"Eloi, Eloi, lema sabachthani?"* (which means "My God, my God, why have you forsaken me?"). 35 When some of those standing near heard this, they said, "Listen, he's calling Elijah." 36 Someone ran, filled a sponge with wine vinegar, put it on a staff, and offered it to Jesus to drink. "Now leave him alone. Let's see if Elijah comes to take him down," he said. 37 With a loud cry, Jesus breathed his last. 38 The curtain of the temple was torn in two from top to bottom. 39 And when the centurion, who stood there in front of Jesus, saw how he died, he said, "Surely this man was the Son of God!"

UNIFYING LESSON PRINCIPLE: All personal relationships encounter problems that result in division and strife. Who can heal the breaches and restore harmony? Mark describes how Jesus' crucifixion forges a new covenant and reconciles God and humankind.

LESSON OBJECTIVES

Upon the completion of this lesson, the students will be able to do the following:

1. Summarize Mark's account of the crucifixion of Jesus.
2. Reflect on the amazing price Jesus paid to establish a new covenant between God and humankind.
3. Pray for a restored relationship with God in light of the reconciliation that Jesus provides.

AGE-LEVEL POINTS TO BE EMPHASIZED
Teachers of ADULTS and YOUTH

—Different aspects of Pilate's character are seen in the various Gospels. In Mark, he seems to be a weak ruler who only seeks to satisfy the crowd. In John 19:1-15, he slyly manipulates the chief priests into confessing that Caesar is their king (see also John 19:21-22).

—*Barabbas* means "son of the father." Is there a

note of irony that this is the name of the man released instead of Jesus, "the Son of God" (Mark 1:1)?

—Jesus' "cry of dereliction" (Mark 15:34) is a quotation (in Aramaic) of Psalm 22:1. This cry is found only here and in Matthew 27:46. Psalm 22 seems to foreshadow the Crucifixion in several details.

—The crowd misinterpreted Jesus' cry as a call for Elijah to come to His aid (verses 35-36). Jewish piety expected Elijah to appear at Passover time to herald the coming of God's kingdom. Even today, a cup of wine is prepared for Elijah at the Passover table.

—The "curtain of the temple" (verse 38) was a partition separating the holy place from the Holy of Holies. Its tearing suggests that Jesus' death opens the way for more intimate divine-human relationship.

—Although God (1:11) and demons (1:24; 5:7) have previously acknowledged Jesus' divine identity in Mark, the centurion's confession that Jesus is God's Son (15:39) is the first time a human character comes to this realization (see 4:41).

Teachers of CHILDREN

—According to Mark 15:6, it was a custom during the time of the Feast to release a prisoner that was requested by the people.

—Crucifixion was punishment from the Roman government for rebellion.

—Jesus was not guilty of a crime under Roman law.

—Pilate did not want to execute Jesus, but the religious leaders did.

—Jesus was crucified between two thieves at the third hour.

—After Jesus cried out and breathed His last breath, "the curtain of the temple was torn in two from top to bottom" (verse 38, NIV).

THE CHRONOLOGICAL SETTING OF THE LESSON

The writing of the gospel of Mark is attributed to John Mark and the apostle Peter. This text is believed to have been written in Rome in AD 50, following the persecutions of the apostles Peter, James, and Paul by Nero, who was against the early church. The gospel of Mark is believed to have been the first of the Gospel books to have been written, giving the narratives about Jesus Christ. The gospel of Mark was originally known as *kata markon*, which means "according to Mark" during the early days of the church (bible.org). Other Gospel books include Matthew, Luke, and the gospel of John.

THE GEOGRAPHICAL AND CULTURAL SETTING OF THE LESSON

There is an agreement among the church fathers that Mark wrote his gospel in the city of Rome and that it was originally intended for the church in Rome. Mark is said to have been in Babylon alongside the apostle Peter on his missionary journey. According to Papias, the Hierapolis bishop, in his historical writings he asserts that John Mark was the interpreter of Peter. Peter is therefore the eyewitness of Mark's accounts, and Mark compiles these memoirs after Peter's death. The population in the ancient Rome spoke predominantly Latin, as it was the official language, but Greek was also one of the languages spoken by the Gentiles in Rome. The Roman culture is prevalent in this text, as we see frequent use of Latin words such as "Praetorium" (Mark 15:16) and "centurion" (Mark 15:39).

The gospel was written after the Jewish revolt and the fall of the Temple of Jerusalem at the hands of the Roman Empire in AD 70 (see Mark 13). This book gives the accounts of the early church and the persecutions that the Gentile believers were going through at the hands of Roman rulers such as Nero for following Jesus Christ and giving testimonies of His messianic work (see Mark 13:9-13). Mark 15 gives the chronological events of the trial of Jesus before Pilate, who ruled Palestine as a praetorian representative of the Roman Empire and was responsible for the verdict against and crucifixion of Christ. Mark tells of his up-close personal experience concerning the life of Jesus Christ as illustrated in Mark 14:51-52, where he becomes known as the young man who fled naked at the Garden of Gethsemane after Jesus was arrested.

The gospel also shows the suffering of the early church and the persecution of the apostles under the rule of Nero of Rome. This is clearly depicted in the Anti-Marcionite Prologue by Irenaeus, who gives the accounts of persecutions of Christians for their faith in Christ (bible.org). The cultural setting also depicts the Jewish community through the illustrations of some common elements that are attributed to Jewish worship practices (see Mark 14:12; 15:42).

PROMINENT CHARACTER(S) IN THE LESSON

Jesus Christ: Most of the events in the gospel of Mark revolve around the character, life, mission, betrayal, and persecution of Christ.

Pontius Pilate: He was a Roman governor of Judea commissioned by the Roman Emperor Tiberius. Pilate was responsible for the trial and crucifixion of Jesus Christ. He declared Christ as innocent, but he bowed to the pressure of the crowd and authorized Jesus to be flogged and crucified.

KEY TERMS IN THE LESSON

Crowd (verse 8)—Greek: *ochlos* (okh'los): a crowd, "multitude" (KJV); the common people.
Crucify (verse 14)—Greek: *stauroó* (stow-ro'-o): to fence with stakes; to crucify.
Cry (verse 37)—Greek: *phóné* (fo-nay'): a sound, noise, "voice" (KJV).
Darkness (verse 33)—Greek: *skotos* (skot'-os): darkness; opposite of light.
Prisoner (verse 6)—Greek: *desmios* (des'-mee-os): one bound; a prisoner; captive.
Released (verse 15)—Greek: *apoluó* (ap-ol-oo'-o): to set free, release.

TOPICAL OUTLINE OF THE LESSON

I. **Introduction**
   A. A Gateway to Suffering
   B. Biblical Background

II. **Exposition and Application of the Scripture**
   A. An Uneven Exchange (Mark 15:6-11)
   B. Pilate's Peer Pressure (Mark 15:12-15)
   C. The Death of Jesus (Mark 15:25-26, 33-37)
   D. The Veil Is Torn (Mark 15:38-39)

III. **Concluding Reflection**

I. INTRODUCTION

A. A Gateway to Suffering

As seen in our previous lesson, chapter 14 of the book of Mark highlights events before the death of Christ, beginning from the Lord's Supper and leading up to the events in Gethsemane. *Gethsemane* means "oil press," and olive oil symbolizes the Holy Spirit. This garden was filled with olive trees and was on a slope referred to as the Mount of Olives. It should be noted that Jesus had frequently visited this spot with His disciples whenever He wanted to get away from the crowds and spend time in prayer (see John 18:1-2; Matthew 26:34).

Mark 15 was written in AD 30 and contains forty-seven verses which continue Jesus' trials before Pontius Pilate and then His crucifixion and death. In Mark 15, Jesus is brought before the authorities of Rome, where He is sentenced to death by crucifixion. This explanation of Jesus' final day is structured carefully according to Roman customs of keeping time in three-hour intervals. Here in Mark 15, we see four critical things happen in the life of Jesus. Here, He was brought to Pilate by the Jews; the soldiers mocked Him; He was crucified, died, and was buried in a borrowed tomb. This chapter brings to light the hardest part of Jesus' life and all the suffering that He was put through and endured.

B. Biblical Background

In Mark 14:32-50, during the Lord's Supper, we see how Jesus showed a great deal of love to His disciples. The symbolism of the Communion received in the upper room was a reminder of His sacrifice and the restoration and strengthening of the relationship with Christ. All was now accomplished in Him, except dying on the Cross. Through the giving of the cup, Jesus laid the foundation of the new covenant in His blood. When He extended the cup and the disciples received it, they symbolically partook in His death and He announced that this was the seal of the new covenant which was well-known to the Jews according to Jeremiah (in Jeremiah 31:31-34).

The death of Jesus was necessary for this new covenant to be established. The breaking of bread and drinking from the cup also represented the dissolution of the bonds of earthly association between Jesus and His disciples. He no longer would drink of the fruit of the vine until the renewal of this association with them in the kingdom of God, for He would be with them again when the kingdom would be established.

Instead of Jesus' death's being the end of His relationship and bond with the disciples, Jesus actually strengthened the relationship. The death of Jesus was a part of God's plan. When Jesus was raised from the dead, He would go before the disciples to Galilee, where this relationship would move to the next level. Death was just a tool that was used to accomplish God's perfect will.

The death of Jesus was a very necessary step in God's plan for humanity to be reconciled to God. The ultimate goal was to restore the relationship between God and people through the sacrificial atonement of Jesus. The relationship between God and humanity was so important that Jesus had to die for reconciliation to occur. Jesus decided to obey God's will and die a sacrificial death for the benefit of humanity (see Mark 14:34-36). It was not Jesus' desire to die, as was made evident by Jesus' prayer to "let this cup pass from me." It is good that Jesus arrived at the place of "nevertheless, not my will but Thy will be done." It is at this place of peace and trust that we become most usable by God and most beneficial to God's kingdom.

II. EXPOSITION AND APPLICATION OF THE SCRIPTURE

A. An Uneven Exchange
(Mark 15:6-11)

Now at that feast he released unto them one prisoner, whomsoever they desired. And there was one named Barabbas, which lay bound with them that had made insurrection with him, who had committed murder in the insurrection. And the multitude crying aloud began to desire him to do as he had ever done unto them. But Pilate answered them, saying, Will ye that I release unto you the King of the Jews? For he knew that the chief priests had delivered him for envy. But the chief priests moved the people, that he should rather release Barabbas unto them.

The Passover was celebrated by the Jews in memory of their deliverance from Egypt. Part of the tradition was to release a prisoner as a part of the feast. This custom may have originated with the Jews and possibly continued through the Roman governors who were also accustomed to periodically allowing amnesty for convicted criminals. The rules for the prisoner release do not seem to have been hard and fast, with some liberal parameters for personal discretion of governmental leadership.

According to Luke 23:19, Barabbas (verse 7) was a rebel and a robber, but Mark alone records the fact that his fellow insurgents were also imprisoned with him. In addition to insurgency, he seems to have also been charged with murder. Pilate appears to have thought that by offering to release someone so notorious and dangerous as Barabbas as a choice instead of Jesus, they would surely opt for Jesus, if for no other reason than the safety of the community. But Pilate miscalculated the level of distaste and pure hatred that the Pharisees, chief priests, and scribes had toward Jesus. The word *Barabbas*, better written "Bar-Abbas," means "son of father."

The tone and words used by Pilate (verse 9) suggest a serious case of faulty leadership, in that he placed something as serious as the decision of a man's life or death into the hands of a mob. Surely, Pilate abdicated his responsibility as a decision maker and left it up to the crowd to choose. According to the *Pulpit Commentary*, "Envy was the low passion that influenced the chief priests. They saw that Jesus was gaining a great and increasing influence over the people by the sublime beauty of his character, by the fame of his miracles, and the constraining power of his words. And hence they concluded that, unless he was arrested in his course, and put out of the way, their own influence would soon be gone. The whole world was going after him. Therefore, he must be destroyed."

Pilate's wife had sent him a message about her dream concerning Jesus. Her stark and cryptic warning is recorded in Matthew 27:19b (NIV): "Don't have anything to do with that innocent man, for I have suffered a great deal today in a dream because of him." Perhaps this occurrence intensified his focus and feeling, but it did not seem to alter the pronouncement of crucifixion. After the chief priests incited the people with lies and insinuations, they chose Barabbas.

B. Pilate's Peer Pressure
(Mark 15:12-15)

And Pilate answered and said again unto them, What will ye then that I shall do unto him whom ye call the King of the Jews? And they cried out again, Crucify him. Then Pilate said unto them, Why, what evil hath he done? And they cried out the more exceedingly, Crucify him. And so Pilate, willing to content the people, released Barabbas unto them, and delivered Jesus, when he had scourged him, to be crucified.

Not only did Pilate relinquish responsibility to choose whom to release (verse 12), but he also allowed the crowd to dictate the sentence for Jesus. This question of what to do with Jesus was not only before the crowd of Jesus' day, but it is also for the people of today. Jesus can be selected or rejected, but one thing that cannot be done is to ignore Jesus. Many seek to choose what they think is a safe option of ignoring Jesus, but we are compelled in life to make a choice. Revelation 3:15-16 (NIV) records, "I know your deeds, that you are neither cold nor hot. I wish you were either one or the other! So, because you are lukewarm—neither hot nor cold—I am about to spit you out of my mouth." Neutrality is not a viable option. Interestingly, those who are "all the way wrong" are closer to finding the right path than those who are in the middle. Even in church, there are those who are lost in the house. They know how to do church well, but they do not know how to do discipleship well.

Joshua 24:15 reads, "And if it seem evil unto you to serve the LORD, choose you this day whom ye will serve; whether the gods which your fathers served that were on the other side of the flood, or the gods of the Amorites, in whose land ye dwell: but as for me and my house, we will serve the LORD." It is important to actively choose God, because failing to decide anything effectively decides against God.

Of all the forms of capital punishment, crucifixion (verse 13) stands as one of the cruelest forms of death known to man. The *Matthew Henry Concise Commentary* notes, "The thought that no one ever was so shamefully treated, as the only perfectly wise, holy, and excellent Person that ever appeared on earth, leads the serious mind to strong views of man's wickedness and enmity to God." It is difficult to grasp why someone so holy, so innocent, and so lowly had to be subjected to such a horrible form of death. The pre-Crucifixion scourging of Jesus was in itself horrendous. The tremendous loss of blood, the deeply damaged flesh, and the sheer exhaustion of the process was enough to kill any man. But Jesus endured the pain and the shame because He was committed to fulfill the purpose for which He had come to earth: the salvation and redemption of the world. What an ironic contrast—that we who deserve death are given eternal life through the death and substitutionary atonement of Jesus.

Pilate's acute lack of leadership was in full bloom when he released Barabbas and handed over Jesus to the murderous mob (verse 15). The trial of Jesus, the sentencing of Jesus, the scourging of Jesus, and the crucifixion of Jesus were all illegal and unwarranted. However, unbeknownst to Pilate and the mob, they were simply cooperating with the powerful plan of God that had been prophesied many years before in Isaiah 53:5—"But he was wounded for our transgressions, he was bruised for our iniquities: the chastisement of our peace was upon him; and with his stripes we are healed."

C. The Death of Jesus
(Mark 15:25-26, 33-37)

And it was the third hour, and they crucified him. And the superscription of his accusation was written over, THE KING OF THE JEWS. . . . And when the sixth hour was come, there was darkness over the whole land until the ninth hour. And at the ninth hour Jesus cried with a loud voice, saying, Eloi, Eloi, lama sabachthani? which is, being interpreted, My God, my God, why hast thou forsaken me? And some of them that stood by, when they heard it, said, Behold, he calleth Elias. And one ran and filled a spunge full of vinegar, and put it on a reed, and gave him to drink, saying, Let alone; let us see whether Elias will come to take him down. And Jesus cried with a loud voice, and gave up the ghost.

Jesus was twice called the "King of the Jews": once at birth by the wise men (see Matthew 2:2), and again at His trial in Mark 15:2. All four Gospels acknowledge that Pilate ordered this title to be inscribed on a sign and placed above the head of Jesus on the cross (see Matthew 27:37; Mark 15:9; Luke 23:38; John 19:3). But only non-Jews used this title to refer to Jesus which, highlighting John 1:11 (NKJV), reads, "He came to His own, and His own did not receive Him." The title "King of the Jews" carries political implications, because He was chosen to lead the people. It also has messianic ramifications, because Jesus was of the lineage of David to serve as the deliverer of the Jewish people.

Jesus was completely divine and completely human. Jesus was the Word that existed from the beginning but became flesh. In His humanity, Jesus questioned God's location and God's assistance during this extreme time of need.

One possibility for the statement in verse 35 is that the words of Jesus were simply misunderstood and misinterpreted. But considering the jocular atmosphere of mockery that existed at the scene of the Cross, the reference to Elijah could have been a sarcastic gesture of disregard for Jesus' pain. Jesus called upon Eli, God, who was alive and could have intervened to rectify the situation, unlike Elias—who was dead and could have done nothing.

Amazingly, despite all the physical, mental, and emotional trauma that Jesus had experienced at the end of His life, He was still able to muster enough strength and energy to utter a loud cry. This isolated incident is a testament to the sheer will of Jesus to press past the pain in order to broadcast the truth.

D. The Veil Is Torn
(Mark 15:38-39)

And the veil of the temple was rent in twain from the top to the bottom. And when the centurion, which stood over against him, saw that he so cried out, and gave up the ghost, he said, Truly this man was the Son of God.

At the moment of Jesus' death, a thick cloud of darkness descended from noon until three in the afternoon. Then, as now, this was a very unusual occurrence. Even a total eclipse of the sun does not last nearly that long. *Matthew Henry's Concise Commentary* records that "the Jews were doing their utmost to extinguish the Sun of Righteousness. The darkness signified the cloud which the human soul of Christ was under, when he was making it an offering for sin. He did not complain that his disciples forsook him, but that his Father forsook him. In this especially he was made sin for us." Even in death, Jesus was a witness. As we develop a clear understanding of the crucifixion of Christ, our faith will be strengthened, and our witness will be effective.

III. CONCLUDING REFLECTION

In John 10:10b, Jesus announced one of the reasons for why He came to the earth: "I have come that they may have life, and have it to the full" (NIV). This fullness of life was made possible when Jesus served as a mediator between the holy God and sinful humanity, and Jesus emptied Himself in crucifixion. This sacrificial act of atonement made possible the restoration of the damaged relationship. When we confess our sins, God is faithful to forgive us and to cleanse us from all unrighteousness, and we can receive the gift of the new covenant. Once we enter God's rest, we can then daily live out our faith in practical ways and share God's love with others in our world of influence.

PRAYER

Lord, thank You for Your unselfish sacrifice on the cross of Calvary. Let us give of ourselves to others as You have laid down Your life for us. In Jesus' name we pray. Amen.

HOME DAILY BIBLE READINGS
(June 3-9, 2019)

Jesus Seals the New Covenant
MONDAY, June 3: "Turmoil at the Last Supper" (Mark 14:26-31)
TUESDAY, June 4: "Jesus Prays while the Disciples Sleep" (Mark 14:32-42)
WEDNESDAY, June 5: "Jesus Is Betrayed and Arrested" (Mark 14:43-50)
THURSDAY, June 6: "Jesus Is Crucified before Friends and Enemies" (Mark 15:16-24)
FRIDAY, June 7: "Two Criminals Are Crucified with Jesus" (Mark 15:27-32)
SATURDAY, June 8: "Faithful Women" (Mark 15:40-47)
SUNDAY, June 9: "New Covenant Sealed with Jesus' Blood" (Mark 15:6-15, 25-26, 33-39)

June 16, 2019 Lesson 3

THE NEW COVENANT'S SACRIFICE

ADULT/YOUTH	CHILDREN
ADULT/YOUNG ADULT TOPIC: **Cleaning Up the Mess** YOUTH TOPIC: **The Gift of Second Chances**	GENERAL LESSON TITLE: **The New Promise's Offering** CHILDREN'S TOPIC: **A Special Offering**

DEVOTIONAL READING
Psalm 50:1-15

ADULT/YOUTH	CHILDREN
BACKGROUND SCRIPTURE: **Hebrews 9:11-28** PRINT PASSAGE: **Hebrews 9:11-22** KEY VERSE: **Hebrews 9:22**	BACKGROUND SCRIPTURE: **Hebrews 9:11-28** PRINT PASSAGE: **Hebrews 9:11-22** KEY VERSE: **Hebrews 9:15a**

Hebrews 9:11-22—KJV

11 But Christ being come an high priest of good things to come, by a greater and more perfect tabernacle, not made with hands, that is to say, not of this building;

12 Neither by the blood of goats and calves, but by his own blood he entered in once into the holy place, having obtained eternal redemption for us.

13 For if the blood of bulls and of goats, and the ashes of an heifer sprinkling the unclean, sanctifieth to the purifying of the flesh:

14 How much more shall the blood of Christ, who through the eternal Spirit offered himself without spot to God, purge your conscience from dead works to serve the living God?

15 And for this cause he is the mediator of the new testament, that by means of death, for the redemption of the transgressions that were under the first testament, they which are called might receive the promise of eternal inheritance.

Hebrews 9:11-22—NIV

11 But when Christ came as high priest of the good things that are now already here, he went through the greater and more perfect tabernacle that is not made with human hands, that is to say, is not a part of this creation.

12 He did not enter by means of the blood of goats and calves; but he entered the Most Holy Place once for all by his own blood, thus obtaining eternal redemption.

13 The blood of goats and bulls and the ashes of a heifer sprinkled on those who are ceremonially unclean sanctify them so that they are outwardly clean.

14 How much more, then, will the blood of Christ, who through the eternal Spirit offered himself unblemished to God, cleanse our consciences from acts that lead to death, so that we may serve the living God!

15 For this reason Christ is the mediator of a new covenant, that those who are called may receive the promised eternal inheritance—now that he has died as a ransom to set them free from the sins committed under the first covenant.

16 For where a testament is, there must also of necessity be the death of the testator.	16 In the case of a will, it is necessary to prove the death of the one who made it,
17 For a testament is of force after men are dead: otherwise it is of no strength at all while the testator liveth.	17 because a will is in force only when somebody has died; it never takes effect while the one who made it is living.
18 Whereupon neither the first testament was dedicated without blood.	18 This is why even the first covenant was not put into effect without blood.
19 For when Moses had spoken every precept to all the people according to the law, he took the blood of calves and of goats, with water, and scarlet wool, and hyssop, and sprinkled both the book, and all the people,	19 When Moses had proclaimed every command of the law to all the people, he took the blood of calves, together with water, scarlet wool and branches of hyssop, and sprinkled the scroll and all the people.
20 Saying, This is the blood of the testament which God hath enjoined unto you.	20 He said, "This is the blood of the covenant, which God has commanded you to keep."
21 Moreover he sprinkled with blood both the tabernacle, and all the vessels of the ministry.	21 In the same way, he sprinkled with the blood both the tabernacle and everything used in its ceremonies.
22 And almost all things are by the law purged with blood; and without shedding of blood is no remission.	22 In fact, the law requires that nearly everything be cleansed with blood, and without the shedding of blood there is no forgiveness.

UNIFYING LESSON PRINCIPLE: People have devised many methods to deal with the sense of moral uncleanness that their misdeeds incur. How can we be definitively cleansed of guilt? Through shedding His blood and dying, Jesus once and for all fulfilled God's new covenant to forgive sins and guarantee eternal life.

LESSON OBJECTIVES

Upon the completion of this lesson, the students will be able to do the following:

1. Explore the symbolism of blood in the Old Testament in relation to the saving work of Jesus on the Cross.
2. Sense their moral shortcomings and the need for definitive cleansing before the holy God.
3. Rejoice in the purification for sins that Jesus accomplished.

AGE-LEVEL POINTS TO BE EMPHASIZED

Teachers of ADULTS and YOUTH

—"Once for all" (Greek: *ephapax*, verse 12) contrasts the various and repeated sacrifices of the Old Testament system with the definitive sacrifice of Christ (see Hebrews 7:27; 10:10).

—The great complexity of the Old Testament sacrificial system is highlighted throughout this passage, with reference to numerous aspects of its sacrificial regulations (see verses 12-13, 19-20).

—The key symbolism in this passage is not strictly "guilt" and "forgiveness" but, rather, "defilement" and "purification." Christ's blood cleanses us from the stain or contagion of sin.

—Verses 15-18 feature a play on the Greek word *diathēkē*, which can mean either "covenant" or "will." Paul does something similar in Galatians 3:15-18.

—"The shedding of blood" is a Greek neologism: *haimatekchysia*. This is more literally the "application" or "sprinkling" of blood, not its shedding. The imagery is not of the moment at which the sacrificial animal is killed but rather the moment at which its blood is applied to the cultic vessels to cleanse them from ritual contamination.

—The writer nowhere explains why blood is necessary for purification. It is enough for him to assert that it is.

Teachers of CHILDREN

—Success is identified as accepting Jesus' sacrifice for our sin, not practicing sinful acts, and allowing the blood of Jesus to cleanse our minds.

—The shedding of blood for the forgiveness of sin in the Old Testament was offered through the sacrifice of animals.

—Jesus is the perfect sacrifice, and no other sacrifice is needed for the forgiveness of sin.

—Jesus' blood sacrifice is a new life and an opportunity to experience living in the will of God.

—In Jesus, spiritual death and our separation from God have been removed.

—Christ's death and resurrection offer all who would believe victory over sin and death.

THE CHRONOLOGICAL SETTING OF THE LESSON

The authorship of the book of Hebrews has not been clearly proven. Some scholars argue that it was written by the apostle Paul, while others claim it was written by Barnabas, who was a close associate of Paul's while on their evangelistic missionary journey. Although there is no absolute certainty as to its authorship, most likely Paul wrote it—as illustrated through the style of writing which depicts Paul's customary use of the closing phrase, "Grace be with you all." However, some argue that the author was a disciple of Paul's (bible.org).

The book of Hebrews is regarded as one of the General Epistles alongside the books of James; 1 and 2 Peter; 1, 2, and 3 John; and Jude. All these letters have one thing in common: they encourage the early Christians to emulate the teachings of Christ despite persecution. They also share the themes of love, hope, and faith (see Hebrews 5:11-14; 10:19-39).

THE GEOGRAPHICAL AND CULTURAL SETTING OF THE LESSON

The book of Hebrews is believed to have been written between AD 60 and AD 65. This was before the destruction of the Temple and the City of Jerusalem in AD 70, as illustrated in Scripture by use of present tense while speaking of the Temple and the activities of the priests (see Hebrews 9:6-13; 10:1; 13:10-11). Hebrews also asserts that Jesus Christ is the High Priest who fulfills prophecies of the Old Testament prophets concerning the Son of God. The letter was originally addressed to Jewish Christians who were tempted to revert to Judaism.

The phrase that is used to introduce the book "to the Hebrews" shows that the original recipients of the letter were the Christian Jews as depicted through continuous arguments and justifications that Jesus Christ is superior to the Jewish institutions and the Old Testament prophets. The author also quotes heavily from Old Testament Hebrew

Scripture, and this implies that the recipients of this letter were Jewish and not Gentile converts. The author of this letter is also passing on greetings from Italy, and he informs the recipients that he may come to visit them along with Timothy (bible .org). The book of Hebrews gives the accounts of persecutions and imprisonment of Christians, and the author encourages the recipients to persevere (see Hebrews 10:32-34; 13:3).

PROMINENT CHARACTER(S) IN THE LESSON

Jesus Christ: He is the revealer of God's will and salvation of the Christians. The letter focuses on Jesus as the mediator between God and the Israelites, and on Jesus as the creator of the new covenant.

Melchizedek: He is the priest forever, predating the tribe of Levi. Originating the priesthood before God, he is also the king of Salem (traditionally believed to be the original name of Jerusalem) and was the one who blessed Abram in the Old Testament.

KEY TERMS IN THE LESSON

Blood (verse 14)—Greek: *haima* (hah'-ee-mah): blood; refers to the seat of life; of those things that resemble blood, grape juice; bloodshed; to be shed by violence; slay; murder.

Eternal (verse 12)—Greek: *aiónios* (ahee-o'-nee-os): eternal; unending.

Greater (verse 11)—Greek: *megas* (meg'-as): large, great (in the widest sense).

Mediator (verse 15)—Greek: *mesités* (mes-ee'-tace): a mediator; intermediary; a go-between; arbiter; agent of something good.

Redemption (verse 12)—Greek: *lutrósis* (loo'-tro-sis): liberation; deliverance; release.

Sanctify (verse 13)—Greek: *hagiazó* (hag-ee-ad'-zo): to make; to create, shape, form; "sanctifieth" (KJV).

Tabernacle (verse 11)—Greek: *skéné* (skay-nay'): a tent; booth; tabernacle; abode; dwelling; mansion; habitation.

TOPICAL OUTLINE OF THE LESSON

I. Introduction
   A. An Acceptable Sacrifice
   B. Biblical Background

II. Exposition and Application of the Scripture
   A. Christ the High Priest (Hebrews 9:11-14)
   B. Christ the Mediator (Hebrews 9:15-18)
   C. Christ's Blood of the Covenant (Hebrews 9:19-22)

III. Concluding Reflection

I. INTRODUCTION
A. An Acceptable Sacrifice

Hebrews 9 tells how worship in the Old Testament could not make worshippers perfect through adherence to drink, food, various washings, and regulations for the body. When Christ came, He entered the heavenly tabernacle and shed His own blood on the mercy seat. His blood was the only acceptable sacrifice, as the blood of bulls and goats would never be able to cleanse the conscience of the worshipper. The blood of Christ is able to completely save and cleanse us thoroughly from every mess of sin and guilt, making us whole and without blemish or accusation before God our Father. Christ's appearance at the consummation of the ages had put away sin by His sacrifice and made the one who trusts in Him blameless.

In verse 1, the old covenant ritual is described, and the author does not make mention of the covenants made with Noah or Abraham in the Old Testament, even though these covenants came first. By "first," the author referred to the covenant made at Sinai (see Exodus 19–24), because this is the covenant that Jesus had replaced with the new covenant. Laws of how people could approach God were contained in the Sinai covenant, which was fulfilled by the death and resurrection of Christ.

B. Biblical Background

The coming of Christ as a high priest brought spiritual advantages and blessings, and now we have forgiveness and direct access to God. When Jesus became flesh in order to fulfill the covenant, He did it better, not by imitation. He became the sacrificial lamb and shed His blood for the remission of sin. There is an important difference between the animal sacrifices of the Old Testament and Jesus, who is the New Testament sacrifice. Whereas the Old Testament sacrifice required sacrifices to be performed continually and yet could not wash away the sins of the people, the New Testament sacrifice needed only to be performed once and for all by Jesus (see Numbers 19:1-22). Christ had willingly offered a perfect and better sacrifice, which cleanses us inwardly from every sin and enables us to worship God with total confidence. The blood of Jesus has washed and purified us, making Christ the mediator of the new covenant—thus our sins are all gone! And our relationship with God is renewed.

In the Old Testament, the Law required that nearly everything be cleansed with blood, without which there is no forgiveness. In the rituals to be performed according to the Law of Moses, blood is a prerequisite for cleansing. Unfortunately, these droplets of blood eventually did not make anything physically clean. To eliminate defilement, imperfection, guilt, sin, and anything that could hinder them from God's presence, the Israelites needed forgiveness—which only the blood of Jesus could provide.

Animal blood had no power to effect spiritual changes, as animal sacrifices could not eliminate sin. Nevertheless, the old covenant still required animal sacrifices for forgiveness. The author further tells us how the earthly tabernacle needed to be ritually purified by animal sacrifices, but the heavenly holy place required a much different and greater sacrifice. For the spiritual relationship between God and people to be restored, there was a need for a perfect sacrifice without guilt and sin.

Christ Jesus did not enter the sanctuary made with human hands, as it was only a copy of the true tabernacle. He entered heaven to appear before God's presence on our behalf. He was dealing with the real spiritual problem, and He did do it in heaven. It is a better place, and a better sacrifice!

Christ's work was both physical and spiritual. He had to become human in order to redeem humans. Jesus' redemption had to be on the spiritual level as well. He was untainted by sin and gave His life willingly for others. Christ is now in heaven, interceding on our behalf. By becoming the sacrificial Lamb, He has eliminated the distance between God and humanity, and this sacrifice is still fully effective for all time.

II. EXPOSITION AND APPLICATION OF THE SCRIPTURE

A. Christom the High Priest
(Hebrews 9:11-14)

But Christ being come an high priest of good things to come, by a greater and more perfect tabernacle, not made with hands, that is to say, not of this building; Neither by the blood of goats and calves, but by his own blood he entered in once into the holy place, having obtained eternal redemption for us. For if the blood of bulls and of goats, and the ashes of an heifer sprinkling the unclean, sanctifieth to the purifying of the flesh: How much more shall the blood of Christ, who through the eternal Spirit offered himself without spot to God, purge your conscience from dead works to serve the living God?

Everything from the past, present, or future that is good is founded on the office of Christ and is accessible through Christ. Through entering heaven, Christ has obtained eternal redemption. The function of the sacrifices in the Old Testament was to make people ceremonially clean according to the Levitical laws of the time. However, that cleansing process was only on the exterior or surface level.

The power of the blood of Christ is rooted in the reality of Christ's sinlessness (verse 12). Since the blood of Christ was sinless, that same blood can cleanse the guilty conscience, and it can cleanse from sinful works.

The ashes of the heifer (verse 13) were to be mixed with water in order to purify those who had been ceremonially defiled by contact with dead bodies (see Numbers 19). The ashes of the sacrifice were for recurring cases of known defilement, and the sin offerings ("goats and bulls") were for situations of unknown defilement (*Pulpit Commentary*). This remedy for sin was in the same class with general sin offerings for the congregation. The Old Testament Levitical system of laws was a complex and sometimes confusing set of rules

and regulations that intimidated people and was a burden to many who felt inadequate to completely obey all the laws. Consequently, when Jesus came to be the ultimate sacrifice, He effectively fulfilled the Law and made it unnecessary to continue many of the strict rituals of the Old Testament. The reality of this did not sit well with the religious aristocracy, but it was good news to the ears of the Gentiles who felt that they had access to the only true God for the first time in their lives.

The substitutionary blood of Christ is unquestionably more valuable than and greatly superior to the natural blood of animals. There is no power or promise in the blood of animals, but there is healing and purpose in the blood of Christ. Verse 14 acknowledges several reasons for this reality. The first reason is the source of the blood which comes through the Spirit. Second, the condition of the sacrifice is that it (Christ) is without blemish or fault. No other human or animal qualifies to serve as the Lamb of God who takes away the sin of the world (see 1 Peter 1:19).

B. Christ the Mediator
(Hebrews 9:15-18)

And for this cause he is the mediator of the new testament, that by means of death, for the redemption of the transgressions that were under the first testament, they which are called might receive the promise of eternal inheritance. For where a testament is, there must also of necessity be the death of the testator. For a testament is of force after men are dead: otherwise it is of no strength at all while the testator liveth. Whereupon neither the first testament was dedicated without blood.

Verse 15 reflects Hebrews 9:11-12. The predominant idea in Hebrews 9 is the establishment of a new covenant, and the old covenant has already been referred to three times in this very chapter (see verses 1, 4, and 15).

The death of Christ was a payment to God for the debt created by our sin. "The covenant and the promise relate to the establishment of the better future. Death was necessary alike for both. The offering of Christ's life (Matt. xx. 28) was a ransom or an offering for sin; it was also a sacrifice inaugurating a new covenant, which contained the promise of the eternal inheritance. See [Hebrews 9:16-18]; also [Galatians 3:13-14], where the thought is very similar" (*The Commentary for Schools*, edited by C. J. Ellicott, p. 156).

The binding spiritual agreements between God and humanity are sometimes called *covenants*. A covenant is different from a contract in that a covenant is based on trust, and a contract is based on distrust. Verses 16 and 17 compare the activation of a spiritual covenant to that of an earthly will. Earthly wills only go into effect when someone dies. (That is one reason it was so disrespectful in the parable of the Prodigal Son for the younger son to ask for his inheritance while the father was still alive.) From a spiritual perspective, Christ had to die in order for salvation to become available to all.

As *Matthew Henry's Commentary* states, all, by sin, had become guilty before God, had forfeited everything that is good; but God, willing to show the greatness of His mercy, proclaimed a covenant of grace.

The shedding of Christ's blood presented a powerful picture of His willingly losing His own life in order to give life to others. Sin made the sacrifice necessary, and God's grace made the covenant possible. First Peter 3:21-22 (NIV) highlights the figurative death through baptism that occurs in the life of everyone who embraces the new covenant through God's grace: "And this water symbolizes baptism that now saves you also—not the removal of dirt from the body but the pledge of a clear conscience toward God. It saves you by the resurrection of Jesus Christ, who has gone into heaven and is at God's right hand—with angels, authorities and powers in submission to him." Galatians 2:20 (NIV) further expresses a sense of figurative voluntary death to self on a regular basis in order to live to Christ: "I have been crucified with Christ and I no longer live, but Christ lives in me. The life I now live in the body, I live by faith in the Son of God, who loved me and gave himself for me."

C. Christ's Blood of the Covenant (Hebrews 9:19-22)

For when Moses had spoken every precept to all the people according to the law, he took the blood of calves and of goats, with water, and scarlet wool, and hyssop, and sprinkled both the book, and all the people, Saying, This is the blood of the testament which God hath enjoined unto you. Moreover he sprinkled with blood both the tabernacle, and all the vessels of the ministry. And almost all things are by the law purged with blood; and without shedding of blood is no remission.

As the hand-picked communicator of God's laws, Moses demonstrated his obedience to God by ensuring that all of God's commands were securely delivered to all the people (verse 19). One incorrect addition or one small omission could have proven disastrous for generations who were to follow God's commands in the future. The Old Testament rendering of this event is found in Exodus 24: "When Moses went and told the people all the Lord's words and laws, they responded with one voice, 'Everything the LORD has said we will do'" (verse 3b, NIV). Matthew 5:18 (NIV) further reflects this concept: "For truly I tell you, until heaven and earth disappear, not the smallest letter, not the least stroke of a pen, will by any means disappear from the Law until everything is accomplished."

The reference to the blood of calves refers to those sacrificed by the young men in Exodus 24:5. The peace offerings were of oxen, and the burnt offerings were possibly goats which were also used on the Day of Atonement. The reference to water here and in many other places in Scripture is related to spiritual cleansing. Also used for ritual purification were scarlet wool and hyssop. *Hyssop* is an herb in the mint family and is useful—having cleansing, medicinal, and flavoring properties. It was commonly used in the Middle East in a wide variety of ways, including for spicing, healing, and cleaning.

The blood of Christ is the immovable foundation of this testament (verse 20), which is reflected in Exodus 24:8. Another Scripture which can be used for comparison and is related to this concept is the Scripture commonly used as a part of Holy Communion: "In the same way, after supper he took the cup, saying, 'This cup is the new covenant in my blood; do this, whenever you drink it, in remembrance of me'" (1 Corinthians 11:25, NIV).

The tabernacle was a structure that was at the center of the worship for the people of Israel (verse 21). This lasted "from shortly after the exodus until it was replaced by Solomon's temple around 960 b.c. The term 'tabernacle' is sometimes used to refer to one part of a larger complex: the tent-like structure that stood within a court enclosed by linen curtains. At other times the term describes the entire complex" (*Baker's Evangelical Dictionary of Biblical Theology*, https://www.biblestudytools.com/dictionaries/bakers-evangelical-dictionary/tabernacle.html).

The Pentateuch does not mention sprinkling of blood on the tabernacle or its furniture. It does, however, acknowledge anointing with oil in Leviticus 8:10. "But the garments of Aaron and his sons are said to have been sprinkled with the blood as well as with the anointing oil (Hebrews 8:30) . . . . [The writer may be following the more] traditional account, with which there is still nothing in the Pentateuch inconsistent. Be it observed again that the force of the argument does not depend on these added details, but on the general principle, abundantly expressed in the original record, which is assorted in the following verse" (*Pulpit Commentary*, http://biblehub.com/commentaries/hebrews/9-21.htm).

The central act during the sacrifice was the pouring out of the blood on the altar (verse 22), as found in Leviticus 17:11. Of course, this pouring of the blood was preceded by the initial slaying of the sacrificial animal. Luke 22:20 connects to this concept: "This cup is the new testament in my blood, which is shed for you." Another favorite phrase the apostle Paul used is "remission of sins." This has a connection with repaying a debt (see Matthew 6:12; 18:27, 32). The imagery is of our sins' being the debts that were paid in full by the death of Christ on the Cross. This idea is captured in the lyrics of the song by Ellis J. Crum entitled, "He Paid a Debt He Did Not Owe." The lyrics are as follows:

He paid a debt He did not owe, I owed a debt I could not pay,
I needed someone to wash my sins away.
And now I sing a brand new song: Amazing Grace,
Christ Jesus paid a debt that I could never pay.
My debt He paid upon the cross,
He cleansed my soul from all its dross,
I tho't that no one could all my sins erase,
But now I sing a brand new song: Amazing Grace.

III. CONCLUDING REFLECTION

The well-known song written by Robert Lowery poses this question: "What can wash away my sin?" The answer is this: nothing but the blood of Jesus. No matter how much moral dirt we may accumulate, no case is beyond the ability of Jesus to reach and to wash. We do not have to live lives burdened by the guilt of sin. The forgiveness and cleansing power offered by the sacrificial Lamb of God is extended to all who believe and receive God's forgiveness.

PRAYER

Dear God, thank You for the precious gift of Jesus, who offers us not only second chances but also multiple opportunities to get it right. Let us never be guilty of taking advantage of that costly grace that was purchased on Calvary's cross. In Jesus' name we pray. Amen.

HOME DAILY BIBLE READINGS
(June 10-16, 2019)

The New Covenant's Sacrifice

MONDAY, June 10: "The People Promise to Obey" (Exodus 24:3-8)

TUESDAY, June 11: "Aaron Performs the Atoning Sin Sacrifice" (Leviticus 16:11-19)

WEDNESDAY, June 12: "Redeemed and Purified" (Titus 2:11-15)

THURSDAY, June 13: "Entering the Sanctuary by Jesus' Blood" (Hebrews 10:19-25)

FRIDAY, June 14: "The Time Has Come" (Hebrews 9:1-10)

SATURDAY, June 15: "Christ, the Final Sacrifice for Sin" (Hebrews 9:23-28)

SUNDAY, June 16: "Christ, Mediator of the New Covenant" (Hebrews 9:11-22)

June 23, 2019   **Lesson 4**

HEARTS UNITED IN LOVE

ADULT/YOUTH	**CHILDREN**
ADULT/YOUNG ADULT TOPIC: Stronger Together	**GENERAL LESSON TITLE: Hearts United in Love**
YOUTH TOPIC: Stronger Together	**CHILDREN'S TOPIC: Team Strong!**

DEVOTIONAL READING
1 Corinthians 3:10-17

ADULT/YOUTH	**CHILDREN**
BACKGROUND SCRIPTURE: Colossians 2:1-15	**BACKGROUND SCRIPTURE: Colossians 2:1-15**
PRINT PASSAGE: Colossians 2:1-15	**PRINT PASSAGE: Colossians 2:1-15**
KEY VERSES: Colossians 2:6-7	**KEY VERSES: Colossians 2:6-7**

Colossians 2:1-15—KJV

FOR I would that ye knew what great conflict I have for you, and for them at Laodicea, and for as many as have not seen my face in the flesh;

2 That their hearts might be comforted, being knit together in love, and unto all riches of the full assurance of understanding, to the acknowledgement of the mystery of God, and of the Father, and of Christ;

3 In whom are hid all the treasures of wisdom and knowledge.

4 And this I say, lest any man should beguile you with enticing words.

5 For though I be absent in the flesh, yet am I with you in the spirit, joying and beholding your order, and the stedfastness of your faith in Christ.

6 As ye have therefore received Christ Jesus the Lord, so walk ye in him:

7 Rooted and built up in him, and stablished in the faith, as ye have been taught, abounding therein with thanksgiving.

8 Beware lest any man spoil you through philosophy

Colossians 2:1-15—NIV

I WANT you to know how hard I am contending for you and for those at Laodicea, and for all who have not met me personally.

2 My goal is that they may be encouraged in heart and united in love, so that they may have the full riches of complete understanding, in order that they may know the mystery of God, namely, Christ,

3 in whom are hidden all the treasures of wisdom and knowledge.

4 I tell you this so that no one may deceive you by fine-sounding arguments.

5 For though I am absent from you in body, I am present with you in spirit and delight to see how disciplined you are and how firm your faith in Christ is.

6 So then, just as you received Christ Jesus as Lord, continue to live your lives in him,

7 rooted and built up in him, strengthened in the faith as you were taught, and overflowing with thankfulness.

8 See to it that no one takes you captive through hollow

and vain deceit, after the tradition of men, after the rudiments of the world, and not after Christ.

9 For in him dwelleth all the fulness of the Godhead bodily.

10 And ye are complete in him, which is the head of all principality and power:

11 In whom also ye are circumcised with the circumcision made without hands, in putting off the body of the sins of the flesh by the circumcision of Christ:

12 Buried with him in baptism, wherein also ye are risen with him through the faith of the operation of God, who hath raised him from the dead.

13 And you, being dead in your sins and the uncircumcision of your flesh, hath he quickened together with him, having forgiven you all trespasses;

14 Blotting out the handwriting of ordinances that was against us, which was contrary to us, and took it out of the way, nailing it to his cross;

15 And having spoiled principalities and powers, he made a shew of them openly, triumphing over them in it.

and deceptive philosophy, which depends on human tradition and the elemental spiritual forces of this world rather than on Christ.

9 For in Christ all the fullness of the Deity lives in bodily form,

10 and in Christ you have been brought to fullness. He is the head over every power and authority.

11 In him you were also circumcised with a circumcision not performed by human hands. Your whole self ruled by the flesh was put off when you were circumcised by Christ,

12 having been buried with him in baptism, in which you were also raised with him through your faith in the working of God, who raised him from the dead.

13 When you were dead in your sins and in the uncircumcision of your flesh, God made you alive with Christ. He forgave us all our sins,

14 having canceled the charge of our legal indebtedness, which stood against us and condemned us; he has taken it away, nailing it to the cross.

15 And having disarmed the powers and authorities, he made a public spectacle of them, triumphing over them by the cross.

UNIFYING LESSON PRINCIPLE: People bind themselves together by mutual bonds of love and commitment. How can communities avoid losing their identities while under attack? Paul urged the Colossians to be united in love in order to fully understand the rich treasures offered to them by faith so that they could resist false teachings and come to appreciate their new spiritual standing in Christ.

LESSON OBJECTIVES

Upon the completion of this lesson, the students will be able to do the following:

1. Contrast the deceptive philosophies of false teachers with the true faith in which the Colossians had been established.
2. Long to be rooted and built up in Christ and more firmly established in the faith we have received.
3. Embrace what Paul teaches about our new standing in Christ as a guard against false teaching.

AGE-LEVEL POINTS TO BE EMPHASIZED

Teachers of ADULTS and YOUTH

—Paul stressed, in this letter, knowledge of God's mystery hidden in Christ Himself because He was refuting heresy that emphasized knowledge as the means of salvation. (Colossians 2:3)

—Paul was counteracting the Colossian heresy which, in part, taught that for salvation one needed to combine faith in Christ with secret knowledge and with man-made regulations concerning such practices as circumcision, eating and drinking, and observance of religious festivals. (Colossians 2:8)

—The declaration that the very essence of deity was present in totality in Jesus' human body was a direct refutation of gnostic teaching. (Colossians 2:9)

—Paul was declaring that the Christian is complete in Christ rather than being deficient, as the Gnostics claimed. (Colossians 2:10-15)

—Paul uses the term *record* as a designation for the Mosaic Law with all its regulations, under which everyone is a debtor to God. (Colossians 2:14)

—Not only did God cancel out the accusations of the Law against the Christian, but God also conquered and disarmed the evil angels who entice people to follow asceticism and false teachings about Christ. The metaphor used here recalls a Roman general leading his captives through the streets, so the citizens could see and celebrate victory. (Colossians 2:15)

—This passage expresses a "Christus Victor" approach to the atonement: through the Cross, Christ vanquishes the spiritual powers arrayed against humanity and sets us free to live for God.

Teachers of CHILDREN

—Paul's letter to the church of Colossae was to be shared with the church of Laodicea, a wealthy community located only a few miles from Colossae.

—Paul encouraged believers to be aware that love brings them together so that they can know and learn more about Christ.

—The churches of Colossae and Laodicea experienced false teachings regarding God's Word.

—Believers must stay united in faith and work together to build up their relationship in Christ.

—The strength of Christ overrides human regulations that bind people to laws that are not of Christ.

—Baptism is the new circumcision that identifies believers as part of the covenant community.

THE CHRONOLOGICAL SETTING OF THE LESSON

The letter to the Colossians was written by the apostle Paul to the church in Colossae around AD 61-62. He wrote the book while in prison in Rome to counter false teaching of the Scriptures and those concerning the person of Christ and His work (see Colossians 2:3, 9, 14-15). Paul warned the church against believing in human philosophies that were based on empty human traditions instead of on the true and divine revelation of Christ. Other letters authored by Paul while in prison include Ephesians, Philemon, and Philippians. (bible.org)

THE GEOGRAPHICAL AND CULTURAL SETTING OF THE LESSON

The city of Colossae was a Graeco-Phrygian town in Asia Minor while under Roman rule. This cosmopolitan city was located a hundred miles to the east of Ephesus in the Lycus Valley. Other cities within this valley were Laodicea and Hierapolis (see Colossians 2:1; 4:13). The city of Colossae had different cultural and religious interactions, and this was the basis of Paul's message to the small church of believers in this city concerning the teachings of Christ. Paul had not visited the church in Colossae at this period, but he trains a young man named Epaphras who went back and established a church in his hometown of Colossae (see Colossians 1:7; 4:12). (bible.org)

PROMINENT CHARACTER(S) IN THE LESSON

Epaphras: Epaphras was the apostle Paul's fellow coworker who was assigned to teach the truth in God's grace and the ministry of Jesus Christ in Colossae (see Colossians 1:7). He was imprisoned alongside Paul in Rome during one of his visits.
Tychicus: He was an Asian Christian who accompanied the apostle Paul to Rome (see Colossians 4:7). He was sent by Paul to deliver the letter to the Colossians to encourage and establish the church in Colossae.

KEY TERMS IN THE LESSON

Faith (verse 5)—Greek: *pistis* (pis'-tis): faith; belief; trust; confidence; fidelity; faithfulness.
Heart(s) (verse 2)—Greek: *kardia* (kar-dee'-ah): the heart; inner life; intention.
Knowledge (verse 3)—Greek: *gnósis* (gno'-sis): a knowing; knowledge.

Love (verse 2)—Greek: *agapé* (ag-ah'-pay): love; benevolence; goodwill; esteem; plur: love-feasts.
Treasures (verse 3)—Greek: *thésauros* (thay-sow-ros'):** treasures; stores.
Wisdom (verse 3)—Greek: *sophia* (sof-ee'-ah): skill; wisdom.

TOPICAL OUTLINE OF THE LESSON

I. **Introduction**
   A. Warning: Danger Ahead
   B. Biblical Background

II. **Exposition and Application of the Scripture**
   A. Encouragement, Enlightenment, and Knowledge
      (Colossians 2:1-4)
   B. Stand Strong on a Firm Foundation
      (Colossians 2:5-10)
   C. Spiritual Circumcision
      (Colossians 2:11-15)

III. **Concluding Reflection**

I. INTRODUCTION
A. Warning: Danger Ahead

In Colossians 2, there is an expression of concern by the apostle Paul regarding the people of Colossae. Although Paul had not met some of the people to whom he was writing, he still expressed his desire that their hearts would be knit together in love, and that they would have the assurance that comes from an understanding of God's mystery revealed through Christ Jesus. He also rejoiced in their orderly conduct and steadfastness, and further encouraged them to be established in Christ firmly, abounding in thanksgiving (verses 1-7).

The apostle's warning in verse 8 summarizes the rest of the chapter as he began to warn the people of the dangers of what he called the deceitful messages being preached. These dangers included being taught vain philosophy and being deprived of their reward by those who show false humility. He expressed concern regarding those who believe in the worship of angels, who tell false visions, and who follow strict regulations according to human commandments and doctrines which really have no value against the indulgence of the flesh. He reminded them that in Christ they are complete, having passed through a circumcision which is not made with human hands. This circumcision is one in which God had made them alive together with Christ. No one could judge them regarding religious observances which were only a shadow that pointed toward the true substance of Christ (verses 8-23).

B. Biblical Background

In Colossians 2:1-3, we see evidence that the sufferings of Paul were not just for himself, but also for the benefit of others. Paul had a true understanding of the wisdom of God's mysteries. Other religions might seem to have part of the truth, but in Christ is contained all truth. There is no need for speculations about intermediate levels of spiritual power. What is needed is a better and deeper understanding of Christ and all that this involves. The essence and purpose of Paul's letter was to focus and direct his readers to Christ and having faith in

Him. We are united through faith in Christ, and through His effective work on the Cross. Christ died for us that our sins would no longer be counted against us, and He paid the price for our sin in full.

Through Christ's death, we have also received new life. God's work through Jesus Christ was not only for Jesus alone, but also for those who have faith in Christ.

In verse 13, Paul described how we were far apart from Christ. In our sinful nature, as we followed the flesh, we were spiritually dead (uncircumcised) and consequently separated from Christ. However, when we accept and yield to Christ, this sin is forgiven and cleansed.

In verse 14, Paul described this forgiveness which has been granted to us. Christ has forgiven us and given us a life without debts, because He cancelled the bill of sin and paid it in full.

In Colossians 2:15, Paul again further illustrated how strategic is the victory we have in Christ, when Christ disarmed the rulers and authorities and made a public show of them. Christ conquered them all. When we have Christ, no power or authority has power over our lives.

II. EXPOSITION AND APPLICATION OF THE SCRIPTURE

A. Encouragement, Enlightenment, and Knowledge (Colossians 2:1-4)

FOR I would that ye knew what great conflict I have for you, and for them at Laodicea, and for as many as have not seen my face in the flesh; That their hearts might be comforted, being knit together in love, and unto all riches of the full assurance of understanding, to the acknowledgement of the mystery of God, and of the Father, and of Christ; In whom are hid all the treasures of wisdom and knowledge. And this I say, lest any man should beguile you with enticing words.

The intense earnestness described by Paul is related to the pervasive spiritual struggle against evil which he was experiencing on behalf of his Colossian and Laodicean congregation. A great amount of energy is also expended by Paul in prayer support for the people who were under his pastoral care and spiritual supervision. Paul did not have to personally know the people in order to pray for them. Likewise, today, our prayers are still effective, regardless of whether we have all the details and firsthand experience in a given situation.

Paul imparted a heart-full in verse 2 as he exhibited great emotional transparency and put on full display his spiritual fervor for the faithful. Paul's purpose was not selfish in its focus but is rightly focused on the spiritual growth and development of the congregation. Paul's goal was spiritual progress and development for God's people, and he could not be satisfied with anything less than their reaching a state of spiritual maturity.

Part of the process of spiritual maturity involves the body of Christ's being united in love. We cannot attain spiritual maturity and sustain it through operating independently. The type and quality of this unity is bolstered by the use of the phrase "in love" (verse 2). The sense of being unified in Christ is also supported in Colossians 2:19 and Ephesians 4:16.

This Colossians 2:2 passage mirrors Philippians 1:9—"I pray that your love may abound (or, overflow) more and more in knowledge, and in all judgment (or, perception)." As he does in Ephesians 3:18-19 (NIV), Paul here encourages the church to "grasp how wide and long and high and deep is the love of Christ, and to know this love that surpasses knowledge—that you may be filled to the measure of all the fullness of God." All too often, individuals join a church but fail to join Jesus. Furthermore, sometimes after being Christians for several years we find ourselves drifting into a state of neutrality and lulled into the ineffective sleep state of comfortable satisfaction. As Christians, we cannot lose our state of urgency for our own spiritual growth, our drive to disciple other Christians, and our calling to share the Good News with those who have never tuned into station G-O-D.

Theologian Charles Ellicott suggests that the word *hidden* (verse 3) is a technical word for a secret kind of teaching which is only available to the initiated. Some aspects of the things of God may be temporarily hidden, and others may require deeper searching and even sacrifice in order to discover. First Corinthians 13:12 further underscores this: "For now we see only a reflection as in a mirror; then we shall see face to face. Now I know in part; then I shall know fully, even as I am fully known."

The "fine-sounding arguments" mentioned in verse 4 refers to the tendency of blending Judaism with Oriental philosophy and then mixing this combination with Christianity. The result is a hodgepodge of spiritual-sounding elements that are not purely anything. The effect of this mixing is to create a semi-authentic appeal for a wider audience and to draw in those who are easily convinced by partial truths. Sometimes, people use enticing words that sound plausible when disguised in pseudo wisdom and false humility (see 2:18, 23).

B. Stand Strong on a Firm Foundation (Colossians 2:5-10)

For though I be absent in the flesh, yet am I with you in the spirit, joying and beholding your order, and the stedfastness of your faith in Christ. As ye have therefore received Christ Jesus the Lord, so walk ye in him: Rooted and built up in him, and stablished in the faith, as ye have been taught, abounding therein with thanksgiving. Beware lest any man spoil you through philosophy and vain deceit, after the tradition of men, after the rudiments of the world, and not after Christ. For in him dwelleth all the fulness of the Godhead bodily. And ye are complete in him, which is the head of all principality and power.

Like a proud father whose children are off in college or away at church camp, Paul expressed his joy in their discipline and confirmed his confidence in their faith despite the miles that separate them. His absence in the flesh did not hamper his presence in the Spirit. Although Paul was imprisoned in Rome, those bars could not incarcerate his spirit (see 1 Corinthians 5:3). A central thing that gives Paul the most joy as a spiritual father is that his mentees walk and grow in discipline (see 1 Thessalonians 4:1 and 5:14). The definition of the word *disciple* is "a disciplined learner." As Christians, our primary responsibility is to be disciples and to make disciples.

The way that we initially receive God is by faith. Likewise, the way that we grow and progress as Christians is also by faith (verses 6 and 7).

Anything that is of significant value also has potential counterfeits. This phenomenon also extends into the realm of discipleship (verse 8). Counterfeit spirituality looks like true faith and may sound like the real thing but, in actuality, only has pieces of truth mixed in with humanistic teaching or worldly rituals.

The theology reflected in verses 9-10 is significant to understand and essential to include in any comprehensive conversation about Christ. This one central point of the deity of Christ is a line of demarcation between truth and untruth. Many people are willing to recognize Christ as a nice, human moral teacher but not as God in bodily form. There are several problems with this approach. One problem is that human moral teachers can be flawed and can be found in error. However, we dare not disagree with God. Another issue is

that if Jesus had just been a nice, moral teacher, He would not have been crucified. The charge against Jesus was not teaching or even preaching. The charge against Jesus was blasphemy, as is reflected in John 10:33. "We are not stoning you for any good work," they replied, "but for blasphemy, because you, a mere man, claim to be God." *Blasphemy* is defined as "the act or offense of using profane talk and speaking sacrilegiously about God or sacred things." A denial of deity is a denial of Christ.

C. Spiritual Circumcision (Colossians 2:11-15)

In whom also ye are circumcised with the circumcision made without hands, in putting off the body of the sins of the flesh by the circumcision of Christ: Buried with him in baptism, wherein also ye are risen with him through the faith of the operation of God, who hath raised him from the dead. And you, being dead in your sins and the uncircumcision of your flesh, hath he quickened together with him, having forgiven you all trespasses; Blotting out the handwriting of ordinances that was against us, which was contrary to us, and took it out of the way, nailing it to his cross; And having spoiled principalities and powers, he made a shew of them openly, triumphing over them in it.

Here in verse 11, the reference to circumcision points to the difference between self-control and Spirit-control. Although circumcision is a physical ritual associated with a spiritual practice of separation, this ritual is only externally effective for the flesh rather than internally effective for the spiritual part of humanity. (Read Romans 2:25-29 for a further clarification of this point.)

The central metaphor employed in verses 13 and 14 is one of a death sentence being commuted by Christ. In this case, being dead means being void of spiritual and eternal life from a Christian perspective (see Ephesians 2:1, 5; 5:14; John 5:24; 1 John 3:14; 5:12; compare John 3:3; 6:53; Genesis 2:17).

God used Jesus to take what seemed to be a devastating defeat and transform it into a resounding victory (verse 15). In combat or conflict, one of the most demoralizing occurrences is to be disarmed. Disarmament immediately transfers one from being in control to being controlled.

III. CONCLUDING REFLECTION

Without constantly sharpening our walk with God through Bible study, prayer, preaching, and teaching, we may likely fall prey to the world's distractions that seem like truth but are thinly veiled half-truths. Jesus is supreme over every spiritual "ruler and authority," and that is why we must reject false teachings and the inadequate focus on Christ and His Cross. With consistency, we must refuse to be swayed by teachings that run counter to the Gospel. Then we can walk in the light of God's Word in order to fulfill God's will and delight in God's ways.

PRAYER

Lord, let us be steadfast, unmovable, and always abounding in Your work so that our labor will not be in vain. In Jesus' name we pray. Amen.

HOME DAILY BIBLE READINGS
(June 17-23, 2019)

Hearts United in Love
MONDAY, June 17: "Christ, the Source of Life" (1 John 5:6-12)

TUESDAY, June 18: "Pursue Unity in the Church" (1 Peter 3:8-12)

WEDNESDAY, June 19: "All Peoples United in Christ" (Ephesians 2:11-22)

THURSDAY, June 20: "Christ, the Image of God" (Colossians 1:15-20)

FRIDAY, June 21: "Paul's Ministry in the Congregation" (Colossians 1:24-29)

SATURDAY, June 22: "Maintain Your Union with Christ" (Colossians 2:16-23)

SUNDAY, June 23: "United with Christ and One Another" (Colossians 2:1-15)

June 30, 2019　　　　　　　　　　　　　　　　　**Lesson 5**

JESUS TEACHES ABOUT RIGHT ATTITUDES

ADULT/YOUTH	CHILDREN
ADULT/YOUNG ADULT TOPIC: Attitude Check	**GENERAL LESSON TITLE: Jesus Teaches Attitudes of Love**
YOUTH TOPIC: Attitude Check	**CHILDREN'S TOPIC: The Right Attitude**

DEVOTIONAL READING
Isaiah 61:1-8

ADULT/YOUTH	CHILDREN
BACKGROUND SCRIPTURE: **Matthew 5:1-12**	BACKGROUND SCRIPTURE: **Matthew 5:1-12**
PRINT PASSAGE: **Matthew 5:1-12**	PRINT PASSAGE: **Matthew 5:1-12**
ADULT KEY VERSE: **Matthew 5:12**	KEY VERSE: **Matthew 5:12**
YOUTH KEY VERSES: **Matthew 5:11-12**	

Matthew 5:1-12—KJV

AND SEEING the multitudes, he went up into a mountain: and when he was set, his disciples came unto him:

2 And he opened his mouth, and taught them, saying,

3 Blessed are the poor in spirit: for theirs is the kingdom of heaven.

4 Blessed are they that mourn: for they shall be comforted.

5 Blessed are the meek: for they shall inherit the earth.

6 Blessed are they which do hunger and thirst after righteousness: for they shall be filled.

7 Blessed are the merciful: for they shall obtain mercy.

8 Blessed are the pure in heart: for they shall see God.

9 Blessed are the peacemakers: for they shall be called the children of God.

10 Blessed are they which are persecuted for

Matthew 5:1-12—NIV

NOW WHEN Jesus saw the crowds, he went up on a mountainside and sat down. His disciples came to him, 2 and he began to teach them. He said:

3 "Blessed are the poor in spirit, for theirs is the kingdom of heaven.

4 "Blessed are those who mourn, for they will be comforted.

5 "Blessed are the meek, for they will inherit the earth.

6 "Blessed are those who hunger and thirst for righteousness, for they will be filled.

7 "Blessed are the merciful, for they will be shown mercy.

8 "Blessed are the pure in heart, for they will see God.

9 "Blessed are the peacemakers, for they will be called children of God.

10 "Blessed are those who are persecuted because of

righteousness' sake: for theirs is the kingdom of heaven.
11 Blessed are ye, when men shall revile you, and persecute you, and shall say all manner of evil against you falsely, for my sake.
12 Rejoice, and be exceeding glad: for great is your reward in heaven: for so persecuted they the prophets which were before you.

righteousness, for theirs is the kingdom of heaven.
11 "Blessed are you when people insult you, persecute you and falsely say all kinds of evil against you because of me.
12 "Rejoice and be glad, because great is your reward in heaven, for in the same way they persecuted the prophets who were before you."

UNIFYING LESSON PRINCIPLE: Our attitudes determine how we view circumstances in our lives. How can our attitudes bring long-term benefits? Jesus' Beatitudes taught the crowd and His disciples those heartfelt values and attitudes required of anyone who seeks to be in a covenant relationship with Him.

LESSON OBJECTIVES

Upon the completion of this lesson, the students will be able to do the following:
1. Explain the irony in the Beatitudes.
2. Marvel at the values taught by Jesus and their complete reversal of the world's values.
3. Pursue the value system taught by Jesus and claim the blessings in belonging to Christ's kingdom.

AGE-LEVEL POINTS TO BE EMPHASIZED

Teachers of ADULTS and YOUTH

—This passage marks the beginning of the "Sermon on the Mount," the first of Jesus' five major discourses in the book of Matthew (the others are found in chapters 10, 13, 18, and 24–25).

—Matthew 5:2-12 is commonly referred to as the "Beatitudes" due to the fact that each statement begins in Latin with *beati*, meaning "blessed" or "happy."

—Contrary to modern usage, Jesus used the word *blessed* to indicate not a receiving of material gifts or a temporary feeling of happiness but, rather, a wholeness and health of one's relationship with God.

—By framing the Beatitudes with the promise of "the kingdom of heaven" (verses 3, 10), Jesus was establishing these statements as a way of life for those who would follow Him and was including each of the promises in verses 3-10 as benefits of doing so.

—The exact location of the giving of the Beatitudes was is uncertain, though it is thought to be at the Tabgha near Capernaum. The "old law" was also given from a mountain (Matthew 5:1; see Exodus 19:3).

—*Blessed* means more than happy or any similar adjective based on outward circumstances. In this context, *blessed* refers to the ultimate well-being and distinctive spiritual joy of those who share in the salvation of the kingdom of God. (Matthew 5:3)

—This beatitude is taken from Psalm 37:11 and refers not so much to an attitude toward people as to a disposition before God—namely, humility. (Matthew 5:5)

—"Heart" is referring to the center of one's being, including mind, will, and emotions. (Matthew 5:8)

—Those who promote peace, as far as it depends on them, are peacemakers (see Romans 12:18). In so doing, they reflect the character of their heavenly father. (Matthew 5:9)
—The "kingdom of heaven" is a present reality *and* a future hope. (Matthew 5:10)

Teachers of CHILDREN
—The word *blessed* means more than happiness and connotes eternal, joyous rewards.
—Believers who live out God's desires for loving and caring for others are blessed.

—"The Beatitudes" is the longest recorded sermon given by Jesus.
—God's kingdom is organized differently than the world's order of happiness, wealth, and various life pursuits.
—Jesus preached the Sermon on the Mount on a hillside near Capernaum over a period of a few days.
—The Sermon on the Mount or the Beatitudes challenged the religious leaders who were opposed to Jesus.

THE CHRONOLOGICAL SETTING OF THE LESSON

The book of Matthew was written during Roman rule in the land of Israel as a narrative that recounts the events in the life of Jesus Christ. The gospel of Matthew is among the four canonical books that show the fulfillment of the Old Testament messianic prophecies which reaffirm the life, ministry, death, and miraculous resurrection of Jesus Christ (see Matthew 3:13–4:11). The other Synoptic Gospels of the New Testament are Mark and Luke. The gospel of John stands alone, as it contains much unique information. A substantial portion of the gospel of Matthew is dependent on the gospel of Mark as a point of reference.

THE GEOGRAPHICAL AND CULTURAL SETTING OF THE LESSON

The early church fathers argued that the gospel of Matthew was written in AD 70 after the fall and destruction of the Temple of Jerusalem by the Roman Empire. The gospel was written by the apostle Matthew for a Jewish Christian congregation. Matthew also went by the name "Levi the son of Alphaeus" and was a tax collector in Capernaum (see Matthew 9:9-13). This gospel was originally written in Greek, the predominant language of the Roman Empire. However, the original audience was Jewish. Most Christian scholars argue that Matthew wrote this gospel in Antioch of Syria or in Palestine (due to the heavy use of Greek dialect). The earliest reference to the gospel of Matthew is by Ignatius the Bishop of Antioch (bible.org).

The main focus of this gospel is the Old Testament prophetic revelations, and this implies that the recipients' background was entirely Jewish, and that they would have had knowledge about Old Testament teachings. Matthew purposely wrote this gospel to remind the Jews that Jesus of Nazareth was the promised Messiah (bible.org).

The Lesson Scripture from the book of Matthew focuses on the Beatitudes, which forms the central message of the Sermon on the Mount. The apostle Matthew places this chronology of events at the beginning of the ministry of Christ and forms the basis of the grand proclamation of the message concerning the kingdom of God. The theme in this section is on righteousness, which is a key feature for the kingdom of Christ. This also forms the narrative framework of the Sermon on the Mount, where Jesus ascended the mountain and began His authoritative proclamation to the disciples and the crowd. The audience for this message was Jesus' disciples and the people. The

Sermon on the Mount also alluded to the Mosaic Law in the Old Testament.

PROMINENT CHARACTER(S) IN THE LESSON

Jesus Christ: He was/is the main evangelist, giving assurance to His followers concerning true virtues of discipleship and the kingdom of heaven.

The Disciples: These were the twelve followers of Christ to whom the message concerning the Beatitudes were given. However, the message on Beatitudes was also meant for everyone, including the crowd that followed Christ to the Mount (bible.org).

KEY TERMS IN THE LESSON

Blessed (verse 3)—Greek: *makarios* (mak-ar'-ee-os): happy; blessed; to be envied.

Heaven (verse 3)—Greek: *ouranos* (oo-ran-os'): heaven; the visible heavens: the atmosphere, the sky; the starry heavens.

Meek (verse 5)—Greek: *praus* (prah-ooce'): mild; gentle.

Mourn (verse 4)—Greek: *pentheó* (pen-theh'-o): to mourn, lament.

Poor (verse 3)—Greek: *ptóchos* (pto-khos'): poor; destitute.

Righteousness (verse 6)—Greek: *dikaiosuné* (dik-ah-yos-oo'-nay): justice; justness; righteousness.

TOPICAL OUTLINE OF THE LESSON

I. **Introduction**
   A. It's What's on the Inside that Counts
   B. Biblical Background

II. **Exposition and Application of the Scripture**
   A. The Leading Spiritual Gift of Jesus (Matthew 5:1-2)
   B. Attitudes Reflecting Humility (Matthew 5:3-5)
   C. Attitudes Reflecting Love (Matthew 5:6-9)
   D. Attitudes Reflecting Perseverance (Matthew 5:10-12)

III. **Concluding Reflection**

I. INTRODUCTION

A. It's What's on the Inside that Counts

The opening verses of our text, which many refer to as the Beatitudes, show how this message deals with the person's inner heart, attitude, and behaviors, which is the core of true Christian discipleship. This text describes the outward displays of the character and conduct of true believers and genuine disciples of Christ Jesus. This life, as described by Jesus, is a life of glory and grace which only God can give.

This kind of life cannot be achieved by human effort alone, as it would amount to an overestimation of people's ability to achieve a high-quality moral life. This message (the longest recorded message of Jesus) in turn cannot be left or assigned to the Jewish lifestyle alone, as this would amount to robbing the church of her greatest statement of true Christian living. As we will explore further, we shall see how important this text is in serving as a guide to check our attitude as children and disciples of God. Matthew 5 contains the first portion of the Sermon on the Mount. It has forty-eight verses and is said to be one of the most discussed passages in the Bible.

B. Biblical Background

The Beatitudes is one of the most loved texts of the Gospels. It is the beginning of the Sermon on the Mount, which is seen in Matthew 5–7. This sermon as it appears in Matthew seems to have taken place sometime later in the chronology of the life of Christ. Matthew chose to place it at the beginning of the ministry of Jesus, as it magnificently frames the proclamation of the kingdom of God and its lifestyle.

Matthew originally intended his text for the nation of Israel and especially the crowds that flocked to Jesus. However, this message was preached directly to Jesus' disciples. While speaking to His disciples and the crowd that followed Him, Jesus focused on the true will of God and righteousness which they all must manifest in order to enter God's kingdom. This message is directed to everyone, both young and old, Jew and Gentile, circumcised and uncircumcised, saved and unsaved. Its dominant theme is righteousness as the standard for the kingdom of God.

The Sermon on the Mount, as stated earlier, is the first and longest message of Jesus ever recorded in the Gospels. As a matter of fact, this sermon tells people the level of righteousness that characterizes the kingdom, and also what that righteous life would look like for the kingdom citizen.

This sermon begins with the Beatitudes, revealing the qualities and character of the true people of God. This sermon gives a perfect picture to Christ's disciples, who are the heirs of the promises of God's kingdom.

The Beatitudes tend to be a little different in content than other passages in the Scriptures. The sermon is proverb-like, precise, and full of interpretation and deep thought. Each one of these verses includes a topic which forms a major biblical theme.

II. EXPOSITION AND APPLICATION OF THE SCRIPTURE

A. The Leading Spiritual Gift of Jesus (Matthew 5:1-2)

AND SEEING the multitudes, he went up into a mountain: and when he was set, his disciples came unto him: And he opened his mouth, and taught them, saying.

In reading the Sermon on the Mount, there is a distinct similarity to a lesser-known passage which might be called the Sermon on the Plain found in Luke 6:20-49. In both passages, the word choice and phrase pattern are similar. There are many other portions of this passage that can be found in various places in Luke's gospel.

In verse 1, Matthew highlights what served as the starting point of this teaching. Jesus was profoundly in touch with His surroundings and with the wants, needs, and motives of the people—even if those desires were yet unexpressed. Both now as well as then, Jesus knows exactly what we need, even when we do not know or express what we need. Not only does God know our needs, but God is also able to supply our needs: "But my God shall supply all your need according to his riches in glory by Christ Jesus" (Philippians 4:19).

Verse 2 presents Jesus as doing what He does better than any other—teaching. Jesus is referred to as "Rabbi" in more than fifteen places throughout the New Testament. The term *Rabbi* and its derivatives are defined as "a Jewish scholar or teacher, especially one who studies or teaches Jewish Law." In eighteen other instances, Jesus is referred to as a teacher or as teaching others. One may wonder why so much emphasis is placed on teaching. Hosea 4:6a affirms that "My people are destroyed for lack of knowledge." Jesus was a master teacher, and He employed several tactics that we can learn from and utilize today in order to become effective teachers. Below are some of the reasons why Jesus was such an effective teacher: 1) Jesus modeled what He taught. 2) Jesus knew and understood the people He taught. 3) Jesus adapted His approach to teaching different kinds of people in different kinds of settings. 4) Jesus used word pictures in the form of parables and sometimes even used objects to help His point to stick with the listener (see Mark 4:34). 5) Jesus spoke in simple, understandable words so that anyone at any level could understand. 6) Jesus spoke the truth with authority (textsource.com).

B. Attitudes Reflecting Humility
(Matthew 5:3-5)

Blessed are the poor in spirit: for theirs is the kingdom of heaven. Blessed are they that mourn: for they shall be comforted. Blessed are the meek: for they shall inherit the earth.

As we delve into the Beatitudes, it is important to understand that its focus is on our inner attitude because that is what makes a difference in our outer life. It is also important to understand the meaning of the word *blessed*. Contemporary concepts of being blessed often relate to financial or material acquisition. *Strong's Exhaustive Concordance* defines this concept translated from the Greek term *makarios* as meaning "extremely blessed, fortunate, endowed, happy, and joyful." This type of felicity comes not from an exterior source, but from an inner resource.

The term *poor in spirit* (verse 3) need not necessarily refer to spiritual or financial poverty. Rather, it is an indication of inner peacefulness and a willingness to receive whatever may occur in life. Paul refers to this state in Philippians 4:11: "I am not saying this because I am in need, for I have learned to be content whatever the circumstances."

The reward of the "poor in spirit" is the kingdom of heaven. The word *kingdom* is a compound word which indicates the domain of a king. The kingdom of heaven, then, is the rule, will, and reign of God. This word is applied twice in the Disciples' Prayer (better known as The Lord's Prayer) as seen in Matthew 6.

Usage of the word *mourn* within the context of being blessed (verse 4) may at first glance seem antithetical. The word *mourn* is usually related to weeping (see Mark 16:10; Luke 6:25; James 4:9; Revelation 18:15-19). Here, however, there is an implied, though not an expressed, limitation. This kind of mourning is not like the sorrow of the world that produces death (see 2 Corinthians 7:10) because of failure, suffering, and the consequences of sin. This kind of sorrow flows out in the tears that cleanse us. This mourning is over sin and the stain it leaves on the soul (*Ellicott's Commentary for English Readers*). The reward of those who mourn is comfort from a supernatural source. Psalm 126:5 (NIV) proclaims that "Those who sow with tears will reap with songs of joy." The promise of those who trust God is God's provision of mercy, peace, and consolation.

There can be no true spiritual ability without personal humility (verse 5). This does not mean false humility but true humility that flows from a connection with God and a healthy fear of God. Meekness is reflected in an attitude that is mild, gentle, longsuffering, forgiving, slow to anger, not easily provoked, not resentful, and not vengeful. Instead, the humble Christian is sweet, affable, courteous, and kind. Humble people seek to reconcile offenses and to win people over to peace and love. It is these individuals who will inherit the earth. What a prize! This does not guarantee a life without problems, but it is a promise of peace even in the presence of problems.

C. Attitudes Reflecting Love
(Matthew 5:6-9)

Blessed are they which do hunger and thirst after righteousness: for they shall be filled. Blessed are the merciful: for they shall obtain mercy. Blessed are the pure in heart: for they shall see God. Blessed are the peacemakers: for they shall be called the children of God.

Jesus employed simple yet powerful imagery to describe the quest to be righteous. As human beings, we are most successful at doing the things that we are passionate about and most internally driven to accomplish. Few things in life are as motivating as the basic need to eat and drink. Since most people can identify with this, Jesus linked this need to the need for righteousness. A similar concept was expressed by the psalmist who declared, "As the deer pants for streams of water, so my soul pants for you, my God. My soul thirsts for God, for the living God. When can I go and meet with God?" (Psalm 42:1-2, NIV).

Righteousness is the state of being morally right and justified. *The Benson Commentary* articulately describes righteousness as when people "sincerely, earnestly, and perseveringly desire universal holiness of heart and life, or deliverance from all sinful dispositions and practices, and a complete restoration of their souls to the image of God in which they were created. [It is a] fervent, constant, increasing, restless, and active desire; of that holy ardor and vehemence of soul in pursuit of the most eminent degrees of universal goodness which will end in complete satisfaction." The strong desire for righteousness is what makes possible the fulfillment of that desire.

"Mercy" (verse 7) is compassion or forgiveness shown to someone whom is within one's power to punish or harm. Jesus took this opportunity to affirm the principle of sowing and reaping, which is also noted in Galatians 6:7 (NIV): "Do not be deceived: God cannot be mocked. A man reaps what he sows." At some points in life, everyone will need mercy. Those who are so affected by the sufferings of others as to be disposed to alleviate them will be the very ones who will receive mercy when the need arises. Matthew 10:42 further expresses this idea: "Whosoever shall give to drink unto one of these little ones a cup of cold water only in the name of a disciple, verily I say unto you, he shall in no wise lose his reward" (see also Matthew 25:34-40).

Verse 8 of the Beatitudes echoes Psalm 86:11 (NIV): "Teach me your way, LORD, that I may rely on your faithfulness; give me an undivided heart, that I may fear your name." When our hearts are purified by faith, the Spirit of God cleans up our "vain thoughts, unprofitable reasonings, earthly and sensual desires, and corrupt passions; [we] are purified from pride, self-will, discontent, impatience, anger, malice, envy, covetousness, ambition; [our] hearts are circumcised to love the Lord [our] God with all [our] hearts, and [our] neighbors as [ourselves], and who, therefore, are not only upright before him, but possess and maintain purity of intention and of affection in all [our] designs, works, and enjoyments; serving him continually with a single eye and an undivided heart" (*The New Testament of Our Lord and Saviour Jesus Christ*, Joseph Benson, p. 59).

The term *peacemakers* (verse 9) suggests that it is possible to create peace even when there is no peace currently in existence. A strong resolve, honorable character, and reliance on the Holy Spirit are all important components in becoming a peacemaker. Peacemakers not only possess an inner sense of personal peace, but they also endeavor to sow seeds of understanding, harmony, and unity among others where there is discord. Peacemakers seek to help "heal the differences of brethren and neighbours, to reconcile contending parties, and to restore peace wherever it is broken, as well as to preserve it where it is" (*The New Testament of Our Lord and Saviour Jesus Christ*, Joseph Benson, p. 59).

Whenever people are called the "children of God" it carries with it a certain sense of responsibility to reflect the attitude, image, and actions of the Father. Children of God are called to reflect God's love, peace, and mercy.

D. Attitudes Reflecting Perseverance
(Matthew 5:10-12)

Blessed are they which are persecuted for righteousness' sake: for theirs is the kingdom of heaven. Blessed are ye, when men shall revile you, and persecute you, and shall say all manner of evil against you falsely, for my sake. Rejoice, and be exceeding glad: for great is your reward in heaven: for so persecuted they the prophets which were before you.

When this text was written, religious persecution was a common occurrence. Although widespread persecution still exists in some countries, most of those who live in the United States have never experienced real persecution on the level experienced by those in the first century.

To be righteous is to be free from guilt or sin. It is to be morally right, justifiable, or godly. During the time this was written, people were being persecuted for the cause of Christ and the Gospel. If they professed Christ, showed concern for His interests, or engaged in preaching or worship, they became targets for rage and persecution.

Jesus was particularly sensitive to persecution. But no matter how much persecution one may experience, no amount of persecution can compare to the reward received from enduring hardship for the cause of Christ. The Jesus kind of response to persecution is the exact opposite of what would be expected. The normal response might be resistance, revenge, or remorse. Jesus recommended rejoicing. It is a great privilege to be persecuted and to suffer. "To those who suffer most, God imparts the highest rewards. Hence the crown of martyrdom has been thought to be the brightest that any of the redeemed shall wear; and hence many of the early Christians sought to become martyrs, and threw themselves in the way of their persecutors, that they might be put to death. They literally rejoiced, and leaped for joy, at the prospect of death for the sake of Jesus. Though God does not require us to seek persecution, yet all this shows that there is something in (faith) to sustain the soul, which the world does not possess" (*Notes, Explanatory and Practical, on the Gospels: with an Index, a Chronological Table, Tables of Weights, Etc.,* Albert Barnes, p. 72).

III. CONCLUDING REFLECTION

In the Sermon on the Mount, Jesus gave clear and detailed instructions on how to think, act, and respond as a Christian. The Beatitudes can serve as a template for the kind of attitudes that are possible and expected of one who claims to be one of the children of God. As we grow in our relationship with God, we will experience various challenges. Problems and hardships in life are inescapable. The question we must ask and answer as Christians is this: "How will I respond when my faith is tested?" As we reject the values of the world, we can embrace the values of the Spirit of God. Although some of the Beatitudes may seem difficult to embody, God gives us the power to fulfill those requirements and expectations of us. We can do all things through Christ who strengthens us. "'For my thoughts are not your thoughts, neither are your ways my ways,' declares the LORD. 'As the heavens are higher than the earth, so are my ways higher than your ways and my thoughts than your thoughts'" (Isaiah 55:8-9, NIV).

PRAYER

Dear God, help us not to depend on the things of this earth to supply our needs. Let us allow the mind which was in Christ Jesus also to be in us. In Jesus' name we pray. Amen.

HOME DAILY BIBLE READINGS
(June 24-30, 2019)

Jesus Teaches about Right Attitudes
MONDAY, June 24: "Living among Wrongdoers" (Psalm 57)
TUESDAY, June 25: "Perfect God's Love among You" (1 John 4:7-21)
WEDNESDAY, June 26: "Great Rewards to Come" (Luke 6:17-23)
THURSDAY, June 27: "Apostles Chosen for Ministry" (Mark 3:7-12)
FRIDAY, June 28: "Do Not Judge" (Luke 6:37-45)
SATURDAY, June 29: "A Life Pleasing to God" (1 Thessalonians 4:1-12)
SUNDAY, June 30: "Right Attitudes for Blessed Living" (Matthew 5:1-12)

July 7, 2019   **Lesson 6**

JESUS TEACHES ABOUT FULFILLING THE LAW

ADULT/YOUTH
ADULT/YOUNG ADULT TOPIC: Be the Difference
YOUTH TOPIC: Be the Difference

CHILDREN
GENERAL LESSON TITLE: Jesus Teaches about Loving and Obeying God
CHILDREN'S TOPIC: Letting Our Light Shine

DEVOTIONAL READING
Psalm 119:105-112

ADULT/YOUTH
BACKGROUND SCRIPTURE: Matthew 5:13-20
PRINT PASSAGE: Matthew 5:13-20
KEY VERSE: Matthew 5:16

CHILDREN
BACKGROUND SCRIPTURE: Matthew 5:13-20
PRINT PASSAGE: Matthew 5:13-20
KEY VERSE: Matthew 5:14a

Matthew 5:13-20—KJV

13 Ye are the salt of the earth: but if the salt have lost his savour, wherewith shall it be salted? it is thenceforth good for nothing, but to be cast out, and to be trodden under foot of men.

14 Ye are the light of the world. A city that is set on an hill cannot be hid.

15 Neither do men light a candle, and put it under a bushel, but on a candlestick; and it giveth light unto all that are in the house.

16 Let your light so shine before men, that they may see your good works, and glorify your Father which is in heaven.

17 Think not that I am come to destroy the law, or the prophets: I am not come to destroy, but to fulfil.

18 For verily I say unto you, Till heaven and earth

Matthew 5:13-20—NIV

13 "You are the salt of the earth. But if the salt loses its saltiness, how can it be made salty again? It is no longer good for anything, except to be thrown out and trampled underfoot.

14 "You are the light of the world. A town built on a hill cannot be hidden.

15 "Neither do people light a lamp and put it under a bowl. Instead they put it on its stand, and it gives light to everyone in the house.

16 "In the same way, let your light shine before others, that they may see your good deeds and glorify your Father in heaven.

17 "Do not think that I have come to abolish the Law or the Prophets; I have not come to abolish them but to fulfill them.

18 "For truly I tell you, until heaven and earth disappear, not the smallest letter, not the least stroke

pass, one jot or one tittle shall in no wise pass from the law, till all be fulfilled.

19 Whosoever therefore shall break one of these least commandments, and shall teach men so, he shall be called the least in the kingdom of heaven: but whosoever shall do and teach them, the same shall be called great in the kingdom of heaven.

20 For I say unto you, That except your righteousness shall exceed the righteousness of the scribes and Pharisees, ye shall in no case enter into the kingdom of heaven.

of a pen, will by any means disappear from the Law until everything is accomplished.

19 "Therefore anyone who sets aside one of the least of these commands and teaches others accordingly will be called least in the kingdom of heaven, but whoever practices and teaches these commands will be called great in the kingdom of heaven.

20 "For I tell you that unless your righteousness surpasses that of the Pharisees and the teachers of the law, you will certainly not enter the kingdom of heaven."

UNIFYING LESSON PRINCIPLE: People express their beliefs through their actions. How do we express what we believe? Jesus teaches us that we are to do good for others and follow God's law.

LESSON OBJECTIVES

Upon the completion of this lesson, the students will be able to do the following:
1. Contrast the kind of righteousness Jesus taught with that of the scribes and Pharisees'.
2. Appreciate the "salty," "light-shining" quality of true righteousness.
3. Make an effort to bring salt and light to their community.

AGE-LEVEL POINTS TO BE EMPHASIZED
Teachers of ADULTS and YOUTH
—Salt adds flavor to food and preserves it. Thus, Jesus' disciples are to improve the condition of the world as well as preserve it from being corrupted by sin. In the book of Colossians, Paul talks about how Christians' words are to be seasoned with salt and beneficial to hearers (see Colossians 4:6).
—Metaphors for "light" and "darkness" abound in the Scriptures, and Matthew 5:14-16 speaks of the importance of a Christian's actions' brightening a world that is enshrouded in the darkness of sin. When this takes place, those living in darkness will take notice and will give God glory.

—Most of the salt in Israel came from the Dead Sea and was full of impurities that caused the salt to lose some of its flavor. (Matthew 5:13)
—"Light of the World" refers to Jesus' disciples having the kingdom life within them as a living testimony to those who do not yet have the light. (Matthew 5:14)
—The typical lamp in a Jewish home was small, was made of clay, burned olive oil, and was placed on a stand in the center of the room to maximize its effectiveness. (Matthew 5:15)
—The "Law" or "Torah" refers to the first five books of the Old Testament. (Matthew 5:17)
—Jesus is confirming the full authority of the Old Testament and demands a commitment to both. (Matthew 5:18-19)

Teachers of CHILDREN

—In the Sermon on the Mount, Jesus spoke of the responsibility of His disciples in the world.

—Followers of Jesus are to make life better for others.

—Jesus affirmed that His role was to bring the Hebrew traditions to fulfillment.

—God's commandments are always to be respected and obeyed.

—Jesus liked to use familiar objects, such as salt and light, in His teachings.

—Jesus urged His followers not to use the current religious leaders as models for their behavior.

THE CHRONOLOGICAL SETTING OF THE LESSON

The book of Matthew is conventionally believed to have been written by the apostle Matthew during the Roman Empire's occupation of Israel as a narrative recounting the events in the life of Christ. This Gospel is among the four canonical books that show the fulfillment of the Old Testament messianic prophecies which reaffirm the life, ministry, death, and the miraculous resurrection of Jesus Christ (see Matthew 3:13-4). The other Synoptic Gospels of the New Testament include Mark and Luke. A substantial amount of the gospel of Matthew is dependent on the gospel of Mark as a point of reference and original sourcing. This implies that the book of Matthew was written after the gospel of Mark had already been written and distributed.

THE GEOGRAPHICAL AND CULTURAL SETTING OF THE LESSON

Jesus Christ used the analogy of "salt" and "light" in the introductory part of this chapter to refer to His disciples and all His followers to describe what they were supposed to do and the kind of influence they had as His disciples in the world (see Matthew 5:13-16). In ancient Roman society, salt formed a basic part of livelihood. This alongside oil and wine were signs of prosperity and survival necessities. Salt was a valuable commodity due to its proximity to the Dead Sea in Palestine; it was mined along the rocky shores and the marshes and used for seasoning food and preserving meat. This was commonly done during the night to prevent the salt from vaporizing during the day due to high temperatures (bible.org).

Salt also serves as the basis for some religious principles and interpretations in the New Testament. For instance, there was scarce vegetation where salt was found, and as a result most of the Old Testament Scriptures allude to salt as a symbol of barrenness and dissolution (see Deuteronomy 29:23; Psalm 107:34, Jeremiah 17:6) (bible.org).

Salt was also a symbol of hospitality, fidelity, and friendship in ancient times in the East. As such, it formed a very significant emblem in the Old Testament Scriptures where it solidified the covenant between God and the Israelites (see Numbers 18:19; 2 Chronicles 13:5).

Disciples of Christ are the salt of the earth; Christ has chosen them to add value to the human experience as they live according to God's Word, purifying the sinful nature of the human beings through the blood of Jesus. Disciples are also seen as the light of the world that shines before people. A deeper study of the Scriptures suggests that ancient Galilee had a small city on a hill known as Safed (pronounced "sah FEHD"), and this might be the same city to which Jesus referred. This small town was set on the part of the hills where it is believed the Sermon of the Mount was given by Christ. This could just be a succinct illustration of light. The Christians are therefore mandated by Christ to shine His glory to the world (bible.org).

PROMINENT CHARACTER(S) IN THE LESSON

Jesus Christ: The teachings and the Sermon on the Mount center on Him as the main masterpiece in Matthew's text. Jesus was teaching His disciples about the righteous life that He desired them to lead in the world, and the need to obey its laws.

The Crowd: The audience forms a significant part of the ministry of Christ. These are the disciples that Christ talks to in a broader sense apart from His twelve chosen disciples. They are the people who follow Him up the mountain to listen to His teachings (bible.org).

KEY TERMS IN THE LESSON

Fulfil(l) (verse 17)—Greek: *pléroó* (play-ro'-o): fill; fulfill; complete.

Good (verse 16)—Greek: *kalos* (kal-os'): beautiful; good; worthy.

Lamp (verse 15)—Greek: *luchnos* (lookh'-nos): source of light; "candle" (KJV).

Light (verse 14)—Greek: *phós* (foce): a source of light; radiance.

Salt (verse 13)—Greek: *halas* and *hala* (hal'-as): a substance used for seasoning and preserving.

Works (verse 16)—Greek: *ergon* (er'-gon): works; labor; actions; "deeds" (NIV).

TOPICAL OUTLINE OF THE LESSON

I. Introduction
  A. Mission Impossible: Keeping the Law
  B. Biblical Background

II. Exposition and Application of the Scripture
  A. You Are Salt and Light (Matthew 5:13-16)
  B. Fulfillment of the Law (Matthew 5:17-20)

III. Concluding Reflection

I. INTRODUCTION

A. Mission Impossible: Keeping the Law

Christ explained the full meaning of the Law, showing how its demands were impossible for people to fulfill (see 5:48). This, however, is the use of the Law with respect to salvation. The Law shows how and why salvation, though given freely, remains not just important but necessary as well. The Law does not provide any possible avenue of merit for humans and leaves sinners totally dependent on nothing but God's divine grace for salvation (see Romans 3:19-20; Galatians 3:23-24).

Christ fulfilled the Law, showing that its true demands were beyond the surface meaning of the words (see 5:28, 39, 44), and He has set a standard that is higher (see 5:20). The events in Matthew 5 are believed to have taken place around AD 27 and contains the first portion of the Sermon on the Mount. It has forty-eight verses and is said to be one of the most discussed passages of the Bible.

B. Biblical Background

Being the "salt of the earth" as described in our text indicates that it is the genuinely born-again person that is the salt and can help meet the needs of other people and the entire world. By so doing, we make a difference in our environment and society at-large. The Beatitudes are followed by a statement which summarizes the basic character of the Christian's life as salt and light: "You are the salt of the earth."

Describing the believer as the salt of the earth is very appropriate with regards to the relationship we ought to have with the world. Salt always makes a difference when added to any substance. In the same way, we always ought to make a difference wherever we are found. Just as salt is a preservative, so the Christian is a preservative to the earth.

In verse 14, we see Jesus explaining that if we are His, then we ought to have His Light dwelling richly in us. This light which we have in Christ should shine so brightly that no one needs to ask whether or not we are saved, but others should at a glance see the glow of this light within us. The light of Christ should go with us and should illuminate wherever we are found.

In verses 17-18, we see Jesus neither giving a new law nor modifying the old, but rather He explains the significance and truth of the moral content found in Moses' Law and also the rest of the Old Testament. After laying down a foundational understanding of the message contained in the Beatitudes, Jesus then began to show how superior His message is to that of the Law of Moses. Jesus here made it clear that He did not come to destroy the Law; this simply means that the New Testament Gospel does not in any way contradict the Old Testament Law; rather, it has come as an ultimate fulfillment of the spiritual intention of the Law. Jesus now takes the Law from a mere legalism among the Pharisees to an inner spiritual intention of God. Christ further affirms absolute authority of the Old Testament as the Word of God even down to the smallest letter. This here suggests that the New Testament should in no way be seen as supplanting, overriding, or dissolving the Old Testament, but, rather, that it is a fulfillment of it (see Colossians 2:16-17). The Old Testament prophesied constantly about Jesus' coming to fulfill prophecy. Jesus is the fulfillment of the Law, and this is not because the Law was incorrect; it was just incomplete. By fulfilling the Law, Jesus reconciled us to God the Father.

Determining rank in God's kingdom is entirely God's prerogative (see Matthew 20:23), and God would hold in low esteem those who hold His Word in lowest esteem (see Matthew 5:19). In communicating the depth of His message, Jesus used a series of contrasts as seen in the outward behavior which the Law demands and the inner attitude of the heart which God desires. We also discover here the practical application of true Christian character to spiritual living.

God does not want us just to have a form of godliness or religion. God wants our hearts and wants us to be the difference. Though the scribes and Pharisees kept the Law, God was still not pleased with them. They had only a surface belief, which had no significant impact on their hearts or on the lives of people around them. It was a mere religion, devoid of a true spiritual belief and worship. God, through His salvation, has called us to make a difference in a world that often seems to be filled with sin and darkness.

II. EXPOSITION AND APPLICATION OF THE SCRIPTURE

A. You Are Salt and Light
(Matthew 5:13-16)

Ye are the salt of the earth: but if the salt have lost his savour, wherewith shall it be salted? it is thenceforth good for nothing, but to be cast out, and to be trodden under foot of men. Ye are the light of the world. A city that is set on an hill cannot be hid. Neither do men light a candle, and put it under a bushel, but on a candlestick; and it giveth light unto all that are in the house. Let your light so shine before men, that they may see your good works, and glorify your Father which is in heaven.

During New Testament times, salt was a necessity of life and had been used since ancient times in many cultures for seasoning, as a preservative, as a disinfectant, for ceremonial offerings, and as a unit of exchange. With eloquence and elegance, Jesus addressed His followers with regards to their spiritual capacity, their potential, and their deficiency. He was keenly aware of what they could do as well as their limitations. In this passage, Jesus called out the best in His disciples and essentially told them that they were as important, valuable, and necessary to the world as salt is to the people of the earth.

Jesus made it clear that disciples were called to a prophetic work of preserving the earth from moral decay. The restorative and antiseptic action of salt is similar to what they were called to do and expected to accomplish, because a thing is not a thing if it ceases to fulfill the purpose of the thing. Consequently, if the salt loses its saltiness it essentially forfeits its purpose.

The metaphorical imagery of light (verse 14) has a long history of being associated with all things divine. One of the values or functions of light is to provide illumination and thus direction for those who are working or moving. Ephesians 5:13 (NIV) observes this: "But everything exposed by the light becomes visible—and everything that is illuminated becomes a light." Consequently, the purpose of light is dual in nature: it exists both to be seen, as well as to assist others with their sight. A city that sits on a hill has the advantage of being easily visible to those in search of it, especially if that search happens at night while travelling along unlit roadways.

The lighting of a lamp (verse 15) within a household provided the illumination necessary for effectively navigating and performing common domestic functions after dark. The higher the light is placed, the wider the light will shine. The opposite is also true. When we cover our light, we forfeit our function. In the natural sense, placing a burning lamp under a basket would not only be impractical, but it would also be quite dangerous in terms of possibly starting a fire. The reason for any disciple of Christ to be enlightened is to walk in the light himself/herself and also to become a light for someone else.

The admonition to "let" one's light shine (verse 16) suggests an inner ability to allow the glow to shine forth or to disallow that glow. This word choice of "let" suggests a choice and a measure of potential control in the matter. If the light of Jesus Christ resides within us, the only thing we must do is not to block or hinder that brilliance. This light shines through our thought life, our spiritual fruit, our pure conversation, our godly treatment of others, our faithfulness, and our obedience to God. The reason that we do good works is not to be seen by others; we do good works as a natural overflow from the abundance of our hearts.

We can declare with confidence that whenever light is introduced to darkness, the light makes a definite difference and more so than when darkness is introduced to light.

Visible good works give praise to God as well as provide a holy, human example of what it means to be moved and motivated by the mighty power of God.

B. Fulfillment of the Law
(Matthew 5:17-20)

Think not that I am come to destroy the law, or the prophets: I am not come to destroy, but to fulfil. For verily I say unto you, Till heaven and earth pass, one jot or one tittle shall in no wise pass from the law, till all be fulfilled. Whosoever therefore shall break one of these least commandments, and shall teach men so, he shall be called the least in the kingdom of heaven: but whosoever shall do and teach them, the same shall be called great in the kingdom of heaven. For I say unto you, That except your righteousness shall exceed the righteousness of the scribes and Pharisees, ye shall in no case enter into the kingdom of heaven.

Besides being a perfect example to be imitated by all of humanity, another purpose for the first coming of Christ was to "fulfill that which was shadowed by the figures of the Law, by delivering men through grace from the curse of the Law: and moreover to teach the true use of obedience which the Law appointed, and to engrave in our hearts the power for obedience" (*Geneva Study Bible,* http://biblehub.com/kjv/matthew/5-17.htm). The Pharisees must have erroneously imagined that Jesus intended to dismantle the Law and the Prophets. Perhaps this can partially explain their volatile and malicious response to His ministry. The problem with laws without a matching life is that laws alone have no real power. But application engenders an internal combustion of spiritual power and progress. The pathway toward the city of holiness is along the highway of obedience. The more we are obedient to the will of God, the more we will reflect the ways of God.

Some African-American elders might have summed up verse 18 by simply saying, "Chile, God will do what He says He will do!" This sense of confidence and even bravado regarding fulfillment of the promises of God are built on years of personal experience with God's faithfulness. When God does a work, it is not half done but well done. Reference to the "jot" is "the Greek iota . . . , the smallest of all the letters of the alphabet. The 'tittle' was one of the smaller strokes, or twists of other letters . . . . Jewish Rabbis used to caution their scholars against so writing as to cause one letter to be mistaken for another, and to give examples of passages from the Law in which such a mistake would turn a divine truth into nonsense or blasphemy" (*Ellicott's Commentary for English Readers,* http://biblehub.com/matthew/5-18.htm).

Verse 19 stresses the importance of perpetual unity between one's teachings and one's actions. One of the biggest problems with the Pharisees is that they often taught one thing and did another. But God's commandments are so important that there is no room for mistakes and misunderstandings surrounding their clarity or accuracy. This is especially so when it comes to teachers of the Law.

The scribes (verse 20) were like secretaries of state, who prepared and disseminated decrees on behalf of the king (see 2 Samuel 8:17; 20:25; 1 Chronicles 18:16). They performed other important public duties and were regarded as men of high authority and influence.

The Pharisees (a Jewish group) are mentioned, either collectively or as individuals, ninety-eight times in the New Testament. "In contrast to the Sadducees, the Pharisees were mostly middle-class businessmen, and therefore were in contact with the common man. The Pharisees were held in much higher esteem by the common man than the Sadducees. Though they were a minority in the Sanhedrin and held a minority number of positions as priests, they seemed to control the decision making of the Sanhedrin far more than the Sadducees did, again because they had the support of the people" (https://www.gotquestions.org/Sadducees-Pharisees.html).

The kingdom of heaven was the bottom line in the life and priority system of Jesus and therefore should also be the central concern of any true disciple. Any kingdom other than God's kingdom is a renegade kingdom. That includes the kingdom of culture and the kingdom of self.

III. CONCLUDING REFLECTION

Jesus taught us to love God and to love others as we love ourselves. We can accomplish this through deciding on radical obedience to God, even when it hurts or when it may be inconvenient. Our radical obedience to God spills over into genuine love and service to others as we love ourselves. We are called not just to live for ourselves, but to impact our world around us as well. Just as salt adds flavor to food, we are called to be spiritual spice to a bland culture and world. The source of our spice and our light is not from ourselves but from the Son of God. As God's light shines through us, we will help others find their way out of the darkness.

PRAYER

Lord, please help us to see Your great light and then to be a bright light to those who desperately need spiritual illumination. In Jesus' name we pray. Amen.

HOME DAILY BIBLE READINGS
(July 1-7, 2019)

Jesus Teaches about Fulfilling the Law
MONDAY, July 1: "Living Wisely" (Colossians 4:1-6)
TUESDAY, July 2: "A Light to the Nations" (Isaiah 42:1-9)
WEDNESDAY, July 3: "Christ's Sacrifice for All" (Hebrews 10:1-10)
THURSDAY, July 4: "Living Humbly" (Matthew 23:1-12)
FRIDAY, July 5: "Applying the Law in New Ways" (Luke 6:1-11)
SATURDAY, July 6: "Deliverance from the Law" (Romans 7:24–8:4)
SUNDAY, July 7: "Interplay of Salt, Light, and Righteousness" (Matthew 5:13-20)

July 14, 2019   **Lesson 7**

JESUS TEACHES US TO LOVE ONE ANOTHER

ADULT/YOUTH	CHILDREN
ADULT/YOUNG ADULT TOPIC: **Love from the Heart**	GENERAL LESSON TITLE: **Jesus Teaches Us to Love One Another**
YOUTH TOPIC: **Love Changes Everything**	CHILDREN'S TOPIC: **Forgiving Others**

DEVOTIONAL READING
Genesis 2:18-24

ADULT/YOUTH	CHILDREN
BACKGROUND SCRIPTURE: **Matthew 5:21-32**	BACKGROUND SCRIPTURE: **Matthew 5:21-32**
PRINT PASSAGE: **Matthew 5:21-32**	PRINT PASSAGE: **Matthew 5:21-25**
KEY VERSES: **Matthew 5:23-24**	KEY VERSES: **Matthew 5:23, 24b**

Matthew 5:21-32—KJV

21 Ye have heard that it was said of them of old time, Thou shalt not kill; and whosoever shall kill shall be in danger of the judgment:

22 But I say unto you, That whosoever is angry with his brother without a cause shall be in danger of the judgment: and whosoever shall say to his brother, Raca, shall be in danger of the council: but whosoever shall say, Thou fool, shall be in danger of hell fire.

23 Therefore if thou bring thy gift to the altar, and there rememberest that thy brother hath ought against thee;

24 Leave there thy gift before the altar, and go thy way; first be reconciled to thy brother, and then come and offer thy gift.

25 Agree with thine adversary quickly, whiles thou art in the way with him; lest at any time the adversary deliver thee to the judge, and the judge deliver thee to the officer, and thou be cast into prison.

Matthew 5:21-32—NIV

21 "You have heard that it was said to the people long ago, 'You shall not murder, and anyone who murders will be subject to judgment.'

22 "But I tell you that anyone who is angry with a brother or sister will be subject to judgment. Again, anyone who says to a brother or sister, 'Raca,' is answerable to the court. And anyone who says, 'You fool!' will be in danger of the fire of hell.

23 "Therefore, if you are offering your gift at the altar and there remember that your brother or sister has something against you,

24 "leave your gift there in front of the altar. First go and be reconciled to them; then come and offer your gift.

25 "Settle matters quickly with your adversary who is taking you to court. Do it while you are still together on the way, or your adversary may hand you over to the judge, and the judge may hand you over to the officer,

26 Verily I say unto thee, Thou shalt by no means come out thence, till thou hast paid the uttermost farthing.
27 Ye have heard that it was said by them of old time, Thou shalt not commit adultery:
28 But I say unto you, That whosoever looketh on a woman to lust after her hath committed adultery with her already in his heart.
29 And if thy right eye offend thee, pluck it out, and cast it from thee: for it is profitable for thee that one of thy members should perish, and not that thy whole body should be cast into hell.
30 And if thy right hand offend thee, cut it off, and cast it from thee: for it is profitable for thee that one of thy members should perish, and not that thy whole body should be cast into hell.
31 It hath been said, Whosoever shall put away his wife, let him give her a writing of divorcement:
32 But I say unto you, That whosoever shall put away his wife, saving for the cause of fornication, causeth her to commit adultery: and whosoever shall marry her that is divorced committeth adultery.

and you may be thrown into prison.
26 "Truly I tell you, you will not get out until you have paid the last penny.
27 "You have heard that it was said, 'You shall not commit adultery.'
28 "But I tell you that anyone who looks at a woman lustfully has already committed adultery with her in his heart.
29 "If your right eye causes you to stumble, gouge it out and throw it away. It is better for you to lose one part of your body than for your whole body to be thrown into hell.
30 "And if your right hand causes you to stumble, cut it off and throw it away. It is better for you to lose one part of your body than for your whole body to go into hell.
31 "It has been said, 'Anyone who divorces his wife must give her a certificate of divorce.'
32 "But I tell you that anyone who divorces his wife, except for sexual immorality, makes her the victim of adultery, and anyone who marries a divorced woman commits adultery."

UNIFYING LESSON PRINCIPLE: Love transforms how we relate to one another. In what form does this transformation come? Jesus taught us how to reflect His light through controlling our anger, being reconciled with others, immediately dealing with sin, and being faithful.

LESSON OBJECTIVES

Upon the completion of this lesson, the students will be able to do the following:

1. Contrast outward conformity to moral rules with the inner purity that Jesus commands.
2. Repent of times when they have obeyed God superficially or hypocritically.
3. Respond to Jesus' call to take practical steps to live righteously.

AGE-LEVEL POINTS TO BE EMPHASIZED

Teachers of ADULTS and YOUTH

—Matthew 5:17-20 details how God values internal righteousness more than external righteousness; Jesus built upon this teaching by focusing on the spirit of the Mosaic Law in regard to its

teachings on murder and adultery in Matthew 5:21-32.

—When Jesus referred to one's controlling his/her anger toward a brother or sister, He was not talking only about a literal family member; instead, He was referring to all members of the family of God.

—The word *hell* in the text comes from the Greek word *gehenna*. The word appears often in Matthew to refer to the eternal destination of the wicked (see Matthew 5:29-30; 10:28; 18:9; 23:15, 33). Hell is not to be confused with Hades (see Luke 16:23), which was the underworld for the dead (known as Sheol in the Old Testament).

—The contrast Jesus set up was not between the Old and New Testaments but, rather, between externalistic interpretation of the rabbinic tradition and His interpretation. (Matthew 5:21)

—The dangerous and destructive effect of human anger, which typically entails a desire to damage or destroy the other person, is stressed throughout Scripture (see Proverbs 20:2; 22:3; 29:22; 2 Corinthians 12:20; Galatians 5:20; James 1:20; etc.). (Matthew 5:22)

—"Looks at a woman with lust" does not refer to a passing glance but to a willful, calculated stare that arouses sexual desire. (Matthew 5:28)

Teachers of CHILDREN

—Jesus spoke to His followers about their need to seek reconciliation with others.

—Jesus reminded His followers of the consequences of anger.

—Jesus wanted the disciples to work out their differences with those who had a grudge against them.

—Jesus urged His followers to make the first move in reestablishing broken relationships.

—Jesus suggested that our gifts to God are meaningless if we have grievances with others.

—Jesus reinterpreted the traditional teachings of God's people in bold new ways.

THE CHRONOLOGICAL SETTING OF THE LESSON

The gospel of Matthew is one of the Gospel letters of the New Testament that is believed to have been written between AD 65 and AD 70. This book was written by the apostle Matthew. The gospel of Matthew traces and recounts the life and ministry of Jesus Christ during the ancient times of the Roman Empire's rule over Israel. These observations are partly based on the gospel of Mark, which was written earlier than Matthew's gospel. The book of Matthew was written one generation after the crucifixion of Jesus Christ and seeks to reaffirm the ministry of Christ as illustrated in Matthew 3 (which took place about AD 30). Mark, Luke, John, and the gospel of Matthew form the four canonical Gospel books of the New Testament that detail the chronological events that shape the life, ministry, death, and resurrection of Christ. All these books approach the narrative of Christ using different styles of writing and different points of emphasis (bible.org).

THE GEOGRAPHICAL AND CULTURAL SETTING OF THE LESSON

The apostle Matthew wrote using Greek or the Aramaic language, and this writing was initially meant for a Greek-speaking Jewish audience. Matthew stresses the point that Jesus is a Jewish Messiah, and to some this indicates that the intended audience was the Jews. This text was possibly written outside of the region of Palestine, and many biblical scholars have argued that it may have been written in the city of Antioch in Syria (see Acts 11:26). The author brings out the growing body of what would become New Testament teachings and contrasts it with the Old Testament; this was common among the religious teachers during the time of Matthew (see Leviticus 19:17; Matthew 5:21-26).

The notion of law and authority is clearly brought out in this chapter with relation to the civil court in Israel as well as God's heavenly court that was the only one competent to deal with the internal issues that cause people to hate and kill one another. It is in this vein that this chapter seeks to correct the ideologies that were common among the scribes and Pharisees and their external observation of sinful acts.

PROMINENT CHARACTER(S) IN THE LESSON

Jesus Christ: He is the main character teaching on observing the laws of the Old Testament, using illustrations about internal anger and hatred that consequently lead people to commit external heinous acts such as murder (see Matthew 5:21). He teaches concerning divine and eternal judgment that is beyond the understanding of the human courts (bible.org).

Pharisees and Scribes: These were the teachers of the people and the interpreters of the Law. In the Jewish community, these individuals were widely respected because they had knowledge of the Scriptures and were dedicated to observing the Law of the Old Testament teachings. They were the main group that Jesus Christ criticized in His teachings (see Matthew 5:20; 12:38).

KEY TERMS IN THE LESSON

Altar (verse 23)—Greek: *thusiastérion* (thoo-see-as-tay'-ree-on): an altar (place for sacrifice).
Gift (verse 23)—Greek: *dóron* (do'-ron): a gift, present.

Heart (verse 28)—Greek: *kardia* (kar-dee'-ah): the heart, mind, character, inner self, will; intention; center.
Judge (verse 25)—Greek: *krités* (kree-tace'): a judge.
Judgment (verse 21)—Greek: *krisis* (kree'-sis): judging; divine judgment.
Reconciled (verse 24)—Greek: *diallassó* (dee-al-las'-so): changed; exchanged; "I reconciled"; changed enmity for friendship.

TOPICAL OUTLINE OF THE LESSON

I. Introduction
   A. Consider the Source
   B. Biblical Background

II. Exposition and Application of the Scripture
   A. Murder, He Wrote (Matthew 5:21-22)
   B. Heavenly Harmony (Matthew 5:23-26)
   C. Avoiding Adultery (Matthew 5:27-30)
   D. Divorce Directives (Matthew 5:31-32)

III. Concluding Reflection

I. INTRODUCTION

A. Consider the Source

In this section of the Sermon on the Mount, Jesus gave an interpretation of the Law and acknowledged how the Law was taught. We see Jesus make a visible distinction between what the Law taught and what He declared by His authority when He says, "but I say unto you." Consider the Source! While speaking, Jesus did not condemn in an outright manner the explanation of the Law. However, He expanded its meaning and also showed how God desires a pure heart filled with love for God. Jesus did not come to abolish the Law, but to fulfill the true purpose of the Law.

Jesus began by addressing the action of murder. He, however, does not stop at the common meaning of murder but extends it to include slander of anyone (see Psalm 101:5; James 4:11). Murder is a sin, but so is slander (which is using the tongue to murder someone). This truly does not proceed from the heart of a Christian who is filled with love. Rather than kill with both hand and tongue, Christians are expected to make peace with those who offend them.

B. Biblical Background

As Christians and ambassadors of Christ on earth, our work must always portray and reflect the love of God. When we are able to show love, then we can truly show remorse and express our regrets to those we might have hurt and equally forgive them of any offense they might also have done to us, just as God has forgiven us (see Colossians 3:14; 1 John 4:7).

Jesus in this passage touched on the subject of adultery, in which lust is included. Lust is a sin and must not be found in the life of any Christian or in the marriage relationship of Christians. Christian marriage is a symbol of the union of Christ and the church. As Christ's union with the church is pure, so also are we expected to show purity in marriage.

From verses 21-22 of our text, Jesus Christ began a contrast when He quoted the Law: "Thou shalt not kill" (Exodus 20:13). As clearly seen and understood in the Old and New Testaments, killing refers to murder. Jesus, however, went beyond this literal, legalistic meaning to bring about an extended view to include anger as an inner intention which could lead to such a sin (see 2 Samuel 6:20; Exodus 10:13; Deuteronomy 5:17). Consequently, Jesus here suggested that verbal abuse proceeds from a heart of sinful motives and anger and hatred, which could lead to murder. Jesus here tried to show that insults and abuses that proceed from the mouth carry the same guilt as murder.

In verses 23-24, after illustrating the similarities between murder and the inner intentions of hatred which produce abusive words, Jesus went on to show an example of one who intended to buy a clear conscience through gifts to God without first clearing his conscience by reconciling with his brother. The latter is actually paramount, since reconciliation is the tool through which forgiveness can be shown and love expressed. Christians, we must love our brothers and sisters in Christ just the way we love ourselves. Any offering made from a bitter heart cannot be accepted by God. We must learn to forgive everyone, including the "opponent at law" (one who is in legal dispute with us). Jesus always wants us to reconcile with our brothers, sisters, or just anyone.

From verses 27-28, we see that Jesus began to discuss the problem of adultery, which also was found in the Law (see Exodus 20:14). And like murder, Jesus once again revealed how adultery was first carried out inwardly (lust) before the physical act took place. Here, we are also brought to the consciousness that glancing or looking could cause adultery even without the physical action. In the Old Testament era, people who indulged in adultery were stoned to death. On Judgment Day, our hearts will first be judged before our deeds and actions. A desire to sin is worse than when the action of sin is committed. Our hearts are intended to produce love and grace (see Romans 10:9-10).

As discussed in verses 29-30, Jesus made an illustration which should not be taken literally. This was the statement of cutting off one's hand or plucking out one's eye. The intent of the illustration was that we ought to recognize that lust comes from within the mind and heart of a man and not the actual physical organ. Consequently, we can separate ourselves from people or places that contribute to our sin as a beginning to cease our sinful behavior. Thus, Jesus was teaching that it would be much better for one to lose his/her body here on earth in order to gain eternity. We must deal with sin in our bodies so that we may gain eternity.

II. EXPOSITION AND APPLICATION OF THE SCRIPTURE

A. Murder, He Wrote
(Matthew 5:21-22)

Ye have heard that it was said of them of old time, Thou shalt not kill; and whosoever shall kill shall be in danger of the judgment: But I say unto you, That whosoever is angry with his brother without a cause shall be in danger of the judgment: and whosoever shall say to his brother, Raca, shall be in danger of the council: but whosoever shall say, Thou fool, shall be in danger of hell fire.

The sixth commandment is "Thou shall not kill" (verse 21). Murder is commonly regarded as one of the worst social infractions known to humanity. Jesus used this egregious act to set the context of the point that He was about to make. Murder happens when a person takes another person's life. But God is the giver and the sustainer of life. It was God who breathed His life into the nostrils of human creation and His creation became a living soul. Since humans cannot create or ultimately sustain life, then they also have no natural right to take another human life.

Anger (verse 22) is a natural human emotion that is usually triggered by an inner or outer sense of deep hurt, fear, or frustration. Today's text is a good example of the fact that the purpose of the Bible was not only to address super-spiritual theological topics, but also to provide practical insight on how to successfully navigate the nuances of everyday life. The text does not address all anger, but it targets being angry for no good reason. The danger of this kind of blind anger is that it could soon turn into harsh actions that one will later regret.

The word *raca* means "vain fellows," as is seen in Judges 9:4; 11:3; and Proverbs 12:11. This term was commonly used to express insolent contempt, a sense of being despised, and basic anger. When we are no longer able to recognize the mere humanity of a person regardless of his or her offense, we sink to "raca" level. The term *council* referred to the great Sanhedrin court, which consisted of seventy to seventy-two members, a president, and a vice president. In addition, there were also priests, elders, and scribes who were part of the Sanhedrin.

Have you ever called someone a fool, or have you ever been called a fool by someone else? The Greek word translated "fool" in today's text is similar to the instance used in Psalm 14:1 and is an expression of utter contempt. Here, the choice of words is not as important as the condition of the heart, and the same word can be acceptably used with a righteously indignant heart, as is seen by the fact that Jesus Himself used this term in Matthew 23:17, 19 (see *Ellicott's Commentary for English Readers*, http://biblehub.com/commentaries/matthew/5-22.htm).

B. Heavenly Harmony
(Matthew 5:23-26)

Therefore if thou bring thy gift to the altar, and there rememberest that thy brother hath ought against thee; Leave there thy gift before the altar, and go thy way; first be reconciled to thy brother, and then come and offer thy gift. Agree with thine adversary quickly, whiles thou art in the way with him; lest at any time the adversary deliver thee to the judge, and the judge deliver thee to the officer, and thou be cast into prison. Verily I say unto thee, Thou shalt by no means come out thence, till thou hast paid the uttermost farthing.

Interestingly, Jesus connected harmony of the heart to the question of inner healing. A prompt offering given while living with a splintered relationship is not as important as a unified relationship and a gift that is brought later (verses 23-24). The emphasis here is beyond personal recognition of internal conflict with a brother or sister. Even if our hearts and consciences are clear, we as Christians also are called to consider and work toward eradicating any negative dispositions that others may have against us. Throughout Scripture, the importance of oneness, unity, and harmony are elevated to top importance. Jesus insisted in Mark 3:25 that a house divided against itself cannot stand. In the high priestly prayer before His betrayal, Jesus prayed that the disciples might be one in heart and spirit.

Jesus realized that harmony was paramount in the work of discipleship to ensure the success of God's kingdom. Distractions caused by common conflict can easily hinder and even immobilize the progress of a local church.

Not only was Jesus concerned about the presence of conflict, but He was also sensitive to the timing of the settlement of disagreements (verses 25-26).

C. Avoiding Adultery
(Matthew 5:27-30)

Ye have heard that it was said by them of old time, Thou shalt not commit adultery: But I say unto you, That whosoever looketh on a woman to lust after her hath committed adultery with her already in his heart. And if thy right eye offend thee, pluck it out, and cast it from thee: for it is profitable for thee that one of thy members should perish, and not that thy whole body should be cast into hell. And if thy right hand offend thee, cut it off, and cast it from thee: for it is profitable for thee that one of thy members should perish, and not that thy whole body should be cast into hell.

Here in verse 27, Jesus turned His attention to the seventh commandment: "Thou shall not commit adultery."

There are at least three well-known instances in which Jesus encountered a woman with a questionable sexual history. One of these encounters is chronicled in John 4, featuring the Samaritan woman that Jesus addressed concerning her living arrangement: "You are right when you say you have no husband. The fact is, you have had five husbands, and the man you now have is not your husband. What you have just said is quite true" (verses 17b-18, NIV). Here, the purpose was not only to expose the sin, but also to propose a remedy. A second instance occurred in John 8 when a crowd brought to Jesus a woman who was caught in the act of adultery, and they asked Jesus what should be done to her. It was a trick to try to trap Him. Jesus' classic response to their question was, "Let any one of you who is without sin be the first to throw a stone at her" (verse 7, NIV). After her accusers left, Jesus addressed the woman: "'Neither do I condemn you,' Jesus declared. 'Go now and leave your life of sin'" (verse 11, NIV). It is almost as important to acknowledge what Jesus did not do as it is to acknowledge what Jesus did do. Jesus did not condemn her. Jesus did not excuse her. Perhaps most significant, Jesus did not ignore her. The third instance concerns the sinful woman who anointed Jesus' feet in Luke 7. Jesus' response to her in verse 47 (NIV) was, "Therefore, I tell you, her many sins have been forgiven—as her great love has shown. But whoever has been forgiven little loves little." In this third setting, Jesus acknowledged her sins and forgave her based on her extravagant and emotional expression of love and repentance, as exhibited by her tears and her acts and attitude of sacrificial love and humility.

Jesus went beyond the scope of the Old Testament definition of "adultery" to include not only the physical act of adultery, but also the attitude of the adulterous heart (verse 28). Most people would acknowledge that pollution of the body is problematic. But what about pollution of the mind?

These graphic descriptions in verses 29 and 30 succeed in capturing the attention of the reader. Jesus used as an example two of the most prominent and useful exterior body parts (the eye and hand) to effectively illustrate the overriding importance of sacrificing the freedom, usage, and pleasure of one body part in order to ensure the salvation of the whole body. Just as with a situation of necessary amputation, as radical as removal may seem, it is the preferable option when it may determine life or death.

D. Divorce Directives
(Matthew 5:31-32)

It hath been said, Whosoever shall put away his wife, let him give her a writing of divorcement: But I say unto you, That whosoever shall put away his wife, saving for the cause of fornication, causeth her to commit adultery: and whosoever shall marry her that is divorced committeth adultery.

Great abuses had arisen in Jesus' time with regards to divorce, which was permitted on very trivial grounds (verse 31). One rabbinical saying was, "If any man hate his wife, let him put her away" (*Cambridge Bible for Schools and Colleges*). The reference to this divorce law (see Deuteronomy 24:1) was probably directed toward the scribes who busied themselves solely about getting the bill of separation into due legal form. They did nothing to restrain the unjust caprice of husbands; they rather opened a wider door to license.

Some of the rabbis allowed divorce to be granted on the grounds that the wife was displeasing to her husband or that the husband was attracted to a more beautiful woman. As we discuss the topic of divorce, it is important to understand that "Christ did not come to be a new legislator making laws for social life. He came to set up a high ethical ideal, and leave that to work on men's minds. The tendency of His teaching is to create deep aversion to the rupture of married relations. That aversion might even go the length of shrinking from severance of the tie even in the case of one who had forfeited all claims" (*The Expositor's Greek Testament*, *Volume 1*, edited by Sir William Robertson Nicoll, p. 110).

But Jesus casted heavenly light on what Moses allowed in verse 32. According to the Law of Moses, if the husband left his wife, there were certain necessary steps in the process: "If a man marries a woman who becomes displeasing to him because he finds something indecent about her, and he writes her a certificate of divorce, gives it to her and sends her from his house, and if after she leaves his house she becomes the wife of another man" (Deuteronomy 24:1-2, NIV). Of course, civil laws and financial responsibilities have significantly changed since the time this ordinance was written. According to Malachi 2:16 (NIV), "'The man who hates and divorces his wife,' says the LORD, the God of Israel, 'does violence to the one he should protect,' says the LORD Almighty. So be on your guard, and do not be unfaithful."

III. CONCLUDING REFLECTION

Love is the transformative factor that informs and impacts the way that we relate to each other in everyday life. We reflect the light of Jesus as we manage our anger, unify from conflicts, become reconciled with others, and eradicate patterns of sin. Outward conformity to spiritual and moral rules is made possible through inward purity that Jesus commands. God calls us to righteous living through controlling our behavior through disciplining our minds, our tongues, our time, and our money. Marriage is a microcosm of life, and it calls us to live in close proximity to another human being. This requires that we become transparent as well as vulnerable and truthful. Not everyone is able to endure the weight and pressure that comes with the territory of a healthy marriage. But those who are considering marriage should submit to a rigorous, spiritual, and competent course of examination, coaching, and counseling in order to help them make the right decisions about the institution of marriage.

PRAYER

Dear God, thank You for giving us the power to fulfill the purpose for which we have been created. Help us to see Your face and to live in harmony with those who walk beside us along the pathway of life. In Jesus' name we pray. Amen.

HOME DAILY BIBLE READINGS
(July 8-14, 2019)

Jesus Teaches Us to Love One Another

MONDAY, July 8: "Obey Judicial Rulings at Once" (Deuteronomy 17:8-11)

TUESDAY, July 9: "Handling Temptations" (Mark 9:42-48)

WEDNESDAY, July 10: "Living with Neighbors" (Leviticus 19:11-18)

THURSDAY, July 11: "Living with Believers" (1 Thessalonians 5:12-18)

FRIDAY, July 12: "The Unbreakable Marital Bond" (Mark 10:2-9)

SATURDAY, July 13: "Let Yes Be Yes—No, No" (Matthew 5:33-37)

SUNDAY, July 14: "Commit to Love Each Other" (Matthew 5:21-32)

July 21, 2019   **Lesson 8**

JESUS TEACHES ABOUT TRANSFORMING LOVE

ADULT/YOUTH
ADULT/YOUNG ADULT TOPIC: **All You Need Is Love**
YOUTH TOPIC: **A Love that Transforms**

CHILDREN
GENERAL LESSON TITLE: **Jesus Teaches Us to Love Our Enemies**
CHILDREN'S TOPIC: **Loving Our Enemies**

DEVOTIONAL READING
Romans 12:9-21

ADULT/YOUTH
BACKGROUND SCRIPTURE: **Matthew 5:38-48**
PRINT PASSAGE: **Matthew 5:38-48**
ADULT KEY VERSES: **Matthew 5:43-44**
YOUTH KEY VERSE: **Matthew 5:44**

CHILDREN
BACKGROUND SCRIPTURE: **Matthew 5:38-48**
PRINT PASSAGE: **Matthew 5:38-48**
KEY VERSE: **Matthew 5:44**

Matthew 5:38-48—KJV

38 Ye have heard that it hath been said, An eye for an eye, and a tooth for a tooth:

39 But I say unto you, That ye resist not evil: but whosoever shall smite thee on thy right cheek, turn to him the other also.

40 And if any man will sue thee at the law, and take away thy coat, let him have thy cloak also.

41 And whosoever shall compel thee to go a mile, go with him twain.

42 Give to him that asketh thee, and from him that would borrow of thee turn not thou away.

43 Ye have heard that it hath been said, Thou shalt love thy neighbour, and hate thine enemy.

44 But I say unto you, Love your enemies, bless them that curse you, do good to them that hate you, and pray for them which despitefully use you, and persecute you;

Matthew 5:38-48—NIV

38 "You have heard that it was said, 'Eye for eye, and tooth for tooth.'

39 "But I tell you, do not resist an evil person. If anyone slaps you on the right cheek, turn to them the other cheek also.

40 "And if anyone wants to sue you and take your shirt, hand over your coat as well.

41 "If anyone forces you to go one mile, go with them two miles.

42 "Give to the one who asks you, and do not turn away from the one who wants to borrow from you.

43 "You have heard that it was said, 'Love your neighbor and hate your enemy.'

44 "But I tell you, love your enemies and pray for those who persecute you,

45 "that you may be children of your Father in heaven.

45 That ye may be the children of your Father which is in heaven: for he maketh his sun to rise on the evil and on the good, and sendeth rain on the just and on the unjust.

46 For if ye love them which love you, what reward have ye? do not even the publicans the same?

47 And if ye salute your brethren only, what do ye more than others? do not even the publicans so?

48 Be ye therefore perfect, even as your Father which is in heaven is perfect.

He causes his sun to rise on the evil and the good, and sends rain on the righteous and the unrighteous.

46 "If you love those who love you, what reward will you get? Are not even the tax collectors doing that?

47 "And if you greet only your own people, what are you doing more than others? Do not even pagans do that?

48 "Be perfect, therefore, as your heavenly Father is perfect."

UNIFYING LESSON PRINCIPLE: Many people believe that retribution is justified when they are mistreated. What is the appropriate response when people are mistreated? Jesus taught His disciples to love their enemies and pray for those who persecute them.

LESSON OBJECTIVES

Upon the completion of this lesson, the students will be able to do the following:

1. Tell what it means for one to love his or her enemy.
2. Desire that those who act contrary to Christ's ethic of love would come to experience Christ's love.
3. Pray that God would work through them to touch and transform the lives of unloving people.

AGE-LEVEL POINTS TO BE EMPHASIZED

Teachers of ADULTS and YOUTH

—This passage echoes a theme found throughout the Beatitudes in which Jesus called His followers to exhibit behavior that exceeds the common wisdom of unbelievers.

—The command to "be perfect" (verse 48) was a call to be more complete rather than be sinless. It was not intended to discourage disciples who make mistakes but, rather, to be an encouragement to adopt God's standards of radical love as our own.

—This is referencing Leviticus 24:19-20, which says to do the opposite of what Jesus is now saying. (Matthew 5:38)

—Jesus' teaching here is very radical and would have been very countercultural to His listeners; being called to love your enemy was rare. (Matthew 5:39-43)

—Love here means *agape* and is a sacrificial love that is unique in its character. (Matthew 5:43)

—Leviticus 19:18 speaks of not doing wrong to your own people, and Jesus is clearly expanding this to not doing wrong to anyone, including enemies. (Matthew 5:43-44)

—Tax collectors and pagans were seen as sinners; so, if we too only love those who love us, then we are not doing that differently. (Matthew 5:46)

—"Perfect" in the Greek means "teleioi," which means to mature and be full grown. (Matthew 5:48)

Teachers of CHILDREN

—Jesus spoke hard words about not retaliating when we are hurt.

—Jesus held up the ideal of returning good for evil.

—Jesus practiced what He preached about loving our enemies.

—Jesus pointed to tax collectors and Gentiles as people who failed to love their enemies.

—Jesus wanted His followers to strive for the perfect love of God, the heavenly Father.

—Nations that claim to follow Jesus forget the ideal of love when they are threatened.

THE CHRONOLOGICAL SETTING OF THE LESSON

The gospel of Matthew was written during the rule of the Roman Empire between AD 65 and AD 70. Matthew was a tax collector and one of the twelve apostles of Christ. This gospel contains the genealogy and the historical events surrounding the life, ministry, death, and resurrection of Jesus Christ. It is one of the four canonical Gospels of the New Testament, which are written collections of sayings and teachings of Jesus Christ in the Greek and Aramaic languages. This gospel was partially based on the earlier gospel of Mark, which is believed to have been written around AD 40 in the form of a narrative recounting the history of Jesus of Nazareth. The other canonical Gospels of the New Testament also recount the life and ministry of Christ, using somewhat varied content and their own forms and style of writing. They include the gospels of Mark, Luke, and John (bible.org).

THE GEOGRAPHICAL AND CULTURAL SETTING OF THE LESSON

The gospel of Matthew was written after the fall of Jerusalem and the destruction of the Temple in the city of Jerusalem in AD 70. Matthew, also known as Levi, was a tax collector and one of the twelve disciples committed to the ministry of Christ. Early church fathers suggested that the book of Matthew was first written in Hebrew, and this may be because the initial audience of this gospel were the Jews who were despaired and shocked after the fall of Jerusalem. However, other biblical scholars have argued that the original composition language remains unresolved (bible.org).

Matthew portrays a nonviolent Savior in his writing of the gospel through his portrayal of the character and the teachings of Christ, who advocates for passivism for the sword-bearing rule of the Roman Empire (see Matthew 5:38-42). Jesus urged His followers to turn the other cheek and give up the garment, which simply implies that Christians were not to engage in physical force for justice in the society but, instead, show counterintuitive strategies that will effect peaceful social transformations (see Matthew 5:38-42).

Jesus taught His disciples and followers that civil retribution has no place in the kingdom of heaven; He, instead, encouraged them to show the ethical virtues of mercy and forgiveness. This provides a framework for appreciation of exegetical conclusion of reformed Christianity rather than retributive justice. The apostle also presents the six antitheses that show how Jesus compared the newness of the Gospel to the Mosaic Law, and how Christ fulfills these laws through His sacrificial death (see Matthew 5:17-20).

PROMINENT CHARACTER(S) IN THE LESSON

Jesus Christ: He is the main masterpiece in Matthew's gospel. Jesus is teaching His disciples concerning the interpretation of the Law and authority of the state. He criticizes how the scribes, Pharisees, and the Sadducees interpret the Law and urges His followers to show mercy and forgiveness instead of judgmental retribution.

The Disciples: Jesus is directing this message to His followers and disciples on the nature of true discipleship, and how they should passively endure their humiliation under Roman rule and show forgiveness. (bible.org)

KEY TERMS IN THE LESSON

Cheek (verse 39)—Greek: *siagón* (see-ag-one'): the jawbone, cheek.

Eye (verse 38)—Greek: *ophthalmos* (of-thal-mos'): the eye.

Give (verse 42)—Greek: *didómi* (did'-o-mee): offer; give; put; place.

Resist (verse 39)—Greek: *anthistémi* (anth-is'-tay-mee): take a stand against; oppose; resist.

Sue (verse 40)—Greek: *krinó* (kree'-no): to judge, decide.

Tooth (verse 38)—Greek: *odous* (od-ooce): a tooth.

TOPICAL OUTLINE OF THE LESSON

I. **Introduction**
  A. Seeing beyond the Law
  B. Biblical Background

II. **Exposition and Application of the Scripture**
  A. Revised Revenge
    (Matthew 5:38-42)
  B. The Hardest Kind of Love
    (Matthew 5:43-45)
  C. The Easiest Kind of Love
    (Matthew 5:46-48)

III. **Concluding Reflection**

I. INTRODUCTION

A. Seeing Beyond the Law

Our Lesson Scripture is Matthew 5:38-48, which is part of the larger section of the Sermon on the Mount that we examined in the previous lessons. This passage provides us with six illustrations of what Jesus meant by fulfilling the Law. These illustrations begin with the Jewish laws: 1) forbidding murder; 2) forbidding adultery; 3) the need for a certificate of divorce; 4) forbidding false swearing; 5) forbidding revenge; 6) loving our neighbors.

In this text, Jesus showed us how to see beyond the observance of the Law to seeing the spirit behind the Law. He showed us how to be children of God who reflect God's love and God's will in our everyday actions and relationships. These verses are strictly about living according to God's standard and that of His kingdom. The difficulty of living up to these standards reminds us that the grace of God has been and still is our only hope. God's grace is sufficient, as is seen in Romans 3:23 and 2 Corinthians 12:9.

B. Biblical Background

Our focal passage begins in Matthew 5:38, which marks the beginning of a review of the law "an eye for an eye." The events in Matthew 5–7 are said to have occurred in AD 27.

Our text opens with the Old Testament saying of "an eye for an eye, and a tooth for a tooth," which expresses the intent for equalization of justice. Jesus, in quoting this law, intended for us to resist and not to retaliate when someone has wronged us. Jesus here was not focusing on revenge, nor did He in any way mean for us to be weak or passive. Rather, He wanted us to look beyond revenge and being vindictive. Jesus here encourages us to respond to evil with good, as this is the standard of God and His kingdom.

In verses 39-42, Jesus provided us with four different examples of what it actually means not to take revenge. In His first example, Jesus illustrated the act of being hit (slapped) on the right cheek and suggested that we offer the other side also to be hit. The whole essence of His illustration is to encourage us (at all times) to never seek revenge and to avoid retaliation. This cannot take place except we learn to love like God, for when we love without limits, we love like God.

In the second illustration in verse 40, Jesus said, "If anyone wants to sue you and take your shirt, let him have your coat also" (NASB). The cloak, as it was known, is an outer robe which is an indispensable part of a clothing that the poor also used in sleeping. The cloak was very important, so much that even if an opponent had won it in court, he had to return it every evening for the one to sleep in. This was the law of the time. In essence, Jesus was speaking to the poor among His followers who, in their persecution, were denied their most basic need and taught that instead of defending themselves or retaliating, they should ultimately let go for the sake of the kingdom and the One in whom they believe.

In the third example in verse 41, Jesus said that if a person forces you to go one mile, go with him two. This illustration demonstrates and encourages us to go the extra mile—put in that extra time, effort, care, and so forth. God's standard requires us to give our best even if it means going an extra length to achieve it. We are to be a blessing continually.

In His fourth and final illustration in verse 42, Jesus said that we are to give to those who ask, and do not turn away those who want to borrow from you. This illustration is linked to the law about lending in Deuteronomy 15:7-11. Jesus here is talking about people with legitimate needs. It is our responsibility to be generous and to discern whether a person has legitimate needs.

Finally, in verses 43-48, Jesus began to speak on unconditional love. He reminded listeners of the Old Testament law when He said, "You have heard that it was said, 'Love your neighbor and hate your enemy'" (verse 43 [NIV]; see Leviticus 19:18)—but He took it to a whole new level far beyond their expectations when, in verse 44, He said, "But I say to you, love your enemies and pray for those who persecute you" (NASB). Love in this context is commanded. This truly requires spiritual strength and dexterity to fulfill. Jesus is not calling us to like our enemies or like whatever they do; rather, the command is to love! And the only love that could satisfy this is *agape* love—the God kind of love.

The sole purpose of exhibiting this kind of love, according to Jesus, is so that we may be sons of our Father who is in heaven. He sends sun and rain to everyone equally, whether they be His child or not. We are here encouraged to show and share the characteristics of our

Father—as it is not just enough to be called His children.

In conclusion, Jesus summarized His teachings by encouraging us to be perfect just as our heavenly Father is perfect (verse 48). This is the goal of Christianity. Until we begin to love like God loves, we may never attain the level of perfection that God wants from us.

II. EXPOSITION AND APPLICATION OF THE SCRIPTURE

A. Revised Revenge
(Matthew 5:38-42)

Ye have heard that it hath been said, An eye for an eye, and a tooth for a tooth: But I say unto you, That ye resist not evil: but whosoever shall smite thee on thy right cheek, turn to him the other also. And if any man will sue thee at the law, and take away thy coat, let him have thy cloak also. And whosoever shall compel thee to go a mile, go with him twain. Give to him that asketh thee, and from him that would borrow of thee turn not thou away.

In verse 38, Jesus discussed the very natural and human subject of revenge. To exact revenge upon someone means to retaliate or to get even by means of verbal, emotional, psychological, or physical injury to the offending party. By using the phrase "you have heard that it was said," Jesus again made an oblique reference to the tendencies of the scribes who usually held strictly to the letter of the Law without much care for the spirit of the Law.

Upon initially reading or hearing this perspective (verse 39), it almost seems unthinkable that any rational person would actually offer his or her face to be slapped a second time. In this passage, Jesus was addressing and explaining the letter of the Law versus the intent of the Law. In this very sentence, Jesus issued a directive that was intended to express a particular attitude, disposition, and response rather than serve as an eternal template for universal replication. Support for this perspective is seen in Jesus' own response when confronted with a similar situation in John 18:22-23 (NIV):

"When Jesus said this, one of the officials nearby slapped him in the face. 'Is this the way you answer the high priest?' he demanded. 'If I said something wrong,' Jesus replied, 'testify as to what is wrong. But if I spoke the truth, why did you strike me?'" Jesus responded to this rude, brute gesture in a humble, nonviolent, and nonretaliatory manner while still maintaining His dignity and His spirituality. We are called to emulate the behavior of Jesus when in similar situations.

This issue of legal revenge (verse 40) is similar to the previously discussed issue of physical revenge. Both are presented as a distraction and a waste of valuable time and energy for the disciple. Paul maintained a similar perspective in 1 Corinthians 6:1-4 (NIV): "If any of you has a dispute with another, do you dare to take it before the ungodly for judgment instead of before the Lord's people? Or do you not know that the Lord's people will judge the world? And if you are to judge the world, are you not competent to judge trivial cases? Do you not know that we will judge angels? How much more the things of this life! Therefore, if you have disputes about such matters, do you ask for a ruling from those whose way of life is scorned in the church?"

After Paul initially identified the problem, he then explained to his readers why suing a brother or sister in Christ may not be the best decision and appealed to the reader's sense of decency and self-respect in 1 Corinthians 6:5-7 (NIV): "I say this to shame you. Is it possible that there is nobody among you wise enough to judge a dispute between believers? But instead, one brother takes another to court—and this in front of unbelievers! The very fact that you have lawsuits among you means you have been completely defeated already. Why not rather be wronged? Why not rather be cheated?"

Some governments utilized a system of forced service (verse 41) in which they used certain citizens as couriers or messengers. The message conveyed in the text is to gladly go beyond the expected call of duty in order to be a good representative of the Gospel of Jesus Christ and the kingdom of God (*Ellicott's Commentary for English Readers*). The inference here is to allow reasonable personal discomfort and inconvenience if such actions bring greater glory to God. Those who act upon the right kinds of principles and values will have the greatest amount of personal peace and comfort.

The spotlight here in verse 42 is on a sense of generosity and hospitality. When it is within one's power to give, one should strive to give to those who ask. However, such principles should always be balanced by the all-purpose principles of wisdom and discernment. Scriptures such as 2 Thessalonians 3:10 (NIV) assist with latitude in this matter: "For even when we were with you, we gave you this rule: 'The one who is unwilling to work shall not eat.'"

B. The Hardest Kind of Love
(Matthew 5:43-45)

Ye have heard that it hath been said, Thou shalt love thy neighbour, and hate thine enemy. But I say unto you, Love your enemies, bless them that curse you, do good to them that hate you, and pray for them which despitefully use you, and persecute you; That ye may be the children of your Father which is in heaven: for he maketh his sun to rise on the evil and on the good, and sendeth rain on the just and on the unjust.

Some teachers of the Law adopted the approach and perspective that only those who were from their own country, their own race, and their own religion were to be deemed as neighbors and friends (verse 43). Jesus had a different perspective and insisted that God, who is Father of all, has a much wider concept regarding kinship, relationship, and responsibility. This is an age-old lesson that was first taught in the Genesis 4:9 Creation narrative: "Then the LORD said to Cain, 'Where is your brother Abel?' 'I don't know,' he replied. 'Am I my brother's keeper?'" (NIV). Although there is no recorded response to this question, the implicit answer is a resounding yes. In Mark 3:35 (NIV), after Jesus was informed that His blood relatives were waiting for Him outside the house where He was ministering, His response was, "Whoever does God's will is my brother and sister and mother."

Jesus taught that our extending kindness must not be limited to those who are kind to us (verse 44). The hardest kind of love is to love those who are unlovable. However, it is often the unlovely who are most in need of love. "Others salute their brethren, and embrace those of their own party, and way, and opinion, but we must not so confine our respect. It is the duty of Christians to desire, and aim at, and press towards perfection in grace and holiness. And therein we must study to conform ourselves to the example of our heavenly Father, [1 Peter 1:15, 16]. Surely more is to be expected from the followers of Christ than from others; surely more will be found in them than in others. Let us beg of God to enable us to prove ourselves his children" (*Matthew Henry Commentary*, http://biblehub.com/matthew/5-45.htm).

C. The Easiest Kind of Love
(Matthew 5:46-48)

For if ye love them which love you, what reward have ye? do not even the publicans the same? And if ye salute your brethren only, what do ye more than others? do not even the publicans so? Be ye therefore perfect, even as your Father which is in heaven is perfect.

The easiest kind of love is love that is equally and automatically reciprocated. Such love makes few laborious demands, and this does not always provide the length and breadth of experiences and conditions necessary to adequately test and prove the reality and durability of love.

Jesus noted that our loving those who love us is so easy that even tax collectors are capable. Tax collectors in New Testament times were much more loathed than our modern-day Internal Revenue Service. The Roman system of taxation was demoralizing to all engaged in it.

People usually reserved greetings and salutations for those who were of the same nation or family, or who were friends (verse 47). The same is often still true today. We have an innate and instinctive tendency to acknowledge and gravitate to those with whom we naturally connect and relate. "By saluting is meant common [offerings] of kindness, such as inquiring of our neighbours' health, wishing them well, etc. The publicans were civil officers appointed by the Romans to gather up public taxes and revenues. The chief commissioners were knights and gentlemen of Rome, who either [assigned] these revenues to others, or employed others

under them in the collecting of them" (*Matthew Poole's Commentary*, http://biblehub.com/commentaries/matthew/5-47.htm). Since these individuals were so hated, they were usually not even greeted in the marketplace. Jesus was preaching and teaching how to let love make a difference in the often-overlooked, everyday matters of life.

The word translated "perfect" (verse 48) comes from the Greek word *teleios*, which means "complete" (*Strong's Exhaustive Concordance*). Another word that is helpful in our ability to process the concept presented here is the word *mature*. Spiritual maturity is an ongoing process rather than a one-time event. Many Christians love to excuse their less-than-stellar behavior by remarking, "Nobody's perfect." This is true, but we are never to give up the quest for spiritual maturity—for that, not flawlessness, is our goal. The text leaves no doubt that attainment to maturity—to perfection according to creaturely limits—is eventually possible.

But when this attainment can be made is not stated. Many will, indeed, affirm that, as our Lord is giving directions to his disciples concerning things in this life, the attainment also is affirmed to be possible in this life. But this by no means follows. Christ gives the command, and by the form of it implies that it shall be carried out to the full. But this is quite consistent with the conception of a gradually increasing development of love which, in fact will attain maturity, a state in which God's love has ever been; but not immediately and not before the final completion of all Christ's work in us. (*The Complete Pulpit Commentary, Volume 7: Matthew to John*, Henry D. M. Spence)

III. CONCLUDING REFLECTION

Jesus desired to have an influence and an impact on the way we interact with our friends as well as our perceived enemies. Although it is often difficult for us to love the unlovable, through Christ it is indeed possible. Nowhere in the Old Testament are the covenant people instructed to hate their enemies. In the current social and political climate, we can learn much from the life lessons of Jesus regarding loving the unlovable. God's expectation is perfection. This state is ultimately possible through travelling the pathway of spiritual maturity. Through commitment to a life of spiritual discipline, we will eventually be able to accept Jesus' call to a higher standard than the world's, hate evil but not evildoers, and imitate God by showing unconditional love.

PRAYER

Lord, thank You for calling us to a higher calling and for equipping us with the power to reach spiritual maturity. In Jesus' name we pray. Amen.

HOME DAILY BIBLE READINGS
(July 15-21, 2019)

Jesus Teaches about Transforming Love

MONDAY, July 15: "Restrain Your Anger" (Leviticus 24:16-22)

TUESDAY, July 16: "Filled with Grace" (Acts 6:8-15)

WEDNESDAY, July 17: "Transformed Giving and Praying" (Matthew 6:1-6)

THURSDAY, July 18: "The Lord Honors Patience" (Lamentations 3:25-33)

FRIDAY, July 19: "Love Your Neighbors" (Romans 13:1-10)

SATURDAY, July 20: "The Greatest Commandments" (Matthew 22:34-40)

SUNDAY, July 21: "Practice Love toward All" (Matthew 5:38-48)

July 28, 2019   **Lesson 9**

JESUS TEACHES ABOUT SPIRITUAL DISCERNMENT

ADULT/YOUTH
ADULT/YOUNG ADULT TOPIC: The Pursuit of Truth
YOUTH TOPIC: Resist Judgment

CHILDREN
GENERAL LESSON TITLE: Jesus Teaches How to Think about Others
CHILDREN'S TOPIC: Judging and Being Judged

DEVOTIONAL READING
Galatians 5:16-26

ADULT/YOUTH
BACKGROUND SCRIPTURE: Matthew 7:1-6, 15-23
PRINT PASSAGE: Matthew 7:1-6, 15-23
ADULT KEY VERSES: Matthew 7:15-16a
YOUTH KEY VERSE: Matthew 7:1

CHILDREN
BACKGROUND SCRIPTURE: Matthew 7:1-6, 15-23
PRINT PASSAGE: Matthew 7:1-6, 15-23
KEY VERSE: Matthew 7:1

Matthew 7:1-6, 15-23—KJV

JUDGE NOT, that ye be not judged.

2 For with what judgment ye judge, ye shall be judged: and with what measure ye mete, it shall be measured to you again.

3 And why beholdest thou the mote that is in thy brother's eye, but considerest not the beam that is in thine own eye?

4 Or how wilt thou say to thy brother, Let me pull out the mote out of thine eye; and, behold, a beam is in thine own eye?

5 Thou hypocrite, first cast out the beam out of thine own eye; and then shalt thou see clearly to cast out the mote out of thy brother's eye.

6 Give not that which is holy unto the dogs, neither cast ye your pearls before swine, lest they trample them under their feet, and turn again and rend you.

Matthew 7:1-6, 15-23—NIV

"DO NOT judge, or you too will be judged.

2 "For in the same way you judge others, you will be judged, and with the measure you use, it will be measured to you.

3 "Why do you look at the speck of sawdust in your brother's eye and pay no attention to the plank in your own eye?

4 "How can you say to your brother, 'Let me take the speck out of your eye,' when all the time there is a plank in your own eye?

5 "You hypocrite, first take the plank out of your own eye, and then you will see clearly to remove the speck from your brother's eye.

6 "Do not give dogs what is sacred; do not throw your pearls to pigs. If you do, they may trample them under their feet, and turn and tear you to pieces."

15 Beware of false prophets, which come to you in sheep's clothing, but inwardly they are ravening wolves.
16 Ye shall know them by their fruits. Do men gather grapes of thorns, or figs of thistles?
17 Even so every good tree bringeth forth good fruit; but a corrupt tree bringeth forth evil fruit.
18 A good tree cannot bring forth evil fruit, neither can a corrupt tree bring forth good fruit.
19 Every tree that bringeth not forth good fruit is hewn down, and cast into the fire.
20 Wherefore by their fruits ye shall know them.
21 Not everyone that saith unto me, Lord, Lord, shall enter into the kingdom of heaven; but he that doeth the will of my Father which is in heaven.
22 Many will say to me in that day, Lord, Lord, have we not prophesied in thy name? and in thy name have cast out devils? and in thy name done many wonderful works?
23 And then will I profess unto them, I never knew you: depart from me, ye that work iniquity.

15 "Watch out for false prophets. They come to you in sheep's clothing, but inwardly they are ferocious wolves.
16 "By their fruit you will recognize them. Do people pick grapes from thornbushes, or figs from thistles?
17 "Likewise, every good tree bears good fruit, but a bad tree bears bad fruit.
18 "A good tree cannot bear bad fruit, and a bad tree cannot bear good fruit.
19 "Every tree that does not bear good fruit is cut down and thrown into the fire.
20 "Thus, by their fruit you will recognize them.
21 "Not everyone who says to me, 'Lord, Lord,' will enter the kingdom of heaven, but only the one who does the will of my Father who is in heaven.
22 "Many will say to me on that day, 'Lord, Lord, did we not prophesy in your name and in your name drive out demons and in your name perform many miracles?'
23 "Then I will tell them plainly, 'I never knew you. Away from me, you evildoers!'"

UNIFYING LESSON PRINCIPLE: In a complex world, many become confused in trying to cope with the diversity in beliefs and lifestyles. How can one maintain a sense of stability given such complexity? Jesus taught His disciples the spiritual disciplines of resisting the use of judgment and using discernment.

LESSON OBJECTIVES

Upon the completion of this lesson, the students will be able to do the following:
1. Understand judgment and discernment and distinguish between the two.
2. Reflect on the consequences of practicing discernment rather than judgment.
3. Model discernment rather than judging.

AGE-LEVEL POINTS TO BE EMPHASIZED

Teachers of ADULTS and YOUTH

—Given the immediate context and other scriptural statements about judgment, verses 1-2 are clearly not condemning divine, civil, or even all forms of interpersonal judgment;

rather, the verses specifically condemn rash and overly harsh judgment between individuals that is generated from pride and a spirit of harsh criticism.

—The exhortation to "first take the log out of your own eye" (verse 5) emphasizes the importance of regularly evaluating our own actions and motives so that we can be in a better position to help our Christian brothers and sisters identify their own shortcomings without hypocrisy.

—In both the balance of verses 1-5 with verse 6 and the teaching of verses 15-20, Jesus emphasized the importance of using discernment in evaluating the behaviors and motivations of others.

—Verses 21-23 extend the use of discernment not only to help identify false disciples, but also, even more importantly, to encourage self-examination to make sure that one is not a false disciple.

—Judging someone refers to hypocritical judging. (Matthew 7:1)

—*Hypocrite* literally means "a stage player; a dissembler, or pretender." (Matthew 7:5)

—"Dogs" is an insult, and "swine" is considered very unclean. (Matthew 7:6)

—"Lord" hints at Jesus' divinity and is used in Scripture as a respectful and worshipful address for God. (Matthew 7:21)

—"In your name" denotes Jesus' authority and sense of power. (Matthew 7:22)

—*Evildoers* literally means "workers of lawlessness." (Matthew 7:23)

Teachers of CHILDREN

—Jesus encouraged His followers not to be judgmental of others.

—Jesus urged His disciples to reflect on their lives before judging others.

—Jesus said that it is important to know with whom you share holy things.

—Jesus spoke of discipleship and the kingdom of God in familiar terms, such as dogs and fruit trees.

—Jesus emphasized the importance of obeying God if we are to inherit the kingdom.

—Jesus suggested that it is dangerous to claim discipleship if we are unwilling to pay the price.

THE CHRONOLOGICAL SETTING OF THE LESSON

The early church fathers argued that the gospel of Matthew was written around AD 65 and AD 70 after the destruction of the Temple of Jerusalem during the Roman Empire reign. It is conventionally agreed by the church fathers that this gospel was written by the apostle Matthew, who also went by the name Levi the son of Alphaeus. Matthew was one of the twelve disciples and a tax collector in Capernaum. The other canonical gospels of the New Testament include Mark, Luke, and John. All these canonical gospels share one thing in common: they all give a narrative concerning the ministry, death, and resurrection of the Messiah. However, the gospel of Matthew uses the gospel of Mark as a point of reference (bible.org).

THE GEOGRAPHICAL AND CULTURAL SETTING OF THE LESSON

It is generally accepted that the book of Matthew was written after the fall of Jerusalem in AD 70 using the gospel of Mark as the source, as suggested by Ignatius and Didache. The apostle Matthew criticized the Pharisaic traditions (which were common after the fall of the Temple in Jerusalem) and sought to separate the church community from these individuals. The gospel of Matthew is believed to have been written in Palestine or in the city of Antioch in Syria, where a significant number of Jews were living. This also suggests that the primary audience of the Gospel were Jewish Christians, as suggested by the wide use of Old Testament references and Jewish-specific messages. The references to synagogues and the Jewish religious authorities are framed negatively in the Gospel. It refers to the synagogues as "their synagogues," which implies that the Jewish Christians were no longer active in the synagogue worship (bible.org).

Matthew 7:15 warns concerning false prophets, as Christ compared them to wolves disguised in sheep's clothing. The images of wolves and sheep are used in the Old and New Testaments. Wolves represent the worst aspects of people and depict callousness and insatiable hunger (see Matthew 7:15; 10:16). The Gospel also warns Christians concerning judging their brothers and the tendency of the Jews to judge other nations. Jesus Christ addressed this idea of retribution through the approach of the messianic law (see Matthew 5:1-12, 19).

PROMINENT CHARACTER(S) IN THE LESSON

Jesus Christ: He is the central focus of the Gospel. Jesus taught concerning the need for His followers to avoid judging others. He criticized the Pharisees for being culpable of being unjust and lacking the spirit of love and tenderness in their judgment.

KEY TERMS IN THE LESSON

Bear (verse 18)—Greek: *pheró* (fer'-o): to bear, carry, "bring forth" (KJV).

Fruit (verse 17)—Greek: *karpos* (kar-pos'): fruit; deed; action; result.

Give (verse 6)—Greek: *didómi* (did'-o-mee): to offer, give; to put, place.

Hypocrite (verse 5)—Greek: *hupokrités* (hoop-ok-ree-tace'): a hypocrite, dissembler, pretender.

Kingdom (verse 21)—Greek: *basileia* (bas-il-i'-ah): kingship; sovereignty; authority; rule; kingdom.

Measure (verse 2)—Greek: *metron* (met'-ron): a measure; measuring rod.

Speck (verse 3)—Greek: *karphos* (kar'-fos): a small, dry stalk; a chip of wood; "mote" (KJV).

TOPICAL OUTLINE OF THE LESSON

I. **Introduction**
   A. The Message in the Message
   B. Biblical Background

II. **Exposition and Application of the Scripture**
   A. Judge Not
      (Matthew 7:1-6)
   B. True and False Prophets
      (Matthew 7:15-20)
   C. True and False Disciples
      (Matthew 7:21-23)

III. **Concluding Reflection**

I. INTRODUCTION

A. The Message in the Message

As we continue to study the various themes in the Sermon on the Mount, we thus have a reminder of the importance of Jesus' teaching as portrayed by Matthew. Matthew wants us to know all the teachings of Jesus Christ even when he cannot fit these teachings into a defined structured series. As can be seen, the Sermon on the Mount does not really fit as a structured text—as each paragraph seemed to be independent, having its own message.

Notwithstanding, Matthew arranged these teachings in a relevant way for his readers. In Matthew 7:1-5, he talked about avoiding external evaluations of people and self-examination.

Matthew 7:7-11 talks about Jesus' promise concerning prayer, expanding the discourse on personal prayer. In Matthew 7:15-23, he brought up Jesus' caution about not trusting all religious claims and about observing a person's behavior (which ultimately tells one's character).

Matthew 7 is the last of the three chapters that make up the Sermon on the Mount. As stated in previous lessons, the events of Matthew 5–7 are said to have taken place in AD 27. Matthew 7 has twenty-nine verses.

B. Biblical Background

Matthew 7:1-12 contains some of the very vital and delicate duties of the Christian life. In the elaborate presentation of these texts, great principles are produced, which are necessities of the Christian race. In Matthew 7:1-5, Jesus talked about judgment. It is worth noting that this judgment does not exactly translate into condemning or judging a person, whether favorably or not. In this context, judgment simply points toward looking unfavorably toward a person's disposition, character, and actions—which consequently results in the pronouncement of unjust, unloving, and rash comments or judgments on them. What our Lord Jesus tried to make noticeable when He said, "Judge not, that ye be not judged" is the spirit out of which these comments and judgments come.

Jesus further expressed the truth when He said in verse 2, "For with what judgment ye judge, ye shall be judged: and with what measure ye mete, it shall be measured to you again." This expression is also used by Jesus in other contexts (see Mark 4:24, Luke 6:38), and it represents a great principle of divine administration. When we make unkind and unloving judgments about others, it will also be returned to us. Another issue brought to the fore by Jesus is the issue of "mote." The mote could represent small faults that we tend to notice and focus on rather than look inward to discover the bigger faults which we harbor in our lives. In light of this, Jesus here referred to such a person as a "hypocrite." The hypocrite pretends to be overzealous and compassionate but, in reality, these services are not without faults; but the hypocrite tends to fit himself as a reproof of the faults of others without judging himself first.

Matthew 7:13-29 begins the final conclusion of the Sermon on the Mount. The righteousness of the kingdom is aptly described in detail and principle. It involves one's self-sacrifice at every step. This consequently would bring about the division of all into two classes of truths: those who will follow self-indulgence and the easy path; and those few who are bent on following the path of eternal safety at whatever cost.

From verse 15, we see Jesus issuing a warning about false prophets. These prophets are those teachers and preachers who come in the guise of expounding on the mind of God and claim to show the right path to heaven and eternal life while inwardly they are ravaging wolves whose actual intentions are to mislead and deceive their followers (see Acts 20:29-30; 2 Peter 2:1-2; 2 Corinthians 11:2-3, 13-15). These false teachers and preachers can only be known by their fruits (verses 16-19). The heart is a true interpreter and determines the actions of life.

At this point, the hypocrisy of teachers leads Jesus to issue a solemn warning against religious hypocrisy in general.

In conclusion, we are always to seek for the truth and abide in it (see Proverbs 23:23). In the last days shall arise various teachings, beliefs, and ways of life. The Bible remains our standard of truth and living. When we continually look into this perfect law of liberty, we shall continually find truth to help us live in this ever-changing world of darkness (see James 1:25).

II. EXPOSITION AND APPLICATION OF THE SCRIPTURE

A. Judge Not
(Matthew 7:1-6)

JUDGE NOT, that ye be not judged. For with what judgment ye judge, ye shall be judged: and with what measure ye mete, it shall be measured to you again. And why beholdest thou the mote that is in thy brother's eye, but considerest not the beam that is in thine own eye? Or how wilt thou say to thy brother, Let me pull out the mote out of thine eye; and, behold, a beam is in thine own eye? Thou hypocrite, first cast out the beam out of thine own eye; and then shalt thou see clearly to cast out the mote out of thy brother's eye. Give not that which is holy unto the dogs, neither cast ye your pearls before swine, lest they trample them under their feet, and turn again and rend you.

Here in verse 1, the word *judge* comes from the Greek word *krino*, which indicates a kind of judging that presumes to self-determine the salvation or lack thereof in others. This same term can also be found in other passages, such as John 12:48; Acts 17:31; and 2 Timothy 4:1. Even Jesus Himself did not adopt this presumptive stance as noted in John 12:47 (NIV): "If anyone hears my words but does not keep them, I do not judge that person. For I did not come to judge the world, but to save the world."

The lure to judge others seems for some people to be too strong to resist. "Some insist on their right to judge others and defend it on the basis of Jesus' words, 'By their fruits ye shall know them' (Matthew 7:20). Discerning and judging, however, are two different things. The Greek term for "accounting," or thinking, with reference to another is *hegeomai*. Making a private, personal, and tentative appraisal of others is not forbidden; but 'judging' is prohibited. One must deplore the conduct of self-appointed 'fruit inspectors' whose flagrant violations of this commandment have worked untold damage in the church" (*Coffman's Commentaries on the Bible, Matthew 7*, https://www.studylight.org/commentaries/bcc/matthew-7.html24).

Verse 2 is reminiscent of the well-known proverb that advises, "Do unto others as you would have them do unto you" (see also Matthew 7:12 and Luke 6:31). The judging and measuring listed in verse 2 are parallel expressions which are repeated for the sake of emphasis and effect. "The thought of these parallel expressions is identical, the repetition being for the sake of emphasis. A censorious, presumptuous preoccupation with other people's destiny encourages a reciprocal judgment from them, resulting in all kinds of bitterness, recriminations, and vindictive hatreds" (*Coffman's Commentaries on the Bible*, Matthew 7, https://www.studylight.org/commentaries/bcc/matthew-7.html17?print=yes).

Jesus ingeniously utilized another set of parallel images to communicate the ageless principle of minding one's own business (verses 3-4). The effect of this construction of words is to present a kind of literary cartoon. In order to see this kind of humor, one need only to imagine a plank sticking out of the eye of a person who is also busy trying to remove a speck of dust from another person's eye. It is sad that someone could be in a sinful and spiritually disadvantaged condition without even realizing it. Sometimes, we can be so close to ourselves that we are unable to see our faults and failures even though they may be glaringly apparent to others who observe us.

The remedy for false pride is acknowledgment of our faults and personal shortcomings (verse 5). "The Pharisees were great at censuring, but slow at amending. Our Lord will not have his kingdom made up of hypocritical theorists, he calls for practical obedience to the rules of holiness. After we are ourselves sanctified, we are bound to be eyes to the blind, and correctors of unholy living; but not till then" (*Commentary on the New Testament*, Charles Spurgeon).

There are many examples throughout the Gospels of where Jesus judged the Pharisees. However, Jesus judged people who were proud, pretentious, and cruel. He also defended those who were the last, the lost, and the least. When it comes to judging, we must make sure to avoid selfish motives and focus on kingdom objectives with love as our leading priority (*Expositor's Greek New Testament*).

The base metaphor using dogs and swine (verse 6) focuses on the idea that things which have been offered sacrificially were no longer to be treated commonly. The reference to dogs in verse 6 described a species that was a far cry from the kinds of dogs commonly seen in the United States. These dogs were ruthless, ravenous scavengers who were avoided and disdained (see Exodus 22:31). To "cast one's pearls before swine" means to intentionally place something valuable in the presence or pathway of something worthless. One example might be publicly arguing with a foolish person regarding the precious truths and promises of almighty God. At the end of the day, it is just not worth it and such activity often does more harm than good.

B. True and False Prophets
(Matthew 7:15-20)

Beware of false prophets, which come to you in sheep's clothing, but inwardly they are ravening wolves. Ye shall know them by their fruits. Do men gather grapes of thorns, or figs of thistles? Even so every good tree bringeth forth good fruit; but a corrupt tree bringeth forth evil fruit. A good tree cannot bring forth evil fruit, neither can a corrupt tree bring forth good fruit. Every tree that bringeth not forth good fruit is hewn down, and cast into the fire. Wherefore by their fruits ye shall know them.

Jesus continued with the graphic metaphors and this time likened false prophets to destructive wolves (verse 15). No doubt many of His listeners could identify with the responsibilities of the shepherd who cares for the sheep and must be on constant watch for predators. Luke 6:43-45 (NIV) enlarged on this metaphor of fruit in verse 16 in relationship to spiritual character: "No good tree bears bad fruit, nor does a bad tree bear good fruit. Each tree is recognized by its own fruit. People do not pick figs from thornbushes, or grapes from briers. A good man brings good things out of the good stored up in his heart, and an evil man brings evil things out of the evil stored up in his heart. For the mouth speaks what the heart is full of."

Jesus was consistent in utilizing common imagery that could easily be understood by those who encountered His teaching (verses 17-18). Not only were these analogies understood, but also, they were more than likely remembered due to the fact that the hearers probably encountered these examples every day. "The two verses state nearly the same fact, but each presents a different aspect. First it is stated as a matter of practical experience, then the general fact is referred to a necessary law. If the tree is corrupt, i.e., rotten or decayed at the core, it cannot bring forth good fruit. If there is falseness in the teaching, or in the man, it will sooner or later show itself in his life, and then, even though we judge of the doctrine on other ground, we should cease to feel confidence in the guidance of the teacher" (*Ellicott's Commentary for English Readers,* http://biblehub.com/commentaries/matthew/7-17.htm).

Verses 19 and 20 provide a picture of a wasteful and unproductive life that once had potential but never truly fulfilled its function. Any life that is disconnected from God is operating below full capacity. Whenever a person fails to bear fruit there is a disconnect in the operation of the Holy Spirit in that life. A lack of self-control yields misplaced priorities, distraction from purpose, and distance from God. Spirit control provides peace, progress, and accomplishment of purpose.

C. True and False Disciples
(Matthew 7:21-23)

Not everyone that saith unto me, Lord, Lord, shall enter into the kingdom of heaven; but he that doeth the will of my Father which is in heaven. Many will say to me in that day, Lord, Lord, have we not prophesied in thy name? and in thy name have cast out devils? and in thy name done many wonderful works? And then will I profess unto them, I never knew you: depart from me, ye that work iniquity.

It is easy to articulate right-sounding religious rhetoric in order to project the impression of personal piety. However, right living always outweighs right speaking. Life service supersedes lip service (verse 21). This same concept is also seen in Luke 6:46 (NIV): "Why do you call me, 'Lord, Lord,' and do not do what I say?" This rhetorical question utilizes the principle of stating a known fact and function. He then applies the known information to the subject matter about which he is speaking. The best-case scenario is for us to address God correctly as well as to live lives of obedience to God. Anyone who has ever watched a film that has a spoken soundtrack that does not match the video movements knows that such an occurrence can be extremely irritating. A similar phenomenon occurs when our verbal "audio" does not coincide with our life action's "video."

There is a short phrase at the beginning of verse 21 that is easily overlooked but is extremely important and critical to a thorough understanding of the identity and authority of Jesus. The phrase is "Many will say to me." Some people only view Jesus as a good, moral teacher who is bereft of divinity. To dismiss the divinity of Jesus would make His sacrificial death in vain and would nullify all that He affirmed regarding His being the Messiah.

Jesus attested to the fact that three highly regarded religious activities are possible to accomplish detached from the power and authorization of Jesus (verse 22). These three activities are prophesying, demonic deliverance, and miracle working. Here, as everywhere in the New Testament, "prophesying" is more than mere prediction of the future. It also includes delivering a message to people as if it were coming directly from God. Demonic deliverance is the freeing from bondage for one who is demonically possessed. Miracle working may take a wide variety of different forms, from physical healing to supernatural provision. Jesus said that all this is quite possible even while operating outside the parameters of a relationship with God.

In verse 23, Jesus continued to articulate and activate the mantle of divinity when He identified Himself as being the one to whom all will answer on the Day of Judgment. On that day, He declared that He would speak plainly, publicly, and revealingly to the ones who have spoken secretively, covertly, and with duplicity. He would reveal whatever has been hidden and will officially separate Himself from those who operated in opposition to obedience. All sin is basically separation from God and from the will and ways of God.

III. CONCLUDING REFLECTION

It is important to understand what it means to judge, as well as what it means to operate in spiritual discernment. One is done in the flesh, and the other is motivated by the Holy Spirit of God. There are consequences in practicing judgment, but there are also rewards for operating in discernment. As we live our lives, there will always be temptation to judge the actions and motives of others and to more readily justify our own behavior rather than that of others. Jesus encouraged and compelled us to first take a look at our own lives before seeking to dissect and correct someone else's life. Through God's powerful Holy Spirit living within us, we would be able to resist the temptation to judge others harshly, avoid operating in hypocrisy, gently help correct the wrong behavior of and attitudes in other believers, and recognize false teaching when it appears.

PRAYER

Dear God, thank You for giving the body of Christ the gift of discernment. Help us to use it in order to live lives to Your glory. In Jesus' name we pray. Amen.

HOME DAILY BIBLE READINGS
(July 22-28, 2019)

Jesus Teaches about Spiritual Discernment

MONDAY, July 22: "Walk by the Word and Prosper" (Psalm 1)

TUESDAY, July 23: "Godly Trust Leads to Fruitful Life" (Jeremiah 17:5-8)

WEDNESDAY, July 24: "Settle Differences Face-to-face" (Matthew 18:15-20)

THURSDAY, July 25: "How Believers Judge Grievances" (1 Corinthians 6:1-6)

FRIDAY, July 26: "Asking and Receiving Fairly" (Matthew 7:7-14)

SATURDAY, July 27: "Hearing and Doing" (Matthew 7:24-29)

SUNDAY, July 28: "Discerning Faith and Action Together" (Matthew 7:1-6, 15-23)

August 4, 2019　　　　　　　　　　　　　　　　**Lesson 10**

A COVENANT BETWEEN FRIENDS

ADULT/YOUTH
ADULT/YOUNG ADULT TOPIC: **A Trusted and Loyal Friend**
YOUTH TOPIC: **Loyalty between Friends**

CHILDREN
GENERAL LESSON TITLE: **A Promise between Friends**
CHILDREN'S TOPIC: **A Friend in Need Is a Friend Indeed**

DEVOTIONAL READING
John 15:12-17

ADULT/YOUTH
BACKGROUND SCRIPTURE: **1 Samuel 18–20**
PRINT PASSAGE: **1 Samuel 18:1-5; 19:1-7**
KEY VERSE: **1 Samuel 18:1**

CHILDREN
BACKGROUND SCRIPTURE: **1 Samuel 18–20**
PRINT PASSAGE: **1 Samuel 18:1-5; 19:1-7**
KEY VERSE: **1 Samuel 18:1**

1 Samuel 18:1-5; 19:1-7—KJV

AND IT came to pass, when he had made an end of speaking unto Saul, that the soul of Jonathan was knit with the soul of David, and Jonathan loved him as his own soul.

2 And Saul took him that day, and would let him go no more home to his father's house.

3 Then Jonathan and David made a covenant, because he loved him as his own soul.

4 And Jonathan stripped himself of the robe that was upon him, and gave it to David, and his garments, even to his sword, and to his bow, and to his girdle.

5 And David went out whithersoever Saul sent him, and behaved himself wisely: and Saul set him over the men of war, and he was accepted in the sight of all the people, and also in the sight of Saul's servants.

.....

AND SAUL spake to Jonathan his son, and to all his servants, that they should kill David.

1 Samuel 18:1-5; 19:1-7—NIV

AFTER DAVID had finished talking with Saul, Jonathan became one in spirit with David, and he loved him as himself.

2 From that day Saul kept David with him and did not let him return home to his family.

3 And Jonathan made a covenant with David because he loved him as himself.

4 Jonathan took off the robe he was wearing and gave it to David, along with his tunic, and even his sword, his bow and his belt.

5 Whatever mission Saul sent him on, David was so successful that Saul gave him a high rank in the army. This pleased all the troops, and Saul's officers as well.

.....

SAUL TOLD his son Jonathan and all the attendants to kill David. But Jonathan had taken a great liking to David

2 But Jonathan Saul's son delighted much in David: and Jonathan told David, saying, Saul my father seeketh to kill thee: now therefore, I pray thee, take heed to thyself until the morning, and abide in a secret place, and hide thyself:

3 And I will go out and stand beside my father in the field where thou art, and I will commune with my father of thee; and what I see, that I will tell thee.

4 And Jonathan spake good of David unto Saul his father, and said unto him, Let not the king sin against his servant, against David; because he hath not sinned against thee, and because his works have been to thee-ward very good:

5 For he did put his life in his hand, and slew the Philistine, and the LORD wrought a great salvation for all Israel: thou sawest it, and didst rejoice: wherefore then wilt thou sin against innocent blood, to slay David without a cause?

6 And Saul hearkened unto the voice of Jonathan: and Saul sware, As the LORD liveth, he shall not be slain.

7 And Jonathan called David, and Jonathan shewed him all those things. And Jonathan brought David to Saul, and he was in his presence, as in times past.

2 and warned him, "My father Saul is looking for a chance to kill you. Be on your guard tomorrow morning; go into hiding and stay there.

3 "I will go out and stand with my father in the field where you are. I'll speak to him about you and will tell you what I find out."

4 Jonathan spoke well of David to Saul his father and said to him, "Let not the king do wrong to his servant David; he has not wronged you, and what he has done has benefited you greatly.

5 "He took his life in his hands when he killed the Philistine. The LORD won a great victory for all Israel, and you saw it and were glad. Why then would you do wrong to an innocent man like David by killing him for no reason?"

6 Saul listened to Jonathan and took this oath: "As surely as the LORD lives, David will not be put to death."

7 So Jonathan called David and told him the whole conversation. He brought him to Saul, and David was with Saul as before.

UNIFYING LESSON PRINCIPLE: Sometimes we are challenged to compromise our loyalty to a beloved authority figure to keep a promise made to a trusted friend. Whom does one choose? Jonathan chose to keep his promise to love and protect David, his intimate friend, despite his father's insane hatred of David.

LESSON OBJECTIVES

Upon the completion of this lesson, the students will be able to do the following:

1. Summarize Jonathan's plan to protect David from Saul.
2. Appreciate how the demands of honesty and friendship can surpass family bonds and civil obedience.
3. Examine their relationships and recommit to pure and honest loyalty in the sight of God.

AGE-LEVEL POINTS TO BE EMPHASIZED

Teachers of ADULTS and YOUTH

—In 1 Samuel 18:1-5, Saul approved of David. Later, he tried to kill David.

—Jonathan struggled to balance his loyalties (see 1 Samuel 19:1-7).

—Jonathan's removal of his robe and putting it on David (18:4) is symbolic of transferring the monarchy from the house of Saul to the house of David.

—The friendship between Jonathan and David was rare. They could have been rivals, but Jonathan seemed to understand that David was destined to become king.

—The traditional, mainstream view of the relationship between David and Jonathan is that it was platonic, brotherly love.

—Jonathan's being bound to David's soul denotes an inseparable devotion. (1 Samuel 18:1)

—The covenant made here was a formal agreement based on friendship and mutual loyalty. (1 Samuel 18:3)

—Some say that by Jonathan giving David his robe and other gear, Jonathan was transferring his claim of the throne to David. (1 Samuel 18:4)

—Jonathan showed that his loyalty was to his friend David by telling David of this plan and helping him hide from his father. (1 Samuel 19:2)

—Jonathan took a risk and spoke with his father, King Saul, concerning David. (1 Samuel 19:4)

—Throughout this story of love, honesty, and commitment, God was faithful to both Jonathan and David.

Teachers of CHILDREN

—King Saul developed a deep resentment toward David because of David's success as a warrior and popularity among Saul's subjects.

—Saul's resentment led him to desire to kill David.

—Jonathan, Saul's son, saw David as Israel's future and so was willing to invest in him wholeheartedly.

—True friendship like the friendship between Jonathan and David takes risks out of love for the other.

—Jonathan intervened by telling his father that David posed no threat to King Saul.

—Jonathan's intervention resulted in a temporary pause in Saul's wrath against David.

THE CHRONOLOGICAL SETTING OF THE LESSON

The book of 1 Samuel is named after Samuel, whom God used to anoint and establish the monarchy in Israel. This representative of God's is significant in the history of Israel because he plays a very critical role in ensuring continuity of the covenant and transition from the rule of judges to the rule of a monarchy in Israel. The books of 1 and 2 Samuel were originally one volume and were referred to as "The First and Second Books of Kingdoms" (Septuagint translators); "First and Second Kings" (Latin Vulgate in AD 400); and finally, "First and Second Samuel" (Hebrew and modern versions).

THE GEOGRAPHICAL AND CULTURAL SETTING OF THE LESSON

The authorship of 1 Samuel cannot be absolutely confirmed. The Talmud and the Hebrew cannon argue that the book was written by the prophet Samuel himself because of the role he played in the history of Israel covered in the first twenty-four chapters. This, however, is subject to criticism because of his death in chapter 25.

There is a possibility that the book of 1 Samuel might have been compiled by the prophets Samuel, Nathan, and Gad (see 1 Chronicles 29:29; 1 Samuel 10:25). The book of 1 Samuel warned the kings of Israel through revelations that the prophets received from God. This happened when Israel and Judah were a divided monarchy (931 BC) and before the fall of the Northern Kingdom of Samaria (722 BC). This is clearly illustrated by the fact that Ziklag, the city of Philistia, was still under the kingdom of Judah (see 1 Samuel 27:6).

First Samuel 18:1-6 narrates the covenant of friendship made between David and Jonathan, the son of King Saul. This is after David had killed Goliath and his fame was renown all over Israel. Jonathan took off his robe and tunic and gave them to David as a sign of their covenant. Their friendship shows real love and commitment to the Lord, which, in itself, is a covenant. However, King Saul became jealous of David's achievements and fame and sought to kill him. He told his son Jonathan and his house to kill David, but Jonathan warned David of the plan and told him to go into hiding (see 1 Samuel 19:1-7). He even took the dangerous step and spoke well of David to his father. (bible.org)

PROMINENT CHARACTER(S) IN THE LESSON

David: He was the eighth son of Jesse. He was born around 1040 BC. He was a shepherd, a musician, and a soldier (see 1 Samuel 16:11, 18; 17:20; 18:16). He endured all the trouble and attempts made on his life by King Saul. He faithfully served and recognized Saul as God's chosen servant (bible.org).

Jonathan: He is the eldest son of King Saul in the Old Testament Scriptures (see 1 Samuel 18:1-4). He made a self-sacrificing friendship with David that mirrored love between individuals and God. He is a biblical model of faithful friendship and fidelity (bible.org).

King Saul: He was the king of Israel. Saul was the most handsome man in the whole of Israel (see 1 Samuel 9:2). He was plagued by an evil spirit that tormented him to madness, and he was envious of David's fame and victory (bible.org).

KEY TERMS IN THE LESSON

Bow (18:4)—Hebrew: *qesheth* (keh'-sheth): weaponry for shooting arrows.

Covenant (18:3)—Hebrew: `berith (ber-eeth'): covenant; agreement.

Gave (18:4)—Hebrew: *nathan* (naw-than'): to give, put, set.

Knit (18:1)—Hebrew: *qashar* (kaw-shar'): to bind; league together; conspire; "became one" (NIV).

Spoke (19:4)—Hebrew: *dabar* (daw-bar'): to have spoken; "spake" (KJV).

Stand (19:3)—Hebrew: *amad* (aw-mad'): to take one's stand; stand.

TOPICAL OUTLINE OF THE LESSON

I. Introduction
   A. A Profile of True Friendship
   B. Biblical Background

II. Exposition and Application of the Scripture
   A. Saul Is Intimidated by David (1 Samuel 18:1-5)
   B. Saul Tries to Kill David (1 Samuel 19:1-7)

III. Concluding Reflection

I. INTRODUCTION
A. A Profile of True Friendship

In 1 Samuel 18, we see that jealousy translates to anger, murder, delusion, and evil meditations. This is expressly exemplified by King Saul. It also shows the trials which young David faced. We see David move from being Saul's most favorite assistant to being his most sought after and worst enemy. This truly is something many of us have faced in the course of friendships. Many friendships are made, and some just make themselves. In life, there is no such thing as waiting for special friendships because they might never happen, and if they do we must be especially thankful and appreciative for such friendships.

After David's interview by Saul before David's battle with Goliath in chapter 17 of 1 Samuel, Jonathan the king's son came to love David like himself, and they became best friends. The phrase "loved him as himself" speaks to the true state of their love for each other and the depth of their friendship. Their friendship was devoid of false motives. This kind of friendship is still very much possible today, although it is rare. It was a joy for Jonathan to discover that his father, the king, has also permitted David to come live at the royal palace.

B. Biblical Background

The events of 1 Samuel 18–20 were said to have occurred between 1018 BC and 1013 BC, and David would have been between the ages of fifteen and twenty-two. He spent approximately seven years living with King Saul before Saul began trying to kill him. Jonathan was born in 1067 BC, when Saul was fifteen years old. David had not been born when Jonathan single-handedly defeated the Philistines at Geba and Michmash, which was shortly after Saul became king in 1046 BC. This twenty-five-year age gap between David and Jonathan did not impede their friendship or love for each other because it was built on faith.

After the defeat of Goliath, Saul decided to keep David full time in his service, and David became very close to Jonathan. They become so close that Scripture records that they became one spirit (see 18:1). In their friendship, three people were involved: David, Jonathan, and God. This combination is still a recipe for successful relationships today. They loved each other and both loved and respected God. Such friendships centered on love for God will always be strong and last long. Jonathan not only loved David but also went on to make a covenant with him. In the covenant, Jonathan removed his robe and gave it to David as well as his military clothes—his sword and belt (see 1 Samuel 18:3-4). These gifts could indicate Jonathan's willingness to give his authority to David and, consequently, submitting his right to the throne. The covenant between Jonathan and David is a true display of friendship based on trust and obedience to God.

After the battle with the Philistines, the Israelites returned home, and their wives and sons came rejoicing. They became so excited that they began to sing David's praises, and this was the beginning of Saul's hatred for David. This song planted a root of jealousy and anger in Saul (see 1 Samuel 18:8-9). From this point on, Saul began to seek to kill David as an evil spirit possessed him (see 1 Samuel 18:12).

As Saul's anger and jealousy deepened, he began to seek every available means to kill David. Saul told Jonathan his son and all other attendants to kill David, but Jonathan loved David and had made a covenant with him, so he warned David of his father's intentions. Jonathan pleaded with his father on David's behalf, after which Saul promised his son Jonathan that he would not harm David (see 1 Samuel 19:1-5).

In serving Saul once more and defeating the Philistines, David went to calm Saul from the spirit that oppressed him by playing his music. Saul once more attempted to kill David with a spear, but David escaped. First Samuel 19:11-12 tells of how Michal, David's wife and Saul's daughter, helped David escape a second time from Saul.

Once again in chapter 20, Jonathan helped rescue David from Saul's grasp. True friendship is not deterred by mistakes, background, age, or social status. In David and Jonathan, we see the definition of true friendship, which is an exhibition of trust, loyalty, and love. As Christians, we should always strive to be exemplary in our relationships, friendships, and lifestyles.

II. EXPOSITION AND APPLICATION OF THE SCRIPTURE

A. Saul Is Intimidated by David
(1 Samuel 18:1-5)

AND IT came to pass, when he had made an end of speaking unto Saul, that the soul of Jonathan was knit with the soul of David, and Jonathan loved him as his own soul. And Saul took him that day, and would let him go no more home to his father's house. Then Jonathan and David made a covenant, because he loved him as his own soul. And Jonathan stripped himself of the robe that was upon him, and gave it to David, and his garments, even to his sword, and to his bow, and to his girdle. And David went out whithersoever Saul sent him, and behaved himself wisely: and Saul set him over the men of war, and he was accepted in the sight of all the people, and also in the sight of Saul's servants.

When the text mentions that the soul or spirit of Jonathan became one with David, the Hebrew phrase means "to be knit together, or to be bound up." This strong term is also used in Genesis 44:30 to describe Jacob's love for his son Benjamin. Some contemporary writers have incorrectly assumed that this bond of unity between David and Jonathan was in some way less than honorable or semi-sexual, but neither the text nor the broad context offer any indication of truth regarding such a wild speculation. A cursory look at David's life will reveal that he was definitely and exclusively attracted to women.

David was somewhat of a man's man, meaning David possessed many character traits that other men would like to see in themselves. Jonathan was also a man of outstanding character. *Ellicott's Bible Commentary, Volume 1: Genesis–Esther* describes Jonathan as "a true warrior of those wild, half-barbarous times—among brave men seemingly the bravest—a perfect soldier, whether fighting as a simple man-at-arms or as the general of an army—chivalrous and generous—utterly free from jealousy—a fervid believer in the God of Israel—a devoted and loyal son—a true patriot in the highest sense of the word, who sealed a devoted life by a noble death, dying as he did fighting for his king and his people." Likewise, the attributes of David went beyond his personal bravery and world-renowned skills on the battlefield. He was also kind, thoughtful, and a man of honor who was quick to acknowledge his wrong and willing to forgive even someone like Saul, who openly demonstrated his extreme malice toward David by attempting to take his life on many occasions. It is safe to say that in the relationship between Jonathan and David, greatness recognized greatness. The mutual attraction was real and unshakable, even after the death of Jonathan.

With a mindset that was primarily focused on war, Saul gladly took on the promising young soldier David to be one of his bodyguards (see 1 Samuel 14:52). From that time forward, David constantly rendered excellent service to Saul (verse 2)—first as a musician, and later as a soldier. The life principle that is evident through David's actions is to aim for excellence in everything attempted. Consistent excellence in small things leads to eventual excellence in all things.

The great friendship between these two men was built on strong faith in God and the mutual admiration of two stalwart personalities (verse 3).

When Jonathan presented David his own robe, tunic, sword, bow, and belt (verse 4), it was possibly because David (as a shepherd) was poorly clad. Earlier, David had refused Saul's armor because it did not fit, but David accepts this generous gift from Jonathan. To receive any part of the dress or weaponry which had been worn by a sovereign was deemed the highest honor that could be conferred on a subject.

The articles given were part of the military dress and added an outward air of impressiveness to David's already-impressive inner resources. Jonathan's generous gift aptly demonstrated his great love and respect for David and provides insight into the character of Jonathan, who possibly had a strong desire to help David feel comfortable in his new surroundings.

Without any formal military training, David was successful in every single assignment given to him by Saul (verse 5). Two primary reasons for this are that, first, God was with David and prospered him; second, David walked by faith and whatever he endeavored to do, he did it with all his might. This attitude and disposition is reminiscent of Ecclesiastes 9:10 (NIV), which states, "Whatever your hand finds to do, do it with all your might . . . ." Another passage emphasizing this same attitude is Colossians 3:23 (NIV): "Whatever you do, work at it with all your heart, as working for the Lord, not for human masters." David's initial expeditions were on a smaller scale, but as he was faithful with smaller tasks, he was elevated in rank and entrusted with greater assignments. As people today, sometimes we are left out of opportunities to do big jobs because of our lackluster track record with smaller jobs. This verse summarizes a long span of time in which many different events took place. As David's responsibilities increased, his success increased. And when his success increased, his acclaim increased. When his acclaim increased, he increased as a figure to be envied by Saul.

B. Saul Tries to Kill David
(1 Samuel 19:1-7)

AND SAUL spake to Jonathan his son, and to all his servants, that they should kill David. But Jonathan Saul's son delighted much in David: and Jonathan told David, saying, Saul my father seeketh to kill thee: now therefore, I pray thee, take heed to thyself until the morning, and abide in a secret place, and hide thyself: And I will go out and stand beside my father in the field where thou art, and I will commune with my father of thee; and what I see, that I will tell thee. And Jonathan spake good of David unto Saul his father, and said unto him, Let not the king sin against his servant, against David; because he hath not sinned against thee, and because his works have been to thee-ward very good: For he did put his life in his hand, and slew the Philistine, and the LORD wrought a great salvation for all Israel: thou sawest it, and didst rejoice: wherefore then wilt thou sin against innocent blood, to slay David without a cause? And Saul hearkened unto the voice of Jonathan: and Saul sware, As the LORD liveth, he shall not be slain. And Jonathan called David, and Jonathan shewed him all those things. And Jonathan brought David to Saul, and he was in his presence, as in times past.

How can one person's attitude toward another person descend so quickly from love to hate (verse 1)? Human nature permits people to move quickly from one emotion to another, as observed in the 1971 song by the New York City-based R&B vocal group The Persuaders, which declared, "It's a thin line between love and hate." Truly, Jesus could identify with this perspective, as on Palm Sunday the people hailed Him and less than a week later they nailed Him. Saul initially believed that he was unjustified in his anger and hatred against David. But as he continued his pattern, he eventually convinced himself of his right to take David's life. Saul's insecurity was also prompted by a powerful spirit, as seen in 1 Samuel 16:14 (NIV): "Now the Spirit of the LORD had departed from Saul, and an evil spirit from the LORD tormented him." One might ask the question, "If God is all good, how can an evil spirit come from God or be

sent by God?" Saul's "evil spirit" is comparable to what happened when Satan came upon Judas to betray the Lord's Anointed (see John 13:2, 27). "God's Spirit did not leave Saul, nor did the evil spirit enter him until after Saul had rebelled against God and God had announced to him that his kingdom was to go to another (1 Samuel 15:28)" (https://bible.org/question/1-sam-199-lord-sent-evil-spirit-saul-if-god-good-why-did-he-send-evil-spirit-people). This evil spirit is something that God permitted due to Saul's decision to rebel. This is somewhat like disobedient children who open the door to hardship when choosing to disobey their parents.

Saul quite likely had a custom of taking a morning walk, and Jonathan devised a plan to discern the level of danger or safety for David in the heart of his father. When Jonathan spoke well of David (verses 3-4), he took a chance with his own life and performed the duty of a true friend by seeking to keep David safe from harm. As Saul's son and a prince, Jonathan served as the voice of reason—speaking sensibly to his father, the king.

Jonathan reminded his father, Saul, of David's unselfish bravery when David took on the Philistine (verse 5). But when David's success against the Philistines brought David popularity among the people, Saul's jealousy was ignited. Meanwhile, because of his pure heart, David continued to be loyal and respectful to Saul.

Most likely at the time of Saul's words in verse 6, Saul intended to keep his promise of not seeking to harm David. But his change of heart was based on fleeting feelings and thus was temporary. Choices and decisions that are only motivated by the emotion of the moment cannot be trusted.

Verse 7 shows the power and importance of right words' being spoken at the right time to the right person. Proverbs 25:11 (NIV) reads, "Like apples of gold in settings of silver is a ruling rightly given." Jonathan could have easily deferred to his father's decision regarding David, but through tapping into godly courage and discernment, he did not allow his age and lower position to silence his truth. First Timothy 4:12 (NIV) supports this: "Don't let anyone look down on you because you are young, but set an example for the believers in speech, in conduct, in love, in faith, and in purity."

III. CONCLUDING REFLECTION

One of life's most valuable possessions is a genuine friend. In the age of reality shows and Facebook friends, it is rare to have someone who will walk with you in good times and in bad times. James Harris and Terry Lewis raised this question in the lyrics of a song: "Sunny days . . . everybody loves them. Can you stand the rain?" Times of sun are associated with times of fun, and times of rain are associated with times of pain. Since life cannot be perpetually sunny, it is a blessing to have a rain-worthy friend. The older one gets, the greater the appreciation for true friendship. The demands of honesty and friendship can surpass family bonds and civil obedience. Jonathan and David could have been rivals, but Jonathan, whether by intuition or revelation, understood that David was destined to become king.

PRAYER

Dear God, thank You for giving us true friends to help us navigate the sometimes-weary waters of life. Also, thank You for giving us a friend who sticks closer than a brother—Jesus Christ, Your Son. In Jesus' name we pray. Amen.

HOME DAILY BIBLE READINGS
(July 29–August 4, 2019)

A Covenant between Friends
MONDAY, July 29: "Saul Fears David" (1 Samuel 18:10-16)
TUESDAY, July 30: "David Marries Saul's Daughter" (1 Samuel 18:20-24, 28-30)
WEDNESDAY, July 31: "Michal Helps David Escape" (1 Samuel 19:8-12)
THURSDAY, August 1: "David and Jonathan Enter into Covenant" (1 Samuel 20:12-17)
FRIDAY, August 2: "Jonathan and David Plan a Rendezvous" (1 Samuel 20:18-23)
SATURDAY, August 3: "David and Jonathan Separate in Peace" (1 Samuel 20:35-42)
SUNDAY, August 4: "A Covenant between Two Friends" (1 Samuel 18:1-5; 19:1-7)

August 11, 2019   **Lesson 11**

A MOTHER-DAUGHTER COVENANT

ADULT/YOUTH	CHILDREN
ADULT/YOUNG ADULT TOPIC: Loyalty and Devotion	**GENERAL LESSON TITLE: A Mother-Daughter Promise**
YOUTH TOPIC: A Mother-Daughter Devotion	**CHILDREN'S TOPIC: Love in Action**

DEVOTIONAL READING
Ruth 4:13-17

ADULT/YOUTH	CHILDREN
BACKGROUND SCRIPTURE: Ruth 1:1-18	**BACKGROUND SCRIPTURE: Ruth 1:1-18**
PRINT PASSAGE: Ruth 1:6-11, 14-18	**PRINT PASSAGE: Ruth 1:6-11, 14-18**
KEY VERSE: Ruth 1:16	**KEY VERSE: Ruth 1:16b**

Ruth 1:6-11, 14-18—KJV

6 Then she arose with her daughters in law, that she might return from the country of Moab: for she had heard in the country of Moab how that the LORD had visited his people in giving them bread.

7 Wherefore she went forth out of the place where she was, and her two daughters in law with her; and they went on the way to return unto the land of Judah.

8 And Naomi said unto her two daughters in law, Go, return each to her mother's house: the LORD deal kindly with you, as ye have dealt with the dead, and with me.

9 The LORD grant you that ye may find rest, each of you in the house of her husband. Then she kissed them; and they lifted up their voice, and wept.

10 And they said unto her, Surely we will return with thee unto thy people.

11 And Naomi said, Turn again, my daughters: why will ye go with me? are there yet any more sons in my womb, that they may be your husbands?

.....

Ruth 1:6-11, 14-18—NIV

6 When Naomi heard in Moab that the LORD had come to the aid of his people by providing food for them, she and her daughters-in-law prepared to return home from there.

7 With her two daughters-in-law she left the place where she had been living and set out on the road that would take them back to the land of Judah.

8 Then Naomi said to her two daughters-in-law, "Go back, each of you, to your mother's home. May the LORD show you kindness, as you have shown kindness to your dead husbands and to me.

9 "May the LORD grant that each of you will find rest in the home of another husband." Then she kissed them goodbye and they wept aloud

10 and said to her, "We will go back with you to your people."

11 But Naomi said, "Return home, my daughters. Why would you come with me? Am I going to have any more sons, who could become your husbands?"

14 And they lifted up their voice, and wept again: and Orpah kissed her mother in law; but Ruth clave unto her.

15 And she said, Behold, thy sister in law is gone back unto her people, and unto her gods: return thou after thy sister in law.

16 And Ruth said, Intreat me not to leave thee, or to return from following after thee: for whither thou goest, I will go; and where thou lodgest, I will lodge: thy people shall be my people, and thy God my God:

17 Where thou diest, will I die, and there will I be buried: the LORD do so to me, and more also, if ought but death part thee and me.

18 When she saw that she was stedfastly minded to go with her, then she left speaking unto her.

.....

14 At this they wept aloud again. Then Orpah kissed her mother-in-law goodbye, but Ruth clung to her.

15 "Look," said Naomi, "your sister-in-law is going back to her people and her gods. Go back with her."

16 But Ruth replied, "Don't urge me to leave you or to turn back from you. Where you go I will go, and where you stay I will stay. Your people will be my people and your God my God.

17 "Where you die I will die, and there I will be buried. May the LORD deal with me, be it ever so severely, if even death separates you and me."

18 When Naomi realized that Ruth was determined to go with her, she stopped urging her.

UNIFYING LESSON PRINCIPLE: When bonded by a strong love and commitment to one another, people who are unrelated by birth may enter into a covenant relationship. What drives and sustains this relationship? Although Naomi begged Ruth to return to her people, Ruth clung to her mother-in-law and vowed her loyalty until death.

LESSON OBJECTIVES

Upon the completion of this lesson, the students will be able to do the following:
1. Identify Ruth and Naomi and tell why they were devoted to one another.
2. Feel compassion for someone in a vulnerable situation.
3. Demonstrate their loyalty and devotion to a spouse or other family member.

AGE-LEVEL POINTS TO BE EMPHASIZED

Teachers of ADULTS and YOUTH

—Naomi urged her daughters-in-law to find new husbands for economic security. Repetition of "return" and "turn back" denotes the real struggle here.

—Because Naomi was a widow whose children had died, she had no one to support her. Therefore, she chose to return to Judah, where the extended family of her late husband would be required by tradition to take her in.

—Naomi urged Ruth and Orpah to remain in Moab because their chances of finding husbands among Moabite men would be greater than among Jewish men (who would likely want nothing to do with Moabite women; see Deuteronomy 23:3).

—Naomi's question in verse 11 relates to the custom of Levirate marriage. (See Deuteronomy 25:5-10.)

—In many other places in Scripture, Moab has negative connotations, but not here. Ethnic prejudices existed between Jews and Moabites. (Ruth 1:6)

—The idea of Ruth, a Moabite, extending such kindness to Naomi likely would have puzzled the ancient hearers. Ruth was not legally obligated to remain with Naomi. Doing so was an act of loyalty, devotion, and love.

Teachers of CHILDREN

—Naomi, an Ephrathite widow in a foreign land (Moab), was vulnerable as a woman with no means of supporting herself.

—The widowed Naomi was left with only two daughters-in-law, who were also widows.

—Naomi, who had decided to return to Judah, urged her daughters-in-law to return to their own people—as she had no other sons for them to marry.

—Orpah, one of the daughters-in-law, left to return to her people, as Naomi had urged.

—Ruth, the other daughter-in-law, was constrained by her love for Naomi to remain with her.

—Ruth's devotion to Naomi is notable, since Ruth would be going to a land foreign to her and without any means of support.

THE CHRONOLOGICAL SETTING OF THE LESSON

The book of Ruth is conventionally believed to have been written during the rule of judges in Israel (see Ruth 1:1). The timing of the events in the book may have been during the later rule of judges, because the genealogy is three generations before the birth of David. This brevity in genealogy may suggest that the book was written during the later days of the judges, because the book of Ruth employs the use of Hebrew idioms that align with the period of the prophet Samuel. This book is also considered to be one of the most beautiful narrations of a short story ever written. Other books that the Jewish tradition maintain were written by Samuel are 1 Samuel and Judges.

THE GEOGRAPHICAL AND CULTURAL SETTING OF THE LESSON

Although there is not total consensus as to authorship, there is a strong leaning in the Talmud that Ruth was written by the prophet Samuel. The events of the book occurred between 1160 BC and 1100 BC. The setting of this book takes place in two venues: Moab and Bethlehem. The events took place during a great famine in Israel, and the story revolves around three women: Ruth, Orpah, and Naomi. The famine had forced Naomi to relocate to Moab with her sons, who ended up marrying two Moabite women: Ruth and Orpah.

The book of Ruth displays the love between God and humankind. Even though these were dark days facing the Israelites as a result of their immorality and apostasy, the book of Ruth plays a major role of shining light on the love that God has for His people (see Ruth 1:6; 4:17).

Moab was a pagan nation located near the Dead Sea and east of Judah, and was the neighboring country where Naomi, Elimelech, and their two sons had fled after a famine struck Judah. Elimelech and their two sons died in Moab. The additional setting of this book is in Bethlehem after Naomi and Ruth returned to Israel, where she encouraged Ruth to seek out her relative Boaz for possible marriage (see Ruth 3:9).

PROMINENT CHARACTER(S) IN THE LESSON

Boaz: He was a wealthy landowner and kinsman to Elimelech in Bethlehem in Judah. He married the widowed Moabite Ruth in order to continue the lineage of Elimelech, hence becoming the direct ancestor to King David and Jesus Christ.

Elimelech: He was an Israelite and husband to Naomi. He succumbed to death in Moab after he had fled the famine in Judah together with his family.

Naomi: She was married to Elimelech. They had relocated to Moab with their two sons from Judah during the great famine. However, she is widowed, and her sons also die, and she decides to return to Bethlehem (bible.org).

Ruth: Ruth was a Moabite woman married to one of Naomi's sons. She followed her mother-in-law back to Bethlehem after they both were widowed. Ruth accepted Yahweh as her God and bound herself to her mother-in-law. She is an example of how God will always reward His faithful servants (see Ruth 2:14-17; Hebrews 11:6).

KEY TERMS IN THE LESSON

Land (verse 7)—Hebrew: *erets* (eh'-rets): earth; land.

Moab (verse 6)—Hebrew: *Moab* (mo-awb): Moab; a son of Lot; also his descendant and the territory where they settled.

People (verse 6)—Hebrew: *am* (am): folk.

Place (verse 7)—Hebrew: *maqom* (maw-kome'): a standing place; a place.

Rest (verse 9)—Hebrew: *menuchah* (men-oo-khaw'): a resting place; rest.

Wept (verse 9)—Hebrew: *bakah* (baw-kaw'): wept; bewailed.

TOPICAL OUTLINE OF THE LESSON

I. **Introduction**
    A. A Special Kind of Love
    B. Biblical Background

II. **Exposition and Application of the Scripture**
    A. Decisions at the Crossroads (Ruth 1:6-11)
    B. The Tie that Binds (Ruth 1:14-18)

III. **Concluding Reflection**

I. INTRODUCTION
A. A Special Kind of Love

The account of Ruth begins during the closing days of Judges. It was a four-hundred-year timeline of anarchy and oppression during which the Israelites were not ruled by kings but rather had judges who were deliverers whom God periodically raised up to deliver Israel whenever the nation of Israel sought Him. Among those who presided over Israel as judges were Gideon, Samson, and Deborah (see Judges 17:6; 18:1; 19:1; and 21:25).

Ruth is a narrative of a love story which also contains some important genealogical information. The timeline of Ruth as stated earlier is intertwined with the era of the judges. Though the author is anonymous, it is believed that the book of Ruth was written by the prophet Samuel. The book of Ruth was written approximately 1046–1035 BC, and its purpose was mainly to show the kind of love, loyalty, and faithfulness that God desires to see us practice.

B. Biblical Background

The first part of our text, verses 1-5, firstly associates the book with the time of judges and goes on to describe the problems of famine which caused a family to move from Bethlehem to Moab. The family included Elimelech, his two sons Mahlon and Chilion, and their mother Naomi. The narrative gradually turns to Naomi and her plight after she loses her husband and two sons to death.

After it is reported that there is food in Israel once more, Naomi is set to return to her people, as a widow and childless. It is important at this point to note the importance of patience and longsuffering as necessary godly virtues. Partakers of God's deliverance learn and abide in the trust and faith that patience and long-suffering teach. It is important to learn to wait and understand God's timing and purpose for every season (see Romans 12:12; Psalm 37:7-9; Isaiah 40:31).

As Naomi got set to return to Jerusalem after the unpleasant tragedy that had befallen her over the years, she instructed her daughters-in-law to go back to their homes, kissed them goodbye, and hoped that God would deal kindly with them and perhaps give them husbands to replace their loss (verses 8-9). She no longer saw the need to care for them as was common at the time (see Deuteronomy 26:12-13; 27:19).

However, Naomi was met with an initial protest and refusal from both daughters-in-law. Naomi was determined and convinced that there was no more reason for them to continue with her. She reminded them of her inability to bear more children or even have someone who could marry them and give them children. As was the custom of ancient Israel, a widow without a son could be taken by her deceased husband's brother who would serve as a kind of surrogate father, providing her with a son in the name of the deceased brother/husband. Naomi expressed her heartfelt grief as she talked of her calamity and her belief that these calamities had befallen her as a result of disobedience, leaving the Promised Land, and also intermarrying with the Moabites. In going back to Israel, Naomi, though not bitter with God, is rather returning in repentance, trust, and submission to the will and purpose of God. Perhaps if Naomi had been bitter, she would have gone a different route rather than return to Israel. When we submit to God in humility, repentance, total reverence, and acceptance of His will, we position ourselves for the many great blessings God would release upon us in the shortest possible time.

After Ruth and Orpah had listened to Naomi, they both wept bitterly: they loved Naomi but were, however, anxious about their future. Orpah decided to leave and kissed Naomi goodbye, but Ruth decided to stay, despite the gloomy situation and unknown future (verse 14).

In our walk with God, sometimes we must move beyond our feelings to actually do and show what we claim to feel or express. Ruth went beyond her feelings to actually show the love she felt for Naomi by her actions and was not deterred even by Naomi's pleading.

In verses 15-18, Ruth expressed one of the most powerful statements of faith and devotion. We see Ruth (as a Gentile woman) go beyond relocation from one city to another to changing her belief system to which she had been accustomed. She did not just want to go with Naomi—she was ready to identify with, accept, and subject herself to an entirely new way of life as well. It was worth noting that Ruth could not have come to a conclusion of this magnitude if she had not been in any way impacted by the godly life of Naomi.

II. EXPOSITION AND APPLICATION OF THE SCRIPTURE

A. Decisions at the Crossroads (Ruth 1:6-11)

Then she arose with her daughters in law, that she might return from the country of Moab: for she had heard in the country of Moab how that the LORD had visited his people in giving them bread. Wherefore she went forth out of the place where she was, and her two daughters in law with her; and they went on the way to return unto the land of Judah. And Naomi said unto her two daughters in law, Go, return each to her mother's house: the LORD deal kindly with you, as ye have dealt with the dead, and with me. The LORD grant you that ye may find rest, each of you in the house of her husband. Then she kissed them; and they lifted up their voice, and wept. And they said unto her, Surely we will return with thee unto thy people. And Naomi said, Turn again, my daughters: why will ye go with me? are there yet any more sons in my womb, that they may be your husbands?

Throughout history, God has proven His love to His people by coming to their aid in their greatest times of trouble (verse 6). Psalm 46:1 (NIV) helps us to understand that "God is our refuge and strength, an ever-present help in trouble." The relationship between Naomi and her two daughters-in-law presents a picture of a tranquil, peaceful, supportive, loving functional family. There are not many things worse than a dysfunctional family. The sincere love, support, and loyalty demonstrated by this trio (verse 7) is a breath of fresh air, especially in a culture of so-called reality shows where family dysfunction is often celebrated and glorified. Quite possibly it was Naomi, the godly matriarch, who anchored the family and exhibited characteristics and tendencies of respect which were in turn reflected within the rest of the family. Love begets love. It has been suggested that if there were more Naomis, then there might be more Orpahs and Ruths. We as people and as Christians are not only living for ourselves, but we are also influencing our family members, our church members, our schoolmates, our work associates, and the community at-large.

In the culture of that time period, whenever a woman married, she would conform and adapt to her husband's faith tradition. But when she returned to her own people as a widow, she returned to her family's religion (verse 8; see also Ruth 1:15). God's influence extended beyond the land of Israel, and Naomi wanted her daughters-in-law to be under the protection of God when they were back in their own land (*Cambridge Bible for Schools and Colleges*). Naomi demonstrated a sublime sense of unselfishness and holy human character. Naomi was consistently more concerned about the future welfare of her two daughters-in-law than she was for her own fate. Naomi had lived her life, and she wanted to see Orpah and Ruth live their lives.

Once again, love is on billboard-sized display in verses 9-10. The raw emotion of the moment takes its toll on all three women at this point of possible departure and the dismantling of the safe and familiar past. The two younger widows had good reason to be concerned about their uncertain future.

Naomi's insistent and consistent advice and directions were for both young women to return and seek a better life without her (verse 11). She pleaded for them to abandon her, even in the face of the fact that an elderly widow travelling alone could prove dangerous and life-threatening. Naomi's resolved insistence for her widowed daughters-in-law was motivated by the perils of a single or widowed woman in the extremely male-dominated culture of the time.

B. The Tie that Binds
(Ruth 1:14-18)

And they lifted up their voice, and wept again: and Orpah kissed her mother in law; but Ruth clave unto her. And she said, Behold, thy sister in law is gone back unto her people, and unto her gods: return thou after thy sister in law. And Ruth said, Intreat me not to leave thee, or to return from following after thee: for whither thou goest, I will go; and where thou lodgest, I will lodge: thy people shall be my people, and thy God my God: Where thou diest, will I die, and there will I be buried: the Lord do so to me, and more also, if ought but death part thee and me. When she saw that she was stedfastly minded to go with her, then she left speaking unto her.

Matthew Henry's Concise Commentary raises an interesting question regarding Naomi's insistence that Ruth and Orpah go back to Moab:

Did Naomi do well, to discourage her daughters from going with her, when she might save them from the idolatry of Moab, and bring them to the faith and worship of the God of Israel? Naomi, no doubt, desired to do that; but if they went with her, she would not have them to go upon her account. (http://biblehub.com/commentaries/ruth/1-8.html)

This perspective has a parallel in the New Testament passage of Luke 14:27-33 (NIV), when Jesus provides criteria to measure the authenticity of one's faith:

"And whoever does not carry their cross and follow me cannot be my disciple. Suppose one of you wants to build a tower. Won't you first sit down and estimate the cost to see if you have enough money to complete it? For if you lay the foundation and are not able to finish it, everyone who sees it will ridicule you, saying, 'This person began to build and wasn't able to finish.' Or suppose a king is about to go to war against another king. Won't he first sit down and consider whether he is able with ten thousand men to oppose the one coming against him with twenty thousand? If he is not able, he will send a delegation while the other is still a long way off and will ask for terms of peace. In the same way, those of you who do not give up everything you have cannot be my disciples."

It is difficult to determine why Orpah decided to leave. Clearly, it was a difficult and emotionally draining decision. On the other hand, Ruth never wavered but continued to cling to Naomi (verse 14). She was singularly focused and resolutely resigned to stake her future with Naomi, even if that meant forsaking her own people, her native country, and her familiar god.

The emotionally charged exchange between Ruth and Naomi (verses 15-16) is among the most sensitive and compassionate dialogues in all of Scripture. Both are sincere, both are unselfish, and both are determined to prevail in the desire to do what is best for the other.

Who shall decide which was the more noble and truly womanly in her self-forgetfulness—the elder, sadder heart, which strove to secure for the other some joy and fellowship at the price of its own deepened solitude; or the younger, which steeled itself against entreaties, and cast away friends and country for love's sweet sake? We rightly praise Ruth's vow, but we should not forget Naomi's unselfish pleading to be left to tread her weary path alone. Ruth's passionate burst of tenderness is immortal. It has put into fitting words for all generations the deepest thoughts of loving hearts, and comes to us over all the centuries between, as warm and living as when it welled up from that gentle, heroic soul. The two strongest emotions of our nature are blended in it, and each gives a portion of its fervor—love and religion. So closely are they interwoven that it is difficult to allot to each its share in the united stream; but, without trying to determine to which of them the greater part of its volume and force is due, and while conscious of the danger of spoiling such words by comments weaker than themselves, we may seek to put into distinct form the impressions which they make.[1]

Ruth's impassioned words reflect a sense of self-sacrifice and forsaking of personal gain in order to love, protect, befriend, and support her mother-in-law. The reason why Ruth chose Jehovah God was because Naomi chose Jehovah God. Naomi's spiritual influence upon Ruth was undeniable. This encounter is a prime example of how God can use everyday relationships as a bridge to allow Him to become leader in someone else's life.

Ruth spoke in ultimate life-and-death terms (verse 17) that exhibit the tremendous depth and seriousness of her commitment to Naomi. She elevated her intentions beyond the human level and appealed to Yahweh God in the form of an oath backed by a self-imposed severe penalty for reneging on her promise. "It was thus that the Hebrews made their most awful appeals to Yahveh. They signified their willingness to suffer some dire calamity if they should either do the evil deed repudiated or fail to do the good deed promised" (*Pulpit Commentary*, http://biblehub.com/ruth/1-17.htm).

One might say that in this beautiful battle of who could out-love the other and who could unselfishly out-care for the other, it was Ruth who won (verse 18). Although this beautiful battle was extremely close, Ruth wore Naomi down with commitment and overwhelmed her with love. Commitment and demonstration consistently overcome pious platitudes and empty emotions. "Those that are but half resolved, and go on in the ways of religion without a steadfast mind, stand like a door ajar, which invites a thief. But resolution shuts and bolts the door, and then the devil flees from us" (*Benson Commentary*, http://biblehub.com/commentaries/ruth/1-18.htm).

III. CONCLUDING REFLECTION

The household of Elimelech emigrated to Moab during a famine in their homeland and were there as Jehovah worshippers in a nation of idol worshippers. Whenever believers are surrounded by unbelievers, that automatically qualifies them to actively serve as missionaries. Through the consistent and powerful influence of Naomi, Ruth became a kind of first-fruits of the Gentiles. One purpose of the book of Ruth that seems not to directly emphasize God is to "show how the believing Gentile was to be incorporated into Israel. Boaz rejoices over her, and especially over her conversion, and prays, 'A full reward be given thee of Jehovah, the God of Israel, under whose wings thou art come to trust.' She is married to him, and becomes the ancestress of David, and, through him, of the Messiah" (*MacLaren Expositions of Holy Scripture,* http://biblehub.com/commentaries/maclaren/ruth/1.htm). We find in the book of Ruth encouragement to build solid, successful, and functional families. To invest in one's family is to invest in his/her future and the future of the entire world. Time is never wasted that is spent loving one's family and encouraging others to do likewise.

PRAYER

Lord, thank You for the gift of family. Help us never to take this gift for granted but to do all we can to grow it into an entity that can be of aid to others. In Jesus' name we pray. Amen.

HOME DAILY BIBLE READINGS
(August 5-11, 2019)

A Mother-Daughter Covenant
MONDAY, August 5: "Protecting Widows" (Deuteronomy 24:17-22)
TUESDAY, August 6: "Continuing the Family Line" (Deuteronomy 25:5-10)
WEDNESDAY, August 7: "Ruth, Mother of David and Jesus" (Matthew 1:2-6, 16)
THURSDAY, August 8: "Naomi Loses Her Husband and Sons" (Ruth 1:1-5)
FRIDAY, August 9: "Ruth and Naomi Return to Bethlehem" (Ruth 1:19-22)
SATURDAY, August 10: "Boaz Welcomes Ruth to His Fields" (Ruth 2:5-13)
SUNDAY, August 11: "Intimate Family Ties" (Ruth 1:6-11, 14-18)

---

1. *MacLaren Expositions of Holy Scripture,* http://biblehub.com/commentaries/maclaren/ruth/1.htm

August 18, 2019   Lesson 12

A COVENANT TO MARRY

ADULT/YOUTH

ADULT/YOUNG ADULT TOPIC: **The Reward of Commitment**

YOUTH TOPIC: **A Promise to Marry**

CHILDREN

GENERAL LESSON TITLE: **A Promise to Marry**

CHILDREN'S TOPIC: **Everything Will Work Out**

DEVOTIONAL READING
Hebrews 13:1-8

ADULT/YOUTH

BACKGROUND SCRIPTURE: **Ruth 1:6-18; 3–4; Matthew 19:1-12**

PRINT PASSAGE: **Ruth 3:1-6, 8-12, 16-18**

KEY VERSE: **Ruth 3:10**

CHILDREN

BACKGROUND SCRIPTURE: **Ruth 1:6-18; 3–4; Matthew 19:1-12**

PRINT PASSAGE: **Ruth 3:1-6, 8-12, 16-18**

KEY VERSE: **Ruth 3:10a**

Ruth 3:1-6, 8-12, 16-18—KJV

THEN NAOMI her mother in law said unto her, My daughter, shall I not seek rest for thee, that it may be well with thee?

2 And now is not Boaz of our kindred, with whose maidens thou wast? Behold, he winnoweth barley to night in the threshing floor.

3 Wash thyself therefore, and anoint thee, and put thy raiment upon thee, and get thee down to the floor: but make not thyself known unto the man, until he shall have done eating and drinking.

4 And it shall be, when he lieth down, that thou shalt mark the place where he shall lie, and thou shalt go in, and uncover his feet, and lay thee down; and he will tell thee what thou shalt do.

5 And she said unto her, All that thou sayest unto me I will do.

6 And she went down unto the floor, and did according to all that her mother in law bade her.

Ruth 3:1-6, 8-12, 16-18—NIV

ONE DAY Ruth's mother-in-law Naomi said to her, "My daughter, I must find a home for you, where you will be well provided for.

2 "Now Boaz, with whose women you have worked, is a relative of ours. Tonight he will be winnowing barley on the threshing floor.

3 "Wash, put on perfume, and get dressed in your best clothes. Then go down to the threshing floor, but don't let him know you are there until he has finished eating and drinking.

4 "When he lies down, note the place where he is lying. Then go and uncover his feet and lie down. He will tell you what to do."

5 "I will do whatever you say," Ruth answered.

6 So she went down to the threshing floor and did everything her mother-in-law told her to do.

.....

.....

8 And it came to pass at midnight, that the man was afraid, and turned himself: and, behold, a woman lay at his feet.

9 And he said, Who art thou? And she answered, I am Ruth thine handmaid: spread therefore thy skirt over thine handmaid; for thou art a near kinsman.

10 And he said, Blessed be thou of the LORD, my daughter: for thou hast shewed more kindness in the latter end than at the beginning, inasmuch as thou followedst not young men, whether poor or rich.

11 And now, my daughter, fear not; I will do to thee all that thou requirest: for all the city of my people doth know that thou art a virtuous woman.

12 And now it is true that I am thy near kinsman: howbeit there is a kinsman nearer than I.

.....

16 And when she came to her mother in law, she said, Who art thou, my daughter? And she told her all that the man had done to her.

17 And she said, These six measures of barley gave he me; for he said to me, Go not empty unto thy mother in law.

18 Then said she, Sit still, my daughter, until thou know how the matter will fall: for the man will not be in rest, until he have finished the thing this day.

8 In the middle of the night something startled the man; he turned—and there was a woman lying at his feet!

9 "Who are you?" he asked. "I am your servant Ruth," she said. "Spread the corner of your garment over me, since you are a guardian-redeemer of our family."

10 "The LORD bless you, my daughter," he replied. "This kindness is greater than that which you showed earlier: You have not run after the younger men, whether rich or poor.

11 "And now, my daughter, don't be afraid. I will do for you all you ask. All the people of my town know that you are a woman of noble character.

12 "Although it is true that I am a guardian-redeemer of our family, there is another who is more closely related than I."

.....

16 When Ruth came to her mother-in-law, Naomi asked, "How did it go, my daughter?" Then she told her everything Boaz had done for her

17 and added, "He gave me these six measures of barley, saying, 'Don't go back to your mother-in-law empty-handed.'"

18 Then Naomi said, "Wait, my daughter, until you find out what happens. For the man will not rest until the matter is settled today."

UNIFYING LESSON PRINCIPLE: Obedience and commitment to others may bring unanticipated rewards. How should loyalty be compensated? Ruth's commitment to Naomi and her efforts to obey were rewarded with favor in Boaz's eyes, marriage to a kinsman-redeemer, and the assurance of a comfortable life in the future.

LESSON OBJECTIVES

Upon the completion of this lesson, the students will be able to do the following:

1. Describe the legal procedure by which Boaz claimed the right to marry Ruth and became kinsman-redeemer for both Naomi and Ruth.
2. Sense the urgency by which Boaz acted in order to marry Ruth.
3. Honor marriage in their actions, whether they are married or not.

AGE-LEVEL POINTS TO BE EMPHASIZED

Teachers of ADULTS and YOUTH

—Ruth needed to marry a kinsman-redeemer (rather than any young man) in order for him to take over the responsibilities of Naomi's dead husband and inherit his land. (Women had no right of inheritance.)

—Spreading the cloak over someone (verse 9) symbolized protection and the intent to marry.

—Six measures of barley were a generous gift for Naomi (verse 17).

—Marriages were arranged by a woman's parents (usually the father). Since Ruth's father was not in the picture, Naomi encouraged a relationship between Boaz and Ruth, and instructed her in what to do (verses 1-5).

—The choice of a husband for Ruth was not hers but driven by the law of Levirate marriage (see Deuteronomy 25:5-10).

—The book of Ruth lifts up the virtue of kindness that goes beyond what is expected or deserved.

Ethnic prejudices existed between Jews and Moabites.

—The story of Ruth reminds us that even desperate circumstances can be redeemed, even when imperfect people are involved.

Teachers of CHILDREN

—Ruth found a source of food for her and Naomi as a gleaner in the fields of Boaz.

—While Boaz was Naomi's kinsman, he was not obligated by Levirate law to marry Ruth.

—Naomi instructed Ruth to approach Boaz in intimacy to propose marriage.

—Boaz was responsive to Ruth's approach and perceived her as an honorable woman because of her commitment to Naomi.

—Boaz's statement to Ruth in 3:11 ("I will do for you all that you ask") indicated that Boaz would indeed marry Ruth.

—Ruth was significant to Naomi, and not just as a companion; her marriage to Boaz made him her "redeemer" when she gave birth to the child Obed, an ancestor of David's.

THE CHRONOLOGICAL SETTING OF THE LESSON

The book of Ruth is a narrative that describes events concerning the genealogy of King David and ultimately Jesus Christ. The narrative is set in two locations: Moab and Bethlehem of Judea. It begins with a painful introduction marred with grief and sorrow and traces the family of Elimelech from a woman's point of view. This story shows a generation that has gone astray from God, and as a result has been subjected to great suffering, civil war, and starvation as punishment for their sins. The children of Israel had sinned against the Mosaic Covenant by practicing divination, sorcery, and incantations (see Judges 2:11-23; Deuteronomy 4). However, the book of Ruth shows the love that exists between God and the children of Israel

even after they had sinned against God. This book shows the love and faithfulness that God has for His people by using three ordinary people: Ruth, Naomi, and Boaz (bible.org).

THE GEOGRAPHICAL AND CULTURAL SETTING OF THE LESSON

The country of Moab is located in modern-day Jordan. Moab was a mountainous region along the Jordan River on the western side of the Dead Sea. Moab was a neighboring country to Bethlehem in Judea. Elimelech and his wife, Naomi, had escaped the famine in Bethlehem and moved to Moab—where her husband and their two sons died—leaving her and her two daughters-in-law, Ruth and Orpah. These two women were Moabites, and according to the Talmud traditions the Moabites and the Ammonites were the sworn enemies of Israel (see Deuteronomy 23:4-5).

The book of Ruth describes the laws concerning levirate marriage which required a close kinsman to carry out the duties of a relative who had died without having a son as his heir. This individual is seen in the character of Boaz, even though he was not the closest male relative of Elimelech (see Deuteronomy 25:5).

The events in the book of Ruth take place in the Southern Kingdom of Judah in the City of Bethlehem, which is part of present-day Palestine. The city of Bethlehem is considered to be the city of King David, because it was his birthplace. This story takes place during the spring harvest of wheat and barley in Judah, which signifies that it was a plenteous harvest (see Ruth 1:6). This period is very significant because Naomi's family had initially left Judah for Moab due to the famine, and she returned with Ruth at the time of a great harvest. The harvest provided Ruth the chance to interact with Boaz under Naomi's instructions while gleaning the grains in his fields (see Leviticus 23:2). This book also portrayed a patriarchal society where the rights of women are below those of men. The notion of levirate marriage and the teachings concerning divorce take the center stage through the character of Boaz, who eventually marries Ruth as a goel or a kinsman-redeemer.

PROMINENT CHARACTER(S) IN THE LESSON

Boaz: He was a rich farmer in the City of Bethlehem and a kinsman to Elimelech. He was made the kinsman-redeemer when he agreed to marry Ruth, and he therefore became the great grandfather to King David and direct ancestor of Jesus Christ.

Naomi: She was a wife to Elimelech and a widow who went through much torment when she lost everything. Naomi was sometimes referred to as the female version of Job, because they both lost everything but remained faithful servants of God.

Ruth: She was a Moabite woman who was initially married to one of Naomi's sons before she was widowed. She returned with her mother-in-law to Bethlehem and accepted Yahweh as her true God. She got married to Boaz, and they became the direct ancestors of David and Jesus Christ (bible.org).

KEY TERMS IN THE LESSON

Daughter (verse 10)—Hebrew: *bath* (bath): daughter; maiden.

Feet (verse 4)—Hebrew: *margeloth* (mar-ghel-aw'): place of the feet; feet.

Night (verse 8)—Hebrew: *layil* or *lel* or *layelah* (lah'-yil): night; opposite of day; "midnight" (KJV).

Rest (verse 18)—Hebrew: *shaqat* (shaw-kat'): to be quiet or undisturbed.

Wash (verse 3)—Hebrew: *rachats* (raw-khats'): to wash, wash off or away, bathe.

Well (verse 1)—Hebrew: *yatab* (yaw-tab'): to be good, well, glad, or pleasing.

TOPICAL OUTLINE OF THE LESSON

I. **Introduction**
   A. The Process of Developing Love
   B. Biblical Background

II. **Exposition and Application of the Scripture**
   A. A Quest for a New Life (Ruth 3:1-6)
   B. Character Counts (Ruth 3:8-11)
   C. Reward for Righteousness (Ruth 3:12, 16-18)

III. **Concluding Reflection**

I. INTRODUCTION

A. The Process of Developing Love

Ruth 3 takes us into what could be referred to as the next stage in our Christian lives and walk with God. In the previous chapters, we saw Ruth's commitment and her determination to follow the true God by sticking with her mother-in-law, Naomi. She grew in her relationship with Boaz, consistently relying upon his favor. Faith is really of little use until it has grown and been tested. This chapter also goes further to the rest and fruit produced when our faith is tried. We can learn from this chapter that God uses processes to bring us closer to Himself.

The events of Ruth are said to have occurred between 1302 and 1250 BC. The book of Ruth features a beautiful love story between Ruth and Boaz, but more than that it is a story about a prodigal nation coming to repentance and God's bringing them back from destruction to the center of spiritual importance.

B. Biblical Background

Chapter 3 begins with Ruth's drawing near to God (verses 1-2). Ruth had already been graced with the provisions of Boaz as she had sought refuge under the wings of God. We also have seen her work in the field of Boaz and have seen his gracious commitment to her in return. Naomi had a greater vision. She had foreseen Ruth's becoming a loved and honored wife but also knew that achieving this would not be easy because it would require Ruth to place herself totally at the feet of Boaz and to rely completely upon his will. In the Christian walk, certain times come when we must be at the threshing floor to be tested and refined. The threshing floor is used to separate the true grain from the chaff. These times purify and strengthen our faith in God.

In verse 3, we see that Ruth received instruction on how to prepare herself for engagement. These three ways also can be found interpreted in the New Testament. They are these: wash yourself (see Ephesians 5:26); anoint yourself (see Ephesians 5:18); and put on new clothes (see Revelation 19:8). Ruth harkened to Naomi and did as she said, going to lay at Boaz's feet. It so happened that at midnight, Boaz noticed Ruth, and this was an answered prayer—as he was willing to marry, redeem, and honor her. Boaz recognized the commitment, kindness, and faith of Ruth when he referred to her as a "woman of excellence." Ruth had shown commitment to Naomi and did not stop there, but also extended the same level of commitment to Boaz, which made him promise to do whatever she asked of him (verses 8-12). When we show so much commitment to God and place our will completely on Him, we will be amazed at His response to our needs—just as Boaz not only accepted Ruth but also gave her gifts (verses 14-18).

Many young people today believe that marriage is only an issue of civil law, but marriage is a commitment involving the couple and God. It is a commitment and must be kept and fulfilled by all measure. When we begin to see marriage as a commitment not only to our spouse but also to God, we are sure to reap the rewards of it.

II. EXPOSITION AND APPLICATION OF THE SCRIPTURE

A. A Quest for a New Life
(Ruth 3:1-6)

THEN NAOMI her mother in law said unto her, My daughter, shall I not seek rest for thee, that it may be well with thee? And now is not Boaz of our kindred, with whose maidens thou wast? Behold, he winnoweth barley to night in the threshing floor. Wash thyself therefore, and anoint thee, and put thy raiment upon thee, and get thee down to the floor: but make not thyself known unto the man, until he shall have done eating and drinking. And it shall be, when he lieth down, that thou shalt mark the place where he shall lie, and thou shalt go in, and uncover his feet, and lay thee down; and he will tell thee what thou shalt do. And she said unto her, All that thou sayest unto me I will do. And she went down unto the floor, and did according to all that her mother in law bade her.

Naomi possessed an intense interest in the welfare of her widowed daughter-in-law, and this powerful sense of responsibility propelled Naomi to be assertive enough to seek a husband for Ruth (verse 1). So, without the benefit of eharmony or matchmaker.com, Naomi activated her trust in God to be able to locate the perfect mate for her daughter-in-law. Perhaps Naomi recognized that time was passing without Ruth's making any definite connections with potential suitors.

As this dramatic scene begins, Naomi, as a seasoned sister, schooled Ruth in an effective way to get the attention of Boaz (verse 2), who was a wealthy, available gentleman. Boaz's relationship to Elimelech and his friendly disposition shown toward Ruth led Naomi to think of Boaz as a great mate for Ruth. "He might be willing to do the kinsman's part; at any rate, she made up her mind to act courageously and in a spirit of faith. In her plan for a next of kin marriage Naomi's only concern is for Ruth's future [and] the perpetuation of the name of her dead childless son" (*Cambridge Bible for Schools and Colleges: The Book of Judges*, p. 10).

The mentor-mentee relationship between Ruth and Naomi is on full display in these verses. It was extremely important for Ruth to carefully follow every detail in this delicate plan (verse 3)—because one error could mean the difference between success and failure.

The specific instructions Naomi gave on how to handle Boaz (verse 4) seem somewhat forward and indiscreet upon first reading and viewed from a contemporary perspective. However, viewed from the Old Testament world perspective, what Naomi told Ruth to do was a simple, practical plan for reminding Boaz of his duty as the kinsman of a deceased relative. "Boaz probably slept upon a mat or skin; Ruth lay crosswise at his feet—a position in which Eastern servants frequently sleep in the same chamber or tent with their master; and if they want a covering, custom allows them that benefit from part of the covering on their master's bed. Resting, as the Orientals do at night, in the same clothes they wear during the day, there was no indelicacy in a stranger, or even a woman, putting the extremity of this cover over her" (*Jamieson, Fausset, and Brown's Commentary on the Whole Bible*).

In contemporary culture, mothers-in-law are often presented in a poor light. They are commonly portrayed as being controlling, judgmental, critical, overbearing, toxic persons. However, that description is for persons who are unhealthy themselves and are also operating in a dysfunctional family environment. Before Ruth went to visit the place where Boaz worked, she washed and anointed herself and kept a low profile while the men were awake, and marked the place where Boaz lay down following his evening meal. In verses 5 and 6, Ruth showed her submission to and appreciation for Naomi's instruction and guidance.

B. Character Counts
(Ruth 3:8-11)

And it came to pass at midnight, that the man was afraid, and turned himself: and, behold, a woman lay at his feet. And he said, Who art thou? And she answered, I am Ruth thine handmaid: spread therefore thy skirt over thine handmaid; for thou art a near kinsman. And he said, Blessed be thou of the LORD, my daughter: for thou hast shewed more kindness in the latter end than at the beginning, inasmuch as thou followedst not young men, whether poor or rich. And now, my daughter, fear not; I will do to thee all that thou requirest: for all the city of my people doth know that thou art a virtuous woman.

This middle-of-the-night incident (verse 8) that occurred while Boaz was sleeping is a test of Ruth's character as well as a test of Boaz's character. The outcome of the incident may have been different for two people with lesser integrity than Boaz and Ruth. The biggest reaction from Boaz was his being startled and earnestly inquiring about the identity of this strange woman he could barely see in the murky shadows of the nighttime.

The symbolic act in verse 9 represented the kinsman's claiming the widow as his wife (see Ezekiel 16:8). Ruth had already placed part of the blanket over her, but she now asked him to participate so that the act might become his own. "To spread a skirt over one is, in the East, a symbolical action denoting protection. To this day in many parts of the East, to say of anyone that he put his skirt over a woman, is synonymous with saying that he married her; and at all the mar-riages of the modern Jews and Hindus, one part of the ceremony is for the bridegroom to put a silken or cotton cloak around his bride" (*Jamieson-Fausset-Brown Bible Commentary*, http://biblehub.com/commentaries/ruth/3-9 .htm).

After Boaz overcomes the initial shock of this midnight female visitor sleeping at his feet, the revelation of her identity and her pure intentions invoke from him a sense of respect, responsibility, and protection (verse 10). If Ruth had exhibited impure intentions and Boaz had responded in kind, this entire scenario would have been a disaster. The spiritually mature and gallant response of Boaz "is in itself a sufficient proof of the view he took of her conduct, and of the integrity of his own. . . . this blessing follows immediately on the avowal of her name. His own feelings had already been attuned to due honour and respect for Ruth; he is prepared not only to discharge the duty of next of kin, but to do it . . . with a sincere loyal affection" (*Ellicott's Commentary for English Readers*, http://biblehub.com/commentaries/ruth/3-10.htm).

Boaz lauds Ruth for her noble character (verse 11), but the character of Boaz is also showing here because he did not attempt to take advantage of Ruth. Boaz also did not allow their class difference to serve as a barrier to his love and kindness toward her.

Boaz did not disdain her as "a poor, destitute stranger, nor suspect her of any ill intentions. He spoke honourably of her as a virtuous woman, made her a promise, and as soon as the morning arrived, sent her away with a present to her mother-in-law. Boaz made his promise conditional, for there was a kinsman nearer than he, to whom the right of redemption belonged" (*Matthew Henry Study Bible—Revised King James Edition*).

C. Reward for Righteousness (Ruth 3:12, 16-18)

And now it is true that I am thy near kinsman: howbeit there is a kinsman nearer than I. . . . And when she came to her mother in law, she said, Who art thou, my daughter? And she told her all that the man had done to her. And she said, These six measures of barley gave he me; for he said to me, Go not empty unto thy mother in law. Then said she, Sit still, my daughter, until thou know how the matter will fall: for the man will not be in rest, until he have finished the thing this day.

The character and integrity of Boaz continues to be on display, as he decided to serve as the kinsman-redeemer for Ruth. He could have disregarded protocol and taken her as his wife, but his heart for doing the right thing in the right way at the right time compelled him to show respect for the other individual who had priority in the family line. Maya Angelou once wrote, "If we lose love and self-respect for each other, this is how we finally die." In a parallel expression regarding respect, Mona Sutphen said that "Most good relationships are built on mutual trust and respect."

Some versions of the Bible translate Naomi's question to Ruth (verse 16) as "Who are you?" This question seems strangely inappropriate. Obviously, Naomi knew well the identity of Ruth, as evidenced by her referring to her as "my daughter" in her salutation. Most likely, Naomi's words beg the question in contemporary vernacular, "What is your status, baby girl? Are you now engaged to Boaz or what?" Surely, Naomi had trouble sleeping that night, wondering how Ruth fared while following her detailed instructions.

The concept of "love language" developed by Dr. Gary Chapman suggests that different people express love in different ways. These ways include 1) Words of Affirmation; 2) Quality Time; 3) Receiving Gifts; 4) Acts of Service; and 5) Physical Touch. Which language relates most to you?

Obviously, Boaz was a man whose love language involved the giving of gifts. The measures of barley that he gave to Ruth (verse 17) weighed about two gallons each and must have been quite a load for one woman to carry by herself. Boaz's generosity may have further indicated to Naomi that he was indeed honorable, and that he would move on Ruth's overture swiftly. As a seasoned woman of wisdom, Naomi advised her daughter-in-law to sit still and wait for Boaz to make the next move (verse 18). Ruth wisely followed Naomi's sage advice.

What great developments might happen today if there was a restoration of wise, spiritually mature women mentoring young women and the young women following their advice? In this day of instant everything, there is strength to be found in learning how to wait. "This narrative may encourage us to lay ourselves by faith at the feet of Christ; He is our near Kinsman; having taken our nature upon him . . . . [He] has the right to redeem.

Let us . . . [seek] to receive from him his directions: Lord, what wilt thou have me to do?" (*A Commentary upon the Holy Bible, from Henry and Scott: Joshua to Esther*, Matthew Henry, p. 121).

III. CONCLUDING REFLECTION

Ruth's need to marry a kinsman-redeemer (rather than any young man) serves as a directive for others today to seek permanent relationships that reward rather than temporary relationships that only momentarily satisfy. When Boaz spread his cloak over Ruth, it was an indication that he intended to marry her. Obedience to God and commitment to God are rewarded with blessings beyond anything we can even ask or think. With marriage being under attack and in decline in the African-American community, it is more important than ever to focus time, attention, and financial resources in efforts and ministries that will help to develop strong and healthy dating relationships, engagements, and marriage relationships. When we have strong marriages, we have strong families, strong churches, strong schools, and strong cities. A healthy marriage provides a template for future generations to emulate. A healthy marriage is the one entity that can make a positive impact on the widest variety of community variables from economics, to education, health and longevity, crime, home ownership, and mental/emotional/spiritual well-being.

PRAYER

Lord, please help us to see the need for healthy marriages and strong homes within our community. Then please give us the strength to build those in our own lives and in the lives of others. In Jesus' name we pray. Amen.

HOME DAILY BIBLE READINGS
(August 12-18, 2019)

A Covenant to Marry

MONDAY, August 12: "God's Chosen Bride" (Ezekiel 16:8-14)

TUESDAY, August 13: "The Status of Divorced Women in Israel" (Deuteronomy 24:1-4)

WEDNESDAY, August 14: "Sustain Marital Love and Fidelity" (1 Corinthians 7:1-11)

THURSDAY, August 15: "Husbands and Wives—Joint Heirs" (1 Peter 3:1-9)

FRIDAY, August 16: "Boaz Buys Naomi's Property" (Ruth 4:9-12)

SATURDAY, August 17: "Ruth and Boaz Marry; Obed Is Born" (Ruth 4:13-17)

SUNDAY, August 18: "Support and Protect Marriage" (Ruth 3:1-6, 8-12, 16-18)

August 25, 2019 — Lesson 13

MARRIAGE: A COVENANT OF MUTUAL LOVE

ADULT/YOUTH
ADULT/YOUNG ADULT TOPIC: **Family Commitment**
YOUTH TOPIC: **Family Commitment**

CHILDREN
GENERAL LESSON TITLE: **Marriage: A Promise to Keep**
CHILDREN'S TOPIC: **All in the Family**

DEVOTIONAL READING
Hebrews 12:7-13

ADULT/YOUTH
BACKGROUND SCRIPTURE: **Ephesians 5:21–6:4**
PRINT PASSAGE: **Ephesians 5:21-33**
KEY VERSE: **Ephesians 5:21**

CHILDREN
BACKGROUND SCRIPTURE: **Ephesians 5:21–6:4**
PRINT PASSAGE: **Ephesians 5:21-33**
KEY VERSE: **Ephesians 5:21**

Ephesians 5:21-33—KJV

21 Submitting yourselves one to another in the fear of God.

22 Wives, submit yourselves unto your own husbands, as unto the Lord.

23 For the husband is the head of the wife, even as Christ is the head of the church: and he is the saviour of the body.

24 Therefore as the church is subject unto Christ, so let the wives be to their own husbands in every thing.

25 Husbands, love your wives, even as Christ also loved the church, and gave himself for it;

26 That he might sanctify and cleanse it with the washing of water by the word,

27 That he might present it to himself a glorious church, not having spot, or wrinkle, or any such thing; but that it should be holy and without blemish.

28 So ought men to love their wives as their own bodies. He that loveth his wife loveth himself.

Ephesians 5:21-33—NIV

21 Submit to one another out of reverence for Christ.

22 Wives, submit yourselves to your own husbands as you do to the Lord.

23 For the husband is the head of the wife as Christ is the head of the church, his body, of which he is the Savior.

24 Now as the church submits to Christ, so also wives should submit to their husbands in everything.

25 Husbands, love your wives, just as Christ loved the church and gave himself up for her

26 to make her holy, cleansing her by the washing with water through the word,

27 and to present her to himself as a radiant church, without stain or wrinkle or any other blemish, but holy and blameless.

28 In this same way, husbands ought to love their wives as their own bodies. He who loves his wife loves himself.

29 For no man ever yet hated his own flesh; but nourisheth and cherisheth it, even as the Lord the church:

30 For we are members of his body, of his flesh, and of his bones.

31 For this cause shall a man leave his father and mother, and shall be joined unto his wife, and they two shall be one flesh.

32 This is a great mystery: but I speak concerning Christ and the church.

33 Nevertheless let every one of you in particular so love his wife even as himself; and the wife see that she reverence her husband.

29 After all, no one ever hated their own body, but they feed and care for their body, just as Christ does the church—

30 for we are members of his body.

31 "For this reason a man will leave his father and mother and be united to his wife, and the two will become one flesh."

32 This is a profound mystery—but I am talking about Christ and the church.

33 However, each one of you also must love his wife as he loves himself, and the wife must respect her husband.

UNIFYING LESSON PRINCIPLE: In an ever-changing and increasingly complex society, the focus on self-indulgence has endangered a healthy concept of family. How do we make commitment to God and family central to our well-being? Paul said that a committed relationship must be sought in which husbands, wives, and children love, honor, and respect both God and one another.

LESSON OBJECTIVES

Upon the completion of this lesson, the students will be able to do the following:

1. Summarize the relationship Paul described as proper between a husband and wife.
2. Appreciate the holy relationship that exists between a husband and wife, which transcends the physical, emotional, and psychological dimensions, and touches the spiritual.
3. Cultivate a climate within the church where marriages can flourish and display the holiness described in this text.

AGE-LEVEL POINTS TO BE EMPHASIZED

Teachers of ADULTS and YOUTH

—The passage highlights love rather than control.

—"Subject to one another" indicates a status that is neither superior nor inferior. It is mutual submission.

—Paul's instructions for family life are set in the context of reverence for Christ.

—Interpretations vary as to what it means for wives to be "subject to your husbands as you are to the Lord" (verse 22). The best interpretations take into account that husbands are similarly called upon to demonstrate self-giving love to their wives following the example of Christ (verses 28-29). At any event, both marriage partners are commanded to "be subject to one another" in verse 21.

—The oneness of a married couple is a metaphor for the oneness of Christ and the church.

—This text should be understood in the context of the larger theme of the book of Ephesians to build up the body of Christ.

—"Household codes" such as this one were common in Greek, Roman, and other cultures of the same era. Their function was to maintain order.

—The relationships in this text all involved unequal power in the minds of the first hearers. The text is lifting up mutuality in unequal power relationships while attempting to retain hierarchical order, the common wisdom of the day, in society and the home.

Teachers of CHILDREN

—All persons in the Christ-led household are to be reverent to one another.

—The relationship between husband and wife is compared to Christ's relationship with the church.

—The male role as head of the family is culturally bound and not intended to be the focus of the teaching.

—This text demonstrates the need for responsibility in relationships of unequal power, wherein the person with the greater power has the greater responsibility for the well-being of the family.

—The background Scripture reminds children of the commandment to honor their parents.

—Verse 4 in the Background Scripture instructs fathers to nurture and provide for their children by teaching them in the word and way of God.

THE CHRONOLOGICAL SETTING OF THE LESSON

The letter to the Ephesians was written by the apostle Paul to the church in Ephesus during his third missionary journey to Antioch (see Acts 18:19-22; 20:31). According to the early church fathers, the epistle to the Ephesians might have been written by Paul during his second Roman arrest. The letter to the Ephesians encourages the Christian Jews and the believing Gentiles to unite as one body in the church. There are also other letters under the authorship of the apostle Paul, including the epistles to the Colossians and Philippians, and the book of Philemon (bible.org).

THE GEOGRAPHICAL AND CULTURAL SETTING OF THE LESSON

The city of Ephesus was a port town located at the mouth of the Cayster River on the eastern side of the Aegean Sea in modern-day Turkey. This was one of the Roman provinces in Asia Minor. This city was home to the temple of the Roman goddess of fertility known to the Greeks as Artemis (see Acts 19:23-28), and this was also a town that practiced sorcery and emperor worship (bible.org). The city of Ephesus was a cosmopolitan town with a population of about 25,000 occupants that included Jews and the Gentiles.

The letter to the Ephesians is believed to have been written by Paul in around AD 60-61. However, prior to this writing, Paul had established the church in Ephesus while on his way to Jerusalem from his ministry in Corinth in AD 53, where he left behind Aquila and Priscilla at the synagogue in Ephesus (see Acts 18:18-22). Paul spent three months in the synagogue, teaching and baptizing both Jews and Gentiles (until he was maligned by the Jews), and he went to lecture at the hall of Tyrannus for two years (bible.org).

PROMINENT CHARACTER(S) IN THE LESSON

Apostle Paul: He was minister of the Word of Christ to Gentile believers in many parts of the Asian continent during the early development of the church (bible.org).

KEY TERMS IN THE LESSON

Body (verse 23)—Greek: *sóma* (so'-mah): body, flesh; the body of the church.

Christ (verse 23)—Greek: *Christos* (khris-tos'): the Anointed One, Messiah, Christ.

Church (verse 27)—Greek: *ekklésia* (ek-klay-see'-ah): an assembly; congregation; church.

Head (verse 23)—Greek: *kephalé* (kef-al-ay'): the head.

Husbands (verse 22)—Greek: *anér* (an'-ayr): male human beings; men.

Reverence (verse 21)—Greek: *phobos* (fob'-os): panic, flight; "fear" (KJV); the causing of fear; terror.

TOPICAL OUTLINE OF THE LESSON

I. Introduction
   A. Work Out Your Salvation
   B. Biblical Background

II. Exposition and Application of the Scripture
   A. Guidelines for Family Life (Ephesians 5:21-24)
   B. Instructions for Husbands (Ephesians 5:25-28)
   C. The Marvel of Marriage (Ephesians 5:29-33)

III. Concluding Reflection

I. INTRODUCTION

A. Work Out Your Salvation

In the beginning of Ephesians, the apostle Paul stated clearly that we are saved by grace, not by works (see Ephesians 2:8). He also helped us to understand that God made us and called us so that we could do good works here on earth (verse 10). In the last chapters of the book, the apostle Paul began to expound on godly behaviors which must be reflected in us as God's children. By the end of chapter 4, Paul began to exhort the believers to forgive as God forgave us, who is our pattern of good examples (see 4:32).

Chapter 5 of this book begins with one of Paul's classic principles—which states that all believers follow the example of God as His dear children (see 5:1-2)—and goes on to talk about the ideal relationship between a husband and wife in the home and the necessary factors which must be present for such a union to excel. He encouraged us to show Christ in us in all our endeavors and dealings. We must emulate Christ—not in authority but in humility, love, sacrifice, and forgiveness (see Hebrews 13:16).

B. Biblical Background

In verses 18-23 of Ephesians 5, we see that Paul gave a form of a command when he said, "Be filled with the Spirit." He went on to say how we ought to act when we are filled with the Spirit when he said, "speaking one to another in hymns, psalms and spiritual songs, singing and making melody in your heart unto the Lord." From Paul's words, it certainly means there ought to be a pattern of life and action which should be seen and expressed in the life of a Christian who is filled with the Spirit. This goes to show that for there to be any form or level of commitment between brothers and sisters in the household of faith, the Spirit of God must fill every one of us.

One of the many results of being Spirit-filled is that the Spirit brings so much humility that we are able to "submit to another out of worship and reverence for Christ." Notice here that the apostle Paul did not recommend that we be half or partially filled. He said, "Be filled with the Spirit," which simply means that our potential to contain the Holy Spirit in us must be maximized so that we practically no longer exist of our own will and volition but according to the dictates of the Holy Spirit in us. Until this is achieved, we may never come to full commitment and submission to one another and may also not be able to seek to meet the needs of others (see Philippians 2:4).

In verse 22, the apostle Paul began his advice to wives, directing them to submit to their husbands as unto the Lord. The yardstick for measuring the standard of submission is "the Lord." Wives should endeavor to submit to their husbands in everything (not to commands contrary to Christ and biblical standards).

The apostle Paul did not stop at the wife alone. He extended directions to the husband when he said, "Husbands, love your wives, just as Christ loved the church and gave himself up for her." In using the word *love*, the apostle Paul simply was encouraging submission to the needs of the wives just as Christ had submitted to the needs of the church. The purpose of Christ's love to the church was to make her holy by cleansing her through the Word and to present the church to Himself as a church radiant and without spot, blemish, or any wrinkle (verses 26-27). Paul encouraged husbands to love their wives as their own bodies (verse 28) and make sacrifices for them as Christ had done for the church. Nothing should be done in selfishness but in humility, regarding their wives more than themselves (see Philippians 2:3). Paul here called for mutual submission and respect (verses 28-30).

Paul's motives are to ensure that husbands and wives are committed and united in one body, as he made reference to Genesis 2:24 (verse 31). He further made it clear that the mystery of oneness of husbands and wives has been solved in the unity and oneness between Christ and the church. We are one in Christ, and our spouses are part of our body and should be treated as such (verse 32).

II. EXPOSITION AND APPLICATION OF THE SCRIPTURE

A. Guidelines for Family Life
(Ephesians 5:21-24)

Submitting yourselves one to another in the fear of God. Wives, submit yourselves unto your own husbands, as unto the Lord. For the husband is the head of the wife, even as Christ is the head of the church: and he is the saviour of the body. Therefore as the church is subject unto Christ, so let the wives be to their own husbands in every thing.

The opening verse in our lesson (verse 21) levels the relationship playing field. Paul moved from addressing our relationship with God to addressing our relationships with each other. This includes natural, civic, and church relationships. We are called to submit ourselves to and give respect to civil magistrates, since they are ordained by God. Respect for human leadership is equated to respect for God. Reverential fear of displeasing God becomes the motive for properly performing our duties as Christians (see 1 Corinthians 10:22; 2 Corinthians 5:11; 1 Peter 2:13).

One of the most misunderstood words and disciplines in Scripture is the word *submission* (verse 22). The dictionary definition for *submission* is "the action or fact of accepting or yielding to a superior force or to the will or authority of another person." This secular definition leans too far toward qualitative differences between two entities rather than the positional differences and the division of labor assignments of two entities. One of the reasons for why the term *submission* has been so maligned and rejected by some wives and some women is because the concept has been abused by some men and husbands. One of the ways that this concept has been misunderstood is that some have elevated the male gender as being superior to the female gender, and females as being answerable to men in general. A closer look at verse 22 reveals that submission is only for wives toward their own husbands rather than for women toward men. The reason that submission is only enacted under the marital covering is because of God's expectation of husbands to live sacrificially with their wives. Any husband who submits to God and regards his wife in a sacrificial manner would be a safe and desirable covering.

Paul uses the relationship between Christ and the church to explain the relationship between a husband and wife (verses 23-24).

The admonition for wives to submit to their husbands "in everything" is a broad stroke which should not be taken in an extremely literal manner. If a husband requires his wife to do something that would bring harm to herself or to someone else, obviously that would not be wise. In this passage, Paul spoke in ideal terms, and the passage should be understood from that perspective.

B. Instructions for Husbands (Ephesians 5:25-28)

Husbands, love your wives, even as Christ also loved the church, and gave himself for it; That he might sanctify and cleanse it with the washing of water by the word, That he might present it to himself a glorious church, not having spot, or wrinkle, or any such thing; but that it should be holy and without blemish. So ought men to love their wives as their own bodies. He that loveth his wife loveth himself.

The duty, calling, and responsibility of husbands to love their wives (verse 25) is not an ordinary, sentimental kind of love but a practical, sacrificial, spiritual kind of love. Sentimental love is surface and conditional. It lasts only as long as the feelings last. The way to discern what is required of husbands in this spiritual kind of love is to go back to verse 25 and ask how Christ loved the church. The answer is that Jesus sacrificed His very life on behalf of the church. Likewise, the husband is called to sacrifice his life for his wife. Interestingly, the wife is only called to submit but never called to sacrifice her life for the husband. One might ask, which one seems more desirable? This call for personal life sacrifice may be hypothetically embraced by some husbands who relish the declaration of their bravado. They may say they would take a bullet for their wives—but a more practical question is if they would be willing to sacrifice a fishing trip with the guys or attendance at a championship ball game in order to meet her needs. The degree of one's willingness to sacrifice is a revealer of one's degree of love and commitment.

There is wide diversity of opinion about the

true meaning of verse 26. Let us approach it phrase by phrase. The words "to make her holy" means to directly assist in the encouragement and development of her spiritual growth and her closeness to God. Some people are intimidated by applying the word *holy* to themselves or to other humans. But 1 Peter 1:16 reads, "Be ye holy; for I am holy." *To be holy* is to be sanctified and consecrated to God's service. It means being conformed to the will of God (see Romans 6:19, 22; Ephesians 1:4; Titus 1:8; 1 Peter 1:15). Personal holiness is not instantaneous but is a gradual work that lasts a lifetime and is enhanced by worship, prayer, service, fellowship, obedience, and exposure to and absorption of the Word of God.

To be cleansed by the "washing with water" through the Word does not refer to baptism. The scriptural concept of "cleansing" in general was related to liquid water as well as to various perfumes and fragrances that were especially applied to a young woman who was preparing for marriage. A spiritual washing with the Word most likely refers to the consistent, unrelenting exposure of the wife to the truth of God's Word and the application of that truth in specific ways to address the individual unique needs or deficiencies of the wife. This might be accomplished through encouragingly quoting relevant Scripture to her, leading her in a targeted study of Bible passages, or other ways of exposing her spirit to the powerful principles of God's Word which do not return void.

The goal of the church is to mature in holiness and blamelessness (verse 27). Matthew 5:48 states, "Be ye therefore perfect, even as your Father which is in heaven is perfect." Literal perfection is obviously impossible as long as we are in the flesh. This concept refers to spiritual maturity and Christlikeness more so than to the ability to be 100 percent without error.

Verse 28 runs parallel to the concept of loving found in Mark 12:31 (NIV): "'Love your neighbor as yourself.' There is no commandment greater than these." If this concept were implemented in every marriage, the divorce rate would instantly and dramatically decrease. The deadly disease that causes most marriages to die is the disease of selfishness. No marriage can survive and thrive when selfishness is present, because healthy marriage consistently asks the question, "What can I do for you?" Godly marriage prompts and empowers the husband to follow the example of Jesus Christ and "not only to protect and cherish his wife, by giving her the necessaries and conveniences of life, but also to cleanse her; that is, to form her mind, and assist her in making progress in virtue. [This shows that he] really loves himself, and promotes his own happiness in the best manner. For his wife, being thus loved and cared for, will be strengthened for performing her duty; and her mind being improved, her conversation will give him the greater pleasure. Withal, having a high esteem for her husband, she will submit to the hardships of her station with cheerfulness" (*Benson Commentary*, http://biblehub.com/commentaries/ephesians/5-28.htm).

C. The Marvel of Marriage (Ephesians 5:29-33)

For no man ever yet hated his own flesh; but nourisheth and cherisheth it, even as the Lord the church: For we are members of his body, of his flesh, and of his bones. For this cause shall a man leave his father and mother,